Office 2003 Timesaving Techniques For Dummies

Readers' Picks

Here's the short list of readers' favorite timesaving techniques and where you'll find them in this book. Tell me what you think! Send me mail: talk2woody@woodyswatch.com.

To Save Time	Find More Info Here
Download and install (and sometimes avoid!) the latest patches and fixes	Technique 6
Organize Outlook for speed	Technique 26
Set up your own letterhead	Technique 23
Reduce your exposure to spam	Technique 30
Send out newsletters and holiday greetings	Technique 70
Build spreadsheets that work right, the first time	Technique 35
Create presentations that run themselves	Technique 48
Protect your privacy by zapping hidden data	Technique 69
Get pictures to stay put	Technique 11
Edit documents quickly, accurately, and easily	Technique 19

Stop Futzing with Mail

You can organize Outlook so it shows your mail in two panes: On the left, you have a list of messages; on the right you see the mail. It's a clean, Spartan, no-nonsense approach to handling large volumes of mail that will boost your productivity enormously. See details in Technique 26:

✔ Most people show the navigation pane (on the left side of the screen) all the time. Usually it gets in the way. Hide it by pressing Alt+F1. Bring it back by pressing Alt+F1 again.

✔ Most people use two or three lines for each message in the message pane. Trim Outlook back to one line per message by choosing View⇨Arrange By⇨Custom⇨Other Settings, clicking the Always Use Single-Line Layout button, and clicking OK.

✔ Microsoft bills Outlook's ability to block pictures attached to messages as a privacy feature. In fact, it's also a great timesaver — if you block pictures, you don't have to wait for them to load. To block pictures, choose Tools⇨Options⇨Security, click the Change Automatic Download Settings button, mark the Don't Download Pictures or Other Content Automatically in HTML E-mail check box, and click OK.

✔ Move quickly through your incoming mail by scanning the one-line list. To delete a message, press Del or Ctrl+D. To move to the next message, press the down arrow or spacebar. To reply, press Ctrl+R.

For Dummies®: Bestselling Book Series for Beginners

Office 2003 Timesaving Techniques For Dummies®

Important Keyboard Shortcuts

All these shortcuts are worth memorizing:

Press This	To Do This
Ctrl+C	Copy selection to the Clipboard
Ctrl+X	Cut selection to the Clipboard
Ctrl+V	Paste from the Clipboard
Ctrl+C+C	Bring up the Office Clipboard (which has 24 cubbyholes)
Ctrl+A	Select everything in the document (except headers and footers)
Ctrl+Z	Undo
Alt+Drag	Move graphics precisely, overriding the snap-to behavior

In Outlook

Alt+F1	Show or hide the navigation pane
F9	Send and receive mail

In Word

Ctrl+''	(Hold down Ctrl, press the apostrophe twice) Make a single curly close quote (for example, '99 or go get 'em)
Click+Shift+Click	(Click, hold down Shift, click again) Select a block of text accurately and quickly without dragging

In Excel

Ctrl+Home	Move to cell A1
Ctrl+End	Move to the last used cell in the spreadsheet (see Technique 10 for details)
F2	Show the formula for the currently selected cell(s)

In PowerPoint

Ctrl+D	Insert a copy of the currently selected slide — Duplicate
F5	Start the slideshow

Wiley, the Wiley Publishing logo, For Dummies, the Dummies Man logo, the For Dummies Bestselling Book Series logo and all related trade dress are trademarks or registered trademarks of John Wiley & Sons, Inc. and/or its affiliates. All other trademarks are property of their respective owners.

For Dummies: Bestselling Book Series for Beginners

Office 2003
Timesaving
Techniques

FOR

DUMMIES®

Office 2003 Timesaving Techniques

FOR DUMMIES®

by Woody Leonhard

WILEY

Wiley Publishing, Inc.

Office 2003 Timesaving Techniques For Dummies®

Published by
Wiley Publishing, Inc.
111 River Street
Hoboken, NJ 07030-5774

About the Authors

Woody Leonhard first described himself as an "Office victim" shortly after Microsoft released the inaugural version of Office. The kvetch stuck. Woody started his computer book writing career more than a decade ago with a compilation of bugs and workarounds in Word for Windows version 1.10, and he's been dishing out advice and digging the 'Softie dirt ever since.

This book continues in the footsteps of *Windows XP Timesaving Techniques For Dummies*, Woody's best-selling compendium of real-world help for the Windows hapless. Woody also wrote the best-seller *Windows XP All-In-One Desk Reference For Dummies*, and dozens of earlier tomes, many of which still rate as required reading on Microsoft's Redmond campus.

Susan Sales Harkins contributed the Techniques on Access. She's written for the *Woody's Access Watch* newsletters on many occasions, and is one of the smartest database people Woody knows. She is also is an independent consultant and the author of several articles and books on database and Web technologies. Her most recent books are: *ICDL Practice Questions Exam Cram 2*, *ICDL Exam Cram 2*, *Absolute Beginner's Guide to Microsoft Access 2003*, *Absolute Beginner's Guide to Microsoft Access 2002*, all from Que; *Mastering Dreamweaver MX Databases*, from Sybex; and *SQL: Access to SQL Server*, from Apress. You can reach Susan at ssharkins@bellsouth.net. Currently, Susan volunteers as the Publications Director for Database Advisors at www.databaseadvisors.com.

Dedication

To Add and her heart of gold, for all she has done for me and Justin over the years.

Author's Acknowledgments

Thanks to Justin Leonhard for his help with this book. Justin lives with his dad and beagle in Phuket, Thailand. Justin co-wrote *Windows XP Timesaving Techniques For Dummies* and frequently helps write computer columns for the local newspaper. He's currently involved in creating a Rotary Interact group on the island. An avid scuba diver and PC game player, Justin was admitted to Mensa International at the age of 14, but occasionally forgets to watch out for monkeys tossing coconuts.

Publisher's Acknowledgments

We're proud of this book; please send us your comments through our online registration form located at www.dummies.com/register/.

Some of the people who helped bring this book to market include the following:

Acquisitions, Editorial, and Media Development

Associate Project Editor: Rebecca Huehls

Senior Acquisitions Editor: Greg Croy

Senior Copy Editor: Teresa Artman

Technical Editor: Lee Musick

Editorial Manager: Leah Cameron

Senior Permissions Editor: Carmen Krikorian

Media Development Manager: Laura VanWinkle

Media Development Supervisor: Richard Graves

Editorial Assistant: Amanda Foxworth

Cartoons: Rich Tennant (www.the5thwave.com)

Production

Project Coordinator: Courtney MacIntyre

Layout and Graphics: Amanda Carter, Andrea Dahl, Beth Brooks, Lauren Goddard, Joyce Haughey, LeAndra Hosier, Stephanie D. Jumper, Michael Kruzil, Kristin McMullan, Heather Ryan, Jacque Schneider

Proofreaders: Laura Albert, John Greenough, Andy Hollandbeck, Carl William Pierce, Dwight Ramsey, Charles Spencer, Brian H. Walls, Ethel M. Winslow

Indexer: Ty Koontz

Publishing and Editorial for Technology Dummies

Richard Swadley, Vice President and Executive Group Publisher

Andy Cummings, Vice President and Publisher

Mary C. Corder, Editorial Director

Publishing for Consumer Dummies

Diane Graves Steele, Vice President and Publisher

Joyce Pepple, Acquisitions Director

Composition Services

Gerry Fahey, Vice President of Production Services

Debbie Stailey, Director of Composition Services

Contents at a Glance

Table Of Contents

Introduction

Do you use Microsoft Office? Or does Office use you?

That is the question.

Most people sit down at a computer, click a couple of times, and start typing. They rarely take the initiative to make Office work better, not knowing (or perhaps not caring!) that a few minutes spent upfront wrangling with the beast can save hours, or even days, down the road.

Chime in any time. Do you spend a lot of time working with Office applications? Have you ever felt the frustration of typing something and having it mangled by a program that thinks it's smarter than you? Maybe you've lost an hour or a day or a week to a PC that just doesn't behave the way any rational machine should. And then wondered why it's all so ludicrously complicated. If you've ever been so mad you could put your fist through the screen . . . this book's for you.

> *Whether 'tis nobler in the mind to suffer*
> *The slings and arrows of outrageous fortune,*
> *Or to take arms against a sea of troubles,*
>
> — Hamlet, III, i

Hey, face it — you or your company paid a bundle for Office. Office is supposed to save you time — not suck it up in voracious gulps. Isn't it about time that you started to get your money's worth?

About This Book

Microsoft says that 400,000,000 people use Office.

Astounding, huh?

If you're like me, you spend most of your working day — indeed, most of your waking hours — wrestling with Office.

Although tamable, the Office beast is getting worse. Trying to capitalize on Office's *familiar* (read: ubiquitous) user interface, Microsoft is attempting to get application program developers to coax Office applications to interact with normal people like you and me. No doubt you've seen demos of ordering systems that look like Word documents or Web pages that act like Excel spreadsheets. In the not-too-distant future, you won't be able to send a handwritten note to school with your kid: You'll have to log on to the school's Web site and submit a Word form.

The simple fact is that you need to know how to use Office in order to get your work done. And the more guff that Office gives you, the harder it is to find time for the important stuff.

Office 2003 Timesaving Techniques For Dummies will save you time, day in and day out, by explaining how to

- ✔ **Customize Office to meet your needs:** These Techniques make Word, Outlook, Excel, PowerPoint, and Access work faster, more like the way you work, with less intrusion than you ever thought possible.

- ✔ **Tame time-sucking everyday tasks and take your skills up a notch:** Like its predecessor, *Windows XP Timesaving Techniques For Dummies,* this book isn't limited to dry *click this, press that* tips. Rather, it goes outside the traditional computer box to solve real-world problems that Office 2003 users encounter every day. Find out which tools work best for specific tasks and dive into some of the more advanced Office skills, like writing macros, setting up templates, and even modifying standard windows.

Although this book is written specifically for Office 2003, most of the Techniques here apply equally well to Office XP and (in many cases) Office 2000. Where differences exist, I point them out, typically at the end of the Technique.

Foolish Assumptions

I assume that you know how to use a computer, how to get Windows running, and how to perform basic mouse functions. In fact, that's the first way I save you time: I won't cover old ground.

I also assume that you're not scared to change Office settings. After all, they're your settings. You can change them any way that you want.

An example. Word, Excel, PowerPoint, and Access all maintain lists of most recently used files. When you open the File menu, the list of files appears at the bottom of the menu. Unless you change each specific program, you'll see only four files listed at the bottom of the File menu. Some people figure that four files are listed by default because some behavioral science genius at Microsoft discovered that four was the optimum number. Ain't so. In fact, the default with a meager list of four files came about years ago when somebody decided that any more than four files (run on an ancient monitor at 640 x 480 resolution) produced a screen too complicated for the average Office user to understand.

That's why you only see four recently used files. Urban legend debunked.

Office comes loaded with dumb defaults that you should change — immediately! — whenever you start working on a new machine. More than anything, I assume that you're willing to take the bull by the horns.

What's in This Book

To save you time, I organized this book into *Techniques* — groups of related tasks that make you or your computer (or possibly both!) more efficient and more effective. Some Techniques are short 'n sweet, tackle one specific topic, and get you in and out of Office in a nonce. Other Techniques depend on a deeper understanding of how Office works. Take your time when you go through the more complex Techniques, and you'll be rewarded with big gains down the road. No two people work the same way. Why should computers?

When a Technique requires you to perform a series of steps, I take you through them in a very direct way. But some big timesavers aren't complicated at all. Keep your eye out for shorter tips, sidebars, and timesavers that are tangentially related to the main topic at hand. Watch for the icons. And don't be surprised if you bump into a tip or two that urges you to change how *you* work, as opposed to making changes to your computer.

This book continues the easy-to-read, two-column format that was pioneered in *Windows XP Timesaving Techniques For Dummies.* It's full of figures and other visual cues that make it easier for you to scan and enter a Technique at the point most appropriate for your circumstances. Linear thinking is good. Non-linear scanning is better: That is, wade in at the topic you need help on . . . no need to read this tome cover to cover.

 Lay this book flat so you that can see exactly what you're doing. Yes, the book was made to stay put.

You can read the book from beginning to end, or you can jump directly into the Technique of your choice. Either way works just fine. Any time a concept is mentioned that isn't covered in-depth in that Technique, you'll find a cross-reference to another Technique to find out more. If you're looking for something specific, check out either the Table of Contents or the index.

The Cheat Sheet at the beginning of this book lists my choices as the most important quick timesaving Techniques. Tear it out, tape it to your monitor, and/or pass it around to other folks at the office. We're all in this leaky boat together.

Here's a quick guide to the meat of the book:

Part I: Knocking Office Into Shape

What you need to do to Office (and Windows!) to take off the training wheels. Here you discover how to make Windows a safe place for Office and get at your Office programs faster. Organize Office documents in ways that make sense for you, and then customize the Open dialog box's Places Bar so that finding files is a snap. Delve into how to set up a backup regimen and stick to it. And don't miss downloading and installing the latest patches — and knowing when *not* to. Go on to disable the really obnoxious IntelliSense setting that converts typed Web address and e-mail addresses into links and use the Office Clipboard with aplomb. Then work with graphics in all the Office applications and streamline your toolbars.

Part II: Saving Time with Word

For most people, timesaving gains in Word have the biggest impact. You gotta read here to discover how to turn off all those stupid IntelliSense settings. Use Word's features to lay out a page that works with you and not against you. Print impressive labels. Read about ways to edit that really work. Use Find and Replace and unleash the truth behind styles. Stick with me to create top-notch letterhead and tame Word's graphics.

Part III: Streamlining Outlook

Do you live in Outlook? Here's what you don't know. I show you here how to set up meaningful search folders and organize with quick clicks. Keep Outlook from autocompleting your way into oblivion. Fight spam before it happens. Finally, look at files attached to e-mail messages — without getting infected — and share Calendars and Contacts.

Part IV: Exploiting Excel

For crunching much more than numbers. Here you navigate creating spreadsheets that check themselves and make spreadsheets look better onscreen and

when printed. Use Excel as a database — er, list —
manager and read the why's and wherefore's of pivot
tables and charts. Finally, calculate sales tax with
the Lookup Wizard.

Part V: Pushing PowerPoint

Making presentations that don't take forever. Still
with me? Don't miss working with the right file type
and making a real presentation template. Eliminate
the middleman with presentations that run themselves. Plan for predictable questions and see how
working backward can save you lots of time.

Part VI: Assimilating Access

A few quick programs go a long way. Discover how to
print cover sheets for all your reports as well as the
skinny on running totals and subtotals. Also read
how to print labels and then set formatting once . . .
and forget it.

Part VII: Combining the Applications

*Some of the Office apps work together, some of the
time.* Here you find my most-requested explanation:
how to print holiday greeting letters. Read on for
how to run an electronic newsletter. And don't miss
converting a Word outline directly into a presentation or animating Excel charts in a presentation.
Cross-app finale: Rotate text in a Word document —
with a little help from Excel.

Part VIII: The Scary (Or Fun!) Stuff

Macros can make your life better. You need this stuff.
Become a power user by inserting unformatted text
in Word, Excel, and PowerPoint. Then make Word's
Show All show you all that you want to see, with
none of that extra junk. Print a folder full of spreadsheets. Strip personally identifiable information out
of Word docs and Excel spreadsheets. Become an
honorary member of Monty Python with spam bust-
ing. In conclusion, create smart documents.

Conventions Used in This Book

I try to keep the typographical conventions to a
minimum:

- ✔ The first time that a buzzword appears in text, I
  italicize it and define it immediately. That makes
  it easier for you to glance back and reread the
  definition.

- ✔ When you see an arrow (➪) in text, it means that
  you should click, click, click to success. For
  example, "Choose Tools➪Letters and Mailings➪
  Envelopes and Labels" means that you should
  click Tools, then Letters and Mailings, and then
  Envelopes and Labels. D'oh!

- ✔ When I want you to type something, I put the
  to-be-typed stuff in bold. For example: In the
  Help Me Now or I'll Suffocate text box, enter
  Send oxygen pronto.

- ✔ I set off Web addresses and e-mail IDs in monospace text. For example, my e-mail address is
  `talk2woody@woodyswatch.com` (true), and my
  newsletter Web page is at `www.woodyswatch.com`
  (also true).

- ✔ I always, absolutely, adamantly include the filename extension — those letters at the end of a
  filename, like `.doc` or `.vbs` or `.exe` — when talking about a file. Yeah, I know that Windows hides
  filename extensions unless you go in and change
  it. That's why you need to look at Technique 1.

Icons Used in This Book

While perusing this book, you'll notice some icons in
the margins screaming for your attention. Each one
has a purpose.

 When I'm jumping up and down on one foot
with an idea so absolutely cool that I can't
stand it any more, I stick a Tip icon in the
margin.

You don't need to memorize the stuff marked with this icon, but you should try to remember that there's something special lurking about.

 Achtung! ¡Cuidado! Thar be tygers here! Any place where you see a Warning icon, you can be sure that I've been burnt — badly. Mind your fingers. These are really, really mean suckers.

 When time is of the essence, this icon emphasizes the point. More than a Tip but not quite a full Technique, this icon points out a quick trick that can save you time — either now or later.

Where to Go from Here

If you want your voice to be heard, you can contact the publisher of the *For Dummies* books by visiting the publisher's Web site at www.dummies.com, sending an e-mail to customer@wiley.com, or sending snail mail to Wiley Publishing, Inc., 10475 Crosspoint Boulevard, Indianapolis, IN 46256.

You can contact Woody at talk2woody@woodyswatch. com. I can't answer all the questions I get — man, there ain't enough hours in the day! — but I take some of the best and write them up in my newsletters every week.

Speaking of newsletters . . . don't forget to sign up for mine! They're free and worth every penny. See www.woodyswatch.com for details.

Confused about where to go next? I have a hint. Start with Technique 1. After Windows has been trained to be a good Office citizen, you can jump around just about anywhere.

Part I

Knocking Office Into Shape

The 5th Wave   By Rich Tennant

"We're much better prepared for this upgrade than before. We're giving users additional training, better manuals, and a morphine drip."

Technique

Making Windows Safe for Office

Every Office user needs to take security seriously. The cretins who make programs that melt down the Internet, pummel sites with bandwidth-clogging pings, or simply diddle with your data, are constantly trolling for unwitting accomplices. Foil their plans by keeping your wits about you.

Security is more than just an ounce of prevention. On rare occasion, viruses can wipe out all your data, and worms can bring your e-mail connection to its knees. Far more insidious, though, are the time-sucking security problems that aren't quite so obvious: the malware that lurks and infects and destroys invisibly or intermittently.

Office rates as the number-one conduit for infections because it's on virtually every desktop. On most machines, Office amounts to a big, wide-open target. Windows might get infected, but frequently the vector of attack goes through an Office application.

 No Office is an island: It's tied into Windows at the shoulders and ankles. To protect Office — and to protect yourself — you must start by protecting Windows, by applying updates, getting Windows to show you hidden information that can clobber you, and installing and using antivirus software and a good firewall.

Updating Windows Manually

Did you hear the story about Microsoft's Security Bulletin MS03-045? Microsoft released the initial bulletin along with a patch for Windows on October 15, 2003. Almost immediately, people started having problems with the patch. A little over a week later, Microsoft issued a patch for the patch. This new patch seemed to take care of most of the problems, but then someone discovered that the program that installed the patch was faulty. A month after the first patch came out, Microsoft issued a patch for the patch to the patch.

Got that?

To protect Office, you need to keep Windows updated. Indeed, some Windows patches — such as the notorious Slammer/SQL patch MS02-020 — are really Office patches disguised as Windows patches. To protect Office, you have to protect Windows. And to protect Windows, you have to protect Office.

Microsoft wants you to tell Windows to heal itself automatically. I think that's a big mistake — and cite Microsoft's track record as Exhibit A. It's a sorry state of affairs, but I believe that every Office user should

✔ **Set Windows Update to automatically notify you when new updates are available.**

✔ **Tell Windows Update that you do *not* want to download — much less install — new patches automatically.** If you need a patch, you can take a few extra minutes and give the go-ahead.

✔ **Follow the major computer publications closely to see whether new patches are stable and effective *before* installing them.**

Some industry observers would have you trust Microsoft and set Windows Update to run automatically. I say hogwash. In theory, a black-hat cretin could unleash an Office-based worm that will destroy your machine while a patch for that very worm was sitting on Microsoft's servers. In practice, Microsoft doesn't work fast enough to release immediate patches. Demonstrably, your risk from a bad patch is far greater than your risk from a ground-zero worm attack. It doesn't make sense to trust your patching to the folks in Redmond.

 I follow Microsoft's patching follies extensively in both *Woody's Office Watch* and *Woody's Windows Watch*. They're free electronic newsletters that go out to more than half a million subscribers every week. Sign up at www.woodyswatch.com.

That said, you *do* need to make sure that you install the patches — after they've been tried and tested by a few million guinea pigs.

To tell Windows Update that you want to do it yourself

1. **Choose Start➪Control Panel➪Performance and Maintenance➪System➪Automatic Updates.**

 In Windows 2000, choose Start➪Settings➪ Control Panel, and go from there.

Windows XP shows you the System Properties dialog box, as shown in Figure 1-1.

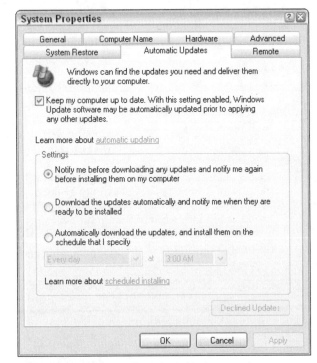

• **Figure 1-1: Windows Automatic Updates settings.**

2. **Mark the Keep My Computer Up to Date check box.**

This allows Microsoft's sniffer program to come in and look at your copy of Windows. The *sniffer program* sends an inventory of Windows pieces and patches back to the Microsoft Mother Ship, but as far as I (and several independent researchers) can tell, it doesn't appear as if Microsoft receives any information that can identify you individually.

3. **Select the first radio button under Settings (Notify Me Before Downloading Any Updates and Notify Me Again Before Installing Them on My Computer).**

That's exactly what you want to do. Microsoft might change the wording of this dialog box slightly. (As this book went to press, there were rumors that the next version of Windows Update would encompass both Windows and Office.) The intent, however, stays the same: You want to be in control of what Microsoft puts on your machine — and when.

4. **Click OK.**

I talk about Windows Update, its implications, and vulnerabilities in *Windows XP Timesaving Techniques For Dummies*. Well worth reading to get the entire Windows perspective.

 Windows and Office are so inextricably inter-woven that a security hole in one frequently shows up as a security hole in the other. It's important to keep both Windows and Office up to date, because Microsoft may have a vital patch for an Office component, and not even realize it, much less warn you about it!

Showing Filename Extensions

 This is the most important Technique in the entire book.

If you're an old DOS fan (or even a young one), you've been working with filename extensions since the dawn of time. Microsoft shows them in all its documentation — Help files, Knowledge Base articles, and white papers. If you're not familiar with exten-sions (see the sidebar "Since When Did Filenames Have Extensions?" for a definition), it's probably because Windows hides filename extensions from you unless you specifically tell Windows otherwise. These hidden extensions are supposed to make Windows more user-friendly. Yeah. Right.

You probably know about EXE (executable) and BAT (batch) files. Windows simply runs them when they're opened. You might not know about VBS (VBScript) or COM files (command files; good old-fashioned PC programs), which run automatically, too. And I bet you didn't have any idea that SCR (screen saver) and CPL (Control Panel add-in) files get run automatically, too.

The bad guys know. Trust me.

 The creators of Windows decided long ago that filename extensions should be hidden from mortals like you and me. I think that's hooey. *Every* Office user should be able to see her filename extensions. If you can't see the filename extensions either in Windows or in Office, you stand a chance of getting zinged — and spending lots of time fixing the damage.

Files attached to e-mail messages rate as the number-one Trojan infection vector, and being able to see filename extensions can make all the difference. For example, that innocent file called `ILOVEYOU` doesn't look so innocent when it appears as `ILOVEYOU.VBS`. You might be tricked into double-clicking a file that's called `Funny Story.txt`, but you'd almost certainly hesitate before double-clicking `Funny Story.txt.exe`.

 If you've been looking around Office trying to figure out how to force Office to show you filename extensions in dialog boxes, you've been looking in the wrong place! Windows itself controls whether Office shows filename extensions.

To make Windows show you the entire filename

1. **Choose Start⇨My Computer.**

2. **Choose Tools⇨Folder Options⇨View.**

Windows shows you the Folder Options dialog box, as shown in Figure 1-2.

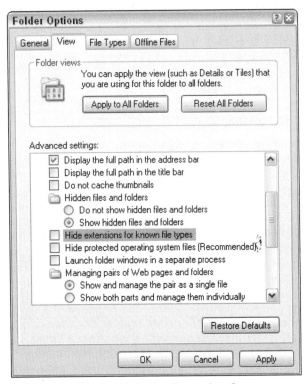

• **Figure 1-2:** Windows hides its view options here.

3. **Clear the Hide Extensions for Known File Types check box.**

   While you're here, seriously consider selecting the Show Hidden Files and Folders radio button and also clearing the Hide Protected Operating System Files (Recommended) check box. You can find a detailed discussion of the implications of both in *Windows XP Timesaving Techniques For Dummies.*

4. **Click OK.**

    All the directions and screenshots in this book (indeed, nearly all of Microsoft's Help files, Knowledge Base articles, and more) assume that you've instructed Windows to show filename extensions.

Since When Did Filenames Have Extensions?

For those of you who haven't been around since ptero-dactyls provided CPU cooling, a *filename extension* is just the last bit of a filename — the part that follows the final *dot-whatever* (like .doc) period in the name. So the file called ILOVEYOU.VBS has a filename extension of VBS; MELISSA.DOC has the extension .doc, and so on.

Office programs are all hooked up to their allotted filename extensions. For example, files that end with .xls are assumed to be Excel spreadsheets; double-click an XLS file (or try to open one that's attached to a message), and Windows knows that it should run Excel, feeding Excel the file. Same with DOC and Word, PPT and PowerPoint, MDB and Access, and even the little-known PST and Outlook.

Using an Antivirus Product

These days, an antivirus package is an absolute necessity — not only to protect your Office files and programs but to protect Windows itself. Antivirus software is cheap, reliable, easy to buy (you can get it online), frequently updated (sometimes with e-mailed notifications), and the Web sites that the major manufacturers support are stocked with worthwhile information. I know people who swear by — and swear at — all the major packages (see Table 1-1).

Every Office user must

✔ **Buy, install, update, and religiously use one of the major antivirus products.** Doesn't matter which one.

✔ **Force Windows to show filename extensions.**

✔ **Be extremely leery of any files with the file-name extensions listed in Table 1-2.** If you download or receive a file with one of those extensions (perhaps contained in a Zip file), save it, update your antivirus package, and run a full scan on the file — *before* you open it

Table 1-1: The Major Antivirus Software Companies

Product	Company	Web Site
F-Secure Anti-Virus	F-Secure	www.f-secure.com
Kaspersky Anti-Virus	Kaspersky Labs	www.kaspersky.com
McAfee VirusScan	Network Associates	www.mcafee.com
Norton AntiVirus	Symantec	www.symantec.com
Panda Antivirus	Panda Software	www.pandasecurity.com
Sophos Anti-Virus	Sophos	www.sophos.com
Trend Micro PC-cillin	Trend Micro	www.antivirus.com

The final filename extension is the one that counts. If you double-click a file named Funny Story.txt.exe, **Windows treats it as an** .exe **file and not a** .txt **file.**

I cover many important details about antivirus software, its care, and feeding in *Windows XP Timesaving Techniques For Dummies*.

Table 1-2: Potentially Dangerous Filename Extensions

.ade	.adp	.asx	.bas	.bat
.chm	.cmd	.com	.cpl	.crt
.exe	.hlp	.hta	.inf	.ins
.isp	.js	.jse	.lnk	.mda
.mdb	.mde	.mdt	.mdw	.mdz
.msc	.msi	.msp	.mst	.ops
.pcd	.pif	.prf	.reg	.scf
.scr	.sct	.shb	.shs	.url
.vb	.vbe/.vbs	.wsc	.wsf	.wsh

Firewalling

The Slammer worm demonstrated, loud and clear, that Office users need to protect any PC that's connected directly to the Internet. Slammer slipped in through a little-used *port* (Internet connection slot), infected a particular type of Access database, and then shot copies of itself out that same unprotected port.

A *firewall* blocks your ports. It ensures that the traffic coming into your PC from the Internet consists entirely of data that you requested. A good firewall will also monitor outbound traffic in order to catch any bad programs that have installed themselves on your machine and are trying to connect to other PCs on the Internet.

Windows XP's Internet Connection Firewall works — and it's a whole lot better than nothing. But it's a big target: If you were writing Internet-killing worms, where would you direct your efforts? The upshot: Enable Internet Connection Firewall (which is in the process of being renamed *Windows Firewall*) by all means, but to guard against all intrusions, you want a third-party firewall as well.

Every Office user needs to ensure that a firewall — some firewall, any firewall — sits between his Office machine and the Internet.

If you have a PC that's connected directly to the Internet, you can enable Windows XP's Internet Connection Firewall by following these steps:

1. **Choose Start➪Control Panel➪Network and Internet Connections➪Network Connections.**

Windows presents you with the Network Connections dialog box.

If you're using Windows 2000, you need to choose Start➪Settings to get into the Control Panel.

2. **Right-click the connection to the Internet and then choose Properties➪Advanced.**

You see the Properties dialog box.

3. **Enable the Protect My Computer or Network by Limiting or Preventing Access to This Computer from the Internet check box.**

4. **Click OK.**

I have detailed instructions for setting up a firewall — including, notably, the free version of ZoneAlarm — in *Windows XP Timesaving Techniques For Dummies.*

 Version notes: Internet Connection Firewall is only available in Windows XP (unless you're running Windows 2003 Server — and if that's the case, you need all the help you can get).

Technique 2

Launching Office Quickly

Save Time By

✔ Activating Windows'
   Quick Launch toolbar

✔ Putting your most-used
   Office programs on the
   toolbar

✔ Changing the ToolTips so
   they don't get in the way

I don't know about you, but I use Outlook and Word about ten times as often as all my other programs combined. And I hate going through the click-click-click routine to start Word, in particular. If I try to choose Start➪All Programs➪Microsoft Office➪Microsoft Office Word 2003 before I've had my first latte in the morning, I'm more likely to run the Calculator than Word. By the tenth time I've clicked all the way through, I'm ready to eat my mouse.

Fortunately, Windows has a dynamite tray immediately to the right of the Start button that's called the *Quick Launch toolbar.* (You might not be able to see it yet. If not, don't worry because I show you how to bring it to life in this Technique.) That piece of oh-so-exclusive Windows screen real estate comes in mighty handy when you want to get a program — most notably, Word — up and running quickly.

Take a few minutes now to get your Quick Launch toolbar set up properly. You'll save at least that much time every day after it's going. If you follow along closely, you might discover a few rather obscure tricks that'll make Quick Launch a key part of your timesaving arsenal.

Empowering Quick Launch

Although the Quick Launch toolbar is the best place in the Windows universe to stick your Office applications, there's a small chance that you can't see it. (Amazingly, Windows XP Professional version, right out of the box, doesn't show the Quick Launch toolbar — whereas Windows XP Home does. Go figger.)

 Version notes: Office 97 shipped with a program called the *Office Shortcut Bar,* which many people still use. OSB had to be installed manually in Office XP, and it disappeared entirely in Office 2003. The Windows Quick Launch toolbar appeared in Internet Explorer 4, and I recommend that you use it rather than the OSB, no matter which version of Office you use. Quick Launch is much easier to configure, and far more stable.

Look immediately to the right of your Start button. Do you see a handful of icons there (as shown in Figure 2-1)? If so, the Quick Launch toolbar is alive and well on your PC. If not:

• **Figure 2-1: The Quick Launch toolbar sits immediately to the right of the Windows XP Start button.**

1. **Right-click any open area on the Windows taskbar, down at the bottom of your screen.**

2. **Select Toolbars and mark Quick Launch.**

Windows XP brings up the Quick Launch toolbar, as shown in Figure 2-1.

At the very least you should see icons for Internet Explorer, Outlook, your desktop (a handy button if a program freezes your machine or if you want to see the desktop without minimizing every window), and Windows Media Player. If you're unlucky, your Quick Launch toolbar will be crammed with junk from the manufacturer of your PC as well as every two-bit program you've ever installed.

 Quick Launch real estate should be guarded jealously. Only put your most-often-used programs on the toolbar. If you see any icons on your Quick Launch toolbar that you don't want, right-click them and then choose Delete. That doesn't get rid of the program, but it does free up room in a key location on your taskbar.

You might see a double chevron (>>) on the right edge of your Quick Launch toolbar (see Figure 2-2). If you do, so many icons are on the toolbar that Windows can't display them all in the space allotted.

• **Figure 2-2: A double chevron on the right indicates that your Quick Launch icons won't all fit.**

To increase the size of the toolbar and get rid of the double chevron

1. **Right-click any empty location on the Windows taskbar.**

2. **Clear the check mark next to Lock the Taskbar.**

3. **Click the dotted pattern at the right edge of the Quick Launch toolbar and drag it to the right.**

That lengthens the area that Windows reserves for the Quick Launch toolbar. Your hidden icons appear as you make more room for them.

4. **When the Quick Launch toolbar is big enough, right-click any empty location on the taskbar and check the line marked Lock the Taskbar.**

 Many people prefer to make their taskbar twice as tall as the default single layer. That doubles the size of the Quick Launch area. To do so, follow Steps 1 and 2 to unlock the taskbar, click the line at the top of the Windows taskbar and drag it up, and then follow Step 4 to lock the taskbar again.

Putting Office Apps on the Quick Launch Toolbar

You have several ways to put an icon for any Office application on your Quick Launch toolbar. This is the fastest, easiest way I know — but you have to follow the instructions carefully:

1. **Make sure that the Quick Launch toolbar is visible.**

See the preceding section.

2. **Choose Start⇨All Programs⇨Microsoft Office; then right-click the Office application that you want to put on the Quick Launch toolbar.**

In Figure 2-3, I right-clicked Microsoft Office Word 2003.

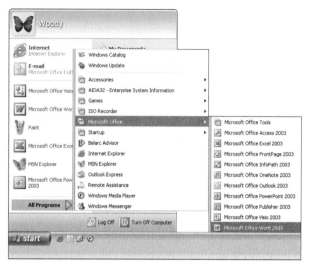

• **Figure 2-3:** Add an app to the Quick Launch toolbar from here.

> 💣 It's important that you *right*-click the Office application. If you *left*-click, you might drag the entry off your Start menu, and it's a monumental pain to put it back.

3. Drag the Office application down to the Quick Launch toolbar.

A thick, black vertical line appears on the toolbar (see Figure 2-4).

• **Figure 2-4:** The thick, black line indicates where Windows will drop your application.

4. Release the mouse button and choose Copy Here.

> 💣 Don't choose Move Here. If you do, you'll have to put the Office application back on the Start menu. (See the sidebar, "What If the Wheels Fall Off?")

Windows responds by placing an icon for the Office app on the Quick Launch toolbar. If you hover your mouse over the icon, you'll see a fabulously long, distracting description of what the application might or might not be able to do (see Figure 2-5). I tell you how to, uh, tone down the rhetoric in the section "Changing Quick Launch Names," later in this Technique.

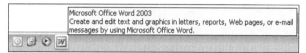

• **Figure 2-5:** You're permitted to snicker at Microsoft's overblown descriptions.

If you play around with the new icon, you'll discover that it works just like all the other icons on the Quick Launch toolbar. You can click it and drag it to a different location on the toolbar. You can even click and drag it off the toolbar, onto your desktop. You can right-click and copy, cut, or delete it. But most of all, if you click it once, Windows starts the application.

What If the Wheels Fall Off?

What do you do if you accidentally remove one of the Office applications from your Start menu? It happens more often than you think, and the cure isn't too bad — if you know the trick.

First, you must find the program associated with the missing application. Choose Start⇨My Computer and in the Windows Explorer window that appears, navigate to C:\ Program Files\Microsoft Office\OFFICE11. Look for one of the programs listed in the following table:

Application	Program Name
Access	msaccess.exe
Excel	excel.exe
FrontPage	frontpg.exe
InfoPath	infopath.exe
OneNote	onenote.exe
Outlook	outlook.exe
Picture Manager	ois.exe

(continued)

Application	Program Name
PowerPoint	`powerpnt.exe`
Publisher	`mspub.exe`
Word	`winword.exe`

After you find the program, follow these steps:

1. **Right-click the program and choose Send To⇨ Desktop (Create Shortcut).**

2. **Click X in the upper-right corner of Windows Explorer and then go back to your desktop.**

3. **Right-click the newly created icon and choose Cut.**

   That puts a shortcut to the Office application on the Windows Clipboard.

4. **Right-click the Start button and choose Explore All Users.**

5. **In the window that appears, navigate to the `Start Menu\Programs\Microsoft Office` folder.**

6. **Right-click the right side (see the following figure) and choose Paste.**

That puts a shortcut to the Office application on the Start⇨ All Programs⇨Microsoft Office menu for anyone who uses the PC. You probably want to change the name that appears on the menu. (*Shortcut to MSACCESS* is a bit, uh, obtuse.) I discuss how to change the name in the next section.

 Although Office 2003 programs are found in the \OFFICE11 folder, Office XP programs are in a similar folder called \OFFICE10, and Office 2000 programs are in one called \Office. The rest of the procedures apply to any version of Office, although the structure of the Start menu is quite different in Office XP and earlier.

 The Windows Quick Launch toolbar isn't limited to programs. In fact, you can put commonly used documents on the toolbar, spreadsheets, presentations — whatever strikes your fancy. Simply navigate to the document you like (either in Windows Explorer or in one of Office's Open or Save As dialog boxes), right-click the document, and drag it down to the Quick Launch toolbar. Release the button and then choose Create Shortcut Here.

Changing Quick Launch Names

Talk about intrusive verbiage! The ToolTips that Microsoft puts on its Office applications read like novels. (A *ToolTip* is the info box that pops up when you hover your mouse over an icon.) When I'm scanning Quick Launch icons, the last thing I need is to wade through an in-yer-face ToolTip such as the one in Figure 2-5, or "Excel / Perform calculations, analyze information, and manage lists in spreadsheets or Web pages by using Microsoft Excel." As my Silicon Valley Girl diction coach would intone, *gag me with a RAM chip.*

Fortunately, it's easy to change the ToolTip. Unfortunately, it isn't quite as simple as you might think: If you right-click (most) Quick Launch icons, choose Rename, and then give the icon a new name, that name appears as the ToolTip. Unfortunately, Office applications aren't so well-behaved. Here's how to change the names and protect the innocent (which is to say, us):

1. **Right-click the icon in the Quick Launch toolbar whose ToolTip you want to eviscerate . . . er, change.**

2. **Choose Properties.**

Windows shows you the Properties dialog box for that particular Quick Launch icon.

3. **Click the General tab.**

You have to start on the General tab because that's where the first line of the ToolTip originates.

4. **In the text box at the top of the General tab, change the wording to a better (shorter/more descriptive) ToolTip.**

In Figure 2-6, I changed *Microsoft Office Word 2003* to read simply *Word 2003.*

5. **Click the Shortcut tab (see Figure 2-7).**

6. **Delete the garbage in the Comment box.**

7. **Click OK.**

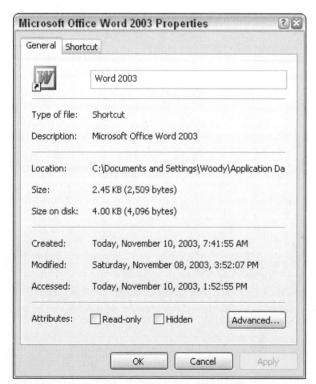

• **Figure 2-6: Make the ToolTip read something short and sensible.**

• **Figure 2-7: All the text in the Comment box gets shoveled onto the ToolTip.**

Now hover your mouse over the icon in the Quick Launch toolbar. Compare Figure 2-8 with Figure 2-5. Much easier and faster to use, wouldn't you say?

• **Figure 2-8: The lean, no-nonsense face of an optimized Word Quick Launch ToolTip.**

Changing Start Menu Names

I don't know why Microsoft insists on using such high-falutin' names on my Start menu. You might be more prescient than me, but it takes my eyes forever to bypass the marketing junk and cut to the heart of the matter. Staring at a Start menu like the one in Figure 2-3 gives me the shivers. I see the name *"Microsoft Office" **12 times*** before I get down to the application I need.

You know, the programmers at Microsoft laugh at all this pretense. It slows you down and serves no purpose but to pay homage to the Redmond Marketing Miracle. Save your eyes and maybe a little time by cutting out the junk.

Fortunately, taking control of all the distracting verbiage is easy. Here's how:

1. **Right-click the Start button and choose Explore All Users.**

Windows Explorer appears, located at the `C:\Documents and Settings\All Users\ Start Menu` folder (see Figure 2-9).

2. **On the left, double-click Programs.**

Windows Explorer shows you folders for the high-level items that appear on the Start⇨ All Programs menu. Compare the folder list here with your Start menu, and you see how the folder names and menu names correspond directly.

3. **Right-click the Microsoft Office folder, choose Rename, and type a better (shorter and/or more descriptive) name.**

You might want to make it MS Office 2003, but you can choose anything you like.

4. **Double-click your newly renamed Office folder.**

Windows Explorer shows you a list of shortcuts to all your Office programs.

5. **One by one, right-click each program, choose Rename, and type in a better (shorter and/or more descriptive) name.**

6. **Click X in the upper-right corner of Windows Explorer.**

7. **Choose Start⇨All Programs and take a look at all your new, shorter, more descriptive Office entries (compare Figure 2-10 to Figure 2-3).**

I find it much easier and faster to crank up the Office programs when I don't have to wade through *Microsoft Office* 12 times.

• **Figure 2-9: The Start Menu structure that compares to the menu items you see in Figure 2-3.**

• **Figure 2-10: The new Start menu consisting of names you choose.**

Technique 3

Organizing My Documents for Speed

Save Time By

- ✔ Thinking through the ways you use documents
- ✔ Setting up My Documents to reflect the way you work
- ✔ Saving documents to the right folder — the first time
- ✔ A place for every thing, and every thing in its place

I can't count the number of hours that I've lost looking for documents that weren't sitting where they should be.

Office gives you many ways to search for documents — complex, sophisticated, needle-in-the-haystack methods that work remarkably well. But the best way to find a document quickly is to look for it in the most obvious place. In order to do that, of course, you must *have* a most obvious place.

No two people organize things the same way. Your closet doesn't look like my closet (thank heaven); your desk doesn't look like my desk (if you can find your desk). But there are a few tricks to organizing yourself — and your computer — that seem to work for most people.

At the heart of it: *a place for everything, and everything in its place.* Your mom was right. I bet she even told ya so.

Understanding Your Requirements

Robert Heinlein invented the perfect term for this technique: to *grok*. In order to grok the way you use documents, you need to understand not only the content of the documents themselves, but you also have to understand their context — that is, the way they fit into the larger scheme of things. In order to get your documents organized in a way that they'll stay organized, you have to grok your requirements.

Most people start by putting everything in My Documents. After a week or a month, My Documents has a few dozen (or a few hundred) documents, so they put a new folder under My Documents, move half the docs over to the new folder, and start flipping a coin every time they save a new doc, trying to decide which folder it goes into.

Weeks turn into months turn into years, and the folders start growing like thistles. Pretty soon, you have folders in one part of My Documents that really should be in another part of My Documents, except they really don't fit there, either, and wouldn't it be easier to put two copies of this document in those folders, and. . . . You get the idea.

 You'll save an enormous amount of time, day after day, if you come up with a framework for storing your data in ways that make it easy to decide where to save your documents and to find where a specific kind of document was saved.

Here's how I suggest you go about thinking through your requirements:

1. **Forget about computers.**

People stumble all over themselves trying to second-guess folder structures and network topologies. Fuhgeddaboutit. For the moment.

2. **Think about what you need to organize.**

Are you mostly concerned about reports? Memos? Products? Courses? Customers?

3. **Take a pen and sketch out the major groups.**

Yes, a real pen. Or use OneNote (see Figure 3-1). (Although OneNote is billed as a member of the Office 2003 System, most people have to pay extra for it.)

4. **Within each group, sketch out what subgroups might be involved.**

For example, in my Books group, I include my recent books. I should also include my older books, but I don't refer to those very often, so they should probably go at an even lower level (see Figure 3-2).

5. **Group and regroup until you get a manageable mess.**

For example, if you have 100 clients, each of whom requires many documents, consider grouping the clients by type.

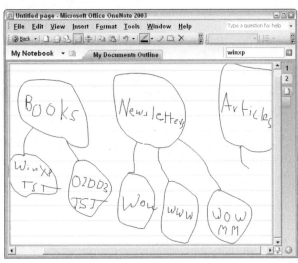

• **Figure 3-1:** A rough sketch of the kinds of things I work with every day.

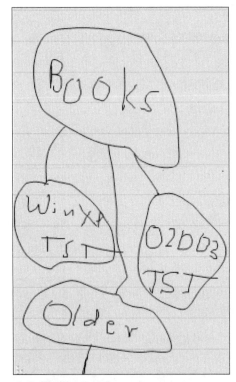

• **Figure 3-2:** Fleshing out the major groups.

6. **Start thinking about computers again.**

When you have an eagle's eye view of your data needs, it's time to start shoehorning all that into a structure for My Documents.

 There's a natural tendency to put all your spreadsheets in one place, all your presentations in another, and all your Word documents in yet another place. Try to avoid prejudging documents based on the application in which you created them. The documents and the Visio drawings that you send to Dr. Jones for her practice should be in the same folder (or group of folders) as the Word documents that you send to her. You'll find it much easier and more efficient to organize documents based on their content — not their appearance.

7. **Don't forget the oddball requirements.**

Everybody needs a folder for taxes. Most people need folders for family, or the house, or the Boy Scout Troop. Think, think, think.

Translating Requirements to Reality

In the preceding section, I talk about figuring out your requirements. In this section, I show you how to translate those requirements into reality. My goal: to make it easy, fast, and a no-brainer to drill down to the correct location for every document that you create as well as every document that you need to retrieve. If it takes you more than a minute to find a document, you're better off using Office's Search window.

With your requirements written down from the previous section

1. **Mark the folders that have to be shared, either with other people on your computer or with other computers on your network.**

Those folders should all go into Shared Documents. Some folks think that's tantamount to being banished to Siberia. Don't worry. It's one-click easy to get into Shared Documents from all the Office dialog boxes when you use the tricks that I discuss in Technique 4.

 If you've identified documents or groups of documents that require ongoing collaboration — that is, if many people are going to be working together to get them whipped into shape — you're a candidate for a SharePoint portal. Setting up a portal isn't easy, but after the beast is in place, it's relatively simple to work with the documents inside. See www. microsoft.com/sharepoint/index.asp for details.

2. **Mark any folders that have to be kept private.**

If you have folders that absolutely must be kept private — even from other people using your computer — and you aren't connected to a Big Corporate Network with protection already in place, you need to look into Windows XP's Simplified File Sharing or Windows 2000/2003's Share capabilities.

You can find an extensive discussion of Windows XP file sharing and its limitations in *Windows XP Timesaving Techniques For Dummies.*

 Don't tell Windows XP to mark any folders as Private until you completely understand the consequences of doing so. The Windows XP documentation is abysmal. If you lose your password, you might never be able to get the data back. Look twice before you leap!

 If you have sensitive files, consider password protecting the individual files (or zipped folders of files) instead of using the Windows method of protection. (To password-protect a file in any of the Office 2003 applications, choose File⇨Save As, click the Tools drop-down menu, and choose Security Options.) Office's password routines work surprisingly well, although they can be cracked.

3. **Choose Start⇨My Documents and start fleshing out the folder structure that you wrote down.**

No doubt you already know that you can add new folders by right-clicking an existing folder and choosing New⇨Folder.

My initial folder structure appears in Figure 3-3.

• **Figure 3-3: The folder structure that I use every day.**

 If you have more than 20 or so folders inside a folder, you have too many. It'll take too long to look through them while you're drilling down. Try to group and consolidate them. It's much faster to click through one extra level and only look at a few folders than it is to scan a bunch of folders all at once.

4. **When you've finished fleshing out My Documents, select Shared Documents on the left (under Other Places) and continue adding folders to Shared Documents.**

Of course, you can click, drag, or right-click and rename any existing file or folder to get it whipped into this new scheme of things.

 Never, ever keep two copies of a document. If you do, your life will be forever more complicated than is necessary. If you bump into a document — or even a folder — that should go into two places at once, stick it in the most likely location and then create a shortcut to the document (or folder) in the second location. To do so, right-click the original document (or folder) and choose Copy. Navigate to the secondary location, right-click on a blank spot, and choose Paste Shortcut.

 The preceding tip applies emphatically for files and folders on networks! If you have a file or folder that needs to be shared among many machines, stick one copy in the Shared Documents folder of the most likely PC and then put shortcuts to the file or folder on all the other machines.

 Need a quick, dirty, easy way to pass text, pictures, Web addresses, and miscellaneous vituperations among users and machines on a network? Because Microsoft doesn't have a Clipboard that lets you copy something on one machine and then paste it on another, I always set up my networks with one special Word document called `Network Clipboard.doc`. I stick that file in the Shared Documents folder of the PC that has the Internet connection. Then I go to each PC and put a shortcut to that file on the desktop of every user on the PC.

Technique 4

Drilling Down with the My Places Bar

Save Time By

- Customizing the bar on the left of the Open and Save As dialog boxes
- Adding locations to the My Places bar
- Deleting locations that you don't need

This Technique rates as a big payoff. By investing just a few minutes now, you can reap dividends every time that you open or save a new file. And unlike similar promises that litter your junk mail, this one is for real.

All the Office applications use the same dialog box when you choose File⇨Open or when you click the Open icon on the Standard toolbar. All the Office applications also use the same dialog box when you choose File⇨Save As or when you save a file for the first time. On the left side of those dialog boxes sits a timesaving aid of the first degree: *the My Places bar*, which you use to drill down to a specific location with just one click.

 Although the My Places bar rates as one of the top timesaving spots in all of Officedom, the method for customizing it will tie you in loops. You could spend a lifetime trying to second-guess how the bar really works. That's where this Technique comes in. Here, I explain how to customize your My Places bar, as shown in Figure 4-1, so that you can jump right to the places you use most often whenever you open or save a file.

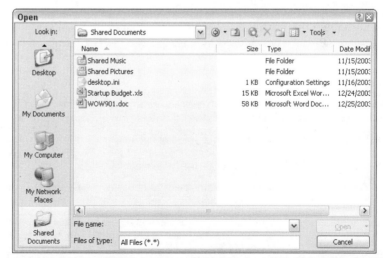

• **Figure 4-1:** This Technique explains how to create a customized My Places bar like this one, which includes a custom icon for the Shared Documents folder.

Checking Out the Default My Places Bar

The My Places bar (refer to Figure 4-1) appears on the left side of the Open and Save As dialog boxes in Word, Excel, PowerPoint, InfoPath, Access, FrontPage, OneNote, Publisher, and Visio. Outlook uses a similar, but subtly different, My Places bar.

 You might bump into discussions about the My Places bar in Windows itself. That's a completely different My Places bar: The Office developers didn't use the Windows dialog boxes, and making changes to the Windows My Places bar won't make any difference at all to the Office My Places bar.

Straight out of the box, Office 2003 has five icons in the My Places bar, as shown in Figure 4-2. As Table 4-1 explains, these aren't always the places that will get you in and out of your maze of folders lickety-split.

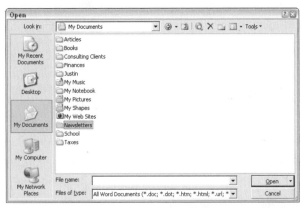

• **Figure 4-2: The My Places bar that Office sets up for you.**

Adding Locations to the My Places Bar

You can start putting the My Places bar to work for you by adding the locations that you use most often, which is easy to do.

TABLE 4-1: WHAT YOU NEED TO KNOW ABOUT THE DEFAULT MY PLACES BAR

My Places Icon	What It Does	Is It Timesaving?
My Recent Documents	This is a list of documents and shortcuts to folders maintained by Office — not by Windows — that you've recently opened.	The list is presented, confusingly, in alphabetical order, with shortcuts to folders jumbled in with the files. Worse, only certain file types (such as the common Office files) seem to be listed: Office can't keep a consistent list of all files that have been opened by non-Office programs. Upshot: Use this icon very much, and you'll lose more time than you'll save.
Desktop	Gives you one-click access to your Windows desktop.	This is very handy for one-off files and temporary storage.
My Documents	Goes straight to your My Documents folder — the same one that you see if you choose Start⇨My Documents.	If you organize your documents well (see Technique 3), this is the main springboard to most of your documents.
My Computer	Goes to the same place as choosing Start⇨My Computer.	Generally, if you find yourself using this icon, you're lost — or at the very least you haven't organized things very well.
My Network Places	If you have a network installed, goes to the same place as choosing Start⇨My Network Places.	Many people store their work on a network drive. If you do, consider adding a My Places icon specifically for the folder(s) on the shared drive that you commonly need.

Don't forget that the main reason for customizing the My Places bar is to speed up the way you use Office. If you have to leaf through too many icons, you'll get bogged down in the minutiae. Keep the list short, sweet, and simple — and don't be afraid to drop an icon the minute it stops pulling its weight.

1. **Bring up the My Places bar by, for example, starting Word and choosing File⇨Open.**

You see the Open dialog box (refer to Figure 4-2).

2. **Navigate to the folder that you want to put on the My Places bar.**

Use any method to get there: the drop-down list at the top of the Open dialog box, click the up-one-level button or the Back button, or even create a new folder.

3. **Select the folder that you want to add to the My Places bar by clicking it. Then in the upper right of the dialog box, choose Tools⇨Add to My Places.**

I almost always put new documents in my computer's Shared Documents folder so that other people working on my computer — or attached to my network — can get at them easily. In Figure 4-3, I click the My Computer icon on the left, click the Shared Documents folder once, and then choose Tools⇨Add to My Places.

• **Figure 4-3: Adding a folder to the My Places bar is enormously convoluted.**

Office responds by adding an icon to the My Places bar for the folder that you selected (see Figure 4-4).

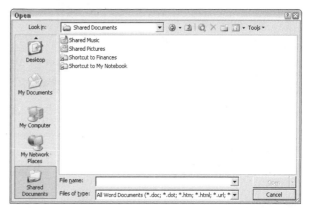

• **Figure 4-4: The new My Places bar entry appears at the bottom of the list.**

4. **Click either the Open or the Cancel button (bottom right), and all the Office applications will show the folder that you chose on the My Places bar.**

You might need to click the down arrow at the bottom of My Places bar to see your new icon. And making more room for those icons is the subject of the next section.

Showing More Icons on the My Places Bar

As soon as you start adding icons to the My Places bar, you'll soon feel claustrophobic. With all those icons bellying up to the bar, you can soon fill up the space allotted and thus can't see all your icons at once. And having to click the up and down arrows kind of defeats the purpose of having shortcuts in the first place. (You can see one of these up arrows above the Desktop icon in Figure 4-4.)

Fortunately, it's very easy to tell Office that you want it to show about twice as many icons — albeit smaller icons — on the My Places bar:

1. **Bring up the My Places bar by, for example, starting Word and choosing File⇨Open.**

You see the Open dialog box (refer to Figure 4-1).

2. **Right-click anywhere on the My Places bar and choose Small Icons.**

The My Places bar shows you twice as many icons — roughly ten at a time, instead of five (see Figure 4-5).

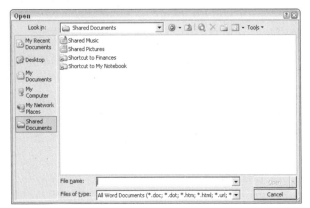

• **Figure 4-5:** My Places holds about five large or ten small icons.

3. **Click either the Open or the Cancel button (bottom right), and all the Office applications will show small icons on the My Places bar.**

Moving Icons on the My Places Bar

Of course, you should put your most frequently used icons at the top of the list. To do so:

1. **Bring up the My Places bar by, for example, starting Word and choosing File⇨Open.**

You see the Open dialog box.

2. **Right-click the icon that you want to move, and then choose either Move Up or Move Down from the context menu that appears.**

3. **Click either the Open or the Cancel button, and all the Office applications will show this new sequence of icons on the My Places bar.**

It's odd that Microsoft hasn't implemented a simple click-and-drag interface for the My Places bar, similar to, oh, the interface on the Start menu or the Quick Launch toolbar. Do you suppose the 'Softies ran out of money?

Removing Icons You Added

Removing icons that you've placed on the My Places bar is also very easy.

1. **Bring up the My Places bar by, for example, starting Word and choosing File⇨Open.**

You see the Open dialog box (refer to Figure 4-1).

2. **Right-click the icon that you want to delete and then choose Remove.**

3. **Click either the Open or the Cancel button, and the icon will be removed from the My Places bar in all the Office applications.**

Hiding Built-In Icons

Although removing your custom icons from the My Places bar is like falling off a log (see preceding section), hiding the $#@! built-in icons — My Recent Documents, Desktop, My Documents, My Computer, and My Network Places — requires a painful, time-consuming trip to the Registry. Yep. No doubt about it. Microsoft ran out of money when it was working on the My Places bar user interface.

 To give any of the built-in icons the heave-ho (personally, I ditch the My Recent Documents and My Computer icons), you should start by saving a backup copy of the existing Registry entries (in case you ever change your mind) before you remove any icons. Otherwise, you screw things up so badly that you want to get back to how things were. I explain how to save a backup later in this section.

 Standard Registry precautions apply. Follow the instructions here. You can look at anything you like, but don't change anything except what you originally went in to change.

Although it's extremely rare that an accidental change in the Registry will mess up anything significant — no matter how many scary warnings you see — you always face a teensy-tiny chance that if you change something, you'll break Windows. So don't change anything, except the entries that I talk about here, okay?

Backing up your My Places settings

First make a backup of your Registry settings for your My Places bar:

1. **Choose Start⇨Run.**

Windows cranks up the Run dialog box (as shown in Figure 4-6).

• **Figure 4-6: This way to the Windows Registry.**

2. **Type** regedit **and then press Enter.**

Welcome to the Registry Editor (as shown in Figure 4-7).

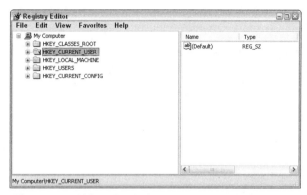

• **Figure 4-7: Although it isn't as scary as you think, you would be well advised not to change things willy-nilly inside the Registry.**

3. **Click the + signs until you navigate down to** HKEY_CURRENT_USER\Software\Microsoft\ Office\11.0\Common\Open Find\Places.

4. **Right-click the Places folder (key) and then choose Export.**

That's called *exporting the Places key* in Registry parlance (see Figure 4-8). The Registry Editor not only exports the key you've chosen, but it also automatically exports every key underneath the one you've chosen. In this example, if you export the Places key, you also automatically export the StandardPlaces and UserDefinedPlaces keys.

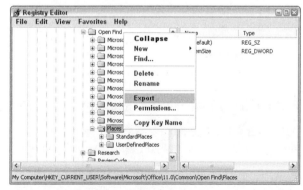

• **Figure 4-8: Export the Places key so you can bring it back if things go sour.**

The Registry Editor responds by showing you the Export Registry File dialog box (see Figure 4-9).

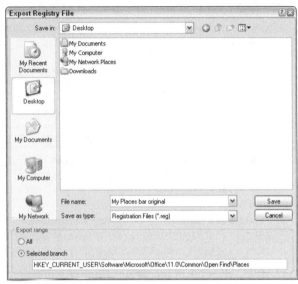

• **Figure 4-9: A Registry backup file ends with the filename extension** .reg.

5. **Give the backup file a good name and choose a location where you can find it. Then click Save.**

In Figure 4-9, I call the file My Places bar original.reg, and I put it on my desktop.

At this point, you have a full backup of all the Registry settings for your My Places bar. If anything goes bump in the night, find that file and double-click it. Your Registry will be magically restored to its original condition.

Tweaking My Places in the Registry

Only after you make a backup should you go in and make changes to the Registry. And I advise you not

to fiddle with any settings other than the ones I mention here. But you know that already.

To take specific built-in icons off the My Places bar:

1. **In the Registry Editor, double-click the Places key (see Figure 4-10), and then click the Registry entry for the icon you want to zap.**

See "Backing up your My Places settings" earlier in this Technique to find out how to open the Registry Editor.

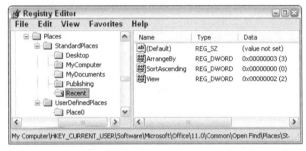

• **Figure 4-10: Settings for My Places bar built-in icons sit under the StandardPlaces key.**

Table 4-2 shows you which Registry entry corresponds to what icon.

TABLE 4-2: REGISTRY ENTRIES FOR THE MY PLACES BAR

My Places Bar Icon	Associated Registry Key
Desktop	Desktop
My Computer	MyComputer
My Documents	MyDocuments
My Network Places	Publishing
My Recent Documents	Recent

2. **If the icon you want to get rid of has an associated key with a value called Show (values are**

on the right-hand side), double-click Show to open the Edit DWORD dialog box, and then go to Step 4.

3. If the icon you want to get rid of has an associated key that does not have a value called Show, do the following:

   a. Choose Edit⇨New⇨DWORD Value. Regedit creates a new value called, disingenuously, New Value #1.

   b. Type Show. (In the process, you're overtyping New Value #1.)

   c. Press Enter twice. The Edit DWORD Value dialog box appears.

In Figure 4-11, the MyComputer key — which is associated with a folder that I want to take off the My Places bar — does not have a value called Show. So I choose Edit⇨New⇨DWORD Value. Then I immediately type **Show** (overtyping Regedit's automatically generated *New Value #1*), creating a new value called Show. Finally, I press Enter twice.

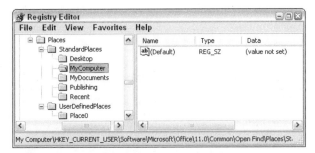

• **Figure 4-11: The MyComputer key doesn't have a value called Show.**

4. In the Edit DWORD Value dialog box (see Figure 4-12), type the numeral 0 (zero) in the Value Data box and then click OK.

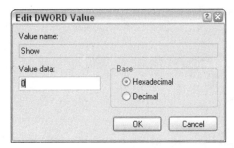

• **Figure 4-12: The Show value should be set to 0 (zero).**

At this point, each icon you want to delete should have a value called Show, which has been set to zero (see Figure 4-13). The data 0x00000000 (0) is, as you probably guessed, just plain zero.

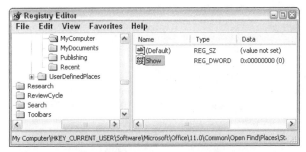

• **Figure 4-13: The MyComputer key now has a Show value that's set to zero.**

5. Choose File⇨Exit to leave the Registry Editor.

 You can't delete all the built-in icons on the My Places bar. If you try, Office will put the Desktop icon on the bar.

Test your settings by starting one of the Office applications. Choose File⇨Open. The offensive icon(s) should be banished from the My Places bar (see Figure 4-14).

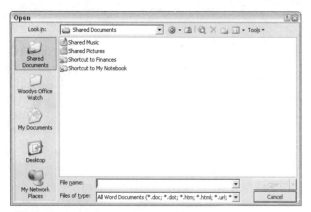

• **Figure 4-14:** My lean, quick My Places bar.

 Version notes: The My Places bar debuted in Office 2000, but there were no tools provided. You couldn't even switch between small icons and large icons. Office XP improved the situation substantially but still left out a number of bells and whistles, and XP wouldn't let you put some specific folders on the bar. If you're using Office 2000 or XP and want the full feature set — and much more — take a look at the $14.95 WOPR (Woody's Office POWER Pack) Places Bar Customizer, from www.wopr.com. Yes, *that* Woody is *this* Woody.

Taking Control of Icons That Won't Move Up and Down

Sometimes adding Show values as described in the preceding procedure will interfere with your ability to move icons up and down on the My Places bar. You know that the navigation has gone awry when you right-click an icon, and the Move Up and Move Down options are grayed out. (Another stellar example of the user interface that Microsoft didn't bother to improve.)

If you find that your Move Up and Move Down options are gone, you can assign locations on the My Places bar manually:

1. **Follow the preceding steps to create a new DWORD value called Index for each icon on the My Places bar.**

    Find Registry entries for any icons that you've manually assigned to the My Places bar in the UserDefinedPlaces key (refer to Figure 4-13).

2. **Set the value of Index to 1 for the icon that you want to appear at the top of the My Places bar.**

3. **Similarly, set the value of Index to 2 for the icon that you want to appear second, 3 for third, and so on.**

Technique

5

Backing Up Quickly and Effectively

Save Time By

- ✔ Choosing a backup program
- ✔ Backing up files the time-saving way
- ✔ Creating a backup
- ✔ Making your backups run at night

In this life, only three things are certain: death, taxes, and hard drive crashes. Yes, you need to back up your Office files. In fact, chances are good that a large percentage of the really, really important data that sits on your computer exists in Office files. You're no, uh, dummy. You know you need to back up.

If you're connected to a Big Corporate Network, there's a fair-to-middling chance that all your files are backed up for you already. Check with your network administrator. But if you aren't on a Big Corporate Network, you're on your own; Office doesn't back itself up.

Most Office users — particularly those with a lot riding on their Office data — would do well to consider buying a third-party backup program. In this Technique, you find out what to look for in a program, what your backup options are (and which ones will save you time), and how to create and schedule backups by using ZipBackup, a $30 package that runs rings around Windows' own.

If your hard drive ever breaks down . . . no, strike that . . . *when* your hard drive breaks down, you'll save hours, days, and weeks of abject fear if you have a good backup at hand.

Been there. Done that.

Backing Up: Why Pay More?

If your backup needs are modest and you don't particularly want to shell out any more cash, Windows XP Backup will do. You can bring up Windows Backup by choosing Start⇨All Programs⇨Accessories⇨System Tools⇨Backup. I talk about Windows XP Backup extensively in *Windows XP Timesaving Techniques For Dummies.*

On the other hand, if you have a lot riding on your Office files and you don't mind spending about $30, you can get a more versatile, easier-to-use backup that's sure to save your data and your time in the long run. But more on that later in this Technique.

What's wrong with Windows XP's Backup?

✔ Windows XP Backup makes you jump through all sorts of hoops to back up to multiple CDs. If your backups are less than 650MB in total, hey, no problem. But if you have an Outlook PST file like my Outlook PST file — along with a zillion graphics files and oodles of big spreadsheets — Windows XP Backup will only back them up into one big, monolithic file — too big to fit on a CD.

✔ Windows XP Backup creates backups in a weird, old-fashioned, tape-friendly format. The only way to pull data from a Windows XP backup is to use Windows XP Backup. And if you can't get Windows XP Backup to work right (for whatever reason), you're completely out of luck.

✔ Setting up Windows XP backup for unattended backups — such as ones that run in the middle of the night — takes a master's degree in computer science. See *Windows XP Timesaving Techniques For Dummies* for all the gory details.

✔ I might be hopelessly hip, and pardon me while I clean my yttrium shades on my NPL Super Black leather cape, Neo, but that tape-like Windows XP Backup interface just gives me the willies.

Choosing a Third-Party Backup Program

If you go looking for an alternative to Windows XP Backup, make sure that the package you buy

✔ Can break backups into chunks of a given size so that you can stick the backup chunks on CDs, Zip drives, multiple hard drives, or any other media that strikes your fancy

✔ Uses a nonproprietary format, such as the ubiquitous Zip format

If you use a backup program that produces normal files, such as .zip files (instead of arcane files meant for backing up to tape), bringing back an old copy of a file can be very quick and easy indeed.

✔ Runs unattended with a minimum of hassle

✔ Doesn't give you the willies

Personally, I use a little program called ZipBackup, which I explain how to use later in this Technique.

If you want to back up your entire hard drive, as I explain in the next section, look for a program like Norton Ghost (www.symantec.com) that will chomp through all the bits to create a complete copy of the hard drive in one step.

Choosing Which Files to Back Up

Here are the two extremes in the backup spectrum.

✔ Some folks believe that you should back up *everything* — that is, take a full snapshot of your hard drive — so you can restore the whole shootin' match in case your drive goes up in smoke.

✔ Others believe that you should select only the important folders for backup, letting the rest hang out to dry. After all, you have a copy of Windows and Office and all your applications on installation CDs already, so why waste the (considerable) space to keep a backup copy?

I used to side with the damn-the-torpedoes-back-it-all-up camp, but I'm starting to believe in a middle way. A backup of your entire hard drive can make it difficult to restore pieces of what you've backed up. Locating and bringing back that two-week-old copy of Financial Statement 2003.xls can take forever.

If you're concerned about saving time, backing up everything might not be the best approach.

 As a timesaving alternative to the full backup, I suggest performing a surgical backup that saves copies of only your Office files and settings (see "Saving your settings" later in this Technique). This minimalist approach makes a lot of sense if you're short on backup storage space or if you screw up a file and want to revert to the version you had last week. Of course, you want to take a snapshot of your entire hard drive occasionally, in case something disastrous happens. But for workaday backups, stick to the important stuff.

Finding your Office files

If you decide to back up only your Office files, make sure that you pick up all the file types listed in Table 5-1 when you create your backup. See "Running ZipBackup" later in this Technique for an example of how to create a backup.

 Read Table 5-1 closely to see that almost all the important Office files are stored in \My Documents, **possibly** \Shared Documents, **and in the** \Documents and Settings **folder associated with your user name. That's what I back up.**

TABLE 5-1: OFFICE 2003 FILES YOU NEED TO BACK UP

Filename	Description	Where They're Usually Located
.doc	Word document	\My Documents, \Shared Documents
.dot	Word template	C:\Documents and Settings\\<your user name>\Application Data\Microsoft\Templates, C:\Documents and Settings\\<your user name>\Application Data\Microsoft\Word\STARTUP
.xls	Excel worksheet	\My Documents, \Shared Documents
.xlt, .xla	Excel template	C:\Documents and Settings\\<your user name>\Application Data\Microsoft\Templates, C:\Program Files\Microsoft Office\Office11\Xlstart, C:\Documents and Settings\\<your user name>\Application Data\Microsoft\Excel\XLSTART
.ppt, .pps	PowerPoint presentation	\My Documents, \Shared Documents
.pot	PowerPoint template	C:\Documents and Settings\\<your user name>\Application Data\Microsoft\Templates
.pst	Outlook file (if you don't have Exchange Server)	C:\Documents and Settings\\<your user name>\Local Settings\Application Data\Microsoft\Outlook
.dic	Custom dictionary	C:\Documents and Settings\\<your user name>\Application Data\Microsoft\Proof
.acl	AutoCorrect entries (unformatted)	C:\Program Files\Microsoft Office\OFFICE11\1033 (US English)
.mdb	Access database	\My Documents, \Shared Documents

Saving your settings

When you back up your data, you should also back up your settings. If something goes wrong, it can take longer to get your settings reestablished than it can to retype a letter or two or twenty.

Office's Save My Settings Wizard (Start⇨ All Programs⇨Microsoft Office ⇨Microsoft Office Tools⇨Microsoft Office 2003 Save My Settings Wizard) saves most (but not all) of your Office settings in an OPS file in the \My Documents folder (see Figure 5-1). I recommend periodically running the Save My Settings Wizard before you do a backup creating a new OPS file so that you can back it up with the rest of your Office data.

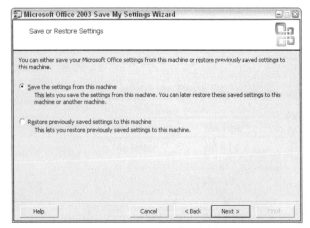

• **Figure 5-1:** Run the Office Save My Settings Wizard every month or so to create a file that contains your Office settings.

Running ZipBackup

Dozens and dozens of backup programs are on the market, ranging from decent routines written by weekend programmers to monster systems scaled back for the individual user.

I use ZipBackup because it has all the characteristics I describe earlier in this technique. Your mileage may vary, of course, but I wanted to take you

through the paces with ZipBackup to give you an idea of how to set up and run a backup program that's more adaptable and more attuned to the typical Office user than Windows XP's backup.

 ZipBackup normally costs $39.95, but *Office 2003 Timesaving Techniques For Dummies* readers can buy it for just $29.95 by going to www.zipbackup.com/partners/tstfd. You can download the trial version of ZipBackup from www.zipbackup.com.

To create a backup using the ZipBackup Wizard

1. **Choose Start⇨All Programs⇨ZipBackup⇨ ZipBackup.**

The ZipBackup Wizard appears.

2. **Mark the Backup Files to a Zip File radio button and then click Next.**

The wizard asks you to choose what kinds of files you want to back up (see Figure 5-2).

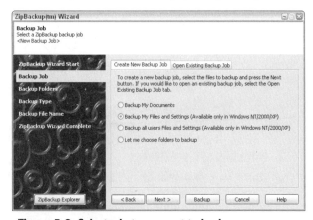

• **Figure 5-2:** Select what you want to back up.

3. **Choose the general category of backup that you want to perform and click Next.**

Don't worry if you don't see exactly what you want. In Figure 5-2, I choose to back up my files and settings.

4. **The wizard gives you an opportunity to add or remove folders from the ones that it chooses** (see Figure 5-3). If you want to change ZipBackup's selected folders, mark or clear the check boxes on the list and then click Next.

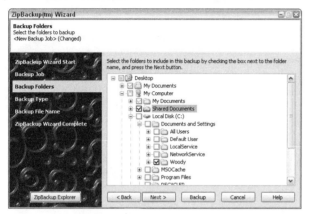

• **Figure 5-3:** Add or remove folders from the wizard's recommended list.

As I explain earlier in "Choosing Which Files to Back Up," you can back up all your files or back up just your Office files for easier retrieval. If you back up only Office files, refer to Table 5-1 for a handy list of files to select.

In Figure 5-3, I added the \Shared Documents folder because that's where I commonly put documents that need to be backed up.

5. **ZipBackup presents you with a choice of which folders to include in the backup (see Figure 5-4). See Table 5-2 and click the appropriate button; then click Next.**

ZipBackup asks what kind of backup you want to make. This is a fairly standard list, and no matter what backup package you use, you'll likely have similar (if not identical) choices. Table 5-2 details the choices and their implications; if you have space, choose Normal.

6. **Choose a filename and location, using the check boxes to append the current date and time, if you like. Then click the Backup button (see Figure 5-5).**

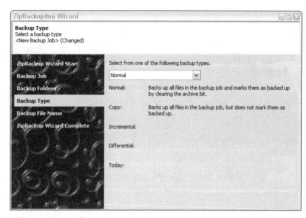

• **Figure 5-4:** Choose a backup type.

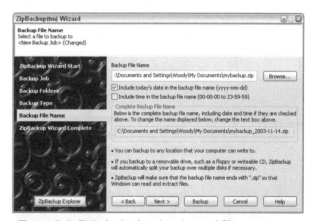

• **Figure 5-5:** Pick the backup location and filename.

 I recommend including the current date in the filename, if only to avoid overwriting older backups.

ZipBackup displays its progress as it performs the backup, which can take a great deal of time if you've selected many files. While the backup is under way, your machine will run like molasses, so this is a good time to download that copy of *War and Peace* or go get a latte.

7. **When ZipBackup finishes, the "tah-dah" window at the end gives you an option to view a summary report. Click View and verify that the backup finished properly. (See the** Completed **line in Figure 5-6.)**

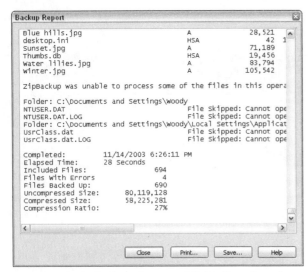

```
Backup Report                                              ⊠
  Blue hills.jpg                     A         28,521  ▲
  desktop.ini                        HSA           42  1
  Sunset.jpg                         A         71,189
  Thumbs.db                          HSA       19,456
  Water lilies.jpg                   A         83,794
  winter.jpg                         A        105,542

  ZipBackup was unable to process some of the files in this opera

  Folder: C:\Documents and Settings\woody
  NTUSER.DAT                          File Skipped: Cannot ope
  NTUSER.DAT.LOG                       File Skipped: Cannot ope
  Folder: C:\Documents and Settings\woody\Local Settings\Applicat
  UsrClass.dat                        File Skipped: Cannot ope
  UsrClass.dat.LOG                    File Skipped: Cannot ope

  Completed:        11/14/2003 6:26:11 PM
  Elapsed Time:      28 Seconds
  Included Files:          694
  Files with Errors:         4
  Files Backed Up:         690
  Uncompressed Size:  80,119,128
  Compressed Size:    58,225,281
  Compression Ratio:        27%                            ▼
  ◄                                                  ►

           [ Close ]  [ Print... ]  [ Save... ]  [ Help ]
```

• **Figure 5-6: ZipBackup gives you full details on how the backup completed.**

The ZipBackup summary report usually says that several system files couldn't be backed up. As long as the files involved are clearly system files, you're okay. (If some other files weren't backed up, try opening them to see whether there's a problem.) When you're happy with the results, click the Close button.

8. **When ZipBackup asks whether you want to save your Backup Job, click Yes.**

9. **In the Save As dialog box that appears, choose a convenient location and click Save.**

It's important to save the job if you want to set ZipBackup to run unattended, which I explain how to do later in this Technique.

 Regular workaday backups can go on the same hard drive as the original files, which makes it easier to retrieve an old version of a file that you accidentally clobber. But from time to time, you should also make copies of all your important data and store that backup on a different drive. In fact, for real disaster recovery, you should store those complete backups in a different building.

10. **Click Close twice to return to Windows. You're done.**

TABLE 5-2: BACKUP CHOICES

Type	Description	Timesaving Bonus Info
Normal	Backs up all files in the folders that have been selected, regardless of when they were last modified. Each file is marked as backed up by setting the *archive bit* of each file to zero. (Windows sets the archive bit to one when the file is modified.)	This option produces the largest backup file, but it also makes it faster and easier to find the latest backup of any particular file because all the files have been backed up.
Copy	Same as Normal but the archive bit is not changed.	Because the archive bit isn't changed back to zero, copying doesn't mark the file as backed up. That leads to unnecessarily big backups.
Incremental	Backs up all the files in the selected folders that have their archive bit set to one. Marks files as backed up by setting the archive bit to 0 (zero).	Produces the smallest backup files, but you might have to hunt through many backups to find the latest version of a specific file.
Differential	Same as incremental but the archive bit is not changed.	Because the archive bit isn't changed to zero, differential backups don't mark the file as backed up. That leads to unnecessarily big backups.
Today	Backs up all the files in the selected folders that were modified today. Does not change the archive bit.	Use this type only if you consistently and reliably run backups every day.

Scheduling ZipBackup

ZipBackup's reliance on standard, old, everyday Zip files, as well as its ability to split files across multiple CDs, are admirable. But its ability to run unattended, while you sleep, will really save you time.

To schedule regular backups

1. **Follow the steps in the preceding section to run a backup and save the settings in a ZB file.**

2. **Choose Start⇨All Programs⇨ZipBackup⇨ ZipBackup.**

The ZipBackup Wizard appears.

3. **On the lower left, click the ZipBackup Explorer button.**

ZipBackup goes into its more-advanced Explorer mode.

4. **Choose File⇨Open and open the ZB file that you created in the preceding section, "Running ZipBackup."**

ZipBackup Explorer shows you all the settings for that particular backup job (see Figure 5-7).

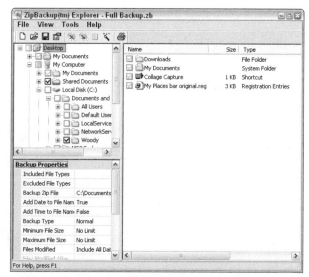

• **Figure 5-7:** Bring back the specific backup job that you want to run periodically.

5. **Verify that you have the correct folders selected in the upper-left pane.**

6. **Choose Tools⇨Schedule Backup Jobs.**

ZipBackup shows you the Schedule Backup Jobs dialog box (as shown in Figure 5-8), with your current job highlighted.

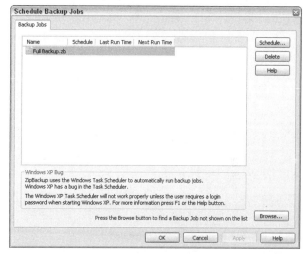

• **Figure 5-8:** Heed the warning at the bottom of this dialog box!

7. **Click the Schedule button, and in the Scheduled Task dialog box that appears, click the Schedule tab (see Figure 5-9).**

8. **Choose a schedule that you like — backups run best when you aren't anywhere near your PC — and click OK.**

Windows XP's scheduler asks you for a password (see Figure 5-10).

9. **Type in your Windows password and then click OK.**

 The password that you type in this step must match the password on your account *at the time the scheduled backup is run*. If you ever change your Windows password, you need to go back into the scheduler and change the password here as well.

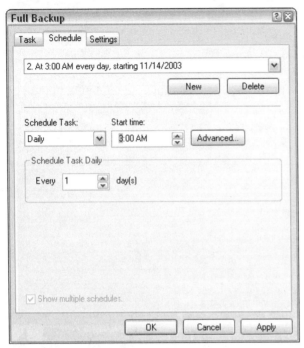

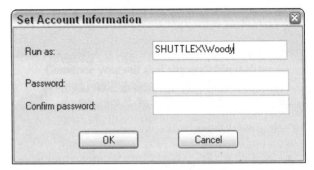

• **Figure 5-10:** The password you provide must match the account's password when the scheduled backup runs.

10. Click OK on the Schedule tab and then choose File⇨Exit to get out of ZipBackup.

Providing that your password matches, the backup will run at the time you specify.

After the first scheduled run, check to make sure your backup ran correctly. Follow Steps 1 through 6 above and verify the Last Run Time entry in the Schedule Backup Jobs dialog box.

• **Figure 5-9:** Set the backup schedule here.

Technique

Keeping Office Up-to-Date

Within two weeks of its official launch date, Microsoft released three major patches to Office 2003. Right out of the starting gate, Office 2003 appears to be the most frequently patched Office version in Microsoft history.

If you run Exchange Server — even a little Exchange Server on a Windows Small Business Server network — and you rely on the automatic Office updater to keep your machine patched, you missed two of the three Office 2003 patches: Outlook 2003 breaks Exchange Server, you have to patch Exchange Server separately (two times!), and those patches aren't available — indeed, aren't even *mentioned* — on the Office update site.

All the Office and Windows components have become so thoroughly intertwined (see Technique 1) that keeping on top of Office and Windows updates makes me feel like Rex Harrison officiating at a pushmi-pullyu Celebrity Death Match.

This Technique shows you when you can trust the automatic Office updater . . . and what to do when you can't. (Although Office 2003 is my prime concern, this Technique also includes specific, hard-to-find details for installing the latest fixes to Office 97, Office 2000, and Office XP.) You can save a lot of time and worry by patching Office, the right way, the first time.

Patching Jargon: A Rose by Any Other Name

You can tell a lot about a profession by looking at its *jargon* — the words that insiders use to convey large amounts of information in a staccato conversation. The chaos surrounding Office (and Windows) patching gets reflected in the jargon of the patchers.

I use the term *patch* to mean a piece of software that alters another piece of software. Patches are supposed to fix problems. I say that in a non-judgmental way. Honest.

The Microsoft Knowledge Base — Quickly

All Microsoft security communication with the vast, unwashed masses goes through the *Knowledge Base*, which is Microsoft's giant collection of accumulated wisdom about all its products (only a small part of which is visible to the public, starting at `http://support.microsoft.com`). Patches are numbered, and those numbers refer to Knowledge Base (KB) articles. If you work with security patches, you use the Knowledge Base extensively.

If you find yourself bobbing in and out of the Knowledge Base frequently, you can set up Internet Explorer so that it goes directly to a specific KB article when so bidden: Type **kb 831527** in Internet Explorer's Address box, for example, and IE hops directly to Knowledge Base article 831527. I give full details in *Windows XP Timesaving Techniques For Dummies.*

Microsoft boasts an entire lexicon of terms revolving around patches and patching. Although the terms have official definitions (see Knowledge Base article 824684), they're more often honored in the breach than in the practice. Here's my best take on the real meaning of the terms that you'll hear most often:

✔ A **Security Bulletin** is a sequentially numbered advisory (such as MS03-050; see Figure 6-1) that Microsoft releases to alert customers to security-related patches. Every Security Bulletin has one or more related Knowledge Base articles that, in turn, refer to the software patch(es) covered by the Security Bulletin.

Microsoft Security Bulletin MS03-050   🖨 Print

Vulnerability in Microsoft Word and Microsoft Excel Could Allow Arbitrary Code to Run (831527)

Issued: November 11, 2003
Version: 1.0

See all Office bulletins released November, 2003

Summary

    Who should read this document: Customers who are using Microsoft® Excel or Microsoft Word

    Impact of vulnerability: Run code of attackers choice

    Maximum Severity Rating: Important

    Recommendation: Customers who are using the affected versions of Microsoft Excel or Microsoft Word should apply the appropriate security update at the earliest

---

• **Figure 6-1: Security Bulletin MS03-050, which refers to Knowledge Base article 831527.**

 Microsoft has been, uh, economizing on Security Bulletin numbers lately — releasing multiple security patches with a single bulletin number — probably as PR damage control. Mainstream press accounts frequently refer to the number of Security Bulletins that Microsoft has released as an indication of Windows and Office's unreliability. Don't be suckered. One Security Bulletin can contain multiple unrelated patches.

The system of bulletins and patches is unnecessarily complex because Microsoft makes it exceedingly difficult to correlate Security Bulletins (MS04-*xxx* numbers) with patches (which rely on Knowledge Base articles, such as 831527), which in turn are completely unrelated to Office version numbers (such as 11.5604.5703), which (do you see a pattern here?) might or might not have anything to do with individual files' version numbers. See the upcoming section, "Identifying Versions to Get Help," for further commiseration.

 Microsoft would have you believe that there's a difference between *Critical, Important,* and *Moderate* Security Bulletins (`www.microsoft.com/technet/security/bulleting/rating.asp`). Horsefeathers. In theory, *Critical* patches fix holes that can be exploited by some cretin without you doing a thing, and *Important* patches fix holes that require you to do something spectacularly dumb — click a file or answer Yes in a dialog box — to get zapped. But in practice, the labels are entirely arbitrary and change from day to day, in spite of all the fancy doublespeak. Don't waste time worrying about it.

✔ An **Update** is a patch that isn't particularly critical and doesn't relate to security. (If the patch were security–related, it'd trigger a Security Bulletin, right? Well, no. The world of Office patches is littered with inconsistencies. See KB articles 822036 and 824938 for examples of Office security updates that don't have Security Bulletins.) Updates are also associated with Knowledge Base articles and are generally referred to by their KB article number.

✔ A **Critical Update** is a patch that keeps Office from crashing, destroying data, or otherwise clobbering your valuable work (see Figure 6-2). Microsoft draws a distinction between a Critical Update and a *hotfix,* but I don't see any difference.

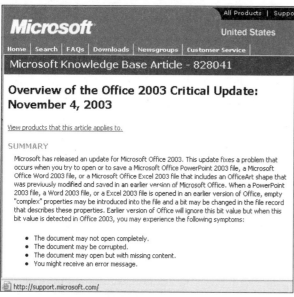

Microsoft All Products | Suppo
United States

Home | Search | FAQs | Downloads | Newsgroups | Customer Service |

Microsoft Knowledge Base Article - 828041

Overview of the Office 2003 Critical Update: November 4, 2003

View products that this article applies to.

SUMMARY

Microsoft has released an update for Microsoft Office 2003. This update fixes a problem that occurs when you try to open or to save a Microsoft Office PowerPoint 2003 file, a Microsoft Office Word 2003 file, or a Microsoft Office Excel 2003 file that includes an OfficeArt shape that was previously modified and saved in an earlier version of Microsoft Office. When a PowerPoint 2003 file, a Word 2003 file, or a Excel 2003 file is opened in an earlier version of Office, empty "complex" properties may be introduced into the file and a bit may be changed in the file record that describes these properties. Earlier version of Office will ignore this bit value but when this bit value is detected in Office 2003, you may experience the following symptoms:

- The document may not open completely.
- The document may be corrupted.
- The document may open but with missing content.
- You might receive an error message.

http://support.microsoft.com/

• **Figure 6-2:** Office 2003's first Critical Update.

✔ **Service Releases** are bunches of patches (and patches of patches to patches) that get released at once to make it easier to fix everything that's gone wrong before. From time to time, Service Releases include minor new features. Supposedly there's a difference between Service Releases, Service Packs, and Update Rollups, but it all sounds like marketing hogwash to me.

Outlook 2003 has a built-in spam filter (see Technique30) that requires constant updating. As this book went to press, it became apparent that Microsoft would release occasional (perhaps *sporadic* is a better term) updates to the spam filter, via the normal Office 2003 Update mechanism.

Finding (And Using) Office Update

Microsoft used to make it easy to find and use the Office Update site (`http://officeupdate.com`). Now you have to click through a page or two of commercials and "Ain't Office wunnerful" self-congratulatory drivel before you can get to the real content.

This is progress.

 Worse, the most important Office updates — including Critical Updates — might not even be directly accessible from the Office Update site.

If you have only one copy of Office 2003 to keep tamed, the fastest and easiest way to make sure that you're up-to-date is to rely on automatic update. Unfortunately, automatic update has some severe shortcomings, but as long as you're wary — and you only have one PC — the update approach works reasonably well:

1. **Start your favorite Office 2003 application.**

For detailed advice on Office 97, 2000, and XP, see the version-specific sections at the end of this Technique.

2. **Choose Help➪Check for Updates.**

Office launches Internet Explorer and takes you to the Office Downloads site (as shown in Figure 6-3). See all those ads? Microsoft is trying to sell you many things — and take some sting out of the fact that you're here to fix a hole in Office.

3. **Click the Check for Updates button.**

The Office Update automatic detection program kicks in, displaying a progress bar.

4. **Follow the instructions onscreen to download and install any outstanding updates.**

Note: You might need your original Office 2003 CD, so have it handy.

• **Figure 6-3: The Office Downloads site, formerly known as the Office Update site.**

Here are (at least) four problems with this one-size-fits-all approach to updating Office 2003:

✔ **You won't find all the pertinent patches.** Many Office problems manifest themselves as problems in other pieces of software (for example, the two Exchange Server patches that I discuss at the beginning of this Technique). You need to be ruthless in your pursuit of all patches — Windows *and* Office — to fix those ugly security holes.

✔ **Office might install patches that you don't want.** It's considered heresy, but the fact is that some patches do more harm than good. You should wait a day or two or three — maybe even a week or two — before installing a new patch, and see how much wailing and gnashing of teeth surrounds the release.

 I follow all new patches very closely (and with a jaundiced eye) at *Woody's Windows Watch,* my free, weekly electronic newsletter. Visit www.woodyswatch.com to subscribe.

✔ **If the updater gets screwed up, you might see wacky results.** The program that detects and installs updates might go bonkers. If the updater offers to install patches that just don't look

right — an Office XP update on an Office 2003 PC, for example — or if it stops working entirely, download and install the patch directly, as I describe in the next section.

✔ **If you have more than one copy of Office to update, you have to download the entire patch file for each one.** That's why Microsoft makes the patches available for download, as I describe in the next section.

Applying Patches Manually

If you have more than one PC running Office, it makes absolutely no sense to use the automatic updater, downloading those humongous patch files over and over again for each PC. Microsoft makes client version patches available for download, so you can clog up your Internet connection just once and then apply the patch on each PC, one by one. (*Client version* is Microsoft-speak for a patch that's applied to regular, old, everyday computers — *clients* as opposed to *servers.*)

The easiest way for Office 2003 users to find and download client version patches is

1. Go to www.microsoft.com/office/ork/2003/ admin/default.htm.

   Microsoft posts a list of all available patches to Office 2003 (see Figure 6-4).

• **Figure 6-4: The hard-to-find list of all patches to Office 2003.**

Do not click the link to the update on this page. If you do, you'll end up downloading an *administrative update* — a (typically huge) full-file version of the patch that you neither need nor want.

2. **Jot down the KB article number(s) of the patch(es) that you need.**

For example, in Figure 6-4, the first critical update to Office 2003 is listed as KB article number 828041.

3. **Bring up the Knowledge Base article associated with the patch.**

In this case, it would be `http://support.microsoft.com/?kbid=828041`; refer to Figure 6-2.

4. **Choose Edit➪Find (On This Page) and search for the phrase *client version*.**

Almost always, you end up at the download link for the downloadable version of the patch (see Figure 6-5).

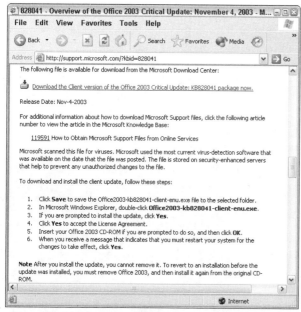

• **Figure 6-5:** The downloadable version of the patch is the *client version*.

5. **Download the patch and follow the instructions in the Knowledge Base to install it.**

The precise method for installing each patch varies a little bit, so make sure you take a few seconds to *RTFM* . . . ahem, read the tips from Microsoft.

 You might find it easier to run Office Update on one machine, jot down the KB article numbers based on that run (see Figure 6-6), and then use Steps 3–5 of the preceding to download and install the individual patch files on all your PCs. Assuming the updater is correctly identifying missing patches, anyway. That way, you'll download the updates twice, but the second download produces a file (a client patch) that you can simply transfer from machine to machine.

> **Office 2003 Critical Update: KB828041**
> The Office 2003 Critical Update: KB828041 offers the highest level of reliability available for Office 2003. This update fixes an issue in Word 2003, Excel 2003 and PowerPoint 2003 that occurs when opening a file last edited and saved in Office 2000. This update is applicable to the following Office 2003 products: Word 2003, Excel 2003, Outlook 2003, PowerPoint 2003, Access 2003, Publisher 2003, InfoPath 2003, FrontPage 2003, and OneNote 2003.
> More information...

• **Figure 6-6:** You can use the Office updater to retrieve a list of KB articles and then manually download and apply the patches.

Identifying Versions to Get Help

It should be very easy for you to tell which version of Office you're running. I don't mean, oh, Office 2003 versus Office 2000. That's easy. I mean you should start Word or Outlook, choose Help➪About, and be able to tell immediately which patches have been installed as well as which version of the program you're using. You can't — and I've been railing about this for years.

When you ask someone for help — more often than not, Microsoft tech support — you have to be able to provide the person who's helping you with specific information about the version you're using. Many times when you go diving through Microsoft's

Knowledge Base, trying to figure out what's wrong with Office and how to cure it, you have to know exactly which version you're running. Sometimes other manufacturers (especially antivirus companies) have problems with specific versions of Office, and you have to know what you're running before you can fix their problems. At this stage in Office's evolution, that means you have to use three separate tools: Office Help, Windows Explorer, and Microsoft's online revision sniffer.

When you start the program that's giving you fits and choose Help⇨About (for example, Help⇨ About Microsoft Office PowerPoint), the About dialog box (see Figure 6-7) reads something like *Microsoft Office PowerPoint 2003 (11.5529.5703)*. Here's what the numbers mean:

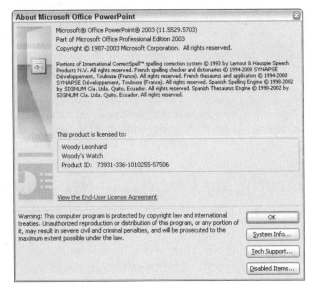

• **Figure 6-7: PowerPoint 2003's About screen.**

✔ The first numeral, 11, denotes Office 11 — what you and I know as Office 2003. If you see a 10, it's Office XP; a 9 represents Office 2000. Office 97's Help doesn't use this numbering system.

✔ The second number is the version number of the specific Office application program that's running. In this example, 5529 means that you're running version 5529 of the file `powerpnt.exe`.

(For a list of the application program names, see Technique 2.)

✔ The third number is the version of `mso.dll` that you're using. `mso.dll` is something of an uber-Office program, which is more or less the glue that holds Office together.

The version numbers listed in the About dialog box corresponds to what you will see if you go into Windows Explorer, right-click the file, choose Properties⇨Version, and look at the File Version number. In this example, if you right-click `powerpnt.exe`, choose Properties⇨Version, and look at the Product Version number, you see 11.0.5529. If you right-click `mso.dll` and choose Properties, the Product version number comes up 11.0.5703 (see Figure 6-8). Combine both of those version numbers and you end up with 11.5529.5703, the number in the Help⇨About dialog box.

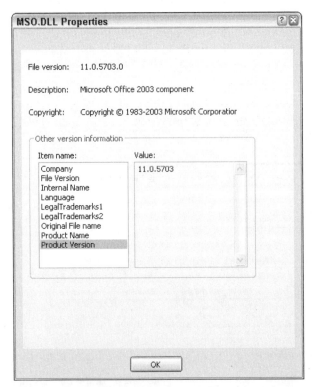

• **Figure 6-8: The About dialog box contains the version number of `mso.dll`.**

Keeping the version numbers straight is very important because certain combinations of Office program versions and `mso.dll` versions can cause untold grief. If you ever find multiple copies of the Office programs or `mso.dll` on your PC and want to know which copies are actually running, check their version numbers in Windows Explorer against the version reported in the Help➪About dialog box. Frequently, Knowledge Base articles will tell you which versions should or should not be running.

Unfortunately, not all patches to Office change the specific version numbers reported in the About dialog box. To get a complete list of revisions made to the version of Office 2003 on your computer, go to the Web site `http://office.microsoft.com/officeupdate/alreadyinstalled.aspx`, and wait for the updater to scan your system. You should be rewarded with a list such as the one in Figure 6-9.

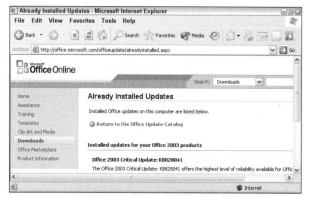

• **Figure 6-9: The only way to retrieve a full list of installed updates is by trusting the Office updater — a dicey proposition at best.**

Updating Office 97

Running Office 97 on Windows 98 (or Me) is like building a house of cards on top of a jackhammer. Still, tens of millions of people slog through that combination every day, and they deserve to get the best that Microsoft has to offer.

Microsoft likes to pretend that it doesn't support Office 97 any more, but it does. Both the November 11, 2003 security patches for Word 97 and Excel 97 and the October 16, 2002 security patch for Word 97 amply demonstrate Microsoft's continuing support for its legions of Office 97 customers.

Or maybe it demonstrates fear of the legions of product liability lawyers. Never mind.

 In spite of what you might read on (many!) Microsoft Web pages, the automatic Office updater doesn't work with Office 97. You have to perform all the Office 97 updates manually.

To make sure you have the latest Office 97 patches

1. **Start Word and choose Help➪About. If you do not see *Microsoft Word 97 SR-2* listed, go to** `http://office.microsoft.com/downloads/9798/sr2off97detail.aspx` **and install Office 97 Service Release 2b.**

Note that you might need to install Service Release 1 first. Check that Web page for details.

2. **Go to** `http://support.microsoft.com/?kbid=830354` **and download and install the Word 97 November 11, 2003 patch.**

This patch includes the MS02-059 October 16, 2002 patch (which was previously available only if you begged somebody at Microsoft to point you to it), the MS02-031 June 19, 2002 patch, and all previous patches.

3. **Go to** `http://support.microsoft.com/?kbid=830356` **and download and install the Excel 97 November 11, 2003 patch.**

Similarly, this patch includes all previous Excel patches.

4. **PowerPoint 97 has been patched since SR-2, but you have to contact Microsoft and ask to have the patch made available to you.**

See `http://support.microsoft.com/?kbid=310364` for details.

If you're still using Outlook 97, you're a better man than I: It drove me nuts. Microsoft distributed free copies of the Outlook 98 upgrade for more than a year. You could download it for free from http://microsoft.com until June, 1999 — around the time Office 2000 appeared. Since then, the only way to get the Outlook 98 upgrade is to buy a book (probably used) with Outlook 98 on the companion CD.

Updating Office 2000

I still think Office 2000 (now at Service Pack 3) represents the sweet spot of the Office suite. It's stable and capable — and it doesn't include all the onerous product activation hassles.

Here's how to bring your Office 2000 system up to date:

1. **Start Word and choose Help⇨About. If you do not see *Microsoft(r) Word 2000 (9.0.xxxx SP-3)*, go to** http://support.microsoft.com/?kbid=326585 **and follow the instructions there to install Service Pack 3.**

The key here is the SP-3 tag; the *xxxx* version number isn't important. If you don't see SP-3, install Service Pack 3.

2. **Run the automatic updater at** http://office.microsoft.com/officeupdate **to see whether you need any more patches, and then install as necessary.**

Chances are good that at the very least, you'll need the Word 2000 November 11, 2003 and Excel 2000 November 11, 2003 patches.

3. **Download and install Ken Slovak's ATTOPT utility, at** www.slovaktech.com/attachmentoptions.htm, **which I explain how to do in Technique 32.**

Outlook 2000 with SP-3 installed hides certain files attached to e-mail messages, and this utility enables you to take back control of attachments. The utility is free, but Ken asks for a $10 donation.

Updating Office XP

Office XP Service Pack 2 has been patched extensively — in fact, Service Pack 3 might have been released by the time you read this.

Here's how to bring Office XP up to speed:

1. **Start Word and choose Help⇨About. If you do not see *Microsoft Word 2002 (10.xxxx.xxxx) SP-2*, go to** http://support.microsoft.com/?kbid=325671 **and follow the instructions there to install Service Pack 2.**

The *xxxx* version numbers aren't important, but the SP-2 is. If you don't see SP-2, install Service Pack 2.

 If Microsoft has released an Office XP Service Pack 3, it should be noted on that Knowledge Base article. It should also be listed at http://support.microsoft.com/default.aspx?scid=fh;en-us;offxpset&product=ofxp.

2. **Run the automatic updater at** http://office.microsoft.com/officeupdate **to see whether you need any more patches, and then install as necessary.**

If you haven't updated them recently, you'll need the Word 2002 November 11, 2003 and Excel 2002 November 11, 2003 patches.

3. **Download and install Ken Slovak's ATTOPT utility, at** www.slovaktech.com/attachmentoptions.htm **(see Technique 32 for details).**

Outlook 2002, like Office 2000 SP-3, hides certain files attached to e-mail messages.

Technique 7

Disabling Automatic Hyperlinks

This is the number-one question I hear from Office users, all over the world, time and time and time again: How do I keep Office from screwing things up when I type a Web address or an e-mail address? I hear the question so often that I decided to devote an entire Technique to the topic.

As you might imagine, several epithets typically get thrown into the mix — and for good reason. Automatic hyperlinks is one of the most intensely stupid settings in all of Officedom.

 If you take a minute or two right now to turn off the ^%$#@! automatic hyperlinks, you'll save untold misery in the future. And it's not just your misery I'm talkin' about. Your readers hate it, too, even if they're too polite to mention it. Guaranteed.

Understanding IntelliNONsense

Once upon a time, somebody in Redmond decided it would be, like, really cool to have Office applications watch while you're typing things, and occasionally swoop in and make what you typed, you know, like better, cooler, and all that stuff, right?

I mean, if you type a Web address like **www.dummies.com**, you really want it to be blue and underlined, don't you? And you want it to be hot, too, so if anybody accidentally clicks it (Ctrl+clicks it in Office XP or 2003), you want them to be sent out to Office Never-Never Land and make them wait for a minute or two or more while Office launches Internet Explorer and IE tries to bring up the www.dummies.com Web page, yeah?

Microsoft calls it IntelliSense. I call it IntelliNONsense.

Unless you go in and change things, Word, Outlook, Excel, and PowerPoint all automatically modify typed Web addresses and e-mail address into underlined, blue links.

I wish I had a nickel for each time I've seen an underlined Web address or e-mail address in a major publication. It's one thing for *National Geographic* to alter the location of one of the pyramids at Giza, to goose things up electronically. It's another thing entirely to see an underlined Web address in print because the editors couldn't figure out how to turn the damnable thing off.

Want to get rid of the link, swiftly and easily? If you catch the transmogrification quickly enough while you're typing, click the Smart Tag that seems to appear immediately whenever Office does something dumb, and choose Undo Hyperlink. If the Smart Tag isn't around any more, right-click the link and choose Remove Hyperlink.

Hijacking a Link

Automatic links aren't just intrusive. If you come to accept them as just another annoying aspect of using Office, they can come back to bite you. Why? The link is more than skin deep.

If I type **www.woodyswatch.com** with automatic hyperlinks enabled, the address is converted into a link to the Web site www.woodyswatch.com. Innocent enough.

The thing is, these links can easily be hijacked and send you to site that's a bit, uh, unsavory, instead. All anyone has to do is right-click the automatically generated link and choose Edit Hyperlink. In the Edit Hyperlink dialog box that appears (see the following figure), someone can type a different Web address, and in the Text To Display box, retype the original Web address, hiding the actual address from the unsuspecting reader. (***Note:*** If you Ctrl+click the link, you can see where it actually leads.)

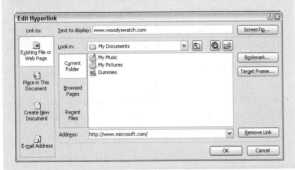

Hyperlinks are always subject to this kind of hijacking; it's not a deficiency in Office, by any means. But if you're inured to the danger because "Office always does that," you might be surprised some day when a suitably modified Web beacon (see Technique 29) finds its way into your Inbox or onto your desktop.

Turning Off Automatic Hyperlinks

All the Office 2003 applications allow you to take back control of your typed Web addresses and e-mail addresses, although details vary.

In Word 2003:

1. **Choose Tools⇨AutoCorrect Options and click the AutoFormat As You Type tab.**

Word has the most intrusive, er, extensive array of automatic formatting capabilities (see Figure 7-1).

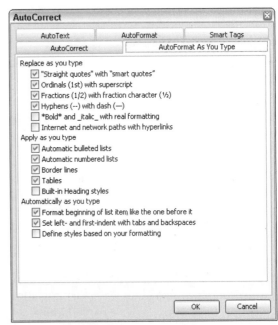

• **Figure 7-1: Take back control from Word's IntelliNONsense.**

2. Clear the Internet and Network Paths with Hyperlinks check box.

3. Click OK.

Word (and Outlook, when you use Word as your e-mail editor, which is the default setting) will no longer hijack your typed Web and e-mail addresses.

 To eliminate automatically generated links when you type e-mail messages, use the preceding steps to turn off automatic hyperlinks in Word. As Word goes, so goes Outlook: You can't have autolinking in one and not the other.

In Excel 2003:

1. Choose Tools➪AutoCorrect Options and then click the AutoFormat As You Type tab.

Excel's automatic formatting functions pale in comparison with Word's (see Figure 7-2).

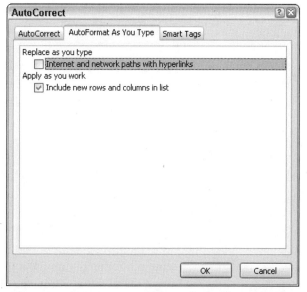

• **Figure 7-2: Eliminate hyperlink autoformatting in Excel.**

2. Clear the Internet and Network Paths with Hyperlinks check box.

3. Click OK.

Excel reverts to a less frenetic state.

In PowerPoint 2003:

1. Choose Tools➪AutoCorrect Options and click the AutoFormat As You Type tab.

PowerPoint stands second only to Word in its intrusiveness (see Figure 7-3).

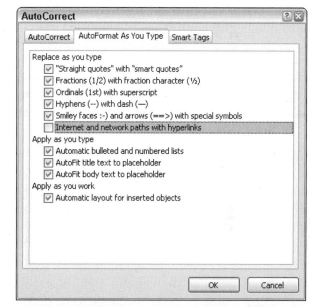

• **Figure 7-3: No more automatically generated links in PowerPoint.**

2. Clear the Internet and Network Paths with Hyperlinks check box.

3. Click OK.

PowerPoint won't take over Web addresses and e-mail addresses any more.

Creating a Manual Hyperlink — Quickly

On the rare occasion that you really *do* want a hyperlink, it's easy to roll your own:

1. Type the Web address (preceded by `http://`) or the e-mail address (preceded by `mailto:`) in your document (see Figure 7-4).

> mailto:woody@wopr.com

• Figure 7-4: To create your own mail link quickly, type **mailto:** followed by the e-mail address.

2. Select the stuff that you just typed.

3. On the Standard toolbar, click the Hyperlink icon (the one that looks like the Earth in chains).

The text that you typed turns into a link, formatted in blue and underlined.

 If you want to get rid of the http:// or the mailto: in the document, right-click the link, choose Edit Hyperlink (see Figure 7-5), and change the Text to Display text box to say whatever you like.

• Figure 7-5: Gussy up your quick link by deleting unwanted display text.

Technique

8

Digging with Research — Quickly

O ffice 2003 brought us all sorts of pains, not the least of which is the Research task pane. The Research pane hooks into Word, Outlook (when you're using Word to view or write a message, which is the default), Excel, and PowerPoint, and at times it hangs on the left edge of Internet Explorer.

Office 2003's Research pane includes some very powerful tools, including a fully functional version of Microsoft *Encarta,* which is the same good-but-not-excellent Microsoft encyclopedia that's available free online (www. encarta.com). (You might have paid big bucks for Encarta a few years ago — D'oh!) Add the 20-minute-delayed stock quotes and historic price charts, and you have the formula for time saving and time wasting on a massive scale.

The Research pane also includes a bunch of advertising fluff, designed specifically to convince you to part with your money — in exchange for information that's readily available on the Internet.

As long as you have a reasonably fast Internet connection, using the Research pane is considerably simpler — and possibly faster — than pulling out your old dictionary or encyclopedia and running the lookup manually. The results won't be as thorough as a trip through Google, say, but if you're looking for quick, adequate definitions and explanations, the Research pane is a decent place to start.

Fixing the Research Pane

Right out of the box, the Research pane is a great advertising tool, fully functional and ready to convince you to spend more money. Before I try to explain how to use the Research pane and its options quickly and efficiently, I strongly urge you to cut out the commercials:

1. **Start Word. Click the Research icon on the Standard toolbar (see Figure 8-1).**

Word brings up the Research task pane.

• **Figure 8-1:** The Research icon.

2. **Click Research Options at the bottom of the Research task pane.**

Office shows you the Research Options dialog box (as shown in Figure 8-2). The remainder of this procedure helps you decide which Research Options you need as well as which will only get in your way.

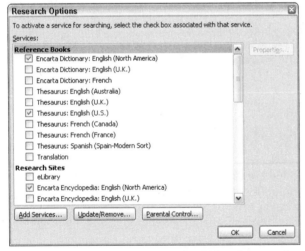

• **Figure 8-2:** This dialog box controls which references the Research pane searches.

3. **If you want Office to suggest translations for individual, common words, keep the Translation check box marked. But if you don't normally use machine translation (or if you're content to work with something like Google's Language Tools,** www.google.com/language_tools**), clear the Translation check box.**

When I use the Research pane, the automatic Translation just gums up the works, reporting that it can't find words that I don't want it to search for anyway. See "Looking in the Dictionary," later in this Technique.

4. **Unless you have an ongoing need to be teased by the first hundred words of a million magazine articles, clear the eLibrary check box.**

eLibrary will tell you that it found your Research task pane search item, show you the first few words of each magazine article, and then offer to show you the full articles for a price. This is not worth your time nor your money unless you really need access to the magazines that eLibrary represents exclusively (see www.elibrary.com). Use http://news.google.com instead.

5. **Unless you have an ongoing need to be teased . . . well, you get the idea . . . clear the Factiva Search check box.**

Dow Jones Reuters Business Interactive LLC operates as Factiva (www.factiva.com). You know the tune.

6. **Seriously consider clearing the MSN Search check box.**

This is a personal preference, I suppose, but why have the Research pane spend time banging against MSN's search engine when, with a couple of clicks and the Google toolbar, you can run against Google's mother lode. (Read more about the Google toolbar in *Windows XP Timesaving Techniques For Dummies.*)

7. **Click OK.**

I leave the Gale Company Profiles and MSN Money Stock Quotes check boxes enabled because they induce little overhead, don't beg incessantly for money, and can actually be useful if you can figure them out. See "Searching for Business" later in this Technique.

Finding Synonyms

Nine times out of ten, when you're using Word, Outlook, or PowerPoint, you won't need or want to use the Research task pane to look for a synonym. Simply right-click the word, choose Synonyms, and choose from one of the six most-common synonyms (or one antonym) on offer.

Right-clicking a word to find a synonym is quick and easy. The Research task pane is slow and cumbersome. Why? Because the synonym entries in the right-click menu are all stored on your computer: You can look up a synonym even if you aren't connected to the Internet.

To save time, don't right-click and choose Look Up. Right-clicking and then choosing Synonyms⇨Thesaurus feeds the chosen word directly into Office's Thesaurus, which is already located on your PC. If you choose Look Up, the word you choose goes into the Encarta Dictionary, which is a Web site away.

If you can't get the synonym you want with a simple right-click, choose Thesaurus, and Office brings up the Research task pane (see Figure 8-3). (***Note:*** Excel doesn't offer synonyms in its right-click contextual menu. You have no choice but to use the considerably slower Research task pane — or start Word, type the word, right-click it, and go from there.)

Here's how you drill down in the Thesaurus — which is to say, to find a synonym of a synonym. In the Research pane, click the word that you want to explore. As long as you continue to search in the Thesaurus, Office's response remains snappy.

When you find the synonym you want, click the down-arrow to the right of the word in the Research pane and choose Insert. Your old word is automatically replaced by the new one.

• **Figure 8-3: The Research task pane searches for synonyms.**

Looking in the Dictionary

Although the Office Thesaurus is swift, the other reference book you're likely to use — the Encarta Dictionary — can be sluggish indeed.

Sometimes a quick look at a word's synonyms will confirm immediately whether you have the right word — and avoid a trip to the dictionary. For example, if you aren't quite sure whether the word *hirsute* means *hairy,* right-click *hirsute* and choose Synonyms.

The primary timesaving trick to using the Encarta Dictionary lies in understanding that the dictionary doesn't include many of the terms that you might expect to find in a dictionary. For example, the names of almost all countries, states, cities, rivers, mountains, people, and zillions of additional proper nouns aren't in the dictionary at all. If you look for them in the dictionary, you're just wasting your time.

For example, if I right-click the word *thailand* and choose Look Up (or hold down the Alt key and click the word — same thing), the Research pane opens, grabs the word *thailand*, looks it up, sits there for a while — and finds nothing.

 If you didn't disable the Translate search service, as I mention in the first section of this Technique, chances are good the Research task pane will get hung up trying to translate the word *thailand* into French or Spanish! Oy.

The problem? Actually, there are two:

- ✔ **Office's Research task pane is hard-wired to repeat the same search that it last performed.** When you right-click a word and choose Look Up — or hold down the Alt key and left-click a word — the Research pane repeats its previous search by using the new word. If your previous search was a dictionary lookup, you go out to the dictionary again.

- ✔ **There's no way to tell the Research task pane that you want it to look in both the dictionary and the encyclopedia.** You get one or the other but not both.

Compounding the problem is the blasted terminology: Only Microsoft would have the hubris to draw a distinction between *Reference Books* (which includes the Thesaurus located on your PC and Microsoft's dictionary out on the Web) as opposed to *Research Sites* (which includes Microsoft's encyclopedia Web site), and prevent you from searching both simultaneously.

Using the Encarta Encyclopedia

In the preceding section, I explain why a search of the dictionary might not produce the results that you expect. You might not realize that the reason why the Research task pane frequently responds to your inquiries with a blank stare is because Office doesn't think of the encyclopedia as a reference book.

Go figger.

The example in the preceding section left the Research task pane high and dry, without a match on the word *thailand*. Here's how to get an answer:

1. **Start Word. Inside a Word document, type** thailand. **Right-click *thailand* and choose Look Up (or hold down the Alt key and then left-click *thailand*).**

   If your last search was a dictionary search — in Microsoft-speak, *All Reference Books* — you see the "blank stare" Research task pane.

2. **Click the down arrow on the box underneath the Search For box and then choose All Research Sites or Encarta Encyclopedia.**

   After more churning and spluttering (which could be slightly less annoying if you're using the world's fastest Internet connection), the Research task pane produces worthwhile results (see Figure 8-4).

3. **Click one of the links in the Research pane.**

   Internet Explorer opens with the Research pane on the left, the appropriate Encarta Web site on the right, and lots and lots (and lots and lots) of advertising (see Figure 8-5).

• **Figure 8-4: At last, on the second try, you strike pay dirt.**

• **Figure 8-5: Clicking through a Research pane encyclopedia hit will take you to the corresponding Encarta Web site.**

It only takes a few more seconds to copy the word to the Clipboard, point Internet Explorer to Wikipedia (www.wikipedia.org), **paste the word into the Wiki search box, and press Enter.** Try it a few times and see whether Wikipedia doesn't give you better results. Best of all, **you can freely use the material that you copy from Wikipedia as long as you acknowledge the source. See** wikipedia.org/wiki/ wikipedia:copyrights **for details.**

Don't forget Google! If you really want to research a topic, as opposed to looking it up in an encyclopedia, head to www.google.com.

Searching for Business

The Research task pane's All Business and Financial Sites offering, found in the drop-down list under Search For, hooks into the Gale Company database of business information as well as MSN stock quotes in several countries.

Although the All Business and Financial Sites option makes for great demos, you need to keep three things in mind to keep from spinning your wheels:

✔ You can look up a company's data in the Gale Company database (see Figure 8-6) by using its name or its stock symbol.

✔ The MSN 20-minute delayed stock quote must be fed the company's ticker symbol (if you type the company name, you come up with nothing).

✔ The basic Gale Company information can be quite helpful (see Figure 8-6), but if you want more-detailed info, you have to pay for it.

If you don't know a company's stock symbol, the Gale database will have it. Just search on the company name.

• Figure 8-6: The Gale Company database understands *Starbucks*.

In some circumstances, the Research pane can be so useful that you really want two panes open. I frequently open two panes to trace down different branches of a synonym search simultaneously. Hopping around encyclopedia entries can be much faster with two panes open, also.

Although you can open only one Research task pane at a time in Excel or PowerPoint, Word lets you work with a different Research pane for each open document. Thus, if you want to have two or more Research panes going at the same time, create a new document (or two or three) in Word, and have at it (see Figure 8-7).

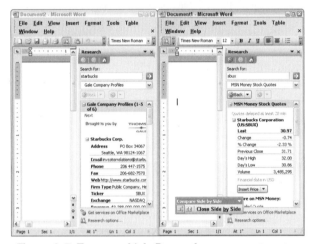

• Figure 8-7: To use multiple Research panes, create multiple Word documents.

 Here is an easy way to see two (or more) Word documents simultaneously, with the panes accessible: Choose Window⇨ Compare Side by Side.

Technique 9

Copying and Pasting in a Nonce

Save Time By

- ✔ Understanding how the Office and Windows Clipboards interact
- ✔ Using the Office Clipboard quickly
- ✔ Making the Clipboard go away when you don't want it — and stay away, if you *really* don't want it
- ✔ Replacing the Clipboard with a shareware clipboard

A good friend once asked me, "I want to copy paragraphs from different parts of a document and put them in a new document. It's easy if all the paragraphs are next to each other — I just highlight them, choose Edit⇨Copy (or press Ctrl+C), move to the new document, and choose Edit⇨Paste (or press Ctrl+V). Can Microsoft build something into Word that makes it easy to do the same thing with paragraphs that aren't next to each other?"

Ah, do I have a Clipboard for you!

The Office 2003 Clipboard — it's really a pane — doesn't solve all the copying and pasting problems most people encounter, but it can save you a lot of time if you can put up with its idiosyncrasies. My friend was disappointed by the fact that it's still fastest and smartest to gather and paste pieces one at a time, rather than trying to set up a massive paste, all at once. But he was delighted to find that he can stick all the copied pieces in one place and work with them *en masse*. The Office Clipboard makes it easy to gather far-flung pieces of text and pictures. Unlike earlier versions of Office, this 2003 flavor of the Clipboard is also easy to turn off.

 If you copy and paste and copy and paste, spending a few minutes now taking control of the Clipboard (or getting a decent replacement for the Clipboard, as I describe in this Technique) can save you time day after day.

Working with the Office Clipboard versus the Windows Clipboard

If you've used Windows or Office for any time at all, you've undoubtedly worked the Windows Clipboard every which way but loose: Select stuff, copy it or cut it, click where you want it to go, and then paste. Easy. The Windows Clipboard consists of a single cubbyhole. You stick stuff in the cubbyhole and bring it out when you need it.

Office has a second, more powerful Clipboard that you can call up and use. You have to explicitly start the Office Clipboard. If you don't start it, the Office Clipboard stays out of the way, and your copying and pasting only takes place on the old-fashioned Windows Clipboard.

The Office Clipboard's main claim to fame? It has 24 cubbyholes. And after it's started, Office's Clipboard works in tandem with the Windows Clipboard. You can tell that the Office Clipboard is running by looking for its little icon down in the Windows Notification Area, next to the clock (see Figure 9-1).

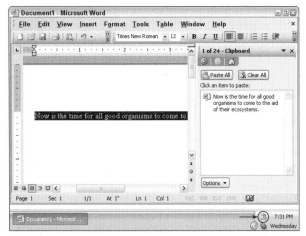

• **Figure 9-1: The Office Clipboard can hold up to 24 items.**

After you start the Office Clipboard, it gathers items pasted onto the Windows Clipboard even if you didn't paste them from Office. The last 24 items that you copied or cut from any program — Notepad, CorelDRAW, Paint, Adobe Acrobat, Uncle Ned's Golf Handicapper — all go onto the Office Clipboard.

The Office Clipboard doesn't interfere with the Windows Clipboard. The Windows Clipboard always contains the contents of the most recently used cubbyhole in the Office Clipboard. The Office Clipboard acts like a packrat, watching the Windows Clipboard to see whether there's anything new, storing away the last 24 items that were put on the Windows Clipboard.

 Word has an old feature called *the Spike* that used to be used to gather text and pictures from many different places and put them all in one place in a document. Don't use it. The Office Clipboard is vastly superior, in no small part because you can actually see what you're doing.

If you clear the Office Clipboard (by clicking the Clear All button), the Windows Clipboard gets zapped out, too.

 Although it's true that Word lets you select *noncontiguous* pieces of text and pictures (that is, pieces of text that aren't physically next to each other), I don't recommend that you select noncontiguous pieces of text if you're going to move or copy. It's much faster and less error-prone to use the Office Clipboard to gather the text, block by block, and then move or copy it where you will.

The contents of the Office Clipboard hang around only as long as you have at least one Office application open. The minute all your Office apps get closed, the Office Clipboard and all its contents go to the big bit bucket in the sky. You can start the Office Clipboard by

- Choosing Edit➪Office Clipboard.

- Bringing up any Office task pane, clicking the down arrow on the pane's title bar, and then choosing Clipboard.

- Pressing Ctrl+C twice. That can happen if you hold down the Ctrl key and press C twice. But it also happens if you press Ctrl+C, get up from your desk to answer the Call of Nature (or any other call, for that matter), come back to your desk, and absentmindedly press Ctrl+C again.

- Copying something to the Windows Clipboard (by pressing Ctrl+C, for example), pasting what you copied (perhaps with Ctrl+V), and then copying something else to the Windows Clipboard. You have to do all that while in the same Office program. The copy-paste-copy combination automatically brings the Office Clipboard to life, and along with it the Clipboard pane, the Clipboard icon in the system tray, and the little message — the whole nine yards.

 This last method of starting the Office Clipboard is a bit obscure, but if you've ever wondered why the Clipboard pane suddenly jumped in your face, you must've copied, pasted, then copied again, in that order, all within the same Office program. Frankly, this is one Clipboard function that I find distracting, and I explain how to turn it off in "Customizing the Clipboard" later in this Technique.

Moving Stuff Onto and Off the Office Clipboard

The best way to get to know the Office 2003 Clipboard is by taking it for a little test drive. You might recognize some of the following functions, but others are lesser-known:

✔ **To start the Office Clipboard and copy something to the Clipboard, select whatever you want to copy (such as text in a Word document), hold down the Ctrl key, press C twice, and release the Ctrl key.** (Ctrl+C is the nearly universal key combination for copying in Windows.) The text that you select is copied to the Windows Clipboard as well as to the Office Clipboard. When you copy something to the Clipboard, Word (or any other Office application) brings up the Office Clipboard pane (refer to Figure 9-1).

✔ **To add something else to the Office Clipboard after you've started it, press Ctrl+C.** Office adds the item to the top of the Office Clipboard and also tells you that a second item has been collected by flashing a small message above the Windows notification area (see Figure 9-2). The message appears only for a few seconds.

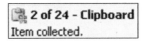

• **Figure 9-2: Notification that a second item is added to the Office Clipboard.**

✔ **To see how many items are on your Clipboard, check the Clipboard pane or the system tray.** The Office Clipboard pane indicates that the first (of 24) cubbyhole(s) contains the text that you just selected and copied. At the same time, Office puts an icon in the Windows system tray notification area, next to the time. If you hover your cursor over that icon, a small message appears that tells you how many items are currently on the Office Clipboard.

✔ **To see all the different elements on your Clipboard, just glance at the Clipboard pane.** For example, in Figure 9-3, you can easily see that the pane contains a picture and two different selections of text.

• **Figure 9-3: A picture and two pieces of text on the Office Clipboard.**

✔ **To insert an element (such as text or a picture) from one of the Office Clipboard's cubbyholes into an Office document, click the down arrow next the element and choose Paste.** The text is pasted into the document wherever you've positioned your cursor, just as you would expect.

✔ **To insert all the elements on the Clipboard, click the Paste All button.** The Office Clipboard pastes each item, in turn, into the document, starting with the item on the bottom (that is, in the first cubbyhole), then the second item, and then the third (the picture on top).

It all works pretty much as you would expect, after you realize that the Office Clipboard cubbyholes go from bottom to top. But there are some interesting timesaving settings that I describe later in this Technique.

 Unless you do something to start the Office Clipboard, it stays out of the way — you get the normal, plain, one-cubbyhole Windows Clipboard, and that's all she wrote. Most of the time, the Windows Clipboard is all you need. But if you're trying to juggle multiple chunks of text or pictures, bring up the Office Clipboard and have at it.

Customizing the Clipboard

Remember Clippit, the not-so-handy Office Assistant, who was always asking questions and getting in the way? Well, like Clippit, the Office Clipboard's habit of popping up while you're copying and pasting can be mighty intrusive. Here's how to trim its wings so that the Clipboard doesn't sidetrack you while you're working and appears only when you really need it:

1. Start one of the Office programs.

Doesn't matter which one: If you change the Office Clipboard in one program, you change it in all.

2. Choose Edit⇨Office Clipboard.

You see the Clipboard pane.

3. At the bottom of the pane, click the Options button.

The Office Clipboard lets you change its settings (see Figure 9-4).

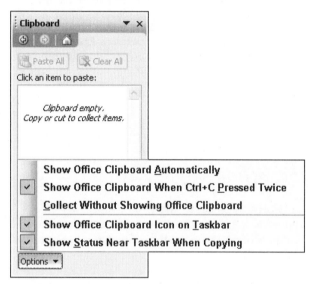

• **Figure 9-4:** All the major Office Clipboard settings appear here.

4. To stop the surprisingly intrusive Clipboard behavior, turn off the Show Office Clipboard Automatically setting.

You can adjust other settings if you like (see Table 9-1).

5. Click anywhere outside the settings area, and Office remembers your choices.

TABLE 9-1: OFFICE CLIPBOARD SETTINGS

This Setting	Means This	My Recommendation
Show Office Clipboard Automatically	Whether the copy-paste-copy sequence in a single Office app will enable the Office Clipboard. (*Note:* This is more than merely showing the Office Clipboard.)	Turn it off.
Show Office Clipboard When Ctrl+C Pressed Twice	Press Ctrl+C twice to enable the Office Clipboard.	Leave it on.
Collect Without Showing Office Clipboard	Puts new items on the Office Clipboard without having the pane appear. (*Note:* You have to turn on the Office Clipboard first!)	Leave it off.
Show Office Clipboard Icon on Taskbar	When Office Clipboard is running, puts the little icon (refer to Figure 9-1) in the Windows notification area, next to the time.	Leave it on.
Show Status Near Taskbar When Copying	When you add an item to the Office Clipboard, the small message (refer to Figure 9-2) appears for a few seconds.	Leave it on.

Replacing the Office Clipboard

So what's not to like about the Office Clipboard?

For starters

- ✔ You're limited to 24 items, and they disappear when the last Office application turns out the lights.

- ✔ There's no way to organize or search through the contents of the Clipboard — and those picture thumbnails can be *mighty* hard to see.

- ✔ None of the items in the Clipboard has a history — you have no way to know where it came from or when it was copied or pasted.

- ✔ You can't edit anything inside the Clipboard — can't take out line breaks, or trim down pictures, or strip extraneous text.

Thornsoft (www.thornsoft.com) makes the ultimate Office (and Windows) Clipboard. For $25, ClipMate fills in all of Office Clipboard's shortcomings and delivers much more. Check out the free, 30-day evaluation version. I swear by it — ClipMate is one of the best shareware products ever made.

Note: Office 2000 put the Office Clipboard on a toolbar, and it just doesn't work. Instead of wrestling with it, get ClipMate. Life's too short. Office XP is a little better, but there's no way to keep the Clipboard pane from bouncing to life, even when you'd rather never see it again.

Technique 10

Keying Combinations Quickly

Save Time By

✔ Memorizing the keyboard shortcuts you need most

✔ Finding the key combinations you need quickly

I don't memorize keyboard shortcuts very often. They kind of grow on me, whether I want them to or not. If you've been using Office since the dawn of time, you already have your own favorite pack of shortcuts. But if you aren't so encumbered, it might be worthwhile to learn a few new tricks — shortcuts that can really save you time.

Although it's true that using keyboard shortcuts can be enormously faster than diving for the mouse, it's also true that my brain hiccups when I ask it to conjure up an obscure key combination. The net effect, in either case, is an abrupt pause in my ability to get work done. So I don't take shortcuts lightly. You shouldn't either.

Forget about memorizing every keyboard shortcut you come across. Life's too short. But some key combinations are so important that every Office user needs to get them down. And that's where this Technique comes in.

Exploiting Vital Shortcuts

The Clipboard shortcuts, which I list in Table 10-1, should become a part of every Office user's repertoire. You will save so much time with these shortcuts that they should become second nature.

 If the Office Clipboard is running (see Technique 9), copying to the Windows Clipboard also places the item in the last cubbyhole of the Office Clipboard. Pasting from the Windows Clipboard is the same thing as pasting from the last cubbyhole. There are no direct keyboard shortcuts for pasting other items from the Office Clipboard or for pasting all or clearing the Office Clipboard entirely.

TABLE 10-1: SHORTCUTS TO TATTOO INSIDE YOUR EYELIDS

Press This	What It Does
Ctrl+C	Copies the selected items and puts them on the Clipboard
Ctrl+X	Cuts (deletes) the selected items and puts them on the Clipboard
Ctrl+V	Pastes the contents of the Clipboard at the current cursor location

The second group of vital Office shortcuts, in Table 10-2, has to do with rescuing Office applications when they hang or when something goes wrong with your computer. These are worth memorizing (or knowing where to look up!) in case Office or Windows goes bump in the night.

 You can use Alt+F4 instead of Alt+F, Alt+X, Enter. I just find it easier to remember the F-X approach when I'm ready to panic.

The third group of Office shortcuts, in Table 10-3, comprises my top picks for the best timesavers in all the applications.

TABLE 10-2: SHORTCUTS TO USE WHEN OFFICE STOPS WORKING

Press This	What It Does	Timesaving Bonus Info
Alt+Tab	Switches among running Windows programs and open documents (see Figure 10-1). Techies call this the *CoolSwitch* — Microsoft's internal code name for the feature.	A fast way to swap among documents; also a convenient way to exit an Office app if it suddenly freezes.
Ctrl+Alt+Delete	The Vulcan Mind Meld brings up the Windows Task Manager (see Figure 10-2), which allows you to shut down individual applications.	If you're trying to kill an ornery Office app, don't forget Office Application Recovery, which might be able to save some of your files: Start➪ Microsoft Office➪Microsoft Office Tools➪ Microsoft Office Application Recovery (see Figure 10-3).
Alt+F, then Alt+X, then Enter	Performs a File➪Exit; then saves changes to open files.	Very useful if your mouse or monitor stops working. Press Enter several times, pausing each time to make sure you save changes in all the files.

TABLE 10-3: TOP TIMESAVING PAN-OFFICE SHORTCUTS

Press This	What It Does	Timesaving Bonus Info
Ctrl+A	Selects everything in the document.	In Word and Excel, pressing Ctrl+A in the body of a document does *not* select the headers or footers.
Ctrl+Z	Undoes the last thing you did.	Pressing Ctrl+Z will also undo the last autoformatting change made by Office itself. Unfortunately, some actions (such as setting the Zoom factor) can't be undone with Ctrl+Z.
Shift+click (Click something, hold down Shift, then click again.)	Selects everything between the clicks: text, cells, slides.	You can use Shift+click to select multiple files and folders in dialog boxes.
Ctrl+click (Select something, hold down Ctrl, select something else.)	Adds to a selection so you can select items that are not next to each other.	This doesn't work all the time in all applications.

(continued)

TABLE 10-3 *(continued)*

Press This	What It Does	Timesaving Bonus Info
Alt+drag (Click a graphic, hold down the mouse button, press the Alt key, drag the graphic.)	Overrides the default snap-to behavior.	In Word, this lets you nudge a graphic, so it doesn't automatically snap to the document's guidelines. In Excel, does exactly the opposite. In PowerPoint, this doesn't have any effect.
Ctrl+P	Print.	Same as choosing File➪Print, so you can adjust the number of copies, send to a different printer, and so on.

• **Figure 10-1:** The Alt+Tab CoolSwitch cycles among running Windows programs.

• **Figure 10-3:** Instead of using Task Manager to stop a frozen Office program, try Application Recovery, which recovers files that might get clobbered (at least in theory).

• **Figure 10-2:** The Windows Task Manager lets you stop any program (at least in theory).

My final list of vital shortcuts, in Table 10-4, comes in handy when you're ready to put your fist through your computer's screen. If you're typing, look up at the screen, and see that what you've typed is all bold or italic or underlined, you can switch back to normal with simple keystrokes. Believe me, we've all been there.

Using Word Shortcuts

Word has a large number of keyboard shortcuts, I'm convinced, because so many touch typists are so anally retentive . . . and I mean that in the kindest possible way because I'm a touch typist, too.

That said, from a timesaving perspective, Word shortcuts fall into four categories:

- ✔ High-payoff timesaving shortcuts, which almost all Word users will want to commit to memory because the mouse versions of the commands are so convoluted or hard to remember (see Table 10-5)

- ✔ Shortcuts for moving around in a document (see Table 10-6)

- ✔ Entire groups of shortcuts, specifically for creating accented and other non-English characters (see Table 10-7)

- ✔ Reams and reams of additional shortcuts that might prove useful, depending on how you use Word

TABLE 10-4: SHORTCUTS TO REDUCE AGGRAVATION

Press This	What It Does	Timesaving Bonus Info
Ctrl+B	Toggles bold formatting on and off.	If you suddenly discover that everything you're typing is bold, press Ctrl+B, and you go back to normal.
Ctrl+I	Toggles italic formatting on and off.	Same as bold.
Ctrl+U	Toggles underline formatting on and off.	Same as bold and italic.
Insert	Toggles Word's and Excel's infamous *Insert mode.*	If what you type overwrites what's on the screen (as opposed to inserting new characters that you type), press the Insert key to go back to normal.

TABLE 10-5: HIGH-PAYOFF TIMESAVING WORD SHORTCUTS

Press This	What It Does	Timesaving Bonus Info
Ctrl+'+' (Hold down Ctrl, then press the apostrophe twice.)	Makes a single curly close quote.	Use for abbreviated dates ('93) or missing initial characters (go get 'em).
Click+Shift+click (Click once at the beginning of a block of text, hold down the Shift key, click at the end.)	Selects all the text between the two clicks.	Beats the living daylights out of trying to select large blocks of text by clicking and highlighting the whole thing while Word or Excel scrolls at lightning speed.
F9	Updates all selected fields.	Don't forget that a Table of Contents in a document is a field. If you change the document, you have to click inside the TOC and press F9 to make sure that it gets updated, too.
Ctrl+Tab	Puts a tab inside a table cell.	If you just press the Tab key, Word moves on to the next cell.
Ctrl+Shift+End	Extends the current selection to the end of the document, including the final paragraph mark.	No mouse equivalent.
Ctrl+Shift+Home	Extends the current selection to the beginning of the document.	No mouse equivalent.

TABLE 10-6: TIMESAVING WORD NAVIGATION SHORTCUTS

Press This	What It Does
Shift+F5	Moves cursor back to the last place you made changes
Ctrl+↑	Moves to the beginning of the current paragraph, or to the beginning of the preceding paragraph if the cursor is already at the beginning of a paragraph
Ctrl+↓	Moves to the beginning of the next paragraph
Home	Moves cursor to the beginning of the current line
End	Moves cursor to the end of the current line
Ctrl+Home	Moves cursor to the beginning of the document
Ctrl+End	Moves cursor to the end of the document

TABLE 10-7: WORD SHORTCUTS FOR TYPING ACCENTED AND OTHER CHARACTERS

Hold Down Ctrl; Type This	Get This
' (apostrophe), then the letter	á ð é í ó ú ý Á Ð É Í Ó Ú Ý
` (accent grave, to the left of the numeral 1), then the letter	à è ì ò ù À È Ì Ò Ù
^ (caret = Shift+6), then the letter	â ê î ô û Â Ê Î Ô Û
~ (tilde = Shift+accent grave), then the letter	ã ñ õ Ã Ñ Õ
: (colon = Shift+semicolon), then the letter	ä ë ï ö ü ÿ Ä Ë Ï Ö Ü Ÿ
& (ampersand = Shift+7), then a o s A O	æ œ ß Æ Œ
@ (each at = Shift+2), then a A	å Å
, (comma), then c C	ç Ç
/ (slash), then o O	ø Ø
Alt+Ctrl+Shift, then !	¡
Alt+Ctrl+Shift, then ?	¿

You can find an enormous list of Word shortcut keys at `www.microsoft.com/enable/products/keyboard/keyboardresults.asp?Product=23`. Although the list is ostensibly for Word 2002, the shortcuts haven't changed much since the days of Word 97.

Using Outlook Shortcuts

Outlook has many shortcuts for working with specific objects (Tasks, Contacts, what have you), but I've only found a few to be worth the bother. They're listed in Table 10-8.

 All the important Word shortcuts (see preceding section) work when you're composing mail.

TABLE 10-8: OUTLOOK SHORTCUT KEYS WORTH REMEMBERING

Press This	What It Does
Alt+F1	Shows or hides the Navigation pane on the left
F9	Sends and receives mail
Ctrl+Shift+A	Creates an Appointment (Calendar item)
Ctrl+Shift+C	Creates a Contact
Ctrl+Shift+K	Creates a Task
Ctrl+Shift+M	Creates a Message
Ctrl+Shift+I	Moves the current message to the Inbox
Ctrl+Shift+O	Moves the current message to the Outbox

You can see a lengthy list of Outlook shortcut keys at `www.microsoft.com/enable/products/keyboard/keyboardresults.asp?Product=24`. Although the list is for Outlook 2002, Outlook 2000 and 2003 behave similarly.

Using Excel Shortcuts

Excel folks don't seem to be as, uh, enamored with keyboard shortcuts as the Wordies. However, big timesaving gains await those willing to memorize a few key combinations (see Table 10-9), but with these notable exceptions, the general Office shortcuts suffice for all but the most persistent Excel hunt-'n-peckers.

TABLE 10-9: EXCEL TIMESAVING SHORTCUTS

Press This	What It Does
Ctrl+Home	Moves cursor to the first cell in the spreadsheet, typically A1
Ctrl+End	Moves cursor to the "last" cell in the spreadsheet — where the right-most used column and the bottom-most used row meet
Ctrl+spacebar	Selects the current column
Shift+spacebar	Selects the current row
Ctrl+Shift+~ (tilde)	Applies the General number format
F2	Allows you to edit the currently active cell by showing the cell's formula (not its value)
Ctrl+` (accent grave, to the left of the 1)	Similar to F2, but for the entire spreadsheet; also brings up the Auditing toolbar

The monster list of Excel shortcuts is at `www.microsoft.com/enable/products/keyboard/keyboardresults.asp?Product=25`. **Again, although the list is officially for Excel 2002 (the version in Office XP), the shortcuts work for Excel 97, 2000, and 2003, too.**

Using PowerPoint Shortcuts

PowerPoint's best timesavers are a handful of quick keyboard shortcuts that perform actions repeated many times in the course of developing a new presentation (see Table 10-10). These shortcuts are well worth your consideration if you spend any time at all creating presentations.

TABLE 10-10: TOP TIMESAVING POWERPOINT SHORTCUTS

Press This	What It Does
Ctrl+M	Inserts a new slide immediately after the current slide
Ctrl+D	Inserts a copy of the currently selected slide(s)
Ctrl+T	Opens the Format⇨Font dialog box
F5	Starts the slideshow

Microsoft's big list of PowerPoint shortcut keys hasn't changed since the days of PowerPoint 97. It's at `www.microsoft.com/enable/products/keyboard/keyboardresults.asp?Product=21`.

Technique 11

Drawing Quickly

Save Time By

- Knowing how Office inserts drawings in documents
- Choosing the right drawing tools — the first time
- Aligning drawings quickly and accurately

You might think that your Office document — Word doc, Excel spreadsheet, or PowerPoint slide — looks and acts a lot like a sheet of paper. In some respects, it does. But the minute you get involved with drawing, that wonderful, flat, reliable piece of paper starts evolving into a multidimensional, snarly beast.

If you think of your document as a flat piece of paper, you're going to get burned, over and over again. I can't even begin to imagine how much time Word users have lost trying to figure out why their clip art (or pictures) does (or doesn't) move (or stay put) the way it should. That's the topic of Technique 24.

It all harkens back to the *drawing layer,* which you need to understand if you expect to save any time at all with Office's drawing tools. This Technique shows you how to coexist with the drawing layer — a kind of warp in the flat-paper, space/time continuum, if you will — and draw on your documents quickly and accurately. Although you might find it faster to buy a box of colored pens.

Drawing on the Drawing Layer(s)

On the surface, Word documents, PowerPoint slides, and Excel spreadsheets look like flat pieces of paper. (Well, okay, a PowerPoint slide is supposed to look like a slide, but you get my drift.) But if you dig below the surface. . . .

Imagine this for a moment. You've sweated and strained for two weeks, and you finally have your résumé formatted precisely the way you want it. You print a copy and take it home. (What? You never worked on your résumé at the office before? Sheeesh.) Somehow, while you're fixing dinner, your three-year-old finds the résumé, pulls out a garish red marker, and makes giant scribbles all over it. That's the drawing layer.

Word doesn't let you draw inside the document itself. You can't mix garish red scribbles with the perfectly formatted 11-point Garamond text on your résumé. But you can draw on top of your résumé, just like your three-year-old. You use the drawing layer like this:

1. **Open a Word document.**

If you have a résumé handy, it'll do.

2. **If you can't see the Drawing toolbar at the bottom (it starts with a button that reads *Draw*), right-click an empty spot on the menu bar and select the Drawing check box (see Figure 11-1).**

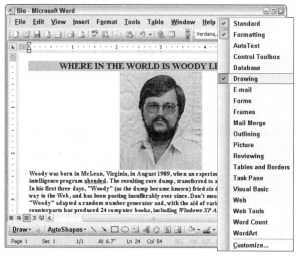

• **Figure 11-1:** My résumé, pre-toddler rampage.

3. **You have to get rid of a particularly obnoxious Word setting before you can scribble on your résumé, so choose Tools⇨Options⇨General and clear the Automatically Create Drawing Canvas When Inserting AutoShapes check box; then click OK.**

See the upcoming sidebar, "Word's Ignominious Drawing Canvas."

4. **On the Drawing toolbar, choose AutoShapes⇨ Lines and pick the Scribble drawing tool in the lower-right corner of the submenu (see Figure 11-2).**

If you aren't already in Print Layout view, Word switches over to it. (Otherwise, you wouldn't be able to see what you're scribbling!)

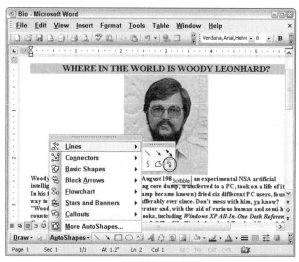

• **Figure 11-2:** Choose the Scribble drawing tool.

5. **Scribble.**

Really. Pretend you're a three-year-old, hold down the left mouse button, and draw loopy scribbles all over the document (as shown in Figure 11-3). When you're done, release the left mouse button.

6. **With the Scribble tool still selected (it has dots all around it, like a selected picture), click the down-arrow next to the Line Color icon on the Drawing toolbar (it looks like a fountain pen) and choose a bright red.**

Of course. You could see it coming, couldn't you?

7. **Click the Line Style tool on the Drawing toolbar (a stack of three solid lines) and choose one of the big, thick lines.**

If you did everything right, you should see a giant red scribble all over your résumé. Of course, the scribble isn't *in* your document at all. Rather, it's sitting in the drawing layer *on top* of your document. That's why you can click the scribble itself and drag it any place you like — it moves around in the drawing layer, out of harm's way.

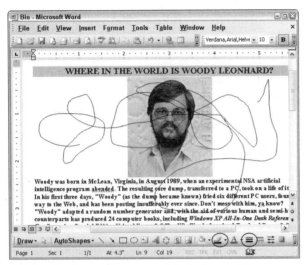

• **Figure 11-3:** I think my résumé looks better this way, frankly.

8. To see what's happening, choose View⇨ Normal.

The scribble disappears. Word doesn't show the drawing layer when you're in Normal view (see Figure 11-4). Scroll up, scroll down. You won't find it anywhere.

• **Figure 11-4:** In Normal view, it's back to the dull same-old, same-old.

9. Print the document (File⇨Print) or just take a look in Print Preview (File⇨Print Preview; see Figure 11-5).

Convince yourself that the scribble *is* there — it's just floating above the document.

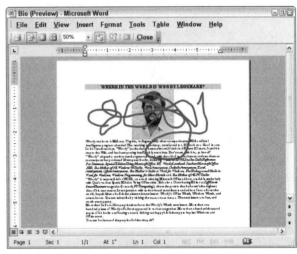

• **Figure 11-5:** Even though you can't see it in Normal view, the scribble exists — just on a different plane.

So far, you have seen the drawing layer on top of your document. In fact, Word maintains two drawing layers — one on top of and one underneath the main layer of the document.

10. If you're in Print Preview, click Close.

11. Go back into Print Layout view by choosing View⇨Print Layout.

You see the document with the scribble on top (refer to Figure 11-4).

12. Click once on the scribble to select it; then right-click the scribble and choose Order⇨ Send Behind Text.

Word dutifully puts the scribble in the drawing layer behind the text on the page (see Figure 11-6).

• **Figure 11-6:** Drawings can live in the drawing layer underneath the main part of the document as well.

13. Choose File⇨Close — and no, you don't want to save changes.

Unless you want to save the scribble, of course.

If you accidentally save a scribble-enhanced version of your résumé, just click the scribble once and then press the Delete key. Drawings are easy to delete.

Word has drawing layers above and below the main text on the page. Excel and PowerPoint have only one drawing layer, and it's on top of the spreadsheet or the slide. (You can't put pictures directly into a spreadsheet or a slide; they always sit on top.)

The drawing layer(s) exhibits all sorts of strange behavior. You can waste a lot of time — days, weeks — trying to figure out why a particular Word feature won't work in the drawing layer. At a minimum, you should realize that

✔ Text that you type in the drawing layer, no matter how it's formatted, will never appear in a Table of Contents, Table of Figures, or any other automatically generated Word reference table.

✔ Automatic caption numbering and style-based numbered paragraphs don't work in the drawing layer.

✔ Many other features that you take for granted (alignment in table cells, for example) might or might not work in the drawing layer.

There's a difference between drawings, which are made with Word's drawing tools, and inline pictures. See Technique 24 for details.

Word's Ignominious Drawing Canvas

Word 2003 has an obnoxious habit — I refuse to call it a feature — of putting a "canvas" in the drawing layer every time you use one of the Drawing toolbar's tools. The idea is sweetness and light itself: If you draw on the canvas, Word will treat everything that you draw as a group, so you can stretch, scale, and move them as a single unit. The items on a canvas all appear on the same page. And so on.

In practice, the drawing canvas is horribly intrusive. It slams the screen around so you can't draw where you thought you were going to draw. It adds an entire layer of settings and potential problems where getting things done is time-consuming anyway. In the end, the drawing canvas gets in the way unless you have a whole bunch of pictures that you want to treat as a single unit — and if that's the case, you should learn about grouping.

I tell you how to turn off the drawing canvas in Technique 15, along with changing all the rest of Word's intrusive settings, but you can just follow Step 3 in the preceding procedure to put Word out of its misery.

Sketching Basic Shapes

The Office drawing tools are phenomenally easy to use, and as long as your drawing needs are modest, you can turn out simple stick figures in a snap.

Constraining a line

Here's all it takes to draw a straight line:

1. **Start the Office application.**

In this example, I work with Excel. (Yeah, yeah, I don't want to mess with the drawing canvas — see the "Word's Ignominious Drawing Canvas" sidebar elsewhere in this Technique. Do you blame me?)

2. **If you can't see the Drawing toolbar (the first button reads *Draw*), right-click an empty spot on the menu bar and mark the Drawing check box (refer to Figure 11-1).**

3. **Click the Line icon on the Drawing toolbar.**

It's immediately to the right of the AutoShapes button.

4. **Click once on the spreadsheet (actually, in the drawing layer on top of the spreadsheet) where you want the line to begin, hold the mouse button down, and release the button where you want the line to end.**

Your line appears on top of the spreadsheet (see Figure 11-7).

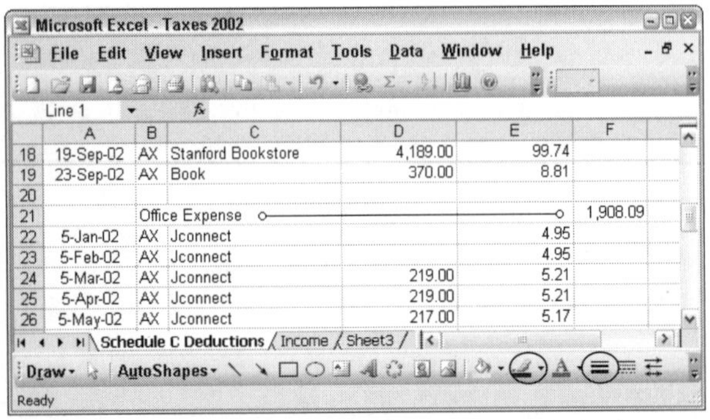

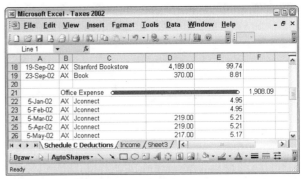

• **Figure 11-7: Drawing a straight line takes a few clicks.**

5. **To change the color and thickness of the line, first click it once to select it.**

▶ **Color:** Choose a color by clicking the down arrow next to the Line Color icon (which looks like a pen).

▶ **Line thickness:** Choose a line size by clicking the Line Style icon (see the results in Figure 11-8).

• **Figure 11-8: Making the line thick takes a couple more clicks.**

You can constrain the line by holding down certain keys while you drag. The mechanics are easy and quick, after you figure out how:

1. **Click the Line icon on the Drawing toolbar.**

2. **Click to start the line and keep holding down the mouse button.**

3. **Press the constraining key (see Table 11-1).**

4. **When the line looks right, release the mouse button and then release the constraining key.**

TABLE 11-1: LINE-CONSTRAINING KEYS IN EXCEL

Press This	To Constrain the Line Like This
Click, Shift, release	The line starts at the first click and then gets constrained to 15-degree intervals from the horizontal.
Click, Ctrl, release	The line is centered at the first click.
Click, Alt, release	The end of the line is constrained to fall at the corner of a spreadsheet cell.

Fletching an arrow

To draw an arrow:

1. **Start the Office application.**

In this case, I'm working in Excel.

2. If you can't see the Drawing toolbar, right-click on an empty spot on the menu bar and mark the Drawing check box (refer to Figure 11-1).

3. Click the Arrow icon on the Drawing toolbar.

4. Click once on the spreadsheet where you want the butt of the arrow, hold down the mouse button, and release the button where you want the arrowhead to appear.

Arrow drawings can be constrained in all the ways that I describe in the preceding section. You can also modify the appearance of the arrowhead — both at the butt and at the point of the arrow:

1. Draw the arrow, using the preceding steps.

2. Right-click the arrow and choose Format⇨AutoShape⇨Colors and Lines.

The Format AutoShape dialog box appears (see Figure 11-9).

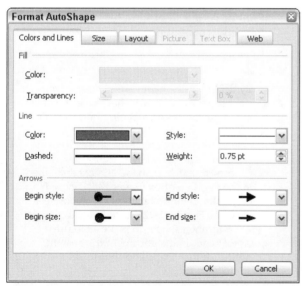

• **Figure 11-9:** Choose arrowhead styles and sizes — even for the butt of the arrow.

3. From the respective drop-down lists, choose a Begin Style and size for the butt of the arrow and an End Style and size for the tip.

Make any other changes that you like in this dialog box, including the color, line size, whether the line is dashed or solid, and so on.

4. Click OK.

The arrow takes on the characteristics that you specify.

 If you want all future items that you draw with the Drawing toolbar in this document to have the characteristics of the arrow that you just formatted (line color, thickness, arrowhead style and size, and so on), right-click the arrow and choose Set AutoShape Defaults.

Rolling your own shapes

If you need to draw your own shapes, the most powerful tool in the Drawing toolbar arsenal is the so-called Freeform tool. With the Freeform tool, you can draw straight lines or curves or even make a single line with both straight and curved segments. You can also connect the ends of the line to form a closed shape. Here's how:

1. Start the Office application. If you can't see the Drawing toolbar, right-click an empty spot on the menu and mark the Drawing check box (refer to Figure 11-1).

2. Choose AutoShapes⇨Lines and choose the Freeform tool, the penultimate icon (see Figure 11-10).

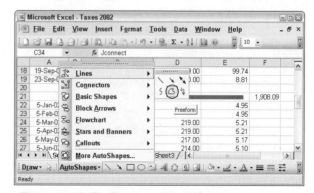

• **Figure 11-10:** The Freeform drawing tool.

3. **Click where you want to start drawing.**

▶ **To draw a straight line:** Release the mouse button and move the mouse to where you want the end of the line to appear; then click again.

▶ **To draw a curved line:** Hold down the mouse button and draw, releasing the button when you want to start a new segment.

It sounds complicated, but if you try it a couple of times, you'll get the hang of it (see Figure 11-11).

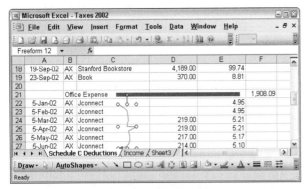

• **Figure 11-11: The Freeform tool lets you mix straight segments and hand-drawn curves.**

4. **If you want a closed shape, click near the place where you started drawing.**

5. **If you want an open shape, double-click where you want the shape to stop.**

Easy. Fast. Not very good-looking, but it'll do.

 To modify a freeform drawing, on the Drawing toolbar, choose Draw⇨Edit Points. Office lets you click and drag the ends of each of the segments of the freeform shape.

 If you close the shape — click near the place where it started — you can fill the shape with a color.

Adding AutoShapes

In the preceding section, I show you how to draw lines, arrows, and freeform lines. All three of those shapes are *AutoShapes* — shapes that the Drawing toolbar provides for you to construct your own drawings. In fact, every shape on the Drawing toolbar (including line, arrow, rectangle, oval, and text box) is an AutoShape.

 The Drawing toolbar includes hundreds of AutoShapes that you can use in a wide variety of situations to save all sorts of time.

✔ Need curly braces and brackets to group together a number of lines of text? Look in *Basic Shapes*.

✔ Want to draw a flowchart? Use the *Flowchart* AutoShapes, of course, but don't overlook the *Block Arrows* that tie them together.

✔ Printing certificates or awards? Look at *Stars and Banners*.

✔ Have a point you want to emphasize? *Callouts!*

 By default, AutoShapes are *opaque* — you can't see through them. That's great for covering up blemishes on a photo (mine doesn't count), but most of the time you want to be able to see what's under the shape. To make an AutoShape transparent, right-click it and choose Format AutoShape⇨Colors and Lines. In the first Color box (under Fill), choose No Fill; in the Color box under Line, choose No Line (see Figure 11-12). Click OK, and you get a see-through shape. To make all future AutoShapes in the document transparent, right-click that shape and choose Set AutoShape Defaults.

Unfortunately, setting AutoShapes defaults that "stick" across multiple documents is a monumental pain in the neck. You'd think Microsoft would've figured out by now that some people want to have all their AutoShapes in all their documents transparent, but nooooooo. . . . See Technique 16 for a workaround.

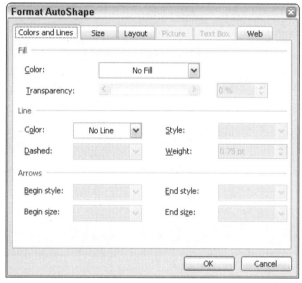

• **Figure 11-12:** To make a shape transparent, set it to No Fill and No Line.

Basic rules for creating an AutoShape are straightforward: Click the shape, click the document, and then drag to draw. Keep in mind that you can

- Put text in almost any AutoShape (except you can't put text along lines). To do so, right-click the shape and choose Add Text.

- Tear off and float individual AutoShape toolbars. Just click and drag the dotted line at the top of the menu.

- Constrain the drawing so that, for example, the Oval tool makes only circles. To do so, you must follow these instructions precisely:

  1. **Click the AutoShape's icon.**

  2. **Click in the document where you want the shape to appear.**

  3. **Continue to hold down the left mouse button.**

  4. **Push and hold down the appropriate drawing constraint key (see Table 11-2).**

  5. **Release the mouse button after the shape looks right.**

TABLE 11-2: SHAPE-CONSTRAINING KEYS

Press This	To Constrain the Shape Like This
Click, Shift, release	The upper-left corner of the shape starts at the first click; then the shape is constrained to be symmetric. (For example, a rectangle becomes a square, and an oval becomes a circle.)
Click, Ctrl, release	The shape is centered at the first click.
Click, Alt, release	Only in Excel, the edge of the shape is constrained to fall along the edge of a spreadsheet cell.

Connecting Shapes

Excel and PowerPoint make it easy to draw lines between shapes and have the lines "stick to" the shapes. They're called *connectors,* and you can use them by first drawing the shapes that you wish to connect, choosing AutoShapes⇨ Connectors, and then choosing the kind of connector that you like. (Good information is available in online Help; search for *Connectors.*)

Unfortunately, Word allows you to connect only AutoShapes that sit on the same drawing canvas. (No, online Help doesn't tell you that.) Save yourself a bunch of time: If you need connectors between your shapes — and you might for complicated drawings and flowcharts — either create the drawing in Excel or PowerPoint, or hold your nose and enable the drawing canvas (see "Word's Ignominious Drawing Canvas" sidebar elsewhere in this Technique).

Grouping, Aligning, and Distributing

You can spend eons trying to line up your drawings — or you can let Office do it. Guess which way is faster? More accurate?

To align a bunch of shapes:

1. **Draw the shapes.**

2. **Select the shapes that you want to align.**

> You might find it fastest to click the first shape, hold down the Ctrl key, and then click each of the other shapes, one at a time. In some cases, it's easier, faster, and more accurate to click the Select Objects icon on the Drawing toolbar (to the right of the Draw button), and lasso the shapes that you want.

3. **On the Drawing toolbar, choose Draw➪ Align or Distribute and choose the alignment method that you wish to apply (see Figure 11-13).**

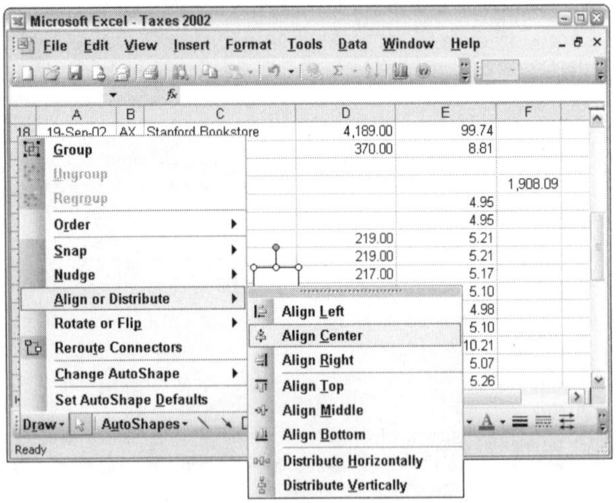

• **Figure 11-13:** Select the shapes and then let Office do the aligning.

When you have your shapes aligned, lock them together so that you can treat them as a single shape:

1. **Select the shapes that you want to treat as a single shape.**

Again, Ctrl+click works, as does lassoing.

2. **Choose Draw➪Group.**

After the shapes have been grouped, you can resize, move, or copy them — or even change their formatting — as if they were one shape.

> You can select an individual shape even if it's part of a group. First click the group to select it. Then click the shape. It will be singled out, and you can work on it independently of the others. That can save you lots of clicks — and the potential for messing up when you regroup.

Shrinking Graphics

Technique 12

Save Time By

- ✔ Getting the flab out of your documents
- ✔ Choosing an appropriate resolution for pictures
- ✔ Squeezing down pictures — quickly

When you need quality prints, it's nice that your new camera can take 2.5MB e-pictures, but when you need to stick a handful of those pics in a document or turn them into a PowerPoint slideshow, those file sizes can make you feel like the ringmaster at an elephant show.

Say your boss calls from Timbuktu and wants you to put together a little PowerPoint presentation with a half-dozen pictures of the main store and the staff, and then e-mail it to him . . . well, there's another day down the drain, trying to get another bloated document slammed together and then crammed down the telephone line.

It's an expensive, time-consuming pain in the neck to wrestle with files that contain 10 or 20MB of data. Your programs don't like to handle all that extra weight, either. The good news is that Office has the tools for cutting the flab out of your documents, and this short Technique explains how to use 'em.

So get real, get slim, and save an enormous amount of time.

Picking Your Compression Battles

If you have a document that consists of screen shots or pictures pulled off Web sites or graphics produced by a "draw" program, chances are pretty good that they're compressed already. But if you're working with photos from a digital camera, or high-resolution stock photography shots, or anything generated by a computer bigger than a breadbox, you probably have a whole lot more data than you need. In this section, you find out how much data your images really require to get the job done.

Office 2003 makes it fast and easy to shrink all the graphics in a document. Why spend hours fighting with huge, high-resolution graphics inside your documents when tiny, only slightly fuzzy shots are more than good enough?

Table 12-1 illustrates how you can reduce the file size of an image and improve download times but still get the image quality that you need for different tasks. Compare the size of a typical picture file when it comes from a plain-vanilla digital camera to the compressed sizes, and notice how much you can compress the file by using Office's tools while maintaining decent quality.

To see how this works, compare a pixel-filled image to a compressed one. Figure 12-1 shows a Word document that I put together for my mom, with a half-dozen vacation pictures. It weighs in at 3.2MB. It would take my mom about 15 minutes to download that document over a dialup connection.

Figure 12-2 shows the same document after I used Office's built-in compression routines to bring the pictures down to Web resolution (which I explain how to do in the next section). It's just 181KB, and my mom could download that in less than a minute.

Can you see any difference in the quality of the shots?

Neither could she.

Customizing Compression with PowerToys

Office offers two levels of compression — Print and Web. They're fast and easy to use if the pictures that you want to compress are already inside a document, spreadsheet, or presentation.

The Windows XP PowerToys, on the other hand, offers five levels of compression and also allows for a customized compression level. The PowerToys compression levels are keyed to the size of the display screen — 640 x 480 image, 1024 x 768, and so on. PowerToys works directly on the picture files. I talk about Windows XP PowerToys and its compression routine in *Windows XP Timesaving Techniques For Dummies*.

To get the PowerToy that deals with picture compression, go to www.microsoft.com/windowsxp/pro/downloads/powertoys.asp and download the ImageResizer.exe file.

 Version notes: Picture compression was introduced in Office XP. There's nothing analogous in Office 2000.

TABLE 12-1: COMPRESSION OF A TYPICAL PHOTOGRAPH

Compression Level	Picture Size	Suitable For	Time to Download on a 56 Kbps Dialup Line
Original (straight from the camera)	1.1MB (= about 1,100KB)	Prints up to 10 x 12 inches. Only use this option if you absolutely must have the best quality picture available.	5 minutes
Print (200 dpi)	250K	Prints up to 4 x 6 inches. More than good enough for most documents and presentations, as well as for e-mailing snapshots.	1 minute
Web (96 dpi)	90K	Graphics on a Web page. Use this option if you have a bunch of pictures you want to send by e-mail. In most cases, the person receiving the pictures will have more than enough detail to choose which pictures are worth sending at higher resolution.	20 seconds

• **Figure 12-1: A Word document assembled by choosing Insert⇨Picture.**

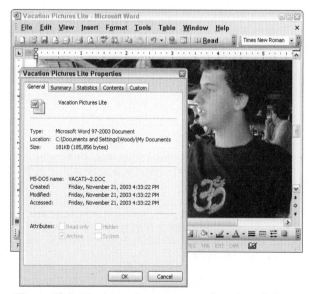

• **Figure 12-2: The same document at reduced resolution.**

Compressing an Image

To compress a picture (or all the pictures) in a Word document, Excel spreadsheet, or PowerPoint presentation, do the following:

1. **Start the application and open the document.**

2. **If you want to compress one specific picture, click it. If you want to compress all the pictures in the document, click any convenient picture.**

> If you want to compress more than one picture — but not all of them — you have to compress each one manually, separately.

3. **Right-click the picture and choose Format Picture⇨Picture.**

The Format Picture dialog box appears (see Figure 12-3).

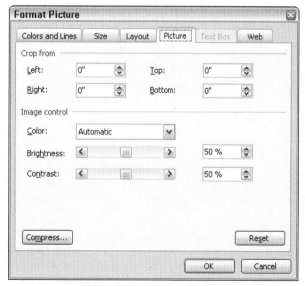

• **Figure 12-3:** Finding the compression feature is a bit difficult.

4. On the lower left, click the Compress button.

Office shows you the Compress Pictures dialog box (see Figure 12-4).

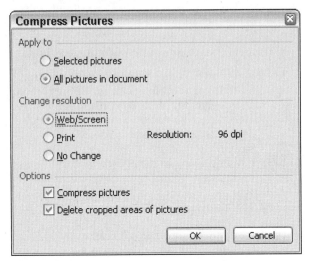

• **Figure 12-4: This dialog box does the work.**

5. Specify whether you want to compress just the one currently selected picture or all the pictures in the document.

6. Choose a resolution.

▸ **Web/Screen** resolution is identified as *96 dpi* (*dpi* being a term that's hard to define precisely because it doesn't translate directly into screen resolution). Suffice it to say that Web/Screen resolution looks good up to 1024 x 768, and reasonably good to 1280 x 1024 and even further. This is the leanest choice.

▸ **Print** resolution is identified as *200 dpi*. In practice, you can get a decent 4-x-6-inch print from pictures at this resolution, but at 6 x 9 and larger, they're too fuzzy. Not as lean as Web/Screen but still significantly squished.

▸ **No Change** means that Office won't change the resolution but will delete cropped-out parts of the pictures, if so instructed (see the next step).

7. Select the Compress Pictures check box if you want Office to compress the pictures.

Leaving this check box clear is the same as choosing No Change in the preceding step. In other words, if this check box is clear, Office will strip off unused (cropped) parts of the pictures, but it won't reduce the resolution.

8. If you want Office to get rid of any cropped out parts of the picture(s), mark the Delete Cropped Areas of Pictures check box.

Normally, Office applications keep the cropped-out sections embedded in the document in case you edit the picture at some point in the future and want to reclaim some of the cropped-out part.

9. Click OK.

Office responds with a warning that's a little confusing (see Figure 12-5). In fact, compressing the pictures only reduces the quality of the pictures inside the document. Your original pictures are untouched.

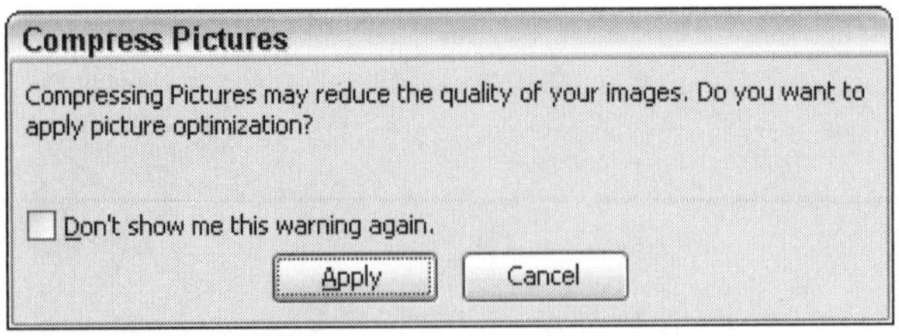

Compress Pictures

Compressing Pictures may reduce the quality of your images. Do you want to apply picture optimization?

☐ Don't show me this warning again.

[Apply] [Cancel]

• **Figure 12-5: A rather confusing warning. Don't worry —
your original pictures are safe and sound.**

10. Click Apply.

Office compresses and/or removes cropped areas from the indicated picture(s) inside the document.

As long as you know where to find the magic Compress button, compressing pictures in a document is fast and easy — and a great way to save time . . . not only for you but for whoever receives the document!

Technique 13

Modifying Toolbars

Save Time By

✔ Taking control of your toolbars

✔ Removing icons that you don't use

✔ Adding icons that will speed up your work

✔ Separating marketing gimmicks from useful features

Microsoft doesn't design the Office toolbars to make your work faster or easier. Microsoft designs toolbars to sell more copies of Office.

Each version of Office wrings out the old toolbars and brings in the new. Office has a frightful tendency to throw out default toolbar icons that have become old hat for the sole and express purpose of bringing in ones that show off new — and in many cases, dubious — features. How else can you explain the fact that, in Word 2003, Microsoft dropped the Search for File icon that appeared in Word 2002 — although, presumably, there's just as much searching in Word 2003 as there was a year previously — and added icons for the Permissions, Research, and Read features, which didn't exist in Word 2002. Looks like a great marketing gimmick to me. Don't be bashful. Save time by making Office work your way.

 After you've had a chance to use an application for a while, choosing your own most-used icons for the toolbars can save you time all the time — click after click after click.

Using Toolbars Effectively

Toolbars are the original Office timesaving technique. Instead of forcing you to hunt and peck your way through layers and layers of menus, the Office toolbars give you one easy, fast, central place to go to perform the tasks that consume your waking, working hours.

All the Office apps have copious quantities of toolbars. Even lowly PowerPoint, which seems to get the short end of the stick so many times, has a dozen of them. The problem doesn't lie in creating more toolbars; the problem is making the toolbars that you use most often do the work you want to do.

If you've spent much time at all with Word 2003, you know that there are more than just two toolbars. The Standard toolbar and the Formatting toolbar — along with the menu bar at the top of the screen — take the lion's share of your workaday clicking. But if you choose Tools⇨Customize⇨Toolbars (see Figure 13-1), you can see a list of 30 toolbars, just waiting to help you with everything from Outlining to inserting Japanese greetings.

• **Figure 13-1: Choose your Word toolbars.**

In fact, Word has dozens of toolbars. Only about half of them can be brought up by using the Tools⇨ Customize⇨Toolbars command. For the rest, you have to hunt around.

 Both the menu bar at the top of the screen — the one that reads File, Edit, View, and so on — and the task pane that appears sporadically on the right of the screen are considered to be toolbars. In fact, it's easy to drag an icon onto the menu bar at the top of the screen, using the steps in this Technique. If you run out of room for icons on your normal toolbars, don't forget that the vast real estate on the right side of the menu bar is always available.

 Unless you're stuck with a horribly tiny screen, you will almost certainly speed up your work by allowing both the Standard and the Formatting toolbars to occupy separate lines at the top of the screen. In fact, this is the very first change I make to any and all Office PCs that I use.

To break free the screen real estate so that the main toolbars can breathe

1. **Start Word.**

2. **Choose Tools⇨Customize⇨Options.**

   You see the Options tab of the Customize dialog box, as shown in Figure 13-2.

• **Figure 13-2: Make Word give the Standard and Formatting toolbars enough room to be useful.**

3. **Enable the Show Standard and Formatting Toolbars on Two Rows check box.**

 While you're here, get rid of those horrible bouncing adaptive menus by enabling the Always Show Full Menus check box. I talk about bouncing menus in Techniques 15, 25, 33, 43, and 52. I'm, uh, rather opinionated on the topic.

4. **Click the Close button.**

Word allots one full line for the Standard toolbar and another full line for the Formatting toolbar — the way the Office gods intended.

5. **Repeat Steps 2–4 for Excel and then likewise for PowerPoint.**

Rearranging Toolbar Icons

Removing icons from any toolbar couldn't be simpler . . . if you know the trick. Permit me to show you how to delete the Permissions icon on the Word 2003 Standard toolbar — an icon that I vow I will never use. You can use these steps in any Office application to remove any other icon that gets in the way of more useful icons, as well:

1. **Start Word.**

2. **Locate the Permissions icon.**

The Permissions icon (see Figure 13-3) allows you to set permissions for a document: who can view it, who can copy it or forward it, and when it will self-destruct. Permissions/Information Rights Management (IRM) strikes me as a half-baked technology poised to bite many people in the butt. Although IRM might improve with time, that isn't going to happen in the near future.

• **Figure 13-3: Your mission: Get rid of this icon.**

3. **Hold down the Alt key.**

4. **Click the Permissions icon and drag it off the toolbar. When the mouse pointer shows an X, just let go of the mouse button.**

That's it. Poof. You'll never see the Permissions icon again unless you intentionally put it back on the toolbar.

 There's a little subtlety here that I'm intentionally glossing over. When you start Word, you see a new, blank document, which is based on the Normal template, `normal.dot`. When you drag an icon off a toolbar, in fact, you're changing the toolbar in `normal.dot`. If you use other templates, things get complicated. But for all intents and purposes, the four simple steps get rid of the icon. Good riddance, I say.

Moving a toolbar icon is every bit as easy as deleting one:

1. **Start the application (Word, Outlook, Excel, PowerPoint, or Access).**

2. **Hold down the Alt key.**

3. **Drag the icon from wherever it is to wherever you want it to be.**

Note that you can drag an icon onto the menu.

4. **When the mouse pointer turns into an I-beam where you want the icon to go, let go of the mouse button.**

 To copy an icon from one toolbar to another (rare, but you might have a good reason for doing so), hold down Ctrl+Alt and then click and drag.

Restoring a Screwed-Up Toolbar

So you played too hard, and now you want to put your toolbar back the way it was? No problem. Of the many ways to do so, here's my favorite.

Choose Tools➪Customize➪Toolbars (refer to Figure 13-1). Click once on the toolbar that you want to revert to its original, pristine state. Then click the Reset button.

Adding Recommended Icons

Microsoft maintains a list of icons that people frequently want to put on their toolbars. As long as the icon that you seek is among this small group of preselected entries, adding the icon to the toolbar is a snap:

1. **Click the down arrow on the far-right end of the toolbar that you want to change.**

2. **Click Add or Remove Buttons and then select the name of the toolbar (for example, Formatting).**

    You see a list of all the preselected icons (see Figure 13-4). A check mark appears next to icons that are already on the toolbar.

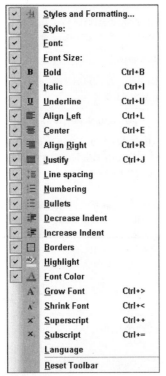

✓	⟋	<u>S</u>tyles and Formatting...	
✓		<u>S</u>tyle:	
✓		<u>F</u>ont:	
✓		<u>F</u>ont Size:	
✓	**B**	<u>B</u>old	Ctrl+B
✓	*I*	<u>I</u>talic	Ctrl+I
✓	<u>U</u>	<u>U</u>nderline	Ctrl+U
✓	≣	Align <u>L</u>eft	Ctrl+L
✓	≣	<u>C</u>enter	Ctrl+E
✓	≣	Align <u>R</u>ight	Ctrl+R
✓	≣	<u>J</u>ustify	Ctrl+J
✓	⌐≣	Line spacing	
✓	⌐≣	<u>N</u>umbering	
✓	⌐≣	<u>B</u>ullets	
✓	⌐≣	<u>D</u>ecrease Indent	
✓	⌐≣	<u>I</u>ncrease Indent	
✓	☐	<u>B</u>orders	
✓	ᵃᵇ⁄	<u>H</u>ighlight	
✓	A	<u>F</u>ont Color	
	A˙	<u>G</u>row Font	Ctrl+>
	A˙	<u>S</u>hrink Font	Ctrl+<
	×	<u>S</u>uperscript	Ctrl++
	×	<u>S</u>ubscript	Ctrl+=
		<u>L</u>anguage	
		<u>R</u>eset Toolbar	

• **Figure 13-4:** Word's preapproved list of icons for the Formatting toolbar.

3. **Click to check any icons that you want to appear on the toolbar.**

    You can clear any check mark by clicking, too, if you want to get rid of a specific icon.

4. **Click anywhere outside the list of icons.**

    The changes that you made show up on the toolbar immediately.

Office has a predefined sequence for new icons: It always puts a new icon in the same location on the toolbar. But, as I describe in the preceding section, it's very easy to drag any icon you like to a new location.

Making Any Command a Toolbar Icon

Although it's a little bit more work, you can put an icon on any toolbar that will perform just about any command. If you can click a menu and get an Office app to do something, you can probably put an icon on a toolbar of your choice that does precisely the same thing.

For example, in all the Office apps, you can choose File➪Save As to bring up the Save As dialog box. For most people, most of the time, that's no big deal. You want to do a Save As maybe once a day or once a week, and it isn't worth cluttering up your toolbar with a specific Save As icon.

Some people, though, use Save As all the time. For those folks, it makes sense to put a Save As icon some place very convenient, like on the main (Standard) toolbar. Say you want to put a Save As icon on Word 2003's Standard toolbar. Here's how:

1. **Start Word and choose Tools➪Customize➪ Commands.**

    Word shows you the Commands tab of the Customize dialog box, as in Figure 13-5.

2. **Make sure that the Save In box at the bottom of the dialog box reads either Normal or Normal.dot.**

    That ensures that any changes you make to toolbars will show up in normal blank documents (that is, ones that you haven't applied other templates to).

• **Figure 13-5:** Drag your choice of commands onto any toolbar from this dialog box.

3. On the left, under Categories, select File. On the right, under Commands, click once on the line that reads Save As.

File⇨Save As is only an example. You can find almost all menu commands — and hundreds of additional commands that aren't on any menu — by scrounging around in the Categories and Commands lists.

4. Drag the line that reads Save As to whatever toolbar location you like.

5. When the mouse pointer turns into an I-beam where you want the icon to go, release the mouse button.

In Figure 13-6, I release the mouse button as soon as the mouse pointer turns into an I-beam to the right of the Save icon.

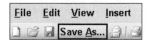

• **Figure 13-6:** Save As goes to the right of the Save icon.

6. If you add an icon with a picture that you don't like, make sure the Customize dialog is still open, right-click the image, choose Change Button Image, and then pick a picture that you like.

In Figure 13-7, I chose a diskette with a down arrow.

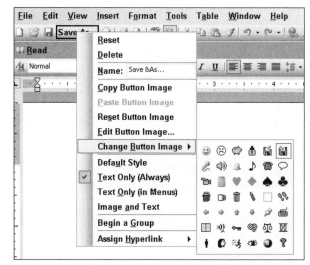

• **Figure 13-7:** Choose a picture from the ones offered.

Sometimes you have to right-click the icon and choose Change Button Image a second time and then pick the new image again. This appears to be a bug (or at least an oddity) in the way Office switches from icons with text into icons with both pictures and text. At any rate, if you don't get the picture you want the first time, try, try, try again.

7. If you add an icon with text that you want to get rid of (Save As, in this case), right-click the icon and choose Default Style.

8. Click Close in the Customize dialog box, and you can use your chosen icon on the toolbar (see Figure 13-8).

• **Figure 13-8: The new Save As icon.**

 You can paste any icon image onto a toolbar icon by using the Paste Button Image command in Figure 13-7. My favorite program for retrieving icon images is Icon Snatcher from Creative Design. To download it, go to `www.cdiware.com`. Click the Software tab, scroll down to find Icon Snatcher, and follow the instructions.

Technique 14

Getting Help

Save Time By

- ✔ Making Office Help more visible
- ✔ Knowing where to look
- ✔ Knowing how to ask

Everybody needs Help sometimes. Master Office Help, and you'll save hours and hours of frustration. But before you delve into this Technique, it helps to know what you're up against. Here are my big gripes about Office Help:

- ✔ **Microsoft keeps changing the way it works.** Office Help is so different from version to version that you have to keep relearning how to use it. Never fear. MS will change it again; it's still not right.

- ✔ **It's hard to find an answer unless you already know the answer.** Major culprits: all the jargon and a lack of links. However, there are some solutions, which I discuss in this Technique.

- ✔ **Help topics toe the Microsoft Party Line.** Too often, Help explains how Office *should* work — not how it really does work. To make things worse, all too often, Microsoft uses Knowledge Base articles, and Security Bulletins manage to obfuscate and not educate.

- ✔ **Topics are poorly connected.** Frequently you find solutions to bits and pieces of a problem, but only rarely is there an explanation of how to solve an entire problem or how the pieces fit together.

Fortunately, I can show you ways to fight those problems — and ways to get help that don't involve Microsoft at all — such as reading this book, for example.

Making Help Visible

I hate the Office 2003 Help interface. Even on a very-high-resolution monitor, the Help pains, er, panes keep getting in the way. With the Help window sitting on top of the main window, I can't get any work done, and if I didn't need to refer to Help, I wouldn't have opened it in the first place. As far as I'm concerned, if you're going to be using Help extensively, the first bit of help that everyone needs is to put Help in its place.

Here's how to access Help and make it visible while you're working:

1. **Start Word (or any other Office app; they all work the same way).**

2. **Press F1.**

Word shows you the Word Help task pane (see Figure 14-1).

• **Figure 14-1:** The Help pane connects to Microsoft's Help Web site.

3. **Type a search term in the Search For box and press Enter.**

Assuming that you're connected to the Internet, the Office Help engine runs out to Microsoft's Web site and returns a list similar to the one in Figure 14-2. (I typed **connector**.) For tips on search terms, see the next section, "Popping the Question."

The list of Help articles that you receive today could well be different from the list that you receive on the same query next week. Microsoft has massive programs that monitor which articles are used and how people respond to them. Based on the results, responses to inquiries get rearranged from time to time.

• **Figure 14-2:** The retrieved list of Help "hits" appears in the task pane.

4. **In the Search Results pane, select the article you want.**

I chose the Draw a Line or Connector Help topic, which appears. After you click a topic, Help becomes unwieldy in one of two ways:

▶ **If Help determines that you have a lot of room on your screen, the topic goes in a task pane-like strip on the right of the screen.** Even on a very-high-resolution monitor, the Help task pane combined with the Help topic on the right wastes a lot of room; nearly half the monitor is taken up with Help, and when you type in a document, the text gets slammed around, trying to avoid the task pane.

▶ **If you're using a smaller screen, the Help topic floats over the top of your document — where you're trying to work (see Figure 14-3).** On a low-resolution monitor, the Help topic floats, but the topic's window is just like any other window: When you start typing in your document, the Help topic goes away. Hardly a good way to get help!

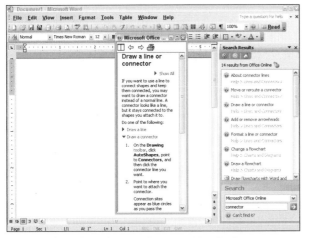

• **Figure 14-3:** This Help window is getting in the way.

 If you're trying to work quickly, both of these results are very intrusive. To streamline your work area, keep Help accessible but out of the way. You only need to follow these steps once: The Office app remembers what you did.

5. **The best solution I've found: Click the column of dots to the left of the term *Search Results* and then drag the task pane onto the document. Then click the Auto Tile icon in the topic window.**

You can resize the Search Results task pane to some extent and tuck it into a little-used corner of the screen (see Figure 14-4). Clicking the Auto Tile icon on the Help topic ensures that the Help topic will continue to be visible even when you're typing in the document.

6. **When you're through using Help, put the task pane back where you got it by clicking and dragging it to the right side of the screen.**

You want to put the task pane back because if you don't, it'll float on top of your document even when you're using it for something other than Help.

• **Figure 14-4:** Drag the Search Results task pane onto the document and click Auto Tile on the Help topic.

If you have trouble dragging it back — the pane has a nasty habit of clinging to the toolbars at the top of the screen — drag it way over to the right of the screen so that it's almost off the screen; then slowly drag it up.

Popping the Question

By far the easiest, fastest way to use Office Help is by simply typing a few words in the Type a Question for Help box at the far upper right of the screen. That does precisely the same thing as bringing up the Help task pane and typing in the Search For box.

Here are some quick tips for successful searches:

✔ **Get connected.** Make sure you're connected to the Internet. If you're unplugged, you only get results from the comparatively tiny database that's installed on your computer.

✔ **Keep it short.** Although it's true that you can phrase your question in the form of a question (to coin a phrase), I invariably find that using keywords in the Type a Question for Help box produces better results.

✔ **Try different keywords.** If you don't find what
you want the first time, use completely different
words the second time.

✔ **Stick with jargon.** If you know the jargon, use the
precise term that describes what you're after. If
you aren't sure of the exact name of what you
want, use very generic terms and try drilling
down (see the next section, "Drilling Down Fast").

✔ **Search the Table of Contents.** When all else fails,
use the Help Table of Contents (see Figure 14-5).
You can go directly to a Table of Contents entry
by clicking the gray link below any result in the
Search Results task pane.

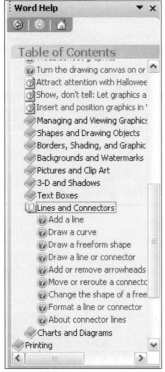

• **Figure 14-5: Help's Table of Contents might point in the
right direction.**

Drilling Down Fast

Office 2003's online Help includes thousands of how-
to articles and animated training sessions, most of
which cover topics quite superficially (see Figure
14-6). You can identify how-to articles by the ques-
tion-mark-on-top-of-a-document icon that appears in
the Search Results task pane (for example, in Figures
14-2 and 14-4).

• **Figure 14-6: A very brief introduction to positioning
graphics in documents.**

Many Office users look at a few how-to articles in
online Help and decide that they really don't cover
the topic at the depth that they need. Most find that
the articles don't solve the specific problem they
have at hand.

Don't give up.

Each one of those articles contains oodles and oodles of Microsoft jargon. If you ever find yourself stuck in Help's Search For box, looking for the right word or words to describe your problem, try running through a how-to article. Even if the article you read is only vaguely related, you can likely pick up the jargon that you need to plug into the search box — jargon that will lead you to the answers you seek. That's the best way I know to find answers to common questions, fast.

Digging Deeper: The Knowledge Base

When you go looking beyond the basics, Office's online Help won't, uh, help. You have to haul out the big guns and refer directly to Microsoft's Knowledge Base (KB).

The *Knowledge Base* is Microsoft's massive reference for everything related to MS products. Whereas mere mortals like you and me can see only part of the Knowledge Base (Microsoft doesn't air its dirty linen in public), the KB that we *can* see includes detailed articles on thousands — hundreds of thousands — of topics.

To put it a slightly different way: Office online Help tells you how Office is supposed to work. Some parts of the Knowledge Base tell you how Office really does work. (Unfortunately, there's plenty of fluff in the KB, too. But it isn't nearly as bad as online Help.)

Using the KB isn't much different from using online Help:

1. **Bring up Internet Explorer and go to**
    `http://support.microsoft.com`.

    This is Microsoft's general support page (see Figure 14-7).

• **Figure 14-7**: A good place to start if you're looking for more help than Office online Help can give.

2. **Click the <u>Search the Knowledge Base</u> link.**

    You get the KB search page (see Figure 14-8).

• **Figure 14-8**: Start your search here.

3. **Pick the product that you're concerned about in the Select a Microsoft Product drop-down list.**

 Specifying a product is a frequently overlooked key step. There's so much in the KB that blindly searching for keywords without limiting the search to a specific product really wastes your time.

4. **Type the keyword(s) in the Search For box and then click Go.**

The KB returns with as many matches as you specified. In Figure 14-9, six articles match my search criteria.

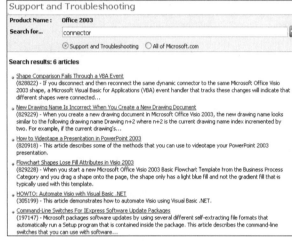

Support and Troubleshooting

Product Name : Office 2003

Search for... connector

⦿ Support and Troubleshooting ⚪ All of Microsoft.com

Search results: 6 articles

○ Shape Comparison Fails Through a VBA Event
(828822) - If you disconnect and then reconnect the same dynamic connector to the same Microsoft Office Visio 2003 shape, a Microsoft Visual Basic for Applications (VBA) event handler that tracks these changes will indicate that different shapes were connected...

○ New Drawing Name Is Incorrect When You Create a New Drawing Document
(829229) - When you create a new drawing document in Microsoft Office Visio 2003, the new drawing name looks similar to the following drawing name Drawing n+2 where n+2 is the current drawing name index incremented by two. For example, if the current drawing's...

○ How to Videotape a Presentation in PowerPoint 2003
(820918) - This article describes some of the methods that you can use to videotape your PowerPoint 2003 presentation.

○ Flowchart Shapes Lose Fill Attributes in Visio 2003
(829228) - When you start a new Microsoft Office Visio 2003 Basic Flowchart Template from the Business Process Category and you drag a shape onto the page, the shape only has a light blue fill and not the gradient fill that is typically used with this template.

○ HOWTO: Automate Visio with Visual Basic .NET
(305199) - This article demonstrates how to automate Visio using Visual Basic .NET.

○ Command-Line Switches For IExpress Software Update Packages
(197147) - Microsoft packages software updates by using several different self-extracting file formats that automatically run a Setup program that is contained inside the package. This article describes the command-line switches that you can use with software...

• **Figure 14-9: Although many KB articles are very technical, some of the how-to articles are readable — and even accurate.**

5. **If you didn't find what you want, click the Back button in your browser and try a different search.**

 Sometimes searching for older versions will ferret out results that apply to later versions. For example, if you search for a keyword in Office 2003 and come up with bupkis, try searching for the same keyword in Office XP. I'm frequently pleasantly surprised.

 Don't limit your searches to the product at hand: if you hit a problem in Word, try searching in Excel. Sometimes searching in another Office application area can return good results, especially when checking an operation error that might have caused Office to not properly function or dealing with some features that are common to all of Office.

When you call Microsoft Tech Support, the technician's first line of inquiry is the Knowledge Base — the same Knowledge Base that you can search, using this Technique. You can save a lot of time (and money!) if you learn to do it yourself.

Every Knowledge Base article has a six-digit number up at the top of the article. That's a mighty handy way to keep track of problems and their solutions; advanced users refer to article numbers (for example, KB123456) all the time. If you want to find an article again, make sure you get the number.

At the bottom of every Knowledge Base article, you'll see a last-reviewed date (see Figure 14-10). The date can give you a feel for whether Microsoft has come up with a new approach to solving a problem or whether you're looking at an article that's been gathering dust for eons. Most have version numbers — a welcome addition that should put to rest lingering ill feelings about Microsoft changing KB articles surreptitiously to cover up stupid mistakes. If you look at a KB article and it's up to, oh, version 2.1, you can bet your bottom buck that Microsoft's been struggling with the problem, too — and might not have it right yet. Ach, the stories I could tell!

Last Reviewed: 11/10/2003 (1.0)

Keywords: kbcode kbprb KB828822 kbAudDeveloper kbAudEndUser

• **Figure 14-10: Glance at the bottom of a KB article to get an idea of how recently it's been updated — and how many times it's been fixed.**

A Word about Connectors

You might have noticed that I use the same example throughout this Technique, searching for help on connectors. There's a reason why. When I was writing Technique 11, I hit a repeated problem trying to get *connectors* — the "stick to" lines between shapes in the drawing layer — to stick to AutoShapes. All the online Help explained precisely how connectors work. Er, how they're *supposed* to work. A Web search through Google came up with zip. I've written about connectors a dozen times and had no problems.

Even the KB produced no results — as you can see in various screen shots throughout this Technique. I lost hours trying to find an answer.

In the end, I got lucky. I finally guessed that the drawing canvas might be the key and, as described in Technique 11, turning on the canvas solves the problem. It's a good example of a simple problem that isn't documented anywhere. Office has zillions of problems like that. Zillions.

Finding Help from Other Users

The best way to get help is to ask someone who knows. Many Office guri work for pizza and beer. They're good people to get to know.

A surprisingly large number of kind-hearted Office folks hang out online, and many of them will tackle problems just for the challenge and an occasional heart-felt thank you.

Many of those good folks — volunteers all — hang out on my message site, the WOPR Lounge. Drop by www.wopr.com/lounge sometime when you're up a creek without a paddle, and see whether one of the people there can lend a hand.

You'll also find lots and lots of help in the Microsoft-run newsgroups. Look on the server msnews.microsoft.com for newsgroups beginning with microsoft.public.

Finally, don't forget to subscribe to my free weekly Office newsletter, *Woody's Office Watch,* www.woodyswatch.com. With more than half a million subscribers, the Watches are the one source of (fiercely independent!) help that all Office users need.

Part II

Saving Time with Word

The 5th Wave   By Rich Tennant

"Oh, Anthony loves working with AppleScript. He customized all our Word documents with a sound file so they all close out with a 'Badda Bing!'"

Technique 15

Getting Word Settings Right

Save Time By

- Keeping Word's mitts off what you type
- Making Word show you vital parts of your documents
- Using Word's options to speed up your work

Right out of the box, Word is designed to make it easy for new users to understand what they're doing. Of course, it fails miserably. Try to explain to your Word-neophyte friends why typing **1.** and a few letters and then pressing Enter suddenly starts adorning paragraphs with phantom numbers that you can't delete — or even *select,* for that matter.

I think that Microsoft underestimates the intelligence of its users and overestimates their desire for whiz-bang, so-called features that only get in the way. Keep it simple, sez I. If you've used Word for more than a few weeks, it's time to take off the training wheels. That's what this Technique is all about.

Word bunches unrelated settings in different dialog boxes with the consistency of a kangaroo on a random walk. For the sake of my sanity (and saving your time) in this Technique, I group recommended changes together based on their location in the Word menus. It's a terribly disjointed approach, but by knocking off all the settings in one fell swoop, dialog box by dialog box, you should be able to breeze through this Technique in minutes.

 If you aren't particularly interested in the *why* and want to cut straight to the *what,* skip the text and set your settings to look like those in the figures.

Blistering the Bouncing Menus

At the top of my most-hated list: the fact that my menus don't stay put. I *hate* adaptive menus — the ones that go boing-boing-boing when you click them. (Microsoft calls them *personalized* or *animated* menus.) Hunting and searching for menu items, trying to find them when they've been moved around, rates as a class-A waste of time. Your eyes and fingers should grow accustomed to menus being in a certain place. Why go looking?

A close second: the fact that Word, straight out of the box, doesn't show me all the buttons on my two most-used toolbars.

Start with the Customize dialog box:

1. **Choose Tools⇨Customize⇨Options.**

Word shows you the Options tab of the Customize dialog box (see Figure 15-1).

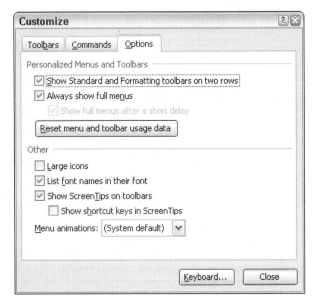

• **Figure 15-1: The Customize dialog box controls the appearance of the menu and toolbars.**

2. **Mark the Show Standard and Formatting Toolbars on Two Rows check box.**

I talk about this setting in Technique 13. You need to be able to see all the icons on your two key toolbars. If you're running a monitor at incredibly high resolution — well beyond 1280 x 1024 — you might be able to see all the icons on one row. But for those of us in economy class, Word needs two rows. It's utterly inconceivable to me why Microsoft doesn't make both toolbars fully visible, right out of the box.

3. **Mark the Always Show Full Menus check box.**

That keeps your menus from bouncing around like a jumping bean in a microwave.

4. **Click Close.**

Seeing Clearly

Microsoft's second greatest design gaffe is trying to hide key information from you. It's time to see all the pieces that are making your life miserable.

To get your View settings straight

1. **Choose Tools⇨Options⇨View.**

Word shows you the View tab of the Options dialog box (see Figure 15-2).

• **Figure 15-2: These settings control what you see onscreen.**

2. **Consider clearing the Windows in Taskbar check box.**

If you frequently tile multiple documents so that you can see them all at once, you probably want to clear this check box. If switching among open documents by clicking the taskbar buttons is more your style, you probably want to leave the box checked.

When the Windows in Taskbar box check box is enabled, Word puts a separate entry on the Windows taskbar for each open document (as shown in Figure 15-3). That can be very handy for switching between open documents. But Word also insists on putting menus, icons, rulers, and more inside the window for *every* open document. That makes it difficult — if not impossible — to work on three or more documents simultaneously. (Tile Word windows automatically by choosing Window⇨Arrange All.)

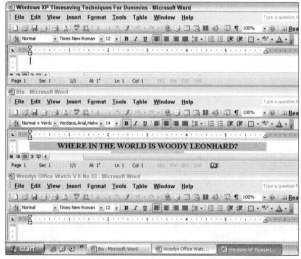

• **Figure 15-3:** Here's how tiled Word windows and the taskbar look with Windows in Taskbar enabled.

When the Windows in Taskbar check box is cleared, Word puts just one entry on the Windows taskbar for all of Word. If you want

to switch among open documents, you have to do it from inside Word itself (see Figure 15-4). On the other hand, Word puts only one set of menus, icons, and rulers in its window, for use by all open documents.

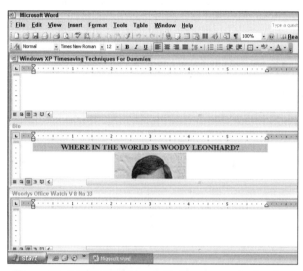

• **Figure 15-4:** With Windows in Taskbar unmarked, only one button is in the taskbar, and you have more breathing room for multiple documents.

Personally, I keep this check box enabled, but then again, I don't arrange multiple documents on the screen all that often. Your mileage may vary.

I dunno why Microsoft doesn't give us the obvious timesaving option — put multiple buttons in the Windows taskbar but only use one set of menus and icons. That's the way Excel has worked for a decade.

3. **Mark the Tab Characters check box.**

If you do any work at all with tabs — in fact, even if you press the Tab key accidentally — you'll be completely lost unless you can see Tab characters on the screen.

4. **Mark the Paragraph Marks check box.**

Word stores all its paragraph formatting in the paragraph mark. If you can't see the paragraph marks in a document, you don't stand a chance of understanding how formatting is being applied. Personally, I won't even look at a Word document unless paragraph marks are showing.

 Word users lose enormous amounts of time trying to track down problems caused by invisible paragraph marks. You probably know that a paragraph's style is stored in its paragraph mark. But did you know that every paragraph's spacing, indent, and tab stop settings are stored there, too? If you have an autonumbered or autobulleted paragraph, all the associated information is stored in the paragraph mark, as are the alignment, boxes and background shading, and a dozen different settings. Heck, even a document's *section* settings — headers and footers, column spacing, and the like — are in the final paragraph mark.

If all your paragraphs suddenly appear right-aligned, or bold, or numbered, or if your tabs aren't working right, or bullets sprout up like dandelions on a brand-new lawn, the paragraph mark is invariably the culprit. The difference between copying a paragraph without the paragraph mark at the end and copying it with the paragraph mark can be devastating. *You need to be able to see your paragraph marks.*

5. **Mark the Object Anchors check box.**

Floating pictures move with the paragraph they're attached to: Move the paragraph, and the picture goes with it. Of course, that begs the question of which paragraph the floating picture attached to. Enable this check box, and Word shows a little anchor symbol next to the paragraph that's attached to a picture. (See Technique 24 for much more about floating and inline pictures.)

6. **Set the Style Area Width to half an inch or thereabouts.**

The Style Area Width comes into play only when you work in so-called Normal view. In Normal view, Word shows you the names of the styles to the left of each paragraph (see the left side of Figure 15-5), providing that the Style Area Width isn't zero. Most of us usually work in Print Layout view and only flip over to Normal view to pay special attention to the text. That's when you're most likely to want to see style names.

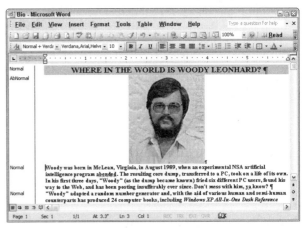

• **Figure 15-5:** In Normal view, if the Style Area Width is not zero, the name of each paragraph's style appears to the left of the paragraph.

7. **Click OK.**

Zapping the Drawing Canvas

Word calls these General settings. I think of them as a miscellaneous-of-the-miscellaneous kind of collection:

1. **Choose Tools➪Options➪General.**

You see the General tab of the Options dialog box (see Figure 15-6).

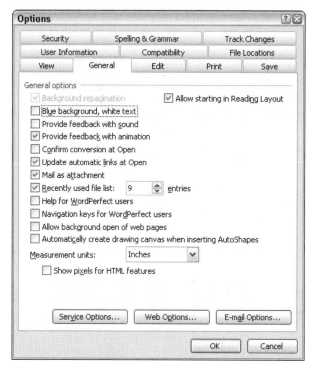

• **Figure 15-6: Get rid of the drawing canvas here.**

2. **Run the Recently Used File List up to 9 entries.**

When you choose File, the list of most recently used files appears at the bottom of the menu. Microsoft originally set the number of files to be displayed on the list at 4 when 640 x 480 monitors were common (to conserve space). There's no reason at all to leave it at 4.

3. **Clear the Automatically Create Drawing Canvas When Inserting AutoShapes check box . . .**

. . . and drive a stake through its heart. I talk about — indeed, rail against — this intrusive setting in Technique 11.

 You'll encounter a few times when you really must have a drawing canvas. Specifically, if you need "stick on" connectors that move when their attached shapes move (as you likely would for a flowchart), Word requires that your drawing go on a drawing canvas.

Unfortunately, Word doesn't have an Insert⇨ Drawing Canvas command or anything similar. The only way that you can put a drawing canvas in your document is by enabling this check box and then using the Drawing toolbar to put an AutoShape in your document, thus automatically generating a drawing canvas.

4. **Click OK.**

Taking Back Your Mouse

The next set of settings deal with editing text:

1. **Choose Tools⇨Options⇨Edit.**

You see the Edit tab of the Options dialog box (see Figure 15-7).

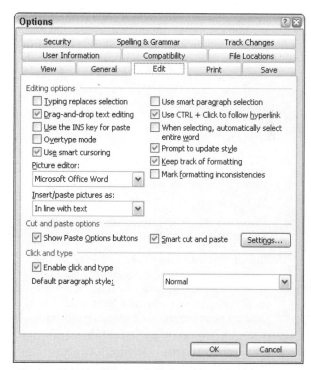

• **Figure 15-7: A plethora of settings for editing.**

2. **Consider clearing the Typing Replaces Selection check box.**

If this check box is marked, when you select text and then type, the first letter that you type replaces all the selected text. Most Windows programs work that way, but I personally don't like it. With the check box cleared, if you have something selected when you type, Word simply moves to the beginning of the selection before putting your typed text into the document.

3. **Clear the Use Smart Paragraph Selection check box.**

This setting exists only because Microsoft doesn't to show paragraph marks on the screen by default. If you select the Use Smart Paragraph Selection box (wink, wink), Word surreptitiously selects the paragraph mark (nod, nod) when you select all the text in a paragraph (nudge, nudge). Why? Quoth Microsoft, "If you include the paragraph mark when you cut and paste a paragraph, you don't leave a blank paragraph, and your formatting automatically stays with the paragraph." This is a very convoluted (and inaccurate) way of saying that *Word stores all its paragraph formatting in the paragraph mark.*

If you can see your paragraph marks — I show you how in the earlier "Seeing Clearly" section — you can decide for yourself whether you want to select a paragraph mark. Don't leave it up to Word. Clear the check box.

4. **Clear the When Selecting, Automatically Select Entire Word check box.**

In fact, this intrusive IntelliNONsense setting does much more than automatically select entire words. Leave this check box enabled, and Word wrests control of the mouse from your hands, making even the simplest selecting jobs much more time-consuming than need be.

If your mousing skills are anywhere near capable — much less proficient — the Automatically Select Entire Word setting eats into your productivity. Dump it.

And don't forget that you can frequently select small pieces of text much more quickly and accurately by simply holding down the Shift key and pressing the right and left arrows.

 If you want to select an entire word, you can double-click it. To a first approximation, anyway. The problem is that double-clicking a word that's followed by a space selects the word and the space. But if you double-click a word that's followed by a punctuation mark or paragraph mark, you get the word without the final punctuation or paragraph mark (even if you can't see the paragraph mark). Life ain't so simple, eh?

5. **Mark the Prompt to Update Style check box.**

In certain circumstances, Word will change the definition of a style without even asking. (You have to change formatting manually and then reapply the style.) Word should always ask before changing things.

6. **Click OK.**

Correcting AutoCorrect

If you haven't yet changed AutoCorrect — most likely by using a Smart Tag to tell Word to keep its hands off — this section alone will pay for the book.

Word has an absolutely infuriating habit of correcting things that shouldn't be corrected. I talk about Word's mangling of typed Web addresses and e-mail addresses in Technique 7. That's just one of the problems. To correct the rest:

1. **Choose Tools➪AutoCorrect Options➪ AutoFormat As You Type.**

Word gives you a list of all the things that it changes while you are sleeping, er, typing (see Figure 15-8).

Most AutoFormat and AutoCorrect settings are infuriating computer-knows-better-than-you time sinks. Stop Word from fiddling with your work and turn off most of these settings.

AutoCorrect

AutoText	AutoFormat	Smart Tags
AutoCorrect		AutoFormat As You Type

Replace as you type

- ☑ "Straight quotes" with "smart quotes"
- ☑ Ordinals (1st) with superscript
- ☐ Fractions (1/2) with fraction character (½)
- ☑ Hyphens (--) with dash (—)
- ☐ *Bold* and _italic_ with real formatting
- ☐ Internet and network paths with hyperlinks

Apply as you type

- ☐ Automatic bulleted lists
- ☐ Automatic numbered lists
- ☐ Border lines
- ☐ Tables
- ☐ Built-in Heading styles

Automatically as you type

- ☐ Format beginning of list item like the one before it
- ☑ Set left- and first-indent with tabs and backspaces
- ☐ Define styles based on your formatting

OK   Cancel

• **Figure 15-8:** Most AutoFormat settings only get in your way.

2. **Consider clearing the Fractions (1/2) with Fraction Character check box.**

It's misleading. Word is only capable of changing three fractions — ½, ¼, and ¾ — into single characters. If you type any other fraction, Word doesn't even try to change it because Windows doesn't have fonts that can handle it. I'd rather have all my fractions look the same, so I clear this check box.

3. **Clear the Internet and Network Paths with Hyperlinks check box.**

I rant about this setting in Technique 7. Get rid of it.

4. **Clear all the check boxes under Apply As You Type.**

If you've ever typed **1.**, some text, and then pressed Enter — only to discover that Word creates bizarre numbered paragraphs with phantom numbers that you can't delete or even select — you've been bitten by these settings. Tell Word to keep its steeeeeenkin' hands off. If you want bullets, you can click the bullet icon. Ditto for numbered lists and border lines, and you can click the Tables and Borders icon to draw your own table, thank you very much.

5. **Clear the Format Beginning of List Item Like the One before It check box.**

This is a bizarre, badly documented setting with almost unpredictable behavior. In Word 2002 (Microsoft didn't even bother documenting the setting in Word 2003), online Help says, "Automatically repeats character formatting that you apply to the beginning of a list item. For example, if the first word or phrase of a list item is bold, Word automatically applies bold formatting to the first word or phrase of the next list item."

One little problem: That isn't the case, and if you spend 30 seconds working with the setting, you'll see that. Get rid of it.

6. **Click OK.**

Making Final Timesaving Changes

I make two additional changes to Word:

1. **Choose View➪Ruler and turn off the rulers.**

Most of the time, the rulers just get in the way. Use the screen real estate to see more of your document as you write. If you need to see the horizontal ruler (the one at the top) for just a second, move your mouse up and hover directly underneath the Formatting toolbar (the one with font names on it). The ruler stays on the screen until you move your mouse.

2. **Choose Tools⇨Macro⇨Security.**

Word responds with the Security dialog box (see Figure 15-9).

• **Figure 15-9: Change macro settings here, but only after you know what the settings do.**

3. **Select the Medium radio button.**

 Make sure you know what you're doing when you change the macro Security Level setting. Unfortunately, when you set Word's macro security to High, all the macro babies get thrown out with the bathwater: Word throws away any macros attached to documents or templates that you receive and *doesn't even ask* whether it's okay to run them. Conversely, if you set it to Low, Word doesn't even scan for viruses.

If you have a decent antivirus package installed and you update it regularly and use it religiously — and you follow my recommendation in the next step — putting Word on Medium security should not incur any significant risk. With security set at Medium, you'll have the advantage of being able

to see and use macros that other people send you — although you will need to approve them every time that you open the macro-enhanced document or template.

4. **Click the Trusted Publishers tab.**

Word shows you a list of software publishers — actually a list of companies or individuals who electronically sign their macros — whom you have given blanket approval to run on your PC.

5. **If any publishers are listed, click each, one by one, and then click the Remove button (see Figure 15-10).**

Why? Because there have been instances where electronic signatures have been hijacked, including a celebrated case where somebody conned VeriSign into issuing two bogus Microsoft signatures (news.com.com/2100-1001-254586.html). Nobody has yet come up with a macro virus that operates under the cloak of a hijacked signature. But it could happen.

6. **Click OK.**

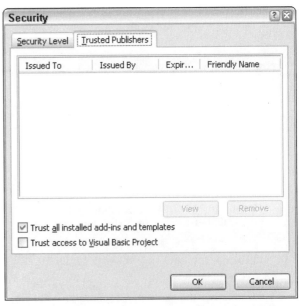

• **Figure 15-10: Make sure you have no trusted publishers. Not even Microsoft. Especially not Microsoft.**

I have an important handful of additional suggestions for changing Word's default behavior, but they all involve modifying a file called `normal.dot`. See Technique 16 for details.

Saving Your Settings

After you have your settings the way that you want them, store them away so they're easy to bring back — or so you can carry them to a new computer:

1. Choose Start➪All Programs➪Microsoft Office➪ Microsoft Office Tools➪Microsoft Office 2003 Save My Settings Wizard.

The wizard appears. It's a rather ordinary look-ing wizard but a worthwhile one for us Muggles.

2. Click Next.

3. Mark the Save the Settings From This Machine check box and then click Next.

You can also use the wizard to restore settings from a different machine.

4. Choose a location for the settings (".OPS") file.

5. Click Finish.

The wizard completes. Tuck away a copy of the file someplace safe.

 To restore the settings, choose Start➪ All Programs➪Microsoft Office➪ Microsoft Office Tools➪Microsoft Office 2003 Save My Settings Wizard. Click Next and then choose Restore Previously Saved Settings to This Machine. Choose the OPS file that con-tains the backup you wish to use and then click Finish.

Technique 16

Changing Your Normal Template

Save Time By

- Setting the font and other properties of all new blank documents
- Making personal privacy settings permanent — once and for all
- Controlling the formatting on all new AutoShapes

When Word creates a new blank document, in fact, it makes a carbon copy of a template file called `normal.dot`. There's nothing particularly normal about `normal.dot`, but it does occupy a pivotal position in the Word hierarchy. As the progenitor of most of your new documents (specifically it's the template on which all new documents are based, unless you apply a different template), if you make a change to `normal.dot`, that change gets picked up whenever you create a blank document.

You can save a lot of time by creating templates for each of your most common types of documents: status reports, sales proposals, internal memos, and on and on. Think of anything that differs from your normal kinds of documents in predictable ways (perhaps some boilerplate text like a *From the desk of* line) as a good candidate for its own template.

This Technique shows you ways to save time by making overarching changes once inside your templates, which carries those changes over into all new documents created based on those templates. After you have the foundation set, you can build templates to solve every problem. For example, Technique 23 shows you how to make a letterhead template — a very specialized and surprisingly difficult task.

Customizing Blank Documents

Every Word document is based on a *template,* which is a proto-document that contains all the settings necessary to grow a new document. When you tell Word to create a new document based on a template, Word basically makes a copy of the template and uses the copy as the new document.

It's a little more complicated than that but not much.

Whatever you add to template will show up when you create a document using that template. If you stick a picture of a gargoyle in a template, every new document based on that template will include the picture of the gargoyle. There's nothing magical about the gargoyle in the new document: You can click it, resize it, drag it, and even delete it. But it's there, right from the get-go.

One template, the *Normal template* (filename, normal.dot), gets pressed into service whenever you create a new blank document. If you click the New Blank Document icon at the beginning of the Standard toolbar (see Figure 16-1), you don't get a blank document, *per se*. You really get a copy of normal.dot. That's also the case if you choose File➪New and choose Blank Document from the top of the task pane or if you choose File➪New➪Templates/ On My Computer➪General and double-click Blank Document.

• **Figure 16-1:** Click here to create a new blank document: actually, a copy of normal.dot.

Microsoft has built a lot of fancy ways to change normal.dot directly from inside various dialog boxes — they're called *tunnels*. But the fastest, easiest, and most reliable way to make changes to normal.dot is to simply open it up and make the changes.

If you make the changes described in this Technique to normal.dot, the new settings propagate to any new templates that you create based on normal.dot. For example, if you change your privacy settings in normal.dot and then create a new template for your weekly status report, those privacy settings get carried across.

To make changes that affect all new blank documents, do the following:

1. **Make sure that Windows is set up to show your hidden folders.**

The easiest way to do that is to choose Start➪ My Documents and then choose Tools➪ Folder Options➪View. Under Hidden Files and Folders, click the Show Hidden Files and Folders button, and then click OK.

2. **Start Word. Choose File➪Open. In the Files of Type box, choose Document Templates.**

3. **In the Look In box, navigate to** C:\Documents and Settings*<your user name>* \Application Data\Microsoft\Templates.

You see the Open dialog box, shown in Figure 16-2.

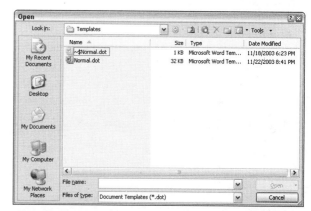

• **Figure 16-2:** Normal.dot **is tucked away in a hidden folder.**

4. **Double-click** Normal.dot.

Word opens the file, just like any other document or template.

5. **Choose Format➪Styles and Formatting.**

Word brings up the Styles and Formatting task pane (as shown in Figure 16-3).

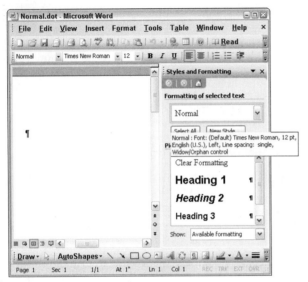

• **Figure 16-3: The list of paragraph styles in** `normal.dot`.

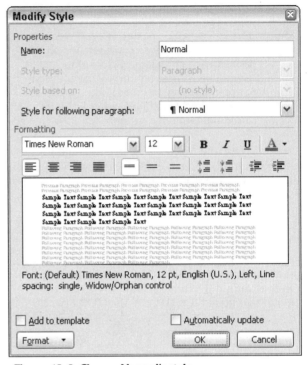

• **Figure 16-4: Change Normal's style.**

6. To change the default font for new blank documents, click the down arrow to the right of Normal and then choose Modify.

The Modify Style dialog box appears (see Figure 16-4).

7. Choose Format⇨Font from the lower left of the dialog box and then choose your new default font. When you're done, click OK.

I'm partial to Garamond, 11 point for business correspondence. No doubt you have your own preference.

8. If you want to change the default paragraph style (perhaps to add extra spacing or to automatically indent the first line of each paragraph), choose Format⇨Paragraph, make the changes, and then click OK.

9. When you're done with the Modify Style dialog box, click OK.

You don't need to mark the Add to Template check box — and for heaven's sake, do *not* select the Automatically Update check box. That'll cause you all sorts of trouble down the road.

If you select the Automatically Update check box, Word automatically redefines the style every time a document is opened, changing the style in the document to match the style in the template. If you never change styles in the template, the automatic update isn't a problem. But the minute a style gets changes — even a little bit — the formatting in a document can get thrown for a loop. And unless you know that this setting is the cause of the problem, it can take ages to figure out why your document suddenly doesn't look right.

10. To change the default page settings — margins, paper size, and the like — choose File⇨Page Setup.

Word shows you the Page Setup dialog box for `normal.dot` (see Figure 16-5). Personally, I think Word's default margin settings are way too wide, so I change them to the settings shown in the figure. After you make the changes that you want, click OK.

• **Figure 16-5: Change any of the default page settings for new blank documents here.**

11. **If you need to make any other changes to all new blank documents, go ahead.**

For example, if you want to have a standard header or footer on your blank documents, choose View➪Header and Footer and have at it. If you want boilerplate text to appear in all your new documents, just type it in the template. If you want to put a subtle watermark on all the pages (perhaps, *From the Desk of Woody Leonhard*), see Technique 71.

12. **When you're done, choose File➪Close.**

Chances are good that Word won't ask whether you want to save changes — but if it does, answer Yes.

Every new blank document that you create will take on all the settings that you apply to `normal.dot`. In addition, any new templates that you create (see the next section) absorb these settings, too. That's a *big* timesaver.

You can go through the same basic steps that I describe in this section to modify any template that you create.

Creating New Templates

Custom templates can save you so much time that you'll wonder how you ever lived without them. Creating a good template is an art — and a *difficult* art, at that. It would take a book this size just to hit the high points. Basically, anything you can do with a document, you can do in a template, and whatever you do in the template applies in all future documents based on that template.

Templates are enormously powerful timesaving tools because they embody all the customizing you need, and you need to perform the hard work only once. For starters, you can have different settings (say, different fonts or boilerplate text) for different templates.

To create a new template:

1. **Choose File➪New. In the New Document task pane, click On My Computer. (It's in the Templates section.)**

Word brings up the Templates dialog box (see Figure 16-6).

2. **Under the Create New heading (lower-right corner), select the Template radio button and then click OK.**

Your new template is ready for customizing. You can set formatting, add text, and whatever else you want just as you would in a regular Word document. See the earlier section, "Customizing Blank Documents," for details on how to use the Modify Style dialog box. See Technique 21 for details about creating new styles.

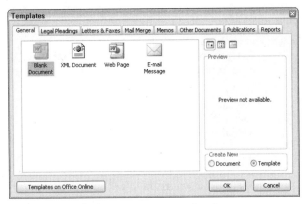

• **Figure 16-6:** Create your own template here.

3. When you're done, either click the Save icon or choose File⇨Close, give the new template a name, and then click Save.

The next time that you create a new document with File⇨New⇨On My Computer, your template will be among the choices.

Making Privacy Settings Stick

Word has two key personal privacy settings that as far as I know, can be set permanently only if you set them in the template. If you want to make them stick for all new blank documents, you have to reach into normal.dot and change the settings there.

The first privacy setting removes a small subset of personal information from inside a Word document.

 Word stores a vast array of potentially embarrassing private information inside documents — your name, the location of the file, and even (in some cases) a log of people who have edited the document. Anyone with a bit of time on his hands can go through and find it. This privacy setting does *not* remove all the personal information from a file. See Technique 69 for important details.

To understand what information gets removed, choose File⇨Properties⇨Summary (see Figure 16-7). This particular setting (that I describe in the following procedure) removes the Author, Manager, and Company information from this dialog box, plus the Last Saved By information on the Statistics tab.

• **Figure 16-7:** These fields are blanked out when you choose the first privacy setting.

The second privacy setting removes a randomly generated number that can be used to trace e-mail messages back to the PC that originated them. For example, if you send a document to a friend and that friend sends the document to another person who sends it to your boss, your boss can determine (if she has access to your PC) that *your* PC sent the document.

Scary stuff. Here's how to fix it:

1. **Make sure that Windows shows hidden folders.**

Choose Start⇨My Documents and then choose Tools⇨Folder Options⇨View. Under Hidden Files and Folders, click Show Hidden Files and Folders, and then click OK.

2. **Start Word. Choose File⇨Open. In the Files of Type box, choose Document Templates.**

3. **In the Look In box, navigate to**
`C:\Documents and Settings\`<your user name>
`\Application Data\Microsoft\Templates.`

The Open dialog box should look like Figure 16-2.

4. **Double-click** `Normal.dot.`

Word opens `normal.dot.`

5. **Choose Tools⇨Options⇨Security.**

You see the Security tab on the Options dialog box (see Figure 16-8).

• **Figure 16-8: The security settings for** `normal.dot.`

6. **Mark the Remove Personal Information from File Properties on Save check box.**

That knocks out the Author, Manager, and Company, and Last Saved By fields.

7. **Clear the Store Random Number to Improve Merge Accuracy check box.**

If you e-mail a document out for revisions and the revisions come back, when you open the returned document, Word isn't be smart enough to ask whether you want to merge changes with the original document. You'll have to do the merge manually — Tools⇨Compare and Merge Documents — assuming that you want to do it at all!

8. **While you're here, consider selecting the Warn Before Printing, Saving or Sending a File That Contains Tracked Changes or Comments check box.**

Personally, I work with tracked changes all the time, and I appreciate a little nudge saying, "you have tracked changes in this document, so make sure that you aren't sending out anything sensitive." Your mileage may vary.

9. **Click OK.**

10. **Close** `normal.dot.`

Setting Formatting for Drawings

One of the enduring problems with using the Drawing toolbar is the default AutoShape format. Every new AutoShape — whether it's a line or a rectangle or a callout — has a white fill and a solid black 0.75-point line.

I *hate* white fill and a solid black 0.75-point line. In about 99 percent of all the situations that I encounter where I need to use Word's Drawing toolbar, it's the worst possible setting. If I'm creating a line, the default is too thin to show up, and it lacks an arrowhead. If I'm working on a callout, I don't want the white fill to obliterate text underneath. If I'm drawing a rectangle, I get both problems at the same time! Blech, blech, and blech.

You can change the formatting on an individual drawing (right-click and choose Format AutoShape), and then set up a document so all future AutoShapes will take on that formatting (right-click a drawing and choose Set AutoShape Defaults). But there's no way to change the default for all new AutoShapes in all new documents — at least, that's what I thought until a few months ago. The trick? Make the change to normal.dot so that all new blank documents take on the AutoShape defaults that you specify:

1. **Make sure that Windows shows hidden folders.**

   Choose Start⇔My Documents, and then choose Tools⇔Folder Options⇔View. Under Hidden Files and Folders, click Show Hidden Files and Folders, and then click OK.

2. **Start Word. Choose File⇔Open. In the Files of Type box, choose Document Templates.**

3. **In the Look In box, navigate to** C:\Documents and Settings\<your user name>\ Application Data\Microsoft\Templates.

   The Open dialog box should look like Figure 16-2.

4. **Double-click** Normal.dot.

   Word opens normal.dot.

5. **Either click the Drawing icon on the Standard toolbar or right-click an empty spot on any toolbar and mark the Drawing check box.**

   Either way, the Drawing toolbar appears.

6. **Choose AutoShapes⇔Callouts on the Drawing toolbar, and pick one of the Line Callouts in the second, third, four or fifth rows. Then click and drag on** normal.dot **to create a callout.**

   normal.dot should look like Figure 16-9.

    I have you work with a callout because it's one of the few shapes that have fill, line, and arrow settings.

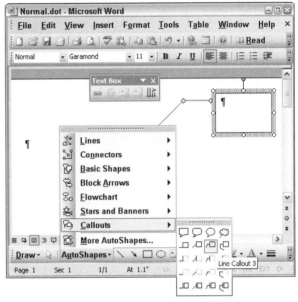

• **Figure 16-9: Start by drawing a simple AutoShape callout.**

 If you get a drawing canvas, review my diatribe in Technique 11 and follow the steps there to get rid of the blasted beast. When you've knocked some sense into Word, come back to Step 6 and try again. It isn't absolutely necessary — you can set the default here without zapping the drawing canvas — but this is as good a time to get rid of it as any.

7. **Right-click the callout and choose Format AutoShape.**

   You get the Format AutoShape dialog box, as shown in Figure 16-10.

8. **Choose the settings that you use the most often so that you never have to reset the default again.**

   I prefer No Fill so that the AutoShape is transparent, with a solid red line at a width (Weight) of 1 pt (point), and a Begin Style arrow. (Play with it a bit and find a combination that you like.) When you're done, click OK.

• **Figure 16-10:** Set your AutoShape defaults here.

9. **Back in** `normal.dot`**, right-click the callout and choose Set AutoShape Defaults.**

With AutoShape defaults set, Word will use the formatting that you choose for all new AutoShapes in all new blank documents.

10. *Important!* **Select the callout and delete it.**

 If you don't delete the callout, every new blank document will contain a callout just like it!

11. **Close** `normal.dot`**. Save changes if asked.**

That is something I've been trying to do for many years.

In Technique 11, I talk about using the Drawing toolbar to make quick sketches, callouts, arrows, and the like in Word documents. (Actually, on top of Word documents; see Technique 11 for details.)

Technique 17

Laying Out a Page — Quickly

Save Time By

- Knowing which Word feature to use for quick layouts
- Doing as little as possible to get the layout right — the first time

Most people catch on to the Word basics pretty quickly — at least, after the intrusive IntelliNONsense settings get axed (see Techniques 15 and 16). You know that you need to select text before applying formatting; you can click and drag to move stuff around; you can put pictures in a document by choosing Insert⇨Picture. Indents and bullets and centering and color. All easy stuff.

The first major stumbling block that most Word users encounter comes when they have to lay out text in an unfamiliar way. Perhaps you need a form where people fill in their name and address — and you can't get the lousy columns to line up. Maybe you're working on a résumé where the dates go on the left and the activities on the right, and it's a hemorrhoid trying to keep them in sync.

My personal trial by fire, many years ago, was a newsletter. The content was easy; in fact, other members of the club wrote most of the text. But the layout! Oy! I spent hours every month getting the columns to line up and keeping the headings in order. Adding a picture or a pull quote was worse than pulling teeth.

It took years, but I finally figured out that I was trying to make Word work the way I thought it should — and that I was doomed to failure. It's as if I decided that my Segway should swim, and no number of calamitous splashes would sway my determination.

If you need to lay out a page, follow this Technique and save yourself days of heartache.

Seeing Word's Way

Word has no problem at all dealing with plain-vanilla reports, memos, letters, and the like. You can right-justify paragraphs or insert a picture and have the text wrap around in a snap (see Technique 24).

When you go beyond standard formatting, Word has four tools that do the heavy lifting. Each tool works well with a certain class of formatting problems — and doesn't work worth squat solving others. Your first job, when confronted with a nonstandard formatting problem, is to find the right tool for the job:

✔ **Tabs and tab stops:** These work well for creating fill-in-the-blanks forms (see Figure 17-1) or in any other situation where you need blank, underlined lines (_____) between aligned columns of text.

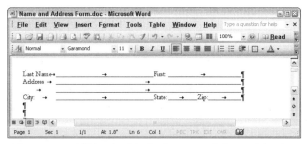

• **Figure 17-1:** Fill-in-the-blanks forms work best with tabs.

 My advice: If you want to print underscores _____ or dots ..... and you need to line up the text around them, use tabs.

✔ **Tables:** These critters are great for keeping columns of text in sync. You might want to use tables for a résumé (see Figure 17-2), a parts catalog, or a list of consultants with their qualifications.

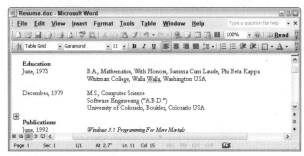

• **Figure 17-2:** Tables make it easy to keep text lined up left-to-right.

 My advice: If you need to line up text or graphics and you aren't sure what to use, try tables first.

✔ **Snaking columns:** These are like the ones in a newspaper, but they aren't used very often by those in the know . . . although you'll see them mentioned many places online and in Word help. Snaking columns work when you have a fairly long list of items that you want to appear in columns on a page (see Figure 17-3), and the list will fit on one page. Microsoft calls these *newsletter columns,* but using them for newsletters is an invitation to disaster. See the sidebar, "Creating Newsletters," elsewhere in this Technique.

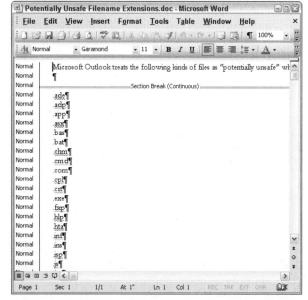

• **Figure 17-3:** Snaking columns work well in a very limited set of circumstances.

 My advice: If you think that snaking columns will solve your problem, they probably won't. Look at linked text boxes, which probably do everything that you need to do with much less headache. I explain how to use linked text boxes later in this Technique.

✔ **Text boxes:** These are AutoShapes that you draw and then fill with text. You can even link text boxes so that if you put too much text in a box, it overflows into the next box. Text boxes are infinitely superior to snaking columns in almost all cases.

 You'd think that with all the advanced capabilities of Word, you could use it to put together a quality newsletter. The reality is that you run into little problems here and there that require you to tinker with the settings, and the process turns into a real time sink. I hate to admit it, but if you have a copy of Microsoft Publisher, it's much, much easier to build a good printed newsletter in Publisher than in Word. If you need real newsletter-publishing capabilities (such as the ability to balance columns easily, a feature to extend Page 1 text onto back pages, and a way to generate a Table of Contents without pulling out your hair) get a program designed for the purpose instead. If your situation does require that you create a newsletter in Word, linked text boxes, which I discuss later in this Technique, are your best bet.

Laying Out Forms with Tabs

If you're working with a monospace font — one like Courier, where all the characters are the same width — it's easy to line up text so that all the columns start in the same location. Just type like you would on a typewriter, count the characters, and it all lines up. No sweat. But the minute you go beyond Courier, you've got problems. Big time.

The good news is that you don't need to revert to Courier and conjure up bad memories of correction tape or (even worse) count characters in the hope of finding a magic formula that will make the text line up (you won't find one).

 If you've ever tried to get a form to line up by typing underlines and spaces, using the methodical approach in the following steps not only gives you a much better-looking form, but it'll do so in record time. Guaranteed.

Here's how to make a form quickly and accurately, the first time:

 Creating a fill-in-the-blanks form is almost impossible unless you have Word show you paragraph marks and Tab characters. Follow the instructions in Technique 15 to have Word display these two crucial characters. Someday, you'll thank me for that.

1. **Open (or create) the document that you want to contain the form. Put your cursor wherever you want the form to appear, pressing Enter once for each line in your form. Then give yourself a little extra breathing room by pressing Enter a couple more times.**

The form in Figure 17-1 is really only four lines long. But because I want to leave a couple of extra clean paragraph marks in the document (following the form), I press Enter a total of six times.

 When creating a fill-in-the-blanks form, you want one separate paragraph for each line. That's because Word stores the tab stop information (along with all other paragraph formatting) *inside the paragraph mark*. When you set tab stops, if there's one line per paragraph, keeping track of what you're doing is easy. If you have more than one line in a paragraph, the situation turns very messy, very quickly.

2. **Determine exactly where each line and each piece of text will begin on the first line of the form.**

You can use a pencil. Measure from the left edge of the text. In Figure 17-1, I decide to start the first underline at 0.75 inches from the left edge of the text, put Last Name at three inches from the left edge of the text, and the final underscore goes all the way out to five inches.

3. **Click the first line of your form and then choose Format⇨Tabs.**

Word shows you the Tabs dialog box for the first paragraph — which is to say, the first line — of your form (see Figure 17-4).

• **Figure 17-4: Set the tab stops for the first line of the form.**

 The so-called *Bar* tab stop alignment (see Figure 17-4) is a useless and confusing throwback to the days of Word 1.0. Don't touch it.

4. **In the Tab Stop Position box, type the location of the first tab stop on the line.**

In the sample form in Figure 17-1, the first tab stop appears where the underline starts, which is at 0.75 inches.

5. **Choose an alignment for the tab stop.**

All the tab stops in the sample form are left-aligned. Word has four usable tab stop alignments (see Figure 17-5):

▶ *Left* means that any text after the Tab character starts immediately after the tab stop.

▶ *Right* means that any text after the Tab character gets right-aligned at the tab stop.

▶ *Center* means that any text after the Tab character gets centered at the location of the tab stop.

▶ *Decimal* means that Word puts the first decimal point (period) following the Tab character at the tab stop location and arranges the other text around the decimal point.

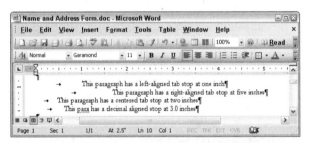

• **Figure 17-5: Tab characters and tab stops interact in predictable (but sometimes hard to visualize) ways.**

6. **Choose a leader for the tab stop.**

The *leader* (pronounced *lee*-der) is the character that Word uses to fill in blank sections on the line. For a fill-in-the-blanks form, you frequently use the underline leader.

If you don't like the underline styles in the Tabs dialog box, you can create a more customized line instead. Select None in the Leader area, select the Tab character in your document (remember to have character marks showing), and then choose Format⇨Font to select from the wider array of underline styles in the Font dialog box instead.

7. Click the Set button to set the tab stop.

8. Repeat Steps 4–7 to set all the tab stops on the line. When you're done with the line, click OK.

The first line of the form in Figure 17-1 relies on the tab stops shown in Table 17-1.

 It's very easy to replicate tab stops that you've already set in the Tabs dialog box. To do so, just copy a paragraph mark with the tabs that you want to a new location. Or press Enter while the cursor is inside a paragraph with custom tab stops that you created, and the new paragraph will inherit the tab stops. This quick and easy method is possible because the tab stops are stored in the paragraph mark. Remember to make character marks visible, or this trick can become very confusing.

9. Repeat Steps 3–8 for each line of your form.

Table 17-1 also shows you the tab stops for the second, third, and final lines of the form in Figure 17-1.

TABLE 17-1: TAB STOPS FOR THE FOUR-LINE FORM IN FIGURE 17-1

Line Number	Tab Stop Location	Alignment	Leader
One	0.75"	Left	None
	3"	Left	Underline
	5"	Left	Underline
Two and three	0.75"	Left	None
	5"	Left	Underline
Four	0.75"	Left	None
	3"	Left	Underline
	4"	Left	Underline
	5"	Left	Underline

Aligning Text with Tables

If you think of Word tables as being just like little Excel spreadsheets without most of the calculating capabilities — or as a neat way to draw horizontal and vertical boxes in a document — you might be missing an important point.

Tables rate as one of the premiere ways to align text on a page. The minute that you need to put text on the left and text on the right — and have the two pieces of text line up — you should think tables.

Figure 17-2 illustrates a classic use for tables: to build a résumé. A typical résumé has headings on the left side and detailed text on the right. You want the headings to line up with the details, and it's *murderous* keeping the two synchronized if you don't use tables.

To set up a document with two synchronized columns of text

1. Create or open the document that you want to lay out.

2. Press Enter five or six times.

It always helps to have some extra, unused paragraph marks hanging around when you're working with tables.

3. Click where you want the table to appear and then choose Table⇨Insert⇨Table.

Word brings up the Insert Table dialog box (see Figure 17-6).

• **Figure 17-6: Put a table in your document the fast way.**

4. Type 2 in the Number of Columns box, type 2 in the Number of Rows box, and then click OK.

Word draws a two-column table in your document (see the results in Figure 17-7).

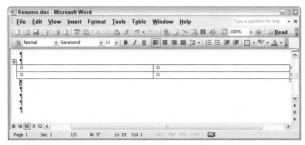

• **Figure 17-7: Start with a standard, everyday two-column table.**

5. If you want a narrower column on the left than on the right, click the vertical line in the middle of the table and drag it to the left.

Don't worry too much about aligning things precisely. It's always easy to move the middle line.

6. Get rid of the border lines on the table cells. First, select the table. (The fastest way is to click the four-headed arrow at the upper left of the table, but you can also choose Table⇨Select⇨Table.) Then choose Format⇨Borders and Shading⇨Borders.

Word shows you the Borders and Shading dialog box (as shown in Figure 17-8).

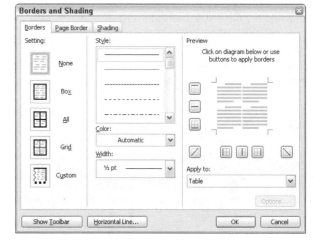

• **Figure 17-8: Take the lines off the table cells.**

7. In the upper-left corner, click None. Then click OK.

Word removes the borders from the table cells.

 If you don't see gray lines around each table cell, choose Table⇨Show Gridlines, and they will appear onscreen. These gridlines are only there to help you visually; they don't print on the final document. If they bug you, turn them off (Table⇨Hide Gridlines), but I generally leave them there while I'm filling out the table.

8. **Fill in the table and watch how it all lines up neatly.**

Add content to the columns as you would normally. You can type text, insert pictures, create bulleted lists . . . just about anything that you would normally do in a document.

Here are some tips for working with tables:

✔ To jump to the next cell in the table, press Tab.

✔ If you press Tab when you're in the last cell in the table, Word creates a new row.

✔ Working with tab stops and Tab characters inside a table cell can get claustrophobic, but if you need to type a Tab character, you have to hold down the Ctrl key: Ctrl+Tab puts a tab in the document.

✔ Because Word needs a paragraph mark outside the table to keep track of section and document formatting, you can't delete the final paragraph mark in a document if it's preceded by a table. If the lingering paragraph mark causes you grief — for example, if it causes Word to add an extra page to your document — remember that you can format the paragraph mark so it's hidden. Just select the paragraph mark and choose Format⇨Font, select the Hidden check box, and then click OK.

Creating Newsletters

Some people use Word for newsletters, but because you have to spend a lot of time tinkering with settings, creating a newsletter in Word becomes time-consuming if you create newsletters on an ongoing basis. Here are some of the major pitfalls you'll run into when using the formatting options that I discuss in this Technique to create newsletters:

Tables: There are plenty of pros and cons, but the biggest problem that I've encountered is with the table cells shrinking or expanding when a little bit of text is added or deleted, throwing the entire layout out of kilter. (If you set the cells to stay exactly at a specific size, it's even worse than letting them shrink and expand because text gets chopped off, or big gaps develop.)

Snaking columns: Microsoft recommends, repeatedly, that you use snaking columns for newsletters. I take this as conclusive proof that the people inside Microsoft who write these things never use their own product. Snaking columns might be useful if your entire newsletter consists of one article that flows continuously from the first page to the last. But snaking columns don't work at all if you have different elements in the newsletter. They're impossible to balance and deucedly difficult to keep from flip-flopping from page to page, destroying any formatting that you've attempted to enforce. This way lies madness.

Linked text boxes: In my experience, the hardest part of setting up linked text box newsletters lies in the process of physically getting the text boxes on the page: where they go, how wide the margins run, and whether to nudge this column here or that graphic there. You can't just paint a couple of text boxes on a page and rely on Draw⇨Align or Distribute to lay out the page. It takes an enormous amount of time to do a good job — and even a lousy job ain't no walk in the park. If you do have to use Word to create a newsletter, however, linked text boxes are the way to go.

Cramming Lists with Snaking Columns

I strongly recommend that you avoid snaking newspaper-like columns (Microsoft's Help calls them *newsletter-style columns*) in all instances save one: when you need to cram a list of items together, and that list will fit on a single page. See a good example of the type of list that I'm talking about in Figure 17-3. I've also seen columns used to fit outlines and other lengthy lists onto a single page.

Why?

✔ **You have very little control** over where and how the columns will break. Performing edits on a document with snaking columns is like trying to pet a hungry moray eel.

✔ **You can't continue text** from one place to another. The text takes up all the space that it wants, and you can do very little about it.

✔ **You can get truly bizarre and buggy behavior** if a snaking list flops over a page break (see break types in Figure 17-9).

✔ **Snaking columns rely on section breaks.** You can see the section breaks themselves only if you work in Normal view. However, you can see the effect of the section breaks only in Print Layout view (or in Print Preview, if you can stand the wait). Flipping back and forth between the views will leave you screaming for mercy.

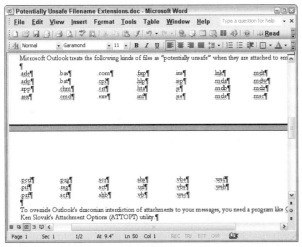

• **Figure 17-9:** The seven snaking columns on the first page produce only six columns on the second page. Go figger.

 If there's any chance that your snaking list will bump over a page break, take the time to turn it into a table.

To lay out a list with snaking columns within a larger document, follow these instructions *precisely:*

1. **Start with a clean, new Word document. Even if you have all the stuff typed and ready for formatting, start with a clean, new Word document.**

   If you start with a document that isn't pristine — say, one with headers and footers — a million things can go wrong when you insert snaking columns.

2. **Choose View➪Normal.**

   Start in Normal view so that you can see the section breaks.

3. **Press Enter a dozen times.**

4. **Click near the top of the document — around the third or fourth paragraph mark — and choose Insert➪Break.**

   Word responds with the Break dialog box (see Figure 17-10).

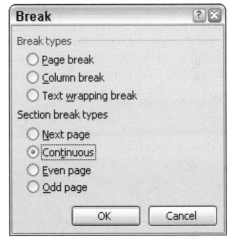

• **Figure 17-10:** You need a section break to tell Word that you want to change the number of columns in the text.

5. **Under Section Break Types, select the Continuous radio button and then click OK.**

   Word puts a Section Break (Continuous) — those are Word's parentheses and not mine — in your document at the beginning of the area that you will use for snaking columns.

6. **Click farther down in the document — say, after a few more paragraph marks — and choose Insert➪Break. Under Section Break Types, select the Continuous radio button and then click OK.**

   You now have two section breaks in your document, with a handful of paragraph marks to work with in between (see Figure 17-11).

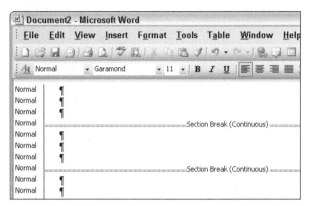

• **Figure 17-11:** The staging area for snaking columns is between the section breaks.

7. Between the two section breaks, copy (or type) all the stuff that you want to appear laid out with snaking columns.

In Figure 17-12, I copy in the list of filename extensions that I want to snake.

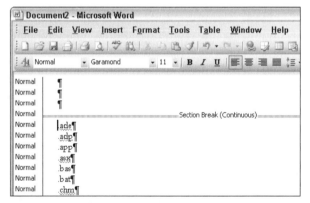

• **Figure 17-12:** Bring in the list that you want to format with snaking columns.

8. Click once somewhere between the two section breaks.

9. Choose Format➪Columns.

Word brings up the Columns dialog box (see Figure 17-13).

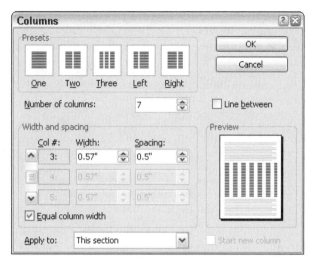

• **Figure 17-13:** Set the number of columns between the two section breaks here.

10. In the Number of Columns box, type the number of columns that you want (or choose from one of the preset options at the top) and then click OK.

Word immediately flips into Page view and shows you the columns (see Figure 17-14).

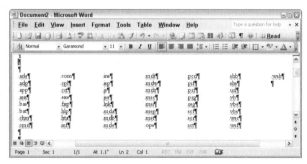

• **Figure 17-14:** Word switches to Page view so you can see the columns.

 Note the section break mark immediately before the first item in the snaking list. Don't delete it! If you do, all of the earlier material in the document will start snaking, too.

11. To be safe, choose View➪Normal.

Don't edit the document in Page view because it's very easy to move, copy, or delete the section breaks. Stay in Normal view (refer to Figure 17-12) to complete your edits. Switch back to Page view only to see the ungodly mess that you've created.

Linking Text with Text Boxes

Anytime you want to arrange text in a complex way, where text can flow from one part of your document to another, you should immediately think of linked text boxes. Snaking columns are unwieldy. Tables work well if the format is regimented — stuff on the left aligned with stuff on the right (or even possibly stuff in the middle). But if you want to flow text through a document, as you would with a newsletter or a flyer or some kinds of reports, linked text boxes hold the key.

 Are you trying to build an electronic newsletter? That's a horse of a different color. See Technique 61 for details. This section deals only with printed newsletters.

On the surface, linked text boxes sound simple:

1. Bring up the Drawing toolbar. Disable the drawing canvas (more on this monster in Technique 11).

2. Carefully draw text boxes where you want text to appear.

3. Construct links among the text boxes, thereby telling Word where to put text when it gets too big for the first text box.

4. Put sentences that read *Continued on page XXX* at the bottom of the text boxes that overflow.

As is so often the case with Word, the devil's in the details.

Here's the general approach that I recommend:

✔ Use the following steps to see how linked text boxes work.

✔ Don't try to build your own newsletter. Instead, take one from Office Online and adapt it to your needs. To look through the Office Online newsletter templates, type **newsletter templates** in the Help box in the upper-right corner of the Word screen, press Enter, and download a few.

To create linked text boxes:

1. **Review Technique 11 to discover how to turn off the drawing canvas and how to use the Drawing toolbar.**

2. **Click the Text Box icon on the Drawing toolbar.**

3. **Click and drag on your document (actually, in the drawing layer of your document) to create a text box.**

   The box should look like Figure 17-15.

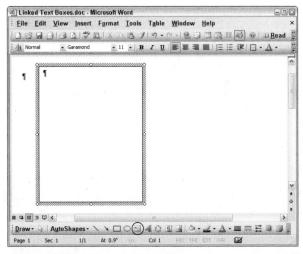

• **Figure 17-15: Draw a text box first.**

4. **Click the Text Box icon again, click and drag again, and create a second text box (see Figure 17-16).**

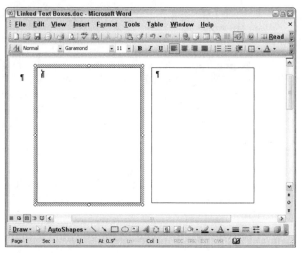

• **Figure 17-16:** The second text box will be linked to the first.

5. **Right-click the outer rim of the first text box and choose Create Text Box Link.**

The mouse pointer turns into a pitcher (!) with letters pouring out of the spout.

6. **Click once inside the second text box.**

The two text boxes are now linked. Any text put in the first box that won't fit will flow to the second box.

7. **Try it. Type (or copy) a few long paragraphs into the first text box.**

The excess flows into the second text box (see the magic in Figure 17-17).

 To insert text that reads *Continued on page XXX* at the bottom of a text box, I suggest that you use *another* text box. Draw it at the bottom of the second text box. Doing so keeps the *Continued on page XXX* text from spilling over into the linked text box if you should edit the contents of the linked boxes.

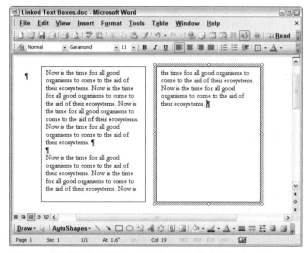

• **Figure 17-17:** Anything that doesn't fit inside the first text box flows into the second.

Word's newsletter support is rudimentary at best, but you can always do better than struggle with snaking newspaper-like columns.

Technique

Making Professional Labels

Save Time By

- ✔ Printing simple labels quickly and easily
- ✔ Setting up fancy labels with graphics
- ✔ Aligning pieces of the label with ease and dexterity

All businesses (and most individuals!) use mailing labels. Printing simple, ugly, text-only labels takes a minimal amount of effort. You can do it in your sleep.

If good-looking labels are important to you, this Technique is for you. I explain how to set up very professional, high-quality labels in an hour or less. And you'll be able to reuse the labels over and over again.

You don't need to spend big bucks at the print shop. If your address changes, you don't need to throw away stacks of old labels. If you want to put a special tag line on Via Airmail or New Price List! labels, you don't need to run out and buy a rubber stamp. All it takes is a little foresight and a few quick clicks. See my handiwork in Figure 18-1.

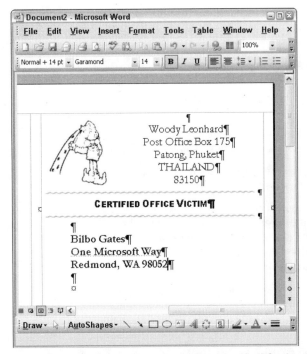

• **Figure 18-1: Use Word to make your own customized and professional labels.**

Creating and Printing Simple Labels

This section covers the typical approach for small, text-only labels — the Avery 5160 (see Figure 18-2) being a prime example. If you don't have enough room on the label for anything but the recipient's address, you're rather limited in appearances, but Word's built-in label printing capabilities can save you time.

If fancier labels are what you're looking for and you don't mind copying addresses into your labels manually (or you're setting up a full-scale merge to print labels for a whole bunch of people), spring for larger labels and follow the quick steps in the following sections in this Technique. Your mailings will look infinitely better.

Printing single mailing labels — or a sheet of identical mailing labels — is a snap:

1. **If the name and address that you want to appear on the mailing label is already in your document, select it.**

Word does a good job of grabbing addresses from the document, but you can make sure the mailing labeler gets precisely what you want if you select it first.

2. **Choose Tools⇨Letters and Mailings⇨ Envelopes and Labels⇨Labels.**

You see the Envelopes and Labels dialog box, as shown in Figure 18-2.

3. **If the correct label isn't showing in the lower-right corner, or if you've never used the Label feature before, click the Options button, pick the label (see Figure 18-3), and make adjustments to the printer setup if need be.**

You can design your own labels and type in custom dimensions (use the New Label button in Figure 18-3), but chances are very good that Microsoft already has your label size nailed.

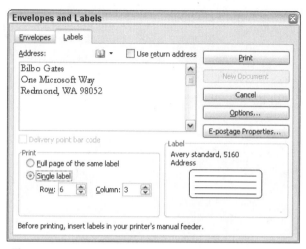

• **Figure 18-2: Preparing to print a single label.**

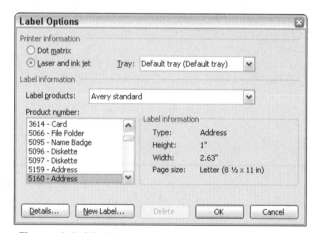

• **Figure 18-3: Word has an enormous list of manufacturers' labels.**

4. **Choose whether you want an entire sheet of labels to be printed that use the same address or whether you want just one label.**

Laser printer manufacturers generally recommend that you *not* print single labels; rather, they want you to run them through a sheet at a time and not try to reuse the sheet. Why? A label that gets dislodged inside the printer's fuser can turn to gooey toast faster than you can say, "Where the %$#@! is the fire extinguisher?" Ink jet and dot matrix printers don't have the same, uh, sense of urgency.

5. **Put a sheet of labels in your printer.**

Do it now because when you click Print, Word prints. Immediately.

6. **Click Print.**

The label(s) come out the back.

Customizing a Template for Fancy Labels

Adding graphics, a return address, or even a tag line or slogan to a mailing label is easy. Unfortunately, you can't use a customized label with Microsoft's automatic label program, so you lose some of the features that I describe in the preceding section. In particular, you can't bring in a name and address directly from your Outlook Contacts list.

You can perform a mail merge to create massive numbers of mailing labels. When merging, you can start with the built-in labels that ship with Word (the text-only kind), or you can start with your own custom-designed labels. The trick to using your own custom labels is to tell Word that you want to merge to a Directory in the first step of the Mail Merge Wizard.

This same procedure works well for printing business cards; disk, CD, or video tape labels; file folder labels; small wedding invitations or birth announcements; name badges; index cards; postcards; Rolodex cards; or in any other situation where you print the same stuff multiple times on a single sheet, and Word has a label size entry that matches the dimensions of what you're printing. (Word appears to include all the labels from AOne, APLI, Avery, Devauzet, ERO, Formtec, HERMA, Hisago, Kokuyo, MACO, PIMACO, Xerox, and Zwekcform — and that covers a lot of ground!)

If your needs for fancy labels don't stray too far from the straight and narrow — or if you're looking for label layout ideas — take a gander at the Avery Wizard and templates at www.avery.com/us/software/index.jsp.

The best and fastest way that I know to set up fancy labels so they're reusable involves using Word's Label routine to create a template and then using the template to print the labels. This section explains how to set up the template, and "Filling In and Printing Labels from a Template" later in this Technique explains how to put the template to use. Here's how to set up a template, based on the Avery 5164, a 3.3-inch (high) x 4-inch (wide) label that I've used for many years:

1. **Choose Tools⇨Letters and Mailings⇨ Envelopes and Labels⇨Labels.**

Word brings up the Envelopes and Labels dialog box, as shown in Figure 18-4.

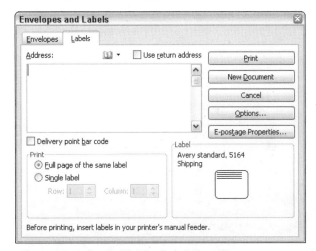

• **Figure 18-4: Start with Word's Label routine.**

2. **If there's any text in the Address box, delete it.**

3. **Click the Options button (refer to the resulting dialog box in Figure 18-3) and pick the label that best matches the size of what you will be printing. If you want to see the full layout description, click the Details button. When you find the right one, click it and then click OK.**

Don't get hung up on the descriptions — a Shipping Label works just as well as an Address Label or a Postcard. You're just looking for a match on the size and how the labels are aligned on a page.

 If you want to print announcements or invitations, take a look at the Avery 3263, 3611, 5389, or 5824.

4. **Back in the Envelopes and Labels dialog box, click the New Document button.**

Word creates a one-page document that consists of a table (see Figure 18-5). That table contains cells, one for each of the labels on the sheet.

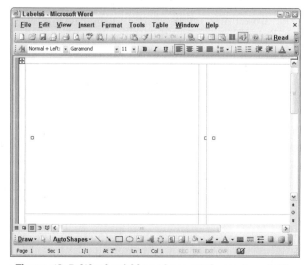

• **Figure 18-5:** Word quickly and accurately creates a table in which each cell corresponds precisely to one label on the page.

5. **Put together the first label. Add graphics, your return address, slogan — whatever strikes your fancy.**

My fancy struck Figure 18-6.

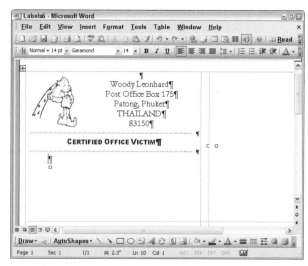

• **Figure 18-6:** Get the first label the way you want it.

 If you put a paragraph mark (that is, press Enter) immediately in front of the end-of-cell marker (the circle with lines emanating from it), select the paragraph mark and apply some sort of distinctive formatting. (I use Garamond 14-point bold in Figure 18-6.) Now making the recipient's address look distinctive when you print the label is easy. See details in the following section.

 Good graphics make all the difference. Try searching the Web for pictures with Google's Image Lookup (www.google.com/imghp). Also, see the section, "Micro-Adjusting Pictures," later in this Technique for advice on getting pictures lined up the right way.

6. **When the first label (which is to say, the first cell of the table) looks right, select everything in the label and copy it.**

Also — if one exists — select the end-of-cell marker in the small (blank) cell to the right of the first cell (see Figure 18-7). That ensures that you pick up the graphic and everything else in the cell.

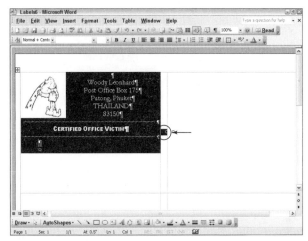

• **Figure 18-7:** Select everything in the first cell. You might need to select the second end-of-cell marker, too.

7. Click once inside each label, in turn, and paste.

You have a full sheet of labels (see Figure 18-8).

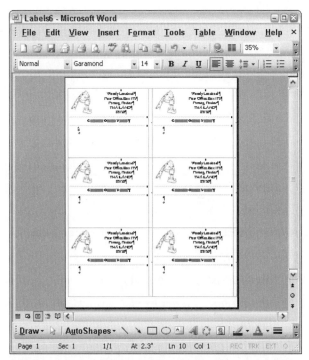

• **Figure 18-8:** Paste the graphics and text into each label.

8. Click immediately in front of the paragraph mark at the end of the first label. (That's where you want to paste the recipient's address for the first label.) Choose Insert⇨Bookmark and then type a name for the bookmark. (I use R1C1 to stand for row 1, column 1 in Figure 18-9, but you're probably much more clever.) Then click Add.

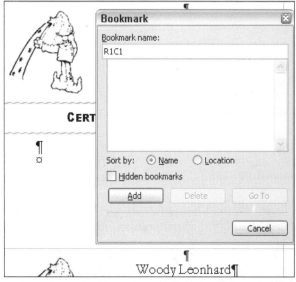

• **Figure 18-9:** Bookmark the addressee location for the label in row 1, column 1.

Bookmarking the addressee location makes it easy to navigate directly to the addressee location for the label in row 1, column 1. When you reuse the label setup, the bookmarks come in handy.

9. Similarly, put a bookmark where the addressee goes for the label in row 1, column 2. Repeat for each label in the document.

In this case, I create six bookmarks: R1C1, R1C2, R2C1, R2C2, R3C1 and R3C2.

10. Choose File⇨Save. In the Save as Type box at the bottom, choose Document Template. Give the label template a descriptive name (in Figure 18-10, I choose `Label AV5164.dot`) and then click Save.

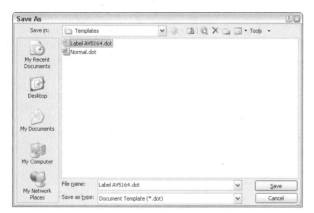

• **Figure 18-10:** Save the mailing label as a template.

If you save the label setup as a template, you can reuse it every time you need to print labels. See "Filling In and Printing Labels from a Template" later in this Technique for details on using the template.

You can make many different mailing label templates. Just give each of them names that you can recognize.

If you always print a full sheet of mailing labels at a time, you're done. On the other hand, if you want to make it easy to print just one label at a time, I suggest that you save a customized copy of the template for each label — one template can be used to print the label in the upper-left corner, the next for the label to its right, and so on. That makes it easy and fast to print each label on a page, one by one. Here's how:

1. **If the template from Step 10 in the preceding procedure isn't open, open it.**

If you need to find it, make sure that Windows shows you hidden folders (see Technique 1), then look in `C:\Documents and Settings\` `<your user name>\Application Data\` `Microsoft\Templates`. Right-click the template (don't double-click it) and choose Open.

2. **Use the Zoom drop-down list on the Standard toolbar and zoom the template for Whole Page.**

This makes selecting entire columns and rows easier.

3. **Select every row except the first and then press Delete.**

4. **Select every column except the first and then press Delete.**

All the text and graphics in the template are deleted except for the first label (see Figure 18-11).

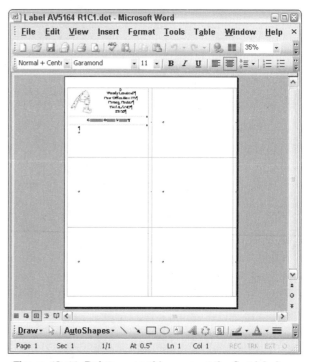

• **Figure 18-11:** Delete everything except the first label.

5. **Choose File➪Save As and save the first label with an easily recognized name.**

For example, I save the template in Figure 18-11 as `Label AV5164 R1C1.dot`.

6. **Click the Undo icon on the Standard toolbar twice.**

That restores the template to its original state.

7. **Repeat Steps 3–5 for each label, saving each one with a different name.**

For example, in Figure 18-12, I save the label in row 3, column 2 as `Mailing Label 6-Up AV5164 R3C2.dot`.

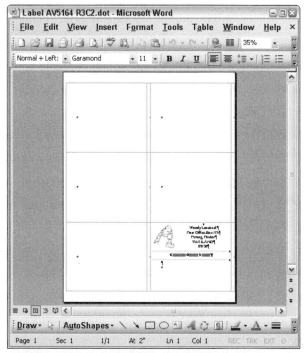

• **Figure 18-12: Row 3, column 2 gets R3C2 in its name.**

In the next section, I describe some shortcuts for using this kind of label.

Filling In and Printing Labels from a Template

If you follow the instructions in the preceding section and create a template for fancy mailing labels, here's how to print one label:

 Unfortunately, Microsoft hasn't built any hooks into the Tools➪Envelopes and Labels feature, so you have to run your homegrown labels manually. Surprisingly, though, the amount of extra work involved is minimal.

1. **Copy the addressee's name and address to the Clipboard.**

You can pick it up from a Word document, in your Contacts list, on a Web page . . . doesn't matter.

2. **In Word, choose File➪New.**

3. **If your mailing label template isn't on the list of Recently Used Templates, click On My Computer (it's in the middle, underneath the line Templates).**

Word responds with the Templates dialog box (see Figure 18-13).

• **Figure 18-13: Your fancy mailing label template appears on the General tab.**

4. **Double-click the appropriate mailing label template.**

Word creates a new document based on the template (see Figure 18-14).

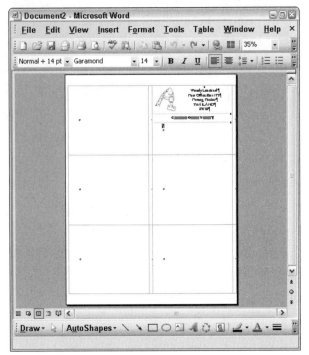

• **Figure 18-14: A new document based on Label AV5164 R1C2.**

5. **Move to the place where you want to put the name and address.**

   You can navigate there, choose Edit⇨Go To, or press F5 twice to move to the appropriate bookmark.

6. **Paste the name and address (refer to Figure 18-1 for the final result).**

   Click the Smart Tag, if need be, and choose Match Destination Formatting to format the copied address to match the formatting that you applied to the paragraph mark inside the label.

7. **Print the label. Click the X in the upper-right corner to close the document. No, you don't want to save changes.**

To print an entire sheet of labels, choose the correct template in Step 4 and then repeat Steps 5 and 6 to paste the names into each label.

Micro-Adjusting Pictures

One weekend, while making a template like the one described in "Creating Fancy Labels" earlier in this Technique, Justin (my writing partner) and I discovered a nifty little trick for adjusting pictures.

Putting a picture in a table cell is easy: Insert⇨ Picture does the trick. You can click the picture and adjust the drag handles to make the picture bigger or smaller with no problem.

Getting the picture down to the bottom of the cell is also easy. Choose Table⇨Properties⇨Cell; under Vertical Alignment, pick Bottom; then click OK. But I wanted the picture to hover just a bit above the bottom of the label. I discovered the hard way that printing a picture too close to the edge frequently chops off the bottom.

You can adjust the paragraph space after settings (choose Format⇨Paragraph and then increase the number in the After box, beneath Spacing), but here's a much faster, more visual way. Use the Word Crop tool to add white space at the bottom of the picture.

Most of the time, I think of the Crop tool as a means for cutting off parts of a picture. But as Justin discovered, it works just as well in reverse, adding white space to a picture, too.

Here's how to crop:

1. **Click once on the picture.**

2. **If you can't see the Picture toolbar (see Figure 18-15), right-click any blank part of a toolbar and then mark the Picture check box.**

Crop tool

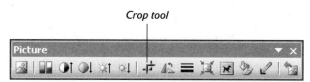

• **Figure 18-15: The Crop tool on the Picture toolbar.**

3. Click the Crop tool on the Picture toolbar.

4. Click one of the picture's drag handles.

I want to add space to the bottom of the picture, so I click the dot in the middle of the picture, at the bottom.

5. Press Alt.

That keeps Word from "snapping" the cropping point.

6. Drag the bottom handle down to make the picture push itself up off the bottom of the cell.

That's a very fast, very visual way to move a picture off the baseline.

Technique 19

Editing Like a Pro

Save Time By

- Convincing your editors to make changes the fast way
- Using Comments and tracked changes quickly
- Reviewing and accepting edits in a snap

I've been writing books for more than a decade now and have turned out tens of thousands of printed pages. I've also written many hundreds of magazine articles and thousands of newsletter articles. Along the way, I've worked with hundreds of editors. Some of them even survived the experience. (Hey, Becky!)

Editing is a tough job. Writing is a tough job. But rolling edits into a document can be an *easy* job — if everybody works the same way.

Twelve years ago, my first computer books were all hand-edited. I typed the pages with Word, printed them out, bundled the printouts with a floppy disk, and sent the whole thing via FedEx to the editorial team. Each of the editors, one by one, would tackle the manuscript with a different-colored pen. After I finished the last pass with a flourish of my telltale red pen, I couriered the final marked-up pages back to the editors. I never did figure out what they did with the bloodstained sheets, but my guess is that they retyped every single word in PageMaker.

Things are different now. Different . . . but I'm not at all sure they're better. Why? Because authors and editors don't use Word's tools properly.

If you edit pages, or if you have editors work on your pages, or even if you edit your own pages, you can save hours and days of frustration — and no small number of errors — if everyone involved will follow a few simple rules. That's what this Technique is about.

Editing in a SharePoint World

Everything begins and ends with doc files.

If you're working on a big project, it's most likely broken into a bunch of smaller documents that are ultimately stitched together to make the final publication.

Typically, the designated author takes a crack at creating a doc file. When the author's satisfied (or just tired of the whole mess), she passes on the doc file to the number-one editor.

That editor tells Word to start tracking changes (see the following section, "Tracking Changes"). (In effect, now whoever fiddles in your document has her handiwork marked in a certain color as well as by a name identifier. Very handy for hunting scoundrels.) The lead editor then passes the document around to other editors and/or posts it to a SharePoint Document Workspace.

 A *SharePoint Document Workspace* holds one in-progress copy of the document, together with information about your co-workers, tasks, scheduling, due dates, and the like. Everyone on the team can get at the document through a Web browser, frequently via an e-mailed pointer to the document, which is updated from the Workspace before you work on it. You can imagine the significant version control problems when more than one person is working on the same document simultaneously, so coordinate what you're doing — and when you do it — with your teammates.

When the number-one editor is happy with the collected modifications, he runs through them, accepts, rejects, changes, or otherwise handles them, and then sends a modified document back to the author.

When the author opens the document, she sees her original submission that was pummeled by the hands of a hundred ham-fisted editors. (Or, if she's a former editor, caressed by the caring observations of a hundred adoring collaborators. I'm a former editor. I know.)

The author's job then is to make final changes, answer any open questions, and send the last, best version back to the number-one editor.

The number-one editor then makes a final run at the changes — accepting, rejecting, or rewriting. He

stops tracking changes and sends the final copy off to a production department or the printer.

 The Track Changes features in Word 2002/ Office XP are so badly botched that you should seriously consider upgrading to Word 2003 if you spend much time at all working with tracked changes. Most of the bugs in Word 2002 appear to be fixed in 2003. At least Word 2003 lets you change formatting for deleted text. (See www.woodyswatch.com/ office/archtemplate.asp?v7-n11 for reams of problems with track changes in Word 2002.) Track Changes in Word 97, in particular, is loaded with bugs, too, and if your writing and editorial staff uses multiple versions of Word, you can expect all sorts of odd behavior.

Give or take a mistake or three — say, forgetting to turn on Track Changes at the right time — and that's how a hearty round of editing should work. In the remainder of this Technique, I show you how to make the process work faster, better, and more accurately for author and editor alike.

Avoiding Master Documents

More advanced Word users have lost more time with Master Documents than any other feature I know. *Master Documents* is Microsoft's smoke-'n-mirrors method of combining smaller documents with hidden section breaks, primarily via the Outline view, to make a big document that can have a single Table of Contents and references between chapters. Although Microsoft swears that Master Documents finally work right in Word 2003, I remain skeptical — and recommend that you avoid them.

Tracking Changes

There comes a point in every document's life where the author finishes with authoring (or, ahem, whatever authors do), and the focus shifts to editing (or, well, you get the idea). That's the point where somebody — author, editor, bit basher in the sky — needs to tell Word to start tracking changes.

Before you start tracking changes, you (and all the other folks who plan to make changes) need to make sure that Word knows who you are. Choose Tools⇨Options⇨User Information and make sure that Word has your name. If you bought your PC with Word pre-installed or if somebody at the corporate office installed it for you, chances are good that the name looks like *Satisfied Dell Customer* or some such. If you don't change the name, Word's tracking doesn't work right.

Yes, even if you edit your own work and nobody ever touches it, as soon as you shift from writing to editing, you need to have Word start tracking changes. It can save you hours of needless rewriting. By telling Word to keep track of your changes, you can go back and change your mind about a particular phrase without disturbing the rest of your work, copying from a day-old backup copy, or clicking the Undo button precisely 113 times.

Turning on Track Changes

To tell Word that you want it to track changes

1. **Choose Tools⇨Track Changes.**

Equivalently, you can double-click the TRK button in the status bar at the bottom of Word's screen. See Figure 19-1.

The TRK box tells you that Track Changes is on.

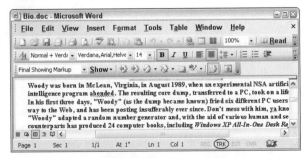

• **Figure 19-1:** The TRK box.

2. **In most cases (see the sidebar, "Track Changes Lockdown"), you want to lock the document so that changes other people make to the document are always tracked. If that applies, immediately choose Tools⇨Protect Document.**

Word shows you the Protect Document task pane on the right (see Figure 19-2).

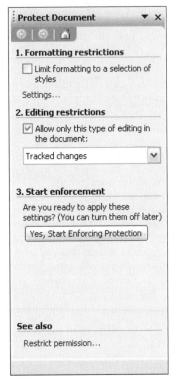

• **Figure 19-2:** As soon as you track changes, make sure that others can't accidentally (or intentionally!) make changes that aren't tracked.

3. **Select the Allow Only This Type of Editing in the Document check box. Then in the drop-down list, choose Tracked Changes.**

This effectively prevents other people from turning off tracked changes — either accidentally or intentionally. That means that you can be reasonably sure that every change made to your original prose will be tracked and noted by Word.

Yes, bypassing this protection is relatively easy. If somebody really, really wants to turn off Track Changes, he can by copying the document to a new document and giving it the original document's name; retyping the document; or taking a screenshot and putting the shot through an OCR scanning program. And even though this isn't heavy-duty security, it is an effective way to keep all but the most determined mitts off.

4. **Click the Yes, Start Enforcing Protection button.**

Word asks you to enter an optional password in the Start Enforcing Protection dialog box (see Figure 19-3).

• **Figure 19-3: You can password-protect tracked change enforcement.**

5. **Enter a password if you must, but if you do, realize that you aren't really protecting much. Then click OK.**

Word advises you that the document is protected and that changes will be tracked.

6. **Make a change or two to confirm that Track Changes is in effect.**

Track Changes Lockdown

When you track changes, most of the time you want to make sure that changes other people make to the document are always tracked. That's why I recommend that you lock the document: When other people make changes to the document, the changes are always tracked. When you lock the document, *you* can turn Track Changes on or off, no problem: Just choose Tools➪Track Changes or double-click the TRK button on the status bar. Being able to turn off Track Changes comes in handy when you need to move a big block of text, for example, or when you have to do some complex juggling and you don't want the details to appear.

Working with Track Changes in Word 2003

Track Changes in Word 2003 is full of surprises, although it's considerably better behaved than the feature in Word 2002/Office XP. Given a choice, experienced Word users frequently switch to Word 2000 or turn off the balloons (see "Reviewing and Finalizing a Document" later in this Technique) to work with tracked changes just because it's so much simpler and more stable.

When Word keeps track of changes, it can show those changes to you in four different ways. First, you can look at the original document as it looked before any changes were made. (That's also how the document would look if you rejected all the changes.) Word calls this *Original*.

Second, you can look at the Original document with changes appearing off to the side. For example, if a word was deleted by an editor, the word still appears in the body of the document but with some sort of indication — probably a strikethrough line — that says the text was deleted. Text that's inserted appears in a balloon off to the side. Word calls this *Original Showing Markup*.

Third, you can look at the final document with the changes appearing off to the side. If a word was deleted by an editor, that word does not appear in the body of the document; rather, it's hung off to the side. Text that's inserted does appear in the main document. Word calls this *Final Showing Markup*.

Fourth, you can look at the document as if all the revisions had been accepted. Word calls this *Final*. And so it is.

With the Revisions toolbar set at Final Showing Markup and working in Print Layout view, here is how edits look onscreen:

- ✔ **Deletions:** These appear by default as balloons on the right side.

- ✔ **New text:** All inserted text is underlined.

- ✔ **All edits:** Wherever changes occur, Word puts a vertical bar in the left margin (see Figure 19-4).

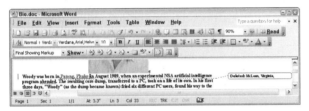

• **Figure 19-4:** Tracked deletions appear in balloons; additions appear underlined and in a different color.

 You can make the text in the balloon appear bigger and adjust words such as Deleted, which appears in Figure 19-4. See the section, "Changing the Font of Tracked Changes and Comments," later in this Technique.

 Do the balloons drive you batty? Man, you should see some of the documents that I work on. They have more balloons on the edge than text in the main part of the document! You can get rid of the balloons by working in the Normal view (choose View➪Normal), or by choosing Tools➪Options➪Track Changes and setting the Use Balloons (Print and Web Layout) drop-down box to Never.

Making Comments

Word makes it easy to put a Comment in a document; just choose Insert➪Comment and type away. If you work in Print Layout view, Comments usually appear in balloons on the right edge of the onscreen page. If you work in Normal view, Comments are highlighted and noted with the commentator's initials in line with the text.

 To see the Comments in Normal view, hover your mouse over the Comment or show all Comments at the bottom of the screen by bringing up the Reviewing Toolbar (choose View➪Markup), clicking the Show button, and selecting Reviewing Pane.

To put a Comment in a Word 2003 document

1. Select the text (or graphic) that you want to make a comment about.

2. Choose Insert➪Comment.

Word responds by putting colored brackets around whatever you selected and setting up a Comment balloon on the right edge of the page (see Figure 19-5).

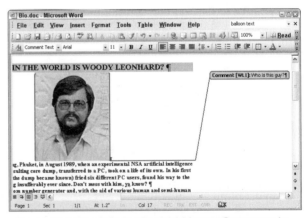

• **Figure 19-5:** By default, Word 2003 puts Comments in balloons to the right of the text.

3. **Type your Comment directly in the balloon.**

Word puts your initials at the beginning. (The initials are drawn from the User Information tab of Tools⇨Options.)

 If you hover your mouse pointer over the Comment, Word shows you when the Comment was last modified.

4. **When you're done, click anywhere in the document and keep going.**

You can modify the font used in Comment balloons by following the steps in "Changing the Font of Tracked Changes and Comments," coming up next.

Changing the Font of Tracked Changes and Comments

In Word 2003, by default, tracked deleted text and Comments appear in balloons to the right of the text. Unfortunately, Word displays that text in an eye-killing, Tahoma 8-point font, which has to be the most ghastly choice of a working font in Office history. Fortunately, you can change the font. Unfortunately, it isn't easy. Follow the rest of the steps in this procedure to bring some relief to your eyes.

1. **Choose Format⇨Styles and Formatting.**

Word shows you the Styles and Formatting task pane.

2. **At the bottom of the Styles and Formatting task pane, in the Show box, choose Custom.**

You see the Format Settings dialog box (see Figure 19-6).

3. **Select the Balloon Text and the Comment Text check boxes (if they aren't checked already) and then click OK.**

Balloon Text now appears in the Styles and Formatting task pane.

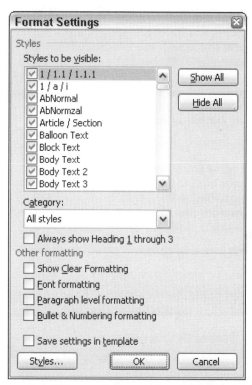

• **Figure 19-6:** To set the font size for text in balloons, you have to dig deep into Word's built-in styles.

4. **Click the down arrow next to Balloon Text and then choose Modify.**

You see Word's standard Modify Style dialog box (see Figure 19-7).

5. **Choose Format⇨Font. Change the font and then click OK.**

The point size here is the important part. (The font itself is used only for the word *Deleted* inside a tracked change balloon and the word *Comment* inside Comments while Word is in Final Showing Markup mode — it's complicated and buggy.) Personally, I use 11 point.

6. **Mark the Add to Template check box (so that all future blank documents will inherit this setting) and then click OK.**

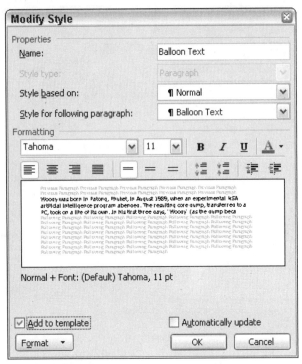

• **Figure 19-7: Change the balloon text style.**

7. Repeat Steps 4–6 for Comment text.

Unlike the Balloon Text style, though, changing the Comment text style's font really does change the font that's used in the Comment balloon. I prefer Arial 11 point.

Reviewing and Finalizing a Document

The mechanics of running through Comments and tracked changes is quite simple. In fact, in most cases, Word identifies documents with changes as you open them and sets everything up for you. In case you want (or need) to do it by yourself, do the following:

1. Open a document with tracked changes and/or Comments.

2. Turn off change tracking by double-clicking the TRK button down on the status bar (refer to Figure 19-1).

3. Choose View➪Markup.

Word brings up the Reviewing toolbar, set for Final Showing Markup, which is the mode that you usually use to review changes (see Figure 19-8).

• **Figure 19-8: The Reviewing toolbar makes it easy to review changes and Comments.**

4. Click the Next button on the Reviewing toolbar to cycle through all the tracked changes and Comments in the document.

The Next button is (confusingly) the second icon on the Reviewing toolbar.

5. If the ping-ponging back and forth between text and balloons bugs you, click the Reviewing pane icon to bring up a pane at the bottom of the screen that contains the text of all Comments and tracked changes.

The Reviewing pane icon is the last one on the Reviewing toolbar. Click it to open the Reviewing pane, as shown in Figure 19-9.

• **Figure 19-9: Follow Comments and changes here.**

If you find the balloons *really* distracting — and many people do — you can get rid of them completely by choosing Tools⇨Options⇨Track Changes; then from the Use Balloons (Print and Web Layout) drop-down list, choose Never (see Figure 19-10). That puts all the document's changes in line with the text and highlights Comments in Page Layout view — making deletions, additions, and Comments look the same in Page Layout view as they always do in Normal view.

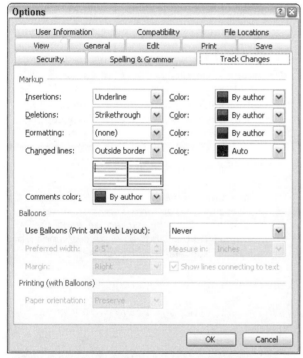

• **Figure 19-10:** Turn off the balloons here. You can always use the Reviewing pane at the bottom of the screen.

6. Accept or reject changes (or delete Comments), one by one by clicking the appropriate icons.

Using Editing Tools the Timesaving Way

Reviewing changes is the easy part. Here's the hard part — the part that can save you and your editors hours, even days, of hard work.

When you have a query or you want to make a comment, insert a Comment. When you want the author (or editor) to make a change, change the text directly.

Why?

The toughest problem that I have as an author (or editor, or author/editor) is understanding precisely what changes the editors want. The process that bogs me down the most during edits is figuring out how to change the text to accurately reflect the editors' concerns.

If I can run through edits quickly, reading Comments and making changes based on them, and accepting (or, occasionally, rejecting) changes that have already been composed, my work goes by in a flash. When I'm done, I know that I have the editors' changes down cold.

But if I have to guess as to the wording that the editor(s) want(s), and bob and weave back and forth in the text, it takes a lot of time — and I'm bound to miss a few key points along the way.

In my experience, editors make their edits in one of five ways. (Rarely does an editor use more than one method in a single document.)

✔ **Change the document with Track Changes turned off.**

Editors who do that should be shot. Figuratively anyway. Ultimately, though, it's the author's responsibility to make sure Word is tracking changes when the document leaves the author's hands. If you should receive a document with untracked changes, use Word's Compare Documents feature (Tools⇨Compare and Merge Documents) to generate a document that resembles one with track changes turned on. And harangue the editor with profuse vituperations.

In my experience, you can't rely on the Compare Documents feature. Specifically, I often get a document that shows the old version completely deleted and the edited version as all new text — not much help.

✔ **Apply highlighting to text he wants to change or ask about and put the query or proposed change somewhere else in the document.**

This behavior, while common, saps so much time for both the editor and the author that it should be outlawed. Word has no features to help authors nor editors look for highlighted text (aside from searching for formatted text directly with the Edit⇨Find dialog box). When an author encounters an edit of this nature, she has to search for the comment or proposed change, hop back and forth in the document between the highlighted text and the changed text, and try to merge the two in some way that makes sense. It's a time-killer of the first degree.

✔ **Make comments or propose changes in paragraphs with special styles.**

This is the most common way for editors in large organizations to make edits. A handful of special styles are set aside for various kinds of edits, and each editor is expected to type his comments and proposed changes in a paragraph with the given style. The approach works, but things could be so much more efficient — with absolutely no additional effort on the editors' part.

✔ **Insert Comments.**

Word's Insert⇨Comment feature works like a champ. Comments are automatically tied to the text that pertains. As long as you change the comment style's font (see "Changing the Font of Tracked Changes and Comments" earlier in this Technique), Comments are very easy to see and use. Word has tools for moving between Comments easily. The only downside comes when an editor uses a Comment balloon to suggest specific changes in the text. In that case, if the author agrees with the Comment, it's a pain in the neck to transfer the Comment to the text itself — which is why editors should feel free to change text directly.

✔ **Make changes directly.**

I don't know whether it's a question of edit etiquette or a predilection for making a job much harder and slower than it should be. But for some reason, many editors have a hard time simply going into the text and rewriting it. The author might not agree with the changes, but when you're in the text, it's easy to accept, reject, or change whatever is on offer — and there's absolutely no question about where or how or what the editor wants to change.

An editor's prime directive and an author's furtive plea: *If you have a comment, insert a Comment. If you have a change, make the change.* Do that, and you make everyone's job easier, faster, and less error-prone.

In my opinion, that's how you edit like a pro.

While I'm on the soapbox, I have two additional requests:

✔ If the change that you want to propose is highly debatable and you don't think that the author will buy it, put it in a Comment with the precise wording that you would like to see in the document.

✔ If you have two alternative changes, make them both in the document itself. That way, the author can accept one or the other or meld the two together in the final document.

Imagine the amount of time we could all save.

Technique 20

Finding and Replacing in the Wild

Save Time By

- ✔ Searching for the text you want — quickly
- ✔ Grabbing the needle in the haystack
- ✔ Avoiding the common — time-consuming — Replace mistakes

One of the first books I ever wrote (no, it wasn't *For Dummies!*) included a lengthy, detailed appendix covering various hardware manufacturers, their products, and their snail mail contact addresses. It took me weeks to compile all that information.

One of the editors decided that my use of the abbreviation *Rd.* in the mailing addresses was too terse. Fair enough. The problem was that the editor opened the appendix in Word and performed a global Search and Replace, replacing every instance of *rd* with *Road.* Ooops. I didn't catch the gaffe until after the book was published. One reader wrote to me and asked whether there was a difference between *video boards* and a *video boaRoads*.

If you wield Search and Replace like a blunt instrument, you're going to smash something in the process. But if you understand the nuances — and use the approaches I discuss in this Technique — Search and Replace can perform the work of a hundred henchmen in the blink of an eye.

Streamlining Text Searches

You might have performed searches before, but you might not be aware of some handy tools tucked into Word's search features. Here's one little trick that will make finding simple text in your document go faster than ever:

1. **Bring up the Find and Replace dialog box (see Figure 20-1).**

• **Figure 20-1:** Finding text starts here.

Of the many ways to make the Find and Replace dialog box appear, the fastest is to press Ctrl+F. You can also choose Edit➪Find. Or, click the Select Browse Object dot (as in Figure 20-2) in the lower-right corner of the screen and then click the Find icon (looks like binoculars).

• **Figure 20-2:** The oddly named Select Browse Object dot in the lower-right corner of the screen leads to the Find icon.

 If you can't remember Ctrl+F for Find, consider putting the Find icon on your Standard toolbar. See Technique 13 for details.

2. **In the Find What box, type the text that you want to find.**

Note: Capitalization doesn't matter in a standard plain-text search. See how to refine this criterion later in this section.

3. **Click the Find Next button.**

4. **Here's the trick. If anything was found, immediately click Cancel.**

If you click Cancel right away, Word not only takes the Find and Replace dialog box off the document (it just gets in the way), but you can repeat your search by clicking the down arrows below Select Browse Object.

 Search upward in the document by clicking the up arrows above the Select Browse Object is much faster and easier than doing the same thing with the dialog box.

To perform fancier searches, click the More button in the Find and Replace dialog box (refer to Figure 20-1). This expands the dialog box to show Search Options and formatting search criteria (see the upcoming Figure 20-3). The Search Options are

- ✔ **Match Case:** Searching for *LaToya* doesn't find *Latoya* or *laToya.*

- ✔ **Find Whole Words Only:** Searching for *gate* doesn't find *stargate* or *gates.*

- ✔ **Use Wildcards:** This is the source of enormous confusion and lost time. See the following three sections of this Technique for details.

- ✔ **Sounds Like (English):** This is supposed to find rhymes, but it doesn't work worth beans. Searching for *time* did not match *lime* or *rhyme.*

- ✔ **Find All Word Forms (English):** This identifies some noun plurals, verb tenses, and adjective variations. Searching for *good* finds *better* and *best.*

With the dialog box expanded, you can also search according to formatting criteria by clicking the Format button; choose from font formatting such as italic, a specific font, or even paragraph formatting or styles. In Figure 20-3, I ran a search for the text *Dummies,* with an initial capital D (by enabling the Match Case check box), all in italic (from a choice offered when I clicked the Format button).

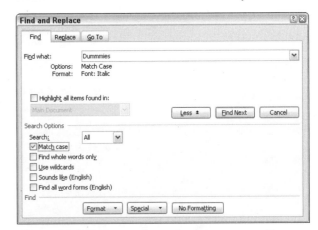

• **Figure 20-3:** Refine your search to be more specific.

If you search for formatting, be sure to click the No Formatting button when you're done to turn off the formatting criterion. Word's search formatting settings are sticky: If you search for bold characters and don't turn off the formatting, your next search is automatically restricted to bold characters.

For details on finding special characters, see the following sections, "Searching for More Than Plain Text" and "Matching Wildcards."

To put the Find and Replace dialog box back to its original svelte shape (***hint:*** save screen real estate while you search), click the Less button, which is a toggle of More. I also recommend clicking Cancel the minute you get a hit.

Searching for More Than Plain Text

If you're just searching for text or formatting, the steps in the preceding section will get you going in no time. But frequently you want to look for more than just text. In that case, you have two choices:

- ✔ Run a fast and easy (but not very versatile) search by using the Special button in the Search and Replace dialog box (refer to Figure 20-3). I talk about that kind of extended search in this section.

- ✔ Run a wildcard search, where you can look for patterns of characters or any of a wide array of ancillary characters. I talk about that kind of search in the next section.

 Unfortunately, the two types of searches are mutually exclusive. If you can't find what you want with the quick extended search described in this section, you have to start all over again, from scratch, with a wildcard search.

When you click the Special button in the Find and Replace dialog, Word gives you the ability to pick individual characters to add to the search. You can mix and match those characters with regular text. For example, if you type *abcd* in the Find What box, click the Special button, choose Paragraph Mark, and then perform the search, Word looks for all occurrences of the characters *abcd* followed by a paragraph mark.

This quick and easy method will find all the characters listed in Figure 20-4 and Table 20-1.

<u>P</u>aragraph Mark
<u>T</u>ab Character
Any <u>C</u>haracter
Any <u>D</u>igit
Any <u>L</u>etter
Ca<u>r</u>et Character
§ Section Ch<u>a</u>racter
¶ P<u>a</u>ragraph Character
Col<u>u</u>mn Break
<u>E</u>m Dash
E<u>n</u> Dash
<u>E</u>ndnote Mark
Fiel<u>d</u>
<u>F</u>ootnote Mark
Grap<u>h</u>ic
Manual <u>L</u>ine Break
Manual Page Brea<u>k</u>
Nonbreaking <u>H</u>yphen
Nonbreaking <u>S</u>pace
<u>O</u>ptional Hyphen
Section <u>B</u>reak
<u>W</u>hite Space

• **Figure 20-4: The items that a standard search is supposed to be able to find.**

TABLE 20-1: FORMATTING CHARACTERS THAT SEARCH CAN FIND

Character	Timesaving Tip
Paragraph Mark	Matches a paragraph mark (you *can* see your paragraph marks, can't you?) but doesn't match manual line breaks (see entry below).
Tab Character	Matches Tab characters.
Any Character/Digit/Letter	Matches any single character (including all the formatting characters mentioned in this table)/any single digit (numeral between 0–9)/any single alphabetic letter (a–z, A–Z).
Caret Character	Matches a caret (the character above the number 6 on your keyboard).
Section Character	Matches the interlocking-ss (§) character only. It has absolutely nothing to do with section breaks or section break marks in a document. Very confusing.
Paragraph Character	Confusingly, this is not a paragraph mark; it's the character in most fonts that looks like a paragraph mark (¶). For example, if you were writing about what the paragraph mark does, you might choose Insert⇨Symbol to insert a printing character that shows what the paragraph mark looks like.
Column Break	Finds breaks inserted by choosing Insert⇨Break⇨Column Break.
Em Dash/En Dash	As expected, finds em dashes (—) and en dashes (–).
Endnote Mark	Finds an autonumbered endnote's number. Does not find manually numbered endnotes.
Field	Finds any Word field code. Only works if field codes (as opposed to results) are visible. Choose Tools⇨Options⇨View, mark the Field Codes check box, and click OK.
Footnote Mark	Finds an autonumbered footnote's number. Does not find manually numbered footnotes.
Graphic	Finds any picture inserted into the document (Insert⇨Picture) that's not in the drawing layer (see Technique 11). Does not find AutoShapes, WordArt, and so on.
Manual Line Break	Matches a soft return, which you create by pressing Shift+Enter.
Manual Page Break	You create a page break by choosing Insert⇨Break⇨Page Break. Confusingly, this choice does not find Next Page, Even Page, or Odd Page section breaks from the same Word dialog box.
Nonbreaking* Hyphen	Matches a nonbreaking hyphen (–), which you insert by pressing Ctrl+Shift+hyphen (-).
Nonbreaking** Space	Matches a nonbreaking space, which you insert by pressing Ctrl+Shift+spacebar (°).
Optional Hyphen	Matches the optional hyphen, inserted by pressing Ctrl+– (minus sign).
Section Break	Finds Next Page, Continuous, Even, or Odd section breaks, which you insert by choosing Insert⇨Break.
White Space	Finds any number of regular or nonbreaking spaces or tab characters, in any combination.

Using nonbreaking hyphens prevents excessive hyphenation at the end of a line and the beginning of the next line. For example, if well-proportioned *fell at the end of a line but needed broken for spacing, without this formatting, you might end up with* well-pro-portioned. *Very ugly.*

**Using nonbreaking spaces prevents paired words/symbols from separating at the end of a line and the beginning of the next line. For example, if you need numerals to stay paired with words, use a nonbreaking space between then, like 150°milligrams, which will always keep* 150 *and* milligrams *together.*

Matching Wildcards

Many people know that Word can search for wild-card patterns. Look for *wo?dy,* for example, and you'll match *woody* and *wordy* but not *wooody.* However, few people realize that checking the Use Wildcards check box in the Find and Replace dialog box actually causes Word to switch to a completely different search engine.

Word uses two separate, completely independent ways of searching, and the wildcards search engine is a vast improvement over the fast and easy (but not very versatile) way of searching. With wildcards, you access a newer, better search database that can save you eons of time. For example, only the wild-card search engine supports the 0-or-more character match commonly denoted as *. Search for *w*dy,* and you match *woody, wordy, wooody,* and *wdy.* You can't do that with a standard search.

 Word's wildcard search capabilities resemble a mini programming language. If you have something specific that you look for over and over again, it would be well worth your while to come up with the precise search string that finds what you want and then save the handi-est search strings in a document or someplace else that's readily accessible.

To perform a wildcard search quickly

1. **Bring up the Find and Replace dialog box (refer to Figure 20-1).**

    Pressing Ctrl+F is fastest, but you can also choose Edit⇨Find. Or, click the Select Browse Object dot in the lower-right corner of the screen and then click the Find icon (looks like binoculars).

2. **Click the More button if the lower half of the dialog box isn't showing; then select the Use Wildcards check box (see Figure 20-5).**

• **Figure 20-5: A wildcard search for *g?n.***

3. **Type the text (optionally including wildcards; see Tables 20-2, 20-3, 20-4, and 20-5) in the Find What box.**

 Feel free to combine any regular text with wild-cards. As long as you avoid the special wildcard search characters (^ ? [ ] < > ! { } @), Word treats the text you type the same way it would in a simple search.

In Figure 20-5, I type **g?n**. This will match *gun* and *gin* and highlight the last three letters of Pa*gan* or the first three letters of *gan*gly or the middle three letters of octa*gon*ally, but it will not match *goon* or *grin* or *bargain.*

4. **Click the Find Next button.**

    Word highlights the first match.

5. **If any match was found, immediately click Cancel.**

    That makes it easy and quick to click the down arrow below the Select Browse Object dot (refer to Figure 20-2) to repeat the search.

Any wildcard search is automatically a Match Case search: Selecting the Use Wildcards check box implies Match Case *even though the Match Case box in Search Options is not enabled*. For example, if you select Use Wildcards and search for A?c, you match Abc and *ABc* but not *abc* nor *ABC*.

The wildcard search engine supports an enormous variety of search characters, only a fraction of which appear when you click the Special button at the bottom of the Find and Replace dialog box (see Figure 20-6). Note that this menu is different from the one shown in Figure 20-4, which is one indicator that the Use Wildcards check box switches Word to a different database.

Any **C**haracter	?
Character in Range	[-]
Beginning of Word	<
End of Word	>
E**x**pression	( )
N**o**t	[!]
N**u**m Occurrences	{ , }
Previous 1 or More	@
0 or More Characters	*
Tab Character	
Ca**r**et Character	
Col**u**mn Break	
E**m** Dash	
En **D**ash	
Graph**i**c	
Manual **L**ine Break	
Page / Section Brea**k**	
Nonbreaking **H**yphen	
Nonbreaking **S**pace	
Optional Hyphen	

• **Figure 20-6:** Some of the vastly superior wildcard search selections.

All the special characters available that I mention earlier in "Searching for More Than Plain Text" (except Word field codes) are accessible in a wildcard search when using the codes in Table 20-2. Be careful to put a caret in front of the number, with no intervening space.

TABLE 20-2: WILDCARD CODES FOR FORMATTING CHARACTERS

Wildcard	Matches
^2	Autonumbered footnote or endnote's number
^5	Annotation mark
^9	Tab character
^11	New line character (Shift+Enter)
^12	Manual page break or section break
^13	Paragraph mark
^14	Manual column break
^a	Comment (but only works in Normal view)
^g	Picture (but doesn't find pictures in the drawing layer)
^s	Nonbreaking space (Ctrl+Shift+spacebar)
^~	Nonbreaking hyphen (Ctrl+Shift+–; hyphen)
^-	Optional hyphen (Ctrl+–; minus sign)

 If you need to perform complex searches, the wildcard codes in Table 20-2 might make it possible to find or change information in your documents in a matter of seconds, whereas searching for or changing the text manually can minutes or even hours. See the example in "Replacing with Care," at the end of this Technique, for one common application — removing extra paragraph marks in a document.

Building on the common characters (letters, numbers, punctuation marks, and the like) and the formatting characters in Table 20-2, you can put together wildcard patterns for your searches. For example, you can look for *1?34* or *a*b*. I list the most common search patterns in Table 20-3.

TABLE 20-3: THE MOST COMMON WILDCARD SEARCH PATTERNS

Wildcard	Description	Timesaving Example
?	Any single character (including punctuation marks, paragraph marks, and so on)	Searching for *b?t?* matches *bite* or *bitter* or *abatement* but not *boot* or *about*.
*	Zero or more characters	Searching for *e*d* matches *every day* or *bled* but not *keen*.
[def]	Matches exactly one of the characters between the brackets	Searching for *r[au]n* matches *ran* or *running* but not *rind* or *ron*.
[m–s]	Matches any single character in the range	Searching for *p[h-u]n* matches *pin* or *pun* but not *pan* or *pUn*.
[!aeiou]	Matches any single character except the ones that are listed	Searching for *b[!iu]n* matches *ben* or *bUn* but not *bun*.
[!k–q]	Matches any single character except the ones that are in the range	Searching for *9[!1-5]9* matches *909* or *999* but not *939*.

You can restrict searches to the beginning and ending of words, as demonstrated in Table 20-4.

TABLE 20-4: MATCHING AT THE BEGINNING AND ENDING OF WORDS

Wildcard	Description	Timesaving Example
<	Look for the following text at the beginning of words	*<gat* matches *gather* and *gateway* but not *begat*.
>	Look for the preceding text at the end of words	*ine>* matches *fine* and *stRine* but not *lined*.

 You can combine the beginning and ending patterns. For example, searching on *<de*ed>* will match *deed* and *deleted* but not *bedeviled*.

The wildcard search patterns can be combined to make it easier and faster to search for certain repeated text or formatting characters in your document. For example, you can tell Word to look for two or more consecutive paragraph marks or to match a specific letter followed by an arbitrary number of numbers. I list the most useful repeating patterns in Table 20-5.

TABLE 20-5: MATCHING ON REPEATING PATTERNS

Wildcard	Description	Timesaving Example
{n,}	The preceding text or expression must appear at least n times.	Searching for *[aeiouy]{3,}* matches *oooops* or *year* but not *meany*. **Note:** n must be 1 or more; you cannot use 0.
@	Same as {1,}; matches one or more occurrence of the preceding text or expression.	*^13@* matches one or more consecutive paragraph marks.
{n,m}	The preceding text or expression must appear between n and m times. m must be larger than n.	Searching for *o{3,4}ps* matches *ooops* but not *oops* or *ooooops*.

 The backslash (\) occupies a pivotal place in wildcard searches, but the blasted character can be completely unpredictable. In general, the \ is a *literal* delimiter: that is, whatever follows a \ is supposed to be, literally, what Word searches for. So if you want to search for a question mark in a wildcard search, you type **\?**. Unfortunately, the backslash is ignored sometimes and doesn't work right other times. Avoid it if at all possible — and if not, test, test, test!

Replacing with Care

Word's Replace works much like Find, but note some a few key differences. To perform a simple replace, do the following:

1. **Bring up the Find and Replace dialog box (see Figure 20-7).**

Press Ctrl+H (if you can remember the shortcut) or choose Edit⇨Replace. Or, click the Select Browse Object dot in the lower-right corner of the screen, click the Find icon (looks like binoculars), and go to the Replace tab.

• **Figure 20-7:** Replacing the text *rd* with *Road.*

2. **Type the text that you want to replace in the Find What box and type the replacement text in the Replace With box.**

In Figure 20-7, I want to replace the characters *rd* (capitalized in any manner) with the characters *Road* (with a capital R).

3. **Click either the Replace or the Find Next button. If you want to replace the selected text with the contents of the Replace With box, click the Replace button. If you want to skip this one and move on to the next, click the Find Next button.**

The first time that Word performs a new replace, both buttons do the same thing: They locate the first occurrence of the text in the Find What box and highlight that text, allowing you to decide whether you want to make the replacement.

After you click Replace or Find Next, Word highlights the next occurrence of the text in the Find What box.

4. **Only when you're satisfied that the Replace operation is set up properly — and you won't get any weird matches — click the Replace All button.**

Otherwise you might find that all your *video boards* change to *video boaRoads.*

Replacing with wildcards

You can click the More button on the Replace tab (refer to Figure 20-7) and use all the tricks that I describe in the preceding sections for setting up wildcard searches. Here are a few significant oddities:

✔ **^13:** Do *not* use ^13 in the Replace With box. You'll end up with a character that looks like a paragraph mark but doesn't act like one. (To see the bug: Format a replaced ^13 mark as Heading 1. See how the height isn't adjusted properly?) You should always use ^p for a paragraph mark in the Replace With box even if you're forced to use a ^13 for the same paragraph mark in the Find What box to perform a wildcard search.

✔ **Capital letters:** If you use capital letters in the Replace With box, Word replaces anything that matches the Find What criteria with precisely what you type in the Replace With box. That's why the lowercase *rd* gets replaced with initial-capped *Road* in the preceding steps.

✔ **Word sez:** If you select the Find All Word Forms (English) check box, Word forces you to choose a word if you click the Replace button.

The Replace With box takes three codes that aren't available in the Find What box:

✔ **^c:** This pastes the contents of the Windows Clipboard, or the last entry in the Office Clipboard, into the current location.

Say you want to replace your company's name with a copy of its logo everywhere in a document. To do so, copy the logo to the Clipboard and then run a Find and Replace. In Find What, type your company's name. In Replace With, type **^c** (see Figure 20-8). Then click Replace All.

• **Figure 20-8: The fast way to put your company's logo many places in a document.**

✔ **^&:** This takes whatever matched the Find What box and pastes it into the current location.

 Say your boss decides that the HR report can't list just Social Security numbers. Every place where a Social Security number appears, the report now has to read SSN 123-45-6789. Easy. Run a Find and Replace. Find What is [0-9]{3}-[0-9]{2}-[0-9]{4}, and Replace With is SSN ^&.

✔ **\1 \2 \3 and so on:** These take a portion of whatever matched in the Find What box and places that portion into the current location. The portions are keyed to parentheses in the Find What box; the first pair of parentheses surround \1, the second set gets associated with \2, and so on. It sounds difficult, but it isn't. See the following example.

Removing extra paragraph marks

Here's an example of the power of Word's Find and Replace. How often do you get documents that have paragraph marks or new line characters (Shift+Enter) at the end of each line?

It's easy to get rid of them with one run of Find and Replace:

1. **Bring up the Find and Replace dialog box (refer to Figure 20-7).**

Press Ctrl+H or choose Edit⇨Replace. Or, click the Select Browse Object dot in the lower-right corner of the screen, click the Find icon (looks like binoculars), and then go to the Replace tab.

2. **Click the More button and select the Use Wildcards check box.**

3. **In the Find What box, type** ([!^13^11])[^13^11] **(see Figure 20-9).**

That bizarre command tells Word to find any character that isn't a paragraph mark (^13) or new line character (^11), followed by a paragraph mark or a new line character. Because the first part is in parentheses, Word saves whatever matched on that part of the Find What box and calls it \1.

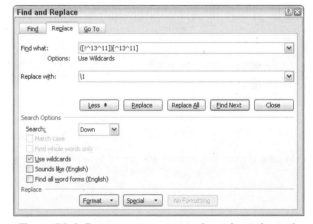

• **Figure 20-9: Remove extra paragraph marks at the end of every line with this simple Find and Replace.**

4. **In the Replace With box, type** \1 **followed by a space.**

The \1 tells Word to insert whatever matched the expression in the parentheses. The space replaces the paragraph mark.

5. **If you're feeling lucky, click Replace All.**

Word takes the document with paragraph marks at the end of each line (and two paragraph marks separating each paragraph) and strips out the extraneous paragraph marks (see Figures 20-10 and 20-11).

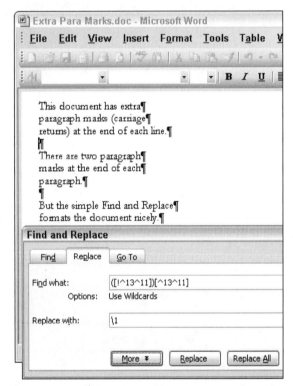

• **Figure 20-10:** A document with extra paragraph marks at the end of each line.

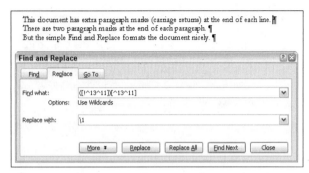

• **Figure 20-11:** The same document after running the simple Find and Replace.

Technique

21

Rapid-Fire Styles

Save Time By

✔ Using styles the right way, every way

✔ Changing Word's built-in styles

✔ Making your own styles

✔ Avoiding some gut-wrenching bugs

The vast majority of Word users never learn about styles. To me, that represents the single greatest global failure in Office education — or *discoverability*, if you look at it from the software's point of view.

At its heart, a *style* is just a collection of formatting settings. You give styles names so that you can remember what the style does, and so you can quickly apply the right style to the right paragraphs or characters.

Styles rate as the original Word timesaving technique. The people who originally designed Word built styles into the very fabric of the program. It's a pity that so much has been done by recent Microsoft designers to subvert the original, clean implementation — everything from format painting to deleted paragraph mark inheritance rules to artificially contrived, incomprehensible style names have chipped away at styles' supremacy. But if you stick with the basics, styles still shine through as a timesaving technique of the first degree.

Getting Styles

If you only use Word to write letters home to Mom, you don't need styles. But boy, howdy, do you need styles if

- ✔ You work on fairly lengthy documents or ones that might have their formatting changed by management edict.

- ✔ More than one person will work on a document.

- ✔ You're putting together a group of documents that need to look more or less the same.

- ✔ You ever need to create a Table of Contents or a List of Figures.

If you use styles, it's easy to

- ✔ **Keep formatting consistent.** Control formatting both internally within one document and among multiple documents. If you have a bulleted list (like this one) with a style applied to it, this bulleted list looks just like bulleted lists everywhere in the document or documents.

✔ **Change formats.** If someone decides that all bulleted lists have to be indented more (or less) on the left, or more (or less) on the right, or that bulleted items should all appear in bold blue underline, you make the change once, and that change is applied consistently, everywhere in the document or documents, in seconds.

✔ **Customize formats.** This book was written with two different sets of styles. The first set was customized to make it easier and faster for the author to write. The second set makes it easier for the editors to see how the page will appear in print. We save hours — maybe days — of hassle because the styles take care of much of the hard work as well as all the translation between what the author needs and what the editors want. (Or is that what the author wants and the editors need? Hmmm.)

✔ **Use Word's built-in tools.** Stick to the styles that ship with Word — even if you modify them — and you can create a Table of Contents with just a couple of clicks. Outlining (View➪Outline) tools help you organize your thoughts. Document Map works automatically (View➪Document Map, see Figure 21-1). Links work in a couple of clicks (see Technique 22). So do a List of Figures and tables and much more.

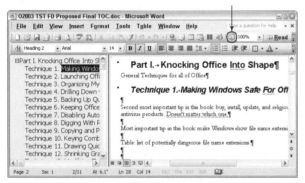

• **Figure 21-1:** Document Map (on the left) is keyed to style settings that are set up automatically if you use Word's built-in styles.

A good set of styles is unobtrusive: You can concentrate on the content, and the format takes care of

itself. A lousy set of styles will keep you going back to tweak the appearance of your work, breaking your concentration and spinning your wheels. Good styles make all the difference. I cover all the details on creating good styles in "Remaking Word's Default Styles" and "Making New Styles" later in this Technique.

 Styles live in documents, and they live in templates. You can define a custom set of styles in a template, and every new document that you create based on that template inherits those styles. Similarly, you can define (or change) styles in `normal.dot`, and all new blank documents receive those styles. See Technique 16 for details.

Applying Styles

Word has four kinds of styles, shown in Table 21-1. Character styles can be applied to individual characters and control the formatting of the characters. The other three kinds of styles are applied to paragraphs and contain formatting not only of the characters in the paragraphs but the paragraph itself.

TABLE 21-1: TYPES OF STYLES IN WORD

Type	Icon	What It Does
Character	a	Sets the formatting for one or more characters or inline pictures.
Paragraph	¶	Sets the formatting for an entire paragraph. (A *paragraph* in Word's world consists of a paragraph mark and all the text up to and including the paragraph mark.)
Table	⊞	A type of paragraph style that also includes formatting information about borders, shading, and cell alignment.
List styles	≔	A type of paragraph style that also includes formatting information about bullets, numbering, and indenting. Numbered list styles might be the buggiest, hardest-to-fathom feature in Word.

Applying a paragraph, table, or list style is a snap as long as you know the rules:

1. **Click once inside the paragraph, select all the text in the paragraph, or select several paragraphs.**

Word creates a jumbled mess of styles if you select just part of a paragraph and apply a paragraph style. Don't do it. Either select the entire paragraph or click once inside the paragraph.

2. **Choose the style from the Style drop-down list on the Formatting toolbar.**

To apply a character style

1. **Select the text that you want to format with the character style.**

2. **Choose the style from the Style drop-down list on the Formatting toolbar.**

Some people find it faster to use the Styles and Formatting task pane rather than the Style drop-down list primarily because the styles in the pane are larger and easier to see. To give the pane a try, click the AA icon on the far left of the Formatting toolbar or choose Format➪Styles and Formatting.

Word ships with 160 predefined built-in styles. I explain how to get at them all in the following section.

Manually applied formatting overrides the formatting in the style. It's a very simple concept but one that can cause some confusion — and wasted time. To see how manually applied formatting works

1. **Bring up the Styles and Formatting task pane by clicking the AA icon at the far left of the Formatting toolbar or choosing Format➪Styles and Formatting.**

I use the Styles and Formatting task pane in this procedure because it's easier to see in the screenshots here in the book. You might find it faster to use the Styles drop-down list on the Formatting toolbar.

2. **Type a few words.**

In Figure 21-2, I type **Methods of Formatting**. Note how the paragraph is Normal style.

• **Figure 21-2: Start typing in a blank document, and you get Normal style paragraphs.**

3. **Select a few characters and then click the U icon on the Formatting toolbar.**

Clicking the U icon formats the characters as underlined. This manually applied formatting (underlining) overrides the Normal style, and you can see the underline onscreen.

4. **Press the right-arrow key to deselect the underlined characters.**

Word really does make a mess of things if you apply paragraph formatting to a bunch of characters inside a paragraph. To prepare for applying a paragraph format, as in the next step, you really must deselect any text that has been selected — or, equivalently, you can select the entire paragraph.

5. **In the Styles and Formatting task pane, click Heading 1.**

Word applies the Heading 1 style to the paragraph, but the manually applied formatting — the underlining — is still there (see Figure 21-3). The manually applied formatting overrides the paragraph's style.

• **Figure 21-3:** Manually applied formatting overrides the paragraph's style.

6. **Select the underlined characters.**

7. **In the Styles and Formatting task pane, click Clear Formatting.**

Word removes the manually applied formatting, and the formerly underlined characters take on the formatting of the paragraph's style — in this case, Heading 1, without underline. (You can

accomplish the same thing — turn off the underline — by clicking the U icon again on the Formatting toolbar.)

In their purest form, styles are really that simple: A paragraph's style controls the formatting for the paragraph (that's also true of table styles and list styles, which are just paragraph styles in wolf's clothing); character styles applied inside the paragraph override the paragraph's formatting; and manually applied formatting overrides everything.

 If you change the paragraph's style, the formatting changes in general, but the original character styles and manual formatting still shine through.

If you send a document to a friend, the formatting that you applied sticks with the document: Even if your friend's Normal paragraph style is 18-point Bodoni, your precious text retains the formatting you gave it unless (and until) your friend has the audacity to apply a new style.

In precisely the same way, older documents that you might have sitting around retain their formatting, too, even if you change Word's built-in styles. So if you wrote a bunch of reports in Times New Roman 12 point and then followed the steps in Technique 16 to change the Normal font to 11 point Garamond, those old documents are still in Times New Roman 12 point. They only change if you open the documents and apply the style once again.

Chances are pretty good that's what has confused you about styles for so long.

 You can put custom styles (or redefine default styles) in a template. If you then send the template to a friend or co-worker who creates a new document based on the template, all the styles that you defined are available in the new document.

Finding Styles

If you can't find the style you want, Word might have a suitable one tucked away. To see more built-in styles

1. **Bring up the Styles and Formatting task pane (see Figure 21-4) by clicking the AA icon at the far left of the Formatting toolbar or choosing Format⇨Styles and Formatting.**

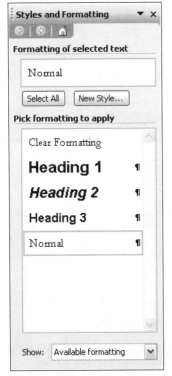

• **Figure 21-4: The only way to get at Word's additional styles is through the Styles and Formatting task pane.**

2. **In the Show drop-down box, choose All Styles.**

    Word shows you a list of most of the built-in styles (see Figure 21-5) but not all of them.

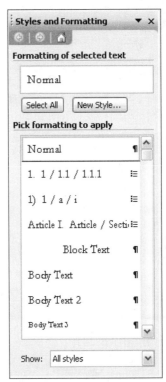

• **Figure 21-5: In spite of the caption, this is not a list of all available Word styles.**

3. **In the Show drop-down box, choose Custom.**

    Word shows you the Format Settings dialog box, with the settings for All Styles selected (see Figure 21-6).

4. **Mark the check boxes next to any styles you want to see in the All Styles list. When you're done, click OK.**

    In particular, you need to work with the Balloon Text style and Comment Text style to change the font used in Word's track changes balloons (see Technique 19).

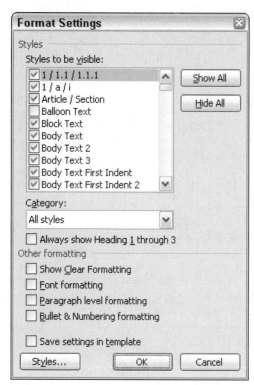

• **Figure 21-6:** This is where you can choose all the built-in styles that Word offers.

Working with all of Word's 160 styles can be more than a bit time-consuming and overwhelming — not just because of the sheer number of styles but also because the styles rarely match the kind of formatting that you probably want to apply.

 As soon as you've scoured Word's built-in styles to see whether you can pull out the style you need, return the Show drop-down box to Available Formatting to avoid wading through mountains of styles.

To see what style has been applied to a specific piece of text, do the following:

1. **Click the text that you want to analyze.**

2. **Choose Format➪Reveal Formatting.**

    Word brings up the Reveal Formatting pane.

3. **Select the Distinguish Style Source check box.**

    Word shows you where the current formatting came from (see Figure 21-7).

• **Figure 21-7:** Word's Reveal Formatting tells you where all the formatting came from.

The Style drop-down list on the Formatting toolbar always contains the name of the style you're currently working with.

If you're trying to juggle many different styles and want to see a list of paragraph style names while you type, go into Normal view (View⇨Normal) and make sure that the Style Area Width is wide enough to display your style's names (Tools⇨Options⇨View; set the Style Area Width).

Remaking Word's Default Styles

To make a good, solid set of consistent styles that work with all of Word's built-in features (including Table of Contents, Document Map, Outlines, and much more), start with the standard styles defined in Word and make modifications to the styles to suit your tastes as well as your documents' needs.

 You can create a set of custom styles in a template (see Technique 16). Any new document based on that template will take on the styles that you defined.

Speaking style-name jargon

Word's major built-in styles have some names that might not be familiar:

- **Heading** *n* styles are for headings (sometimes called *heads* in the print trade). *Heading 1* is the highest-level heading — typically, a chapter name. *Heading 2* is the next lower level and so on. Few documents use more than Heading 4. Heading *n* styles are tied into all sorts of timesaving Word features. Stick with them unless you have an overwhelmingly compelling reason to give them the heave-ho.

- **Emphasis** and **Strong** are character styles for italic and bold, respectively.

- **Header** and **Footer** are the styles that Word automatically uses for document headers and footers.

- **List Bullet** *n* and **List Number** *n* are for bulleted lists and numbered lists, respectively. Note that Word does not include predefined styles for the last bulleted paragraph in a series or for the last numbered paragraph. (Many people create styles for the last bulleted or numbered paragraph to add extra space before the main text resumes.) The List Continue *n* styles are indented like their associated List Bullet and List Number styles, but they lack the bullet or number.

- **Body Text** styles were created to be the main styles in documents that don't want to rely on Normal style. (Normal style, as you might guess, is the style that Microsoft sets up to be the default style in new blank documents.) The formatting settings that Microsoft has given Body Text are a bit odd, so make sure that you understand them (or change them!) before working with them.

- The **Table** styles exist primarily to tie into Word's Table AutoFormat dialog box (Table⇨Insert Table⇨AutoFormat). I don't know anyone who tries to modify them.

Modifying a style

Redefining an existing Word style is easy:

1. Bring up the Styles and Formatting task pane (refer to Figure 21-4) by clicking the AA icon at the far left of the Formatting toolbar or choosing Format⇨Styles and Formatting.

2. Click the drop-down arrow to the right of the style that you want to change.

In Figure 21-8, I want to change the Heading 2 style. Why? Because it's bold italic, and that offends my Typography 101-entrenched sensibilities, which state clearly that no text should *ever* be both bold and italic.

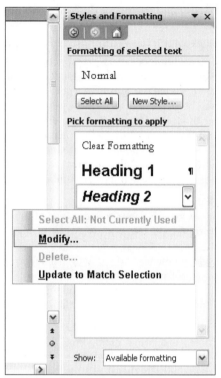

• **Figure 21-8:** Click to the right of the style name and then choose Modify.

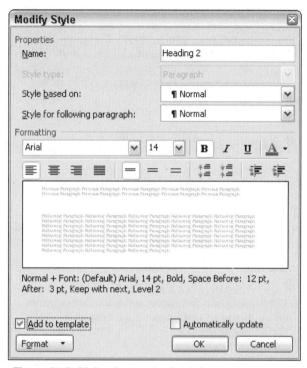

• **Figure 21-9:** Make changes to the style here.

3. Choose Modify.

Word shows you the Modify Style dialog box, as shown in Figure 21-9. Several settings in that dialog box are difficult to understand — and one is down-right dangerous. See Table 21-2 for some insight.

4. Make any changes that you need to the style.

In Figure 21-9, I click the italic icon (*I*) to toggle it off. I also mark the Add to Template check box because I want `normal.dot` to be modified so that all new blank documents will have a Heading 2 style that is bold but not italic (see Technique 16).

5. Click OK.

Word modifies the style and, in so doing, modifies every paragraph in the document formatted with that style. (If you modify a character style, all the text that has been formatted with that character style changes to conform to the new formatting settings.)

Numbering headings automatically

As long as you don't try to do anything fancy, it's easy to get Word to automatically number headings. For example, you might want to modify the Heading 1 style so that it puts the word *Chapter* at the beginning of every Heading 1 paragraph and numbers the paragraphs automatically. That way, you could type three lines in a document:

I Started Out as a Child

Life in a Small Town School

The Liberation That is Graduation

Apply the Heading 1 style to each of the three lines and get this:

Chapter 1. I Started Out as a Child

Chapter 2. Life in a Small Town School

Chapter 3. The Liberation That is Graduation

Because the numbering system is keyed to the Heading 1 style, you can add a new chapter and rearrange all the chapter numbers by simply applying the Heading 1 style to a paragraph. Similarly, you can click and drag the Heading 1 paragraphs to any place in the document, and chapters are renumbered automatically with absolutely no effort on your part.

To set up simple, sequential numbering for one Heading style

1. **Bring up the Styles and Formatting task pane (refer to Figure 21-4) by clicking the AA icon at the far left of the Formatting toolbar or choosing Format⇨Styles and Formatting.**

2. **Click the drop-down arrow to the right of the style that you want to start numbering and then choose Modify.**

I pick the Heading 1 style and choose Modify. Word responds with the Modify Style dialog box (see Figure 21-10).

3. **In the lower-left corner, click the Format button and then choose Numbering.**

Word brings up the Numbered tab of the Bullets and Numbering dialog box, as shown in Figure 21-11.

4. **Click once on the numbering scheme in the lower-right corner and then click Customize.**

I always choose the scheme in the lower right because I never use it for anything else. (Word overwrites the scheme when you customize it.) Word shows you the Customize Numbered List dialog box, as shown in Figure 21-12.

TABLE 21-2: THE STYLE BUZZWORDS IN THE MODIFY STYLE DIALOG BOX

Setting	Explanation
Style Based On	The selected style (shown in the Modify Style dialog box's Name text box) inherits all the formatting in the Style Based On box. You specify which formatting in the selected style differs from the formatting in the Style Based On style — everything else stays the same. This setting defines a hierarchy of styles. If you change one style, all the styles that are based on that style change, too. That's why changing the Normal style's font from Times New Roman to Garamond, for example, also changes the font in the Header and Footer styles.
Style for Following Paragraph	When you're typing and press Enter, the next paragraph appears in whatever style is listed in the Style for Following Paragraph box. Note this a confusing exception: If your cursor is anywhere but at the end of the paragraph when you press Enter, the new paragraph is in the same style as the old paragraph.
Add to Template	If you select this check box, any changes that you make not only take effect in the current document but are in the document's template. Thus, every new document that you make based on the template will include this modified style.
Automatically Update	Beware this, one of the most dangerous settings in Word. Enable this check box, and Word changes styles based on formatting that you apply manually. So if you manually format a paragraph and this box is checked, every paragraph in your document with the same style name is changed. Avoid this cause of accumulated eons of gray hair and bad karma.

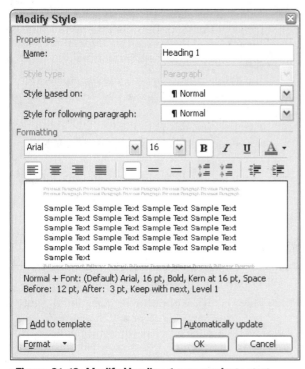

• **Figure 21-10:** Modify Heading 1 paragraphs to start autonumbering.

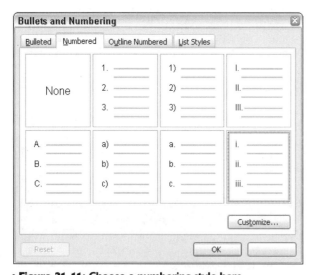

• **Figure 21-11:** Choose a numbering style here.

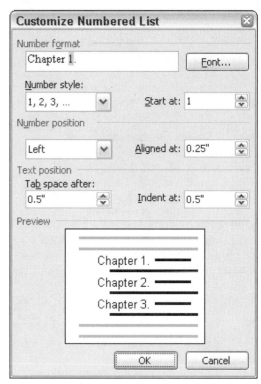

• **Figure 21-12:** One of the most inscrutable dialog boxes in Word.

5. In the Number Style drop-down box, choose the kind of number that you want (Roman numerals, letters, and so on). Then in the Number Format box, type the text that you want to appear before or after the number. Finally, set the Number Position box (which is actually the position of the entire phrase in the Number Format box) to Left.

In the Number Format box in Figure 21-12, I put the text *Chapter* before the number and a period after the number.

6. Click OK.

Word returns to the Modify Style dialog box (refer to Figure 21-10).

Do *not* select the Add to Template check box. If you do, you're on a collision course for screwed up numbering in all of your documents.

7. **Click OK again.**

Word returns to the document, with your new style ready (see Figure 21-13).

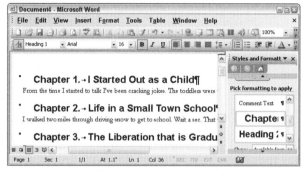

• **Figure 21-13:** All Heading 1 paragraphs are now numbered sequentially, with the word *Chapter* at the beginning.

 If you want to do anything more complicated than simple, sequential numbering of one particular style — the procedure I talk about here — you are treading on thin ice and begging for a time-consuming headache that will never quit. Shauna Kelly wrote the best discussion I have seen about outline numbering (and more complex numbering) in Word. Follow her instructions closely at www.shaunakelly.com/word/numbering/OutlineNumbering.html or resign yourself to spending days fighting Word's problems.

Automatic style numbering is a tremendous time-saver as long as you keep it simple.

Making New Styles

Creating a new set of styles is a time-consuming task but one that can bring large rewards if they're used consistently.

 There are as many different opinions about styles as there are about football teams; no one approach is clearly superior to another. But if you're attempting to set up a group of styles for a large organization, make sure that you read Bob Blacksberg's *Laws of Styles*, www.woodyswatch.com/office/archtemplate.asp?v4-n20. **Bob's** words of wisdom apply specifically to legal firms — the last, most desperate bastion on the style frontier — but they're important guidelines for anyone who needs to come up with a robust set of styles that will survive many generations of writers.

Creating a single new style, on the other hand, is quite easy:

1. **Bring up the Styles and Formatting task pane (refer to Figure 21-4).**

To do so, click the AA icon at the far left of the Formatting toolbar or choose Format⇨Styles and Formatting.

2. **Click the New Style button.**

Word shows you the New Style dialog box, as shown in Figure 21-14.

3. **Type a name for the style and then select the Style Type. Set the formatting that you want.**

In Figure 21-14, I create a paragraph style called Query, which I use to flag items for follow-up while I'm writing. It only takes a couple of clicks to set the Query style to red and bold formatting (from the <u>A</u> and the **B** icons, respectively). See Table 21-1 earlier in this Technique for details about different types of styles.

 If you're creating a new list style that will automatically number paragraphs, you are treading on thin ice. Word's bugs will drive you nuts. See the preceding section.

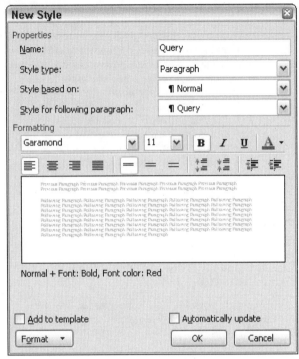

• **Figure 21-14:** Creating a new style takes only a few seconds.

• **Figure 21-15:** The new, custom Query style is just a click away.

4. If you want to put the new style in the document's template (so that you can use it in other documents based on the same template), select the **Add to Template** check box. Click **OK**.

 Don't ever enable the Automatically Update check box. That gives Word licence to kill your styles.

Your new style is ready for use in the Styles and Formatting pane (see Figure 21-15) and the Styles drop-down list on the Formatting toolbar.

 You can save a lot of time by associated keyboard shortcuts of your choosing to the styles that you use most frequently. To do so, in the Styles and Formatting pane, click the down-arrow to the right of the style and choose Modify. In the Modify Style dialog box, choose Format⇨Shortcut Key, and set the keyboard shortcut from there.

Refreshing Styles to Match a Template

If you ever want to refresh the styles in a document so that they match the styles in the document's template, do the following:

 If you ever apply a style and you don't get the formatting you expect, chances are good that the style definition in the document got munged somehow. That's a good time to reach back into the template and refresh the style . . . assuming that you have an up-to-date template, of course.

1. **Choose Tools➪Templates and Add-Ins.**

Word brings up the Templates and Add-ins dialog box (see Figure 21-16).

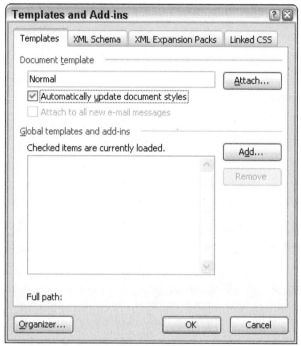

• **Figure 21-16: Refresh the style definitions in a document here, but be careful.**

2. **Enable the Automatically Update Document Styles check box and then click OK.**

Word first copies settings from the template for all the styles currently in the document and then applies those styles throughout the document.

3. **Immediately choose Tools➪Templates and Add-Ins. Clear the Automatically Update Document Styles check box and then click OK.**

Automatically Update Document Styles is a sticky setting, and if you leave this check box selected, you'll waste hours and hours trying to figure out why your styles change for no apparent reason.

Fast Links inside Documents

Save Time By

✔ Creating one-click links to navigate inside your documents

✔ Linking to headings via a Table of Contents

✔ Creating custom links

One of the incredible timesaving features that lies at the core of the Web is the ability to create *links,* which are embedded elements that are specially constructed so that you're automatically transported somewhere else when you click them.

Many Word users don't realize that you can build the same kind of links inside Word with just a few clicks. I'm not talking about links to Web sites; those are easy and a bit old-hat. (And unless you follow my advice in Technique 7, every time you type a Web address, you automatically create a link that'll zoom you off to the World Wide Wait.)

I'm talking about links inside the document itself: links that you can build that transport your readers to places you feel are important, such as chapters, sections, figures, glossary entries, and references. If you know the rules and follow them, Word builds some of the links automatically. If you want to go it on your own, Word has a handful of very powerful features that make it easy.

Save your readers some time. Put links in your documents.

Creating a Linked Table of Contents Automatically

In Technique 21, I talk about the many benefits of using Word's built-in heading styles — Heading 1, Heading 2, and so on, down to Heading 9. If you have a document that uses Word's Heading *n* styles, creating a Table of Contents with links couldn't be simpler:

1. **Click once where you want the Table of Contents (TOC) to appear.**

2. **Choose Insert⇨Reference⇨Index and Tables⇨Table of Contents.**

   Word shows you the Table of Contents tab of the Index and Tables dialog box, as shown in Figure 22-1.

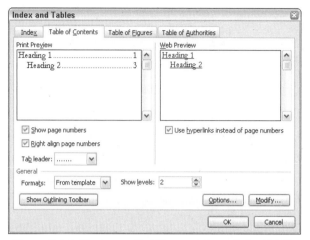

• **Figure 22-1: If you use Heading *n* styles, a linked Table of Contents takes a couple of clicks.**

3. **Use the Show Levels box to set the Heading *n* level that you want to appear in the TOC.**

In Figure 22-1, I set Show Levels to 2, thus telling Word that I want the Table of Contents to include only Heading 1 and Heading 2 entries.

4. **Click OK.**

Word creates a Table of Contents links, as shown in Figure 22-2.

• **Figure 22-2: A Table of Contents with linked entries for all Heading 1 and Heading 2 styles.**

 If your reader is using Word 2003 or 2002 (the version of Word in Office XP), it takes a Ctrl+click to follow the link, as noted in Figure 22-2. On the other hand, if your reader uses Word 2000 or Word 97 to read the document, any stray click of the link will take her zooming off to the linked location. Many people find the one-click-an'-yer-gone behavior disconcerting, so take the version of Word that will be used to view the document into consideration before festooning your documents with many links.

Links created automatically with a Table of Contents move with the heading. If you drag a heading to a new location, Ctrl+clicking the Table of Contents link takes you to the new location. If you cut and paste a heading to a new location, Ctrl+clicking in the Table of Contents finds the new location, too.

Unfortunately, if you copy the heading to a new location and then delete the old heading, Word isn't smart enough to find the new copy. Ctrl+clicking in the Table of Contents just takes you to the beginning of the document.

 If you move a heading in a document with a linked Table of Contents, rebuilding the TOC — to ensure that the links still work — is a good idea. Rebuilding the TOC is easy: Just click once inside the TOC and then press F9 (which updates the TOC field). Alternatively, you can right-click inside the TOC and choose Update Field.

Linking Text to Headings in a Document

Word's strong support of Heading *n* styles isn't confined to the Table of Contents. You can use them to link whatever text you want to a heading, too. So if you have a long document, you can insert a link in one section that takes the reader to a related section. Here's how:

1. **Select the text inside the document that you want to be linked.**

2. **Click the Insert Hyperlink icon on the Standard toolbar.**

The Insert Hyperlink icon is the one that looks like the Earth in chains. Word responds by showing you the Insert Hyperlink dialog box (see Figure 22-3).

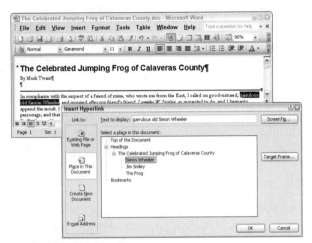

• **Figure 22-3:** Linking to a Heading *n* style from anywhere in the document is a snap.

3. **In the Link To bar on the left side, click Place in This Document.**

Under the Headings category, Word gives you a list of the Heading *n* formatted paragraphs in the document.

4. **Pick the Heading *n* paragraph that you want to link to and then click OK.**

Word sets up a link to whichever Heading *n* paragraph that you picked. Ctrl+click the linked text, and you're immediately sent to that paragraph.

This kind of linking suffers from the same problems that plague the Table of Contents links: If you play around with the heading too much, the link can get broken.

Creating Custom Links That Are Hard to Break

Earlier in this Technique, I describe one easy and fast way to create links inside a document by using Word's built-in Heading styles. If you want a linked, automatically generated Table of Contents, it's the only game in town. The procedure works well, but

it's error-prone because headings can get moved around in a document. Unless you take care to maintain the links, they can break.

Here's a better way. It takes a bit more time, but the links are hard to break:

1. **Click a chunk of text (and/or picture) that you want to link to.**

Make it a good-sized piece of text . . . several words at least.

The link actually goes to the beginning of the text that you select. Click the link, and Word's insertion point jumps to the beginning of the bookmarked area. I recommend selecting a reasonable amount of text because a bookmark that covers a large area is harder to delete accidentally — thus clobbering the link — than a tiny bookmark.

You can also bookmark text inside table cells, entire cells, or groups of cells. You can even bookmark and link to items in the drawing layer (see Technique 11).

2. **Choose Insert⇨Bookmark.**

Word brings up the Bookmark dialog box, as shown in Figure 22-4. (A *bookmark* is a location in a Word document that's given a name so that referring to the location is easy.)

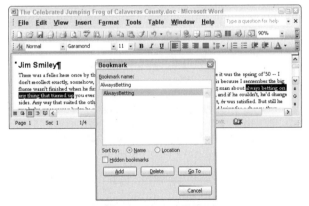

• **Figure 22-4:** Bookmark the Link To location first.

If you're working extensively with bookmarks, have Word show you where they are. Choose Tools⇨Options⇨View, mark the Bookmarks check box, and click then OK. Word shows light gray brackets around all bookmarks. You don't get much information — for example, the name of the bookmark isn't displayed; and if you have overlapping bookmarks, it's hard to tell where one ends and the other begins — but having the gray brackets onscreen will alert you to Link To locations that already exist.

3. Type a name for the bookmark (no spaces allowed) and then click the Add button.

Word sticks a bookmark on the text (and/or pictures) that you selected.

4. Select the text that you want to link to the bookmark.

Items in the drawing layer (see Technique 11) can be linked and also link to locations in the underlying document. That can come in handy if you want to link to a figure that appears in a distant part of the document.

5. Click the Insert Hyperlink icon on the Standard toolbar.

Word brings up the Insert Hyperlink dialog box (see Figure 22-5).

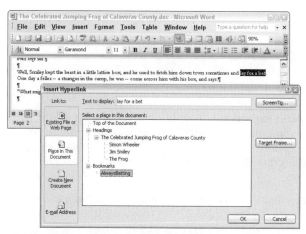

• **Figure 22-5:** Linking to bookmarks is easy, too.

6. In the Link To bar on the left, click Places in This Document.

7. On the right, click the bookmark that you want to link to, and then click OK.

Word sets up a link, underlines it, and turns it blue, as shown in Figure 22-6.

• **Figure 22-6:** The link set up via the dialog box in Figure 22-5.

Seeing all the bookmarks in your document is easy. Choose Edit⇨Go To; this brings up the Go To tab of the Find and Replace dialog box. In the Go To What box, choose Bookmark (see Figure 22-7). Word dutifully lists all the bookmarks in the document. Pick one and click the Go To button, and Word selects the entire contents of the indicated bookmark.

• **Figure 22-7:** Keep track of your bookmarks here.

Technique 23

Setting Up Your Own Letterhead

Save Time By

✔ Making Word work around your company letterhead

✔ Using Word to create your own letterhead

✔ Setting up a letterhead template that works right — all the time

If you write letters, this Technique will pay for this book many times over.

I'm forever amazed — nay, *astounded* — at how many people in the business world jury-rig ways to get around preprinted letterhead. Some people hit Enter precisely 13 times whenever they start a letter to get past the stuff preprinted on top. Others try to use the Tab key (the *Tab* key, for heaven's sake!) to bypass their partners' list on the left side of the page. Almost everyone has trouble when a letter goes beyond one page — the baling wire and chewing gum that works on page one gets all kinked up and gummy on page two.

I'm also amazed at how much money (and time!) gets wasted when companies inevitably move, or change their phone numbers or mailing addresses. If you or your company have a high-quality printer, you should never be in a position of throwing away thousands (or hundreds of thousands) of sheets of perfectly good letterhead.

A little bit of letterhead planning can save a ton of time and money. This Technique shows you how.

Making Letterhead Decisions

The world of letterhead is divided into three camps:

✔ **Those who preprint everything** on their letterhead, not worrying (or caring) about the fact that one small change renders everything useless and wasted. (These are the same folks who paste labels over the top of their changed telephone numbers, hoping nobody will notice. *News flash:* We do.)

✔ **Those who figure that a computer printout is good enough** and print their letterhead as part of the letter itself. (These are the ones who print their business cards on inkjets, ripping down the perforations, hoping nobody will notice. *News update:* I do.)

✔ **Those who preprint a key piece of their letterhead** — perhaps a logo or maybe the company name — and then use the computer to print the stuff that can change. (Yeah, I decided to join that camp about 10 years ago. Didja guess?)

The people who use preprinted, colored, computer letterhead paper from the corner stationery store tend to fall in the second camp, although I've seen a few minimalist designs that aren't too bad and verge on the third. Two problems: They all seem to look the same after a while, and you can probably get a custom print job for about the same price if you use more than a few boxes of paper.

Although this Technique covers all three camps, if you're ever in the position of trying to decide what to have preprinted on your company (or your personal!) letterhead, consider the following:

✔ **Color quality:** Unless you have an absolutely gorgeous color printer, color-print quality from a print shop runs rings around anything that you can produce from your computer's printer.

✔ **Print quality:** Unless you have a remarkably lousy printer, the quality of normal-size text on your company (or personal) letterhead will be comparable whether you have it run at the print shop or through your inkjet or laser printer.

✔ **Paper quality:** When you order new letterhead, try feeding a few sheets of the paper that the printer will use through your own printer *before* you place the order. Print normal text and pictures and then fold and crease the paper in the printed area. Some printer's papers these days are notoriously bad with inkjets (particularly those that wick water-based ink), and other papers (highly textured) are bad with lasers. You want a clean print, and you don't want it to smear.

Creating a New Letterhead Template

Here's a quick, easy, fast way to create your own letterhead.

Before you start, you *must* have the following:

✔ **A handful of copies of your preprinted letterhead (that is, if you're using preprinted letterhead).**

 In this Technique, I assume that you only use preprinted letterhead for the first page of your correspondence and that all subsequent pages are on blank sheets.

✔ **A very good idea of how you want to lay out the letterhead.** If you're going to print your name and address, for example, you should have a good idea of the font and size that you want and where it'll go, as well as any artwork you want.

✔ **A pencil with a very, very good eraser and a ruler.**

No, you don't need to know anything about templates or sections or anything weird.

Here's how to start setting up your letterhead template:

1. **Start with a new, blank document. Choose View➪Print Layout to go into Print Layout view.**

2. **Choose File➪Save.**

I always save new templates immediately. Word shows you the Save As dialog box, as shown in Figure 23-1.

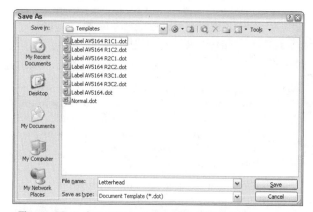

• **Figure 23-1: Save the new template right away.**

3. **In the Save as Type box, choose Document Template (*.dot). In the File Name box, type something sensible (such as, oh, Letterhead). Click Save.**

You now have a new letterhead template. Scary, huh? Don't do anything for now. You will need the template in the section, "Altering Template Settings."

Laying Out the Letterhead

Here's the hard part:

1. **Step away from your computer.**

Figure out what you're going to do before you touch anything.

2. **Pull out a blank sheet of paper — *not* your letterhead — and the ruler and pencil.**

Start by laying out the second page of your template. Not the first.

3. **Figure out reasonable margins and draw them on the blank sheet of paper.**

The *margins* are the boundaries for your typing on the second (and subsequent) pages of the letter. If you want a page number or a date on the second (and subsequent) pages, they go above or below the margins.

 I think new pages look best with the margins at 1 inch on top, 0.75 inch on the sides, and 0.5 inch on the bottom.

4. **Figure out whether you want anything printed in the margins on the second (and subsequent) sheets — your name, page number, date, whatever. Write down what you want and where you want it. Yes, using a pencil. Yes, on a real piece of paper.**

I like to put the page number in the upper-right corner although your sense of the aesthetic might vary greatly from mine.

 Having Word automatically put dates in your documents is problematic. I've been struggling with this for years . . . and finally came to the conclusion that it just isn't worth the time-consuming hassle. I talk about the problem in "Making Dates — With a Macro" later in this Technique. At this point, I would recommend against putting a date on the second (and subsequent) pages of your documents.

5. **Pull out a sheet of letterhead. If you don't have any preprinted letterhead, get another sheet of plain paper.**

Don't put away the ruler or pencil (or eraser). You still need them.

6. **Draw the same margins around the preprinted letterhead that you drew on the second (and subsequent) page(s) of plain paper.**

Yes, I know you have to work around some of that preprinted stuff, and you want your company's name on the first page. Patience, Grasshopper.

7. **Draw rectangles around any additional areas that need to be blocked off.**

For example, if you have a preprinted logo in the upper-right corner, draw a box around it. Got a list of fuddy-duddies (sorry . . . *board members*) on the left? Box 'em. Artistic swoosh at the bottom of the page? Draw a rectangle around it, too.

8. **Measure the boxes and write down the dimensions.**

Yes, with a pencil. Yes, on the sheet of paper. You want the dimensions inside the margins. Any preprinted areas that fall outside the margins — out on the edges of the page — don't count because you won't be printing out there anyway. So write down the additional amount of space that you need to reserve, above and beyond the margins, for each blocked-off preprinted area.

9. **Block off locations for all the other computer-printed letterhead stuff.**

These are items that will be identical in every letter: company name, address, phone number, smarmy slogan, and so on. Don't include the date, the recipient's name, or anything along those lines. That all comes later.

No doubt you have writer's cramp and black fingers, with your carpal tunnels twitching for the keyboard. That's okay. You're now ready to go back to Mother Microsoft.

Altering Template Settings

At your disposal are a thousand different ways to transfer the settings that you sketched in the preceding section into a Word template. I believe that the following is the fastest and most foolproof:

1. **Bring up the letterhead template,** Letterhead.dot, **that you made in the earlier "Creating a New Letterhead Template" section of this Technique.**

 Word sticks templates in weird places. To see where yours are, choose Tools⇨Options⇨ File Locations and look at the setting called User Templates. If you just finished creating the letterhead template, though, you might be able to find the .dot file at the bottom of your File menu.

2. **Choose Tools⇨Options⇨View, select the Text Boundaries check box, and then click OK. Then click the Zoom drop-down box on the Standard toolbar and set it to Whole Page (if you have a high-resolution monitor) or Page Width (if you don't).**

It's much easier to see what's going on if you have the whole page in front of you. Word shows you dotted lines around the margins on the page (see Figure 23-2).

If you notice the boundaries disappear or otherwise act strangely as you work on the template, it's not your vision. It's a bug in Word.

• **Figure 23-2: Have Word show you text boundaries while you're laying out the template.**

3. **Choose File⇨Page Setup and type the Top, Bottom, Left, and Right margins that you drew with your ruler. Click OK.**

The settings in Figure 23-3 are good enough for me.

4. **If you have a header or footer that you want to put on second and subsequent pages, choose View⇨Header and Footer and type the header or footer that you want. When you're done, click the Close button on the Header and Footer toolbar.**

In Figure 23-4, I click inside the header, click the right-align icon on the Formatting toolbar, type the word **Page**, and then click the first icon on the toolbar, which inserts the page number.

• **Figure 23-3:** Set your margins here.

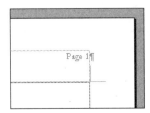

• **Figure 23-4:** Putting the page number in the upper-right corner of the header.

5. Choose File⇨Page Setup⇨Layout and mark the **Different First Page** check box. Click OK.

If you created any second/subsequent page headers and/or footers in Step 4, they now disappear, but don't panic. Word has saved them safely away. (In fact, you're done with all the settings for second and subsequent pages.) What you see is the "different" first page, which needs some work.

6. Block off rectangles so that Word won't print on top of your preprinted letterhead.

This is where your upfront work in the earlier section, "Laying Out the Letterhead," comes in play. If you don't have any such rectangles, skip down to Step 18.

7. If you can't see the Drawing toolbar (the one with Draw on the left), right-click any blank spot on any toolbar and select the Drawing check box.

8. Turn off the %$#@! drawing canvas by choosing Tools⇨Options⇨General and clearing the **Automatically Create Drawing Canvas When Inserting AutoShapes** check box.

While you're at it, make a note to read Technique 11.

9. Click the Rectangle AutoShape icon on the Drawing toolbar (the one to the right of the down-pointing arrow) and then draw a rectangle where you don't want Word to print (what I call a *no-print rectangle*) roughly the same size and location as the one you drew in pencil.

In Figure 23-5, I draw such a no-print rectangle in the upper-left corner of the page, where my preprinted logo appears.

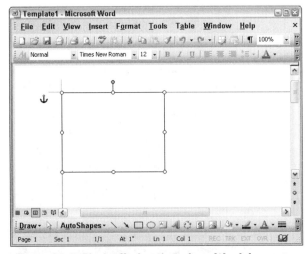

• **Figure 23-5:** Block off a location where Word dare not tread.

10. Right-click the no-print rectangle that you just drew and then choose Format AutoShape. On the Colors and Lines tab, make sure that you have a Line Color and that Weight is not 0 (zero).

You want to be able to see the outline of the no-print rectangle for the moment so that you can print the page and get it to line up with your preprinted letterhead.

11. Click the Size tab. In the Height and Width boxes, type the height and width of the rectangle — the height and width you wrote down in pencil, of course. Make sure that both Scale spinners are set at 100%.

12. Click the Layout tab. Click the Tight icon — assuming that you want Word to wrap text tightly around the box — and then click the Advanced button.

You see the Advanced Layout dialog box, as in Figure 23-6.

• **Figure 23-6:** Force Word to line up the no-print rectangle with the page so it doesn't go scurrying around.

13. On both Absolute Position lines, choose Page from the drop-down boxes. Select the Lock Anchor check box in the Options area, and then click OK twice to return to your document.

Don't worry about the measurements for the moment. What's important is that you lock the rectangle to the page itself (see Figure 23-7) so that it won't flip-flop all over the place even if you change your mind about the other parts of the template someday.

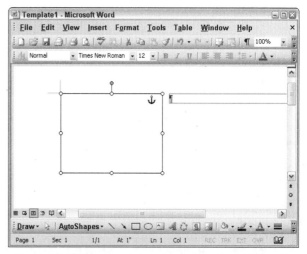

• **Figure 23-7:** The no-print rectangle is anchored to the page.

Hanging or left indents may not work when combined with blocked off sections. If you absolutely must have hanging indents or left indents to the right of a blocked-off preprinted part of your letterhead, you can use multiple sections and adjust the margins in each section, but that turns very ugly, very fast.

14. Carve out as many rectangular no-print zones as you need, following Steps 10–13.

15. Print a test page.

The page at this point consists of rectangles surrounding no-print areas. Print it, stick the sheet of paper that came out of your printer on top of your preprinted letterhead, and hold both of them up to a strong light. How close did you get on the first try?

16. **Click and drag the no-print rectangles in the document until they line up with your preprinted letterhead.**

Remember that you can drag the rectangles just a smidgen by clicking the rectangle, holding the mouse button down, pressing Alt, and then dragging the rectangle. Holding down Alt lets you nudge the rectangle very tiny distances without Word's snap feature getting in the way (see Technique 11).

17. **When you're happy with the no-print rectangles, right-click each rectangle in turn, choosing Format AutoShape and then setting the Color box (under Line) to No Line (see Figure 23-8).**

• **Figure 23-8: When the no-print regions are lined up properly, make the rectangles invisible.**

You now have all the preprinted regions on your letterhead well and truly blocked off, and no telltale lines will print.

18. **Choose File➪Save and save the template.**

You need it in the following section.

Adding Text to Your Letterhead Template

With the no-print areas blocked off (see the preceding section), you're ready to put your own text — and drawings, if you wish — in your letterhead template. This is the text that you want to appear over and over, each time you use the letterhead.

With two exceptions, there are no hard-and-fast rules for laying out the text in your document. You can

✔ **Put text or drawings in the body of the document.** This is a particularly good option if you want to center text on the page, taking into account a no-print rectangle (see Figure 23-9). In that case, just type and format your name and address, select the paragraphs, and click the Center icon on the Formatting toolbar — and you're done in under a minute.

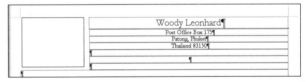

• **Figure 23-9: My name and address, centered between the preprinted logo (blocked out on the left) and the right margin.**

✔ **Put text or drawings in the header or footer.** Add as much as you like, anywhere you like.

Putting a lot of text in the header will drive down text in the body of the document. (That's how Word's headers work: If they get too big, they push down whatever is in the main part of the document.) However, feel free to chuckle to yourself, knowing that sticking gargantuan amounts of text in the header won't budge your no-print rectangles because they're anchored to the page itself.

Keep an eye on the text boundary line at the bottom of the template, however, particularly if you add anything to the footer. Unlike Word's headers (which push text down as they get larger), Word's footers aren't smart enough to push text up if they get too big.

The only way to make more room for Word's footers is by increasing the bottom margin (File➪Page Setup➪Margins) or lowering the footer itself (File➪Page Setup➪Layout).

Use Word's Print Layout view to line up everything. Don't be distressed by all the bogus text boundary lines to the right of any no-print areas (which you can clearly see in Figure 23-9). Think of them as Word's *bugs in action*.

✔ **Insert WordArt or a watermark.** Insert WordArt in the main body of the document or in its header or footer; insert a watermark (which goes in the header, see Technique 71); or insert any other kind of drawing or picture.

This template has different first page headers and footers, so if you put something in the first page header or footer, it only shows up in the final document on the first page. That includes watermarks.

✔ **Format however you like.** Format fonts, lines, boxes, columns, tables, highlights, and arrows to your heart's content.

With two exceptions, whatever you put in this template appears in all documents that you create based on it. The two exceptions are

✔ **Today's date:** If you want to include today's date in the template, you should not put it in a header or footer.

✔ **Final paragraph mark:** The very last paragraph mark in the template should be the location where you want to start typing the letter — typically, where you want to put the recipient's name and address.

To put an automatically updated date (typically, the date that you will type the letter) in the template

1. **Click inside the template where you want the date to appear.**

2. **Choose Insert➪Date and Time.**

Word shows you the Date and Time dialog box (see Figure 23-10).

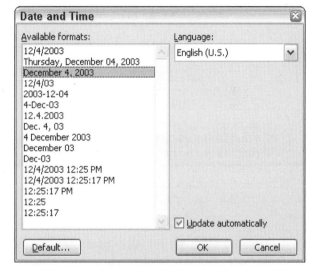

• **Figure 23-10: This dialog box tells Word to use the current date.**

3. **Make sure that the Update Automatically check box is selected, pick the format that you like, and then click OK.**

Enabling Update Automatically is imperative if you want the current date to appear when you open the template.

Don't worry about the autoupdate feature messing with your date; I explain how to write a macro that takes care of the problem later in this Technique.

Word inserts the date into your template (see Figure 23-11).

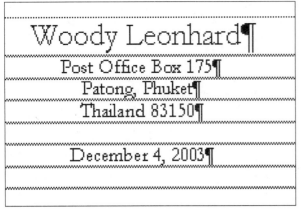

Woody Leonhard¶
Post Office Box 175¶
Patong, Phuket¶
Thailand 83150¶

December 4, 2003¶

• **Figure 23-11:** The current date — actually a field that retrieves the current date — gets inserted into the template.

4. **Format the date any way you like — font, centering, and so forth.**

With the text, drawings, no-print rectangles, formatting, and date in your template, you're now ready to save it:

1. **Make sure that everything is hunky-dory.**

The last paragraph mark is at the location where you want to start typing your letters, right? You might want to print a test sheet on your real preprinted letterhead.

2. **Make sure that your view settings are how you like them.**

▶ In particular, choose Tools⇨Options⇨View and clear the Text Boundaries check box.

▶ If you use Print Layout view, choose View⇨Print Layout.

▶ If you don't like the rulers hanging around, choose View and make sure that Rulers is not marked.

▶ Toggle off any toolbars that you don't want (perhaps the Drawing toolbar?) by

right-clicking any blank area on any toolbar and clearing the appropriate check box.

▶ Adjust your Zoom.

Take your time. If you're like me, you'll live with this template for a long, long time (see Figure 23-12).

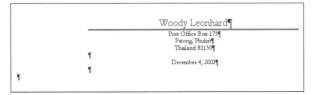

• **Figure 23-12:** My personal letterhead template. Really.

3. **Choose File⇨Close.**

If Word asks you whether it's okay to save changes, be sure to say Yes! If Word gives you a privacy warning, click OK.

Making Dates — With a Macro

In the preceding sections, I talk about creating a letterhead template (`Letterhead.dot`), closing it, and then saving all the changes. If you haven't done that yet, do so now.

You now need to record a macro to make the template work better. This macro runs every time that you create a new document based on the template, and it runs immediately when the document gets created. This macro

✔ Creates a new document with all of your text and no-print rectangles, headers and footers, on the first page and on the second and all subsequent pages.

✔ Selects the entire document.

✔ Updates the Use the Current Date field (and any other field that might be in the body of the document).

✔ Converts the date (and any other fields) to text. After the macro runs and the fields are converted to text, they'll never be updated again, so the date that appears in the letter will be the date on which the macro was run, even if you open the letter five years from now.

✔ Positions the cursor in front of the last paragraph mark in the document.

Fast, quick, and easy — and you'll use it over and over again.

 Although Word makes it easy to display the current date, the autoupdating has all sorts of anomalies that make it difficult to make the date when you created the letter the date that you see every time you open the file. I've struggled with this problem for a decade, and the only decent solution that I can come up with is the one outlined here: Have Word use the current date but then immediately select the date and turn it into plain old text so that it won't ever be updated again. That's why you get to record a macro. There's no easy way to have a recorded macro search in the headers and footers in a document. (You can *write* a macro to do it, but that's a lot of work.) So I recommend that you put the date in the body of the document and keep it all simple.

Here's how to record the macro that makes your letterhead template complete:

1. **Choose File➪New. In the New Document task pane (on the right, about halfway down), click On My Computer.**

Word brings up the Templates dialog box (see Figure 23-13).

2. **Double-click the Letterhead.dot icon.**

Word creates a new document based on Letterhead.dot. You see all the text and drawings that you put into the template in earlier sections of this Technique. You don't see the no-print rectangles (which protect preprinted sections of your letterhead), but they're there. You also don't see the second and subsequent page headers and footers, but they're there, too.

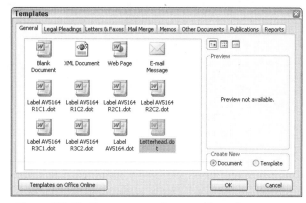

• **Figure 23-13:** Create a new document based on your `Letterhead.dot` **template.**

3. **Choose Tools➪Macro➪Record New Macro.**

Word shows you the Record Macro dialog box, as shown in Figure 23-14.

• **Figure 23-14:** Record an AutoNew macro for `Letterhead.dot`.

4. **In the Macro Name box, type** AutoNew **(all one word; the name is very important). In the Store Macro In drop-down box, choose Documents Based on Letterhead.dot. In the Description box, type any identifying information that you like. Then click OK.**

Word responds with the funny, stunted Recording toolbar shown in Figure 23-15.

• **Figure 23-15: Your macro-recording tools, such as they are.**

5. **Press Ctrl+A.**

That selects the whole document (but not the headers or footers).

6. **Press F9.**

That updates any Use the Current Date fields.

7. **Hold down Shift and Ctrl, press and release F9, and then release Shift and Ctrl.**

That turns any fields into plain, old everyday text.

8. **Press the right arrow.**

That puts the cursor immediately in front of the final paragraph mark in the document — right where you want to start typing.

9. **Click the Stop Recording button (the first button on the Recording toolbar).**

You now have a macro called AutoNew in the Letterhead.dot template. It fires every time that Word creates a new document based on Letterhead.dot.

10. **Choose File⇨Close. When Word asks whether you want to save changes to Document2, click No. When Word asks whether you want to save the changes to** Letterhead.dot, **click Yes. If you get a Privacy warning, click OK.**

Congratulations! You just built a template and macro that should work for a long, long time.

To see your new template in action, choose File⇨New and click Letterhead.dot (which is probably at the top of the Recently Used Templates list on the right). Any time you want to change it, open Letterhead.dot, make your changes, and save. It's really that fast and easy.

Distributing the Letterhead Template

I know. You're so proud of your new letterhead template you can't wait to let everybody else use it. Fortunately, that's very easy and quick, too:

1. **Locate the template on your PC.**

Chances are good it's in
```
C:\Documents and Settings\
<your user name>\Application Data\
Microsoft\Templates.
```

If you can't see the \Application Data folder, Windows is hiding folders from you. Follow the instructions in Technique 1 to show hidden folders — and make Windows safe for Office.

2. **Copy** Letterhead.dot.

You can put it on a floppy disk, e-mail it, copy it onto a network drive, burn it on a CD, or stick it on paper tape and attach it to a homing pigeon's leg.

3. **Put** Letterhead.dot **in the template folder on your friend's PC.**

It's probably C:\Documents and Settings\ <their user name>\Application Data\ Microsoft\Templates, too, but you might have to use Windows Search (Start⇨Find or Start⇨Search) to locate other .dot files.

4. **Have your friend crank up Word and create a new document based on** Letterhead.dot.

Even in older versions of Word, your buddy should have no problems at all.

If you do have a problem — most likely the macro doesn't run, so the date isn't right — choose Tools⇨Macro⇨Security and lower the security setting to Medium.

Technique 24

Positioning Pictures Just Right

Save Time By

- Moving pictures where you want them — and making them stay there
- Understanding how Word tries to help by moving pictures around without your consent (or knowledge)
- Working with the (often inscrutable) program, not against it

Tell me whether this has happened to you. You spend five or ten minutes sticking a picture in a Word document, getting it set up just right. Then you go somewhere else in the document, make a few changes, and when you come back . . . the picture's all screwed up.

Then you spend another half hour trying to figure out what in the $#@! Word thinks it's doing and another half-hour trying to figure out how to make Word stop. In the end, you get lucky — something, somewhere worked right — and you print and save the document, praying that the next time you open it, nothing else gets jostled.

This Technique should help you understand what Word's trying to do, and why. Lest Word exsanguinate you, stick with me here for your garland of garlic and a timesaving wooden stake to make sure that Word stays in its coffin when you bid.

Working with the Drawing Layer

If you haven't read Technique 11 recently, now's the time to do so. There, find out how the drawing layer — actually, drawing layers — float above and below every Word document.

If you want to come to terms with the pictures that you put in Word documents, you must understand the drawing layer and how it interacts with the text layer. Specifically

- **The drawing layers float above and below the text layer in a document.** Think of them as individual transparency sheets, with the text layer in the middle. You can put *drawings* (items created with the Drawing toolbar) or *pictures* (graphic files inserted into your document) on a drawing layer and then move the layer up and down (above or below the text layer, or above or below any other drawing or picture on a drawing layer).

✔ **The text layer is unique: There's only one.** You can put a picture in the text layer — in which case, it's *in-line with text*. You can put a picture in a drawing layer — in which case it's *floating*. You can't put a drawing in the text layer, but you can put text in the drawing layer (for example, with a text box or a callout).

Confused? I don't blame ya. It took me the better part of a decade to figure this out. It isn't documented comprehensibly any place I've seen.

✔ **Pictures in the text layer are treated just like characters — big characters, in most cases.** If you type in front of a picture, it gets pushed farther down the current line and then onto the next line, just like a character. If you select a paragraph that contains an in-line picture, the picture gets selected, too.

 If you have a picture in a document but you can see only a sliver of the bottom of it, chances are good that somebody (not you, of course) inserted the picture into a paragraph that has a Line Spacing setting of Exactly. To see the entire picture (and also expand line spacing enormously in the paragraph), click once inside the paragraph, choose Format➪ Paragraph, and set Line Spacing to Single.

✔ **Pictures in the drawing layer are treated just like drawings in the drawing layer — with one exception.** Pictures in the drawing layer are *anchored* — typically to a paragraph, although you can manually anchor a picture to the page itself. If a picture is anchored to a paragraph, whenever the paragraph moves, the picture goes with it. See "Working with Anchors" later in this Technique, for details.

 If you work with pictures in the drawing layer, you absolutely *must* have Word show you the anchors that go along with the pictures. Otherwise, you don't stand a snowball's chance of figuring out where your pictures are going or why. To see picture anchors, choose Tools➪Options➪View and mark the Object Anchors check box.

 You can't see *anything* in the drawing layer(s) unless you work in Print Layout view. Choose View➪Print Layout.

✔ **Pictures in the drawing layer can affect the location of text in the text layer.** That's how Word wraps text around a picture: The picture floats over the text, and you tell Word to have the text layer wrap around it.

✔ **Beware the drawing canvas.** As if all this weren't complicated enough, Microsoft introduced a new concept in Word 2002: the *drawing canvas*. The drawing canvas (see Figure 24-1) is like a little piece of drawing layer, stuck in-line with text. Apparently the drawing canvas was an attempt to make the drawing layer more understandable, but in the end, I find its hybrid nature far more confusing than either pure in-line pictures or floating pictures.

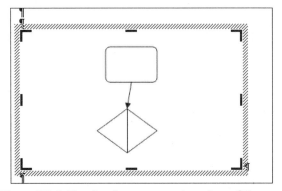

• **Figure 24-1: The drawing canvas puts a piece of the drawing layer in line with text.**

If you run into a feature that requires you to use the drawing canvas, here's the only way to insert a drawing canvas into a document: Turn on the automatic drawing canvas setting (choose Tools➪ Options➪General; select the Automatically Create Drawing Canvas When Inserting AutoShapes check box), and then click one of the AutoShapes on the Drawing toolbar. The minute you have your drawing layer, go back and clear the Automatically Create Drawing Canvas When Inserting AutoShapes box.

 The drawing canvas is another half-baked Microsoft idea that you should only use under extreme duress. (To me, that's when you must draw snap-to connectors, like you would in a flowchart, but Microsoft has lousy support for flowcharts anyway — there isn't even a decision diamond . . . ah, don't get me started.) If you want to get your drawings and pictures off the drawing canvas and into the drawing layer, just click and drag them off the canvas.

That's a 5-minute distillation of 12 years of frustrating experience with graphics in Word. If you ever get stuck trying to figure out why your picture won't go where you want it to go, chances are good the answer is in this section.

Making a Picture Float

When you insert a picture into a document, it always goes in-line with text.

Okay. I lied. Here are two exceptions:

✔ If you click inside a drawing canvas and insert a picture, the picture goes in the drawing canvas. The drawing canvas itself is in-line with text, but . . . I'm going to assume that you follow the instructions in Technique 11 and in the preceding section to get rid of the %$#@! drawing canvas.

✔ Also, you can tell Word to insert pictures in the drawing layer by altering the default insertion method. Choose Tools⇨Options⇨Edit and choose one of the options for Insert/Paste Pictures As.

Ahem. When you insert a picture into a document, it always goes in-line with text. If you want the picture

to float — to live in the drawing layer — you have to tell Word. Here's how:

1. In a document, place the cursor where you want to insert the picture, and then choose Insert⇨Picture⇨From File.

In Figure 24-2, I insert a picture after some text. I can tell that the picture is in-line with text because

▶ The picture appears between paragraph marks. I have paragraph marks showing (see Technique 15).

▶ I can move the cursor in front of the picture by pressing the left-arrow key.

▶ If I put the cursor to the immediate left of the picture, the text goes in front of the picture, and the picture gets shoved to the right.

The point is that an in-line picture acts just like a big character. Nothing particularly magical about it.

The Mon people of Myanmar (Burma) were the first people known to live on the Burmese peninsula. They are widely credited with bringing both Buddhism and writing to Burma. In 573 AD, Prince Samala and Prince Wimala, founded the first Mon kingdom, near present-day Pegu. In 1757, the Burmese destroyed the capital and massacred tens of thousands of Mon. Oppression continues to this day, with many thousands of ethnic Mon seeking refuge in Thailand. ¶

• **Figure 24-2: An in-line picture is nothing more than an overstuffed character.**

2. Levitate the picture into the drawing layer. Right-click the picture and choose Format Picture⇨Layout.

Word shows you the Format Picture dialog box, as shown in Figure 24-3.

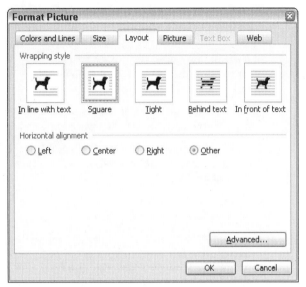

• **Figure 24-3:** Any Wrapping Style choice other than In Line with Text sends the picture into the drawing layer.

3. **Click the text wrapping style of your choice and then click OK.**

See Table 24-1 for a description of the various wrapping styles.

I chose the Square icon (Rover number 2). Word doesn't move the picture. Instead, it wraps the text around the picture, in different ways, depending on the size of the picture and its location. (see Figure 24-4). The picture gets a rotation handle (the green dot above the top of the picture) and is anchored to the closest paragraph (the anchor symbol appears).

4. **You can now move the picture by clicking and dragging the picture. Note how the anchor moves with the picture.**

In Figure 24-5, I move the picture up into the middle of the text, and the picture is anchored to the first paragraph in the document, as indicated (sorta) by the location of the anchor icon. Word wraps the text on the left and right.

• **Figure 24-4:** The picture's anchor symbol appears next to the paragraph closest to the picture.

• **Figure 24-5:** The anchor moves to the first paragraph, and Word dutifully wraps the text.

 If the paragraph containing the anchor moves, the picture moves along with it, although predicting precise placement can be a bit dicey because Word allows the picture to move a little bit when the paragraph itself moves.

5. **You can rotate the picture by clicking the rotation handle — the green dot on top — and dragging your mouse.**

When Word rotates text around in the Square wrapping style, it reserves an entire rectangular area around the picture and flows the text outside of that rectangle (see Figure 24-6).

• **Figure 24–6: With the picture in Square wrapping style, Word gives it a wide berth.**

Word wraps the text much more carefully around the picture after I right-click the picture, choose

Format Picture⇨Layout, click the Tight icon (sorry, Rover), and click OK. See Figure 24-7.

• **Figure 24–7: Changing to Tight wrapping style brings the text in much closer.**

If you ever want to put the picture back in-line with text (perhaps to get rid of any weird drawing layer residue, so you can try all over again), right-click the picture, choose Format Picture⇨Layout, click the In Line with Text icon, and then click OK.

TABLE 24-1: PICTURE WRAPPING STYLES

Style	What It Means	Timesaving Tip
In Line with Text	Text isn't wrapped at all: The picture appears in-line with text, not in the drawing layer.	To simulate text wrapping without floundering in the drawing layer, set up a two-cell table. Put the picture in one cell and the text in the other.
Square	Text is wrapped around the picture in a rectangle.	To adjust how closely Word wraps the text, click Advanced in the Format Picture dialog box and then click the Text Wrapping tab. If your picture is a rectangle that hasn't been rotated, Tight doesn't wrap text any tighter.
Tight	Text is wrapped according to wrapping points, which you can edit.	Click the picture and bring up the Picture toolbar (right-click an empty spot on any toolbar and select Picture). Click the Text Wrapping icon (which looks like a dog) and choose Edit Wrap Points. Click and drag vertices. To add a new vertex, click the red wrapping line.
Through	With properly constructed wrap points (see Tight above), this option is supposed to wrap text inside the picture.	As far as I can tell, this option doesn't work. It appears only in the Advanced dialog box.
Behind Text	This sends the picture to the drawing layer behind the text layer.	Text does not wrap.
In Front of Text	This sends the picture to the drawing layer above the text layer.	Text does not wrap.

Rotating pictures can inflame a few bugs in Word. Here are some tips for avoiding them:

- **Avoid turning rotated pictures back into in-line pictures:** If you float a picture, rotate it, and then put the picture back in-line with text using the preceding tip, you end up with a weird, rotated picture that's not exactly in-line with text and not exactly in the drawing layer. It's as if the picture spun around for 15 minutes and is now trying to walk a straight line. As best I can tell, the problem is because of a(nother) bug in Word. If you need to reset a picture as in-line, you might save yourself a bit of time and aggravation if you just start from scratch by deleting the dizzy picture and reinserting a new copy instead.

- **Watch out for version differences:** Three of my favorite Word guri (Suzanne Barnhill, Dave Rado, and Bill Coan) wrote a paper about that weird half-floating, half in-line state. It can cause problems if people with earlier versions of Word open your documents. Before you distribute a document with a rotated in-line picture, make sure you understand the nuances at `www.mvps.org/word/FAQs/DrwGrphcs/RotatedInline.htm`.

Working with Anchors

All floating pictures have anchors. As long as a picture is anchored to a paragraph and you haven't changed anything, moving the paragraph moves the picture. That's both a blessing and a curse, so it's best for you to be keenly aware of how and why Word is trying to help. Keep in mind the following:

- **You can tell Word to not move the picture even if the anchored paragraph moves.** Right-click the picture, choose Format Picture➪Layout➪ Advanced, and then clear the Move Object with Text check box.

- **If you click the picture and move it somewhere, Word moves the anchor to the nearest paragraph.** *Nearest* here is hard to define or predict, but Word makes a valiant effort.

- **You can move the anchor to a different paragraph manually.** Click the picture. Then click the anchor and drag it to whatever paragraph you like. That can come in handy if Word puts the anchor on a paragraph that isn't related to the picture at all.

- **You can lock the anchor to a specific paragraph.** That way, even if you move the picture, its anchor stays in place. (It's particularly helpful if you're nudging the paragraph around, and the anchor keeps flip-flopping to unrelated paragraphs.) To lock the anchor, make sure that you first have the anchor where you want it. Then right-click the picture, choose Format Picture➪Layout➪Advanced, and select the Lock Anchor check box.

- **You can effectively override all this anchor folderol.** Simply lock the picture down at a specific place on the page. (I use this approach in Technique 23, for no-print rectangles that keep Word from printing on top of preprinted letterheads.) To make a floating picture stay well and surely put, first make sure that you have the picture where you want it. Then right-click the picture, choose Format Picture➪Layout➪Advanced, and set both Horizontal and Vertical Absolute Positions to Page. That nails the sucker to the floor, so to speak.

Moving Pictures Small Distances

Word maintains an invisible *grid,* which it uses to snap pictures so that they more or less line up, even when you don't quite put them in the right place. To move pictures ever so slightly, you have to override the snapping feature:

1. **Make sure you have a floating picture sitting in the drawing layer of your document (see Figure 24-8).**

   I explain how to do this in the section, "Making a Picture Float," earlier in this technique.

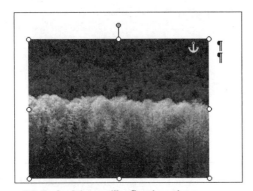

• **Figure 24-8:** A plain-vanilla, floating picture.

2. **To override the snap, click the picture, hold down Alt, and then drag the picture. Release the mouse button and then release Alt.**

You can click and drag the picture any place that you like with the Alt key override.

If you prefer to override the snap with the keyboard, click the picture once, hold down Ctrl, and use arrow keys on the keyboard.

Most people like to have their drawings snapped to the grid, most of the time. But if you want to turn off the snapping behavior completely, make the Drawing toolbar visible and then choose Draw➪Grid. In the Drawing Grid dialog box that appears, clear the Snap Objects to Grid check box.

25 Technique

Typing Fractions Fast

Save Time By

✔ Knowing when Word will make fractions for you

✔ Building your own good-looking fractions quickly

I get messages all the time from people asking me why Word won't type fractions for them. They know that if they type the three characters **1/2**, Word turns that into a single character: ½. And if they type **1/4**, Word produces ¼, and likewise 3/4 becomes ¾. But why won't Word do the same thing to 1/3 or 4/5? Surely, something must be broken. After all, their mother's podiatrist's receptionist's nephew is *sure* that Word makes all sorts of fractions for him. Why won't it work right on their machine?

You can easily waste a lot of time trying to figure out what Word is doing wrong with fractions — when in fact, Word is only doing as much as it can. The secret: Most normal fonts have built-in characters for ¼, ½, and ¾, but no other fractions. Some fancy fonts (specifically Unicode fonts) include a bunch of additional fractions, but in most cases, the font itself can only provide these three fractions. When you type those fractions, Word is actually replacing what you type with the built-in characters, which you can find by choosing Insert⇨Symbol.

That's why Word only autocorrects ¼, ½, and ¾. Word doesn't even try to autocorrect any other fractions — even if the underlying font has built-in fractions that match what you type, Word won't use them. You can stop looking through Help now.

In this Technique, I present a way for producing fractions — any fraction — quickly and accurately.

Creating Consistent-Looking Fractions

When it comes to fractions in Word documents, you have three basic approaches:

✔ Use the (default) AutoCorrect option to change ¼, ½, and ¾ to single characters and manually enter all other fractions. This approach leads to a situation where you might have ½, 1/3, ¼, 2/3, and ¾ all on the same line. It's a jumbled mess that looks really, really bad.

✔ Disable the AutoCorrect option (which I strongly recommend) and enter all your fractions manually.

✔ Build your own good-looking fractions and create AutoCorrect entries for them.

 To save time with fractions, I suggest either of the last two options, depending on how important good-looking fractions are to you. Although using "larger" fractions isn't elegant, it's fast and not too jarring to the eye. If you have 1/2, 1/3, 1/4, 2/3, and 3/4 on the same line, people will be able to read what you've typed without getting eye whiplash (which we presbyopes eschew). Building your own fractions takes a bit of upfront time, but after the fractions are built and stashed away in AutoCorrect, Word takes over, and using the fractions is very fast indeed.

Building Your Own Fractions

By building your own fractions and then inserting them in AutoCorrect, you can make fractions like 2/5 turn into ⅖ as you type. Before you dive into the following steps, you do need to keep a couple of caveats in mind:

✔ The fractions that ship with a font are meticulously hand-tuned to go with the font: somebody, somewhere spent days getting that ½ to look like a fraction, and to look something like tiny versions of the numbers in the font as well. You'll never be able to match the font builder's masterpieces when using the clumsy tools in Word. But you can get remarkably close.

✔ You have to build each fraction for each font separately. (If you want a ⅓ in Times New Roman 11 point, you have to create it separately from the ⅓ in Arial 12 point, for example.)

 Here's the best timesaving solution that I've found: Choose a font and font size for a correspondence font and a heading font (if you haven't already), and create a set of fractions for each font. I explain how to switch between the two sets using AutoCorrect later in this Technique.

Creating the fractions you want to use

This is my favorite way to build a good-looking fraction by using Word's tools:

1. **Start with a blank document. From the Font box on the Formatting toolbar, choose the font that you want for the fraction.**

2. **Choose Insert⇨Symbol, select the a built-in fraction, click the Insert button, and then run the Zoom factor up to 500% (see Figure 25-1).**

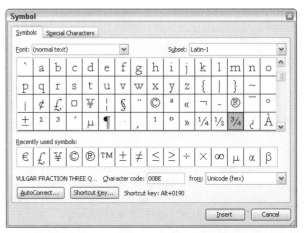

• **Figure 25-1: The 3/4 character is a symbol in the font.**

3. **Press the spacebar, type the new fraction that you wish to create, and press the spacebar a few more times.**

In Figure 25-2, I type **1/5**.

• **Figure 25-2:** Preparing to construct the fraction ⅕.

4. **Select the first number in the new fraction, type 6 in the Font Size box on the Formatting toolbar, and then press Enter.**

In Figure 25-3, I select the 1, type a **6** in the Font Size box, and then press Enter. (It takes a bit of practice to get the font size changed this way.) The idea is to make the first number in your new fraction about the same size as the *numerator* — the top number — in the built-in fraction. 6 points is a good place to start for most fonts.

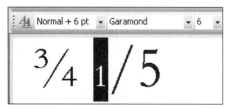

• **Figure 25-3:** Adjust the point size of the first number in the new fraction.

5. **With the first number in the new fraction still selected, choose Format⇨Font⇨Character Spacing. In the Position box, choose Raised. In the By box, type 4 and then click OK.**

Word raises the first number — the numerator-to-be — as shown in Figure 25-4. The intent is to raise the first number to roughly the same level as the numerator in the built-in fraction. You might find that raising the character(s) by 3 points looks better.

6. **Select the second number in the new fraction, and then type 6 (or whatever point size you used in Step 3) in the Font Size box of the Formatting toolbar. Press Enter.**

That scrunches down the *denominator* — the second number.

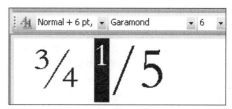

• **Figure 25-4:** Raise the numerator.

7. **Select the first number, forward slash, and second number. Then choose Format⇨Font⇨Character Spacing. In the Spacing box, choose Condensed; in the By box, type 1.**

That squishes the fraction together, making it look more like a fraction. My final fraction (see Figure 25-5) won't win any typesetting awards, but it looks pretty good in text.

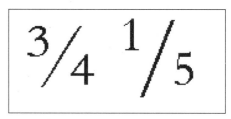

• **Figure 25-5:** The hand-made fraction is on the right.

8. **Juggle the settings — font size, raised position, and condensed spacing — until you're happy with them.**

9. **Write down the settings. You can use them again to make other fractions for this font, at this point size.**

When you're done building fractions, put them in AutoCorrect so that they'll appear automatically as you type. The next section, "Entering fraction sets in AutoCorrect," explains how.

If you aren't happy with the slash in your fractions, first try making it italic. If that doesn't work, try using the slash from the Symbol font (Insert⇨Symbol; and in the Font box, choose Symbol). Thanks to *Woody's Office Watch* readers SB and LL for those suggestions!

You can find many Word macros on the Internet that will produce decent fractions with a few clicks. (Use Google to look for *Word fraction macro*.) Unfortunately, I haven't found one yet that comes close to the quality that you can achieve by simply laying out the fractions by hand, as I describe in this section.

Entering fraction sets in AutoCorrect

After you have a fraction you can live with, it makes a lot of timesaving sense to stick it away in AutoCorrect so that you can use it over and over again. A bit of warning, though: You can create a fraction in, say, Times New Roman 11 point, and it'll work pretty well if you're typing in Times New Roman 10 point or 12 point. But it'll look really bad if you stick it in the middle of a line of Arial text.

My solution is to create two sets of fractions: one in my favorite correspondence font (Garamond 11 point) and another set in my typical heading font (Arial 12 point). I then assign each fraction a name that includes both the fraction and its font — 1/5g for the Garamond fraction ⅕, 2/3a for an Arial ⅔, and so on. That way, if I need the fraction ⅕ in Garamond, I just type **1/5g**, and Word autocorrects it to my custom-built Garamond 11 point fraction ⅕.

Here's how to quickly make your own AutoCorrect entries:

1. **Follow the steps in the preceding section to create the fraction you wish to immortalize.**

2. **Select the fraction.**

In Figure 25-6, I select my Garamond fraction ⅕ (but not the surrounding spaces).

Sometimes it's hard to figure out exactly where the fraction begins and ends. In Figure 25-6, for example, when I select the three characters in the fraction, the highlighting ends before the right edge of the 5. You might need to use the arrow keys to make sure that you get the entire fraction — and only the fraction.

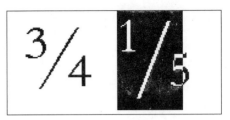

• **Figure 25-6: Select the entire fraction but not any surrounding spaces.**

3. **Choose Tools⇨AutoCorrect Options.**

Word shows you the AutoCorrect dialog box (see Figure 25-7).

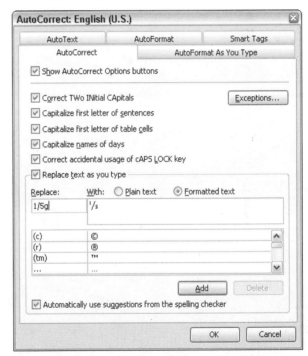

• **Figure 25-7: Make sure you tell Word to create a Formatted Text entry.**

4. **Select the Formatted Text radio button, and then type in the Replace box the code that you want to trigger an AutoCorrect.**

Note that the fraction you selected in Step 2 appears in the With box automatically. In Figure 25-7, I type **1/5g** because that's the code I want to type to get a formatted Garamond fraction ⅕.

5. **Click Add and then click OK.**

Word takes you back to the document.

6. **Test your AutoCorrect entry by typing the code and then pressing the spacebar.**

Every computer has exactly one set of AutoCorrect entries. (There aren't separate entries in different templates, for example.) You can move AutoCorrect entries among computers with a utility that Microsoft shipped with your copy of Office. See http:// support.microsoft.com/?kbid=269006 for details. Unfortunately, the tool mentioned there doesn't always work, so if you have problems, refer to www.mvps.org/word/FAQs/ Customization/ExportAutocorrect.htm.

Part III

Streamlining Outlook

The 5th Wave   By Rich Tennant

KEVIN ACCIDENTALLY E-MAILS HIS OUTLINE FOR A MYSTERY NOVEL IN PLACE OF HIS RÉSUMÉ.

Yes, we received your résumé. Can you tell us more about the period you spent handcuffed in the hull of the Russian freighter?

Technique

26

Getting Outlook Settings Right

Save Time By

- ✔ Making Outlook show you just the info you need
- ✔ Blasting through piles of e-mail
- ✔ Showing Calendars and Contacts separately

If you're like me, you live and die by e-mail. I get about 700 e-mail messages a day, on average. A good 90 percent of that is spam. But most of the rest of it requires a response or at least an acknowledgment, so every little bit of timesaving I can squeeze out of Outlook counts big-time.

Outlook comes festooned with time-sinks. I don't use Journals (which automatically track documents), and I bet you don't either — Microsoft buried the feature in Outlook 2003. I don't want to be reminded with a ping-ping-ping every time a message arrives. Oy. And those little yellow sticky notes look great in demos, but they don't do much to save me time.

Give me an e-mail viewer that lets me deal with messages quickly and accurately, a message editor that doesn't get in the way, a calendar that I can get into and out of quickly, and a contact list that's at least as usable as a phone book. That's what I need. That's what this Technique delivers.

Strolling through the Panes

When you first start Outlook 2003, you see your e-mail. Outlook breaks the e-mail window into three panes (see Figure 26-1).

You see the same three panes when you click the Mail shortcut button:

- ✔ The **navigation pane** on the left has a Favorite Folders list, an All Mail Folders list, and a set of shortcut buttons that transport you to other Outlook applications.

- ✔ The **message list** down the middle shows high-level information from all the messages in whichever mail folder you've selected.

- ✔ The **reading pane** on the right (Outlook stalwarts still call it the *preview pane*) shows you the message selected in the message list.

Rigging Outlook for speed primarily involves granting the reading pane all the screen space you can find. Being able to read (or at least scan) your messages without scrolling is an enormous timesaver.

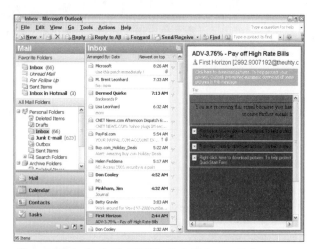

• **Figure 26-1:** Outlook 2003 in its initial e-mail view.

Controlling the Navigation Pane

The number-one e-mail timesaving technique for Outlook 2003? Getting the navigation pane — that strip down the left side of the screen — out of the way. Compare Figure 26-1 with Figure 26-2.

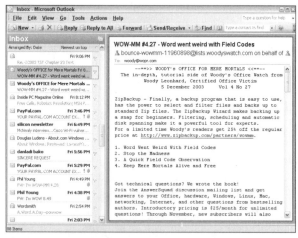

• **Figure 26-2:** Blast the navigation pane out of the way and get some work done.

 If you spend most of your time reading and responding to mail in your Inbox or in one of a small handful of folders, you need the navigation pane only occasionally. Far more

important are the message list in the middle and the reading pane on the right: The navigation pane just sits there looking dumb while you're trying to get some work done. To hide the navigation pane, press Alt+F1. To toggle it back, press Alt+F1 again.

For those occasions when you do need the navigation pane while working on e-mail, remember the following:

✔ Outlook has two fundamentally different mail navigation panes: the Mail list (which is the default; see Figure 26-3) and the Folder List (see Figure 26-4), which includes mail folders plus the Calendar, Contacts, and so on. To see the Mail list, click the Mail shortcut (the line that reads Mail) near the bottom of the navigation pane. To see the Folder List, click the Folder List icon (the one that looks like a folder) at the bottom of the navigation pane.

• **Figure 26-3:** The Mail list is what you normally see when you start Outlook.

• **Figure 26-4: The Folder List resembles the list in Outlook 2002 and earlier.**

✔ Adding mail folders to the Favorite Folders list is easy; either drag the folder to the list and drop it or right-click any mail folder and choose Add to Favorite Folders. Removing folders from the Favorite Folders list is also a snap; right-click and choose Remove from Favorites List.

Although you can remove all the folders from the Favorite Folders list, you cannot remove the list itself. You're stuck with the bar that reads Favorite Folders whether you want it or not.

 You can add only mail folders to the Favorite Folders list. In particular, you can't put your Contacts there nor your Calendar.

✔ To move items around on the Favorite Folders list, just click and drag to the desired location.

Displaying Your Contacts and Calendar in Separate Windows

Many people find it much easier and faster to have Outlook put the Contacts list and the Calendar in their own, separate windows. That minimizes the amount of flip-flopping that you have to do in the navigation pane. To switch from Mail to the Contacts list, for example, you use the Windows taskbar — and when you're ready to return to Mail, a quick run through the taskbar brings you immediately back to where you left off.

To get the Calendar and Contacts running in their own windows

1. **Click the Folder List icon (it looks like a folder) at the bottom of the navigation pane.**

   Outlook shows you the Folder List (refer to Figure 26-4).

2. **Right-click the Calendar folder and choose Open in New Window (see Figure 26-5).**

• **Figure 26-5: Open a separate window in Outlook for the Calendar application.**

   Outlook starts the Calendar application and sets it up in a brand-new window (see Figure 26-6).

3. **In Mail's Folder List, right-click Contacts and choose Open in New Window.**

   Outlook starts the Contacts application in its own new window.

• **Figure 26-6:** The Calendar runs just like a separate application.

4. **Choose among the running applications from the Windows taskbar (see Figure 26-7).**

• **Figure 26-7:** Outlook has three applications running in the Windows taskbar: Inbox, Calendar, and Contacts.

 Old Windows hands will no doubt recall that you can switch among running Windows applications by using the Alt+Tab CoolSwitch. Holding down the Alt key and pressing Tab repeatedly (see Figure 26-8) is a very fast way to cycle among the various Outlook programs.

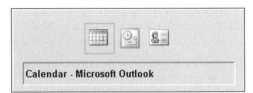

• **Figure 26-8:** Even though the Calendar, Inbox, and Contacts are all Outlook applications, you can use Alt+Tab to cycle among them.

5. **To shut down a single application, click the X in the upper-right corner. To shut down all Outlook applications, switch to any one of them and choose File⇨Exit.**

If you used the Open in New Window feature in earlier versions of Outlook, you might recall that Outlook forgot about its multiple applications unless you shut it down gently by choosing File⇨Exit. Fortunately, Outlook 2003 isn't so forgetful, and you can shut down any of the running programs any way you wish.

Moving More Mail Faster

When it comes to shoveling e-mail bits, I need all the timesaving help I can get.

It all boils down to putting as little information as you can get away with on the screen and clearing the way for as big of a reading pane as possible. By giving yourself more room for the reading pane, you increase your chances of being able to see entire messages without scrolling — and without killing your eyes.

 Although Outlook has oodles and oodles of security holes, the reading pane isn't one of them. As of this writing anyway, it doesn't appear to be possible to create a virus that can crack into your system when you simply view a message in the reading pane.

You might like the way Outlook gives you a big, two-line "landing strip" with information about each message (see Figure 26-9). Personally, I prefer much more, uh, compact entries on the Message list pane.

If I'm really curious about the precise (long-winded) subject, or the size, of a message, I can always hover my mouse over the message and give it a leisurely gander. But when I'm running through a hundred messages, hellbent for leather, I only want enough info to decide — quickly — whether I really need to read the message.

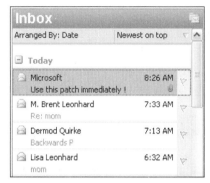

• Figure 26-9: Outlook's more-than-ample landing strip for each message takes up a lot of room.

Slimming down the Message List pane

For me, the two-line entry is overkill, and if you try the one-line version, I bet you'll agree (especially if you press Alt+F1 and sack the navigation pane while you're working). Here's how to limit Outlook to one line per message in the Message list pane (or make the landing strip bigger, if you must):

1. **If you can't see e-mail, choose Go⇨Mail.**

2. **Choose View⇨Arrange By⇨Custom.**

   You see the Customize View: Messages dialog box. (Microsoft really buried this setting.)

3. **Click the Other Settings button.**

   You see the ambiguously named Other Settings dialog box (see Figure 26-10).

4. **Clear the Use Multi-Line Layout in Widths Smaller Than check box, and select the Always Use Single-Line Layout radio button. Then click OK twice.**

   Outlook summarizes your messages in the Message pane, one on a line, so they're much easier to scan (see Figure 26-11).

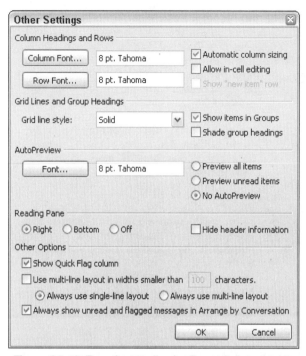

• Figure 26-10: Turn the two-line landing strip into a svelte one-liner.

• Figure 26-11: With one line per message, it's much easier to scan your way through tons of e-mail.

Some people like to see the date and time received, but I find that this gets in the way on smaller screens, particularly if you sort by date received anyway. When you sort by date, the date appears above each day's crop of messages, so why repeat it? To move the Received field, click Received in the title bar and drag it to the right. Then click and drag the edge to scrunch it down to a tiny sliver. (See it smashed between Size and the follow-up flag in Figure 26-11.) If you ever need to see the entire field, just drag the left edge to make it bigger. If you ever sort one of the other fields (From, Subject, Size, and so on), you can go back to sorting by Received date and time by clicking that little sliver.

 What? You *like* the big landing zone? In that case, consider widening it to three lines so that you can see more details about each incoming message. To do that, choose View➪Arrange By➪Custom, click Fields, and bump up the box marked Maximum Number of Lines in Multi-line Mode.

Navigating the Message list in a flash

With the navigation pane stowed and the message list stunted, with a little practice, you can move very quickly through miles of messages. (Um, remember that you have to have a message selected to take any action with it).

✔ **Scan messages in the message list on the left.**

✔ **To delete a message, click it, and then either press Ctrl+D or press the Delete key.**

You can delete sequentially down your message list by pressing Ctrl+D or the Delete key multiple times, and Outlook will catch up with you.

✔ **If you see a message or a subject of interest, scan it in the reading pane on the right.**

✔ **To skip over a message and do nothing, press the spacebar or the down arrow.**

✔ **To reply to a message, press Ctrl+R (or Alt+R).**

✔ **To reply to all recipients of a message, press Ctrl+Shift+R (or Alt+L).**

✔ **To forward a messsage, press Ctrl+F (or Alt+W).**

✔ **To flag a message for follow-up, click the flag icon.**

That gives the message a literal red flag and automatically adds the message to the For Follow Up Search folder.

 Unfortunately, you cannot flag a message for follow-up by using the keyboard.

 See an extended discussion on flagging and follow-up in Technique 28. It's a very powerful feature worthy of your consideration.

✔ **Tell Outlook to display only the images that you want to see, which I explain how to do next.**

Downloading only the images you want to see

Finally, to move through messages quickly, don't download pictures stored on the Web that are referenced in formatted (HTML) e-mail messages (so-called *Web beacons;* see Technique 30). If you really need the pictures to understand the message, you can always right-click the specific pic and let Outlook go retrieve it. But when you're scanning as quickly as you can, waiting for Outlook to grab pics rates right up there with watching grass grow — or watching your hard drive activity light.

To make sure that pictures don't arrive unless you ask for them

1. **Choose Tools➪Options➪Security.**

2. **Under Download Pictures, click the Change Automatic Download Settings button.**

Outlook shows you the Automatic Picture Download Settings dialog box, as shown in Figure 26-12.

3. **Mark the Don't Download Pictures or Other Content Automatically in HTML E-mail check box.**

As I explain in Technique 30, that's the best setting to keep your name off spammers' lists, too. You have plenty of good reasons to keep this setting enabled.

4. **Click OK twice.**

Some of your messages will be hard to, uh, scrute (see Microsoft's Insider Update in Figure 26-13 for an example), but without the pics, you'll still be able to separate the e-mail wheat from the chaff. And if you really, really want to see a message's pictures, click where indicated at the top to get the whole bunch.

• **Figure 26-13: Outlook 2003 mangles picture-laden e-mail, which is probably a good thing.**

• **Figure 26-12: The place to turn off the time-draining download of pictures inside your messages.**

Adjusting the E-Mail Editor Settings

Unless you do something to change it, Outlook 2003 uses Word as its e-mail editor.

I've railed against WordMail (that is, the use of Word as Outlook's e-mail editor) for almost as long as the feature has been available. Outlook and Word are tied together with bailing wire and chewing gum, and the combination has had a tendency to disintegrate in a gooey, wirey way. But with Outlook 2003, it seems as though Microsoft has finally made the two coexist peacefully. Most of the time.

 Here's one indisputable fact: If you can use Word as your Outlook e-mail editor, you'll be able to work faster and more confidently than with the under-aspirated native e-mail editor. Two of the big reasons why are that you already know how to use Word, and that most of Word's features are available when you're writing e-mail.

Outlook 2003 uses only Word 2003 as its e-mail editor, so if you bought Outlook 2003 alone (without the rest of Office 2003), expecting that you would be able to use Outlook fully, you're in for a rude awakening.

Word has been trimmed down in many ways for its WordMail persona — when it's acting in its capacity as e-mail editor for Outlook. One of the big differences between Word and WordMail is the emphasis on styles: In WordMail, it's very difficult to work with styles. (The fact that the default font in WordMail is Arial 10 point manually applied on the Normal style from `normal.dot` should make experienced Word users cringe.) I'd love to be able to use styles to, for example, set off monospaced macro code or quotes from incoming messages. Many other features in Word are mutated extensively for the Outlook environment.

At a minimum, I suggest that you make the following changes to WordMail. Explanations parallel those given in Technique 15, where I have you make similar changes in Word itself:

1. **If you can't see your e-mail, choose Go⇨Mail.**

2. **Click New to start a new e-mail message.**

   This also fires up WordMail — in Microsoft parlance, Outlook starts a *hidden instance* of Word, which is used to edit e-mail messages.

3. **Choose Tools⇨Options⇨View. Enable the Tab Characters, Paragraph Marks, and Object Anchors check boxes. Don't click OK just yet — more changes need to be made.**

   The View tab of the Options dialog box should look like Figure 26-14.

4. **Click the General tab. Clear the Automatically Create Drawing Canvas When Inserting AutoShapes check box. Then click OK.**

As far as I can tell, WordMail picks up the remainder of the Tools⇨Options settings from Word itself. We're treading in the Twilight Zone here because Microsoft doesn't document any of this stuff, but I believe that's what's happening.

5. **Choose Tools⇨AutoCorrect Options⇨ AutoFormat as You Type.**

   WordMail shows you the AutoCorrect in Email dialog box, as shown in Figure 26-15.

6. **Clear all the check boxes under Apply as You Type. Also clear the Format Beginning Of List Item Like the One Before It check box. Click OK. Close out of the e-mail message.**

   WordMail is now safe to use.

• **Figure 26-14:** Keep track of the inner workings of your e-mail messages.

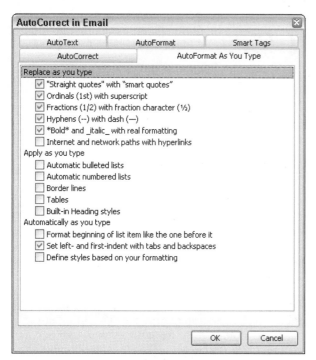

• **Figure 26-15:** These IntelliNONSense settings are just as infuriating in WordMail as they are in Word itself.

Making Other Timesaving Changes

After I put copies of the Calendar and Contacts list in their own windows (see the procedure in "Controlling the Navigation Pane," earlier in this Technique), I make two more changes to Outlook. You might find these to be big timesavers, depending on how you use Contacts and the Calendar:

✔ In the Contacts window, I choose View⇔Arrange By⇔Current View⇔Phone List. That puts the Contacts in phone list view, which crams many names on the screen.

✔ In the Calendar window, I click the 5 Work Week button on the main toolbar. That shows each of the five working days in the current week, each in its own strip.

Technique 27

Searching with Folders

Save Time By

- ✔ Creating search folders that make sense
- ✔ Avoiding search folders for easily found items
- ✔ Using search folders to get what you want — quickly

If you've used Outlook for any time at all, you're accustomed to folders: There's an Inbox folder, a Junk E-mail folder, a Sent Items folder, and so on.

Search folders are different because they don't hold any real messages: They're just collections of pointers to messages. The messages themselves reside in normal folders. If you've ever used Windows' Search function (Start➪Search), you've seen the same thing — except in Outlook 2003, the results are always available.

Most people, at first, tend to set up search folders for everything under the sun. In other words, search folders turn from timesavers to time-wasters in the blink of an eye. The trick with search folders is to use them sparingly and strategically — and to avoid using them when better, less persistent alternatives are available.

That's what this Technique is all about.

Using Search Folders

Although Windows searches look for files and folders, and Outlook searches look for stuff inside Outlook, they surprisingly have something important in common.

When you perform a search in Windows, Rover — bless his pointy little Bobbed ears — delivers a list of files that match your search criteria (see Figure 27-1). The files aren't moved anywhere: They're still sitting in the same place they've always been. Searching merely gathers a list of all the files that match your criteria and presents them in a single window so that you can work with the found files.

You might not realize it, but Windows searches are updated continuously. For example, if you search for music files on your computer (as in Figure 27-1), leave the Search Results window open, and then copy a new music file to your computer, that new file appears in the Search Results window, although it might take a few seconds for Rover to update the list.

• **Figure 27-1: Results of a Windows search. Go, Rover, Go.**

On the downside, Windows searches aren't saved — and indeed, aren't savable. If you close a Search Results window or shut down Windows itself, you have to laboriously reenter the search. Windows gives you no alternative.

Outlook's search folders work a lot like Windows Search Results windows, with two notable exceptions:

✔ Search Folders (yup, it's a folder) automatically saves the search. Because Outlook Search Folders results get updated continuously, just as in Windows Search, you can set up an Outlook search folder and look at it a week from now and rest assured that it has an up-to-the-second list of all the e-mail messages that match the criteria that you established a week earlier.

✔ Search Folders searches only for Outlook e-mail messages and only in a very narrowly defined set of locations.

 Whereas a Windows Search can look for just about anything, anywhere, Outlook Search Folders is restricted to looking only for e-mail messages (no Contacts or Calendar entries or Tasks) and only in the current folder's Mail subfolders. You can tell Outlook to look in a folder and all its subfolders but you can't tell Outlook to look inside two different high-level folders. For example, if you have two main folders — say, Personal Folders and Archive Folders (see Figure 27-2) — you can create a search folder that looks for e-mail messages in Personal Folders or a search folder that looks for e-mail messages in Archive Folders. However, you can't create a single search folder that pulls messages out of both Personal Folders and Archive Folders.

Another limitation is that Outlook refuses to create search folders for the Hotmail folder. For example, if you set up a search folder to keep track of orders, any orders sent to your Hotmail account won't go in the search folder.

• **Figure 27-2: Outlook Search folders can look only in a single main folder at a time.**

When you first start Outlook, two of the five default Favorite Folders in the navigation pane (two of the four if you don't have a Hotmail account; see Figure 27-3) are, in fact, search folders:

• **Figure 27-3: Two of these folders are search folders.**

✔ **Unread Mail** searches for unread messages in the Inbox folder and any folders underneath the Inbox folder as well as the Sent Items folder and any custom mail folders you might have created. This search folder does not include any messages from the Deleted Items or the Junk E-mail folders.

✔ **For Follow Up** searches for messages with follow-up flags (of any color) in the Inbox; folders underneath Inbox, Outbox, Sent Items, and Drafts; and any custom mail folders. See Technique 28 for ways to save time with follow-up flags.

 For Follow Up doesn't include any messages in the Deleted Items folder nor in Junk E-mail, so if you accidentally delete a flagged message (or mark it as Junk E-mail), you'll never find it in the For Follow Up search folder.

Outlook also automatically creates a search folder (of dubious value, frankly) called Large Mail. That folder appears down in the Search Folders list at the bottom of the navigation pane but doesn't appear in Favorite Folders.

 Note that these definitions are quite stringent, and if you try to customize one of the built-in search folders (right-click and choose Customize This Search Folder), the information Outlook provides is inaccurate. For example, if you try to customize Unread Mail, Outlook tells you that it's looking in all mail folders underneath Personal Folders. That, demonstrably, isn't true.

Creating Search Folders

Microsoft's help and training encourage you to create a search folder by choosing File➪New➪ Search Folder, but that approach doesn't give you the advantage of seeing the results before setting the criteria in search folder concrete. Here is a far better way to create your own search folder:

1. **If you don't see e-mail messages, choose Go➪Mail.**

2. **Choose Tools➪Find➪Advanced Find.**

Outlook shows you the Advanced Find dialog box (see Figure 27-4), ready to search for e-mail messages.

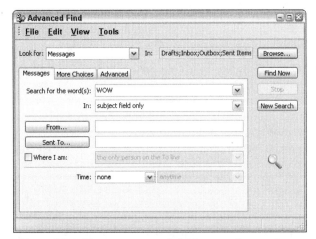

• **Figure 27-4: To create a search folder, start by running a search.**

3. **Click the Browse button in the upper-right corner.**

Outlook presents you with the Select Folder(s) dialog box (see Figure 27-5). Think carefully about which folders you wish to search. In most (but not all) cases, you want to avoid the Junk E-mail folder. In some cases, you want to avoid Deleted Items. Only rarely would you want to search every mail folder because you're bound to come up with a bunch of junk. Literally.

4. Mark the check boxes for the folders that you want to search. If you want Outlook to search in subfolders of the chosen folders, mark the Search Folders check box. Then click OK.

Outlook returns to the Advanced Find dialog box.

5. Type your search criteria. Click the Find Now button and let Outlook run the search.

You see the results at the bottom of the Advanced Find dialog box (see Figure 27-6).

6. If the search didn't produce *precisely* the results you wanted, go back and change the search criteria.

 Spend some time to get it right. The Advanced tab, in particular, has an enormous array of criteria that you can use to force Outlook to deliver the exact messages that you seek.

7. When the search works exactly the way you want it, choose File⇒Save Search as Search Folder.

Outlook asks you to name the search folder.

• **Figure 27-5: Choose your folders wisely.**

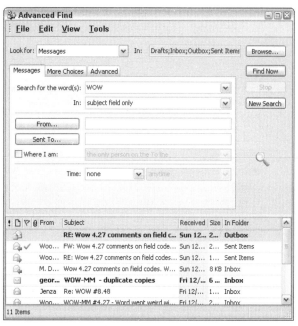

• **Figure 27-6: Take a very close look at the results of the search.**

8. Give your new search folder a name, click OK, and then close the Advanced Find dialog box.

Outlook takes the search criteria that you established, saves it, immortalizes the results of the search — and keeps it up-to-date! — by creating a search folder (see Figure 27-7). Search folders appear with little magnifying glasses on them.

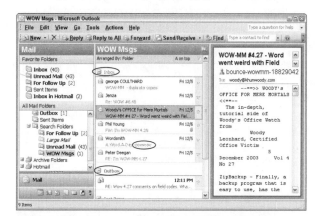

• **Figure 27-7: A new search folder called WOW Msgs.**

Three details illustrated in Figure 27-7 affect your ability to use search folders to save time:

- ✔ **Find the source:** The source folder — the place where the message actually resides — appears as a group heading above the listing for the message itself. In Figure 27-7, there are messages from both the Inbox and the Outbox.

- ✔ **Change the view:** The search folder has its own view settings. If you want the search folder to use only one line for each message in the message list (the middle pane), you have to go in and tell Outlook. (Choose View⇨Arrange By⇨Custom, click Other Settings, and clear the Use Multi-Line Layout In Widths Smaller Then check box, select the Always Use Single-Line Layout radio button, and click OK twice.) See Technique 26 for more details about view settings.

- ✔ **Bogies at 1 o'clock:** No matter how hard you try, you're going to get some bogus entries in your search folders. For example, *Powwow* in Figure 27-7 matches the WOW search criteria.

 You can change the search criteria that a search folder uses by right-clicking it and choosing Customize This Search Folder.

What Happens When I Delete a Message

Microsoft's Help files gleam with hogwash trying to explain what happens when you delete a message that you get to via a search folder. The actual process is quite simple. If you look at a message while you're in a search folder (as in Figure 27-7) and you press Delete, Outlook moves the message from whatever folder it's in to the Deleted Items folder. That's what Outlook always does.

If your search folder doesn't look at items in the Deleted Items folder, the message disappears from the search folder. Remember that Outlook keeps the search folders updated continuously. So if you move the message (as is the case when you press Delete), Outlook updates the search folder according to whatever criteria you've established.

That's the whole story. Nothing magical. The message goes where it always does. Your search folder gets updated the way it always does.

Rationalizing Search Folders

Before you start creating search folders by the dozen, sit back and think about whether they'll save you time. Although it's true that creating a search folder doesn't take much effort, creating a good, targeted search folder can be arduous indeed. And if you have dozens of search folders, every time you need one, you'll have to search for the right search folder (how's that for an irony?). Pile enough on, and your machine's performance will take a hit.

Chances are good that you *don't* need a search folder for

- ✔ **Your boss or any other specific individual:** This is the prototypical demo of search folders — the one used to sell Outlook to the unwashed masses — and it's usually a waste of time.

  You can easily create a list of all the messages sent by a specific individual by right-clicking a message from that person and choosing Find All⇨Messages From Sender. Doing so triggers the Advanced Find dialog box (see Figure 27-8), and you can either double-click each of the messages listed to bring them up one at a time or choose File⇨Save Search as Search Folder to create a search folder on-the-fly and see them in the reading pane.

- ✔ **Anything that should be moved with a rule:** Outlook lets you create *Rules* (custom filters) that shuffle e-mail messages to specific folders. If you want to manage a bunch of messages as a group (for example, to keep track of specific projects or individuals), you should be using rules and custom folders. See the "Rules" sidebar.

 Search folders are great for keeping track of cohorts of messages that are shuffled to different "real" folders by rules. For example, if you have separate folders for different projects and you want to keep track of all the status reports in all the projects, create a search folder for the status reports.

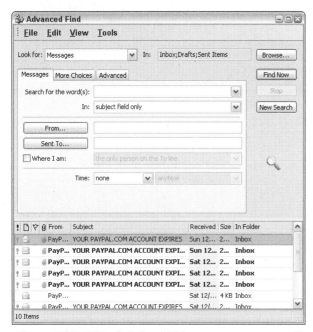

• **Figure 27-8: A list of all the phishing messages supposedly from PayPal (see Technique 33).**

✔ **Big messages. Or small messages. Or messages with attachments:** Most people look only in specific folders for messages with specific attributes. Look in your Deleted Items for big messages, for example. Or look in your Inbox for messages with attachments. You can do that kind of searching just as well by sorting the appropriate column in the message list.

 Get rid of your unused search folders. Outlook will run faster when you do.

 Outlook ships with one more built-in search folder, above and beyond the two that I mention at the beginning of this Technique: Large Mail. It's hard-wired to look for messages larger than a specific size (100KB unless you change it). I figure that this search folder only exists as demo-ware: Microsoft put it there to look good in demos. It's hard to imagine any real-world use for it (unless you're downloading e-mail headers with Exchange Server and want to delete big messages so they don't hog your bandwidth). Right-click it and delete it.

Rules

Outlook contains an entire programming subsystem: *Rules*. In the simplest case, you write Rules to look at and then act on messages as they arrive, shuffling them into folders or flagging, forwarding, or deleting them. Rules can even play a little tune on cue. Cute.

Outlook Rules are notorious for interacting in completely unpredictable ways, particularly as the number of Rules goes up and the volume or rate of incoming mail increases. Although recent versions of Outlook seem to do a better job of keeping rules from stepping all over each other, the introduction of junk mail filtering in Outlook 2003 added a new problem: The Rules kick in before the junk mail filter does, and you can do precious little about it. Thus, any message that matches the criteria in a Rule bypasses spam filtering entirely.

If you want to try your hand at Rules, start with the Outlook Help topic *About managing messages with rules*. But as with all Help, don't believe anything you hear and only half of what you read.

Technique

28

Organizing with Flags

Save Time By

✔ Moving quickly — flag it and forget it

✔ Following up on flags

✔ Making color choices that work for you

So I get a message from one of my newsletter subscribers, and he wants to know about the best way to find a tiny message needle in an Outlook haystack. It's an interesting question, but one that's going to take some research.

In the not-so-good old days, I would drag that message into a special folder full of similar messages, in the hope that some day Congress would legislate 28-hour days and 8-day work weeks. Then I would no doubt have enough time to go back through the folder and tackle the most interesting, or pressing, problems.

Nowadays, with Outlook 2003, I give the message a purple flag. (Purple reminds me of *indigo,* which reminds me of *interesting.* Pretty lame, huh?) The message stays in my Inbox — at least until I go through and do some spring cleaning — and I know I can find it again from the For Follow Up search folder.

This Technique shows you how to flag and flog mail in the fastest possible way.

Marking Mail

You can add flags to incoming and outgoing messages and tack on reminders, too. It's all pretty quick and easy, and this section shows you how flags can help you get in and out of your Inbox without missing a message.

Flagging mail you've received

While you're reading e-mail messages, you can flag a message — typically, so you can return to the message later. Microsoft calls these *Quick Flags,* and that they are.

1. Click the flag icon in the right-most column of the message list to flag the message with the default color (probably red). Right-click the flag icon to flag the message with a different color.

In Figure 28-1, I flag a message as indigo . . . er, purple . . . because it's interesting to me. See "Choosing Flag Colors" later in this Technique for details on working with the colors that work for you.

When you add the flag, Outlook assumes that you want to follow up on the message later and adds the message to the default For Follow Up search folder.

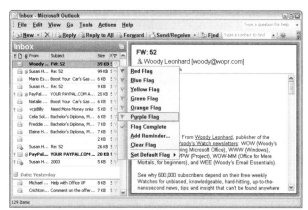

• **Figure 28-1:** Right-click the flag icon to choose a colored flag.

2. Press the down arrow to go on to the next message.

You can add additional info to the flag if you want. See "Tacking other information to a flag" later in this Technique.

Flagging mail before you send it

You can flag a message before you send it by clicking the red flag on the main toolbar in the message window (see Figure 28-2).

• **Figure 28-2:** The red flag in WordMail allows you to set reminders for the message's recipient.

When you click the flag, you get a dialog box that enables you to add additional information for the person you're sending the message to, such as Do Not Forward. See the next section for details.

Tacking other information to a flag

Outlook lets you hang a bunch of information on the follow-up flag in the Flag for Follow Up dialog box, shown in Figure 28-3. The dialog box springs onto your screen if you

✔ Right-click a flag in the right column of the Mail list and then choose Add Reminder.

✔ Click the flag icon on the toolbar of a message you're sending (refer to Figure 28-2).

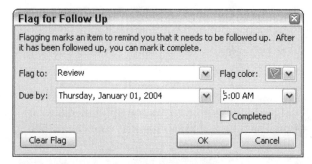

• **Figure 28-3:** Set a reminder to yourself.

In the Flag To box, you can choose from Call, Do Not Forward, Follow Up, For Your Information, Forward, No Response Necessary, Read, Reply, Reply to All, and Review. You can also set a date and time.

After you set a reminder, it shows up at the top of the corresponding e-mail message (see Figure 28-4).

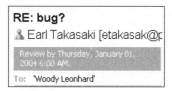

• **Figure 28-4:** The consequences of the settings in Figure 28-3.

 You need to realize that setting a reminder in this way does *not* create a Task, nor does it create a Calendar entry or appointment. You won't receive notification that the e-mail reminder comes due in 15 minutes. Instead, after the due date and time pass, the color of the flag changes to the default flag color — probably red.

 If you want to use a message as the basis for an appointment, drag it onto the Calendar icon in Outlook navigation pane's shortcuts. If you want to use it for a Task, drag it onto the Tasks icon.

Following Up on Flags

When you're ready to view all the e-mail messages that currently have flags, click the For Follow Up folder in the Favorite Folders part of the Mail navigation pane. (Read Technique 26 for more on these Outlook features.) Outlook shows you the contents of the For Follow Up search folder (see Figure 28-5).

You can customize the For Follow Up folder just like any other search folder. See Technique 27 for details.

If you can't find your For Follow Up folder, first look in the All Mail Folders list. For Follow Up should appear underneath the Search Folders entry (folder). If you still can't find it, choose File⇨New⇨Search Folder. In the New Search Folder dialog box (see Figure 28-6), choose Mail Flagged for Follow Up and then click OK.

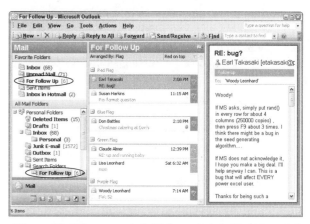

• **Figure 28-5:** In true search folder style (see Technique 27), For Follow Up lets you leaf through flagged messages.

• **Figure 28-6:** Re-create the For Follow Up folder if you lose it.

You aren't restricted to viewing flagged messages by the color of their flags. To view them by date, sender, or a dozen other criteria, click Arranged By directly beneath the For Follow Up header, and choose your preferred sort field.

Typically you flag messages in order to remind yourself to follow up on them. Sooner or later, you have to get some work done (at least theoretically), and in spite of your best attempts, you might actually complete the work associated with a message. In that case, you should change the message's flag to show that it's complete. To flag an item as complete, right-click it and choose Flag Complete. When you do, the For Follow Up folder no longer sees the message.

Choosing Flag Colors

Outlook lets you choose among six different colors of flags. Unfortunately, that's about as far as it goes: You can't tell Outlook that red means *panic,* blue means *cool,* orange is for your *cat,* and indi . . . er, purple is *interesting.* You have to make those decisions for yourself, write them down on sticky notes, and tack them on your computer. High tech.

One option you do have is the default color. Before you go changing it, however, let me tell you why it's important:

 ✔ It's the fastest and easiest color to apply; just click the flag, and it turns red.

 ✔ When you go past your reminder date, the flag changes to the default color (unless it already *is* the default color).

Use flag colors to form the backbone of a quick, rudimentary tracking system. If you normally operate in panic mode (and I certainly fall into that category), red (the universal color for *Hey!*) is a great choice for your default. (It's the color that I want most often when I'm flagging messages and what I want flags to turn to when I miss a deadline.) You might want to consider changing the default color, though,

for different flagging needs. For example, maybe you want to flag your messages as blue to indicate *just starting.* Presumably you would change the color of the flag as the message's status changes. *Remember:* If you don't have a reminder date assigned to the message, it never automatically changes back to the default color.

To set the default color, right-click any flag, choose Set Default Flag, and pick the color.

Moving the Flag Column

The flag column at the right of the message list exhibits one really irritating oddity: It's locked to the right edge there. You can move the other fields around — drag them, resize them, and reverse their order — but you can't usurp the flag column from its chosen position.

That is, unless you know the trick. To make the flag column act like a normal message list column

1. **Right-click any of the fields at the top of the Message list (From, Subject, Size, and so on) and choose Customize Current View.**

 Outlook shows you the Customize View: Messages dialog box (see Figure 28-7).

• **Figure 28-7: Customize the Message list.**

2. **Click the Other Settings button.**

You see the Other Settings dialog box (see Figure 28-8).

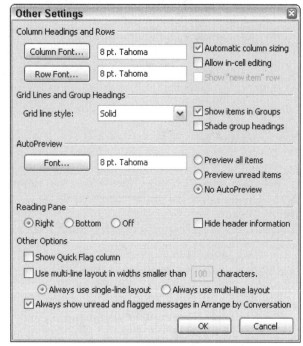

• **Figure 28-8:** Turn the follow-up flag into just another field.

3. **Under Other Options, at the bottom of the dialog box, clear the Show Quick Flag Column check box.**

That unlocks the flag status column from the right of the message list.

4. **Click OK twice.**

The flag status column becomes a field on the message list, just like any other field. Because you changed its status, you now have to add it as a field instead.

5. **To add a flag status column, right-click any field at the top of the message list, and choose Field Chooser.**

6. **From the Field Chooser dialog box (see Figure 28-9), click and drag Follow Up Flag onto the list of fields.**

Now you can move the column anywhere you want.

• **Figure 28-9:** Drag the Follow Up Flag field to the message list bar.

Technique

29

Taming AutoComplete in Outlook

Save Time By

- ✔ Typing part of a name in a message To or Cc box — and getting the right result
- ✔ Changing the list of AutoComplete names
- ✔ Working around Outlook's infuriating bugs

My attorney's name is John. A good friend of mine is named John, too.

Not long ago, I wrote an e-mail message to John, my attorney, railing about . . . well, let's just say I wasn't pleased with certain aspects of a, uh, legal matter. I wasn't angry with Attorney John, mind you, but I spewed fire and venom about various embarrassing situations.

I typed John's name in the To box of my Outlook e-mail message. You probably guessed the punch line already.

Outlook sent the message to the *other* John, my friend John. No warning. No hiccup. I'd sent mail to Attorney John by typing **John** in the To box a hundred times before. But on this particular day Outlook, in its infinite wisdom, decided that mail to Attorney John should go to Friend John.

Some days I want to kill Outlook.

Understanding AutoComplete

If you've used Outlook to write e-mail messages for more than a few days, you undoubtedly know that there are two different, competing ways to put an e-mail address in the To box:

- ✔ **Click the To button.** When you do, Outlook brings up the Select Names dialog box (see Figure 29-1). This is a clunky old dialog box (Microsoft ran out of money again, I guess) that's very hard to configure and use. In particular, you see the list of names sorted by first name, you can't re-sort on the fly, and you only get four fields: Name, Display Name, E-mail Address, and E-mail Type.

 You can coax Outlook into sorting in File As sequence — typically, last name, first name — but only by applying considerable elbow grease. See "Setting the Address Book Straight" later in this Technique for details.

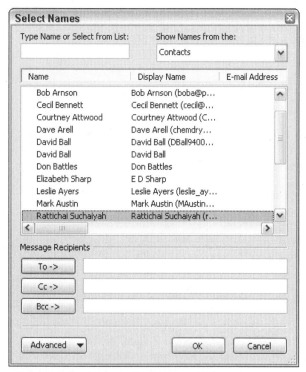

• **Figure 29-1:** Outlook offers slim pickin's when you want to put an e-mail address in a message.

Want to search for a Contact using anything other than their name? Fuhgeddaboutit. Neither the Type Name or Select from List box at the top nor the Advanced⇨Find option will look for, say, a city name or an e-mail address. To perform a real search, you have to switch over to the Contacts application itself.

✔ **Start typing in the To box and see what Outlook drags in.** Outlook uses a complex series of steps to try to *resolve* what you've typed into a usable e-mail address. That is, it tries to be helpful and guess whom you want, filling in the address for you. If and/or when the address is resolved, Outlook underlines it in the To box (see Figure 29-2). Outlook uses the same method for resolving addresses in the To box, the Cc box, and the Bcc box.

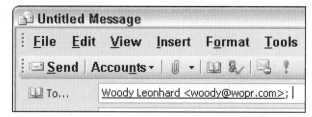

• **Figure 29-2:** A resolved address, in the wedgie style.

Unfortunately, if you want to figure out how to peacefully co-exist with Outlook's AutoComplete feature, you really need to understand where Outlook goes to find addresses.

As best as I can tell (Microsoft doesn't document this stuff), here's how Outlook 2003 resolves what you type in the To box:

The problem with AutoComplete is that it relies on the Nickname cache, which is independent of the Contacts list and relies on a history of addresses and names that you've typed in the address boxes to come up with entries such as the ones in Figure 29-3. Although you can press Ctrl+K to go to the Contacts list and select a name if Outlook can't find a name in the Nickname cache, everything that AutoComplete does happens so fast that you can all too easily end up with the wrong address in the Message. If the address resolves incorrectly milliseconds before you click the Send button, the message goes to the wrong person, and you'll never even know.

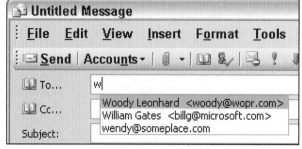

• **Figure 29-3:** Type w, and all the entries from the Nickname Cache beginning with *w* appear.

AutoComplete in Outlook is a real mixed bag. It's an enormous timesaver, without any doubt. But Outlook's headlong dash to the exits when you click Send can mean that you send the right message to the wrong person.

Understand now, John?

Cleaning Up the Cache

In the preceding section, I show you the supremacy of Outlook's Nickname Cache. It's a very helpful tool, but it can bite you, too. The primary problem? The Nickname Cache gets loaded with all sorts of garbage. For example

✔ Every time you send a message, the recipient's e-mail address gets added to Outlook's Nickname Cache.

✔ Every time you reply to a message (or reply to all, or forward), the recipient's e-mail address gets added to Outlook's Nickname Cache.

There's no Nickname Cache Sunshine Law. After an address gets in there, Outlook keeps it forever — unless you delete it. You can do so by deleting individual entries or cleaning out the whole cache.

 If (or when) AutoComplete starts spitting out bad entries that you don't want and that get in the way, clean out the cache so that AutoComplete starts working in your favor again.

✔ **Want to delete unwanted entries from the Nickname Cache?** This is good when you know of an entry or two that's tripping you up all the time and might one day cause you to accidentally send mail to the wrong address. Type the first letter or two of the bad name or address in the To box, use the arrow keys to get to the name, and then press Delete.

Note: If only one entry in the Nickname Cache is showing, you can't delete it! Microsoft's completely bogus solution to this problem is at `http://support.microsoft.com/?kbid=289975`. Yep, you guessed it. Microsoft ran out of money while fixing Outlook.

✔ **To start your Nickname Cache all over again:** That probably isn't such a bad idea, especially if you've been answering a lot of e-mail from people whom you'll never talk to again. To delete the existing cache completely, simply delete the file `C:\Documents And Settings\<your username>\ Application Data\Microsoft\Outlook\ Outlook.nk2`.

Ditching AutoComplete Altogether

If Outlook's AutoComplete really bugs you — and it might, if you've been bitten a few times — you can turn it off. However, I don't recommend that you turn it off because it's such a great timesaver. Far better to come to grips with the beast. But if you want to give it the heave-ho, here's the scoop:

1. **If you can't see Mail, choose Go⇨Mail.**

2. **Choose Tools⇨Options.**

3. **Click E-mail Options.**

4. **Click Advanced E-mail Options.**

   (Did I mention that this setting is buried deep?) Outlook shows you the Advanced E-mail Options dialog box.

5. **Clear the Suggest Names While Completing To, Cc, and Bcc Fields check boxes.**

6. **Click OK three times.**

Setting the Address Book Straight

I tend to think of the Address Book — the place where Outlook goes to look for addresses — and the Outlook Contacts list as being pretty much the same thing. They aren't exactly the same thing; if you're attached to a corporate network, you might know that already.

 If you've been using Outlook Express and you have entries in your Windows Address Book, you need to export them and bring them into Outlook. In spite of the similarities in names, an Outlook Express Windows Address Book isn't anything at all like an Outlook Address Book — or a Contacts list, either, for that matter. To pull your addresses over, go into Outlook, choose File➪Import and Export, choose Import Internet Mail and Addresses, click Next, and follow the wizard.

I've encountered two common time-sucking problems with Outlook Address Books.

✔ Sometimes when you start a new e-mail message and click the To button, you get a message from Outlook that reads:

"The address list could not be displayed. The Contacts folder associated with this address list could not be opened; it may have been moved or deleted, or you do not have permissions. For information on how to remove this folder from the Outlook Address Book, see Microsoft Office Outlook Help."

Help has a short ditty on removing Address Books, but it doesn't tell the whole story.

✔ Sometimes I put up with scanning the list of names/e-mail addresses (refer to Figure 29-1) by first name, but usually I want to look at it in File As order, which looks just like Figure 29-1 but shows the names in alphabetical order. (After all, that's what File As is supposed to do, right?) You can tell Outlook to show the list in File As order — but it ain't easy.

Here's what you need to know:

1. **If Word is running, bring it up, choose File➪Exit and get out of Word completely.**

This is one of the few times I've had problems with Word interfering with Outlook (or, more precisely with Word interfering with WordMail — Word running as Outlook's e-mail editor). It's sporadic, and the simplest solution is to just close down Word entirely.

2. **In Outlook, choose Go➪Folder List.**

That lets you see all the folders in all your open Outlook files.

3. **Right-click each Contacts folder, in turn, and choose Properties➪Outlook Address Book.**

You might have only one Contacts folder. That's fine. Outlook shows you the Contacts Properties dialog box.

4. **Mark the Show This Folder as an E-mail Address Book check box and then click OK.**

That signals Windows that you have an E-mail Address Book, here in this Contacts folder.

5. **Choose Tools➪E-mail Accounts.**

Outlook shows you the E-mail Accounts Wizard.

6. **Select the View or Change Existing Directories or Address Books radio button and then click Next.**

Outlook shows you a list of all major types of Address Books (see Figure 29-4).

7. **Choose Outlook Address Book and click the Change button.**

Outlook lists each of your available Contacts folders (see Figure 29-5).

8. **If you get the *address list could not be displayed* error that I describe at the beginning of this section, and you have more than one Contacts folder in this list, select the first one and then click the Remove Address Book button.**

The error message appears when the first Contacts folder you're trying to access is empty or otherwise messed up.

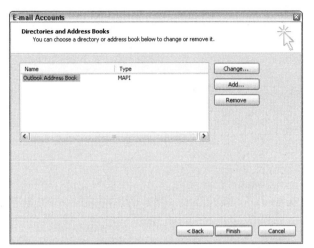

• **Figure 29-4: Every Outlook user has at least one Outlook Address Book.**

9. Click the other Contacts lists, one by one, and select the radio button for whether you want the names in the Select Names dialog box (refer to Figure 29-1) to appear sorted by first name (First Last) or by File As (typically last name, first name).

I bet you find that scanning in File As order is much, much faster than looking by First Name.

10. Click Close and then click Finish.

• **Figure 29-5: The available Contacts folders appear here.**

Dealing with Spam

Technique
30

Save Time By

- Staying off spammer's lists
- Using Outlook's spam filter wisely
- Extinguishing Web beacons

S pam is the bane of my existence.

I get a lot of it — no doubt because my e-mail address adorns Web sites from here to eternity.

My newsletters suffer because of spam, too. People complain when they don't get an issue because rogue spam blocking programs gobble 'em up. Some corporate spam-eaters don't have the good sense to let my newsletters through. Even Outlook 2003's junk mail filter has been known to misfire. Such is my life.

The effort to fight spam also causes problems when people you know get new e-mail addresses:

> Me: "Hi honey. How's it going?"
>
> Her: "Why didn't you answer my e-mail?"
>
> Me: "Huh? What e-mail?"
>
> Her: "I just sent you something from my new ID at work."
>
> Me: (click, click, click, click of my mouse) "Oh. Here it is in my Junk folder. Sorry."

This Technique helps you minimize your exposure to spam and maximize the chances of letting good mail through. It's a mighty fine line, but even a little bit of effort can save you enormous amounts of time.

Employing an Ounce of Prevention

The fastest way to deal with spam? Don't get it in the first place. Fly under the address-catcher's radar:

- **Be discreet.** Never post your address on a Web site or in a newsgroup. E-mail address-gathering spiders go everywhere. If people have to get in touch with you, based on something you posted on the Web, use something that's hard for a spider to decipher: *woody (at) wopr (dot) com* or *talk 2 woody at woodyswatch . . . com.*

- **Never respond to spam.** Ever. You should feel comfortable unsubscribing from mailing lists from reputable companies. But if `DownInDaDirtBoomBoom.com` sends you a message with an unsubscribe button at the bottom, fuhgeddaboutit. You can bet they'll sell your address to somebody else — and at a good-as-gold price because you've verified that you read the junk they sent.

- **Never open an attachment to an e-mail message.** Nope, not even if the message appears to come from Microsoft or PayPal or Citibank (*especially* if the message appears to come from Microsoft or PayPal or Citibank). Reputable companies don't send files attached to messages any more. Before you open an e-mail attachment, you need to contact the person who sent the file to you and make sure he intended to send it, save the file to disk, scan it with your just-updated antivirus program, and only then open the beast. See my detailed advice on dealing with e-mail attachments in Techniques 1 and 32.

- **Never trust a site that you arrive at via an e-mail message link.** (For that matter, you should be cautious about clicking through from Web pages!) If a message that looks like it came from PayPal tells you to click a link to log on to PayPal, you can bet your Aunt Louise's El Dorado that the link won't go anywhere near PayPal. If you need to log on to a Web site, find the site's location from an independent source.

- **Use disposable e-mail addresses.** Spamex, among others, offers a disposable e-mail address service (`www.spamex.com`, free 30-day trial, $10 per year). You get 500 e-mail addresses, which you can use in any way you like. *Cool factor:* Keep track of who gets what address, and you'll be able to nail down where spammers found your ID. If you start getting too much spam, just move on to a new address.

- **Nuke Web beacons.** Tell Outlook 2003 to block automatic downloading of pictures inside e-mail messages. That cuts off *Web beacons* — see the sidebar, "What's a Web Beacon?" — which are a powerful way of gathering e-mail addresses.

Outlook 2003, right out of the box, blocks automatic downloading of pictures (and certain other items, including sounds) inside messages. Blocking pictures makes good sense, and not just from a security point of view. (See the sidebar, "What's a Web Beacon?") By skipping the pictures, you can skim through your e-mail faster, too, particularly if you don't have a hefty Internet connection (see Figure 30-1).

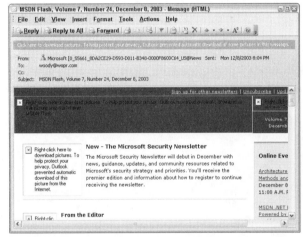

- **Figure 30-1:** Many e-mail newsletters are poorly formatted for Outlook 2003, but you can usually get the gist without the pics.

 Even if you block pictures with this Outlook setting, *you will still see pictures in your incoming e-mail!* That's a good thing. Really. If someone puts a picture inside a message — which is quite common if you, say, copy and paste a picture into the body of a message you're typing — that picture goes through Outlook 2003 and arrives on the other side, no problem. Outlook's picture blocking only applies to messages that are trying to download pictures (or sounds) from the Internet.

To keep Outlook 2003 from reaching out to the Internet and downloading pictures automatically

1. **Choose Tools⇨Options⇨Security.**

2. **Under Download Pictures, click Change Automatic Download Settings.**

Outlook shows you the oddly worded Automatic Picture Download Settings dialog box in Figure 30-2.

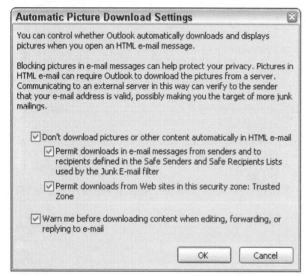

• Figure 30-2: If you really need the pictures, they're just a click away.

3. **Mark the Don't Download Pictures or Other Content Automatically in HTML E-mail check box.**

That prevents Outlook 2003 from downloading pictures (or sounds) referenced from inside the message when you view a message in the reading pane, or when you double-click a message and open it for real. (There are two exceptions; see Steps 4 and 5.)

 If you block pictures and then reply to a message, forward it, or print it, Outlook 2003 shows you the dialog box in Figure 30-3.

Then, if you approve, it downloads the pictures before continuing. (If you don't approve, Outlook refuses to reply, forward, or print.)

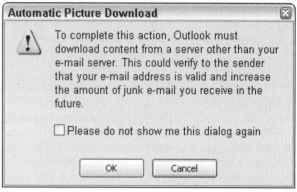

• Figure 30-3: Outlook won't let you reply to, forward, or print a message without downloading the pics (or sounds).

4. **Mark the (hold your breath) Permit Downloads in E-mail Messages from Senders and to Recipients Defined in the Safe Senders and Safe Recipients Lists Used by the Junk E-mail Filter check box.**

This incredibly obfuscating bit of text means that if you receive a message and the e-mail address of the sender is on your Safe Senders or Safe Recipients list, the pictures (and sounds) in the message should be downloaded automatically.

 The easiest way to put an e-mail address or domain such as woodyswatch.com on your Safe Senders or Safe Recipients list is to right-click a message from (or to) the address you want to add, and choose Junk E-Mail⇨Add Sender (or Recipient) to Safe Senders List, as in Figure 30-4.

• Figure 30-4: The fast way to add an address to your Safe Senders or Recipients list.

Anybody in your Contacts list (or global Address Book, if you're on a big corporate network) is automatically included in the Safe Senders List.

Because it's very easy to *spoof* a message's return address — make it appear as if, oh, Microsoft sent you the message, or PayPal, or even Woody Leonhard — you should use this feature with some care and discernment.

 Many pieces of spam these days appear to originate from the same person who received the spam. I call it *Mini-Me-spoofing*. For that reason, you should not put your own e-mail address on the Safe Senders or Safe Recipients list, and you shouldn't put your e-mail address in your own Contacts list!

5. **Mark the Permit Downloads from Web Sites in This Security Zone: Trusted Zone check box.**

Why the weird wording? Because your network administrator (if you have one) can change *Trusted Zone* to *Trusted Zone, Local Intranet Zone, Internet Zone.* If you enable this check box, Outlook 2003 downloads only those pictures (and sounds) that are stored on Web sites in your Trusted Zone. The setting has nothing to do with the e-mail address of the sender.

6. **Click OK twice.**

Any time you want to see a blocked picture, click at the top of the message or right-click an individual picture.

To understand precisely why you want to keep Outlook from automatically downloading pictures (and sounds) from the Web, see the sidebar, "What's a Web Beacon?" But don't fall for the revisionist history. Microsoft itself used to use Web beacons (see Figure 30-5). (See www.internetnews.com/ IAR/article.php/12_584741 among many others.) And the company refused to put any meaningful spam protection into any version of Outlook prior to Outlook 2003.

• **Figure 30-5: Comments like this make me see red.**

A contrarian view. Although Web beacons, in theory, are potentially quite powerful, there's been very little concrete evidence that they lead to increased spamming. In fact, Brian Livingston, in his e-book *Spam-Proof Your E-mail Address* ($9.95 from http://briansbuzz.com), comes to the conclusion that 97 percent of all spam is aimed at e-mail addresses posted on the Internet and that Web beacons really don't matter at all. He might be right.

If you're willing to accept Brian's position and you have a fast Internet connection, you might well want to allow Outlook 2003 to download pictures for all e-mail messages. The downloading doesn't occur until you see the message in the reading pane (or open the message, which few people do nowadays), so you won't have zillions of spammy pictures floating around in Outlook's files.

What's a Web Beacon?

You have two ways to put pictures inside e-mail messages. Most of the time, you simply copy the picture into the message and let Outlook sort it all out on the recipients' end. But you can also put a link to a picture inside a message, using a code that looks something like this:

```
<IMG SRC= "http://cheapcheapills.com/
    somepic.gif">.
```

When Outlook sees a code like that, it knows that it needs to reach out to `cheapcheapills.com` and pick up the picture called `somepic.gif`. Using a link makes the message much smaller, and that's what spammers (and legitimate newsletter publishers, such as yours truly!) like: We don't have to send out zillions of huge messages, all containing the same image, over and over and over again. Sending out a lot of large e-mail messages costs a fortune. Using links costs comparatively little.

Unfortunately, linked pictures can be used by unscrupulous companies to determine whether a specific e-mail message has been viewed. Here's how. The company buys a list of e-mail addresses. (You can buy millions and millions of raw e-mail addresses — most of them useless — for a fistful of yen.) A program then generates unique ID keys for each e-mail address. For example, my address, `woody@wopr.com`, might come up with the key ABYoAEhouX. The company then sends a message to `woody@wopr.com` with a link to a picture that looks like this:

```
<IMG SRC= "http://cheapcheapills.com/
    cgi-bin/flosensing?x=ABYoAEhouX">
```

When I get the message, and if Outlook is allowed to pull down pictures, it goes to the Web site `cheapcheapills.com` and asks for the picture called `flosensing?x=ABYoAEhouX`. The Web site is smart enough to match up the key with my e-mail address before returning the picture. So the unscrupulous company can verify that the message sent to `woody@wopr.com` was in fact viewed — and that means the e-mail address is good and ready to be spammed.

When you tell Outlook to block pictures in e-mail messages, Outlook Help refuses to download pictures in Help topics, and Web sites referenced by Help (including demos) don't get any pictures, either. This is probably a bug.

Deploying a Pound of Cure

Okay, so you're on so many spam lists that your e-mail address gets spray-painted on New York subways. What can you do?

- ✔ Set Outlook 2003's junk mail filter to High and scan your Junk E-mail folder religiously.

- ✔ Change your e-mail address, although I see this option as a last resort.

- ✔ Install a different kind of spam filter (a Bayesian filter) from a manufacturer other than Microsoft. Although you can train these filters to reflect what you think is and isn't spam, these filters probably won't be worth the considerable expense, both in time and money.

Junk mail (or spam) filters, in Outlook or from another source, strive to minimize two kinds of mistakes: false negatives and false positives.

False negatives are cases where junk slips through into the Inbox. They're kind of a pain in the neck, but rarely do any harm — you just have to delete the message to get rid of a false negative.

False positives are a different story altogether. With a false positive, the junk mail filter inaccurately identifies a good message as being junk, discarding it to the Junk E-mail folder.

If you get a lot of junk (and I do), false positives can ruin your day, week, month — or your business.

With Outlook's Junk E-mail filter, you can deal with false negatives and false positives in one of two ways:

✔ If you run the Junk E-mail filter at Low, you need to scan all the messages in your Inbox and delete the junk (false negatives) accordingly. Then you need to scan all the messages in your Junk E-mail folder to see whether the filter misdirected anything (look for false positives).

 If you find a message in the Junk E-mail Folder that should be in your Inbox, right-click it and choose Junk E-mail⇨Mark as Not Junk⇨OK. Outlook will place it in the Inbox.

✔ Likewise, if you run the Junk E-mail filter at High, you need to scan all the messages in your Inbox and delete the junk accordingly. Then you need to scan all the messages in your Junk E-mail folder to see whether the filter misdirected anything.

See a pattern here? Hear the echo?

 With the filter on Low, you delete junk messages many, many times while working on your Inbox, but you almost never find misidentified mail in your Junk E-mail folder.

On High, you go through your Junk E-mail folder, right-clicking and choosing Junk E-mail⇨Mark as Not Junk⇨OK many times. But you only manually delete a few times in your Inbox. In my experience, you save a lot of time if you can live with the High setting.

To set Outlook 2003's junk mail filter

1. **Choose Tools⇨Options.**

2. **On the Preferences tab, click the first button (Junk E-mail).**

You see the Junk E-mail Options dialog box, as shown in Figure 30-6.

3. **Select the radio button that begins with High. (Trust me, the whole name is way too long.)**

A complete description of the options and their timesaving implications is in Table 30-1.

4. **Make sure that you do NOT enable the Permanently Delete Suspected Junk E-mail Instead of Moving It to the Junk E-mail Folder check box.**

This might be the most foolish option in all of Office.

5. **Click OK twice.**

• **Figure 30-6: Set Outlook's spam-filtering level here.**

 Some industry pundits would have you start at Low and then move to High after a week or two. However, because the Outlook filter doesn't learn, I don't see any benefit in telling people to start at Low and then move to High.

TABLE 30-1: WHAT THE JUNK E-MAIL LEVELS MEAN

Setting	Meaning	Timesaving Tip
No Automatic Filtering	Outlook doesn't put anything in the Junk E-mail folder.	Waste of time.
Low	In my experiments, roughly 40 percent of all junk mail gets shunted to the Junk E-mail folder.	Use this option only if your life depends on it. For some people, the effect of a false positive — where a piece of good mail ends up in the Junk E-mail folder — is devastating. They have to use this setting.
High	About 90 percent of all junk mail gets moved to the Junk E-mail folder, but about one-half of 1 percent of good messages ends up in the Junk E-mail folder, too.	If you can afford to miss an occasional "good" message, this setting will save you a lot of time.
Safe Lists Only	This is a traditional *white list* (a list of acceptable e-mail senders) that only allows messages from people on your Safe Senders list or Safe Recipients list through.	You gotta be kidding.

Which brings me to the primary complaint about the Outlook 2003 junk mail filter: It doesn't learn from your settings and actions, and you can't train it to recognize your particular likes and dislikes — or precisely what *you* consider to be spam.

The Outlook 2003 spam filter has some capabilities that aren't built into any Bayesian filter that I've seen. For example, the Outlook filter takes into account the domain of the sender (spam rarely comes from .edu addresses), the presence of attachments (most traditional spam doesn't have attachments, but that might be changing), and the time of day the mail gets sent (most spam goes out at night).

Both Bayesian and Outlook filters take into account formatting in the messages. I was surprised to find one researcher who claims that the presence of bold red text in a message is a better indicator of spamminess than the presence of certain, uh, four-letter words.

Ultimately, the best solution is to make spamming simply *not worth the effort.* Please. Don't ever respond to spam. If you really want to buy an amazing remote-controlled mini-cam that increases the size of your pineal gland and takes off all that horrible sagging cellulite in one week or triple your money back, hop onto one of the Web search engines and find something better.

Please.

Technique

31

Preventing Infection

Save Time By

- Identifying bogus messages
- Avoiding scammers' traps
- Improving your BS meter

This Technique differs from all the other Techniques. My goal: to improve the sensitivity of your internal BS meter.

Many of the most famous — and most effective — worms and viruses on the Internet slithered their way into the record books by effective human engineering. Some convinced you to click an attachment that read ILOVEYOU or contained a picture of a sexy tennis star. Others convinced you to run an attachment with the latest Windows patch. One got you to sign onto a Web site to update your PayPal account. And all were bogus.

Increasingly, the biggest threats on the Web are coming from two different directions: the high-tech stuff that goes whizzing around without you having to lift a finger; and the down-home stuff that convinces you to click something when you know you shouldn't. We have to rely on others to protect us from the former. But for the latter, if you get scammed or infected, you have only yourself to blame.

Understanding the Classic Hooks

Viruses, worms, and other creepy-crawlies (which I shall call *malware*) have long traveled attached to e-mail messages:

- **Melissa** (March, 1999) was the first macro virus that hooked into Outlook. If you opened a Melissa-infected document in Word, copies of Melissa went out to everyone in your Contacts list.

- **Bubbleboy** (November, 1999) and its more prolific soul mate, Kak, were the first viruses that propagated simply by previewing an e-mail message. You didn't even have to open the message — and there was no attachment: The virus did all the work silently.

- **ILOVEYOU** (Love Letter; May, 2000) brought down Microsoft's e-mail servers as well as a large percentage of all the major computer sites in the world. People couldn't keep themselves from double-clicking the file called LOVE-LETTER-FOR-YOU.TXT.vbs attached to a message with the subject ILOVEYOU. Of course, the .vbs exten-sion is a dead giveaway that the attachment was a program — if you can see it. See Technique 1.

✔ **Anna Kournikova** (January, 2001) apparently came from a *script kiddie* — someone who used a virus-building kit downloaded from the Internet. This represents a new low, both in terms of the difficulty in creating a virus and in the security-consciousness of those who got bit.

✔ **Nimda** (September, 2001) is an all-but-the-kitchen-sink piece of malware that infects in a half-dozen different ways. Among them, it attaches itself to an e-mail message, masquerading as a piece of music. On some systems, Outlook would play the music automatically when previewing the mes-sage, thus infecting the machine. Nimda looks everywhere — absolutely everywhere — on your computer to harvest e-mail addresses.

✔ **Klez** (February, 2002) had many of the same annoying characteristics as Nimda, but it included one that drove many Outlook users nuts: Klez *spoofs* the From e-mail address, pick-ing up a random e-mail address from the infected computer. A spoofed message might look like it came from your Mom, but it didn't.

✔ Starting with **Slammer** (January, 2003), the enor-mously destructive pieces of malware shifted from propagation by attachment to e-mail mes-sages toward direct infection via holes in Windows and various kinds of servers.

We're now in an era where most of the malware-writing "talent" (I shudder to use a term like that) looks more toward bringing down the Internet in the first ten minutes of a worm's life and less toward infecting individuals' machines.

 As Microsoft gradually — some say far too gradually — plugs the holes in Outlook and Internet Explorer (in the past, IE frequently helped Outlook infect machines), old-fashioned malware writers are turning toward *social engineering* — telling a convincing story — to entice you to click something you normally wouldn't. That's where your internal BS meter comes into play.

A surprisingly large number of people — a *distress-ingly* large number of people — double-clicked the attachment to the message in Figure 31-1. Note the message about the patch.exe attachment under the toolbar.

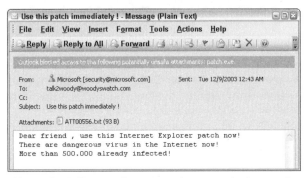

• **Figure 31-1: Beware dangerous viruses on the Internet!**

If you're running Outlook 2003 and you haven't installed Ken Slovak's ATTOPT utility (see Technique 32), you can't even get at the attached file, patch.exe. That's good. But in spite of the fact that the person who wrote this piece of malware proba-bly has an IQ approaching room temperature — Celsius — the bad guys are going to get smarter.

 In the particular, the person who wrote the malware in Figure 31-1 only needs to zip the patch.exe file prior to attaching it to the mes-sage, and it'll go right through Outlook, directly onto your desktop. Instead of double-clicking to get infected, you have to double-click twice and answer a couple of warning messages.

By the way, that message in Figure 31-1 made it right past Outlook 2003's spam filter. No problem. The bad guys are going to get smarter about that, too.

 Very few companies ever send files attached to e-mail messages any more, specifically because of all the problems with malware. If you receive a patch file from Microsoft attached to an e-mail message, you can be absolutely sure that you, uh, didn't receive a patch file from Microsoft (see Figure 31-2).

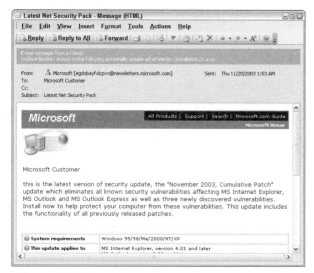

• **Figure 31-2:** One guess which company did *not* send out this message.

Follow the steps in Technique 32 to make Outlook 2003 show you all the files attached to your messages. But use some common sense. The time is coming when malware writers will be smart enough to bypass the security traps in Outlook 2003. When that time comes, the presence of a Zip file attached to an e-mail message could well be a warning that the attachment is infected. Beware!

Phishing for Fun and Profit

As the focus for serious malware writers shifts away from Outlook, the scam artists come rushing in. Stumbling all over themselves, in fact.

Enter *phishing*, the (ahem) technical term for sending out e-mail messages — generally spam — that attempt to extract valuable information from recipients: credit card numbers, financial and shopping site passwords, and the like. It's a lucrative business, and it's going to get bigger.

Part of the problem is that a well-crafted phishing message (such as the one in Figure 31-3) can get through Outlook 2003's junk mail filter.

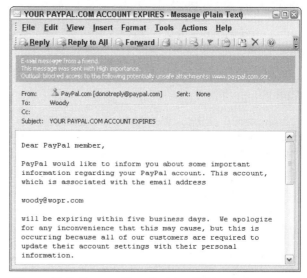

• **Figure 31-3:** Reasonably articulate phishing messages can get through Outlook 2003's spam filter.

Another part of the problem: If the phisher (for want of a better term) is willing to pay for a little extra bandwidth, he can include official-looking pictures with his messages, like the one in Figure 31-4.

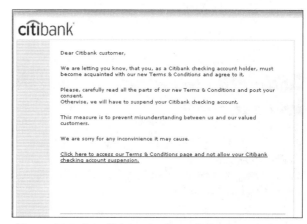

• **Figure 31-4:** An official notice from Citibank — which, of course, isn't from Citibank.

The phishing message in Figure 31-4 looks very, very much like a Citibank missive — logo and all. The language would never make it past a Citibank proofreader ("We are letting you know, that you, as a Citibank checking account holder, must become acquainted with our new Terms & Conditions and agree to it. . . . We are sorry for any *inconvinience* it may cause."), but if you glance at the message and don't read it carefully, you'll be very tempted to click through.

The supposed Citibank Web site you are sent to (which looks mighty professional, too!) only gathers your e-mail address in order to confirm that you viewed and clicked the message that was sent to you. The no-goodniks were phishing for your e-mail address. Fortunately, the site was closed down shortly after the messages came out. I checked the Web address with the official registry (whois.net) and found that the company was registered to Hangzhou Silk Road Information Technologies Co., Ltd. in China.

 If you're curious about who's behind a potentially nasty link in an email message, *don't* click it. Hover your mouse over the link and wait until Outlook shows you the address. Copy the domain name and hop over to whois.net. Although WHOIS doesn't have all the domain names all over the world on file, if you start there, you can almost always find the registered owner of the domain.

Taking the Necessary Precautions

The preceding sections make you aware of what you're up against, and this section explains the best ways to respond to attachments, spoofs, phishers, and their slimeball brethren.

Safeguarding against attachments

Before you double-click any file attached to an e-mail message

1. **Contact the person who sent you the file and make sure that she intended to send it.**

You can reply to the incoming message. Attachments aren't activated, opened, or run when you reply.

2. **Judge for yourself whether the sender is computer-savvy enough to avoid sending infected files.**

3. **Save the file to disk — never open it directly from the message.**

You could save it someplace convenient on your hard drive, but it's best to avoid places like your desktop, where you could double-click the file accidentally.

4. **Update your antivirus software and scan the file manually before opening it.**

See Technique 32 for more about working with attachments.

Keeping phishers at bay

If you receive a message saying that your account is overdue or expiring, or you're going on a long extended holiday, use some simple, common-sense precautions:

✔ **Don't click any attachments, even if they look official or innocuous.**

Phishing and malware go hand-in-hand in exploits like *Mimail*, which contains a virus that replicates the phishing message.

✔ **Don't click through from the message onto the Web.**

Either pick up the phone and call the company or use Internet Explorer to go to the company's Web site.

✔ **Don't give out any information — not even your account number or name — unless you contact the company directly.**

If you initiate the contact — either by calling a telephone number that you found in the phone book or by going to the company's Web site through a search engine — you're safe.

✔ **If it smells, uh, phishy, it probably is. Notify the company being ripped off immediately. *Don't try to trace down the culprit by clicking through.***

Historically, there have been ways to infect PCs directly from Web pages. The last thing you need is to discover that someone has found a new way.

✔ **Send a copy of the message to the Feds by forwarding it to** uce@ftc.gov. **And if you think somebody is zooming you, zoom him back at** www.ftc.gov.

Working with E-mail Attachments

Technique 32

Save Time By

- ✔ Seeing all the files sent to you
- ✔ Controlling which files get blocked
- ✔ Using some not-so-common sense with file attachments

This Technique is all about unraveling some of the safety nets that Microsoft built into Outlook 2003. Straight out of the box, Outlook 2003 prevents you from getting at certain kinds of files that arrive attached to e-mail messages. Unless you change things, many files that people send you are blocked by Outlook, and you can spend a huge amount of time trying to get at a file that should've come through the first time.

In this Technique, I show you how to override Outlook's default settings. It'll save you time — but you must have the discipline to avoid double-clicking potentially dangerous files!

Before you dig into this Technique, make sure that you and your settings are ready for it:

- ✔ If you can't train your clicking finger to avoid clicking e-mail attachments, skip this Technique. See Technique 31 for tips on what to do instead of clicking away.

- ✔ If you haven't told Windows to show you filename extensions, follow the steps in Technique 1 and then come back to this Technique. (Or if you doubt the need to see filename extensions, skip this Technique altogether because without extensions showing, you'll only invite viruses into your computer).

I figure I just lost about 25 percent of you fair readers as well as 90 percent of the brass at Microsoft. Fair enough.

Understanding Draconian Blocks

Outlook 2003 (and Outlook 2002 and Outlook 2000 Service Pack 3 or later) keeps you from getting at certain files attached to incoming e-mail messages. The intent is to keep you from getting infected. The actual effect is to slow file transfer down to an infuriating snail's pace.

It's for your own good. But it's awfully heavy-handed. I use the term *draconian,* and I believe that's accurate.

Here's how the blocking happens:

1. **Before Outlook shows a message in the reading pane or opens it, Outlook examines it to see whether it has a file attached.**

2. **Outlook compares the filename extension on any attached files with the so-called *Level 1* list (see Table 32-1).**

 There's absolutely no intelligence involved: no scanning for viruses, and no comparison with known infected files. Outlook simply compares the filename extension with the Level 1 list.

3. **If the filename extension appears on the Level 1 list, Outlook tells you that it "blocked access to the following potentially unsafe attachments" (see Figure 32-1), and then it gives you the name of the file.**

The specific message in Figure 32-1 was created by a worm called Dumaru, which was a *key logger* that circulated widely in 2003 and 2004. If you double-click the attached file, Dumaru plants a program on your PC that records every key you press and sends that information to a Web site. It also scans most files on your PC, searching for e-mail addresses and then mailing a copy of itself to every address that it finds. Dumaru has its own *SMTP engine,* which means that it can send mail without using Outlook or any other e-mail program.

4. **Outlook won't let you get at the blocked file, no way, no how. You can't save it. You can't forward it. You can't do anything with it.**

Unless you use ATTOPT. See the following section for details.

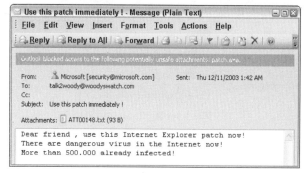

• **Figure 32-1:** `patch.exe` **has a Level 1 filename extension.**

 As of this writing, all the Level 1 lists in the Microsoft Knowledge Base and the Microsoft Office Resource Kit are incorrect. Table 32-1 is correct.

Cynics (present company most certainly included) note that

✔ **Outlook doesn't try to block** `.doc` **(Word document),** `.xls` **(Excel spreadsheet), or** `.ppt` **(PowerPoint) files.** Why? Those kinds of files certainly can harbor viruses and other kinds of malware. Is it possible that MS didn't put them on the banned list because users would scream if they couldn't send documents or spreadsheets to each other? And why are Access databases blocked when docs aren't?

✔ **Outlook only looks at the filename extension.** For example, you can easily and successfully send an `.exe` file attached to an e-mail message just by renaming it before you send it. You could call the offensive file `.exeremoveme` or `.exeee` — but if it's named `.exe`, it won't pass muster.

✔ **Zip files aren't banned.** You can send a virus inside a `.zip` file, and Outlook will never be the wiser.

✔ **SharePoint Portal Server lets you post any kind of file.** Outlook doesn't care about the file or the filename extension — even if you use Outlook to post the file!

TABLE 32-1: OUTLOOK 2003 DEFAULT LEVEL 1 FILENAME EXTENSIONS

Extension	What It Is	Extension	What It Is
.ade	Access project	.mde	Access MDE database
.adp	Access project	.mdt	Access workgroup information
.app	Visual FoxPro application	.mdw	Access workgroup information
.asx	Windows Media audio/video	.mdz	Access wizard program
.bas	Visual Basic class module	.msc	Common Console document
.bat	Batch file	.msi	Windows Installer package
.chm	Compiled HTML Help file	.msp	Windows Installer patch
.cmd	Windows command script	.mst	Windows Installer transform; Visual Test source file
.cer	Outlook Express Certificate	.ops	Office XP settings
.com	DOS program	.pcd	Photo CD image; Visual compiled script
.cpl	Control Panel applet	.pif	Program info file for DOS program
.crt	Security certificate	.prf	Outlook profile settings
.csh	Unix shell script	.prg	Visual FoxPro program
.exe	Program	.pst	Outlook data store
.fxp	Visual FoxPro compiled program	.reg	Registration entries
.hlp	Help file	.scf	Explorer command
.hta	HTML program	.scr	Screen saver
.inf	Setup information	.sct	Script component
.ins	Internet Naming Service	.shb	Shell scrap object
.isp	Internet communication settings	.shs	Shell scrap object
.js	JScript file	.url	Internet shortcut
.jse	Jscript-encoded script file	.vb	VBScript file
.ksh	Unix shell script	.vbe	VBScript-encoded script file
.lnk	Shortcut	.vbs	VBScript file
.mda	Access add-in program	.wsc	Windows Script Component
.mdb	Access program	.wsf	Windows Script file

If somebody sends you a file and it's blocked by Outlook, you have four options.

- ✔ Write to the person who sent the file and ask her to zip it and resend it.

- ✔ Write to the person who sent the file and ask her to rename the file with a filename extension that isn't on the Level 1 list — and then resend it.

- ✔ Write to the person who sent the file and ask her to either put it on a network share or in a SharePoint portal that you can both get to.

- ✔ Install Ken Slovak's ATTOPT utility. (See the following section.)

If you want to save time, Ken's utility is the only way to go.

Bypassing the Blocks

Microsoft won't let you completely free the Level 1 files that I describe in the preceding section, but it does let you move them to Level *2*. (Doncha just love this descriptive terminology?) A file with a Level 2 filename extension is still trapped by Outlook, but you're allowed to save the file onto your hard drive (see Figure 32-2). From that point, you can do what you will — presumably scanning the file would be your first order of business.

• Figure 32-2: A filename extension on the Level 2 list elicits an Outlook response like this.

 The file in Figure 32-2, `patch.exe`, is the same file that's attached to the message in Figure 32-1. It triggered the warning in Figure 32-2 after I moved `.exe` files to Level 2.

So how do you move Level 1 filename extensions to Level 2?

You can do it the hard way by manually editing some very strange keys in the Registry (details at `http://support.microsoft.com/?kbid= 829982`). Or you can download the free (donation requested) Attachment Options utility from Ken Slovak.

 ATTOPT is a crucial, must-have download for any Office 2003 user who wants to save time — and has the discipline not to run programs that come in from the Internet without scanning them first.

To install and use ATTOPT

1. **Choose File⇨Exit to get out of Outlook.**

2. **Go to Ken's Web site at** `www.slovaktech.com/ attachmentoptions.htm`.

3. **At the bottom of the page, click the <u>Download Attachment Options</u> link and save the setup file** `AOsetup.exe` **to disk.**

4. **Double-click** `AOsetup.exe`.

   The installer takes you through the steps.

5. **Start Outlook again. Choose Tools⇨Options⇨ Attachment Security & Options.**

   You see the Attachment Security & Options tab of the Options dialog box, as shown in Figure 32-3.

6. **If you want to hunt and peck through the filename extensions, by all means, go ahead. However, I recommend that you click the Move All button and move every filename extension from Level 1 to Level 2.**

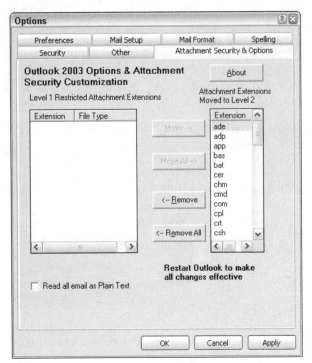

• **Figure 32-3: Move filename extensions from Level 1 to Level 2.**

7. **Click OK and then restart Outlook.**

If you try to open a file attached to a message with a filename extension on the Level 2 list, you get a warning message like that in Figure 32-2.

 Yes, you have to be careful. Yes, you should scan *every single file* that comes in attached to an e-mail message with antivirus software. But at least at Level 2, you have a choice.

 If you can't get Ken's utility to work, it's possible that your network administrator has locked you out of the Level 1/Level 2 part of the Registry. (Outlook has an installation setting that allows this.) You'll have to get permission from your network admin. Good luck.

After you restart Outlook, messages with attached files that used to be on the Level 1 list look like Figure 32-4. You can get at the attached file.

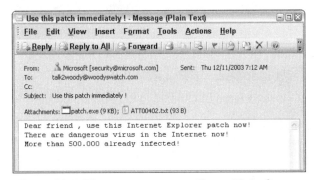

• **Figure 32-4: The same message as Figure 32-1, after** `.exe` **has been moved from Level 1 to Level 2.**

Securing Your Mail

I f the National Security Agency wants to crack one of your messages, it can. It might need an hour on a supercomputer, but it can be done. On the other hand, if you send out messages that you don't want every Tom, Dick, and Harry to read, *encrypting* — scrambling the message — is a very good, surprisingly quick option.

Your e-mail messages are broken into packets, and anybody who can read the packets can reassemble the messages, even changing the messages while en route, much like slathering correction fluid on a postcard. By encrypting the message before you send it, each packet contains a piece of the scrambled puzzle. Reuniting the packets is comparatively easy. Unscrambling the message isn't.

In this Technique, I show you how to encrypt your messages as well as how to digitally sign messages so that the person who receives the message can be reasonably confident that you sent it. They both go hand-in-hand.

Save time. Save gray hair. Encrypt when it makes sense.

Getting a Digital Certificate

To a first approximation, a digital certificate resembles an electronic passport or identity card. You can use a *digital certificate* to

✔ Tell the recipient of an e-mail message that you sent the message. In this case, only you — the sender — need a certificate.

✔ Encrypt a message so that only the intended recipient can read it (give or take a crack on a supercomputer). In this case, both the sender and the recipient need digital certificates.

Digital certificates work very well with Outlook, and they aren't dependent on any other software. If you send and receive e-mail with Outlook, you have everything that you need to encrypt and decrypt messages.

To get your own digital certificate (free for a 60-day trial; $14.95 per year)

1. In Outlook, choose Tools⇨Options⇨Security.

You see the Security tab of the Options dialog box.

2. In the lower-right corner, click the Get a Digital ID button.

Outlook fires up Internet Explorer and takes you to one of Microsoft's Marketplace sites (see Figure 33-1).

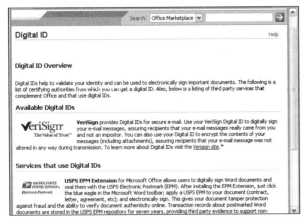

• **Figure 33-1: Microsoft points you to VeriSign.**

3. Click the link to the VeriSign site.

You see information about the Class 1 Digital ID (see Figure 33-2). That's the one you want.

4. Click the link for a 60-day free trial.

You see VeriSign's sign-up form.

5. Fill out the form and then click Next.

The application procedure requires you to download an RSA key generation program, and you might go through a few additional questions. (*RSA* is an encryption method that's used widely on the Internet. Details are available at http://rsasecurity.com.) Ultimately, you are asked to check your e-mail for the Digital ID.

• **Figure 33-2: A Class 1 Digital ID is free for a 60-day trial or $14.95 per year (as this book went to press).**

6. Go back to Outlook and click Cancel on the Security tab of the Options dialog box. Then wait for a confirmation e-mail from VeriSign.

 When I signed up for a VeriSign certificate, Outlook identified the confirmation message as junk mail. Be sure you watch your Junk E-mail folder!

When the message arrives, it looks something like Figure 33-3.

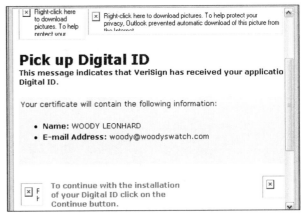

• **Figure 33-3: Watch that your confirmation doesn't end up in your Junk E-mail folder.**

7. **In the message, click the link that says <u>To Continue With the Installation of Your Digital ID Click on the Continue Button</u> and follow the instructions onscreen.**

Specifically, click Install, click OK twice, and then the *cert* (that's in-the-know cool talk for a digital certificate) gets installed.

As your free 60-day trial nears an end, VeriSign sends you a message telling you how to switch to the paid version.

Using a Digital Certificate

Your freshly minted digital certificate will identify you to people who receive your messages, but the preceding section should make you well aware of two facts:

✔ Anybody can request, and receive, a Class 1 digital certificate with any name on it. The fact that you receive a message digitally signed by Bill Gates should give you pause — not because it came from the world's richest person, but because it came from someone with the *chutzpah* to apply for a cert with Bill's name on it.

✔ Despite efforts for years, Microsoft hasn't ironed out the kinks in digital signatures.

Although a person receiving a Class 1 digitally signed message can't be sure of the sender's identity, he *can* be sure that the message hasn't been tampered with. The certificate guarantees that what you got is what was sent.

Most people attach signatures to messages only occasionally. To digitally sign a particular message

1. **In Outlook, create the message normally.**

2. **On the main toolbar, click the Options button (see Figure 33-4).**

You see the Message Options dialog box.

3. **At the top of the Message Options dialog box, click Security Settings.**

Outlook shows you the Security Properties dialog box (see Figure 33-5).

4. **Select the Add Digital Signature to This Message check box. Click OK and then click Close.**

Note the slight change in terminology. *Digital signature* here is the same thing as *digital certificate* and *Digital ID*.

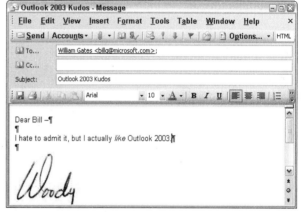

• **Figure 33-4: Attach a certificate from the Options button.**

• **Figure 33-5: Enable adding a digital certificate here.**

5. **Send the message normally.**

Outlook warns you that something is trying to use your digital certificate.

 Don't be confused. *Private Exchange Key* and *CryptoAPI Private Key* are the same as *digital signature, digital certificate,* and *digital ID* earlier in this Technique. Microsoft's terminology runs all over the place.

6. **Click OK.**

The message goes in the Outbox, as usual.

When you receive a message with a digital certificate, you can identify it by its gold-and-red ribbon, both on the message in the message list and at the upper-right of the reading pane (see Figure 33-6).

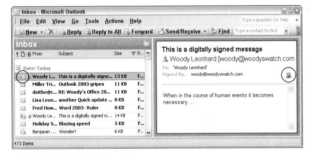

• **Figure 33-6: A signed message.**

If you want to see the details of the certificate itself (which are rarely of any interest, at least for a Class 1 ID), you can click the gold-and-red ribbon (see Figure 33-7).

• **Figure 33-7: The digital certificate is good, although you really don't know who sent the message.**

Encrypting Messages

Before you can *encrypt* (intentionally scramble) a message, both you and the person to whom you send encrypted messages must follow all the steps in the two preceding sections. You must both obtain and install a digital certificate, and your correspondent must send at least one digitally certified message to you. It all has to do with *public key encryption:* You have to receive his *public* key from him before Outlook can combine it with your *private* key and scramble the message. The best description I've seen of public key cryptology is at www.howstuffworks.com/encryption1.htm. It ain't perfect, but it's pretty good.

To send an encrypted message, you must first put your correspondent's digital certificate in that person's record in your Contacts list. You need to do that but once. Here's how:

1. **Make sure that you have a digital certificate installed.**

2. **Have the person to whom you're going to send an encrypted message (your correspondent) send you a message with a digital certificate.**

 Your correspondent has to follow all the steps in the two preceding sections.

3. **When you receive the message from your correspondent, right-click the name in the reading pane and then choose Add to Outlook Contacts.**

You see his Contact record.

4. **On the Contact record, click the Save and Close button.**

You might receive a Duplicate Contact Detected message. If you do, select the Update New Information from This Contact to the Existing One radio button and then click OK.

At this point, your correspondent's digital certificate is stored in his record in Outlook's Contacts.

After your Contact has a digital certificate safely stored away, you can easily send an encrypted message to him:

1. **Create a new message and write it normally.**

2. **On the main toolbar, click the Options button (refer to Figure 33-4).**

Outlook shows you the Message Options dialog box.

3. **At the top of the Message Options dialog box, click Security Settings.**

You get the Security Properties dialog box (see Figure 33-8).

• **Figure 33-8:** Encrypt the message here.

4. **Select the Encrypt Message Contents and Attachments check box. Click OK and then click Close.**

5. **Send the message normally.**

Outlook warns you that something is trying to use your digital certificate.

6. **Click OK.**

The message goes in the Outbox, as usual.

When you receive an encrypted message, only a warning appears in the reading pane (see Figure 33-9).

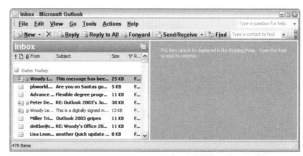

• **Figure 33-9:** You can't preview an encrypted message — and it thus won't show up in the reading pane.

To see the message, you have to double-click it in the message list. When you do so, you see a warning about a program trying to access your digital certificate. Click OK, and the message appears with a blue lock signifying that it was encrypted (see the lower-right corner Figure 33-10).

• **Figure 33-10:** An encrypted message bears a lock.

Part IV

Exploiting Excel

The 5th Wave

By Rich Tennant

@RICHTENNANT

"Unless there's a corrupt cell in our spreadsheet analysis concerning the importance of trunk space, this should be a big seller next year."

34 Technique

Getting Excel Settings Right

Save Time By

✔ Keeping Excel out of your hair

✔ Formatting a default worksheet

✔ Getting Excel to help

I won't mince words about it. Excel drives me nuts. I live in a Word/ Outlook world. Numbers kind of come along for the ride — yes, I confess I was a math major, and I know that a *standard deviation* isn't a guest on *Jerry Springer*. But my world doesn't revolve around spreadsheets. I use Excel to keep my business going, make investment decisions, keep track of taxes, and lots of other stuff. But my day doesn't start with spreadsheets. Alas, often it does *end* that way. If you know what I mean.

If you're like me, you want to get into Excel, get your numbers figured out, and scoot — in time to go home for dinner. That's where this Technique comes in.

Bagging the Bouncing Menus

Excel, like most of the other Office 2003 applications, has an annoying habit of moving your menus around. Today, you find Replace on the Edit menu. Tomorrow, it's gone, and Delete Sheet appears in its stead. You have to double-click or hover your mouse around a menu to get it to appear in its full splendor.

Microsoft calls them *personal menus.* I call them *time-sucking fluff* as well as other, less printable things. To make your menus stand up and take their punishment without cowering

1. **Choose Tools⇨Customize⇨Options.**

   Excel shows you the Options tab of the Customize dialog box, as shown in Figure 34-1.

2. **Mark the Always Show Full Menus check box.**

3. **While you're here, select the Show Standard and Formatting Toolbars on Two Rows check box, too.**

   Might as well get all the icons you paid for.

• **Figure 34-1: Get your full menus back.**

> *4.* **Click Close.**
>
> Aside from a persistent, ineffectual startup task pane (which I dispatch in the next section), Excel is ready to use.

Making Key Changes

Unlike Word — which abounds with spectacularly ridiculous default settings — many of the changes that Excel guri make to their systems have more to do with personal preference than spiritual realignment.

Almost everyone who uses Excel exhaustively agrees on a small handful of changes:

> ✔ **Increase the number of undo levels.** Excel 2003, out of the box, allows you to undo only your preceding 16 actions. It's ludicrous, but Microsoft insists that this limitation exists to protect you from using too much memory! (These guys have never heard of 512MB machines and swap files,

I s'pose. Or maybe Microsoft just ran out of money again.) You can modify the Registry to increase the number of undo levels, but Microsoft sternly recommends that you not allow more than 100 undo's.

> ✔ **Maximize the number of files remembered on the File menu.** The so-called *MRU* (Most Recently Used) list shows your most-recently opened files at the bottom of the File menu. It starts at four. There's no penalty at all in increasing it to nine.

> ✔ **Make more AutoRecover saves.** Excel 2003 automatically saves an AutoRecover file — to recover from crashes — every ten minutes. If you work with excruciatingly huge spreadsheets, you might want to leave that setting at ten minutes because a save can take a long time. If you work with spreadsheets that encompass something less than the national debt, get Excel to spin a safety net more frequently.

> ✔ **Don't let Excel automatically convert Web addresses and e-mail addresses to links.** This is a bit of IntelliNONsense borrowed from Word. I talk about it in Technique 15.

> ✔ **Show page breaks all the time.** Maybe you're disciplined enough to run a print preview every time you change a spreadsheet, but I'm not — and I have a dumpster full of misprinted pages to prove it. Excel can show you the dotted-line page break indicators all the time if you simply tell it.

In addition, I have three pet changes that I always make. You can take 'em or leave 'em, but I find each quite valuable:

> ✔ **Change how Enter works.** When you type something in a cell and press Enter, Excel usually moves to the cell below the one that you're working on. I rarely want to go down one cell. I've played with this for years and come to the conclusion that if I want to move to a new cell, I can use the arrow keys. I prefer to have Enter just accept what I typed and stay at the current cell.

You have the potential to save a lot of time here, particularly if you start using the number pad on your keyboard. A second Enter key is right there next to the numbers — and the arrow keys sit waaaaay over in the lower back 40. (Or down in Soho if you're a city girl.) Pay attention to how you normally enter data, figuring out whether it's best for you to have Excel stay put, move down, or move right (the three most common choices) when you press Enter.

✔ **Get rid of the startup pane.** This is the Getting Started task pane that appears when you start Excel, with options like Get the Latest News About Using Excel. If Microsoft has a more sorry excuse for a task pane, I've never seen it.

✔ **Put the Formula Auditing toolbar at the top.** This toolbar, shown in Figure 32-4, has saved my bacon so many times that I always give it a place of prominence. See the sidebar, "The Formula Auditing Toolbar."

• **Figure 34-2: The Excel save-your-tail Formula Auditing toolbar.**

Setting up the Options dialog box and AutoCorrect

Here's how to get the easy changes knocked out. If you don't want to read the *why,* just follow the *what* in the figures:

1. **Choose Tools⇨Options⇨View.**

You see the View tab of the Options dialog box (see Figure 34-3).

2. **Clear the Startup Task Pane check box and select the Page Breaks check box.**

The task pane won't appear the next time you start Excel, and Excel will automatically show you dotted lines at all page breaks, all the time.

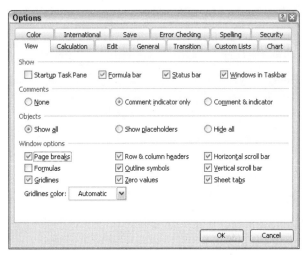

• **Figure 34-3: My recommended View options.**

3. **Click the Edit tab.**

Excel shows the Edit tab of the Options dialog box (see Figure 34-4).

4. **Either clear the Move Selection After Enter check box, or (if your work habits are different from mine) change the Direction that Excel should move after you press the Enter key.**

See the preceding Clock Is Ticking suggestion.

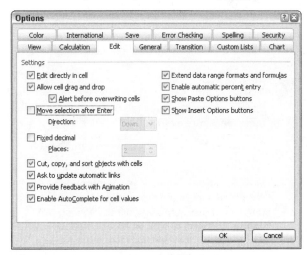

• **Figure 34-4: My recommended Edit options.**

5. **Click the General tab.**

You get the General tab of the Options dialog box (see Figure 34-5).

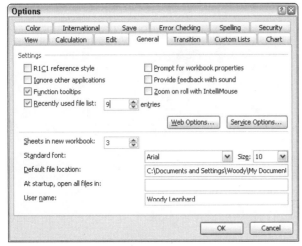

• **Figure 34-5: My recommended General options.**

6. **Run the Recently Used File List up to 9.**

I have no idea why Microsoft limits this to 9.

 If you have an IntelliMouse (or work-alike) and want to zoom in and out quickly while looking at your spreadsheets, also consider selecting the Zoom on Roll with IntelliMouse check box. If you leave this setting cleared, rolling the mouse wheel scrolls through the spreadsheet.

7. **Click the Save tab.**

Excel displays the Save tab of the Options dialog box (see Figure 34-6).

8. **Put the AutoRecover cycle between 3 and 5 minutes.**

It's a question of time: If you commonly work with large spreadsheets, you probably want the interval higher, just so you aren't constantly competing with AutoSave for control of your spreadsheet. (Conversely, though, if something goes bump in the night, you folks with big spreadsheets have more to lose!)

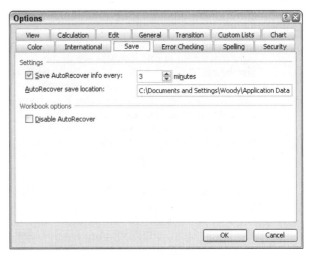

• **Figure 34-6: My recommended Save options.**

9. **Click OK.**

Not quite done yet.

10. **Choose Tools⇨AutoCorrect Options⇨AutoCorrect.**

You see the AutoCorrect tab of the AutoCorrect dialog box, as shown in Figure 34-7.

• **Figure 34-7: Confusingly, Microsoft can't keep its Option buttons/Smart Tag terminology straight.**

I don't recommend changing AutoCorrect settings — they're pretty innocuous — but I do want to warn you about a particularly lousy bit of terminology here. The Show AutoCorrect Options Buttons check box at the top *should* read Show AutoCorrect Option Smart Tags (or something along that line). The check box controls whether Excel shows a Smart Tag each time it applies AutoCorrect. I find it almost impossible to find the Smart Tags in most cases, but unless you're congenitally indisposed to Smart Tags, I suggest you leave it enabled.

11. **Click the AutoFormat As You Type tab.**

Excel shows you the AutoFormat tab of the AutoCorrect dialog box, as shown in Figure 34-8.

• **Figure 34-8: My recommended AutoFormat As You Type options.**

12. **Clear the Internet and Network Paths with Hyperlinks check box. Then click OK.**

Almost done.

13. **Choose View⇨Toolbars and enable the Formula Auditing toolbar.**

Excel brings up the Formula Auditing toolbar (refer to Figure 34-2). See the sidebar "The Formula Auditing Toolbar" for the reasons why the Formula Auditing toolbar comes in handy all the time. You might want to click and drag it someplace handy. You can even dock it on the left or right edge of the screen, if you like.

14. **Choose File⇨Exit.**

Just to be sure, exit Excel and start it again. All your changes should take.

The Formula Auditing Toolbar

Excel 2003 includes a remarkable collection of error-catching and correcting tools. Unfortunately, most Excel users *never see them* because many of them sit on a toolbar that isn't exactly a household word.

To see how this toolbar works, follow the procedure in this section to make the Formula Auditing toolbar (refer to Figure 34-2) visible. Then open a spreadsheet — any spreadsheet. In the spreadsheet, click in a cell that's calculated based on the contents of other cells — a simple sum, say, or a product. Click the second icon (Trace Precedents) on the Formula Auditing toolbar. Excel draws a box around all the cells that are used to calculate the value in the chosen cell, showing you very quickly and easily whether the formula you used includes all the cells you expected it to. To remove the precedent arrows, click the next icon: Remove Precedent Arrows.

Similarly, you can click a cell and see arrows point to where that cell is used in formulas in the spreadsheet. Excel calls those *dependencies.*

Formula auditing rates as one of the most powerful, quick, easy ways to check a spreadsheet for errors — if you know the toolbar is there!

Increasing the levels of undo

There's one difficult change to Excel that I highly recommend. If you never make mistakes, you needn't bother. But if you occasionally make a big blooper and you don't discover the error until 16 or more edits down the line, you can save a huge amount of time by simply undoing whatever you did wrong . . . that is, providing you remove Excel's 16-level amnesia.

Here's how to increase the number of undo levels in Excel:

> The usual Registry editing warnings apply: Don't change things willy-nilly inside the Registry because you really can screw things up. Just go in, get the job done, and get out, okay?

1. **Exit Excel.**

2. **Choose Start➪Run, type** regedit, **and click OK.**

Windows brings up the Registry Editor.

3. **On the left, double-click your way down to** HKey_CURRENT_USER\Software\Microsoft\ Office\11.0\Excel\Options.

Office 11.0 is the internal code name for Office 2003 (see Figure 34-9).

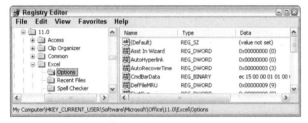

• **Figure 34-9: Edit the Excel\Options key.**

4. **Make sure that Options is selected on the left. Choose Edit➪New➪DWORD Value.**

regedit creates a new DWORD value called New Value #1. The name New Value #1 should be highlighted.

5. **Type** UndoHistory.

That creates a new DWORD value called UndoHistory (see Figure 34-10).

6. **Double-click UndoHistory.**

regedit shows you the Edit DWORD Value dialog box, as shown in Figure 34-11.

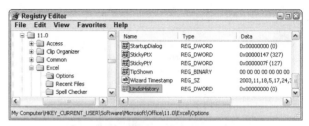

• **Figure 34-10: Add a new DWORD value called UndoHistory.**

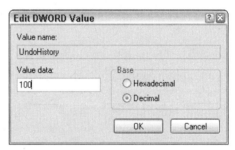

• **Figure 34-11: Set UndoHistory to 100.**

7. **Under the Base heading, select the Decimal radio button. In the Value Data box, type** 100. **Click OK and then exit the Registry Editor.**

8. **Start Excel.**

Excel remembers up to 100 actions for the Undo function.

Modifying Your Default Spreadsheet

When Excel creates a new, blank spreadsheet, it actually creates a copy of the spreadsheet called book.xlt, which is almost always located in C:\Program Files\Microsoft Office\OFFICE11\ XLSTART.

If you want to make changes to your default spreadsheet — the one that appears every time you create a new, blank spreadsheet — the easiest way is to modify `book.xlt` directly. Here's how:

1. **Check whether you already have a** `book.xlt` **file by choosing File➪Open and navigating to** `C:\Program Files\Microsoft Office\OFFICE11\XLSTART`. **If you find a file called** `book.xlt`, **open it.**

Unless you've been modifying Excel, you won't find a `book.xlt`. That's fine. Just start with a clean new workbook by clicking the New icon at the far left on the Standard toolbar.

2. **If you want to change the default font, alignment, borders, and the like, choose Format➪ Style, make any changes you like, and click OK.**

Excel shows you the Style dialog box (see Figure 34-12).

• **Figure 34-12:** Change the Normal style to modify default fonts and so on.

3. **If you want your new workbooks to appear with just one or two sheets, right-click the Sheet3 tab at the bottom of the screen and choose Delete.**

You can have as many or as few as you like.

4. **To create a default header or footer (generally a good idea), choose View➪Header and Footer.**

Excel shows you the Page Setup dialog box, as shown in Figure 34-13.

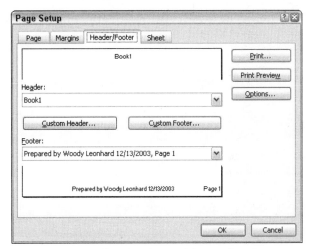

• **Figure 34-13:** Default headers and footers for all my new, blank workbooks.

5. **Select the header or footer that you want. Or, click Custom Header and/or Custom Footer and put together precisely the header and/or footer you wish.**

In Figure 34-13, I choose to put the name of the workbook in the header, and my name, date, and page number in the footer.

 It might look like you're hard-coding Book1, for example, into the header, but that isn't the case. If you stick with the choices on offer, Excel is smart enough to swap the name of the spreadsheet when it comes time to print. The header in a new workbook won't appear as Book1 but will (as you might hope) reflect the actual name of the spreadsheet.

6. **Click OK to return to the spreadsheet.**

7. **When you finish your customizing — and you can customize just about anything — choose File⇨Save. In the Save as Type box, choose Template. In the Name box, type** book. **Finally, navigate to the** C:\Program Files\Microsoft Office\OFFICE11\XLSTART **folder and then click Save.**

   That saves your customized normal template in the place it needs to be (see Figure 34-14).

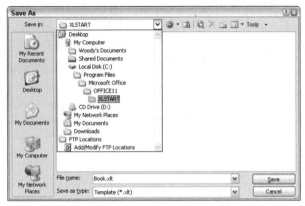

• **Figure 34-14:** Save book.xlt **in the XLSTART folder.**

Technique 35

Building Self-Verifying Spreadsheets

Save Time By

- Formatting bad data to stick out like a sore thumb
- Setting up calculations that warn you about errors
- Cross-footing totals to flag spreadsheet problems

What? Your spreadsheets are always right the first time? Cool. You don't need this Technique at all.

For the other 99.999 percent of us, slapping together anything more than a trivial spreadsheet is a mind-numbing experience. Heck, I've had more than a few trivial spreadsheets turn out bad, too.

It isn't a question of being careful and thoughtful. Rather, it's a question of banging and clanging away at a spreadsheet until something breaks — then it's a question of realizing that something's broken — and *then* it's a question of figuring out what and where and how to fix it.

This Technique brings some powerful verification tools to bear, quickly and effectively.

Highlighting Conditionally

Most of the time, spreadsheet formatting is something you do after the numbers look right and you're getting bored — or you want to impress somebody.

But I'm here to show you one type of formatting — *conditional formatting* — that can help you quickly catch errors in your spreadsheet and errors in your data.

As its name implies, conditional formatting kicks in when a certain condition is met. Although conditional formatting can be used to make a spreadsheet pretty, it's also a dynamite method for alerting people to errors: for example, if your annual sales go over a hundred billion dollars, or the amount of a payroll check goes negative. You tell Excel what conditions apply and, within some surprisingly stringent limits, how to format the results. When the conditions are met, your chosen formatting is applied — for example, a number turns bold blue, or a cell background erupts in fuchsia.

The following example serves double duty: I show you how to apply conditional formatting to point out bad numbers in a spreadsheet. At the same time, I give you a tool for determining whether your copy of Excel 2003 suffers from a bad bug in the RAND() random number generator, which came to light a couple of months after Excel 2003 shipped.

Here's how to set up a potentially buggy spreadsheet, apply conditional formatting, and check for the RAND() bug, all in one fell swoop:

1. **Start with a new, blank workbook.**

2. **In cell A1, type** =RAND().

That's the formula for a random number (see Figure 35-1). In theory, =RAND() is supposed to generate a pseudo-random number between zero and one. In the original version of Excel 2003, there's a bug in =RAND(): When you run it enough times, the values turn negative. Not good.

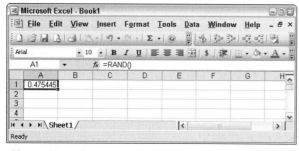

• **Figure 35-1: The formula for a random number.**

3. **Click the drag handle (the lower-right corner) of cell A1, hold down the mouse button, and drag the =RAND() formula down to cell 1000 or so.**

Don't worry if you overshoot or undershoot by a hundred cells or so. What you want is about a thousand copies of the =RAND() function (see Figure 35-2).

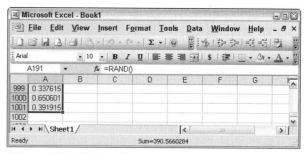

• **Figure 35-2: Make a thousand copies or so. It's quick and easy with the drag handle.**

4. **Click the A column to select it, and then use the drag handle (now in the upper-right corner of cell A1) to drag the =RAND() formula to columns B, C, D and on out to Z or thereabouts.**

You should see a whole lotta =RAND()s (see Figure 35-3).

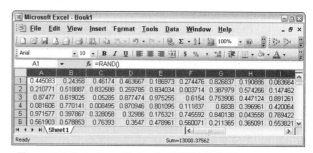

• **Figure 35-3: Lots and lots of =RAND() fields.**

5. **Press F9 a few times to make Excel recalculate the random numbers.**

At some point, if you have the original, unpatched version of Excel 2003, a bunch of those numbers will turn negative. But looking for negative number-needles in this haystack will give you a headache in no time: The only way you can tell that you're looking at a negative number is by squinting hard and looking for a teensy-tiny minus sign. It's much easier on the eyes to apply conditional formatting.

6. **Select the entire spreadsheet.**

The fastest way to select the whole spread-sheet is to click in the rectangle to the left of the A column and above the 1 row.

7. **Choose Format⇨Conditional Formatting.**

Excel shows you the Conditional Formatting dialog box (see Figure 35-4).

• **Figure 35-4: Tell Excel that you want to apply special formatting if the value in a cell is less than 0.**

8. **In the first box, choose Cell Value Is. In the second box, choose Less Than. In the third box, type the number 0 (zero). Then click the Format button.**

Excel brings up the Format Cells dialog box (see Figure 35-5).

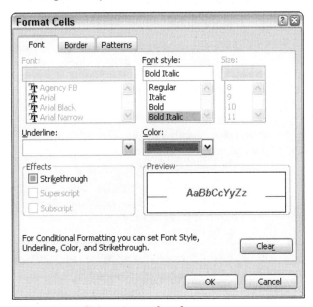

• **Figure 35-5: Pick an in-yer-face font.**

9. **Choose a font treatment that really stands out — something you can see from 30,000 feet. When you have made a literally outstanding selection, click OK twice to return to the spreadsheet.**

The details are up to you, but note that you can't change the font itself or its size. Choose a font style. If you like, add an underline, a color, and strikethrough formatting. Click the Border tab and pick a border. Or, click Patterns and pick both a cell-shading color and a pattern.

10. **Set the Zoom setting on the Standard toolbar to 50% or smaller so that you can see a big chunk of the spreadsheet. Then keep pressing F9.**

If you have a buggy version of Excel 2003, sooner or later, you see a pattern such as the one in Figure 35-6.

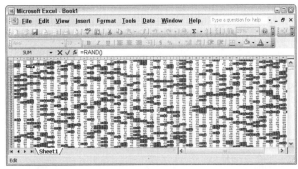

• **Figure 35-6: The specially formatted cells are negative — a very graphic demonstration of the =RAND() bug in Excel 2003.**

If you have a buggy copy of Excel 2003, drop me a line, and I'll point you to the patch (which wasn't available for download as this book went to press): talk2woody@woodyswatch.com.

Running Self-Verifying Cross-Totals

In the preceding section, I show you how to tell Excel that you want to apply a specific format, dependent on the value of the cell. In this section,

I take conditional formatting one step further and show you how to create self-verifying totals in spreadsheets, complete with warnings if something goes out of kilter.

If you build giant spreadsheets for a living, day in and day out, you've probably amassed a complete arsenal of tools to help make sure that your spreadsheets balance properly and that they don't get knocked out of whack by someone absent-mindedly entering data in the wrong place.

Those of us who build small spreadsheets, primarily for our own use or for folks in our immediate workgroup, don't need (or want!) those battleship solutions. Fortunately, though, Excel has a handful of very powerful tools that we mere mortals can use every day.

 In Technique 34, I talk about the Formula Auditing toolbar, which is a very powerful and easy-to-use tool to track how cells are being used in a spreadsheet. That toolbar should be your first line of defense in building a spreadsheet. If you can't see the Formula Auditing toolbar, choose View➪Toolbars and mark the Formula Auditing check box. I discuss how to use it a little later in this Technique.

The most common kind of misbalanced spreadsheet that I encounter involves taking totals horizontally and vertically — *cross-totals* — and the totals don't add up. Argg. Typically, the spreadsheet starts out okay, but when I add a row or a column, the totals get thrown off. Sometimes, somebody (and I won't mention him by name) types over the top of a total — and when one of the numbers later changes, the totals don't.

Here's a fast and easy way to verify totals in a spreadsheet and throw a red flag if they don't balance. The example that I use here is quite simple, so you don't have to type a lot of numbers. But the approach

works — and works well — on spreadsheets that are far larger and more complex.

Here's how to make mortal-proof cross-totals:

1. **Create a simple table, like the one in Figure 35-7.**

You need a few columns and a few rows. Figure 35-7 lists production figures for my fruit farms in four Southeast Asian countries. (And if you've never tasted — much less smelled — a durian, count yourself lucky.)

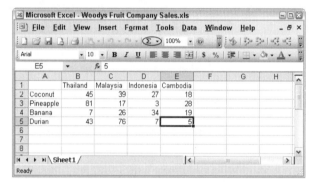

• **Figure 35-7:** Woodys Fruit Company production in four countries.

2. **Create a cross-total in the first row by clicking the final cell (F2), clicking the AutoSum icon (looks like a sigma, Σ) on the Standard toolbar, and then pressing Enter.**

A total appears in the cell.

3. **With the total cell still selected, click the Trace Precedents icon (the second one) on the Formula Auditing toolbar.**

You can immediately see that the sum covers the four numbers that it should (see Figure 35-8). See, I told you this is a very powerful toolbar!

4. **Click the drag handle in the lower-right corner of the total (cell F2 in my example) and copy the =SUM() formula all the way down to the end of the last data row.**

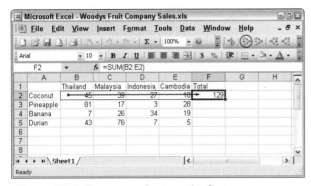

• **Figure 35-8:** Trace precedents on the first row sum.

5. **Click at the bottom of the first data column, click the AutoSum icon on the Standard toolbar, and then press Enter.**

   You get a column sum, like the one in cell B6 of Figure 35-9.

![Microsoft Excel - Woodys Fruit Company Sales.xls, B6 =SUM(B2:B5)]

• **Figure 35-9:** The sum for the first column.

6. **Click the drag handle on cell B6 and copy the =SUM() formula all the way to the last data row, cell E6 (see Figure 35-10).**

7. **Click in the grand total cell (cell F6 in my example).**

   In this cell, I want to tell Excel, "If the total of all the columns and the total of all the rows is equal, use that total. But if it isn't equal, something's wrong, so scream real loud." Here's how to, uh, scream. Real loud.

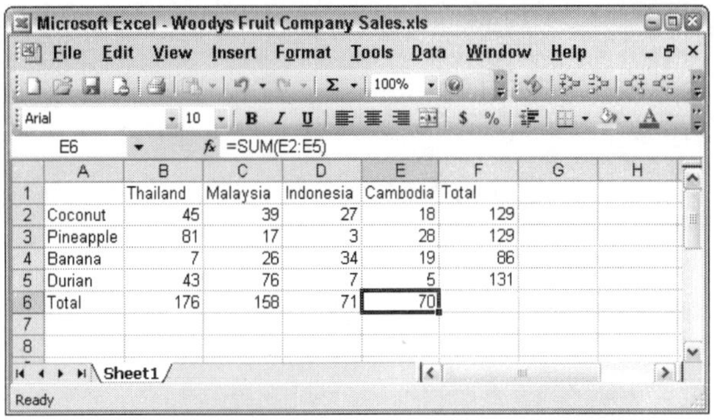

![Microsoft Excel - Woodys Fruit Company Sales.xls, E6 =SUM(E2:E5)]

• **Figure 35-10:** Cross-foot totals in both directions are complete.

8. **I could use the Insert Function icon (the one that looks like *fx* next to where you type stuff for the cells), but this formula is easy enough to type directly. Type this, with no spaces:**

   =IF(SUM(F2:F5)=SUM(B6:E6),SUM(F2:F5), "OUT OF BALANCE")

   That tells Excel that if the sum of the column totals and the sum of the row totals is equal, use the row totals. But if it isn't equal, put in the text OUT OF BALANCE.

   Figure 35-11 shows totals that are okay, and Figure 35-12 shows what happens when I throw the totals out of balance by typing 3 in cell E6.

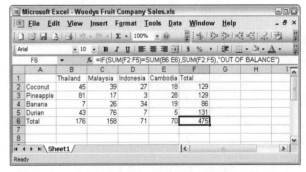

• **Figure 35-11:** If the totals balance, use the number; otherwise, use the text.

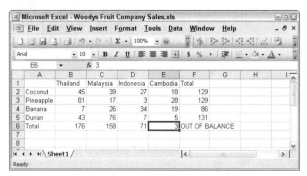

• **Figure 35-12:** If somebody accidentally types over a total, the spreadsheet reports that it's out of balance.

9. If you test the spreadsheet by stomping on a total, click Undo on the Standard toolbar to bring everything back to its full, upright position.

10. Apply conditional formatting to the text OUT OF BALANCE. Start by clicking the grand total cell (F6 in my case).

11. Choose Format⇨Conditional Formatting.

Excel shows you the Conditional Formatting dialog box (refer to Figure 35-4).

12. In the first box, choose Cell Value Is; in the second box, choose Equal To; and in the third box, type precisely the text that appears when the cross-totals are out of balance (OUT OF BALANCE, in this example).

13. Click the Format button and set the formatting that you want for the OUT OF BALANCE warning: bold italic red font, perhaps. Click OK twice to get back to the spreadsheet.

14. Test the conditional formatting by clicking a total cell — say, E6 again — typing 3, and pressing Enter.

And the crowds go wild (see Figure 35-13).

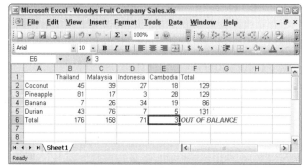

• **Figure 35-13:** Conditional formatting applied to OUT OF BALANCE.

Practice once or twice, and I guarantee this will become your timesaving method of choice for ensuring that cross-foot totals balance.

Technique 36

Freezing Columns and Rows

Save Time By

- ✓ Freezing column headings onscreen so you know what you're seeing

- ✓ Printing headings on every page

- ✓ Hiding rows and columns so you can scan faster

- ✓ Making an elbow in the upper-left cell

How many times have you scrolled down in a spreadsheet and then had to scroll back to the top to figure out what in the %$#@! you were looking at? Do you have the same problem with printouts, where the column headings for page 327 appear on page 1 . . . and page 1 alone?

It's easy to get Excel to show and print column and row headings precisely the way you want them. It's also easy to hide rows and columns so your eyes don't get distracted by meaningless detail. A few quick clicks, and you can be concentrating on what the data means — not wondering what in the heck you're looking at. So much time has been lost over something so simple.

Freezing Column Headings

Any spreadsheet with column headings that has enough rows to extend below the bottom of the screen is a good candidate to have its headings frozen. To freeze column headings so that they stay in place onscreen, do the following

1. **Click the row underneath the column heading(s) that you want to freeze.**

In Figure 36-1, I want to freeze the first row, so I click the second row.

• **Figure 36-1:** The trick to freezing row headings is to click underneath the row(s) you want to freeze.

	A	B	C	D	E	F
1	Date	Supplies	Other	Description	From Bank	Balance
2	1-Dec-03			Balance Forward		462.25
3	3-Dec-03				30,000.00	30,462.25
4		830.00		Gasoline		29,632.25
5		472.50		Lotus		29,159.75
6		2,291.00		Promphan		26,868.75
7		515.00		The deli		26,353.75
8		100.00		Patong best team		26,253.75

Microsoft Excel - Operating Expenses.xls

A2   12/1/2003

Sheets: 2003 10 / 2003 11 / 2003 12

Ready   Sum=7-Mar-05

2. Choose Window⇨Freeze Panes.

From that point on, the headings stay put while you scroll the data up and down (see Figure 36-2).

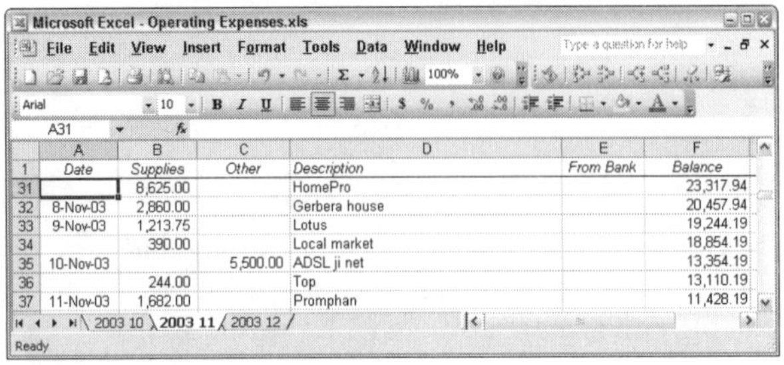

• **Figure 36-2:** The data scrolls while the headings stay frozen onscreen.

  Freezing the screen doesn't affect what's printed.

To freeze row headings (that is, to make specific columns appear onscreen while the rest of the data scrolls), click the column to the right of the headings that you want to freeze and then choose Window⇨ Freeze Panes.

To freeze both column headings and row headings, click the cell immediately to the right and below the headings you want to freeze (which is to say, click the upper-left cell that you want to be able to move) and then choose Window⇨Freeze Panes.

You can't freeze arbitrary rows or columns: Excel only allows you to freeze the row(s) on top and/or the column(s) on the left.

To unfreeze all the frozen columns and rows in a spreadsheet, choose Window⇨Unfreeze Panes.

Splitting the Screen

You can split the Excel screen into two or four panes, and each pane can be scrolled to any part of the spreadsheet. That can come in very handy if you need

to be in two places at once — er, if you want to look at two or four parts of a spreadsheet simultaneously.

Although splitting the screen is inherently a little different from freezing headings (see the preceding section), Excel doesn't allow you to freeze headings and split the screen at the same time.

To split the screen, first choose how many panes you want and how they will appear:

✔ **To split the screen horizontally into two panes (one on top of the other):** Select the row that you want to become the top row of the lower pane.

✔ **To split the screen vertically into two panes (side by side):** Select the column that you want to become the leftmost column of the right pane.

✔ **To split the screen into four panes (like a 2 x 2 paned window):** Click a cell, which becomes the upper-left cell of the lower-right pane.

Then choose Window⇨Split, and Excel splits the window into two or four panes, depending on your choice. Figure 36-3 shows a split into two horizontal panes, top and bottom. Each pane can be scrolled independently.

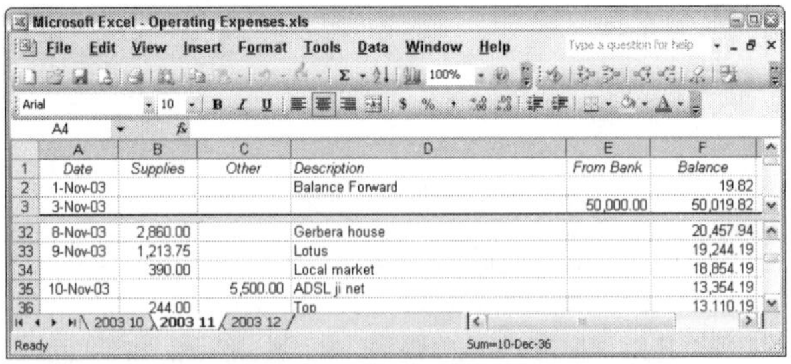

• **Figure 36-3:** Split panes work differently from frozen headings because each pane can be scrolled anywhere in the spreadsheet.

To get rid of the split, choose Window⇨ Remove Split.

Printing Repeating Column Headings

Frequently, you want to repeat column headings at the top of every page in a printout — for precisely the same reason why you might want to freeze column headings onscreen. It's easy:

1. **Choose File⇨Page Setup⇨Sheet.**

Excel shows you the Sheet tab of the Page Setup dialog box, as shown in Figure 36-4.

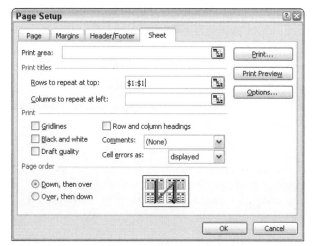

• **Figure 36-4: Set repeating column headings here.**

2. **Click once inside the Rows to Repeat at Top box.**

Your cursor turns into a right-pointing arrow.

Note: The Row and Column Headings check box in the middle of the Page Setup dialog box is very confusing. If you enable this setting, Excel prints the A/B/C column identifiers and the 1/2/3 row identifiers along with the data in the spreadsheet. You don't get row or column headings that you've entered.

3. **Back in your spreadsheet, click once anywhere in the row that you wish to repeat on every page.**

If you want to repeat more than one column heading, click and drag the right-pointing arrow cursor over all the rows with column headings that you want to print.

You can have row headings repeated on every page, too, by using a similar approach. In Step 2, click in the Columns to Repeat at Left box (refer to Figure 36-4) and make your selection. The same click-and-drag method mentioned in Step 3 works here, too.

4. **Click Print Preview.**

You should look at the printout at least once before wasting paper.

5. **When the print preview appears (see Figure 36-5), click Next in the upper-left corner.**

That puts you on to page 2 — the first place where you can see whether your repeated column headings are working.

• **Figure 36-5: Make sure you preview the printout at least once.**

6. **If it looks good, click Print.**

If it doesn't look good, click Close and try again.

> If your page doesn't look right, you need to go back to the Page Setup dialog box; clicking the Setup button in Print Preview won't get you to the settings you need.

Hiding Rows and Columns

Inevitably, any large spreadsheet grows rows and columns that you really don't want to look at: interim calculations, extraneous details, and sort fields can all slow you down when you really want to look at the meat of the report.

 When you hide a row or a column, it doesn't appear on printouts or onscreen. You must unhide the row or column before it will appear on the printed page.

 Hiding is not a security measure. Anybody vaguely familiar with Excel will notice that a column is missing — for example, when a spreadsheet jumps from column B to column D, it's a dead giveaway. In addition, there's a visual cue — a slightly widened line between columns when the column in between has been hidden.

It's easy to hide a row or column:

1. **Select the row or column.**

2. **Right-click it and choose Hide.**

In Figure 36-6, I hide column C. Note that the calculations remain the same — Excel still acknowledges that there's data in the hidden cell and uses it appropriately.

• **Figure 36-6:** Column C has been hidden. Notice the slightly thickened line between columns B and D.

To unhide a row or column

1. **Select the rows or columns surrounding the hidden row or column.**

In Figure 36-7, I select both columns B and D.

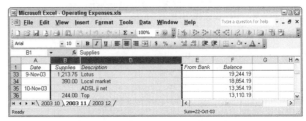

• **Figure 36-7:** To unhide, select the columns before and after the hidden column.

2. **Right-click in one of the selected areas and choose Unhide.**

The prodigal column C returns (see Figure 36-8).

• **Figure 36-8:** Column C gets unhidden.

Bending an Elbow at A1

Excel titles can look so hokey. Frequently, all I want to do is put a short label in the upper-left corner of a spreadsheet that identifies both the columns and the rows. It's called an *elbow,* and you can make one very quickly:

1. **In the cell, type the column heading label, press Alt+Enter, and then type the label for the row headings. Adjust the height and width of**

cell A1 by clicking and dragging its edges until the column label appears on top and the row label appears on the bottom.

In Figure 36-9, I pressed Alt+Enter and then typed **Fruit**. I jimmied the width and height of cell A1 until the labels looked about right, adding a few spaces to balance it all out.

2. **On the Drawing toolbar, click the Line tool (to the right of AutoShapes) and draw a diagonal line in cell A1.**

After a little more dragging and cajoling, and bold formatting for the text, my final elbow looks like Figure 36-9.

• **Figure 36-9:** The final elbow.

37 Technique

Ripping through Lists

Save Time By

✔ Setting up lists so they work right — the first time

✔ Using forms to create and maintain lists fast

✔ Enlisting AutoComplete to do your work

Excel makes a great flat-file database program.

No, I'm not supposed to say that. The Party Line dictates that Access takes the accolades for databases, which is great if you need third-normalized-form linked databases with robust query capabilities, sophisticated data integrity features, and reporting sliced and diced through an electronic Veg-o-Matic. But if you just need to keep track of the inventory in your small business, monthly budgets, kids in your Scout troop, or CDs in your collection, a flat-file database works well enough.

In Excel-speak, a *flat-file database* is called a *list*. Excel lists can hold enormous volumes of information, which you can manipulate in a New Yawk minute. If you have a list, subtotaling and totaling is easy and near invisible (see Technique 38). They form the foundation for well-behaved pivot charts (see Technique 41).

If you have a lot of data, use a list.

Making a List, Checking It Twice

A *list* is just a bunch of data in an Excel spreadsheet. Each column (analogous to a *field* in the database world) contains a specific kind of data — a salesperson's name, the date, or the amount sold, for example. Each row (analogous to a *record* in the database world) contains a single entry in the database. Er, list. The only real restriction in Excel is that you should never have a completely blank row or column. (When Excel hits a blank row or column, it thinks that you might be trying to start a new list.)

In earlier versions of Excel, you had to set up a list manually, putting a row of headings — field names, if you will — at the top. Starting with Excel 2003, Excel can do it all for you.

1. Start with a new spreadsheet.

2. Type the column headings — the field names — for your list in the first row.

I start a list for Woodys Fruit Company Sales Log by typing headings in A1, B1, and so on until F1.

Each column heading must be unique — you can't use the same text for two different headings.

3. Choose Data⇨List⇨Create List.

Excel responds with the Create List dialog box, also shown in Figure 37-1.

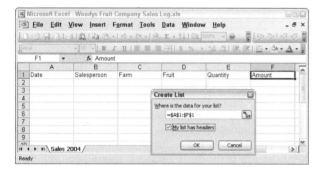

• **Figure 37-1:** Define where the list is.

4. Excel probably chose the row of headings for you. If it didn't, click and drag across all the headings.

The Where Is the Data for Your List? box should show the cells that you select.

5. Mark the My List Has Headers check box. Then click OK.

Excel responds by creating the list, as shown in Figure 37-2.

The list in Figure 37-2 is remarkable for two reasons. One, the headings are set up with AutoFilter drop-down arrows (see the final section in this Technique). Two, Excel reserves one row at the bottom of the list — the *insert row*, with an asterisk placeholder — for new data. Both are great timesavers. The AutoFilter lets you select and sort quickly; the insert row lets you put more data in the list, adjusting the range automatically.

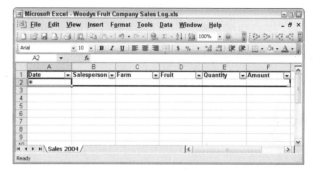

• **Figure 37-2:** The list appears in a flash.

6. To apply formatting to any columns that need it, select the column and then choose Format⇨Cells.

In this example, I format the Date field to appear as Month-Year (Mar-01), the Quantity field as a number with one decimal place, and the Amount field as currency with two decimal places and a dollar sign.

7. Click row 2 (just click the numeral 2) to select the entire second row.

8. Choose Window⇨Freeze Panes.

The column headings are frozen onscreen. (See Technique 36 for more on freezing headings.)

That's all it takes to create a heavy-duty list.

You can start entering data directly in the list, or you can follow the steps in the next section to have Excel build a custom data entry form for you.

If you enter data manually, you can resize the list by clicking any cell in the list, choosing Data➪List➪Resize List, and then dragging the pulsating outline to extend the size of the old list.

Entering Data Manually with a Form

Excel's custom-built data entry form can be an enormous help if you need to enter different data in each row or if most of the data that you enter isn't text.

By far the simplest, fastest, and least error-prone way to enter data in an Excel list is by using a data entry form created by Excel itself. Here's how:

1. **Use the procedure in the preceding section to create a list. Click once anywhere inside the list.**

2. **Choose Data➪Form.**

Excel constructs a data entry form on-the-fly, using the list's column headings for field names.

3. **Type the data for a record on the form.**

In Figure 37-3, I type a record for Justin selling durian from the farm in Thailand in January, 2004.

• **Figure 37-3:** Entering the first record (row) for the list.

4. **Press the down-arrow key, press Enter, or click the New button of the data entry form.**

Excel enters the record into the list, as you might expect, but it also expands the list by one row, moving the asterisk-marked insert row down by one (see Figure 37-4).

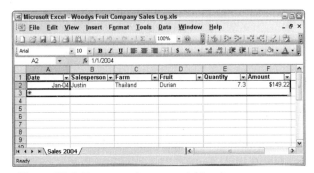

• **Figure 37-4:** Data goes in very quickly when you use Excel's form.

If you press the up- and down-arrow keys, you quickly discover that the data entry form moves from record to record — which is to say, row to row — in the list. You can use the data entry form to make changes or delete records.

If you delete a record, be very aware of the fact that you can't undo the delete: When you use the form, deleted rows are well and truly gone.

Filling In Data with AutoComplete

If you have text entries that repeat in several columns — say, a name that appears over and over again, or a city — you'll find it faster to type data directly into the list via Excel's AutoComplete capability.

Here's how to use AutoComplete to add a new record:

1. **Choose Tools⊏>Options⊏>Edit. Select the Move Selection After Enter check box. Choose the direction Right and then click OK.**

If you're entering data in a list, you probably want Excel to move to the next cell to the right every time you press Enter. Excel is smart enough to realize when it reaches the last column in a row, automatically jumping to the first cell in the next row.

2. **Click the cell with the asterisk.**

That's the first cell in the row that Excel automatically maintains to add new items to your list.

3. **Type the data for the first cell and then press Enter.**

Excel goes to the next field in the record, er, column in the row.

4. **Start typing.**

If you're typing in a column that contains text and the text that you're typing matches another entry in the column, Excel suggests an AutoComplete for you (see Figure 37-5). The AutoComplete appears in white on a black background.

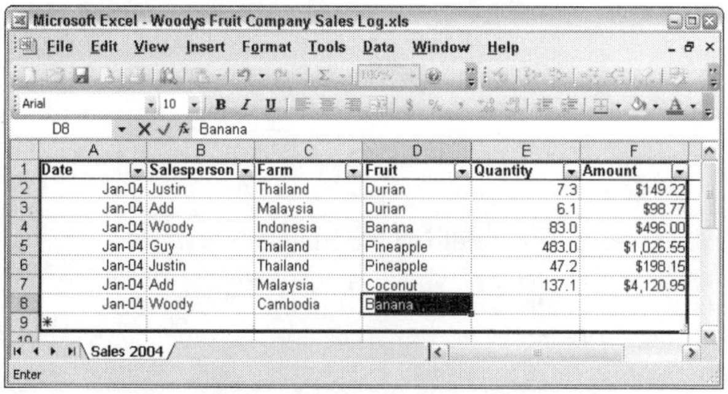

• **Figure 37-5:** AutoComplete suggestions appear if you begin to type text that matches some other entry in the list.

5. **If you want to accept the AutoComplete suggestion, press Enter or any directional arrow.**

Excel moves on to the next cell.

 If you want to choose from among the AutoComplete entries without typing anything, press Alt+↓. Use the up- and down-arrow keys to choose from the list and then press Enter when you find the one you want.

 Unfortunately, AutoComplete doesn't work in data entry forms. It also doesn't work for numbers or dates. But when it works, it's a time-saver of the first degree.

AutoFiltering to Find Stuff Fast

When you create a list from the method in the first section in this Technique, Excel 2003 also creates AutoFilters on all the columns. That's what those down arrows on the right side of the headings are for.

In earlier versions of Excel, or if you didn't follow the directions here, you can create AutoFilters on all the columns by clicking inside the list and then choosing Data⊏>Filter⊏>AutoFilter.

AutoFilters let you restrict the visible portion of the list:

1. **Click the down arrow next to the field (column) that you want to limit.**

You see a list of available AutoFilters. In Figure 37-6, I click the down arrow next to Salesperson.

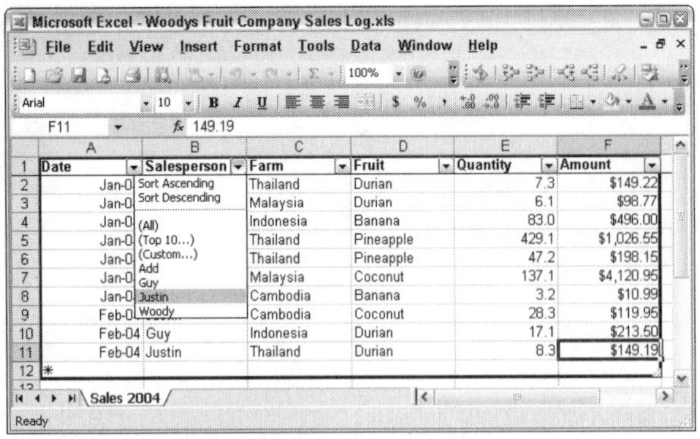

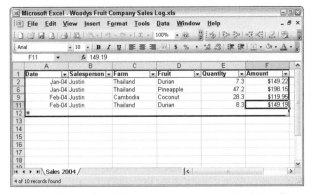

• **Figure 37-6:** AutoFilters allow you to restrict the visible list to the items listed in Table 37-1.

2. Choose one of the AutoFilter options described in Table 37-1.

Excel restricts the list to the option you choose. In Figure 37-7, I show only those sales made by Justin.

Note the row numbers on the left, which correspond to the full list's row (record) numbers.

3. You can further restrict the list by clicking the down arrow on a different heading and choosing another AutoFilter criterion.

• **Figure 37-7:** I filtered this list to show only Justin's sales.

4. To remove AutoFiltering on a particular column, click the down arrow and choose (All).

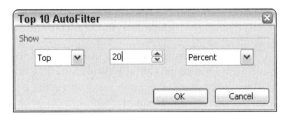

• **Figure 37-8:** Even Excel has to have a Top Ten.

TABLE 37-1: AUTOFILTER CHOICES

Choice	What It Means	Timesaving Tip
(All)	Don't autofilter this column.	When you remove autofiltering, the records reappear in their original order.
(Top 10)	Show the largest or smallest numbers.	When you choose this AutoFilter on a column of numbers, Excel shows you the Top 10 AutoFilter dialog box (see Figure 37-8), from which you can choose the largest (or smallest) numbers, either by number (such as Bottom 5) or percent (such as Top 20 Percent).
Blanks	Show only records with blanks in the indicated field.	Use this to clean up a list.
Non-blanks	Show only records without blanks in the indicated field.	Use to ignore blank (presumably bad) records.
(Custom)	Use Excel's custom AutoFilter settings to compare values in two columns.	See Custom AutoFilter in online Help.

Running Subtotals

Save Time By

- ✔ Creating totals and subtotals with a few quick clicks
- ✔ Filtering data to restrict totals and subtotals
- ✔ Re-sorting and totaling quickly and accurately

Anybody with a long list of data will, at some point, wonder about subtotals and totals. How many widgets did each of your top salespeople peddle? Which store had the most charitable donations?

If you try to use Excel's native SUM() and SUBTOTAL() functions, you'll get the right result. Eventually. If you try hard enough.

But if you set up your data properly — in a list, as I describe in Technique 37 — and use the tools that Excel provides, running totals and subtotals (and Averages and Max's and Min's) by this or by that, including these things or excluding those things, takes just a few clicks.

Very powerful. Almost always accurate. And fast, fast, fast.

AutoFiltering Totals

If you just want a total, click the AutoSum button (look for the sigma, Σ) on the Standard toolbar, drag the flashing selection to cover the numbers you want, press Enter, and you're done.

But what if you want to look at totals for different groups of data — say, total sales for a particular salesperson, or total sales for a specific product, or total sales for a specific product by a particular salesperson? I know a fast, easy way that doesn't involve pivot tables or any particularly obtuse magic.

The trick lies in turning your data into a bona fide, Excel-recognized list. After that, cranking out a total is easy.

Setting up data for AutoFiltering

To make a list, you have two choices:

- ✔ **Build a list from the ground up.** If you have Excel 2003, follow the steps in Technique 37.

- ✔ **Convert your existing data into a list.** This is the only option in Excel 2002 and earlier.

Here is the fastest and cleanest way to convert existing data into a list:

1. **Use File⇨Save As to save the current spreadsheet with a new name (so you don't clobber the current spreadsheet). If you prefer, you can copy the data into a new spreadsheet.**

In Figure 38-1, I copy a bunch of sales data for Woodys Fruit Company into a new spreadsheet.

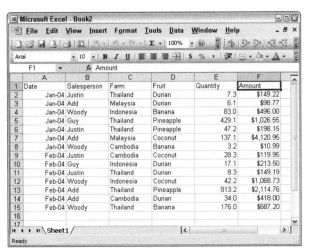

• **Figure 38-1: Start by selecting raw data to convert into a list.**

2. **Delete any empty rows. Delete any empty columns. If possible, type the correct data in any empty cells.**

To delete a row, select the whole row and then choose Edit⇨Delete. I need to delete the two empty rows (rows 4 and 10) in Figure 38-1.

3. **Put headings at the top of every column (see Figure 38-2).**

If you need to insert a new row at the top for the headings, select the top row and then choose Insert⇨Rows.

Each column heading must be different. For example, you can't have two columns called *Name*.

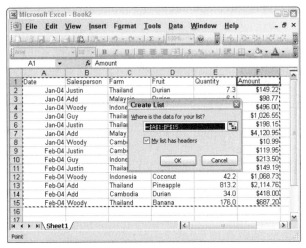

• **Figure 38-2: Add column headings to every column.**

4. **Choose Data⇨List⇨Create List.**

Excel shows you the Create List dialog box (see Figure 38-3).

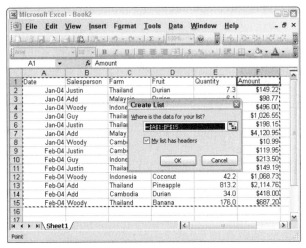

• **Figure 38-3: Convert the data to a bona fide list.**

5. **If Excel didn't select the correct region for the list, click and drag the outline to cover the list that you want. Select the My List Has Headers check box and then click OK.**

Excel creates a real list, with AutoFilter drop-down arrows for each column (see Figure 38-4).

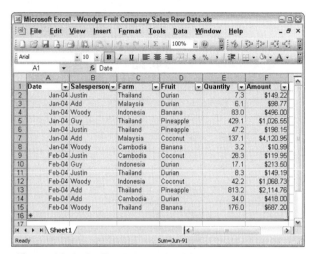

• **Figure 38-4:** An Excel-recognized list.

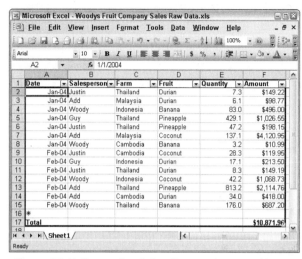

• **Figure 38-5:** If your data is in a list, running a total is easy.

6. Select the second row (click the numeral 2 on the far-left column) and then choose Window⇨ Freeze Panes.

That freezes the column headings so that they're always visible, even if you scroll way down in the list.

Generating the totals

After your data is in a bona fide list — with those drop-down arrows next to each column heading — running totals (Averages, Max's, Min's, and so on) couldn't be simpler. Now you can also easily autofilter a list and see totals of any combination of criteria that you choose:

1. Click inside the list.

2. Choose Data⇨List⇨Total Row.

Excel adds a row at the bottom of the list, entitled Total, that includes a decent guess at exactly what you wanted to total (see Figure 38-5).

3. If you want any other columns totaled, click the appropriate cell in the Total row, click the down arrow that appears to the right, and then select the function that you like.

In Figure 38-6, I put the sum of the Quantity column on the Total row, too.

E	
▼ **Quantity** ▼	Amc
7.3	
6.1	
83.0	
429.1	
47.2	
137.1	
3.2	
28.3	
17.1	
8.3	
42.2	
813.2	
34.0	
176.0	
1,832.1 ▼	$

None
Average
Count
Count Nums
Max
Min
Sum
StdDev
Var

• **Figure 38-6:** Add more columns to the Total row, if you like.

4. To see a subset of the data, use the AutoFilter arrows to the right of each column's heading (see Technique 37).

In Figure 38-7, I select Justin from the Salesperson drop-down AutoFilter list. Note how the sum changes from 1,832.1 to 91.1 to reflect only the sum of the quantity of fruit that Justin sold.

• **Figure 38-7:** Totals for Justin only.

Showing Subtotals

Although the simplest, fastest method of displaying totals and filtered totals revolves around bona fide Excel lists, the quickest way I know to see subtotals and totals requires you to get rid of the "official" list and turn it into a plain, old everyday Excel range. Subtotals are a pain in the neck with bona fide lists. They're easy as can be with a plane range.

 If your data is in an official list, you can see drop-down arrows next to the heading on each column. To convert it to a range, just click once inside the list and then choose Data➪ Lists➪Convert to Range. It's that simple. Excel changes the formatting when you go back and forth, but the data remains the same.

When the data you want to subtotal is in a range, here's how to get the subtotals you want:

1. Figure out which column(s) you want to subtotal. Sort the column by clicking once in the column and then clicking the Sort Ascending icon (looks like an A stacked on a Z, with a down arrow on the right) on the Standard toolbar.

In Figure 38-8, I sort by Fruit.

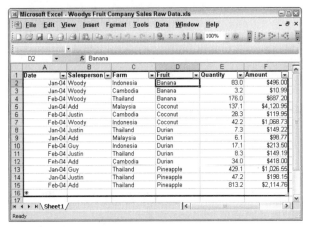

• **Figure 38-8:** Sort on the column that you want to subtotal.

 You can create subtotals within subtotals. To do so, you need to sort by the major column and then by the minor column. In this example, to produce subtotals by Farm within Salesperson, you need to first sort by Salesperson; then, within each Salesperson, sort by Farm. Although Excel has lots of fancy ways to sort by anything under the sun, the fastest way to sort for Salesperson/Farm subtotals is to use the Sort Ascending icon to first sort by Farm and then by Salesperson.

2. Choose Data➪Subtotals.

Excel shows you the Subtotal dialog box in Figure 38-9.

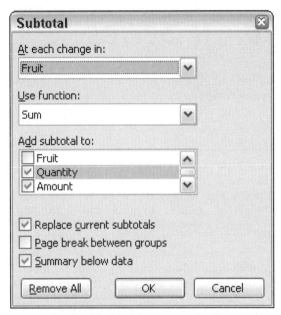

• **Figure 38-9: Set subtotals here.**

3. **Choose the breakpoint where you want subtotals to appear in the At Each Change In dropdown list.**

   In this case, I want a subtotal to show up every time the Fruit field changes.

4. **Pick the function from the Use Function dropdown list.**

   You can choose from Sum (which is the subtotal), Count, Average, Max, Min, Standard Deviation, and more. I want the sum.

5. **Pick the columns that you wish to subtotal by marking the check boxes in Add Subtotal To.**

   I want subtotals on the Quantity and the Amount. If you mark the Summary Below Data box, Excel puts the subtotal at the end, which is where you

usually see subtotals. Leave the check box cleared to get the subtotals at the top.

6. **Click OK.**

   Excel shows you both subtotals for each kind of Fruit and a Grand Total at the bottom (see Figure 38-10).

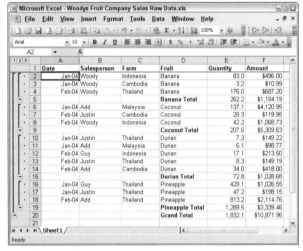

• **Figure 38-10: Subtotals and grand totals are that fast and easy.**

 To hide or expand groups of data, click the + and − signs on the far left (refer to Figure 38-10).

 To remove all the subtotals in a list, choose Data⇨Subtotals; in the Subtotal dialog box (see Figure 38-9), click Remove All.

Pivot tables (see Technique 40) give you much more flexibility, but they're also much more difficult to set up and substantially harder (and slower) to use, particularly if you're not accustomed to how they work. For many situations, lists, and subtotals give you the most timesaving bang for the buck.

Technique 39

Creating Custom AutoFill Series

Save Time By

- ✔ Knowing how to coerce Excel's click-and-drag, built-in AutoFills
- ✔ Making your own AutoFill series when Excel's won't do
- ✔ Combining a little experience and treachery to fill data fast

No doubt (okay, almost little doubt) you've used Excel's AutoFill feature to fill cells with a range of numbers or dates, or maybe the names of days of the week or months. If your list was anything more complex than a sequence of numbers, no doubt you've also had quite a time explaining to Excel exactly what you wanted to do.

Excel makes it very, very easy to convert any sequence into a custom AutoFill series if you've already typed the sequence in a spreadsheet. If you're a teacher, you can make an AutoFill series type the names of all your students — one simple click-and-drag does all the work. If you're forever typing all your branch office names, a custom AutoFill series means that you type it once, click, and drag . . . and it's done. Need a list of house addresses? Names of the U.S. Senators? All the teams in the NFL? Numbers from one to a hundred in pig Latin? Got it, done it, angbay, angbay, angbay.

This Technique shows you how.

Using Fill Lists

Before you consider building your own custom AutoFill series, take a moment to see whether Excel already has one for you:

1. **Start with a clean spreadsheet.**

2. **In cell A1, type** Mon.

   Mon, of course, stands for Monday (see Figure 39-1). Other valid text entries are listed in Table 39-1.

3. **Hover your mouse over the lower-right corner of the cell and jiggle it around until it turns into a big bold + sign.**

TABLE 39-1: TEXT AUTOFILL RECOGNIZES

Enter This	AutoFill Produces This
January	The full month name; February, March, April, and so on.
Jan	An abbreviated month name; Feb, Mar, Apr, and so on.
Monday	The full day name; Tuesday, Wednesday, Thursday, and so on.
Mon	An abbreviated day name; Tue, Wed, Thu, and so on.
Almost any date	AutoFill also recognizes dates in just about any form: Mar 28 autofills into Mar 29, Mar 30, Mar 31, Apr 1, Apr 2, and so on. June 2004 (which Excel interprets as June 1, 2004) autofills to June 2, 2004 and so on, but if you click the AutoFill Options Smart Tag, you can tell it to increment by months or years.
Q1	Q2, Q3, Q4, Q1, Q2, and so on.
Qtr 1	Qtr 2, Qtr 3, Qtr 4, Qtr 1, and so on.
Quarter 1	Quarter 2, Quarter 3, Quarter 4, Quarter 1, and so on.
1st	Ordinals; 2nd, 3rd, 4th, 5th, and so on.
Any text with a number (such as Part 1)	The text stays the same, but the number is incremented; Part 2, Part 3, Part 4, Part 5, and so on.

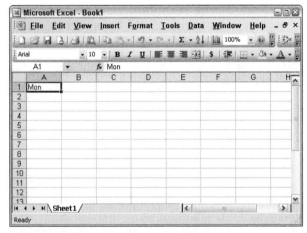

• **Figure 39-1:** Just another manic Monday.

4. **Left-click and drag down for a dozen cells or so.**

   Note that Excel displays a small screen tip (in Figure 39-2, it reads Thu) that tells you what will be filled.

5. **Release the mouse button.**

   Excel autofills the series for you (see Figure 39-3), using its best guess for what you wanted.

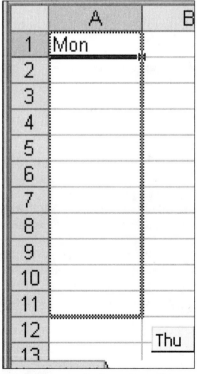

• **Figure 39-2:** The screen tip shows the value that will be filled.

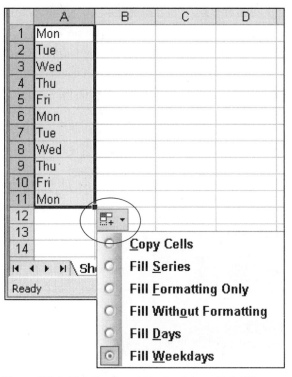

• **Figure 39-3:** Excel guesses that you wanted days of the week.

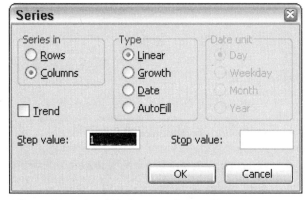

• **Figure 39-4:** Use the Smart Tag to change AutoFill characteristics.

6. **Immediately after you let go of the mouse button, Excel shows you an AutoFill Options Smart Tag. If you didn't get the AutoFill series that you wanted, click the Smart Tag to see whether Excel has the one you want.**

In Figure 39-4, I tell Excel that I really only want Fill Weekdays. AutoFill goes back and fills Mon through Fri, skipping over Sat and Sun.

Numbers can be incremented many ways. If you want greater control over how a number series gets autofilled, either start by selecting two or more numbers in a series (for example, selecting two adjacent cells with the values 1 and 3 and then autofilling produces 5, 7, 9, and so on), or right-click to autofill and choose Series. If you choose Series, the Series dialog box appears (see Figure 39-5), and you can choose from a large number of options.

• **Figure 39-5:** AutoFill can even do trend lines.

Excel's built-in AutoFill series are remarkably adaptable, if you care to push them a little bit. Table 39-1 should give you a hint at the kinds of things that you can do without typing much at all. If you think that Excel might be able to autofill something, give it a try! It's fast.

Making Your Own AutoFill Series

If you ever type the same series of values more than once, take a second and turn that series into a custom AutoFill series. You'll never have to type it again!

Before you create a custom AutoFill series, you should pause for a minute and think about how you'll use it. There's a trick with custom series, and it can make a big difference as to how quickly you can use the series.

Here's the dilemma: Excel identifies a series by the first item in the series. The only way you have to tell Excel which series to use is by typing out the first item in its entirety. For example:

✔ If you have a series of NFL football teams that starts with *Broncos,* all you have to do is type **Broncos**, click the AutoFill handle, drag, and the list appears in your spreadsheet. Ingobay.

✔ But if you have a nasty, long series — something like company departments that starts out *Human Resources and Personal Achievement Recognition Department of Redundancy Department,* you have to type *all* that text before Excel can find the AutoFill series that you want. Ukyay.

Before you create your series, you need to decide whether you can arrange the list so that a short, unique name appears at the top of the series. I stress *unique* because no two custom AutoFill series can start with the same name.

 If you can't put a short name at the top of the series, consider sticking a *list handle* there — a short, easy-to-remember, easy-to-type word that will make your custom listing, uh, experience a bit less tedious.

 The problem with using a list handle is that the list handle itself gets inserted into the spreadsheet, so you either have to delete it, move the series over the top of the list handle, or figure out some way to ignore it.

After you decide whether you need a list handle, here's the fast way to convert an already typed bunch of text into a custom AutoFill series:

1. **If you have a list handle, put it at the top of the list.**

In Figure 39-6, I have a list of student's names. At the top, I type **Students** in the first cell. By putting a list handle in the first cell, it's easy to remember and use the custom AutoFill series. (It will also be easier than remembering to type **Mary M**, and I can continue to use Students even if Mary M leaves my class.)

	A
1	Students
2	Mary M
3	Panthip
4	Bill
5	Dina
6	Aretha
7	James
8	Henry
9	Jose
10	John
11	Alyssa
12	Nicole
13	Stephen A
14	Stephen R
15	Ling

• **Figure 39-6: The prospective custom AutoFill series, with a name for the series on top.**

2. Select all the names in the custom AutoFill series.

3. Choose Tools⇨Options⇨Custom Lists.

You see the Options dialog box, as shown in Figure 39-7.

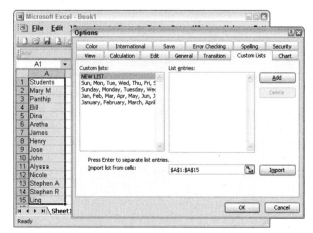

• **Figure 39-7:** Your custom AutoFill series is ready to import.

4. Click the Import button.

Excel adds the series to the Custom Lists box on the left (see Figure 39-8).

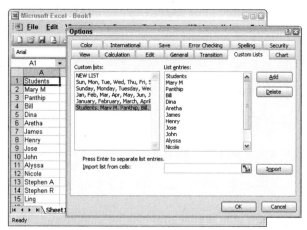

• **Figure 39-8:** The series is imported and ready to use.

5. Click OK.

Excel returns to the spreadsheet.

6. Type the first name in the new AutoFill series and then click the drag-and-fill handle to make sure that it works.

Amazing, eh?

Technique 40

Grabbing the Best with Pivot Tables

In Techniques 37 and 38, I show you fast, easy ways to create lists (read: flat-file databases) in Excel as well as how to sort, filter, total, and subtotal the lists. Although the methods in those Techniques can be mastered by anyone who isn't terrified of numbers, they aren't very flexible. For example, refiguring subtotals for a list takes several steps, and each time that you slice data a different way, you have go back to square one.

To get the most flexibility, you have to invest some time and gray matter in learning how to use pivot tables. They take a while to set up, but after a pivot table is in place, reslicing and dicing the data takes just a click and a drag. Admittedly, it's easy to drag the wrong field to the wrong place, especially when you're just starting, but it's easy to drag the wayward field back.

In this Technique, I take you through the process of creating a pivot table and show you a few ways to use one that might surprise you. The learning curve isn't all that bad — think of it as a speed bump — but the results can save you hours — even days — of work.

Creating a Pivot Table

Pivot tables work with lists. A *list* is just a flat-file database: Each column represents a *field* in the database (such as a name, a part number, or a sales amount); each row represents one *record,* or entry, in the database (say, one record for each sale, each inventory count, or each charitable donation).

You can start with a bona fide Excel-recognized list — one with drop-down AutoFilter arrows next to each column's heading — or you can simply create a list with a heading row at the top and no blank rows in the middle.

✔ If you use Excel 2003 and don't have a list yet, follow the steps in Technique 37 to build a list from scratch.

✔ If you use any other version of Excel, or you already have something that looks like a list, follow the steps at the beginning of Technique 38 to make sure that the heading row is in place and that any blank rows have been deleted.

If you just want to practice, you can download a *big* bunch of sample lists at http://office.microsoft.com/search/redir.aspx? AssetID=DC010554411033.

To create a pivot table

1. **Click once inside a well-formed list.**

2. **Choose Data⇨PivotTable and PivotChart Report.**

Excel's PivotTable and PivotChart Wizard kicks in (see Figure 40-1).

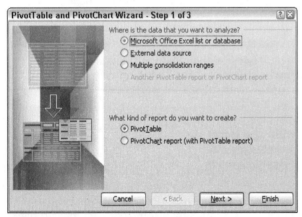

• **Figure 40-1: The wizard takes much of the tedium out of creating a pivot table.**

3. **Select both the Microsoft Office Excel List or Database and the PivotTable radio buttons and then click Next.**

Step 2 of the wizard should identify your list and show marching lines around the column headings and the list itself (see Figure 40-2).

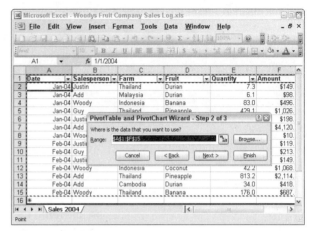

• **Figure 40-2: If you have a list with no blank rows, the wizard identifies it.**

4. **If the wizard found your entire list, click Next. If not, something is likely wrong with the list; click Cancel, fix the list, and start again at Step 1.**

When you click Next, the wizard moves on to its final panel (see Figure 40-3).

• **Figure 40-3: The last step in the wizard.**

5. **Make sure that the New Worksheet radio button is selected and then click Finish.**

Always put the pivot table in a new worksheet. That way, if something goes wrong, you just delete the worksheet and start all over again.

Excel creates a new pivot table on a new sheet. It also brings up the PivotTable toolbar and a list of all available fields (see Figure 40-4).

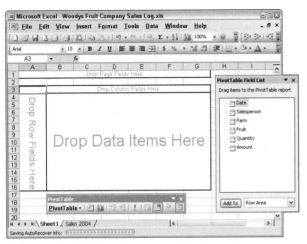

• **Figure 40-4: A pivot table ready for populating.**

6. **To see how a pivot table works, think of how you might want to view the data in the list.**

In this example, I want to look at the amount of sales for each salesperson, broken out by fruit. To do that, I drag Salesperson from the PivotTable Field List and drop it on the block marked Drop Row Fields Here. Then I drag Fruit to Drop Column Fields Here. Finally, I drag Amount into the middle, Drop Data Items Here.

The result is a rather standard-looking spreadsheet showing sales by salesperson by fruit, as shown in Figure 40-5.

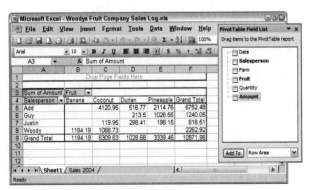

• **Figure 40-5: Drag and drop three fields to create a simple spreadsheet.**

In the next section, I go into detail about slicing and dicing the data.

Manipulating a Pivot Table

After you have a simple pivot table set up as I describe in the preceding section, it's incredibly easy to look at your data in myriad ways.

For example

✔ You want to see how much of the sales in Figure 40-5 occurred for each farm. Drag the Farm field from the field list immediately to the right of the Salesperson field on the pivot table. The result is in Figure 40-6.

✔ You want to look at just Add and Woody's sales. Click the drop-down arrow next to Salesperson and select the boxes marked Add and Woody.

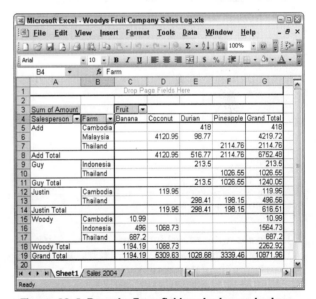

• **Figure 40-6: Drag the Farm field, and sales are broken out by farm.**

The Page box at the top of the spreadsheet is a special location: Drop a field in that box, and Excel creates a separate page for each value of the field. Here's how:

1. **Start with the pivot table in Figure 40-5.**

   It shows sales by salesperson and farm, for each fruit.

2. **Click the Date field in the Field List box and drag it to the location that reads Drop Page Fields Here.**

   Excel shows all the dates initially, so the sales figures don't change (see Figure 40-7).

	A	B	C	D	E	F	G
1	Date	(All)					
2							
3	Sum of Amount		Fruit				
4	Salesperson	Farm	Banana	Coconut	Durian	Pineapple	Grand Total
5	Add	Cambodia			418		418
6		Malaysia		4120.95	98.77		4219.72
7		Thailand				2114.76	2114.76
8	Add Total			4120.95	516.77	2114.76	6752.48
9	Guy	Indonesia			213.5		213.5
10		Thailand				1026.55	1026.55
11	Guy Total				213.5	1026.55	1240.05
12	Justin	Cambodia		119.95			119.95
13		Thailand			298.41	198.15	496.56
14	Justin Total			119.95	298.41	198.15	616.51
15	Woody	Cambodia	10.99				10.99
16		Indonesia	496	1068.73			1564.73
17		Thailand	687.2				687.2
18	Woody Total		1194.19	1068.73			2262.92
19	Grand Total		1194.19	5309.63	1028.68	3339.46	10871.96

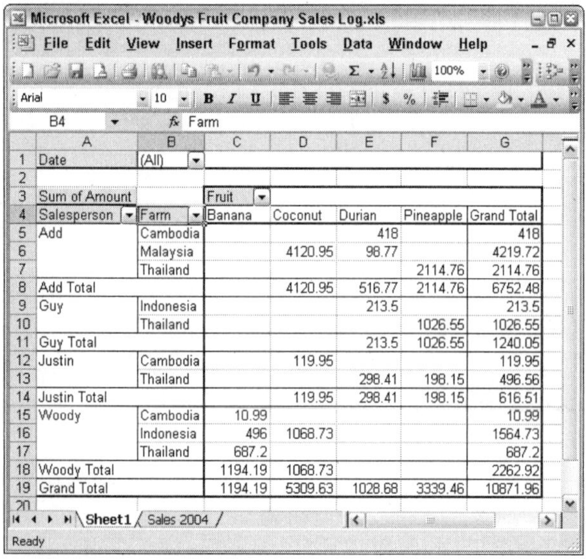

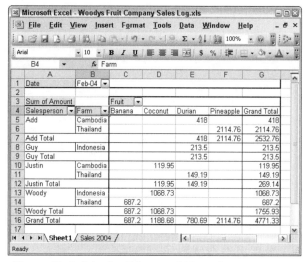

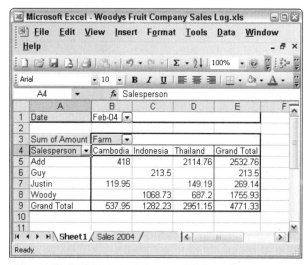

• **Figure 40-7: Sales for all dates.**

3. **To show the report for a specific date, click the down arrow next to (All) in cell B1 and then choose the date.**

   In Figure 40-8, I choose Feb-04.

	A	B	C	D	E	F	G
1	Date	Feb-04					
2							
3	Sum of Amount		Fruit				
4	Salesperson	Farm	Banana	Coconut	Durian	Pineapple	Grand Total
5	Add	Cambodia			418		418
6		Thailand				2114.76	2114.76
7	Add Total				418	2114.76	2532.76
8	Guy	Indonesia			213.5		213.5
9	Guy Total				213.5		213.5
10	Justin	Cambodia		119.95			119.95
11		Thailand			149.19		149.19
12	Justin Total			119.95	149.19		269.14
13	Woody	Indonesia		1068.73			1068.73
14		Thailand	687.2				687.2
15	Woody Total		687.2	1068.73			1755.93
16	Grand Total		687.2	1188.68	780.69	2114.76	4771.33

• **Figure 40-8: Sales for February, 2004 only.**

4. **To show sales for Feb-04 by salesperson and farm, click and drag away the cell that reads Fruit from the spreadsheet. You can drop it anywhere as long as it's off the spreadsheet.**

   Now there's a simple spreadsheet showing sales for February, 2004 (see Figure 40-9).

	A	B	C	D	E
1	Date	Feb-04			
2					
3	Sum of Amount	Farm			
4	Salesperson	Cambodia	Indonesia	Thailand	Grand Total
5	Add	418		2114.76	2532.76
6	Guy		213.5		213.5
7	Justin	119.95		149.19	269.14
8	Woody		1068.73	687.2	1755.93
9	Grand Total	537.95	1282.23	2951.15	4771.33

• **Figure 40-9: Sales by salesperson by farm, for February 2004.**

I hope this little demo gives you a feel for the kinds of data mining that a pivot table can provide — quickly.

There's much, much more. See the next section.

Making a Pivot Table Boogie

In this section, I want to give you a feel for the incredible power of pivot tables by showing you some pivot table functions that aren't obvious, even after you've played with them for a while.

It's easy to have a pivot table give you a count of how many times a particular data item appears. For example, here's how to tally how many sales each salesperson made in the sample list from this Technique:

1. **Clear the pivot table created in the first section of this Technique by clicking and dragging all the fields from the four drop areas: Drop Page Fields Here, Drop Column Fields Here, Drop Row Fields Here, and Drop Data Items Here. You can drop them anywhere as long as it's off the table.**

   The cleared table looks similar to a new, blank table (refer to Figure 40-4).

2. **Click and drag Salesperson from the field list, dropping it on the Drop Row Fields Here box.**

3. **Click and drag Salesperson from the field list again, but this time, drop it on the Drop Data Items Here box.**

   When you drop a text field like Salesperson in the Data Items box, Excel gives you a count of how many times a specific entry (for example, a specific salesperson) appears. See Figure 40-10.

4. **If you want to know the number of sales for each salesperson by farm, click and drag the Farm field to the Drop Column Fields Here box.**

   You get the report in Figure 40-11.

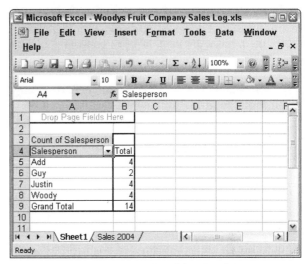

• **Figure 40-10: How many sales did each salesperson make?**

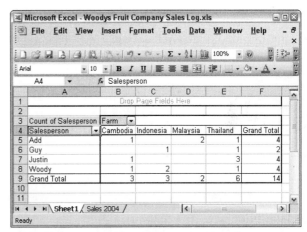

• **Figure 40-11: How many sales did each salesperson make by farm?**

Pivot tables aren't limited to totals or counts in the Drop Data Items Here box. In fact, there's an entire world of options for showing precisely the kind of information you want to find.

For example, say you're interested in learning more about the largest sale made by each salesperson. Here are a few different ways of looking at it.

1. **Clear the pivot table created in the first section of this Technique by clicking and dragging all the fields from the four drop areas.**

Your pivot table should look like Figure 40-4.

2. **Click and drag the Salesperson field, dropping it on the Drop Row Fields Here box. Drag the Amount field to the Drop Data Items Here box.**

Your sheet should look like Figure 40-12.

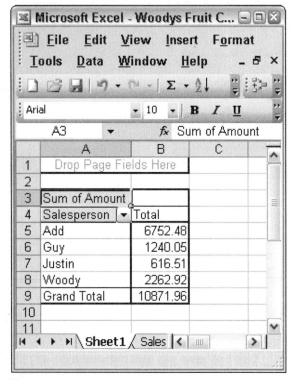

• **Figure 40-12: Sales by salesperson. Ho-hum.**

3. **Double-click the box that reads Sum of Amount.**

You see the PivotTable Field dialog box, as shown in Figure 40-13.

4. **Choose Max (in the Summarize By list) and then click OK.**

The pivot table now shows you the maximum sale for each salesperson (see Figure 40-14).

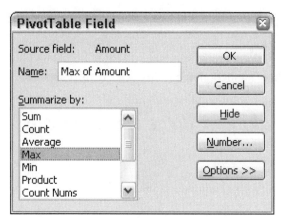

• **Figure 40-13: Tell the pivot table to show you the maximum sales amount.**

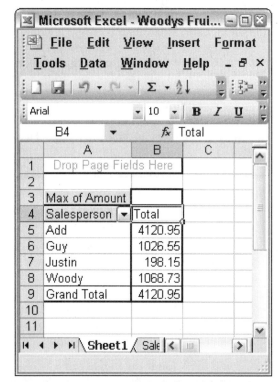

• **Figure 40-14: The maximum sale for each salesperson.**

The line marked Grand Total in Figure 40-14 is a misnomer. It isn't the grand total. Rather, it's the maximum of all maximum sales. Because Add's highest sale is 4120.95 and Add had the single highest sale of all the salespeople, the Max of the Max is 4120.95, which is the number erroneously reported as the Grand Total.

5. Say you want to know which farm accounted for the largest sale for each salesperson. Start by clicking and dragging the Farm field from the field list, and dropping it immediately to the right of the Salesperson box.

The pivot table now shows you the maximum sale for each salesperson for each farm (see Figure 40-15).

Once again, Grand Total is a misnomer. It's the Max of the Max.

• **Figure 40-15:** Maximum sales for each salesperson for each farm.

6. Double-click the Farm cell.

Excel brings up the PivotTable Field dialog box, as shown in Figure 40-16.

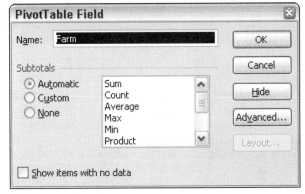

• **Figure 40-16:** Modify how the pivot table looks at the field.

7. Click the Advanced button.

Excel shows you the PivotTable Field Advanced Options dialog box, as shown in Figure 40-17.

• **Figure 40-17:** Limit the number of different values shown for the field.

8. Under the Top 10 AutoShow heading, select the On radio button, set Show to Top, and set the counter at 1. Click OK twice.

The pivot table report now looks like Figure 40-18.

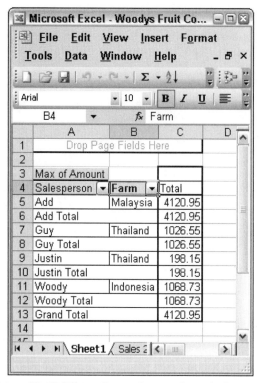

• **Figure 40-18:** Where the maximum sale took place.

Figure 40-18 shows you both the maximum sale for each salesperson and also (in admittedly a rather obtuse way) which farm was associated with the sale: Add's biggest sale was for the Malaysia farm, Woody's was for the Indonesia farm, and both Justin and Guy had their best sales for the Thailand farm.

Pivot tables are incredibly powerful. It takes a bit of effort to get them set up, and the reports can be a bit hard to interpret. But you can save enormous amounts of time sifting through piles of data by simply dragging and dropping.

Technique 41

Creating Pivot Charts That Work Right

Save Time By

- ✔ Knowing when to use a pivot chart
- ✔ Setting up the first chart the right way
- ✔ Using pivot charts to understand the data

How many times have you put together some interesting data, created a chart, run it up the corporate flagpole — or shown it around your Tuesday Lunchtime Investment Club, for that matter — and discovered that somehow, you didn't plot the most important data?

Happens all the time. What's boring to you might be utterly insightful to me. Or (sorry to say) vice versa.

Excel pivot charts let you dash back to your computer, lick your wounds, regraph your data in a new and exciting way, print it, and run it back to the group. The slowest part of the whole process is the lousy color printer, which can't keep up with your breakneck pace.

 I don't talk about regular Excel charts very much. There's a reason why. If you want to save time, don't bother with regular charts. Any time you think about creating a chart in Excel, you really should think about doing a pivot chart instead. Pivot charts do have a slightly higher learning curve — a speed bump with a pimple, if you will — and they aren't quite as pretty as regular Excel charts. But the very first time you have to redo a chart for any tiny reason, you'll thank your lucky stars if you originally built it as a pivot chart.

Starting with a Good List

Every pivot chart starts out as a pivot table.

You don't have to work with the pivot table — the Pivot Table and PivotChart Wizard can let you skip over working with the pivot table directly — but the pivot table exists, nonetheless.

That's why it's important for you to get your data in order — making sure it's in the form of a *list,* which is Excel's version of a flat-file database — before you try to draw a pivot chart.

✔ If you're feeling lucky, you can build the list manually. Remember that the top cell in each column should contain a label for the column, and that every entry in the column should follow suit. For example, if you have a column of telephone numbers, you don't want one cell in that column to contain a date. Also remember that you should have no blank rows.

✔ If you use Excel 2003 and need to create a list, refer to Technique 37 for fast, easy, and foolproof instructions on building a list from scratch.

✔ If you don't use Excel 2003, you can still employ many of Excel's built-in tools to help you create a list. See Technique 38 for details.

After you have a list in place, I strongly recommend that you run through Technique 40 to get a feel for how pivot tables work. To a first approximation, the same drag-and-drop methods that work with pivot tables also work with pivot charts.

Building a Pivot Chart

If you have a good list, here is how to build a pivot chart:

1. **Click inside a well-formed list.**

2. **Choose Data⇨PivotTable and PivotChart Report.**

The Pivot Table and PivotChart Wizard appears.

3. **Choose both the Microsoft Office Excel List or Database and the PivotChart Report (With PivotTable Report) radio buttons and then click Next.**

If the wizard was able to find your list, Step 2 of the wizard highlights the column headings and the list (see Figure 41-1).

4. **If the wizard recognizes your entire list, click Next. If not, you might have a bad (which is to say, blank) row. Click Cancel, find the problem and correct it, and then go back to Step 1.**

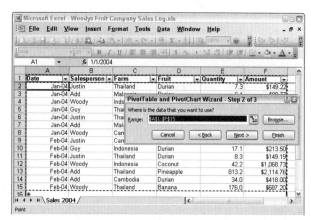

• **Figure 41-1: The wizard should be able to find your list.**

After you click Next in Step 2 of the wizard, the wizard segues to its last step.

5. **Select the New Worksheet radio button and then click Finish.**

You don't want to put the pivot table on the same sheet as the main data. Selecting New Worksheet helps you avoid stomping all over yourself.

After you click Finish, Excel creates a new pivot table on a new sheet (called Sheet1, unless you already have a Sheet1). Excel also creates a new pivot chart on another new sheet (called Chart1; see Figure 41-2). It also shows the Chart toolbar and the PivotTable toolbar as well as a list of all available fields.

6. **Pivot charts work a lot like pivot tables. If you follow the example in Technique 40, try something similar by clicking and dragging an item from the field list to the box marked Drop Category Fields Here. Drag and drop another field onto Drop Data Items Here. Finally, drag and drop a third field onto Drop Series Fields Here.**

It's really that easy to create a pivot chart. In Figure 41-3, I created a chart that shows how many dollars worth of fruit each salesperson sold.

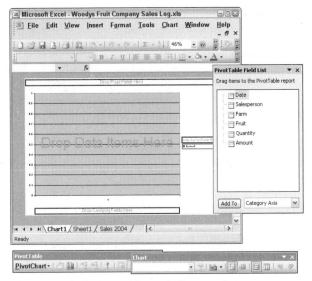

• **Figure 41-2:** A pivot table ready for populating.

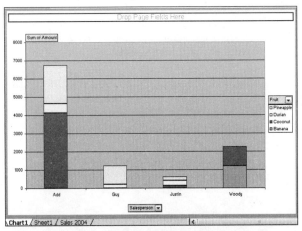

• **Figure 41-3:** Drag and drop three fields, and you have a serviceable (albeit a bit, uh, homely) pivot chart.

Pivot charts can be modified quickly by clicking and dragging — just like their pivot table brethren.

Re-Creating a Pivot Chart

If you have a pivot chart such as the one I create in the preceding section, modifying the chart couldn't be simpler. For example:

✔ If you want to see sales by farm instead of sales by fruit, click the Fruit box from the Series fields location (in Excel-speak, it's the top line of the Legend) and drag it off the chart: make sure you grab the entire drop-down list at the top of the legend, and drop it just about anywhere. Then click Farm in the fields list and drop it on the box that reads Drop Series Fields Here (see Figure 41-4).

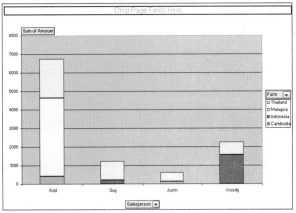

• **Figure 41-4:** Change the pivot chart to sales by salesperson by farm — elapsed time, about five seconds.

✔ If you want to see how much of each fruit was sold at each farm, click and drag Salesperson from the chart (drop it anywhere you like); then click Fruit from the fields list and drag it to where it reads Drop Category Fields Here (see Figure 41-5).

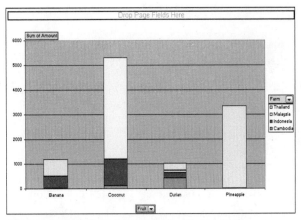

• **Figure 41-5:** Fruit by farm, another five seconds.

✔ As is the case with pivot tables, you can use Page fields to create different reports for different slices of data. For example, if you

  ▶ Remove all the fields from the chart.

  ▶ Drag Salesperson back to Drop Category Fields Here.

  ▶ Drag Fruit to Drop Series Fields Here.

  ▶ Drag Quantity to Drop Data Items Here.

  ▶ Drag Farm to Drop Page Fields Here.

  ▶ Click the down arrow next to Farm.

  ▶ Select just the farm in Thailand.

You get the result in Figure 41-6.

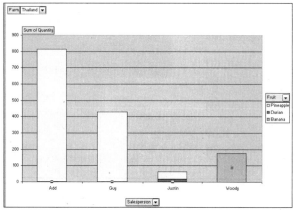

• **Figure 41-6: The quantity of fruit sold in Thailand. Elapsed time: 30 seconds.**

 If you alter the data in a pivot table, you need to update the chart so that it reflects the data.

✔ **If you added rows to your list,** those new rows might not be included in the pivot chart. To be sure, go back to the pivot table that your chart is based on (perhaps in the sheet called Sheet1), click inside the pivot table, choose Data⇨ PivotTable and PivotChart Report, and move back in the wizard to Step 2, where you choose the location of your list. Update the location

information and click Finish. Your pivot table and pivot chart will be updated.

✔ **If you change the underlying data in the list,** your pivot chart won't update automatically. To update the data, right-click inside any of the fields in the pivot chart and choose Refresh Data.

Changing the Chart Type

Although the Pivot Table and PivotChart Wizard creates stacked bar charts by default, you aren't limited to column-style charts. If you right-click any data element (such as a bar) in the pivot chart and choose Chart Type, Excel allows you to switch to any of its standard types.

 Excel won't let you build an XY scatter chart, a bubble chart (very similar to a scatter chart), or a stock market-style (high/low/close) chart from data in a pivot table. Because pivot charts are built on pivot tables, those three types of charts aren't available.

Continuing with the example in this Technique, drag all the fields off the chart, drop Salesperson on Drop Categories Here, and drop Amount on Drop Data Items Here. Then right-click one of the bars and choose a pie chart. The result is in Figure 41-7.

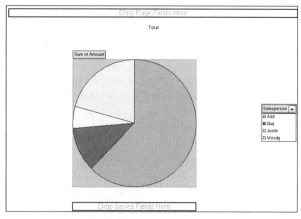

• **Figure 41-7: Pie charts are very easy and quick, too.**

Gussying Up Pivot Charts

The number-one complaint about pivot charts: They're ugly. Ugly, ugly, ugly.

After you have a pivot chart that you can live with, your first order of business should be to get rid of those (did I say U-G-L-Y?) field buttons — the ones with names like *Salesperson* and *Sum of Amount*.

To get rid of the field buttons, right-click one of them and choose Hide PivotChart Field Buttons. The field buttons disappear.

 With the field buttons gone, you probably want to put a title on the chart as a whole and also on the X and Y axes. To do so, right-click a blank location in the chart and choose Chart Options⇨Titles (see Figure 41-8), type the titles, and click OK. When the titles are in the chart, right-click each and choose Format Title to apply your own formatting.

To bring back the field buttons

1. **Choose View⇨Toolbars⇨PivotChart.**

Excel brings up the PivotChart toolbar.

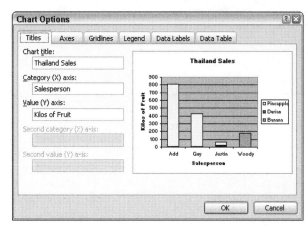

• **Figure 41-8: Type your own titles after the buttons are gone.**

2. **On the PivotChart toolbar, click the button marked PivotChart, and then clear the Hide PivotChart Field Buttons check box.**

You get the buttons back as well as the PivotTable Field List.

Technique 42

Setting Scenarios and Seeking Goals

Save Time By

- ✔ Running scenarios to explore trade-offs — quickly
- ✔ Compiling a list of options so you can choose
- ✔ Using Excel to find solutions to tough problems

It's time to buy that condo. The whole family's excited. You have a price in mind, the lady at the bank said you could get a 30-year, fixed-rate loan at a great percentage rate, and the only question is whether you can afford the payments.

You spend an hour at the bank, run the numbers, and get the good news: You have just barely enough income to cover the house payments — if you can talk the seller into shaving $30,000 off the sales price.

You talk to your agent, who talks to their agent, and the other agent says he doesn't think they'll take it, but you're ready to roll the dice and make an offer when . . . something happens. Maybe you see an ad for a cheaper loan, or you see a house that you like better, or Great Aunt Tillie decides that because you're such a grand niece, she'll give you $10,000. The big question: How much will your payments be if this happens, or that happens, or something else comes hurtling down the pike?

 If you need to figure out a loan payment, here's a huge timesaving tip: Don't bother with Excel. Hop on the Web, type in the numbers, and get the result — the *correct* result — in no time. Loan payment calculating programs abound on the Web. Go to Google and search for *loan amortization*. Or try www.amo-mortgage.com/amortization.html or www.hsh.com/calc-amort.html.

Here's the hook — the way that Excel can really help. Nobody (at least nobody I know) runs an amortizing program just once. Excel is a fantastic timesaving tool when you need to play *what if?* When you're curious about amortization, you want to know how much your payments will be if the rate goes up or down, or if the length of the loan gets longer or shorter. In some cases, you know how much you can afford to pay every month, but you need to work backward to figure out how much you can borrow or what percentage rate you need to fight for. Excel can do that. And how.

In this Technique, I show you how to

- ✔ **Compare multiple *scenarios*.** These are different sets of conditions so that you can tell at a glance what the effect of, say, different interest rates or shorter loan periods will be.

- ✔ **Tell Excel to work backward.** Also called *goal seeking*, you do this to determine what set of initial conditions will lead to a specific result. In the case of loan amortization, you can tell Excel how much you want to pay and ask Excel to figure out how much you can borrow.

Building a Loan Amortization Spreadsheet

To demonstrate both the scenario and goal-seeking capabilities, I use the loan amortization calculation spreadsheet in Figure 42-1. Here's how to build it:

• **Figure 42-1: The Loan Amortization spreadsheet used as an example in this Technique.**

1. **Start with a new, blank spreadsheet.**

2. **In cell A1, type** Amount of Loan. **In A2, type** APR. **In A3, type** Years. **In A5, type** Monthly payment. **In A6, type** Total payments. **In A7, type** Total interest.

Your budding spreadsheet looks like column A in Figure 42-1.

3. **In cell B5, type** =-PMT(B2/12,B3*12,B1).

The formula's basic structure, if you're curious, is =PMT(Rate, Nper, PV, FV, Type).

Cell B5 calculates the monthly payment by using Excel's infamous PMT( ) function.

 You have to put an equal sign *and* a minus sign (in that order) in front of the PMT( ) function because that function returns a negative number. Yes, there's a reason. No, you don't want to hear it.

You can read all about PMT( ) in online Help. In the box that reads Type a Question for Help, just type **PMT**, press Enter — and strap on your hip-waders.

4. **In cell B6, type** B5*B3*12.

That's the monthly payment times the number of months. Easy.

5. **In cell B7, type** B6-B1.

This is the total amount paid minus the original amount of the loan. The spreadsheet looks like Figure 42-2.

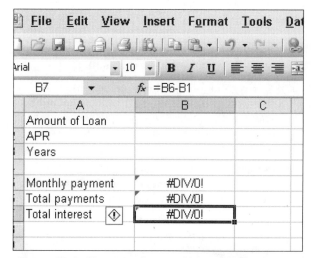

• **Figure 42-2: Almost ready — everything but the data.**

6. **To make the spreadsheet more legible, select cells B1, B5, B6, and B7 (hold down the Ctrl key while you click), choose Format➪Cells, choose Currency, and set them for two decimal places and your favorite currency symbol. Click cell B2 and choose Format➪Cells, choose Percentage, and set it to two or three decimal places.**

7. **In cells B1, B2, and B3, enter data for the loan you want to amortize.**

   Don't forget that B2 is a percentage. So, for example, if you want to run an amortization at a 4.50% interest rate, you must enter the APR as **.045**. Figure 42-1 shows the amounts for a $200,000 loan at 4.50% over 30 years.

8. **Check your results.**

   Your spreadsheet should match the result in Figure 42-1.

Establishing Scenarios

Amortizations are like potato chips. Nobody can run just one.

If you want to compare many different combinations of numbers — multiple *scenarios*, in the parlance — Excel provides an excellent tool for the job. Here's how to use it:

1. **Figure out which numbers you want to change each time you rerun the calculation.**

   The obvious choices for an amortization are the amount, APR, and length of the loan. But you can run scenarios on any spreadsheet, and the choices for variables might not be so obvious. Give it some thought.

2. **Set up your spreadsheet with your first scenario — a *baseline,* if you will. Then select all the cells that you want to be able to change.**

   I use the spreadsheet in Figure 42-1 for my baseline, selecting B1 through B3 as the cells that will change.

 If the cells aren't next to each other, hold down the Ctrl key while you click each one.

3. **Choose Tools➪Scenarios.**

   Excel brings up the Scenario Manager (see Figure 42-3). The Scenario Manager notes that you haven't set up any scenarios yet.

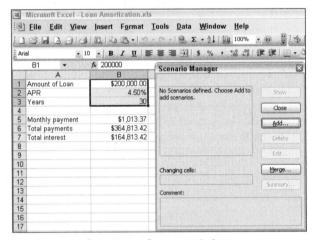

• **Figure 42-3:** Set up your first scenario here.

4. **Click Add.**

   The Scenario Manager invites you to add a new scenario (see Figure 42-4).

5. **Type a name for the scenario, make sure the Changing Cells box correctly lists the cells you want to change in each scenario, and then click OK.**

   In Figure 42-4, I type **Bigger Loan** so that I can identify the scenario easily. The Scenario Manager asks for values for each of the cells that are allowed to change (see Figure 42-5).

6. **Type the values for each of the cells that are allowed to change; then click OK.**

   The Scenario Manager reappears, this time with your first scenario listed.

7. **Repeat Steps 4, 5, and 6 to put as many scenarios in the Scenario Manager as you wish.**

   In Figure 42-6, I run three different scenarios.

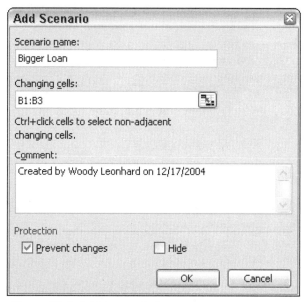

• **Figure 42-4:** Add a scenario here.

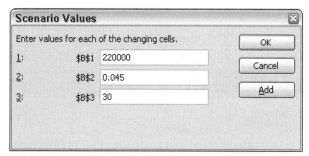

• **Figure 42-5:** Set the values for the scenario. Note that the numbers aren't formatted, so don't let their odd appearance throw you.

8. When you have enough scenarios to start looking at the results, click the Summary button (at the bottom).

The Scenario Manager brings up the Scenario Summary dialog box, as shown in Figure 42-7.

9. Select the Scenario Summary radio button and make sure that the Result Cells box refers to the cell or cells that help you make the best comparison. Then click OK.

• **Figure 42-6:** Three scenarios, ready to compare.

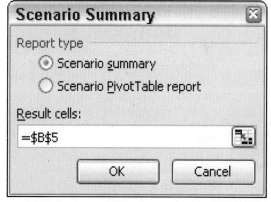

• **Figure 42-7:** Choose the cell or cells with results that you want to analyze.

In Figure 42-7, I choose cell B5 — the monthly payment amount. Excel comes up with a Scenario Summary, as shown in Figure 42-8.

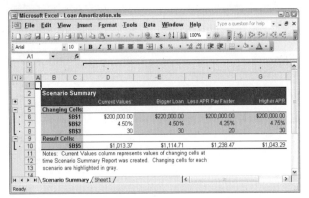

• **Figure 42-8:** You might be surprised to see the effect of shortening the length of the loan or increasing/decreasing the APR.

The Scenario Summary produced by the Scenario Manager is a genuine spreadsheet in all respects. You can add or delete columns or rows, graph it, or do anything that a normal spreadsheet can handle.

Working Backward: Goal Seeking

Scenarios work forward from different starting points: You tweak a few numbers, run the spreadsheet, and see how the results change.

What if you want to work backward? That is, what if you know the results, but you want to see what it takes to generate those results?

In this Technique's loan amortization example, you might know the maximum amount that you can afford to pay every month, and you might know the APR, but you need to know how much you can borrow. Or perhaps you know how much you want to borrow but need to know where the APR has to go in order to hit monthly payments that fit your budget.

That's where goal seeking comes in.

Sometimes you can just reconstruct your spreadsheet. In the case of working backward from payments to borrowed amount, all you have to do is figure out what the PMT() function has to look like. I figure it'd take me, oh, about an hour and a half to make sure I got that right.

But if you have a spreadsheet that does the forward calculation correctly, getting Excel to work backward only takes a few clicks. Here's how:

1. **Start with a spreadsheet that calculates the end result correctly.**

For a loan amortization, the spreadsheet in Figure 42-1 works just fine.

2. **Click the cell that you want to set — your goal.**

In this example, you know how much you can afford to spend per month, which is cell B5.

3. **Choose Tools➪Goal Seek.**

Excel brings up the Goal Seek dialog box, as shown in Figure 42-9.

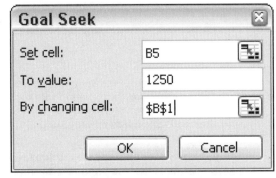

• **Figure 42-9:** Goal Seek lets you work backward.

4. **Tell Goal Seek what value you want to achieve and which cell can be modified to achieve the goal.**

In this case, the most I can afford to pay every month (cell B5) is $1,250. I want Excel to find how big of a loan will necessitate $1,250/month payments, given a 4.50% APR and a 30-year term.

5. **Click OK.**

Goal Seek takes less than a second to come up with the correct answer — a loan of $246,701.45 at 4.50% for 30 years will result in monthly payments of $1,250 (see Figure 42-10).

 Of course, you can ask Excel to Goal Seek a percentage rate or a loan term by using the same technique. Goal Seek is amazingly powerful, fast, and very easy to use.

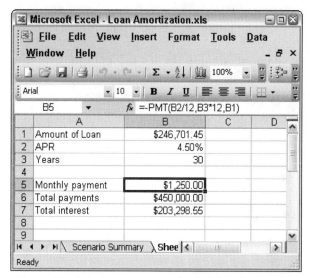

• **Figure 42-10:** In less than a second, Excel tells you how big of a loan you can afford.

Technique 43

Using the Lookup Wizard

Save Time By

- Knowing when to use a lookup table
- Creating lookups that work every time
- Getting Excel to perform lookups quickly and accurately

Excel lookup tables make it easy to reach into a list and extract information. (I talk about lists in Techniques 37 and 38.)

When most people think of lookups, the prototypical situation that springs to mind is a part number lookup: Somewhere in your spreadsheet you have a part number, and you want to look up the name of the part. Equivalently, you might have Customer numbers and want to look up the customer's name, or Department numbers and want to grab the name of the department. Look up a number. Get a description. You get the idea.

Most people don't realize that they can use lookups to cover spans of data, too. My favorite example: tax tables. (Tax tables are those tables of tax rates that any self-respecting, bureaucratic government uses to decide how much you owe in taxes, depending on how much the stuff you buy costs or how much money you make.) Instead of confining yourself to a one-to-one lookup, you can have Excel cruise through a tax table and pick up the tax associated with a certain sales amount or (ugh!) income level.

This Technique shows you how to set up VLOOKUP and INDEX functions the fast way (in other words, using the Lookup Wizard) so that you can enter the known data and Excel fetches what you need automatically. I explain how to search for a less-than-or-equal-to match (entries that are less than or equal to a value you enter) or an exact match (entries that equal a certain value). Yes, most people use a lookup for exact matches. But you should remember that Excel is equally adept at gliding through tables, which could save you a lot of time some day.

Setting Up the Lookup Wizard

Excel lookups fall into two categories:

- ✔ **A less-than-or-equal-to match:** Tax tables work that way. You might also find a *comparative* match useful if you need to look up times or dates. (See "Running a Comparative Lookup.")

- ✔ **An exact match:** This kind of lookup works great if you have a list of part numbers and part names, for example, or customer numbers and customer names. Just feed the lookup a number, and you get back a description. (See "Running an Exact Lookup.")

If you've never used Excel's Lookup Wizard, you might need to install it. To find out, in Excel, click Tools and look for an entry called Lookup (probably at the bottom of the Tools menu). If it's there, the Lookup Wizard is already installed, and you can skip to the next section. If you can't find Tools➪Lookup, you need to install the Lookup Wizard. Make sure that you have your Office 2003 CD, and then follow these steps:

1. **Choose Tools➪Add-Ins.**

Excel shows you the Add-Ins installer dialog box (see Figure 43-1). If you installed Excel with default options, you didn't get any of the add-ins shown in this dialog box.

 An *Excel add-in* is an adjunct to Excel that solves a specific problem or group of problems. Microsoft doesn't install the add-ins by default because they take some room, and they can clutter up Excel's otherwise-svelte appearance (ahem). You might want to consider installing the Conditional Sum Wizard while you're here to make it easier to calculate sums based on specific criteria.

2. **Select the Lookup Wizard check box and then click OK.**

You get a rather, uh, intelligence-inhibited message that says the feature isn't installed, asking whether you want to install it. (D'oh! Why else would you ask to install it?)

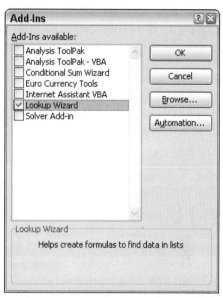

• **Figure 43-1: Begin installing the Lookup Wizard here.**

3. **Click Yes to begin the installation.**

Excel whines and whirs for a minute or so — it might ask you to provide your installation CD — and then nothing happens, and you automatically go back to Excel. That's a good sign. It means that the Lookup Wizard has been installed. You can make sure by clicking Tools: Lookup is undoubtedly now at the bottom of the list.

Primping a List for Lookup

Before you can run either an exact or a comparative lookup, you must make sure that you have a well-formed list ready for Excel to use:

- ✔ **Headings:** The first row should contain headings — text labels that describe the contents of the column.

- ✔ **Blank rows:** The list can have no blank rows.

✔ **Sorting:** If you're going to look up individual entries in the list (such as part numbers or customer numbers), you want an exact match, and the columns don't need to be sorted. But if you're going to look up a range of numbers using a less-than-or-equal-to comparison (as you would in a tax table) — looking for a comparative match — you must sort the column that will be used for the comparisons. (To sort a column, click once anywhere inside the column, and click the Sort Ascending icon on the Standard toolbar.)

In Figure 43-2, I show the sales tax table for Fort Collins, Colorado, whipped into a list that Excel can work with.

	A	B	C
1	From	To	Tax
2	0.00	0.17	0.00
3	0.18	0.22	0.01
4	0.23	0.37	0.02
5	0.38	0.52	0.03
6	0.53	0.67	0.04
7	0.68	0.82	0.05
8	0.83	0.97	0.06
9	0.98	1.11	0.07
10	1.12	1.26	0.08
11	1.27	1.41	0.09
12	1.42	1.56	0.10
13	1.57	1.71	0.11
14	1.72	1.86	0.12
15	1.87	2.01	0.13

• **Figure 43-2: A sales tax table ready for Excel to use.**

 Tax tables are excellent candidates for Excel comparative lookups because taxes are frequently hard to calculate precisely. Many locales have a set sales tax rate — say, 4.7% or 6.3% — but use odd round-off points, particularly for smaller sales amounts. The IRS has tax tables that confound those who create them — much less those of us who have to pay Uncle Sam's piper. If there's any chance for confusion, use Excel's Lookup Wizard on a tax table rather than attempting to calculate a tax directly.

With your lookup table in place, you're ready to use the Lookup Wizard.

Running a Comparative Lookup

In the preceding sections, I show you how to get the Lookup Wizard installed and how to ensure that you have a list that the wizard can understand.

In this section, I show you how to use the Lookup Wizard to run a *comparative lookup:* that is, how to have Excel look up a value in a list that is less than or equal to an entry in the list. The example that I use is a sales tax table — you type the amount of a sale into the spreadsheet, and the lookup function returns the amount of sales tax — but the same approach works in many other situations.

If you want to run an exact lookup, follow the steps in the next section.

In Figure 43-3, I set up a very simple spreadsheet for use with the wizard. (I just took the spreadsheet in Figure 43-2 and added text in cells E1 and E2, for the wizard to use.) Anyone using the spreadsheet just needs to type a sales amount in the indicated box, and the tax table provides the appropriate tax.

	A	B	C		E
1	From	To	Tax		Sales Amount:
2	0.00	0.17	0.00		Tax:
3	0.18	0.22	0.01		
4	0.23	0.37	0.02		
5	0.38	0.52	0.03		
6	0.53	0.67	0.04		
7	0.68	0.82	0.05		
8	0.83	0.97	0.06		
9	0.98	1.11	0.07		
10	1.12	1.26	0.08		
11	1.27	1.41	0.09		
12	1.42	1.56	0.10		
13	1.57	1.71	0.11		
14	1.72	1.86	0.12		
15	1.87	2.01	0.13		

• **Figure 43-3: Type in the amount; retrieve the tax.**

Unfortunately, the Lookup Wizard is one of the worst wizards in Office. It's exceedingly difficult to understand. Follow along closely.

Here's how to use the wizard:

1. **Select the list that you want the wizard to use.**

Using the list in Figure 43-3, I select the From, To, and Tax columns of the list, starting at the headings on the columns, down to the last row.

 The From column is the one that drives the lookup because Excel always matches the largest number that is less than or equal to the amount that it's looking up. For example, in Figure 43-3, a sales amount of 0.22 that's compared with the From column matches 0.18, so the lookup will return a value of 0.01 in the Tax column. An amount of 0.23 returns 0.02. An amount of 0.24 also returns 0.02. And so on.

2. **Choose Tools⇨Lookup.**

The Lookup Wizard identifies the list that you chose in Step 1 (see Figure 43-4).

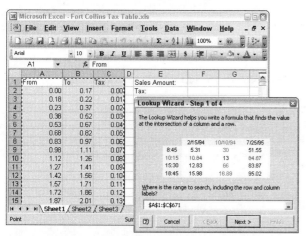

• **Figure 43-4: The wizard picks up the tax table.**

3. **Change the range if necessary and then click Next.**

You see Step 2 of the Wizard, which could be the most confusing wizard step anywhere in Office (see Figure 43-5).

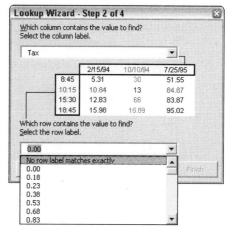

• **Figure 43-5: The tough Lookup Wizard step.**

4. **At the top, choose the column that contains the value to find.**

In this case, I want to look up the amount of tax, which is in the column with the label Tax.

5. **At the bottom, if you want to have Excel look for a range of numbers (as you do with a tax table), choose the entry marked No Row Label Matches Exactly.**

Immediately, the Lookup Wizard hits you with the Lookup Wizard dialog box (I'm not kidding; see Figure 43-6) that asks you to type the value to match. This is a ridiculously confusing dialog box. Hold your nose and follow along.

• **Figure 43-6: The wizard uses the number 99999 as a placeholder.**

6. **For now, trust me by typing** 99999 **and clicking OK.**

You go back to Step 2, but now the bottom box shows New Value – 99999 (see Figure 43-7).

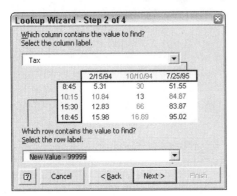

• **Figure 43-7: The placeholder goes into the wizard.**

7. **Click Next.**

You see Step 3 of the Wizard (see Figure 43-8).

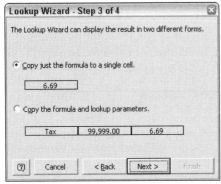

• **Figure 43-8: You don't want the wizard to show all the details.**

8. **Tell the wizard that you want it to copy just the formula to a single cell (select the radio button of the same name); then click Next.**

The final step of the Lookup Wizard appears (see Figure 43-9).

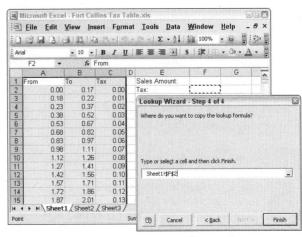

• **Figure 43-9: Tell the wizard where to put the results.**

9. **Click inside the cell (F2 in this example) that will contain the lookup formula (it's a monster), and then click Finish.**

The wizard does the dirty work, depositing the lookup formula in the cell that you specify (see Figure 43-10).

`=VLOOKUP(99999,$A$2:$C$671,MATCH("Tax",$A$1:$C$1,))`

	C	D	E	F	G
	Tax		Sales Amount:		
0.17	0.00		Tax:	6.69	

• **Figure 43-10: The formula that the wizard produced.**

10. **Go into the lookup formula that the wizard created and change the placeholder — the 99999 that you typed in Step 6 — so that it points to whatever cell you want to use for input.**

In this case, VLOOKUP(99999, . . .) should read VLOOKUP(F1, . . .) because you want to use whatever gets typed in the cell above to be used to look into the table. The result should look like Figure 43-11.

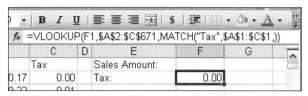

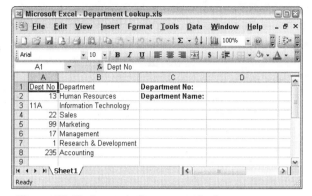

• **Figure 43-11: Change the placeholder to point to the actual input cell.**

If you play with it a bit, you'll see that this lookup formula works.

 The Lookup Wizard is a bear — but it beats the living daylights out of trying to create the VLOOKUP() formula by hand.

Running an Exact Lookup

In this section, I modify the procedure in the preceding section just slightly so the VLOOKUP function that you get matches entries in the list precisely.

Here's how:

1. **Use the instructions in "Primping a List for Lookup" earlier in this Technique to come up with a list.**

I have a sample list in Figure 43-12, consisting of department numbers and names. Note that exact lookup lists don't need to be sorted and that the department numbers can appear in any order at all. Indeed, they may not all be numbers!

2. **Select the list, including the headings.**

In the example, I select cells A1 to B8.

3. **Choose Tools⇨Lookup.**

You get Step 1 of the Lookup Wizard, as shown in Figure 43-13.

• **Figure 43-12: A sample for an exact lookup.**

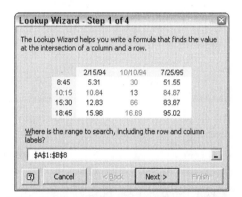

• **Figure 43-13: Establish the range of the lookup list.**

4. **Make sure that the wizard got the list right and then click Next.**

You see Step 2 — as in the preceding section, this is an enormously confusing step (see Figure 43-14).

5. **At the top, choose the heading from the column that you want to appear as the result.**

In this case, I want to feed the lookup a department number and get back a department name, so I choose Department.

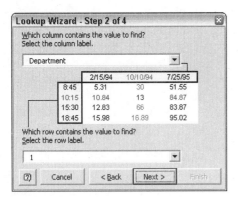

• **Figure 43-14: The confusing step.**

6. At the bottom, make a mental note of what appears in the box but don't bother changing it. Click Next.

The value that appears in the lower box is a placeholder, and you will replace it later in this section.

The wizard moves on to Step 3 (the options are similar to those in Figure 43-8).

7. Select the Copy Just the Formula to a Single Cell radio button. Then click Next.

The final step of the wizard appears.

8. Click once inside the cell that you want to hold the looked-up value; then click Finish.

The lookup formula — actually an INDEX() function — should look like Figure 43-15.

9. Go into the formula and replace the placeholder value that appeared in Step 6 with the cell that you want to use to perform the lookup.

In this case, I replaced the MATCH(1, . . .) function with MATCH(D1, . . .) (see Figure 43-16).

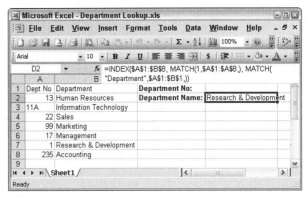

• **Figure 43-15: That horrendous function performs the lookup.**

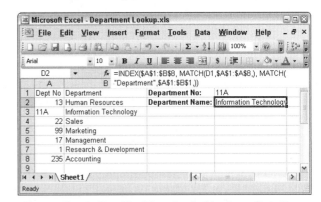

• **Figure 43-16: Get rid of the placeholder from Step 6.**

That's how an exact lookup works.

Part V

Pushing PowerPoint

The 5th Wave   By Rich Tennant

DAD ADDS MULTIMEDIA SOUND AND GRAPHICS TO THE TRADITIONAL CAMPFIRE GHOST STORY.

Technique

44

Getting PowerPoint Settings Right

Save Time By

✔ Scaling back PowerPoint's, uh, exuberant attempts to get in the way

✔ Turning off an antiquated privacy-busting feature

✔ Getting all the templates you paid for

Like all the other Office programs, PowerPoint ships with the training wheels down and locked. However, unlike the other Office programs, one of PowerPoint's default settings can leave old remnants of presentations hanging around, so anyone with a text editor can go digging around inside your presentation file, unearthing earlier versions of what you wrote. That's something they didn't tell you in PowerPoint school, eh?

With more and more companies relying on PowerPoint to summarize and convey information (and more and more truly awful PowerPoint presentations rushing in to fill the void), it's time for PowerPoint power users to take their destiny into their own hands. In this Technique, I show you how.

Working through the Changes

PowerPoint scatters its settings through a handful of dialog boxes with no rhyme nor reason that I can discern. So instead of trying to bring some order to this inherently chaotic situation, in this Technique, I step you through the dialog boxes and show you the changes that you need to make to work more efficiently.

If you're concerned about the *why*, read the text. If you're only concerned about the *what*, run through the setting changes in the figures.

 Most of all, keep one thing in mind: PowerPoint is a great tool to help you communicate your ideas in a concise, focused way. If your ideas aren't concise or focused, your presentation will show it.

Spend your time on getting the content right:

✔ No amount of multimedia pizzazz or glitzy transitions can compensate for the lack of substance.

✔ Don't waste your time — or your audience's — on a PowerPoint slide show that merely parrots your speech.

✔ If you have something worth saying, perhaps you should just say it. In many cases, a PowerPoint presentation *detracts* from the point you're trying to get across (see Figure 44-1).

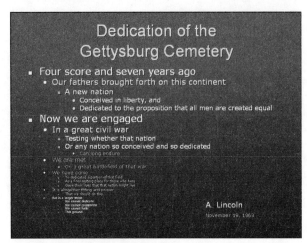

• **Figure 44-1: Seminal PowerPoint presentation, November 19, 1863.**

Blistering the Bouncing Menus

PowerPoint suffers from the same congenital defect that afflicts Word, Excel, and Outlook: menus that don't stay put. If your menus are bouncing around, do the following:

1. **Choose Tools⇨Customize⇨Options.**

PowerPoint brings up the Customize dialog box (see Figure 44-2).

2. **Select the Show Standard and Formatting Toolbars on Two Rows check box.**

I talk about this setting in Technique 13. If you're running a monitor at 2048 x 1024 resolution and you wear high-power reading glasses, you might be able to see all the buttons on one row. Anybody else needs two rows.

• **Figure 44-2: The Customize dialog box controls the bouncing menus and squished toolbars.**

3. **Select the Always Show Full Menus check box.**

I rail against *adaptive* menus (*personalized* menus in Microsoft-speak) — the ones that go boing-boing-boing — every chance I get. Consider the topic railed again.

4. **Click the Close button.**

Setting the View

The *startup task pane* — the pane that appears on the right when you start PowerPoint — doesn't do much, particularly if you follow the advice in Technique 46 and change your blank default presentation. I say get rid of it:

1. **Choose Tools⇨Options⇨View.**

PowerPoint brings up the View tab of the Options dialog box (see Figure 44-3).

2. **Clear the Startup Task Pane check box.**

• **Figure 44-3: My recommended View options.**

• **Figure 44-4: My recommended General options.**

3. Consider clearing the End with Black Slide check box.

When you give a presentation, you generally want to end with a black screen. However, using an extra black screen only takes up time.

4. Click OK.

Showing More Files

Like the other Office apps, PowerPoint shows you only four files on the Most Recently Used list, which appears at the bottom of the File menu. There's no reason to keep it so limited:

1. Choose Tools➪Options➪General.

PowerPoint shows you its General tab of the dialog box (see Figure 44-4).

2. Run the Recently Used File List number up to 9 entries.

3. Click OK.

Taking Back Control

PowerPoint borrows Word's infuriating habit of automatically guessing what you want to select, whether you selected it or not. In addition, PowerPoint is limited to 20 undo's — heaven only knows why. Here's how to take back control:

1. Choose Tools➪Options➪Edit.

PowerPoint brings up the Edit tab of the Options dialog box (see Figure 44-5).

The Show Paste Options Buttons setting in this dialog box controls whether PowerPoint shows you a Smart Tag every time you paste. That Smart Tag lets you strip off formatting from text before inserting it, or apply formatting from the presentation's design template. Unless you have a genetic antipathy to Smart Tags, keep the Tags.

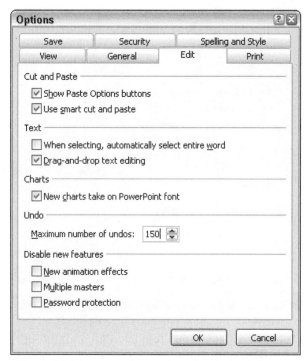

• **Figure 44-5: Increase the number of undo levels here.**

2. **Clear the When Selecting, Automatically Select Entire Word check box.**

I talk about this heinous setting in Technique 15.

3. **Run the Maximum Number of Undos up to 150.**

It makes absolutely no sense for you to skimp on the number of times that PowerPoint can undo your actions.

4. **Click OK.**

Reversing a Privacy-Busting Setting

This one really gets my goat.

Years ago, Word used to enable Fast Save by default. When you save a file and Fast Save is turned on, PowerPoint doesn't save the whole file — just the

changes to the file . . . the *deltas,* as it were. So any text that you delete, for example, remains in the file; with Fast Save turned on, PowerPoint just makes a note that you deleted the text. When you open the file again, PowerPoint scurries along, gathering up all these notations about what was changed during the Fast Saves and modifies the file accordingly before presenting it to you.

Back when people frequently saved their files to floppy disks, Fast Save could save quite a bit of time: PowerPoint wasn't required to rewrite the entire file when you asked to save it. Rather, the program could just post these little notes on the end of the file, knowing that it would all be put back together when necessary.

 Of course, anybody who opens a Fast Save presentation with a text editor (or even using Word's Recover Text from Any File option; see Technique 69) can read all the text inside the file — including anything you thought you had deleted.

Nowadays, the presence of a Fast Save option should send shivers down the spine of anyone who deals with sensitive information — and the fact that PowerPoint enables a Fast Save *by default* is a ringing condemnation of Microsoft's commitment to protecting your privacy.

Sorry. My soapbox seems to be a bit well-worn.

To restore some sanity to PowerPoint:

1. **Choose Tools⇨Options⇨Save.**

You see the Save tab of the Options dialog box, as shown in Figure 44-6.

2. **Clear the Allow Fast Saves check box.**

3. **Send a letter to your Congressional delegation complaining about this ludicrous setting.**

I'm exaggerating. But only a little bit.

4. **Click OK.**

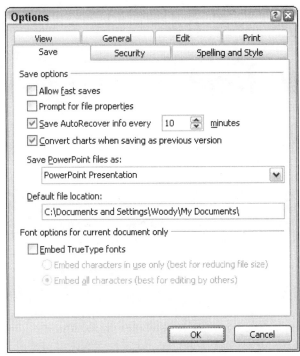

• **Figure 44-6: PowerPoint's truly offensive Fast Save setting.**

Installing All Your Templates

PowerPoint ships with more than 100 design templates. Unless you're running very, very low on hard drive space, you can save yourself a bunch of time by simply installing them all. To do so

1. **Grab your Office 2003 installation CD.**

You probably won't need it, but you might.

2. **Choose View➪Task Pane to bring up the PowerPoint task pane.**

It appears on the right side of the screen.

3. **Click the down arrow to the right of the task pane's title and choose Slide Design.**

PowerPoint shows you the Slide Design task pane.

4. **Scroll to the bottom of the list of Design Templates, and click the box that reads Additional Design Templates (see Figure 44-7).**

• **Figure 44-7: The rest of your design templates are buried here.**

The Windows Installer kicks in, tells you that it's Installing Components for Microsoft Office PowerPoint, and then disappears — and nothing happens. That's good. It means that all your design templates have been installed.

 Click the Microsoft Office Online button in the Slide Design task pane to search for design templates online. If you can't find a template there that you like, try using Google. Of the vast number of presentations on the Internet, Google should be able to help find a design out there that matches your needs.

Choosing the Right PowerPoint File Type

Save Time By

- Knowing what kind of PowerPoint file to use — and when
- Recovering a presentation from a slideshow
- Putting your own presentations in the AutoContent Wizard

We had 12.9 gigabytes of PowerPoint slides on our network. And I thought, "What a huge waste of corporate productivity." So we banned it. And we've had three unbelievable record-breaking fiscal quarters since we banned PowerPoint. Now, I would argue that every company in the world, if it would just ban PowerPoint, would see their earnings skyrocket. Employees would stand around going, "What do I do? Guess I've got to go to work."

— *Scott McNealy, CEO, Sun Microsystems*
San Jose Mercury News, August 5, 1997

The fact that Scott McNealy banned PowerPoint throughout his company makes me wonder whether Microsoft did something right for a change. (I'm not a big fan of Mr. McNealy; if he told me the sky was blue, I'd go out and check.) But then I think back on all the utterly abysmal PowerPoint presentations I've seen — the same ones, over and over again, give or take a bullet point here or there — and it's hard not to sympathize with Scott's position.

PowerPoint can suck up your time, bogging you down in seductive but meaningless minutia. Or it can help you organize your thoughts, get the words out, and get on with your working life. In this quick Technique, I show you how to work with PowerPoint's files — the first step to PowerPoint recovery.

Understanding PowerPoint File Types

If you want to understand what's happening with your presentations, you have to understand what PowerPoint does with your files.

These are the three different kinds of PowerPoint files that most folks bump into:

- .ppt: These are normal PowerPoint presentation files. Double-click a .ppt file, and PowerPoint opens the file so that you can edit it.

✔ .pps: These are PowerPoint show files. Double-click a .pps file, and PowerPoint runs the slideshow immediately.

✔ .pot: These are PowerPoint template files. Template files are typically used to create new presentations (via the AutoContent Wizard) or to apply formatting to an entire presentation (via design templates). However, the templates work just like regular presentation files. Double-click a .pot file, and PowerPoint opens that file, too, so that you can edit it.

Confused? No? Wait a second. You will be.

There's really no difference between the three different kinds of files. Sort of. See the following section.

 If you go into Explorer, right-click a .ppt file, and rename it with a .pps filename extension, the resulting file is a perfectly legitimate, complete PowerPoint show file.

To make things even more confusing, in different places, you see PowerPoint refer to four different kinds of .pot files — when in fact, they're all basically the same:

✔ **Content template,** which is just a presentation, but the presentation typically contains only text for some slide titles and bullets (see Figure 45-1).

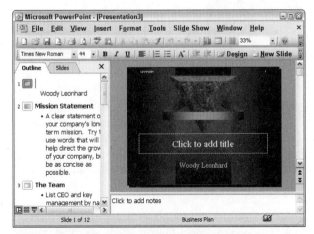

• **Figure 45-1: The Business Plan content template.**

✔ **Presentation template,** which is identical to a content template in every respect.

✔ **Design template,** which usually contains fancy master slides but no real presentation (see Figure 45-2).

• **Figure 45-2: The Globe design template.**

✔ **Presentation design,** which is identical to a design template in every respect.

 If you use PowerPoint very much, I bet you've lost hours trying to figure out what's going on with all the different kinds of templates and files. The fact is that there's no real difference: They're all the same kind of file, just used in slightly different ways.

You can waste a lot of time fretting over the different kinds of files. Or you can save a lot of time by using the file types to your advantage.

Saving Files to Run Automatically

In the preceding section, I explain that there is no difference between plain PowerPoint .ppt files and PowerPoint .pps show files. And now, the obligatory exception: When you double-click a .ppt file in Windows, PowerPoint comes up with the file, ready to be edited. When you double-click a .pps file in Windows, PowerPoint runs the slideshow.

You can use that distinction to minimize the amount of hunting and pecking that you need to do when launching presentations:

1. **Create your PowerPoint presentation as usual.**

2. **When the presentation's ready, choose File➪Save, saving it as you normally do.**

That saves your presentation as a .ppt file.

3. **Choose File➪Save As.**

PowerPoint brings up the Save As dialog box (see Figure 45-3).

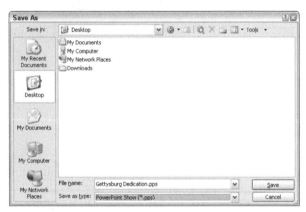

• **Figure 45-3: The easy way to save a slideshow.**

4. **In the Save as Type box, choose PowerPoint Show (*.pps).**

I usually stick ready-to-run presentations on my desktop.

5. **Click Save.**

You now have a second copy of the presentation, saved as a show file. Double-click that file, and PowerPoint runs your presentation immediately.

 Realize that you have two copies of the same presentation. If you make changes to one copy, they won't be reflected in the other. For that reason, I adopt the general rule to not open .pps files — I only open .ppt files.

 If you ever lose your original .ppt file but you still have a .pps file floating around (or if someone sends you a .pps file), you can re-create the .ppt file quickly and easily. Make sure that Windows shows you filename extensions (see Technique 1). Right-click the file, choose Rename, and change the .pps extension to .ppt. That's all there is to it.

Adding a Custom Presentation Skeleton to the AutoContent Wizard

PowerPoint's AutoContent Wizard (see Figure 45-4) walks you through creating a presentation. You can launch the AutoContent Wizard anytime you start working on a new presentation by clicking From AutoContent Wizard in the New Presentation task pane.

• **Figure 45-4: The AutoContent Wizard.**

The only problem with the AutoContent Wizard is that you and about 200,000,000 other PowerPoint users start with the same set of canned Microsoft-endorsed presentation skeletons — and you inevitably end up with a presentation that looks like about 200,000,000 others.

 If you create enough presentations or enough people in your company create presentations, sooner or later, you'll come up with a skeleton of your own. That is, you'll have a presentation that hangs together the basic parts of what you want to say in a way that won't leave your victims snoring. If you use this basic structure for different presentations, you can save yourself the task of revising the same file over and over and instead store the presentation skeleton in the AutoContent Wizard, ready to fill in.

Putting that perfect custom presentation skeleton in the AutoContent Wizard is surprisingly easy:

1. **Make sure that Windows shows you hidden files and folders.**

See Technique 1. You have to put the skeleton in a hidden closet. I mean, folder.

2. **Strip the presentation down to a skeleton: what points should go on which slide, where to put graphs, and so on.**

Be sure that you put any pieces that you always want included — pieces of text, logos, or any special formatting — into the skeleton (see Figure 45-5).

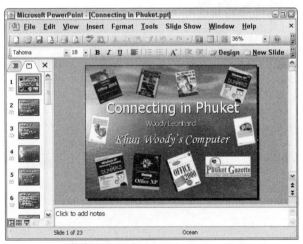

• **Figure 45-5: A skeleton (what you might call a real template) ready to be saved.**

3. **When you're happy with the skeleton, choose File⇨Save As.**

PowerPoint shows you the Save As dialog box (see Figure 45-6).

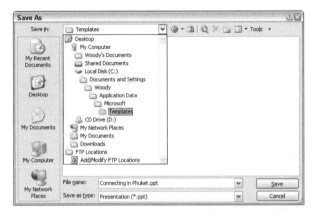

• **Figure 45-6: Save it in your Office 2003\Templates folder.**

4. **Navigate to your Templates folder.**

On most machines, the Templates folder is located at `C:\Documents and Settings\` `<your user name>\Application Data\` `Microsoft\Templates`.

 If you can't find the Application Data folder, you didn't tell Windows to show you hidden folders (see Step 1)!

5. **Click Save.**

6. **Choose File⇨New; in the New Presentation task pane, choose From AutoContent Wizard (see Figure 45-7).**

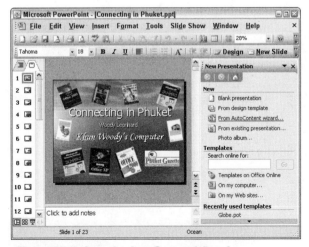

• **Figure 45-7: Start the AutoContent Wizard.**

The AutoContent Wizard appears (refer to Figure 45-4).

7. **Click Next.**

The AutoContent Wizard moves to the Presentation Type step (see Figure 45-8).

• **Figure 45-8: Pick the type of presentation here.**

8. **Click the presentation style button that you feel best describes your custom presentation (Corporate, Projects, and so on). Then click Add.**

The wizard responds with the Select Presentation Template dialog box (see Figure 45-9). Don't let the terminology throw you. As I describe in the first section of this Technique, there's no difference between a presentation template and a plain, old, everyday .ppt file.

9. **In the Files of Type box at the bottom, choose Presentations (*.ppt).**

10. **The presentation that you saved in Step 5 should be visible. Click it and then click OK.**

Your presentation appears in the AutoContent Wizard's list (see Figure 45-10).

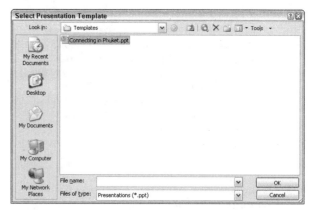

• **Figure 45-9: There's nothing special about a presentation template.**

• **Figure 45-10: Your custom presentation gets slapped into the AutoContent Wizard.**

11. **Click Finish.**

Every time you use the AutoContent Wizard, your presentation will be available in the second step.

Changing Your Blank Presentation

Technique 46

Every Office 2003 (and Office XP) user needs to create a custom, blank PowerPoint presentation.

Why? Because it's the only method that Microsoft gives you to ensure that all your new PowerPoint 2002/2003 presentation files are automatically scoured to remove personal data. It's a helluva note, but it's true. PowerPoint 2000 and earlier don't even have the setting.

While you're creating that new presentation, you might as well fill it with whatever else you need in all your new presentations — a particular design, a company logo, and even the last-edited date and slide numbers that appear on each side.

Take the time to make these changes once and then rest assured that all your new blank presentations will include the settings that you want — and *won't* include your personal information.

Understanding Blank Presentations

You create a new blank presentation in one of three ways:

- Click the New icon, which is the first icon on the Standard toolbar.
- Choose File⇨New (or bring up the New Presentation task pane in some other manner) and then choose Blank Presentation from the top of the task pane (see Figure 46-1).
- Bring up the New Presentation task pane, click the line that reads On My Computer (under Templates), and choose Blank Presentation.

• **Figure 46-1: One way to create a blank presentation.**

No matter how you create a new blank presentation, PowerPoint might or might not create a truly *blank* presentation.

When you tell PowerPoint to create a new blank presentation, PowerPoint looks in your `Office\Templates` folder for a presentation called `Blank.pot`. If it's there, PowerPoint creates a clone of that presentation, delivering that clone as your blank presentation. (If you have no `Blank.pot`, you really *do* get a blank presentation.)

 Every PowerPoint 2003 (or 2002) user needs to create a `Blank.pot` file. Microsoft goofed. There's a very important privacy setting called Remove Personal Information from File Properties on Save. Unfortunately, the 'Softies didn't think of any way to make that setting apply to all your new presentations. You have to remember to go into each presentation as soon as you create it and mark this check box.

The only way that you can permanently mark this check box for all new blank presentations is to save your own `Blank.pot`, with the box checked. Dang it. I'm *sure* that Microsoft ran out of money when building Office 2003.

Creating a Bare-Bones Blank Presentation

In the preceding section, I explain what a blank presentation is and where your blank presentation lives. In this section, I show you how to create and save your own custom blank presentation — an exercise that every PowerPoint 2003 (or 2002) user should undertake.

 If you have specific content — bullet points, entire slides, canned text — that goes into most of your presentations, consider adding that presentation to the AutoContent Wizard by using the steps in Technique 45. But if you have a common layout, background picture, color scheme, title, and the like that appears in most of your presentations, you can save the most time by making all those changes once and saving the result as your blank presentation.

Here's how:

1. **If you don't have a blank presentation showing, click the New icon on the left end of the Standard toolbar to create a, uh, new blank presentation.**

The prototypical blank presentation looks like Figure 46-2.

2. **If you want to use a specific design as your default design, click the Design button on the Formatting toolbar and choose a design from the ones offered in the Slide Design task pane.**

In Figure 46-3, I apply the `Mountain Top.pot` design. That will become the default design in all of my new blank presentations.

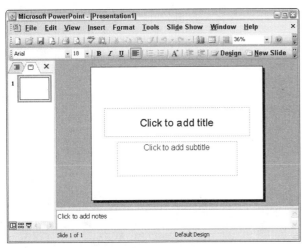

• **Figure 46-2: PowerPoint's original blank presentation.**

3. **If you have a specific piece of text, a picture (such as a logo), or some other common element that you want to appear on all the slides in new blank presentations, follow the instructions in the next section to modify the slide master.**

Changes made to the slide master affect all slides in all new blank presentations.

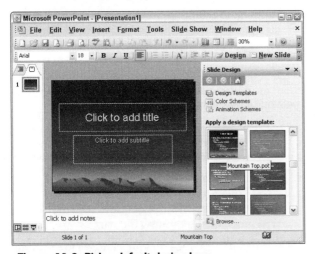

• **Figure 46-3: Pick a default design here.**

4. **Choose Tools➪Options➪Security.**

PowerPoint brings up the Security tab of the Options dialog box (see Figure 46-4).

5. **Select the Remove Personal Information from File Properties on Save check box.**

This keeps PowerPoint from saving personally identifiable information in the PowerPoint file for this presentation and every new blank presentation that you create (because this one will be cloned for all new blank presentations).

• **Figure 46-4: Security is the most important part of this Technique.**

 Although the setting implies that PowerPoint will remove information from File Properties, in fact, selecting the check box here removes some (but not all) information from inside the file. For detailed information, see http://support.microsoft.com/?kbid=314800.

6. **Click OK.**

7. **Choose File➪Save.**

PowerPoint brings up the Save As dialog box (see Figure 46-5).

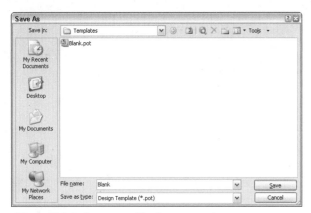

• **Figure 46-5: Save your blank presentation.**

8. In the Save as Type box, choose Design Template (*.pot). In the File Name box, type Blank. Then click Save.

PowerPoint saves the presentation as Blank.pot, in the correct location. (The name Blank.pot is not case-sensitive.)

Using Slide Masters

Slide masters allow you to simultaneously change title and other text fonts, bullets, and so on in all the slides in a presentation. You can use slide masters to format a single presentation in no time. Or make changes to the slide master in Blank.pot to make the changes stick in your current presentation and all the slides in all new blank presentations, too.

Every presentation has a slide master. To make changes to it

1. Choose View➪Master➪Slide Master.

To see the slide master, you might need to click the slide next to the number 1 on the left side. PowerPoint brings up the slide master for the presentation, along with the Slide Master View toolbar (see Figure 46-6).

To make the changes to Blank.pot, make sure you have it open.

2. Click within the Title Area for AutoLayouts box and make changes there to the format of the title on every slide.

For example, you could change the font, make it bold, or click and drag the box to resize it.

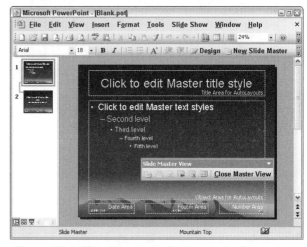

• **Figure 46-6: The slide master for** Mountain Top.pot.

3. Click within the Click to Edit Master Text Styles box and make changes there to the format of the body text on every slide.

You can change font formatting (Format➪Font), or the bullets (Format➪Bullets and Numbering), or any other character or paragraph formatting.

4. If you want a picture or drawing to appear on all slides, choose Insert➪Picture or bring up the Drawing toolbar (View➪Toolbars➪Drawing) and put the picture or drawing on the slide.

Note that you can use this approach to place text in a text box on every slide: Just click the Text Box icon on the Drawing toolbar.

5. When you're done making changes to the slide master, choose View➪Normal and you return to the presentation.

If you're working on `Blank.pot`, resume at Step 7 in the preceding section to save the presentation.

 Every presentation has a slide master that contains pictures, formatting, and other items that appear on each slide. Most presentations also have title masters, which control the formatting on title slides. For 99 percent of the people, 99 percent of the time, the fastest way to get your work done is to ignore the title master. If you want to change all the slides in a presentation, change the slide master. If changing the slide master messes up your title slide (or any other slide in the presentation), just bring up the offending slide and change it manually. Avoid title masters. Avoid multiple slide masters. You'll get home earlier because of it.

Technique 47

Recording a Sound Track

Save Time By

- Shipping a finished presentation with a built-in narration
- Recording an exact transcript of your presentation
- Setting up self-running presentations with a sound track

Uh, honey, I need to give this presentation to the Board tomorrow morning. Could you help me practice? Would you do that for me? All you need to do is sit and listen and tell me where I screw up. . . .

No, I don't expect to screw up all that much, but it helps if somebody listens while I practice so. . . .

Yes, I'm going to be talking about convertible subordinated debent. . . .

Oh, but you *do* know a *lot* about convertible subordinated debent. . . .

Uh, no, I don't think it will put you to sleep. At least, I hope it doesn't put you to. . . .

No, you can't listen to Norah Jones while I. . . .

Wait a sec. It says here in this book that I can record the presentation and play it back. Never mind.

Using Recorded Narrations

If you *really* want to save time with PowerPoint, record a sound track so that you don't have to be present to give the presentation!

Recording a narrative to go along with your presentation is easier than you think. Although you might not be interested in carrying the concept to its natural conclusion — having the presentation deliver itself, writing yourself out of the presentation entirely — recording a sound track can save you time in several ways and hone your presentation:

- Recording a practice presentation is a great way to go over the details and work out the bugs. Every "ummm" and "uhhh" that you utter goes into the recording, and the words that you speak get synchronized to the slides. When you play the narration back, you can tell precisely where you need to apply a bit o' the blarney.

✔ You really *can* record the entire presentation and have it run all by itself — although you need a fair amount of storage to hold the sound file, and you probably don't want to try running it over the Internet.

✔ If you have a presentation that delivers itself — typically in a kiosk (see Technique 48) — even a little bit of recorded sound can improve the presentation tremendously.

If you have a microphone that Windows recognizes, you have all the equipment that you need to record a narrative for your presentation.

Creating a Narration

Here's how to put together a narration for a slideshow:

1. **Get the presentation set up the way that you want it.**

After you start the presentation, you can pause the recording, but PowerPoint might have a hard time keeping up if you pause recording and then jump around to a slide that's out of sequence. Far better to keep it simple from the beginning.

2. **Click the first slide in the presentation.**

3. **Choose Slide Show⇨Record Narration.**

PowerPoint brings up the Record Narration dialog box, as shown in Figure 47-1.

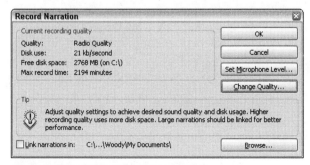

• **Figure 47-1:** Settings for the recording.

4. **Click the Change Quality button.**

You see the Sound Selection dialog box, as shown in Figure 47-2.

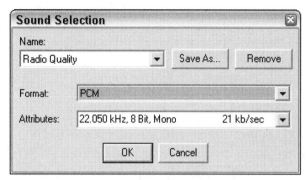

• **Figure 47-2:** Select a sound quality here.

5. **Select a sound quality from the Name drop-down list box and click OK to go back to the Record Narration dialog box.**

If you're going to play the sound through tinny computer speakers, so-called Telephone Quality — the lowest quality on offer — is good enough.

Choose CD Quality — the highest quality — only if you have to compensate for a bad acoustic situation — and you have a lot of disk space to hold the sound file. See the sidebar, "Recording CD Quality Sound," for more details.

Radio-quality sound suffices in all but the most demanding (read: big auditorium, bad sound system) circumstances.

6. **Click the Set Microphone Level button.**

PowerPoint brings up a Microphone Check dialog box, as shown in Figure 47-3. (Surprisingly, PowerPoint doesn't use Windows' microphone tools.)

7. **Follow the instructions onscreen, speak directly into the mike at a distance that you can maintain while narrating the presentation, and then click OK when you have the microphone working right.**

The sensitivity slider at the bottom of the Microphone Check dialog box adjusts itself to pick up your voice. The position of the mike matters most. Get it close to your mouth and don't vary the distance from your mouth to the mike when you test.

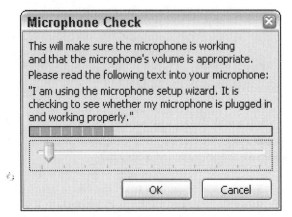

• **Figure 47-3:** Make sure that your microphone is working.

 PowerPoint doesn't use any of the built-in Windows microphone tools. This box is the only chance that you have to adjust sensitivity of the mike for recording a presentation narrative (er, slideshow narration).

 If you're going to do a lot of slide narrations, it's worth investing a few bucks to buy a high-quality headset with a microphone. You can more easily maintain the distance from mouth to mike, which frees your hands and allows you to sit back and relax while doing the narration.

8. Leave the Record Narration dialog box onscreen until you're ready to go through your entire presentation.

9. When you're ready, click OK and give your presentation, speaking into the microphone.

 Allow a second or so of idle time at the beginning of each slide to ensure that PowerPoint associates what you say with the correct slide. When you're through narrating a slide, allow two or three seconds before you click to go to the next slide. Depending on the speed of your computer, PowerPoint might clip the sound at the end of the slide.

10. Finish the presentation normally.

When you're done, PowerPoint asks whether you want to save *slide timings* along with the narrations. Slide timings are an indication of how long you spend on each slide while you're practicing (see Figure 47-4).

• **Figure 47-4:** Choose to save slide timings.

11. Click Save or Don't Save.

▶ **Click Save** if you want PowerPoint to run your presentation automatically (that is, if you want PowerPoint to be able to advance through the slides without your intervention) or if you want to keep track of how long you spend on each slide.

▶ **Click Don't Save** if you aren't worried about how long you're spending on each slide and you plan to run the presentation manually.

PowerPoint shows your presentation in Slide Sorter view. If you saved the slide timings, each slide's duration appears to the lower left of the slide, as you can see in Figure 47-5.

12. Save your presentation by choosing File⇨Save.

The narration gets saved, too.

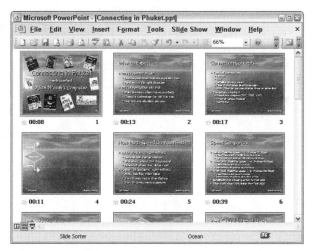

• **Figure 47-5: Slide timings appear below each slide.**

Recording CD Quality Sound

If you're recording CD Quality sound, select the Link Narrations In check box at the bottom of the Record Narration dialog box. If you don't select this check box, PowerPoint stores the recording for each slide inside the slide itself. Although that leads to large .ppt file sizes, it also means that your recording can't get lost. If you do select the check box, each slide's recording is stored in a separate .wav file.

The names of these separately maintained sound files are quite odd. Recordings for the PowerPoint file called myshow.ppt, for example, are stored in files with names myshow.ppt256.wav (for the first slide), myshow. ppt257.wav, and so on. If you re-record the first slide, the narration is stored in myshow.ppt256-0.wav.

Playing a Narration

To play back your narration

✔ If you told PowerPoint to save your slide timings, choose Slide Show➪View Slide Show and stand

back. PowerPoint goes through the entire presentation, precisely the way you recorded it.

✔ If you didn't have PowerPoint save your slide timings, choose Slide Show➪View Slide Show. The first slide appears, and your narration begins to play. PowerPoint waits for you to advance to the next slide by clicking normally before playing the narration that goes along with it.

Editing a Narration

To re-record a narration for an entire presentation, use the steps in the preceding section, starting at the beginning.

PowerPoint also makes it easy to re-record the narration for a single slide, but with a trick:

1. **Select the slide that you want to re-record.**

You can do that in Normal or Slide Sorter view.

2. **Choose Slide Show➪Record Narration.**

PowerPoint responds with the Record Narration dialog box. (Refer to Figure 47-1.)

3. **Adjust the recording quality, if desired; when you're ready to re-record the narration for the slide, click OK.**

PowerPoint shows you a smaller Record Narration dialog box that gives you the option of re-recording the narration for the entire presentation, or just for the specific slide (see Figure 47-6).

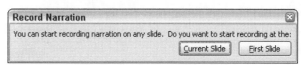

• **Figure 47-6: You can pick up the recording at the beginning of any slide.**

4. **Click the Current Slide button.**

   PowerPoint throws away the narration for the current slide (as well as its slide timing), displays the slide that you selected, and starts recording.

5. **Re-record the narration for the slide.**

6. **Here's the tricky part: You have to press the Esc key** *before* **you move on to the next slide.**

   If you mess up and advance to the next slide (which is easy to do if the re-recorded slide has animations) and then press the Esc key,

PowerPoint records over the beginning of the narration for the next slide. Blech.

When you press Esc, PowerPoint asks whether you want to save the slide timings. (Refer to Figure 47-4.)

7. **Click Save to save the new timing for the re-recorded slide.**

8. **Save the presentation.**

   The re-recorded narration is saved along with it.

Technique 48

Making a Presentation Run Itself

So the boss wants to have a TV at the entrance to the annual Board Meeting, showing off all the company's great achievements for the year. Or your daughter accumulated a bunch of information for her Science Fair project, but it looks really hokey scrawled out on a piece of flimsy whiteboard. Perchance the folks at the local museum are showing a great new exhibit, and they want you to come up with an audiovisual (dare I say, *multimedia?*) teaser so that people don't walk right by, thinking that it's more of the Same Old Stuff. Or maybe you have an extra table at the local trade show, but nobody to stand there and give the same presentation, over and over.

Why shell out the money — and spend the time — to get a television with a continuous-looping tape or DVD player? You have all the tools that you need with PowerPoint. And in this Technique, I show you how.

Choosing Self-Running Transitions

People think of self-running PowerPoint presentations as *kiosk* slideshows — the kind of simple touch-screen application that you've no doubt run into (and cursed over) in your local airport or mall. In fact, self-running presentations work great in many settings that have nothing to do with kiosks.

Every PowerPoint presentation can be coerced into running itself. If you can get PowerPoint to do something, you can tell PowerPoint to do it without any interaction at all — from you or anyone else. In effect, your presentation turns into a super screen saver, capable of running animations, playing sounds, even running the voice-over narrations that I describe in Technique 47.

On the other hand, you can create a PowerPoint presentation that's controlled by the person viewing the presentation, limiting him to very simple controls over when slides advance — or even which slide comes up next. In this case, too, the presentation can take full advantage of all the features that PowerPoint has to offer. On the third hand, you can easily create a presentation that freezes and can't be unstuck without, in effect, pulling the plug.

The trick lies in specifying a transition for each slide:

- ✔ You can tell PowerPoint to move on to the next slide after a specific amount of time passes — the *slide timing.*

- ✔ You can put one of PowerPoint's predefined *action buttons* on a slide to allow the viewer to choose which slide to see next.

- ✔ If you forget to assign a slide timing and you don't put an action button on the slide, the presentation freezes on the unendowed slide: You can't move forward or backward!

Looping a Presentation Continuously

To create a PowerPoint presentation that runs itself

1. **Make sure that you have the presentation itself in good working order.**

2. **Ensure that every slide either has a slide timing (see the next section) or an action button (see the concluding section in this Technique).**

    Every slide must have a way to move on to the next slide. Otherwise, the presentation freezes.

 PowerPoint doesn't warn you or have any tools that will reliably trap these black hole slides. Some tricks do exist (see the next section), but you're basically on your own.

3. **Choose Slide Show⇨Set Up Show.**

    PowerPoint shows you the Set Up Show dialog box, as shown in Figure 48-1.

4. **Select the Browsed at a Kiosk (Full Screen) radio button.**

    PowerPoint immediately selects and grays out the Loop Continuously Until Esc check box. That has three effects:

- ▶ It disables all the mouse functions during the presentation — except clicking action buttons.

- ▶ It disables all the PowerPoint keyboard functions during the presentation except pressing the Esc key, which stops the presentation.

- ▶ It tells PowerPoint to treat the first slide of the presentation as the next slide after the final slide. For example, if you put a Next action button on the final slide of a presentation, when you click it, PowerPoint loops back to the first slide. If you put a Back action button on the first slide of a presentation, click it, and PowerPoint moves to the last slide.

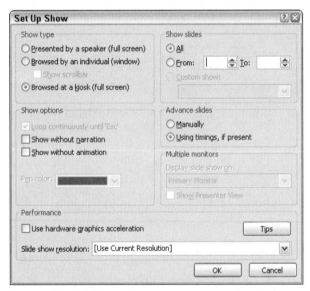

• **Figure 48-1: Self-running presentations are *kiosk presentations.***

5. **Click OK.**

    Your presentation is ready to run itself.

To run the presentation in kiosk mode, choose Slide Show⇨View Show.

 The only way to stop a continuously looping presentation from inside PowerPoint is by pressing Esc. You can, however, invoke a higher authority: Press Alt+Tab to use

Windows to switch between running programs. Alternatively, press Ctrl+Alt+Del to use Windows Task Manager to quash the runaway program.

Getting the Slide Timings Just Right

I explain in the preceding section why every slide in a self-running PowerPoint slideshow must have either a slide timing or an action button. The slide timing setting for a slide tells PowerPoint how long it should wait before advancing to the next slide automatically.

You have three absolutely foolproof ways to make sure that every slide in a presentation has a valid slide timing:

- ✔ **Add a narration** to every slide in the presentation (see Technique 47), and make sure that you click Save when asked whether you want to save slide timings.

- ✔ **Run a rehearsal timing** all the way through the presentation. During a rehearsal timing, PowerPoint keeps track of how long you take to go through each slide and saves that timing along with the slide.

- ✔ **Manually apply a slide timing** to each slide. This is the least desirable approach because it's hard to guess how long each slide will take — and because you might forget to assign a timing to one slide, thus stopping your continuously looping presentation dead in its tracks.

Applying slide timing manually

To manually apply slide timing

1. **Click the slide to which you want to apply slide timing.**

2. **Choose View⇨Task Pane, click the down arrow at the top of the task pane, and then select Slide Transition.**

PowerPoint brings up the Slide Transition task pane, as shown in Figure 48-2.

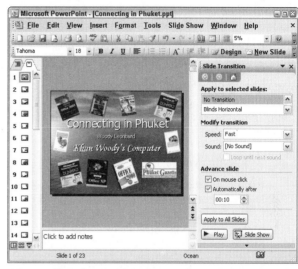

• **Figure 48-2:** Set the slide timing here.

3. **Under Advance Slide, select the Automatically After check box; then set the number of seconds in the list box there.**

In Figure 48-2, I set the slide to advance automatically after 10 seconds.

 Slide timings and action buttons can work together: You can tell PowerPoint to move on to the next slide either when the viewer clicks an action button or after a specific amount of time has passed. If you want to allow both, select both check boxes under Advance Slide.

4. **In most cases, you want to set the timing for only one slide. However, to be absolutely sure that every slide in your presentation has a slide timing, you should click the Apply To All Slides button at least once.**

 I recommend clicking the Apply to All Slides button once as kind of slide timing safety net. That way, you can make sure that every slide in a self-running presentation has an assigned slide timing.

5. Click the X in the upper-right corner of the task pane to get it out of the way. Or, select another slide and repeat Step 3 to assign a timing to that slide.

Adding timing settings with a rehearsal timing

When you run a *rehearsal timing* while you make the presentation, PowerPoint keeps track of the amount of time you spend on each slide. Follow these steps to run a rehearsal timing:

1. Be sure that your presentation is in its final form.

If the presentation is only half-baked, the timings you record won't reflect how the final presentation should unfurl. At the very least, every slide that will appear in your final presentation should be present before you run the rehearsal timing.

2. Wait until you're ready to go through the slide show, allowing sufficient time for each slide.

If the slides have no action buttons, you must allow enough time for a very slow reader to slog through your brilliant prose.

3. Choose Slide Show➪Rehearse Timings.

PowerPoint starts the slide show, placing a Rehearsal dialog box in the upper-left corner, as shown in Figure 48-3. The Rehearsal timer shows you the elapsed time for this slide as well as for the entire presentation. As you go through the presentation, PowerPoint keeps track of how much time you spend on each slide.

• **Figure 48-3: The Rehearsal timer.**

4. To pause the timer (and freeze the presentation), click the Pause button on the Rehearsal dialog box — the one with two parallel lines.

When you pause the presentation, PowerPoint simply stops the clock, so you can get up and walk around before proceeding with your rehearsal. You can resume the presentation (and continue the timer) by clicking anywhere on the slide.

5. To start all over again on a specific slide, click the Repeat button — the one with the left-curbed arrow.

Doing so resets the timer for the current slide to zero, resets the elapsed time for the presentation to nullify the effects of the current slide, and restarts the slide's animation from the beginning. Repeating doesn't affect the timings for other slides in the presentation.

6. Finish the presentation normally.

When you leave the last slide, PowerPoint asks whether you want to save the new slide timings (see Figure 48-4).

• **Figure 48-4: Make sure that you save the results of at least one timing run.**

7. If this is a good timing run, click Yes. If you want to ignore the results of this run, click No.

 A missing slide timing will cause your presentation to grind to a halt. You should click Yes for at least one timing rehearsal to make sure that each slide in your self-running presentation has a slide timing safety net.

PowerPoint returns to Slide Sorter view with each slide's timing showing below the slide, as you can see in Figure 48-5.

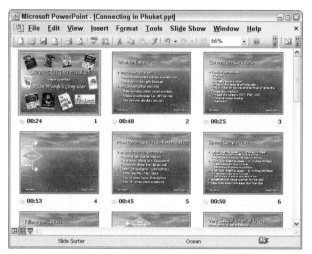

• **Figure 48-5:** Slide timings appear below and to the left of each slide.

Adding Navigation Action Buttons

If you want to allow the person viewing a self-running presentation to move to the next slide or back to a previous slide, the fastest and easiest way is via action buttons.

 Combine action buttons with lengthy slide timings (see the preceding section) to give a viewer the best of both worlds — either the ability to move through your self-running presentation quickly on command, or to view at a more leisurely pace in a completely hands-off way.

To place a navigation button on a slide

1. **Click the slide that you want to contain the action button.**

To place the same action button(s) on all slides in a presentation, put them on the slide master: Choose View➪Master➪Slide Master and follow these steps.

2. **Choose Slide Show➪Action Buttons.**

PowerPoint brings up a panel of AutoShapes (see Table 48-1). I talk about AutoShapes in Technique 11, and all the tricks there apply here.

 If you click and drag the bar with the dots at the top of the panel, you can tear off the action buttons and keep them on your desktop.

3. **Click one of the six action buttons listed in Table 48-1.**

By default, the buttons in Table 48-1 work in self-running presentations.

4. **Click and drag the cursor on the slide to draw the button.**

You draw action buttons just like any other AutoShape (see Figure 48-6).

• **Figure 48-6:** Like AutoShapes, you can draw action buttons anywhere on the slide.

The moment that you release the mouse button while drawing, PowerPoint brings up the Action Settings dialog box (see Figure 48-7). The specific action that you get is keyed to the button. For example, if you select the Back button, Previous Slide appears in the Hyperlink To drop-down list, as shown in Figure 48-7.

5. **Unless you have a burning desire to make your life very complicated, click OK.**

Yes, you can create a link to anyplace you like, but in a self-running presentation, you almost always want to accept the default action.

6. **Repeat Steps 3, 4, and 5 to draw additional action buttons on the slide.**

In Figure 48-8, I drew Previous and Next action buttons — standard fare for self-running presentations that permit viewer interaction.

• **Figure 48-7:** You can override the default settings but only at your own peril.

• **Figure 48-8:** Previous and Next buttons have to be drawn separately by mouse.

TABLE 48-1: ACTION BUTTONS THAT WORK IN SELF-RUNNING PRESENTATIONS

Button	Button Name	Where It Moves You To
🏠	Home	The first slide in the presentation
◁	Back/Previous	The preceding slide in the presentation
▷	Forward/Next	The next slide in the presentation
◁|	Beginning	The first slide in the presentation
|▷	End	The last slide in the presentation
↩	Return	The previously viewed slide

Answering Predictable Questions

Technique 49

So you've given the same presentation a dozen times. Half the time, someone in the audience asks about one specific point in the presentation — a detail that isn't important enough to put in the presentation itself, but one that pops up often enough. You wish you had a few slides that you could show to answer the question. Sound familiar?

Maybe you're going to pitch a proposal to the boss's boss's boss, and you just *know* that she's going to ask to see the details about a particular point in the proposal. You don't want to stick an extra slide in the show to answer the question just because it's so nit-picky and having a slide like that as part of the presentation would slow down the pace. But, man, if she asks that one question, you really want to have one super slide in your hip pocket that nails the point beyond any question. PowerPoint can do that. It's easy. This Technique shows you how.

Planning for the Predictable

PowerPoint has come under a lot of criticism for making us stupid. Yale professor Dr. Edward Tufte, the preeminent academic authority on presenting information, wrote an extended essay on the topic that damns PowerPoint's infuriating insistence on reducing

- everything
- to stunted
- information-poor
- bullet points

which, I hasten to add, are usually read verbatim by the presenter to a far too-uncritical audience (www.edwardtufte.com).

NASA's Columbia Accident Investigation Board placed part of the blame for the space shuttle's failure and loss of seven astronauts' lives on excessive reliance on PowerPoint: "When engineering analyses and risk assessments are condensed to fit on a standard form or overhead slide, information is inevitably lost" (CAIB report volume 1 page 191, www.caib.us).

PowerPoint doesn't have to be that way. Your presentation doesn't have to be that way. With a bit of planning and no small amount of care, you can create a presentation that includes all the detail you need to make a point or explain a complex situation. And you can pull up that information if you need it in the middle of a presentation, go through the supporting information until your audience is satisfied, and then return to the main presentation with a mere click.

 More than that, if you hand out printed slides or notes, all that supporting information on the hidden slides can be included, in sequence, even if it wasn't delivered live in the presentation. Your audience can refer to the supporting detail any time by looking at the handouts.

PowerPoint doesn't make people stupid. Stupid presentations make people stupid. You know what I mean.

In general terms, here's how to handle predictable questions:

1. **Identify abridged slides in your presentation that need additional supporting information.**

2. **Create a supporting slide (or slides) that provides the additional information.**

3. **Put a clickable link on the abridged slide that hops to the supporting slide.**

4. **Put a clickable link on the supporting slide that goes back to the last slide viewed.**

5. **Hide the supporting slide so that it doesn't show up in the presentation unless you specifically click the link and bring it up.**

If you follow this approach

✔ **Displaying the supporting slide (or slides) is easy and fast.** However, if you don't need the

supporting slide, it's also easy to ignore it completely. When you're done with the supporting material, it takes only a click to return to the main presentation.

✔ **When you print presentation handouts, you can print the hidden slide** (and any notes associated with the slide) so that it shows up in the order that you would've shown it if the slide had been necessary.

✔ **You can't lose what's on the supporting slide.** It's part of the presentation; it's in the file. If you distribute the presentation, the supporting slide goes along.

 Keeping supporting data available in the PowerPoint file is particularly important for crucial details (such as engineering data) that might not make the cut for an executive presentation but should nonetheless be available for future reference. If you look at the Columbia Accident Investigation Board report cited at the beginning of this Technique, you'll see how supporting slides could've made a world of difference.

Creating the Supporting Slide

Here's how to ensure that the crucial explanatory slide always sits in your (virtual) hip pocket:

1. **Identify a slide that needs additional supporting information.**

   I call such slides *abridged*. In Figure 49-1, I have a slide that asks "Where do you live?" as one step in determining the best Internet connection for people living in Phuket. Having details about the affected locations would be very helpful if anyone in the audience should ask.

2. **Click the New Slide button on the Formatting toolbar.**

   PowerPoint adds a new slide to the presentation immediately after the abridged slide (see Figure 49-2).

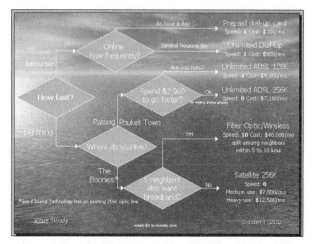

• **Figure 49-1:** Create a supporting slide from the original.

3. Fill in all the necessary supporting information.

If you need more than one slide to hold all the information, see the next section.

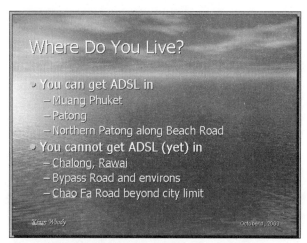

• **Figure 49-2:** The new slide becomes the hidden, supporting slide.

4. Add a Return action button that leads back to the last slide you viewed.

I explain how to add action buttons in Technique 48. Last Slide Viewed is the default action for the return action button.

 Right-click the return action button and choose Format AutoShape. You can format it however you like. Usually you want the button to be very visible and easy to find when you're delivering the presentation. You can put text on the button by right-clicking and choosing Edit Text. Then click OK to exit Format AutoShape.

Figure 49-3 shows what my return action button looks like.

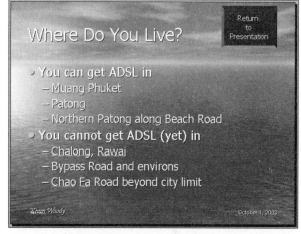

• **Figure 49-3:** Make the action button as conspicuous or subtle as you like.

5. Choose Slide Show➪Hide Slide.

When you hide a slide, PowerPoint doesn't show the slide during a normal presentation, but the slide stays inside the presentation nonetheless. You can tell that a slide has been hidden because of the diagonal strikethrough icon on the slide number in Normal and Slide Sorter view (see Figure 49-4.)

6. Click the abridged slide — the one that needs this supporting slide.

7. If the abridged slide already has a picture, drawing, or block of text that you would like to make into a link, right-click the picture, drawing, or text placeholder, and then choose Action Settings.

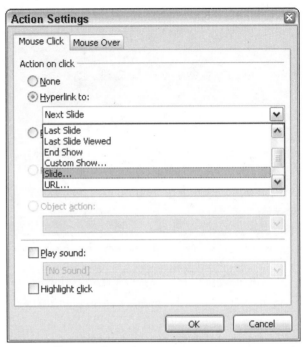

• **Figure 49-4: In Normal and Slide Sorter views, a hidden slide has a slashed slide number.**

If the abridged slide doesn't have a suitable picture, drawing, or block of text available, you can always put one on the slide. Alternatively, you can make any text on the slide hot. (See the procedure at the end of this section.) If you want to use PowerPoint's built-in AutoShapes to create a link, choose Slide Show➪Action Buttons, draw an action button on the slide, and then continue with Step 11.

PowerPoint shows you the Action Settings dialog box that you see in Figure 49-5.

8. **Select the Hyperlink To radio button and then select the Slide option in the drop-down box.**

You see the Hyperlink to Slide dialog box, as shown in Figure 49-6.

9. **Pick the hidden supporting slide from the list of slides on offer.**

When creating a link to a hidden slide, the slide number is in parentheses.

10. **Click OK twice.**

11. **Save your presentation.**

If you run the presentation, you see that the hidden supporting slide never appears unless you specifically click the link (created in Steps 7 through 9) on the abridged slide. When you're done showing the supporting slide, you can simply click the return action button to return to the abridged slide in the presentation.

• **Figure 49-5: Create a link to a hidden slide in the presentation.**

• **Figure 49-6: Choose the supporting slide here.**

Unless you make the link on the abridged slide stand out, you might forget that a hidden supporting slide is available! The only visual cue that PowerPoint gives you during the presentation is the mouse cursor: When you move the mouse over a link, the cursor turns into a pointing finger.

In lieu of Step 10 in the preceding procedure, you can turn plain text on the slide into a link for a hidden supporting slide:

1. **Select the text on the abridged slide that you want to make hot.**

You can choose any text, anywhere, anytime.

2. **Choose Insert➪Hyperlink.**

PowerPoint shows you the Insert Hyperlink dialog box that you see in Figure 49-7.

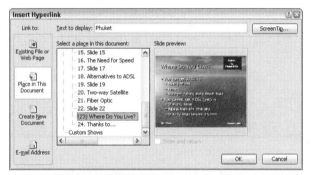

• **Figure 49-7:** You can also create a hyperlink to the hidden supporting slide.

3. **On the left, in the Link To section, click Place in This Document.**

4. **In the Select a Place in This Document list box, select the hidden supporting slide (look for the parentheses).**

5. **Click OK.**

The hyperlink that you create behaves precisely the same way as the link generated via the Action Settings dialog box.

Running Several Supporting Slides

In the preceding section, I talk about creating a single hidden supporting slide that connects to an abridged slide in a presentation. That begs the obvious question: What if you have too much stuff to put on a single supporting slide? You might need an entire supporting presentation.

The easiest and fastest way that I know to set up a hidden sub-presentation involves creating a *custom show,* taking care to tell PowerPoint that you want to show the custom show and then return to the abridged slide that kicked it off.

To create a custom show and use it as a hidden supporting show, follow these steps:

1. **Create all the slides in the supporting show. Select each in turn and choose Slide Show➪ Hide Slide to mark each of the slides in the show as hidden.**

Because the slides have been hidden, none of the slides in this supporting show will appear if you run the normal slideshow.

 Keeping track of a hidden custom show is easier if you group all the slides for the show together and stick them all at the end of the presentation.

2. **Choose Slide Show➪Custom Shows.**

PowerPoint brings up the Custom Shows dialog box.

3. **Click New.**

You see the Define Custom Show dialog box, as shown in Figure 49-8.

• **Figure 49-8:** Pick the slides and put them in order.

4. In the Slide Show Name field, type a name for the custom slideshow. Then, one by one, click the hidden support slides that you've created and click the Add button to add them to the custom show.

 Rearrange individual slides in the show by clicking them in the Slides in Custom Show list box and moving them up or down, clicking the up-arrow or down-arrow buttons on the far right.

5. When you complete the hidden supporting presentation, click OK, and then exit.

6. Click the abridged slide — the slide that you want to link to the hidden sub-presentation.

7. Right-click the picture, drawing, or text in the abridged slide that you want to make hot, and then choose Hyperlink.

You can make just about anything hot. You can also draw action buttons or put AutoShapes or drawings on the slide that can then be made hot. See all the examples in Step 10 in the preceding section.

PowerPoint brings up the Insert Hyperlink box, as shown in Figure 49-9.

8. In the Link To section on the left, click Place in This Document. In the Select a Place in This Document list box, select the hidden custom show that you want to run when you click the link.

 If you forget to select the Show and Return check box, when you reach the end of the hidden support presentation, PowerPoint forgets that it was running a sub-presentation and just ends everything!

9. Click OK.

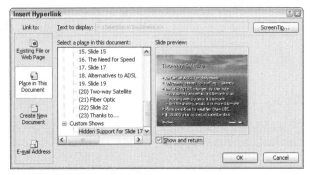

• **Figure 49-9:** Create a link here.

When you click the link on the abridged slide, your hidden presentation runs, following the slide sequence that you chose in Step 4. When the hidden support presentation finishes, PowerPoint returns to the abridged slide.

Slick. Fast. Easy.

Not all PowerPoint presentations are stupid.

Technique 50

Building toward a Goal

Save Time By

- ✔ Creating a goal slide once — the right way
- ✔ Modifying the goal slide to use repeatedly
- ✔ Keeping your viewers alert, anticipating the result

This Technique is all about content.

When you've seen as many bad PowerPoint presentations as I have, they start aligning themselves into categories. I think Dante reserved the seventh slide of PowerPoint hell for presenters who

- ✔ Read ev-er-y stu-pid syl-la-ble directly from the slide. Presenters who parrot their own pap don't seem to realize that the audience skims the important part of the presentation in the first three seconds each slide appears and then promptly goes to sleep.

- ✔ Give the entire presentation in the first two slides and then spend 40 minutes trying to fill in the gaps, haphazardly, jumping from topic to topic.

> *Lasciate ogni speranza, voi ch'entrate. . . .*
> *(Translation: Abandon hope, all ye who enter . . .)*
> *Inferno*, Dante Alighieri, ca. 1308

I don't think there's any cure for the slide readers. Short of euthanasia, anyway.

But there is a cure for the presentation that blasts all its thunder at first, and then slowly, painfully fades away. You need to turn those presentations around; you need to build to a crescendo. Most presentations lend themselves to gradually building up to one key slide, whether it's a flowchart, a graph, or just another bunch of dull bouncing bullets.

 The trick to building up to a finale? Create the *goal* slide first — the slide you want to build up to — and then sprinkle copies of the goal slide throughout the presentation, deleting the pieces that shouldn't appear in the penultimate version, then the preceding version, and so on. By working backward, you not only focus your audience — you focus your presentation.

Reducing the Goal Slide

Take a minute and just think. Think about the point that you want to make. Cut through the bull and the explanations and the arguments. When your audience leaves the room, what do you want them to remember? What do you want them to do?

That's what goes on the goal slide.

If you can't think of any straightforward, unambiguous conclusion to your presentation, you haven't thought enough about what you need to say. Do yourself and your audience a favor and call the whole thing off.

When you do know what you want to say, cut to the chase and create that goal slide. Here's a great way to make a goal slide with impact:

1. **Create the whole slide, lock, stock, and barrel. Don't worry about transitions. Don't worry about how you're going to explain it. Just put the slide together so you can work on it.**

In Figure 50-1, I have one of my favorite slides — a decision tree for choosing the best Internet connection in Phuket, Thailand. Your goal slide might consist of a graph or a sequence of bullet points. The more visual, the better.

2. **Think backward. What part of your presentation leads to this point? Which pieces of the goal slide will be discussed in the final slide or two of your presentation?**

You need to find a piece of the goal slide that can be removed.

3. **Choose Edit➪Duplicate.**

That puts a copy of the goal slide in your presentation (see the left task pane of Figure 50-2), so your entire presentation now consists of two copies of the goal slide.

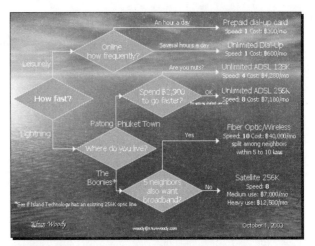

• **Figure 50-1:** Create your goal slide first.

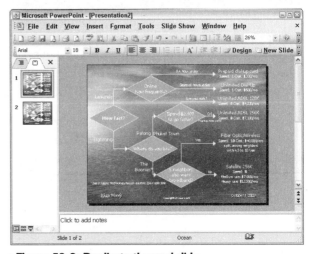

• **Figure 50-2:** Duplicate the goal slide.

4. **Click the first slide in the presentation.**

5. **Select the pieces of the goal slide that can be removed and then delete them.**

In Figure 50-3, I delete the lower-right corner of the goal slide. That becomes the part of the goal slide that I talk about in the presentation between the two slides.

If your goal slide is just a list of bullet points, you probably want to remove the last bullet point. Typically, the last bullet point is what you want to talk about before the complete goal slide appears onscreen.

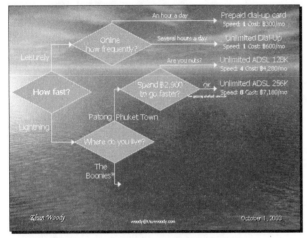

• **Figure 50-3:** I remove the part of the slide that I want to talk about between the two slides.

6. **Again, think backward. What part of your presentation leads to this snapshot of the goal slide?**

   You need enough material to cover two or three traditional bullet-point slides in order to provide the transition to this slide.

7. **Choose Edit➪Duplicate.**

   You now have three slides in the presentation.

8. **Click the first slide in the presentation.**

9. **Select the pieces on this slide that can be removed and then delete them.**

   Figure 50-4 shows how I worked backward.

10. **Repeat Steps 6–9, each time removing a piece of the goal slide while you plot how you're going to get from slide to slide.**

Figures 50-5 and 50-6 trace back the genesis of this presentation.

11. **Save your presentation (if you haven't already).**

I discuss a second half to this building-backward approach in the next section.

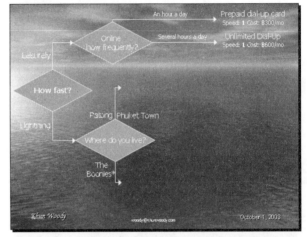

• **Figure 50-4:** Remove the next part of the goal slide.

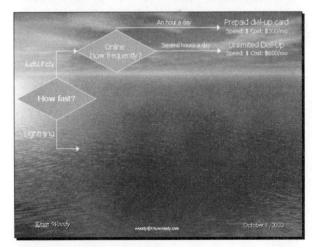

• **Figure 50-5:** The earlier slide.

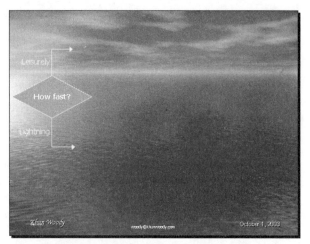

• **Figure 50-6:** The first incarnation of the goal slide.

Building Forward to the Goal Slide

In the preceding section, I show you how to build your presentation backward from the goal slide. Before you start adding all the slides with bullet points, you can make the trip to your goal slide a bit more appealing by adding simple animations. Here's how:

1. **Click the second slide and choose Slide Show⇨ Custom Animation.**

In Figure 50-7, I select the second slide in the series that leads to the goal slide and get ready to animate it.

If you animate the transitions between these slides that lead up to the goal slide, your audience will remember what you've said before, they'll understand how the intervening slides relate to the whole presentation, and they might even see how you're building to a specific goal.

2. **Think about moving from the preceding slide to this one: what elements get added? (Answer: the ones you removed when you created the preceding slide.) In which order should they appear to emphasize that you're building toward a goal slide?**

Looking at Figure 50-7, I decide that the best way to move from the previous slide (shown in Figure 50-6) to this one is by first showing the diamond with the question Online How Frequently? and then by showing each of the two given answers.

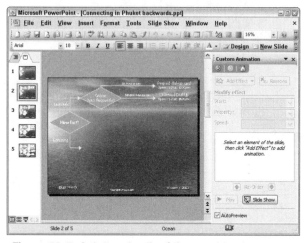

• **Figure 50-7:** Animate details of the transition between slides.

3. **Select the first element that you want to appear on this slide.**

In Figure 50-8, I select the diamond with the question Online How Frequently?

• **Figure 50-8:** Animate the first item that changes between the slides.

4. Click the Add Effect button, choose Entrance, and then choose an Entrance effect that appeals to you.

In Figure 50-8, I use the Glide effect, which rapidly moves the diamond in from the left.

5. Repeat Steps 3 and 4 for each element that appears first on this slide.

In Figure 50-9, after applying the Glide effect to the diamond, I choose all the elements on the top and apply the Glide effect to them. Then I choose all the elements on the lower branch and apply the Glide effect to them.

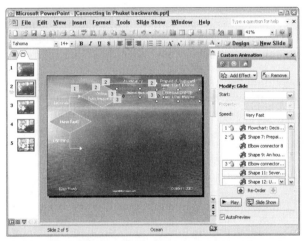

• **Figure 50-9:** First the diamond comes in, then the top branch, and then the bottom branch.

6. Click the Play button in the Task pane to make sure the animation works the way you want.

7. Save your presentation.

8. Repeat Steps 1–7 for every slide in the series.

After you have the sequence leading up to the goal slide, you're ready to fill in the missing pieces: typically bullet-point slides that move from slide to slide in a more-or-less orderly and understandable way.

If you follow this Technique, your audience will stay with you — unless they fall asleep — and they should walk away with a good idea of what you want them to remember and how you came to recommend it.

 Don't hand out a copy of the goal slide until you show it on the screen. You'd just be giving your audience good reason to ignore what you say throughout the presentation.

Technique 51

Tripping the Light Fantastic with Multimedia

If your fondest memories of PowerPoint multimedia date back to the time of postage stamp-size pictures that never managed to play right during a presentation — well, you must've been working with Office 2000. How retro.

PowerPoint 2003 has the ability to bring Windows Media Player (WMP) pictures — and audio tracks, too for that matter — directly into your slides. Instead of relying on PowerPoint to play your movies, WMP itself can take over.

The differences between native PowerPoint and Windows Media Player formats are not nearly as substantial as you might imagine, and the Windows Media Player implementation inside PowerPoint leaves much to be desired. But WMP does have a reputation for being much more stable than PowerPoint's player, and you might see a difference in quality, particularly for high-resolution playback.

This Technique helps you choose the right player for the right job.

Choosing the Right Player

PowerPoint has a built-in media player that can handle most of the common file types, including most video standards (including MPG, AVI, WMV, and animated GIF) and audio standards (including MP3, WMA, WAV, and MIDI).

Windows Media Player, on the other hand, plays all of those kinds of files and many more — so many, in fact, that if you have an odd file format, you really need to try to open the file in Windows Media Player itself to see whether it can figure out how to read the file.

You can put movies (and audio clips) inside your PowerPoint presentation with either of the two players. When you choose, keep these points in mind:

✔ **Speed and ease:** Using the native PowerPoint player is much easier and faster. In fact, Microsoft's first attempt to graft Windows Media

Player into PowerPoint (in PowerPoint 2003) has the look and feel of an amateurish rush job.

✔ **Reliability:** On the other hand, WMP has a reputation for being far more robust than the internal PowerPoint player. Whereas PowerPoint might lock up or crash, WMP should keep cruising.

✔ **Video clips with a slide:** If you want to play a video clip immediately when a slide appears, you have no choice but to use the native PowerPoint player — WMP movies have to be started manually. More than that, if you use WMP, the initial shot of the movie on the slide looks bizarre, and you get a distracting sliding bar across the bottom of the clip.

✔ **Compatibility issues:** If you take a presentation from one machine to another and the versions of Windows Media Player are different, you might have compatibility problems, particularly if the other machine uses WMP 8 (the version that shipped with the original version of Windows XP) or earlier.

For most people on most PCs, I recommend using the native PowerPoint player, even though I've spent years swearing at it. Microsoft hasn't put much effort into integrating WMP with PowerPoint, and it shows.

When you put a movie in a slide, the movie is *not* embedded in the presentation. PowerPoint keeps a link to the movie file. If you take the presentation to a different machine, you have to move the movie file — and put it in the same folder location as on the original machine. (Pack and Go, described in Technique 52, moves the files for you.)

The fact that the movie is linked — not embedded in the presentation — should also give you a hint about the best way to speed up a herky-jerky movie: Stick the movie on some fast media that's immediately accessible to the PC that's running the presentation, even if you have to haul along a USB 2-based CD or external hard drive. If you put the movie on a network drive or a slow CD, you're just begging for jerkiness.

Inserting Multimedia with Native PowerPoint Tools

To run an MPEG (`.mpg`) movie in a PowerPoint slide and let PowerPoint control how it's shown, do the following. You can use this same procedure to put any other kind of multimedia content on a slide, including sounds and GIF/JPEG pictures — even animated GIFs.

To download an MPEG file from the Internet (instead of playing it), right-click the link and choose Save Target As.

1. **Create a new slide to hold the movie.**

You can click the New Slide button on the Formatting toolbar or choose Insert⇨New Slide.

2. **If the Slide Layout task pane does not appear, choose View⇨Task Pane and choose Slide Layout from the drop-down list at the top of PowerPoint's task pane.**

3. **Click one of the layout formats.**

In Figure 51-1, I choose the Title and Content layout.

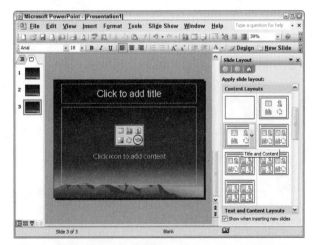

• **Figure 51-1:** Apply one of PowerPoint's built-in layouts that include *Content* (what a lousy name!) or *Media Clip.*

4. Add any text you like to the slide. When you're ready to bring in the movie, click the Insert Media Clip icon in the lower-right corner. (It looks like a video camera.)

PowerPoint brings up its Media Clip dialog box. This dialog box is sluggish (bordering on comatose) because PowerPoint reaches out to Microsoft's Web site to haul in pictures.

 PowerPoint ships with some truly insipid pictures but an enormous collection of wonderful sounds. Fans of the www.tucows.com shareware site might get a special kick out of the audio clip Two Cows Moo.

5. Click the Import button.

PowerPoint brings up the Add Clips to Organizer dialog box.

6. Navigate to the movie that you want to use and then click Add.

Sooner or later, the Media Clip dialog box comes back. Your movie should be the first item in the organizer.

7. Double-click the movie in the Media Clip dialog box.

PowerPoint inserts the movie into the slide and then immediately asks "How do you want the movie to start in the slide show?"

8. Assuming that you want the movie to start as soon as the slide comes up, click Automatically.

The opening shot of your movie appears on the slide, and it's set to run as soon as the slide appears during a presentation (see Figure 51-2).

 You can pause the movie while it's playing by clicking it. Click again to resume play. After the movie finishes, the last shot appears. If you want to start the movie all over again, click it.

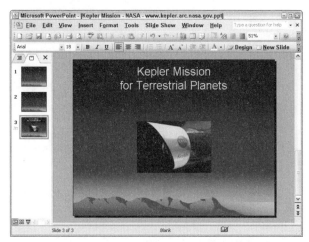

• **Figure 51-2:** This movie clip is from the NASA Kepler Mission site, www.kepler.arc.nasa.gov/downloading.html.

Inserting a Media Player Movie

If you decide to use Windows Media Player to run your PowerPoint movie, here's how to get the movie into a slide:

1. Create a slide for the movie.

The most common ways to make a new slide are to choose Insert⇨Slide or to click the New Slide button on the Formatting toolbar.

2. Type any text that you want to appear on the slide.

The layout for the slide isn't critical unless you need to put text on the slide in addition to the movie. In my example, I simply type a heading on the slide and leave the rest of it blank.

3. Choose Insert⇨Object.

PowerPoint shows you the Insert Object dialog box (see Figure 51-3).

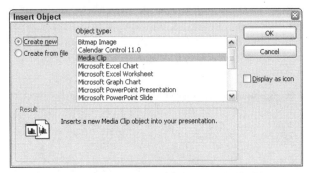

• **Figure 51-3:** To connect to the Windows Media Player, you have to create a Media Clip object.

4. **In the Object Type box, choose Media Clip and then click OK.**

The slide gets a grotesque placeholder, and a Windows Media Player-like control bar appears above the slide (see Figure 51-4).

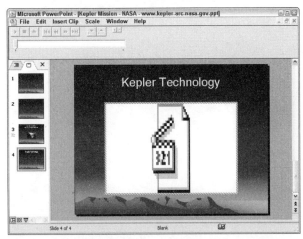

• **Figure 51-4:** The Windows Media Player face painted on PowerPoint.

5. **Choose Insert Clip⇨1 Video for Windows.**

WMP presents you with a variation of the standard Open dialog box.

6. **In the Files of Type box at the bottom, choose All Files (*.*) and then navigate to the movie that you want to put in the presentation. Click the movie; then click Open.**

Windows Media Player, working on top of PowerPoint, comes back with an odd superimposition of the movie on top of the slide (see Figure 51-5).

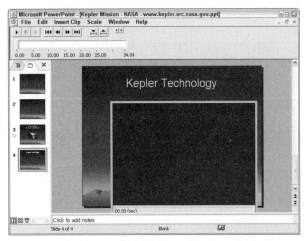

• **Figure 51-5:** The movie has almost been assimilated into the slide.

7. **Click outside the movie panel to have the movie brought into the slide.**

PowerPoint takes back control, but the panel that contains the movie might be out of kilter, falling off the slide (see Figure 51-6).

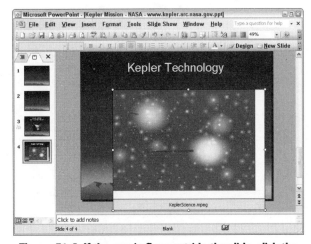

• **Figure 51-6:** If the movie flops outside the slide, click the dragging handles and resize it.

8. **Resize and then click and drag the movie to position it where you want on the slide.**

When you deliver the presentation, the slide with the Windows Media Player movie object comes up looking like Figure 51-7.

• **Figure 51-7:** WMP movies tacked onto slides look funny.

When the slide with the movie appears, you can play the movie by clicking it. Windows Media Player provides you with Play, Pause, and Stop buttons as well as a slider that you can drag to specific locations in the movie (see Figure 51-8).

• **Figure 51-8:** Very abbreviated WMP controls on a slide.

Taking a Presentation on the Road

Save Time By

- Putting the whole presentation on CD
- Using fail-safe backups
- Running presentations without PowerPoint

Y ou're making a tight connection en route between New York and San Francisco, and for some inexplicable reason, you leave your laptop behind on the plane. And by the time you notice, the plane's on its way to Sydney. No big deal. The airline can radio the plane, and your laptop will find its way back . . . except your PowerPoint presentation — the reason *why* you're flying from New York to San Francisco — is on the laptop. Ooops.

A million things can and do go wrong with the best-laid plans. Your hard drive crashes; Windows starts hiccuping with Blue Screens of Death; somebody accidentally grabs your laptop and heads out the door; PowerPoint just won't start. You name it. Somebody's suffered through it.

This Technique shows you how to get your presentation ready for any eventuality . . . except the CEO who inevitably snores.

Packaging for CD

Any PowerPoint presentation that you take on the road should be backed up in a very specific way. PowerPoint calls it *Package for CD*. I call it *Package for CYA*. Microsoft did a good job with the latest version of Package for CD, and it's well worth your consideration.

Packaging a presentation for CD brings together all the parts of the presentation (including linked pictures and weird fonts) in one quick operation. Even if you aren't headed out on the road, Package for CD is a good way to make sure that you have everything backed up in your presentation.

 Although this feature's name is Package for *CD*, you can bundle all the files together in a folder, whether you have a CD burner or not. I talk about an important application of this approach in the section, "Covering Your B...ases."

To package a presentation for CD

1. **Open the presentation.**

In Figure 52-1, I have one of my favorite presentations open and ready to back up. All the pictures show up in the presentation, and the file has just been saved.

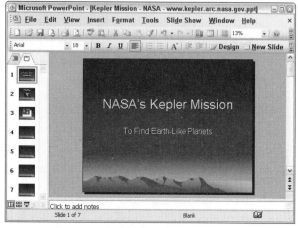

• **Figure 52-1: Start with the final presentation.**

2. **Choose File⇨Package for CD.**

PowerPoint responds with the Package for CD dialog box (some would call it a wizard), as shown in Figure 52-2.

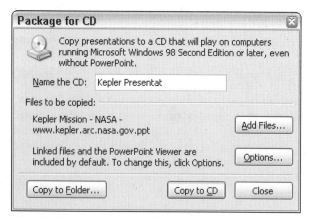

• **Figure 52-2: A very quick and capable wizard.**

3. **Type a name for the CD (or for the folder, if you're copying to a folder) in the Name the CD text box.**

4. **If you want to put additional PowerPoint files on the CD, click the Add Files button.**

I recommend keeping presentations separate, just so they're easier to find. But if you need to burn one massive CD, you can accumulate many presentations by clicking Add Files.

Although you can add a virtually unlimited number of PowerPoint files (.ppt and .pps files), you cannot remove the presentation that you open in Step 1 of this procedure from the list of files.

5. **Click the Options button.**

The Package for CD Wizard shows you the Options dialog box, as shown in Figure 52-3.

• **Figure 52-3: Pick and choose only the files you need.**

6. **If you know for an absolute fact that the PC you will use to view the backed-up presentation(s) has a copy of PowerPoint 2002 or 2003, you can clear the PowerPoint Viewer (To Play Presentations without Using PowerPoint) check box.**

PowerPoint 2002 is the version of PowerPoint in Office XP. Because your presentation might not look right with the older versions of PowerPoint, I recommend including the Viewer if the destination PC is running PowerPoint 2000 or 97.

7. **If you choose to include the PowerPoint Viewer, you might set the CD to *autoplay* — that is, you might want the presentations to start as soon as the CD is inserted in the destination machine's drive. If you do want the presentation(s) to autoplay, select Play All Presentations Automatically in the Specified Order from the drop-down list under the PowerPoint Viewer check box.**

For most people, autoplay is overkill: The choice Don't Play the CD Automatically leads to less confusion.

8. **Make sure that the Linked Files check box is enabled.**

This is one of the truly great features of the Package for CD feature. If you select this check box, the Package for CD routine goes out and picks up all the media files (pictures, movies, sound files, whatever) and sticks them in with the presentation bundle. It also automatically modifies all the links so the whole thing runs correctly the first time.

9. **When you've made all your choices, click OK.**

PowerPoint returns to the Package for CD dialog box (refer to Figure 52-2).

10. **If you want to burn the files to a CD, click the Copy to CD button. (Otherwise, click Copy to Folder.)**

The wizard asks you to insert a CD and then burns the files. You see the progress in the Copying Files to a CD dialog box.

When the wizard finishes burning the files, it asks whether you want to burn another copy to a different CD.

11. **Click No if don't want another copy; then click Close to exit the Package for CD Wizard.**

Playing the Burned CD

In the preceding section, I describe how to burn your PowerPoint presentation on a CD.

If you choose to include the PowerPoint Viewer and tell PowerPoint to autoplay the CD (Steps 6 and 7 in the preceding section), all you have to do is insert the CD in any Windows computer, and the presentation starts immediately.

If you didn't include the Viewer, or if you didn't choose autoplay, or if autoplay is disabled on the destination PC, when you insert the CD in the drive, you get the Windows AutoPlay dialog box, as shown in Figure 52-4.

• **Figure 52-4: Windows doesn't know how to handle the CD.**

The PowerPoint Viewer will not show linked or embedded objects — including, most emphatically, any multimedia video clip that uses the Windows Media Player (see Technique 51). If you need the PowerPoint Viewer, change your presentation to use PowerPoint's built-in multimedia player.

Here's how to get the presentation going:

1. **In the dialog box in Figure 52-4, click Open Folder to View Files Using Windows Explorer; then click OK.**

Windows Explorer shows you a list of the files, similar to an Open dialog box.

2. **If the PC you're using has PowerPoint 2002 (in Office XP) or 2003, just double-click the presentation file — the one with the** `.ppt` **extension.**

PowerPoint on the destination machine kicks in, with the presentation loaded and ready to go.

 You *do* have filename extensions showing, don't you? If you can't see the `.ppt` in the filename, refer to Technique 1 to see how to get Windows to show filename extensions to you.

3. **If the PC you're using has an older version of PowerPoint or no PowerPoint at all, double-click the PowerPoint Viewer, file** `pptview.exe`.

The PowerPoint Viewer appears with its legendary 250,000-line End User License Agreement (okay, I'm exaggerating a little bit). Click Accept, and the Viewer's Open dialog box appears (see Figure 52-5).

4. **Click the presentation you want to see and then click Open.**

The PowerPoint viewer shows your slideshow.

All your linked multimedia files come through intact. They might run a little slow and herky-jerky — you're pulling the data off a CD — but all the pictures should be there.

 The old Viewer — which shipped with PowerPoint 97 and was used as late as Office XP/PowerPoint 2002's Pack and Go Wizard — couldn't handle any animation effects, high quality graphics, picture bullets, automatic numbering, or dozens of additional features. To display these effects in PowerPoint 2000 or later, you need the new viewer. If you use PowerPoint 2003's Package for CD Wizard, the new Viewer comes along for the ride. You can also download a free copy to run on systems without Office 2003 by visiting Microsoft at `www.microsoft.com/downloads/details.aspx?FamilyId=428D5727-43AB-4F24-90B7-A94784AF71A4`. The new Viewer doesn't support any linked or embedded objects in your presentations — even if the linking simply runs out to Windows Media Player to run a video clip.

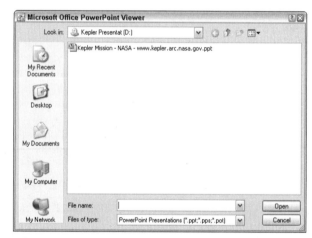

• **Figure 52-5: Another incredibly poorly designed PowerPoint dialog box.**

Covering Your B...ases

If you're headed out on the road with a presentation, make sure that you have several fail-safe copies of your presentation at hand:

- ✔ Run the Package for CD Wizard, burn a CD, and stick the CD in your suitcase along with your socks — anyplace that's nowhere near your laptop.

- ✔ Run the Package for CD Wizard again but this time, choose Copy to Folder (Step 10 in the procedure in the first section of this Technique). Zip the folder and then e-mail the zipped folder to yourself. You get bonus points if you create a free Hotmail account specifically to hold the presentation.

- ✔ If you're going to a location that's on your company network, run the Package for CD Wizard a third time, use Copy to Folder, and copy the folder someplace where you can get at it. Alternatively, if you can use a Virtual Private Network (VPN) or SharePoint to get at a folder when you're on the road, tuck away a copy there.

Things go wrong. Remember the old admonition *two logs crossing?* With PowerPoint, it doesn't hurt to have three.

Part VI

Assimilating Access

The 5th Wave
By Rich Tennant

"Your database is beyond repair, but before I tell you our backup recommendation, let me ask you a question. How many index cards do you think will fit on the walls of your computer room?"

Getting Access Settings Right

As you use Access, you discover just how easy it is to get your work done. Queries, forms, and reports make quick work of maintaining, viewing, and printing out your data. However, you might need to reset a number of default options each time you launch Access, and setting things up can take as much time as the actual work.

Fortunately, Access lets you change default settings so that it looks and responds the way you want from session to session:

✔ **Startup options** control how Access looks each time you launch a specific database.

✔ **Environmental options** determine how Access looks and responds to your actions in general.

Setting Access Startup Options

For the most part, Startup options allow developers to customize a database, and you can set different options for each database. You don't need to make changes to the defaults, but in many cases, the folks using the database can get their work done more quickly and accurately if you do. If you're building a database that only you will use, most of the Startup options are overkill.

To set an Access Startup option

1. **Open the database with options you wish to set.**

2. **Choose Tools⇨Startup.**

Access opens the Startup dialog box (see Figure 53-1)

• **Figure 53-1: The Startup dialog box controls how the database acts.**

3. If you want the database to open with a specific form or page showing, choose that form or page from the Display Form/Page drop-down box.

4. **If others will use the database, consider making changes as described in Table 53-1.**

The Use Access Special Keys check box controls whether the key combinations described in Table 53-2 will work.

5. **Click OK, and the database will use your settings.**

TABLE 53-1: IMPORTANT STARTUP OPTIONS

Option	Explanation	Timesaving Tips
Application Title	Displays text in the title bar.	If you leave this blank, Access displays `Microsoft Access` in the title bar. Fill it in, and people using the database will be able to see its name at the top of the screen.
Application Icon	Displays a specific icon (`.bmp` or `.ico` file) on the Windows taskbar when you minimize Access.	This isn't worth the effort unless you need to differentiate quickly among many open databases.
Menu Bar	Select the default menu bar. The default option refers to the built-in menu bar. Any custom menu bars you add to the database will be in this list.	Unless you have a specific reason to change this setting, I recommend leaving it alone.
Allow Full Menus	Clear this option to disable built-in menus and tools that allow users to modify database objects.	Clear the check box if you want to keep others' hands off your code.
Display Form/Page	Enter the name of an existing form or page in the database. Access automatically opens the specified form or page when you launch the database.	Pick a good opening page now, and you'll save yourself lots of time fishing around every time you open the database.
Display Database Window	Clear this option to inhibit the Database window. By default (selected), Access displays the Database window when you launch the database.	See Table 53-3 to see how this setting interacts with Use Access Special Keys.
Display Status Bar	Enable this to display the status bar at the bottom of the screen.	Feel free to give it the heave-ho if you need more screen space.
Shortcut Menu Bar	Select the default shortcut menu that Access displays when you right-click a database object. The default specifies a built-in shortcut menu. Any custom shortcut menus you add to the database will be in the property's drop-down list.	Keep it.
Use Access Special Keys	Clear this option to inhibit the keystroke combinations listed in Table 53-2.	If you don't want users to accidentally break into your custom programs, disabling this setting is a good idea.

TABLE 53-2: USE ACCESS SPECIAL KEYS OPTIONS

Combination	Result
Alt+F11	Displays the Database window.
Ctrl+F11	Toggles between a custom menu and the built-in menu.
Ctrl+Break	Interrupts the current code and displays the current module in the Visual Basic Editor (VBE).
Ctrl+G	Displays the Immediate window when working in the VBE.

TABLE 53-3: HOW THE KEYS INTERACT

Display Database Window	Use Access Special Keys	Response
Selected	Selected	Access displays the Database window when you launch the database; pressing F11 displays the Database window.
Selected	Deselected	Access displays the Database window, but pressing F11 won't display the Database window.
Deselected	Selected	Access doesn't display the Database window when you first open the database, but pressing F11 still displays the Database window.
Deselected	Deselected	Access won't display the Database window when you open the database, nor can you access the window by pressing F11. Use this combo with great care because without the proper interface in place, you could inadvertently and permanently block access to the database objects.

Changing Access Defaults

Access does a good job of anticipating what the average user will need. However, the default settings won't please everyone. When you find yourself repeatedly changing a particular setting, consider changing it permanently.

 Settings in the Options dialog box are sticky: That is, Access continues to act that way until you change them. These options don't customize a single database: they customize Access itself, affecting both new and existing databases.

To make the key timesaving changes

1. **Choose File⇨Open and open a database.**

2. **Choose Tools⇨Options.**

Access brings up the Options dialog box (see Figure 53-2).

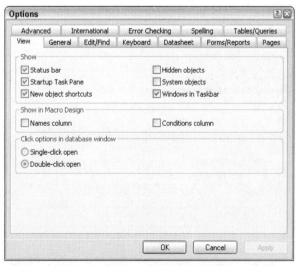

• **Figure 53-2: The Options dialog box settings are sticky.**

3. **Pick your options from the various tabs.**

In particular, look at the Recently Used File List and Compact on Close settings on the General tab (see Table 53-4), which everyone should change. Access should show you all of your most recently used files so you that can get at them quickly. And the best time to compact most databases is when you close them.

Table 53-4 explains what the various options do:

▶ **View:** These control what you see onscreen.

▶ **General:** These options comprise an unrelated jumble that just doesn't fit anywhere else. See Figure 53-3.

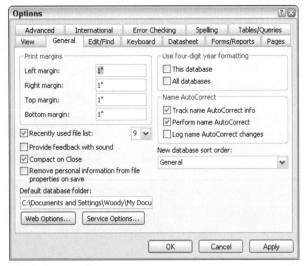

• **Figure 53-3: General settings.**

▶ **Edit/Find:** These control editing and search tasks. See Figure 53-4.

▶ **Keyboard:** These control how the Enter and arrow keys work. See Figure 53-5.

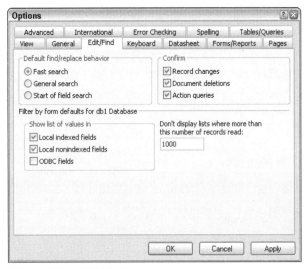

• **Figure 53-4: Edit/Find options.**

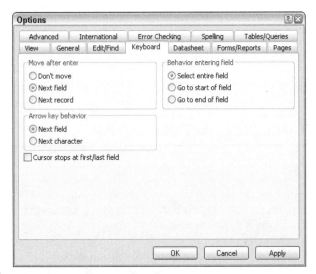

• **Figure 53-5: Keyboard options.**

▶ **Datasheet:** These affect only new tables. You must use Format options to set these attributes for an existing table.

▶ **Forms/Reports:** To create a form or report template, simply create a form or report as you normally would. No special Save as Template command exists. A template is just another form or report. You might want to name the form or report appropriately, using a name such as Form Template or Report Template.

▶ **Advanced:** The casual user has no reason to alter Advanced options, which establish connection and locking settings. Only database administrators and developers with a serious attitude problem will reset these options.

▶ **Tables/Queries:** These settings affect only new tables and queries. A few of these options are available at the table or query level. You can check the object's properties if you want to update an existing table or query.

4. **Click OK.**

TABLE 53-4: IMPORTANT TIMESAVING OPTIONS

Tab	Setting	Explanation	Timesaving Tip
View	Status Bar	Select this option to display the status bar at the bottom of the screen.	Selecting the Status Bar option won't display the status bar if the bar has been disabled via Startup options.
View	Startup Task Pane	Select this option to display the Startup task pane each time you launch Access.	The task pane helps speed things up a bit by showing the most recently used databases.
View	Windows in Taskbar	Select this option to display an icon in the Windows taskbar for each minimized object.	This can come in handy when you work with several open objects at the same time.
General	Left, Right, Top, Bottom Margin	Set the default left margin for new datasheets, modules, forms, reports, and pages.	These margin settings determine the amount of space between controls and code and the object's margins; they have nothing to do with report margins.
General	Recently Used File List	Select this option to display the most recently opened files on the File menu. Four is the default.	Run it up to 9.
General	Compact on Close	Select this option, and Access compacts and repairs the current database when you close it.	Enable this one. The Compact on Close option kicks in only if the compact stands to reduce the file's size by at least 256 kilobytes.
Keyboard	Cursor Stops at First/Last Field	Prohibits the cursor from selecting either the next or previous records in a table when pressing the right or left arrow keys, respectively.	This doesn't truly lock the cursor to the current record. It only inhibits the right and left arrow keys. You can't select the next or previous records by clicking either arrow key.

Technique 54

Adding a Cover Sheet to an Access Report

Save Time By

✔ Creating a cover sheet from the report header section

✔ Formatting the new cover sheet

Most users and developers agree that Access has the best report generator of any relational database management system (RDBMS). With a little practice, it's easy to use and can almost always generate just the right format. Options aren't always automatic, but you can produce amazing results with just a few clicks.

For instance, many reports include a cover sheet that contains the report's title and other pertinent information to the report, such as the date the report was run, the report's author, and so on. You could go to the trouble of creating a cover sheet in Word. That would require that you print the appropriate number of copies and then manually insert a copy of the cover sheet into each printed report.

However, you can save a lot of time and effort by adding the cover sheet to the actual Access report, which is what I show you in this Technique.

 The *Northwind database* is the sample database that Microsoft includes with Access. If you would like a database to tinker with as you follow this technique and haven't yet installed the Northwind database, choose Help⇨Sample Databases⇨Northwind Sample Database. When Access asks whether you want to install the feature, click Yes. You might need to put the Office 2003 CD in the drive.

Generating a Report

Before you can create a cover sheet, you have to have a report. The cover sheet gets tacked on to the front of the report itself. To create a custom report:

1. **Choose File⇨Open.**

   Access displays the Open dialog box.

2. **Open the database file that you want to use to generate the report.**

If you want to use the Northwind database (`northwind.mdb`), it's probably located in `C:\Program Files\Microsoft Office\ OFFICE11\SAMPLES`. Click through the security warnings. (In particular, you have to click Open when Access warns that "This file may not be safe if it contains code. . . .") If you get the fancy lighthouse splash screen, click OK.

3. **Click Display Database Window (or press F11).**

You see the Database window, as shown in Figure 54-1.

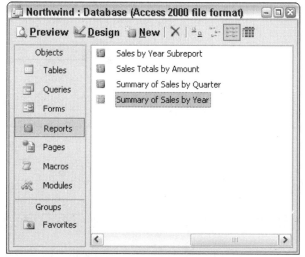

• **Figure 54-1: The Database window for Microsoft's sample Northwind database.**

4. **On the left, under Objects, click Reports. Then click the New button on the toolbar.**

Access shows you the New Report Wizard (see Figure 54-2).

5. **At the top right, choose Report Wizard. From the drop-down list, choose the table you want to use. Then click OK.**

In my example, I choose the Shippers table. You see the first pane of the Report Wizard (see Figure 54-3).

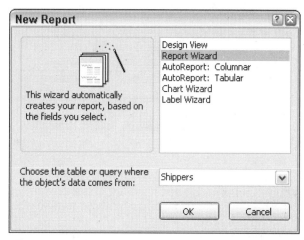

• **Figure 54-2: Create a new report with the wizard's help.**

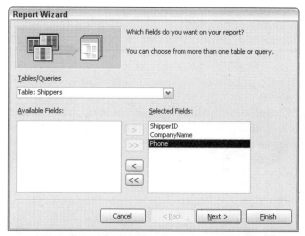

• **Figure 54-3: Include all the fields in the Shippers table in the report.**

6. **Click the right-pointing arrow to move the Available Fields that you want to include in the report to the Selected Fields column.**

In my example, I click the double-pointing arrow. That puts all three fields in the report.

7. **Click Finish and then choose File➪Save to save the report.**

Access zooms through all the defaults in the wizard and generates a report (see Figure 54-4) based on the data in the Shippers table.

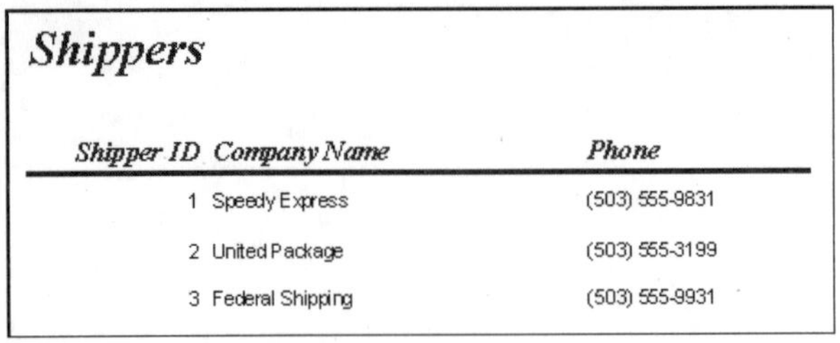

Shippers

Shipper ID	Company Name	Phone
1	Speedy Express	(503) 555-9831
2	United Package	(503) 555-3199
3	Federal Shipping	(503) 555-9931

• **Figure 54-4:** The Shippers report, with a heading but no cover sheet.

Creating the Cover Sheet

When you create a report, the Access Report Wizard automatically grabs a report title from the report's data source, using the table or query's name, and then prints the title at the top of the report's first page. It's a start, but you can do better with a cover sheet — and produce a far more professional report. Quickly.

The information at the top of the report — in this case, the title `Shippers` — is the *report header.* Now that you have a simple one-line header, the next trick is to transform that one-liner into a full-page cover sheet, worthy of the name.

Here's how:

1. **Choose View⇨Design View to take Access into design view.**

The Shippers report from the preceding procedure looks like Figure 54-5.

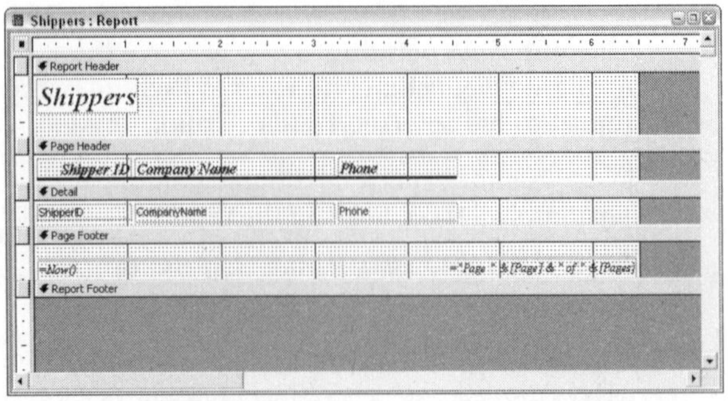

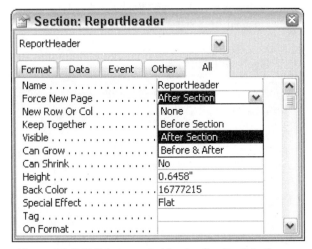

• **Figure 54-5:** The Shippers report in design view.

2. **Double-click the report header section title bar (anywhere on the line that reads** `Report Header`**). Click the All tab of the resulting ReportHeader dialog box.**

Access shows you the report header's Properties dialog box (see Figure 54-6).

• **Figure 54-6:** Tell Access what to do after it prints the report header.

3. **In the Force New Page drop-down box, choose After Section.**

After Section has four possible settings. Choosing After Section forces Access to start a new page after all the information in the report header section is done — which is precisely what any good cover page should do.

4. **Click the Print Preview icon (the one that looks like a sheet of paper with a magnifying glass) on the Report Design toolbar.**

You see the report's first page (see Figure 54-7), which contains just the report's title from the report header section.

5. **Click the Close button.**

Access goes back to design view.

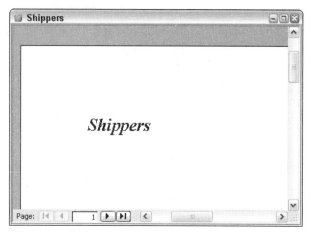

Page: |◀ ◀ [1] ▶ ▶| <

• **Figure 54-7:** The data in the report header is now on a page of its own.

In the following section, I talk about turning that nascent cover page into an editorial wonder.

Formatting the Report Cover Sheet

After you have a custom report with a cover sheet (see the preceding section), modifying that cover sheet is quite easy.

Centering the report title

Say you want to center the report title:

1. **Make sure that Access is in design view (choose View⇨Design View).**

   You should be able to see the report header.

2. **Click once on the text box that holds the report's title.**

   In the example from the preceding section, that text box contains the word Shippers.

3. **Click the Center icon on the Formatting toolbar.**

   That centers the title inside the text box.

4. **Click the right edge of the text box and drag the text box so that it touches the right margin of the report.**

5. **Similarly, click the left edge of the text box and drag it just a smidgen so that it touches the left margin of the report.**

   The report header is centered, as in Figure 54-8.

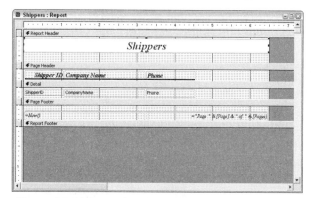

• **Figure 54-8:** Center the report header.

6. **Click Print Preview on the Report Design toolbar.**

   The word Shippers is centered, as in Figure 54-9.

• **Figure 54-9:** The report title is centered.

7. **Click the Close button.**

   Access goes back to design view.

 You can use this technique to quickly center any content between the left and right margins. You can modify the text, font, or almost any property, and Access will center it properly. However, if you change the report's margins, you must adjust the width of the text box accordingly.

Adding text to the cover sheet

To add new text to the cover sheet, simply insert a new label. Here's how:

1. Make sure that Access is in design view (choose View➪Design View).

You should be able to see the report header.

2. Click at the bottom of the report header (just above the Page Header line) and drag it down.

That opens up more room for you to work on the report header.

3. If you can't see the Toolbox (see Figure 54-10), choose View➪Toolbox.

The Toolbox contains all the Access controls — in this case, the items you can put in an Access report.

• **Figure 54-10:** The Access design-time Toolbox.

4. In the Toolbox, click the Label control (it looks like *Aa*).

5. Click and drag inside the report header to create a new label.

6. Type something in the new label

In Figure 54-11, I type **John Smith** and then I create a second label by entering **February 2004**.

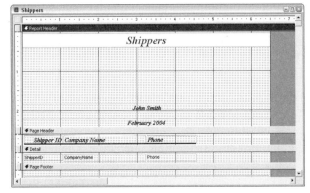

• **Figure 54-11:** Add your own labels to the cover sheet and type whatever you wish.

7. To center the text, click the Center icon of the Formatting toolbar, and then click and drag both ends of the label box to the margins of the report.

8. Click Print Preview.

Your budding cover page looks like the one in Figure 54-12.

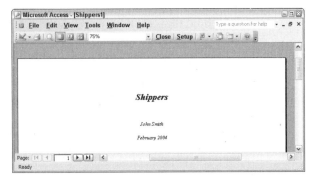

• **Figure 54-12:** The beginnings of a brilliant cover page.

9. **Click the Close button.**

Access goes back to design view.

You might have to rearrange the controls a few times before you get them all just where you want them.

 You can put pictures on the cover sheet, too, by choosing Insert⇨Picture, navigating to the picture you want and choosing OK. Click and drag to resize or crop the picture or to position it wherever you like. Right-click the picture and choose Properties to fine-tune details.

55 Technique

Including Totals in an Access Report

Access reports aren't just for printed reports. They can also help you analyze and summarize data — quickly — whether you ever print them or not.

This Technique shows you a fast, easy way to put *running totals* in a report. (A running total is the sum of the current record's value plus similar values in all preceding records.) Running totals often help pinpoint data discrepancies or trends, and they're a great way to get a feeling for why a specific total turned out so high — or so low.

Access makes it very easy to display running totals, subtotals, and totals in a report based on criteria that you choose. With a little extra work, you can create reports that others can use to identify, and possibly even solve, problems quickly.

Adding a Running Total

Displaying a running total is a simple way to track the progress of a particular value from record to record. You can also use groups to have even more control over how the totals appear.

Setting up the totals

To add a running total to a report

1. **Create or open the report that needs the subtotal.**

See Technique 54 for details on generating a report.

The Northwind database is the sample database that Microsoft includes with Access. If you'd like to follow these exact steps and haven't yet installed the Northwind database, choose Help⇨Sample Databases⇨ Northwind Sample Database. When Access asks whether you want to install the feature, click Yes. You might need to put the Office 2003 CD in the drive. Then follow the steps in Technique 54 for generating a Shippers report.

Using the Orders table in the Northwind database, the example report shown in Figure 55-1 includes the OrderID, ShipCountry, and Freight files.

Orders

Order ID	Ship Country	Freight
10248	France	$32.38
10249	Germany	$11.61
10250	Brazil	$65.83
10251	France	$41.34
10252	Belgium	$51.30
10253	Brazil	$58.17
10254	Switzerland	$22.98

• **Figure 55-1: The bare-bones Orders report with the three chosen fields.**

2. **Choose View⇨Design View to put Access in design view.**

Access shows you the report layout for Orders (see Figure 55-2).

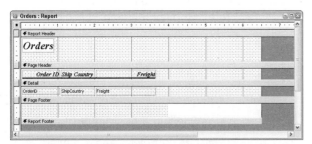

• **Figure 55-2: Design view for the Orders report.**

3. **If you can't see the Toolbox (Figure 55-3), choose View⇨Toolbox.**

The Toolbox lets you draw a text box, which you need to hold the running totals.

• **Figure 55-3: Use the Toolbox to add the running total.**

4. **Click the Text Box icon in the Toolbox (the one that looks like ab|). Then in the Detail section, click and draw a new text box to the right of column where you want to add the totals.**

I drew the text box next to the Freight box in the Detail section.

5. **Immediately click the box that reads** Text11 **and then press Delete.**

The Text11 box is a label, and it only gets in the way. Your new text box looks like the one marked Unbound in Figure 55-4.

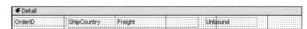

• **Figure 55-4: The new, unbound (and thus not yet functional) running total text box.**

6. **Right-click the Unbound text box and choose Properties.**

Access shows you the Properties dialog box for this text box (see Figure 55-5).

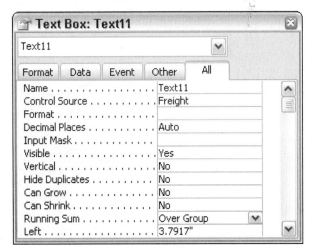

• **Figure 55-5:** Use the Properties dialog box to link this text box to the Freight field and tell Access that you want a running total.

7. **On the All tab, click the box to the right of Control Source and then choose the name of the column you want to add running totals to (Freight, in my example).**

8. **Click the box to the right of Running Sum and then choose Over Group.**

Here's what all the Running Sum options do:

▶ **No:** This default setting displays only the specified control's current value.

▶ **Over Group:** Displays a running sum within the current group. To use this setting, you need to set a group, which I explain later in this Technique.

▶ **Over All:** Displays a running sum over the entire report.

9. **Choose View⇨Print Preview.**

Access shows you the running totals in the final column (see Figure 55-6).

Orders

Order ID	Ship Country	Freight	
10248	France	$32.38	$32.38
10249	Germany	$11.61	$43.99
10250	Brazil	$65.83	$109.82
10251	France	$41.34	$151.16
10252	Belgium	$51.30	$202.46
10253	Brazil	$58.17	$260.63

• **Figure 55-6:** The Freight Running Sum Over Group tally is in the final column.

Setting up groups

The Over Group setting evaluates all the Freight values in a group. But in this report there are no groups: You haven't set any. So, in this report, selecting Over All and Over Group have the same results.

The running total behavior changes if, for example, you have Access group the Freight charges by country. In that case, you get a subtotal for all the Freight charges for shipments going to Brazil, another for France, another for Germany, and so on. Groups can help you run subtotals very easily after you have the overall report set up. It's also easy to change which fields get subtotals by simply changing the groups.

To see the effect of adding groups

1. **Choose View⇨Design View.**

That puts you back in design view.

2. **Choose View⇨Sorting and Grouping.**

Access brings up the Sorting and Grouping dialog box (see Figure 55-7).

3. **Click in the box below Field/Expression and choose the field that you want to use to group the running totals (ShipCountry in my example).**

That tells Access to run the report by country. Access automatically chooses to sort in ascending order (from A to Z).

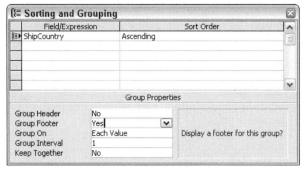

• **Figure 55-7: Tell Access to group the orders by country.**

4. **Click in the Group Footer box (under Group Properties) and choose Yes.**

You must create either a group header or footer in order for Access to act on group behaviors — including running totals. Without a group header or footer, the running sum won't evaluate values within each group.

5. **Choose View⊅Print Preview.**

Access restarts the running total at the end of each country (see Figure 55-8).

Order ID	Ship Country	Freight	
10782	Argentina	$1.10	$1.10
10916	Argentina	$63.77	$64.87
10409	Argentina	$29.83	$94.70
10531	Argentina	$8.12	$102.82
10937	Argentina	$31.51	$134.33
10898	Argentina	$1.27	$135.60
10958	Argentina	$49.56	$185.16
10881	Argentina	$2.84	$188.00
10521	Argentina	$17.22	$205.22
10716	Argentina	$22.57	$227.79
10986	Argentina	$217.86	$445.65
10448	Argentina	$38.82	$484.47
11019	Argentina	$3.17	$487.64
10828	Argentina	$90.85	$578.49
11054	Argentina	$0.33	$578.82
10819	Argentina	$19.76	$598.58
11008	Austria	$79.46	$79.46

• **Figure 55-8: Running subtotals appear by country.**

The modified report displays a running sum, which restarts at zero for each new country. Notice in Figure 55-8 that the first group is Argentina, and the final tally for that country is $598.58. The next record is the first Freight record for Austria, so the running sum control resets itself and starts over, evaluating only those Freight values in the Austria group.

Displaying Subtotals and Totals

Many reports require subtotals and totals. In Access-speak, these *aggregate functions* look at all the data in a group or a report to produce a result. Adding the numbers and counting the records are the two most common aggregate functions.

The most peculiar thing that you'll notice about aggregate functions is that the same aggregate function returns different results depending on where you put it within the report:

✔ **To evaluate all the values in each group:** Place an aggregate function in a group's header or footer.

✔ **To evaluate all the values in the report's data source (table or query):** Place an aggregate function in the report's header or footer.

Make sure you position the aggregate function in the right place to get the results you want.

To see how aggregate functions (including subtotals and totals) work, start with a report that contains running totals with groups, which I explain how to setup in the preceding sections. Then add a sum() function thusly:

1. **Choose View⊅Design View to go into design view.**

Access shows you the report layout as modified to this point (see Figure 55-9).

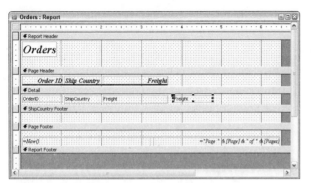

• **Figure 55-9:** Display view for the Orders report.

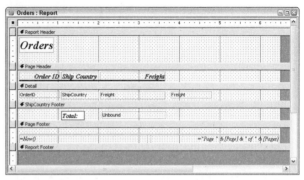

• **Figure 55-10:** The new, unbound subtotal box.

2. **If you can't see the Toolbox (refer to Figure 55-3), choose View▷Toolbox.**

The Toolbox lets you draw a text box, which you need to hold subtotals and totals.

3. **Click the Text Box icon on the toolbar (the one that looks like ab|), and then click and draw a new text box in the appropriate footer.**

In this case, I want the subtotal to appear for each country, so I draw a text box in the ShipCountry footer, directly below the first Freight box in the Detail section.

Make sure you don't put an aggregate function in the Page section header or footer because the function will return an error.

4. **Immediately click the box that reads** Text12 **or** Text13, **delete the text, and type** Total:.

The Text*xx* box is a label. Your new text box looks like the one marked Unbound in Figure 55-10.

5. **Click once inside the Unbound box and type** =sum(Freight).

6. **Choose View▷Print Preview.**

The report (see Figure 55-11) contains totals for each country.

10716	Argentina	$22.57	$227.79
10986	Argentina	$217.86	$445.65
10448	Argentina	$38.82	$484.47
11019	Argentina	$3.17	$487.64
10828	Argentina	$90.85	$578.49
11054	Argentina	$0.33	$578.82
10819	Argentina	$19.76	$598.58
Total:		598.58	

• **Figure 55-11:** With the =sum() aggregate function in the ShipCountry footer, you get subtotals by country.

The Freight cost for Argentina is $598.58. Notice that the =sum() function's results matches the value in the running total column for the last record in the same group.

To change the formatting of the amount, right-click the text box, choose Properties, and choose Currency from the Format drop-down box.

As you might imagine, the same =sum() aggregate function in the report's footer will return a different total. Here's how to create one quickly.

1. Choose View⇨Design View to go into design view. Click and drag down the area immediately below the Report Footer line.

That gives you room for a text box (see Figure 55-12).

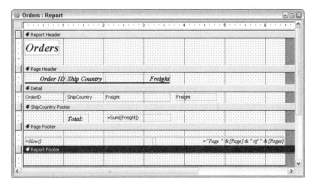

• **Figure 55-12:** Make room for the grand total in the report footer.

2. Create a Total text box and a text box with the =sum(Freight) formula in the Report Footer, as described in the preceding steps.

You can copy and paste the text boxes if you prefer. In my example, click the =sum(Freight) box in the ShipCountry footer to select both text boxes. (Yeah, that isn't how good Windows applications are supposed to work, but what the hey.) Press Ctrl+C and then press Ctrl+V to make and paste a copy. Then drag the two new text boxes down to the Report Footer.

Reposition them if you like (see Figure 55-13).

3. Choose View⇨Print Preview.

Your grand total appears on the final page (see Figure 55-14).

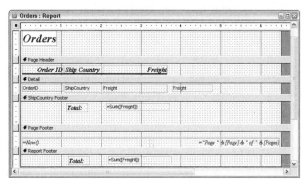

• **Figure 55-13:** Copy the two text boxes to the report footer.

Order ID	Ship Country	Freight	
10476	Venezuela	$4.41	$2,735.06
10296	Venezuela	$0.12	$2,735.18
	Total:	2735.18	
	Total:	64942.69	

• **Figure 55-14:** The first total is for Venezuela; the second is for the entire report.

The first value at the bottom of the report, $2,735.18, is the subtotal for the last group, Venezuela. That's the first sum( ) function in the ShipCountry group footer at work. The second value is the result of the sum( ) function in the report's footer. That value represents the grand total of all the Freight values in the report.

The same expression, =sum(Freight), returns different totals in the same report depending on whether the aggregate function is in a group's footer (for a subtotal) or the report's footer (for a grand total).

Technique

56

Printing Labels in Access

Save Time By

- Printing labels in Access — accurately and quickly
- Making your own custom labels work right the first time
- Reuse your own label designs

You might be showing your age if you remember when creating mailing labels was the untamed office beast. After label sheets came out, the task was somewhat easier because you could simply type up a template and then run the label sheets through the copier. Unfortunately, you had no way to keep a list in strict order: New items and updates had to be added to the end of the list because you couldn't insert them between existing items. Consequently, labeled envelopes usually required additional sorting — particularly if you needed them in ZIP code order. A small mailing wasn't that horrible, but a large mailing could take a full day.

Thanks to Microsoft Office, labels are no longer a problem. Access includes a Label Wizard that turns your data into almost any label format in seconds. The wizard hosts a variety of predefined labels based on manufactured labels and also supports custom labels. You might already be printing labels with Word, but if the data that you want to use is in Access, it's much faster and easier to print them.

Running the Access Label Wizard

The Label Wizard walks you through the process of creating labels step-by-step. Before launching the wizard, you should know the label dimensions, brand name, and product number.

 The Label Wizard isn't just for mailing labels. You can also use this wizard to produce labels for name tags, file labels, DVD labels, and so on.

Here's how you print labels of any sort from an Access database:

1. **Choose File⇨Open.**

Access displays the Open dialog box.

2. **Open the database that you want to use.**

If you want to experiment with these steps by following the examples in the figures, you can use the Northwind sample database file that's included with Access, `northwind.mdb`. Click through the security warnings. (In particular, you have to click Open when Access warns that "This file may not be safe if it contains code. . . .") The Northwind database is probably located in `C:\Program Files\Microsoft Office\ OFFICE11\SAMPLES`.

 The Northwind database is the sample database that Microsoft includes with Access. If you haven't yet installed the Northwind database, choose Help➪Sample Databases➪ Northwind Sample Database. When Access asks whether you want to install the feature, click Yes. You might need to put the Office 2003 CD in the drive.

3. **Click Display Database Window (or press F11).**

You see the Access main window.

4. **Choose Insert➪Report.**

Access shows you the New Report wizard.

5. **From the list on the right, choose Label Wizard. At the bottom, choose the table from the drop-down box. Then click OK.**

You see the first window in the Label Wizard (see Figure 56-1).

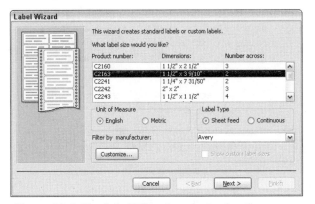

• **Figure 56-1: The Label Wizard supports all major manufacturer's labels by name and number.**

6. **Select the label product number that matches the labels you're using and then click Next.**

In my example, I choose C2163 (the name tag label from Avery), which I'm using to create name tags.

The Label Wizard's second window appears.

7. **Choose the font you want and then click Next.**

I choose Arial 20 point — a reasonable (if perhaps small) choice for name tags.

The wizard moves on to the fields you want to include (see Figure 56-2). Note that you can have only one font for the entire label run, but the next section explains how to override this.

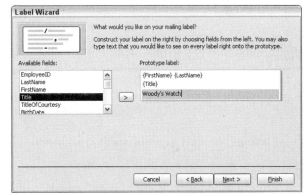

• **Figure 56-2: Choose fields and add text that you want to appear on your labels.**

8. **One by one, click each entry under Available Fields that you want to appear on the labels, and then click the right arrow (or double-click the entry and it moves itself). Type any text that you want to appear on all labels (including, for example, a space between the first and last name). When the labels look right, click Next.**

The wizard asks for sort criteria (see Figure 56-3).

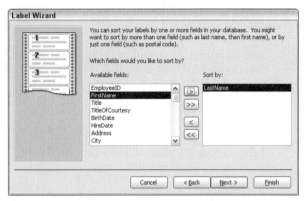

• **Figure 56-3:** Sorting by multiple fields is easy.

9. **Select the fields you want to sort by and then click Next.**

Sorting the labels is especially handy when you need to sort items by ZIP codes to take advantage of bulk mailing rates (in the US, see www.usps.com/businessmail101). Simply sort by the ZIP code or appropriate postal code field, and the labels are printed in order.

You get the final pain, er, pane in the wizard.

10. **Type in a name and then click Finish.**

Access generates the report (see Figure 56-4).

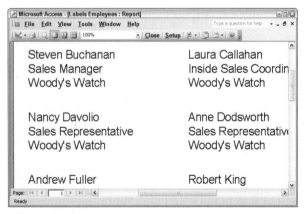

• **Figure 56-4:** The name tags are ready to be printed.

If you give the report a name, you'll be able to find it in the Database window in the future.

Fast, eh? But wait! You can make them look better. See the next section for details.

Tweaking the Label Wizard's Results

Sometimes the Label Wizard does such a good job that you can immediately print the report. Often, though, a little of bit of tweaking goes a long way. For example, the name tags might look better with the names and titles centered. And it might help to reduce the size of the title so that the name is more distinctive.

After you use the Label Wizard to create a report (read the preceding section and refer to Figure 56-4), here's how to make these changes:

1. **Click the View icon (the first icon on the left: the one that looks like a triangle, pencil, and ruler).**

I know, I know. Sometimes View is this icon, and sometimes it's a magnifying glass. See the upcoming Step 10. And don't blame me.

Outlook shows you the report in design view (see Figure 56-5).

2. **To select a line, click anywhere inside it (=Trim([FirstName] & " " & [LastName] for example). To select multiple lines, hold down Shift while you click the lines.**

Access selects the whole line — in Access parlance, the *control*.

3. **Press and hold down the Shift key while you click the second and third lines.**

That selects all three lines.

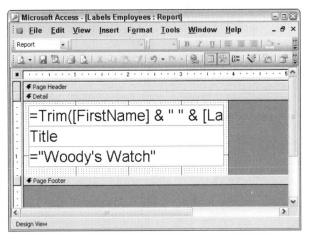

• **Figure 56-5: The name labels in design view.**

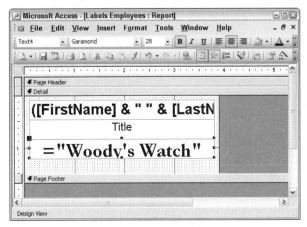

• **Figure 56-6: Center the three label lines.**

 Arggh. In every Office application except Access, you Ctrl+click to select multiple items or Shift+click to select all the items in a list. However, in Access design view (bless its pointed head), you have to Shift+click to select multiple items.

4. **Apply any formatting you want by using the Formatting toolbar.**

   I select all the lines and click the Center icon to center the contents of all three lines. I then select the lines individually and apply bold, change the point size of the title, and make Woody's Watch appear in Garamond instead of Arial (see Figure 56-6).

5. **To move down the text on the label, press the down arrow on the keyboard a few times.**

   It's hard to judge precisely, but pressing the arrow a few times should line up the label on the page reasonably well.

 You can add a graphic to all the labels at this point by choosing Insert⇨Picture and then picking the picture.

6. **Click Detail (immediately above the top label line in design view) to deselect the text when you're done applying any formatting.**

   That deselects the three lines.

7. **Click the first line and apply whatever formatting you like to the name.**

8. **Click the second line and format the Ttitle.**

9. **Click the third line and format the company name.**

10. **Click the View button (the first button on the left, which looks like a sheet of paper with a magnifying glass).**

    Access shows you the newly reformatted name tags (see Figure 56-7).

The labels look much better — and it only takes a few clicks.

 Print just the first page of the report on plain paper (File⇨Print, Pages From = 1, To = 1). Then hold the printout over a blank page of labels (or name tags) to see whether they line up correctly. If they don't, use the preceding steps to move them around.

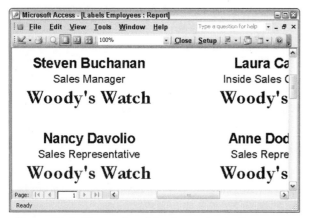

• **Figure 56-7: The results of the formatting in Figure 56-6.**

 When you're ready to print, be sure to load the label sheets before clicking the Print button or choosing another Print command. Nothing worse than a runaway printer.

Creating Custom Labels and Reports

In the preceding sections, I show you how to create and modify a report that relies on a common Avery label. That isn't your only option. You might want to print full sheets of labels and trim them to a size that the Label Wizard doesn't accommodate. You might want to print a report, like a phone book or a stock inventory list, with dimensions of your own choosing.

If you need custom labels or want to print a report that doesn't conform to the wizard's preconceived notions, don't fret. The wizard can be coerced into doing what you wish:

1. **With your database open, choose Insert➪Report.**

2. **In the New Report Wizard, choose Label Wizard and then pick the table or query that you want to use for printing labels. Click OK.**

I'm using the Northwind database with the Employees table, as I describe earlier in this Technique.

3. **In the first pane of the Label Wizard, click the Customize button (refer to Figure 56-1).**

Access shows you the New Label Size dialog box, as shown in Figure 56-8.

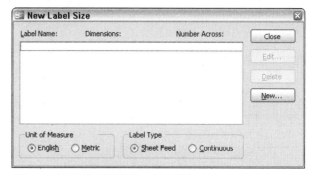

• **Figure 56-8: Establish sheet and label dimensions here.**

4. **Click New.**

You get the New Label dialog box (see Figure 56-9).

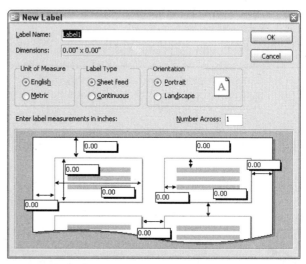

• **Figure 56-9: You can adjust every detail of the sheet's layout here.**

In this example, I want to print labels that are 3 x 3 inches, two labels across, on a letter-size page. The distance from the top of the first label to the top margin of the paper is 0.3 inch; left and right distances are 0.5 inch, with a 0.5-inch gutter all around each label. Inside each label, I want to reserve 0.1 inch of white space at the top and left. (I don't have any direct control over the bottom or right.)

 You need to measure from the print margin of the paper to the edge of the label. If the printer is set up with a 0.5-inch margin on the left and you tell Access that you want the labels to appear 0.5 inch from the left margin, the label itself lies 1 inch from the left edge of the paper.

5. Type a name for your label project in the Label Name box. In the Number Across box, type the number of labels that you want to appear in a row.

For my example, I name the labels Custom Name Tags and type **2** as the number across.

6. Fill in each of the dimension boxes (marked 0.00; refer to the bottom half of Figure 56-9) with the appropriate dimensions.

Figure 56-10 shows the dimensions that I need for this example. In particular, note that the left, right, and top measurements are the distances to the margin — not the distances to the edge of the paper.

7. Click OK and then click Close to go back to the wizard.

8. Continue with the wizard from Step 7 in the first section in this Technique to finish the labels. Modify the labels, if you like, as I explain in "Tweaking the Label Wizard's Results" earlier in this Technique.

When I finish, my name tags should look like those in Figure 56-11.

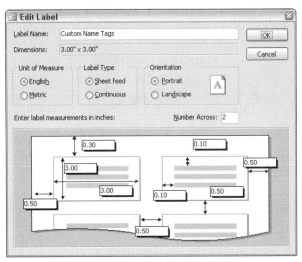

• **Figure 56-10:** Carefully enter the dimensions that you can control; Access takes care of the rest.

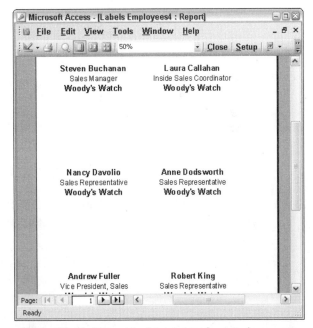

• **Figure 56-11:** Name tags in a custom layout, six per page.

 You might need to adjust the margins of the paper. To do so, choose File⇨Page Setup and type the correct margins in the boxes.

Reducing Repetitive Formatting Tasks

Save Time By

- Making Access use your formatting preferences
- Reusing custom forms and report templates

How much time have you lost applying the same formatting, over and over again?

Depending on your personal preferences — or your boss's, for that matter — formatting forms and reports can take longer than building a database itself. It's like a $10 horse with a $20 saddle: The database might be trivial or strung together with baling wire, but if it looks good, everybody will love it.

Time to turn things around. Time to get the fluff out of the way, so you can concentrate on more important things.

This Technique shows you how to make broad, effective changes in minutes. Best of all, you can reuse what you've built for future projects with similar requirements. Get the formatting right once, and you don't have to futz with it so much with your next project.

If you know the tricks.

Understanding Access Formatting

You can reduce the amount of time that you spend formatting forms and reports by setting custom defaults and by using templates. With a little thought, you can almost eliminate individual formatting tasks completely.

In a typical project, most time gets soaked up formatting forms and reports. That's what people see; that's what has to look good. Access gives you two broad approaches to go beyond typical line-by-line formatting:

- You can change the default formatting for a specific kind of control.
- You can create a custom form or report template that contains all the formatting settings you need.

In either case, you can save a lot of time by applying bunches of formatting in one fell swoop.

Setting Custom Defaults

All controls have a few default properties that determine their general appearance and behavior. For example, all text boxes start out with the same font and font size by default. Here's how to see your current defaults:

1. **Start Access and choose File⇨New. In the New File task pane, click Blank Database.**

You see the File New Database dialog box, as shown in Figure 57-1.

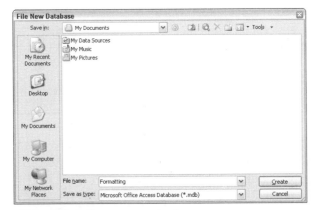

• **Figure 57-1:** Create a new database.

2. **Type a name for your new database and click the Create button.**

Your new database appears.

3. **On the left, on the Objects bar, click Forms. Then double-click the line that reads Create Form in Design View. Choose View⇨Toolbox.**

Access displays an empty form in design view, with the Toolbox (see Figure 57-2).

4. **Click the Text Box icon in the Toolbox (it looks like ab|) and then click and drag the cursor on the form to create a new text box.**

You get two boxes on the form, as shown in Figure 57-3. For more on unbound text boxes, read Technique 55.

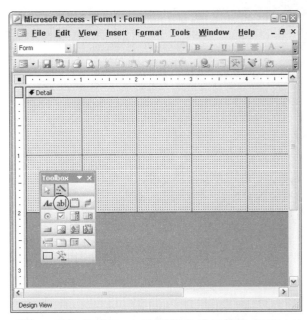

• **Figure 57-2:** Setting custom defaults starts here.

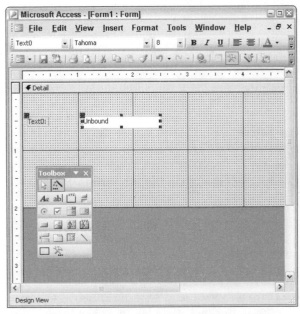

• **Figure 57-3:** An unbound text box, with its tag-along label.

5. **Right-click the text box and choose Properties.**

You see the default properties for this new text box form (see Figure 57-4). Take a little time to look at all the different properties that every text box has. (Might as well look at the All tab; the other tabs don't have much.) Consider whether you want to change any of the properties.

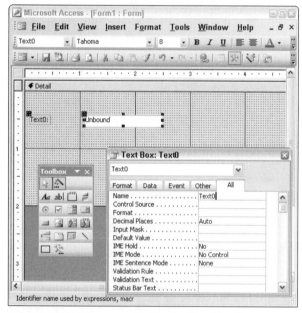

• **Figure 57-4:** The properties for text box Text0.

Don't close this form; you'll be working with it in the next section.

Changing defaults via the Properties window

Can you imagine resetting a number of those properties for each text box in a form? If there's only a few, it's not that big of a deal, but a form with many text boxes can consume a lot of time — unnecessarily.

You can change a default setting temporarily for just the current form or report via the Properties sheet (the box in the lower-right corner of Figure 57-4). Subsequent controls of the same type, inserted into the same form, apply your default setting, and not the application's defaults.

Although the example that I use here is with a form, precisely the same approach can be used with reports.

Fortunately, you can easily reset a control's default properties for the current form (or report). Starting with the form that you created in the preceding section

1. **Click the Text Box icon on the Toolbox.**

The Properties window turns into a Default Text Box dialog box (see Figure 57-5).

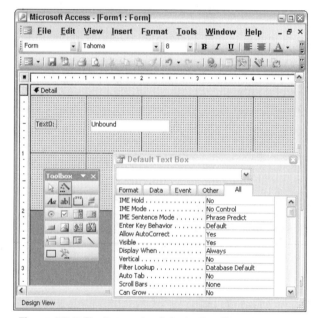

• **Figure 57-5:** To change the defaults for all new text boxes, click the Text Box icon in the Toolbox once again.

2. **On the All tab, get rid of one of Outlook's most annoying settings by scrolling down to Auto Label and changing it to No (see Figure 57-6).**

This gives the heave-ho to the tag-along label that Access insists upon inserting every time it creates a new text box.

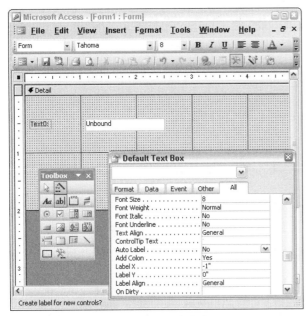

• **Figure 57-6:** Getting rid of Auto Label.

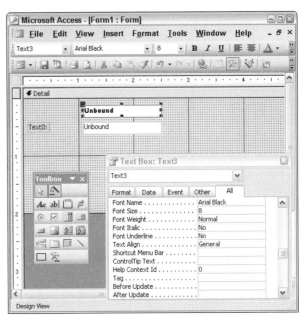

• **Figure 57-7:** Customize text box defaults how you want.

3. **Make any other changes you like.**

For example, I turn the Border Color property from 0 to 255, and the font name from Tahoma to Arial Black.

4. **Click and drag inside the form to create a text box with the new properties.**

The results of my twiddling are in Figure 57-7. The new text box looks very different from the old one. All new text boxes after this point reflect the new defaults.

 You have to change the default properties before you insert the text box. After the text box is on the form, it's too late: You have to adjust the properties manually.

5. **Close the form when you're done with it. If you want to verify that the new default properties stick, choose File⇨Save to make sure that you save your changes.**

 Remember to save changes to the form. If you close the form without saving changes, Access deletes all the custom default properties you've set.

 If you find yourself facing a form full of controls that need the same property change or changes, click the first control, hold down the Shift key, and then click all the others one by one. After the selection includes every control you need to modify, open the Properties window and make the appropriate changes. Access assigns the new settings to all the selected controls. Don't worry about resetting an inappropriate property because the Properties window will only display properties that are common to all selected controls.

Changing defaults using an existing control

In the preceding section, I talk about setting default properties by working with the default properties dialog box.

Here's a different, usually faster, way.

If you make a control that has precisely the formatting that you want for all future controls of the same type, simply click the control and choose Format⇨ Set Control Defaults.

Similar to setting default properties via the Properties window, this technique works for only the current form or report. However, you can share the custom defaults with another form or report by copying the formatted control into another form or report. Then, with the copied control selected, choose Format⇨ Set Control Defaults.

Default changes made via the Properties window or by using the Set Control Defaults command do not change an existing control. Both techniques work only for controls added after you modify the default settings.

Creating a Form Template

If you're modifying default settings for one form or report, you might need to do so for all the forms and reports in the database. Copying the necessary formats from one form to another is more work than necessary. When a database uses the same form and control formats throughout (and most do), you can save yourself a lot of time by creating an appropriately formatted template.

To create a form template

1. **Bring up the Database window.**

Of the many ways to do this, the simplest is to click Window and choose the window with the database's name.

2. **On the left, under Objects, choose Forms. At the top, double-click Create Form in Design View.**

You see a new, blank form in design view.

3. **If you can't see the Toolbox, choose View⇨ Toolbox. If you can't see the Properties window, choose View⇨Properties.**

Access should look something like Figure 57-8.

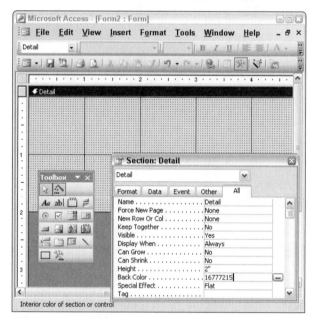

• **Figure 57-8: A new form with the properties window for the background of the form itself.**

4. **Change whatever background properties you like.**

In Figure 57-8, I change the Back Color setting to 16777215 — Access programmer's jargon for white.

You needn't memorize any weird color numbers. All of Access's color properties boxes allow you to click an ellipsis (...) and choose from a wide array of colors. You can also set very specific colors by using standard Windows Red/Green/Blue or Hue/Saturation/Luminosity numbers.

5. **Click the Text Box icon in the Toolbox and then change whatever text box properties you want to modify.**

Predictably, I change Auto Label to No.

6. **Click any other icon in the Toolbox to also change that control's properties.**

The sky's the limit.

7. **When you're done, choose File⇨Save As.**

You get the Save As dialog box, as shown in Figure 57-9.

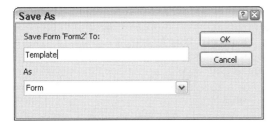

• **Figure 57-9:** Give the form the name *Template*.

8. **In the Save Form 'Form*xx*' To box, type Template.**

Template is just a handy name that's easy for you to remember. In fact, it can be anything.

9. **Click OK.**

Access saves the new form.

10. **Choose File⇨Close.**

Access closes the new form.

11. **Choose Tools⇨Options⇨Forms/Reports.**

Access brings up the Forms/Reports tab of the Options dialog box, as shown in Figure 57-10.

12. **In the Form Template box, type the name of the form that you used in Step 8.**

In my case, it's Template.

13. **Click OK.**

You now have a template. See the following section for a description of how to use it.

 I change only a few properties in this procedure. You can change hundreds. There's no limit to the customization, and you can do it for both forms and reports.

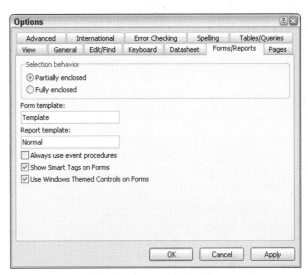

• **Figure 57-10:** Establish a template for forms.

Using a Form Template

In the preceding section, I show you how to create a new form template called, uh, Template. (And who says we aren't creative around here?) This new template made the background on all new forms white, and it neuters text boxes so they don't have tag-along labels.

Here's how to put the template called Template to use:

1. **Bring up the Database window.**

Just click Window and choose the window with the database's name.

2. **On the left, under Objects, choose Forms. At the top, double-click Create Form in Design View.**

You see a new, blank form in design view. Notice that the new form is white (with polka dots) — not gray.

3. **If you can't see the Toolbox, choose View⇨Toolbox.**

4. **Click the Text Box icon in the Toolbox (it looks like ab|), and then click and drag on the form to create a text box.**

Voilà! No tag-along label (see Figure 57-11).

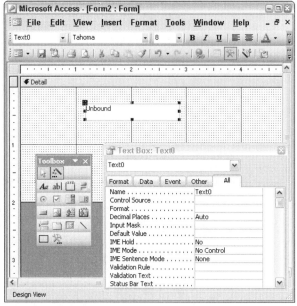

• **Figure 57-11: A white form and a label-less text box. Ah, heaven!**

Every form you create hereafter (in this database) will look like the one in Figure 57-11 until you do one of the following:

✔ Alter the template called Template (the current template form) by opening the form in design view and making changes.

✔ Change the database's default form template to Normal.

✔ Create and specify a new template form.

The template in this example becomes the template for all forms, but a database can contain more than one template. Create a form or report with just the right formatting and name it appropriately. When you need that specific set of formats, open the template form and immediately save it with a new name. Then make changes to the renamed form. That way, the template remains a template, and you get the custom look you need for your new form.

 You might create several databases that share the same custom format styles. When this is the case, don't create new forms and reports for each new database. Simply import the form and report templates from an existing data. To import a database object from another database, choose File⇨Get External Data⇨Import. Navigate to the appropriate database file, select the database file, and click Import. In the Import Objects dialog box, click the appropriate object tab, highlight the form or report, and then click OK. Access will then import each selected item into the current database. At that point, you need only to specify the correct form or report as the database template.

Technique 58

Recycling Forms for Browsing and Data Entry

U sing an Access AutoForm feature makes it easy to create a form that displays existing data and also lets you change existing data or enter new data in a database. You can make forms that give you complete control over the contents of your database. All it takes is a couple of clicks. That's great . . . as long as you don't make any mistakes.

Unfortunately, in the real world, having an omnipotent form like that can be dangerous. More often than not, all you really want to do is look at your data without changing it. Or you want to set up a form for data entry that doesn't let you trounce on any existing data.

You might think that you'd have to come up with those more-specialized (and safer) forms by hand, in some sort of complicated process. Not so. In fact, with a few clicks and a couple of lines of code (which I promise to go through in minute detail!), you can set up one form to do all of that and more.

This Technique shows you how.

Understanding the Forms

As long as you're comfortable working with a form that can change the contents of your database with a sloppy keystroke, nothing is wrong with using that form. But if you're a little less than perfect — or if you want to give the form to someone else so that they can enter new data or review existing data — you might not be so sanguine. And in many cases, you might want to create a data entry form that doesn't allow the entry clerk to look at, or change, existing data.

If you use Visual Basic for Applications (VBA) — and I show you how in this Technique — it's easy to set up a single form that

✔ Starts out with full capabilities; you can add, delete, and edit data. I call this form *omnipotent*.

✔ With one click, turns into a read-only form for the main entries, with no possibility of modifying existing data or accidentally adding new data.

✔ With another click, turns into a data entry-only form, which can't even be used to view existing data.

In order to create the form, you must

1. Start with the omnipotent form, bound to the data in the database. (A *bound* form is one that directly affects data in the database: Access updates the database immediately when you add, delete, or change data in the form.)

2. Add a button to the form which, when clicked, turns the main part of the form into a read-only form.

3. Add another button to the form which, when clicked, turns the form into a data entry-only form.

Creating the Omnipotent Form

In this section, I work with a sample form based on (what else?) the Northwind sample database that Microsoft ships with Access. To create an omnipotent form in which you can add, delete, or edit data, do the following:

1. **Choose File➪Open.**

Access displays the Open dialog box.

2. **Open the database file you want to use.**

If you want a database to experiment with, open the Northwind database file, `northwind.mdb`. The database is probably located in `C:\Program Files\Microsoft Office\OFFICE11\SAMPLES`. Click through the security warnings; for example, click Open when Access warns that "This file may not be safe if it contains code. . . ."

 If you haven't yet installed the Northwind database, choose Help➪Sample Databases➪ Northwind Sample Database. When Access asks whether you want to install the feature, click Yes. You might need to put the Office 2003 CD in the drive.

3. **Click Display Database Window (or press F11).**

You see the Access main Database window, as shown in Figure 58-1.

• **Figure 58-1: The Database window for the Northwind database.**

4. **Under Objects, on the left, click Tables. Then click whichever table you want to use.**

In this example, I choose the Shippers table.

5. **Choose Insert➪AutoForm.**

Access creates an AutoForm based on the fields in the Shippers table. This first form — the omnipotent one, Figure 58-2 — includes all the orders that the selected shipper sent out.

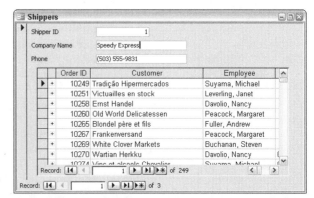

• **Figure 58-2: Use the first AutoForm to make any changes to the database.**

6. **Choose File⇨Save.**

Access brings up the Form Save As dialog box.

7. **Type a name for the form and then click OK.**

In Figure 58-3, I name the form *Shippers*.

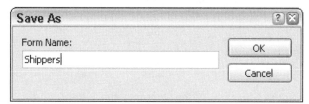

• **Figure 58-3: Name your AuroForm here.**

If you have never used an AutoForm, you might want to take this one for a spin:

✔ **To see how data entry works,** click the navigation buttons at the bottom of the form. In particular, note that the two right-wedge-with-asterisk buttons at the bottom of Figure 58-2 add new records. You can see that the form allows you to change any data in the database, or to add or delete records. The user interface in Figure 58-2 is anything but intuitive, but note that there are three shippers, and the first one, Speedy Express, has 249 orders.

✔ **To see what data entry mode looks like,** choose Records⇨Data Entry. Figure 58-4 shows the Shippers form in data entry mode. Note that both the Shipper ID (at the top) and the OrderID (in the left column) will be generated automatically by Access.

✔ **To leave data entry mode,** choose Records⇨ Remove Filter/Sort. This returns your form to its original, omnipotent capabilities.

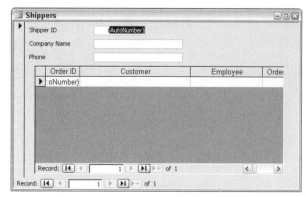

• **Figure 58-4: Shippers form in data entry mode.**

Modifying the Form

In the preceding section, I show you how to create an omnipotent form that you can use to modify, add, or delete any data in your database. In this section, I show you how to put two buttons on the form — one for read-only and another for data entry-only — that curtail its powers in very specific timesaving ways.

To put these buttons on the form's header

1. **Use the steps in the preceding section to bring up the Northwind database's Database window. On the left, under Objects, click Forms. On the right, right-click Shippers and choose Design View.**

Access brings up the Shippers form in design view (see Figure 58-5).

2. **Choose View⇨Form Header/Footer.**

A Form Header area opens at the top of the form (see Figure 58-6).

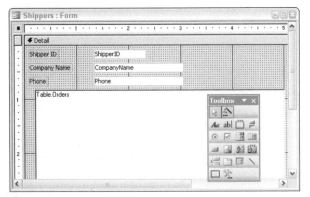

• **Figure 58-5:** Customize the Shippers form here.

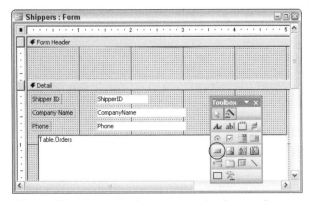

• **Figure 58-6:** Draw the form-constraining buttons here.

3. In the Toolbox, click the Command Button (it looks like a rectangle), and then click inside the form's header section and draw a command button on the left.

4. When the Command Button Wizard appears, click Cancel.

The new command button looks like the Command7 button in Figure 58-7. (Command buttons get sequential default names.)

5. If you can't see the Properties dialog box for the new command button, right-click the button and choose Properties. Click the All tab on the Command Button Properties dialog box.

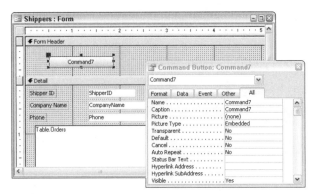

• **Figure 58-7:** One of the two command buttons.

6. In the Name field, type cmdReadOnly. In the Caption field, type Lock Down *Table.* Click once inside the form's header.

Replace *Table* with the table's name, such as Shippers.

Your form looks like Figure 58-8.

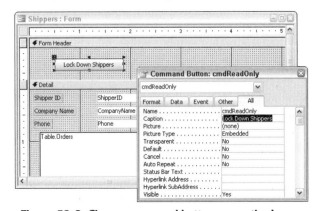

• **Figure 58-8:** Change command button properties here.

7. Repeat Steps 3–6 and put a second command button to the right of the first. Type cmdDataEntry as the name and Enter New Records Only as its caption.

The form looks like Figure 58-9.

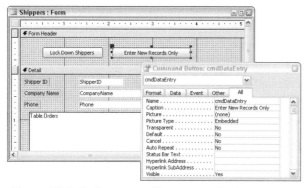

• **Figure 58-9: Both command buttons are in place.**

8. **Choose View➪Code.**

Access brings up the Visual Basic Editor (VBE), ready for you to start writing programs for the Shippers form (see Figure 58-10).

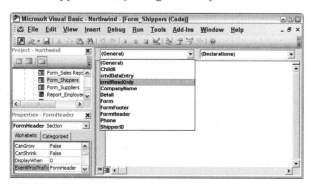

• **Figure 58-10: Write the form-limiting programs in VBA.**

9. **In the left drop-down list, pick cmdReadOnly.**

Access gets ready for you to write a VBA program that runs when someone clicks the cmdReadOnly button (the one now named Lock Down Shippers). Two lines are generated automatically. They look like this:

```
Private Sub cmdReadOnly_Click()
End Sub
```

10. **Add two program lines inside the program — after the first and before the last — so that it reads like this:**

```
Private Sub cmdReadOnly_Click()
Me.AllowEdits = False
Me.DataEntry = False
End Sub
```

Details about the settings are in Table 58-1.

11. **Repeat Steps 9 and 10 similarly for cmdDataEntry (the Enter New Records Only button) and create this program:**

```
Private Sub cmdDataEntry_Click()
Me.DataEntry = True
End Sub
```

The programs should look like Figure 58-11.

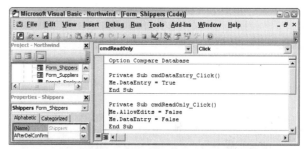

• **Figure 58-11: Tell Access that the form cannot be used to edit existing shipper records.**

12. **Choose File➪Close and return to Microsoft Access. When you're back in Access, choose File➪Close to close the modified form. Yes, now you do want to save changes to the design of the form.**

At this point, the form is ready to use.

TABLE 58-1: VIEWING AND DATA ENTRY PROPERTIES

Property	Setting	Default	Result
Data Entry	No	Default	Displays any underlying data in a bound form.
	Yes		This setting restricts the form to only the new record — a blank record.
Allow Additions	Yes	Default	Allows users to add new records.
	No		You can't enter new records.
Allow Edits	Yes	Default	The user can change existing data.
	No		The user can view data but can't modify it.
Allow Deletions	Yes	Default	The user can view and delete an existing record.
	No		The user can view existing data but can't delete the record.

Using the Modified Form

After you add the two buttons that restrict your form's capabilities (which I explain how to do in the preceding sections), the form is ready to use. Here's how:

1. **Use the steps in the preceding section to bring up the database's Database window. On the left, under Objects, click Forms. On the right, double-click the name of the form.**

   Access brings up your modified Shippers form (see Figure 58-12).

   As the form is now, you can edit data, enter new records, or delete records at will.

2. **Click the Lock Down Shippers button.**

   Access will not allow you to modify the shipper's Company Name or Phone number. Everything else can be modified — including, surprisingly, the Shipper ID — and you can add new shippers at will.

3. **Click the Enter New Records Only button.**

   Access goes into data entry mode, where you can't see any existing records, but you can add new shippers (see Figure 58-12).

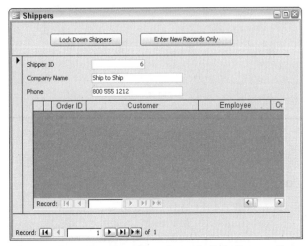

• **Figure 58-12: The Enter New Records Only button allows you to create new shipper records, but that's it.**

Creating Your Own AutoFormat

Technique 59

Save Time By

✓ Using predefined AutoFormat styles to quickly format an object

✓ Hijacking existing AutoFormat styles to create your own

Formatting can really have an impact on a reader. For example, when you read a financial report and you see a red number, you know exactly what it means. (You must be looking at my checking account.) Format a number red, and readers react even before they know the whole story. They feel it before they see it and see it before they understand it. Or sometimes formatting is just a matter of convention — some companies or departments require certain types of data to look a specific way.

In Access, an *AutoFormat* is a set of predefined formatting attributes or styles — fonts, colors, backgrounds, box borders, and the like. Applying an AutoFormat to an object assigns all those attributes to the object.

Regardless of why you need to format your data, don't spend more time than you must. Use the built-in AutoFormat feature to quickly apply any number of format settings to a form or a report — and steal them when you can. This Technique shows you how to pick the lock.

Applying an AutoFormat

Few AutoFormats will meet all your requirements, but they can greatly speed up the way you format reports and forms. In general terms, the fast way to formatting enlightenment goes like this:

1. Create your form or report.

2. Apply the AutoFormat that comes closest to what you want.

3. Tweak the AutoFormat.

4. Save it so that you can apply it again.

To start your career in AutoFormat larceny, do the following:

1. **Inside Access, choose File⇨New. In the New File task pane, click Blank Database. Give your new database a scintillating name and then click Create.**

In Figure 59-1, I create a database called Steal AutoFormats.mdb.

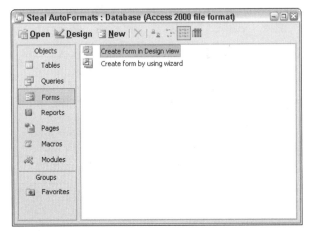

• **Figure 59-1:** Access's Database window.

2. **On the left, under Objects, click Forms. On the right, double-click Create Form in Design View.**

Access creates a new form and swings into design view (see Figure 59-2).

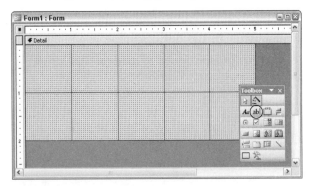

• **Figure 59-2:** Start with a new form.

3. **Click the Text Box control on the Toolbox (it's marked ab|); then click the form and draw a text box.**

The text box looks something like Figure 59-3. The Text0 box to the left of the new text box is an annoying label that's automatically generated by Access. *Unbound* signifies that the text box has not been tied into the database yet.

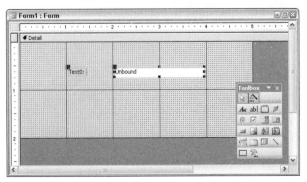

• **Figure 59-3:** A thoroughly uninspired, wimpy, unformatted text box.

4. **Choose View⇨Form View.**

Access shows you the uninspired, wimpy, unformatted form in all its glory (see Figure 59-4).

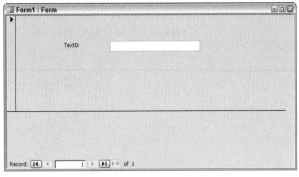

• **Figure 59-4:** A thoroughly uninspired, wimpy form with Standard formatting.

5. **Choose View⇨Design View.**

You have to be in design view in order to apply an AutoFormat.

6. **Choose Format⇨AutoFormat.**

Access shows you the AutoFormat dialog box (see Figure 59-5).

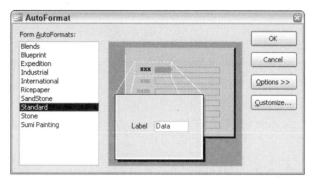

• **Figure 59-5: An AutoFormat wizard, of sorts.**

7. Click the first AutoFormat on offer, the one called Blends, and then click OK. Back in Access, choose View➪Form View.

 Blends (see Figure 59-6) has a graduated color in the background, a special shadow on the text box, and simple (sans serif) font formatting.

• **Figure 59-6: The Blends AutoFormat.**

 You're only changing the formatting here — not the function of the text box nor or the function of the form. It's only skin deep.

8. Choose File➪Close to close the newly formatted form. Yes, you want to save changes to the design of Form1. In the Save As box, give the form a name (such as AutoBlends) and then click OK.

Customizing AutoFormat Styles

In the preceding section, I tell you how to apply an existing AutoFormat style. Applying an AutoFormat can save you a lot of time if you can find one that fits most of your needs.

Fortunately, you can add custom AutoFormat styles by modifying one of the predefined styles or by creating a new one.

 Any custom AutoFormat style that you create will be available via the Form and Report wizards. That means you can format objects while you create them by using your custom AutoFormats.

Customization is the way to go if you have several personalities to please or conventions to satisfy. You can create as many custom AutoFormats as you need and then quickly apply the appropriate style accordingly.

 Although you can modify the built-in AutoFormat styles, I strongly recommend that you don't. Aside from reinstalling Access, you can't reset an AutoFormat to its original settings after you modify it.

 You aren't required to take all the pieces of an AutoFormat. You can pick and choose while you are modifying an element. From the AutoFormat dialog box, click Options to make the Font, Color, and Border check boxes appear (see Figure 59-7); then clear the check box next to whichever attribute of the AutoFormat style you want to ignore.

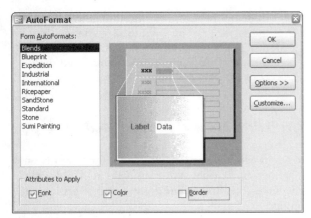

• **Figure 59-7: You don't have to accept all the pieces of an AutoFormat.**

To create your own AutoFormat style

1. **Follow the steps in the preceding section to create a form with the formatting you like.**

   You can start with an existing AutoFormat, as I did in Step 7 of the preceding section, or you can tweak formatting manually.

2. **With the form open, choose View➪Form View to see how the form looks. Change the existing formatting to create the look you want by right-clicking the element and choosing colors or alignments — or even choosing Properties and setting whichever property amuses you.**

   For example, in Figure 59-8, I took the AutoBlends form that I created in the preceding section, right-clicked the Unbound text box, and chose Special Effect➪Chiseled. That changed the appearance of the box around the text box.

    Go back and forth between form view and design view, making sure that you have the formatting you want for your new AutoFormat.

3. **When you're satisfied, choose View➪ Design View.**

• **Figure 59-8: Change formatting by modifying an existing style.**

4. **Choose Format➪AutoFormat➪Customize.**

   Access brings up the Customize AutoFormat dialog box, as shown in Figure 59-9.

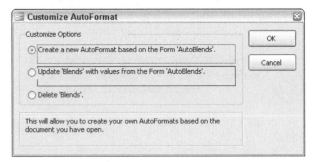

• **Figure 59-9: Create your new AutoFormat here.**

5. **Select the Create a New AutoFormat Based on the Form *<the name of the current form>* radio button and click OK.**

   You see the New Style Name dialog box (see Figure 59-10).

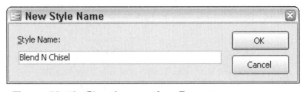

• **Figure 59-10: Give the new AutoFormat a name.**

6. **Type a name for your new AutoFormat and click OK.**

Access returns to the AutoFormat dialog box, and your new AutoFormat is available for use (see the top addition to the list on the left of Figure 59-11).

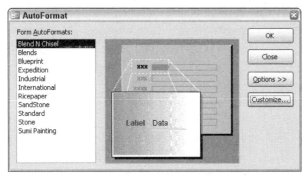

• **Figure 59-11: Your new AutoFormat now works precisely the same way as the built-in AutoFormats.**

 The Form and Report wizards use the current AutoFormat styles, so changes that you make to an AutoFormat will be reflected when you next use one of the wizards.

Deleting Old Styles

After awhile, you might acquire a rather large list of AutoFormat styles and want to delete obsolete styles. To delete an AutoFormat style, open any form in design view. Then do the following:

1. **Choose Format⇨AutoFormat.**

Access opens the AutoFormat dialog box (refer to Figure 59-11).

2. **Click the AutoFormat that you want to delete.**

3. **Click Customize.**

You see the Customize AutoFormat dialog box (see Figure 59-12).

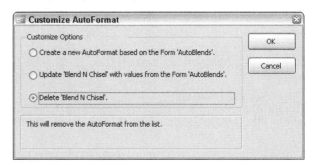

• **Figure 59-12: Delete any AutoFormat (even a built-in one) here.**

4. **Select the Delete *<style name>* radio button and then click OK.**

The AutoFormat is gone for good.

 Because Access allows you to delete a built-in style, be careful! Access won't ask you to confirm the selection (er, deletion), so after you click OK, the style is truly gone.

Part VII

Combining the Applications

The 5th Wave   By Rich Tennant

Technique 60

Inserting a Spreadsheet in a Document

Save Time By

- ✔ Picking the best, fastest way to get spreadsheet data into a doc
- ✔ Getting the right hunk of spreadsheet — the first time
- ✔ Resizing the spreadsheet and formatting data for legibility

If you've never tried to put a piece of an Excel spreadsheet in a Word document, you're in for a bit of a surprise. You'd think it would be easy to get the right piece of the spreadsheet into the document and that little things, like resizing the spreadsheet and its contents, could be accomplished with a minimum of fuss and bother. Well, you'd be wrong.

Word and Excel get along like dogs and cats. You have a few key decisions to make that basically determine whether cats rule and dogs drool, or vice versa, if you know what I mean. In most cases, it's probably best to avoid mixing the cats and dogs entirely, and just copy and paste. But that has its problems, too.

There are four quick ways to get the job done, and this Technique helps you choose a method that will give you the right results.

Choosing an Insertion Method

The four basic ways to put Excel spreadsheet-like data in a Word document are

- ✔ **Forget about Excel completely.** Use a Word table instead. The big advantage to this approach is that it's easy to use Word's extensive formatting and content-management tools if you go native. (For example, you can draw new cells in the table with the Draw Table command; or you can use table data in an index or cross-reference.) The big disadvantage is that you don't have any of Excel's tools, including such simple things as reliable totals (which are abysmal in Word) — not to mention all the great charting and data analysis capabilities.

 If your data is already in an Excel spreadsheet, you have quick ways to get it out and into Word. If you put your data in a Word table, you can move it over to Excel fairly reliably and easily, although stray cells can cause enormous headaches.

✔ **Take a picture of a spreadsheet and put the picture inside the doc.** Word and Excel make it very easy to stick a picture of a piece of a spreadsheet inside a document — you don't need to take a screenshot or use any other intermediary program. The advantage to this approach is that you know exactly what the spreadsheet will look like inside the document. Any formatting that you apply with Excel gets transferred faithfully to the picture — and thus into Word. After the picture is inside Word, you can use Word's tricks to resize the picture, crop it, make it move with text, float in the drawing layer (see Technique 11), and so on. The big disadvantage is that you can't get at the data at all — to show updated data in the Word doc, you have insert a new picture.

✔ **Build an Excel spreadsheet inside the doc.** Microsoft calls this *embedding* because the Excel data lives inside the Word document. The only way to get at the data is by going through Word and then into Excel. The big advantage to this approach is that you can use anything and everything available in Excel to massage the spreadsheet inside the document. Also, the data travels with the document, so it can't get lost. The big disadvantage is that you have to crank up Word and then go into Excel before you can get to the data — and formatting the Excel spreadsheet inside the doc can be a pain in the neck.

 Word documents with embedded spreadsheets can get huge. When I embed my sample 45K Tax Table spreadsheet (see Technique 43) in a 20K Word document, the resulting document balloons to 500K in size. Big documents like that not only slow down everything, they also tend to make Word unstable. You can mitigate the problem by building the Excel spreadsheet inside the document from scratch (see "Embedding a Spreadsheet" later in this Technique).

✔ **Put a link to the Excel spreadsheet inside the doc.** In this approach, the spreadsheet is just like any other Excel spreadsheet (er, workbook) — you've just set up a link between the Word doc and the spreadsheet that enables you to view the spreadsheet in the Word doc. The link from the document to the spreadsheet is *live* in the sense that every time you update the spreadsheet, Word draws data from the current version. Microsoft calls this approach *linking,* for obvious reasons. This approach is great if you already have a spreadsheet with the information that you want to stick in your doc. It's also the only game in town if you want to manipulate the data directly in Excel without having the hassle and overhead of going through Word, and then have the results of your shenanigans show up immediately in the doc. But using linking also means that you have to move the spreadsheet whenever you move the document if you want the latest version of the data. And formatting the data inside Word can be an enormously frustrating, time-consuming, uh, user experience.

No one method is inherently better than the other. Save yourself some time and heartache by taking a close look at the examples in this Technique. Chances are good you will find something that works — but keep the noted problems in mind when something goes bump in the night.

No, you aren't going crazy. Word works this way.

Copying Data

 If you don't need to reuse the data inside Excel and have the changes reflected directly inside the doc, you'll save a tremendous amount of time if you keep it simple: Copy the numbers across either as a Word table or as a picture.

Here's the easiest way to copy Excel data into Word and have the results appear in Word as a plain, ol' everyday table:

1. **Open the Word document that will hold the data.**

2. **Open the Excel spreadsheet that has the data.**

   I bring up my Woodys Fruit Company Sales spreadsheet.

3. **Select the data you want to copy and press Ctrl+C (or choose Edit⇨Copy).**

Excel outlines the data with its marching ants (see Figure 60-1).

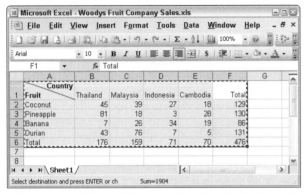

• **Figure 60-1: Selected data gets placed on the Clipboard.**

4. **Click inside the Word document where you want the table made with the Excel data to go.**

5. **Press Ctrl+V (or choose Edit⇨Paste).**

Word makes a valiant attempt to turn the Excel data into a Word table (see Figure 60-2).

Note: The cell borders that you see in Figure 60-2 are table gridlines; they *do not* appear on the printed page. I made Word show gridlines in this figure — just choose Table⇨View Gridlines — so you can see the individual cells.

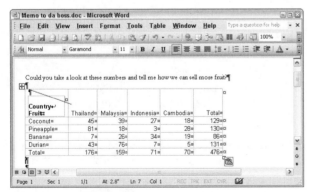

• **Figure 60-2: A fair — but far from exact — copy of the Excel data.**

If you compare Figures 60-1 and 60-2 closely, you see many of the good and bad points about copying data from Excel into a Word table. Notably

✔ The character formatting and table cell border formatting carried over from Excel to Word with no problems at all.

✔ Cell size formatting, on the other hand, got knocked for a loop. The height of the first row in Word is twice that in Excel.

✔ The slanted diagonal line — the *elbow* — in cell A1 wasn't translated into a diagonal line in Word, and the contents of cell A1 got mushed together.

 In fact, the Country/Fruit entry in Excel's cell A1 was transformed into a table inside a table in Word — a potentially very confusing situation.

If you work with the table a bit, you find that you can format it in all the usual Word ways: borders, alignment, centering on the page, and so on. You can also draw inside the table with Word's table drawing tool.

 Entries in the table cells are numbers — Excel's formulas don't survive the leap to Word. If you overtype one of the numbers in the table, Word isn't smart enough to recalculate totals.

The second way to copy data from Excel into Word is to simply bring it across as a picture. Here's how:

1. **Open the Word document that will hold the data.**

2. **Open the Excel spreadsheet that has the data.**

3. **In the Excel spreadsheet, select the data that you want to copy and press Ctrl+C (or choose Edit⇨Copy).**

Refer to Figure 60-1.

4. **Click inside the Word document where you want the table made with the Excel data to go.**

5. **Choose Edit➪Paste Special.**

Word brings up the Paste Special dialog box, as shown in Figure 60-3. The Paste radio button is selected by default.

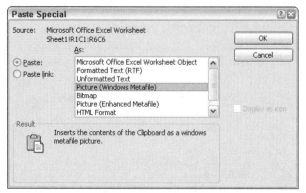

• **Figure 60-3:** Choose from various kinds of formatting for the pasted data.

6. **From the As list, choose Picture (Windows Metafile) and then click OK.**

Word pastes a picture-perfect copy of the spreadsheet into your document (see Figure 60-4).

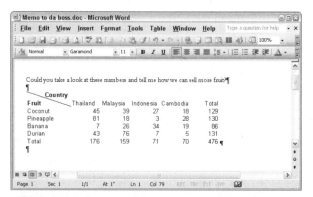

• **Figure 60-4:** An amazingly accurate rendition of the original.

If you compare Figures 60-1 and 60-4 closely, you should be most impressed with the fidelity of the copy.

How good is the copy? If you print the original spreadsheet and the copy in the document, and then examine the two side-by-side, you won't be able to tell the two apart. It's that good.

The problem? The data didn't make it into Word. The copy in Word is a picture: You can click it, drag the resizing handles, crop it, put it in the drawing layer, and rotate it (see Technique 11), and generally do anything to it that Word can do to a picture.

However, you can't change the font size, or put borders around the cells, or add a new row, or do anything that Word can do with tables. If you want to reformat the data or redo calculations, you have to change the data in Excel and copy the picture all over again.

Note the option in Figure 60-3 to paste a link to a picture of the Excel spreadsheet. If you choose that option, you don't get a picture — you get a full-fledged link. See the "Linking a Spreadsheet" section later in this Technique for details.

Embedding a Spreadsheet

In the first section of this Technique, I talk about the four approaches to putting Excel data in Word documents. Embedding is often the fastest approach if you need to update the spreadsheet data, although struggling with formatting might make you change your mind.

Microsoft favors the embedded approach: Word's designers even put a button on the Standard toolbar that lets you create embedded Excel spreadsheets with a couple of clicks.

Of the many ways to embed spreadsheets in Excel, these are the most common:

✔ Create the spreadsheet from scratch from inside Word (the method demonstrated in this section).

✔ Choose Insert⇨Object, choose Microsoft Excel Chart, and either enter the data manually (Create New) or copy data from an existing spreadsheet (Create from File).

✔ Copy the spreadsheet cells to the Clipboard, choose Edit⇨Paste Special (refer to Figure 60-3), choose Microsoft Office Excel Worksheet Object, make sure the Paste radio button is selected (in the Paste Special dialog box), and finally click OK.

 Embedding an Excel spreadsheet inside a Word document using any method other than the build-from-scratch approach can produce enormous .doc files. Big .doc files not only make your machine work slower, but they also make Word significantly less stable.

To create a new embedded Excel spreadsheet from scratch

1. Click the Insert Microsoft Excel Worksheet icon on the Standard toolbar.

It looks like a spreadsheet with a big X on it.

2. Move your mouse to cover the number of cells that you want to appear in the document.

Initially, Word limits you to four rows and five columns (see Figure 60-5).

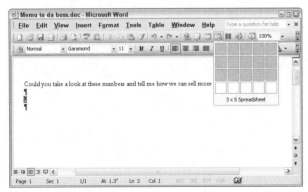

• **Figure 60-5: Embed a 3 x 5 Excel spreadsheet in a Word document.**

3. Click when you have the correct number of cells.

The spreadsheet appears inside your document.

4. To resize the spreadsheet inside Word so that you can work in it, click and drag the sizing handles, just like you would a picture.

In Figure 60-6, I tell Word to show six columns and seven rows by simply dragging the resizing handle on the lower-right corner.

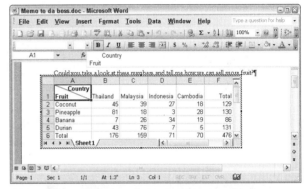

• **Figure 60-6: Use the resizing handles to make the embedded spreadsheet bigger.**

5. At this point, you can work inside the spreadsheet as if you were working in Excel itself — albeit in a cramped tiny sliver.

In Figure 60-6, I copied data across from my Woodys Fruit Company sample spreadsheet, using the same Ctrl+C/Ctrl+V method that I would use to copy data between any Excel spreadsheets.

Oddly, the status bar from Excel doesn't appear when an embedded spreadsheet is active. If you want to use Excel's fast calculation capability (where you select a bunch of numbers and their sum appears at the bottom on the status bar), you're outta luck.

 When you work inside the embedded spreadsheet, Excel icons go on all the toolbars.

6. To see the spreadsheet inside Word, click any-where inside the document but outside the blocked-out Excel area.

In Figure 60-7, I click in the main part of the docu-ment, and the enlarged 6 x 7 spreadsheet appears.

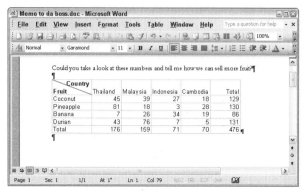

• **Figure 60-7:** Click outside the spreadsheet to show the results.

7. If you want to work on the spreadsheet again, double-click inside the spreadsheet area.

Excel comes back up, as in Figure 60-6.

If you want to resize the spreadsheet on the printed page without changing the number of cells that appear, you have two choices:

✔ **Resize the spreadsheet from Word, as if it were a picture.** Click inside the document (outside the spreadsheet) to return control to Word; then click the spreadsheet once to select it. Use the resizing handles to make the spreadsheet appear larger or smaller (see Figure 60-8).

 Resizing the spreadsheet as if it were a picture distorts the characters inside the spreadsheet — this isn't the same thing as increasing or decreasing the font size, and your readers will notice the difference.

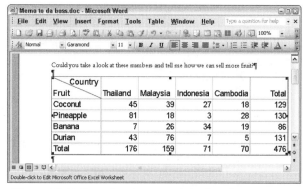

• **Figure 60-8:** Drag the picture resizing handles to make the image larger or smaller without affecting the number of cells appearing inside Word.

✔ **Resize the contents of the spreadsheet inside Excel.** Double-click the spreadsheet to give con-trol to Excel; then select and format any cells that you wish. In Figure 60-9, I made the contents of the cells larger, but because I didn't change the size of the cells (and they don't resize auto-matically), the text gets clipped.

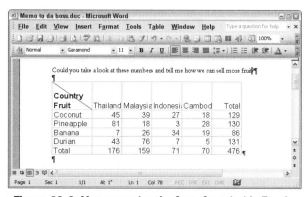

• **Figure 60-9:** You can resize the fonts from inside Excel, but then text can get clipped.

If you resize the text as in Figure 60-1 and then attempt to make the columns wider by clicking and dragging the column markers (without expanding the width of the spreadsheet in Word), Excel *makes the columns narrower.* There are dozens of hard formatting bugs like this one in embedded Excel spreadsheets, and they can drive you up a wall.

Linking a Spreadsheet

In the preceding section, I talk about embedding Excel spreadsheets in Word documents. Linking is similar to embedding, but here are the two big differences:

- ✔ **The data remains in a traditional** .xls **spreadsheet file.** If you move the document to a different machine, you have to take the spreadsheet along with it. At the same time, though, you don't get the elephantine embedded spreadsheet bloat.

- ✔ **You can't edit the data from inside Word.** If you double-click the data, Word starts Excel, and you work in Excel. Sometimes, changes made in Excel are immediately reflected in Word; other times, you have to click the linked spreadsheet image and press F9 (which updates the link).

Linking to a spreadsheet makes sense when

- ✔ You need to get the data updated automatically. In other words, you don't want to spend the time to manually copy the data when it changes, and paste it as a picture in the Word document.

- ✔ The file size bloat associated with embedding an entire spreadsheet inside a Word document is just too much to take.

- ✔ The document doesn't need to travel — or if it does, you're willing to go to the trouble to make sure the spreadsheet travels along with it (and that the destination computer has Excel up and running).

To link a spreadsheet to a Word document

1. **Open the Word document that will hold the data.**

2. **Open the Excel spreadsheet that has the data.**

3. **Select the data that you want to copy and press Ctrl+C (or choose Edit➪Copy).**

   Refer to Figure 60-1.

4. **Click inside the Word document where you want the table made with the Excel data to go.**

5. **Choose Edit➪Paste Special.**

   Word brings up the Paste Special dialog box (refer to Figure 60-3).

6. **In the As list, choose Microsoft Office Excel Worksheet Object. Select the Paste Link radio button. Then click OK.**

   Word pastes a link in your document. You also get a highly accurate picture of the spreadsheet, just like the one in Figure 60-4.

When you want to modify the data, either start Excel and open the spreadsheet that supplied the data, or double-click the picture of the spreadsheet inside the document (in which case, Word starts Excel and opens the spreadsheet that supplied the data). When you're done making changes to the data, exit Excel.

To update the picture in the Word document, click it and press F9. Word automatically updates the picture whenever it updates fields — typically when you open the file and just before you print it.

 You can click and drag the picture, resize it, put it in the drawing layer, rotate it — do anything that Word will let you do with a picture.

You cannot tell just by looking at the picture in the document whether you have a link. The easiest way to work with all the links in a document is to choose Edit⇨Links. That brings up the Links dialog box (see Figure 60-10), which lets you manipulate each link individually.

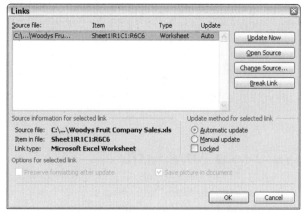

• **Figure 60-10:** Work with the links in your document individually.

Technique 61

Managing an Electronic Newsletter

Save Time By

✔ Keeping in touch with your customers, quickly and cheaply

✔ Setting up the newsletter the right way — the first time

✔ Knowing when it's time to move on to new technology

With the rise of spam as the world's number-one electronic threat, the bloom is off the newsletter rose. Still, if you have compelling information that people want to read, starting your own electronic newsletter rates as a first-class way to keep people informed.

I know. In October 1996, I launched the *Woody's Office Watch* newsletter primarily (if you'll pardon the plug) as a timesaving technique. Peter Deegan, a long-time friend and correspondent, suggested that instead of answering Office users' questions one-by-one, as I had for years, starting a newsletter and sending the answers out to a lot of people, all at once, would be whole lot more efficient.

Back in 1996, *a lot* meant maybe a hundred Office users. I couldn't even conceive of a thousand people being interested in Office tips and news. Man, was I in for a rude awakening. Within five years, WOW and its sister newsletters grew to more than 500,000 subscribers and heaven only knows how many readers.

You can change the world with your newsletters. You can keep customers informed, troll for new business, preach to the converted, or hound any hallowed hall you choose. But running a newsletter takes bunches of time — and a bit of money. That's where this Technique comes in.

Choosing to Start a Newsletter

If you're looking for new customers, trying to motivate a sales force, or reaching out to the public at large, your newsletter will live and die by content, content, content.

If you want to keep a newsletter vibrant and alive, you have to include material that subscribers (even that captive audience — *especially* that captive audience!) will devour, talk about, and pass along to others. The best way to do that is to think like a subscriber. Because you probably already subscribe to a few (dozen? hundred?) electronic newsletters, you know what keeps subscribers reading:

- ✔ More information that makes a difference
- ✔ Better writing that draws people in
- ✔ Less overhead — advertising, notices, corporate Pablum, and the like — that turns off people.

The problem with creating successful newsletters — even newsletters that exist primarily to advertise — stems from the fact that it isn't sufficient to write a compelling story every now and then. You have to produce great material day after day, week after week. If you don't, people stop reading, unsubscribe, or otherwise ignore your work, and all that hard effort goes to naught.

Don't leap into launching a newsletter until you're ready to keep it stoked. In particular, as alternatives to starting a newsletter, consider

- ✔ **Becoming more active on an existing Internet newsgroup or discussion board.** Lending an experienced hand to those seeking help won't make you rich, but it can get you noticed.
- ✔ **Creating your own discussion group.**
- ✔ **Running a moderated mailing list.**

Unmoderated groups tend to degenerate into drivel rather quickly. On the other hand, moderated groups can be very useful for keeping customers posted on the latest product developments.

The advantage to all three of these approaches is that you won't be responsible for writing all the sizzling material that will draw and keep new subscribers — or motivate and energize your captive audience. Other folks can pitch in. If you do decide that starting a newsletter is the way to go, the following sections can get you started.

Starting Small with Outlook

If you have a stable audience — say, fewer than a couple hundred customers, or employees, or a similar group that doesn't change all that much — it's easy and fast to maintain your e-mail newsletter subscriber list in Outlook.

When the time comes to send out a newsletter, you write the newsletter in Word and then use Outlook to send copies to all subscribers. There are several tricks.

Before you put any work into building your Outlook Contacts list, send a message to your Internet service provider (ISP). Some ISPs are so paranoid about junk mail that they limit outbound e-mail messages to 25 or even fewer addressees per message. If you want to set up an Outlook-based newsletter for 100 subscribers, you better make sure that your ISP will allow you to send out one message with 100 addresses in the Bcc (blind carbon copy) field. Otherwise, you'll spend far too much time futzing around with multiple outbound messages for a single issue of the newsletter. If your ISP won't let you send one message to all the people on your subscriber list, get a better ISP.

Creating and maintaining a subscriber list

Here's how to set up the subscribers in Outlook Contacts:

1. **Make sure that you have accurate subscriber information — most importantly, the correct e-mail address — in your Outlook Contacts list.**

    In many cases, most (if not all!) of your new subscribers will be in the Outlook Contacts list anyway.

2. **Add a new category for newsletter subscribers to Outlook. Choose Edit➪Categories. In the Categories dialog box, click Master Category List.**

Outlook shows you the Master Category List dialog box, as shown in Figure 61-1.

• **Figure 61-1:** Create a new category for newsletter subscribers.

3. **Type a name for your newsletter subscriber category and then click Add.**

In Figure 61-1, I type **Newsletter** and then click Add. That adds a new category — Newsletter — to Outlook's master list.

4. **Click OK twice.**

5. **One by one, go through each of your newsletter subscribers in Outlook. Right-click each entry in the Contacts list and choose Categories.**

Outlook brings up the Categories dialog box (see Figure 61-2).

6. **Mark the check box for the Newsletter category and then click OK.**

The Contact gets assigned to the Newsletter category.

• **Figure 61-2:** Assign each Contact who's a subscriber to the Newsletter category.

 Also assign yourself to the Newsletter category. That way, you receive a copy of each newsletter when it goes out, thus confirming that the mail got through.

7. **When you're through assigning the Contacts to the Newsletter category, double-check your work by clicking By Category on the left pane under Current View, or by choosing View⇨ Arrange By⇨Current View⇨By Category.**

Outlook shows you a compact list of everyone who's assigned to your Newsletter category.

Managing your newsletter mailing list becomes a matter of keeping Contacts updated:

✔ To add a person to your newsletter mailing list, add him to your Contacts and then right-click that entry and assign it to the Newsletter category (Steps 5 and 6 in the preceding procedure).

✔ To drop a person from the mailing list, either delete the person from your Category list or (if you want to keep a record of that person) remove the Newsletter category from that entry by right-clicking the entry and clearing the Newsletter Subscriber category.

Creating and sending the newsletter

If your subscriber list is up-to-date and you know that your ISP will allow you to send a message to many Bcc addresses, creating and sending the newsletter couldn't be simpler — if you know the tricks:

1. **Write the newsletter in Word.**

Some people will tell you that Word creates absolutely lousy formatted e-mail. They're right. Anybody who speaks HTML as a foreign language and looks at the code underlying your newsletters will have a well-deserved cow. But unless you're sending out tens of thousands of newsletters, or your subscribers insist on using really buggy e-mail readers (I've had no end of problems with Pegasus), Word is fast, easy, flexible, reliable — and it's the devil ye know.

2. **Choose File⇨Send To⇨Mail Recipient.**

Word sprouts a To and a Cc (carbon copy) box at the top of the newsletter.

3. **Click the down arrow next to Options and then choose Bcc.**

That puts the Bcc field on the screen underneath the Cc field (see Figure 61-3).

Because subscribers don't want their e-mail addresses broadcast with your newsletter, it's vitally important that you stick all your subscriber's e-mail addresses in the Bcc box and not the Cc box. When you do so, nobody (except your ISP) will ever know that the message went out to those destination addresses.

4. **Move over to Outlook and bring up your Contacts list. Get a list of newsletter subscribers by clicking the By Category button on the left pane under Current View (or choose View⇨Arrange By⇨Current View⇨By Category) and then scrolling down to your newsletter subscribers.**

Your screen should look like the upcoming Figure 61-4.

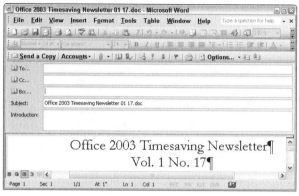

• **Figure 61-3:** All the recipients' e-mail addresses go in the Bcc field.

5. **In the Contacts list on the right, click the Categories entry for your newsletter subscribers.**

You don't need to select all your subscribers. Simply clicking the Categories heading suffices (see Figure 61-4).

• **Figure 61-4:** Bring up your newsletter subscriber list.

6. **Choose Actions⇨New Message to Contact.**

If Outlook responds by telling you that the action will apply to all items in the selected groups, click OK. If Outlook tells you that some of these Contacts do not have e-mail addresses, your subscriber list is out of whack. You can proceed by clicking OK, but then you need to go back and type in valid e-mail addresses for the missing subscribers before sending out the newsletter.

Outlook creates a new e-mail message, called *Untitled Message,* with all — *all* — the newsletter subscribers' e-mail addresses in the To box (see Figure 61-5).

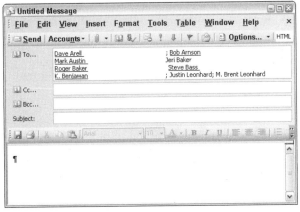

• **Figure 61-5:** A list of e-mail addresses for all of your newsletter subscribers.

7. Click once inside the To box of Untitled Message. Press Ctrl+A to select all the addresses and then press Ctrl+C to copy all the addresses to the Clipboard.

8. Move back to Word and the newsletter. Click once inside the Bcc box. Then press Ctrl+V to paste all the addresses into the Bcc box.

Your newsletter message looks like Figure 61-6.

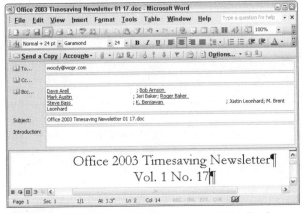

• **Figure 61-6:** All your subscribers appear in the Bcc box.

9. Type your own e-mail address in the To box.

 Many e-mail systems go bonkers if both the To and Cc boxes are blank.

10. Click the Send a Copy button.

The newsletter gets deposited in your Outlook Outbox. The next time you send messages, the newsletter wings its way to all your subscribers — and you, too.

In my experience, after your newsletter subscriber base grows to more than a couple hundred of addresses, the Outlook-based approach gets unwieldy. Word and Outlook can handle the load — indeed, you can easily send out messages to thousands of people — but the process of updating the subscriber list takes a lot of time, particularly with subscribers sending you notifications of address changes. It might be time to employ a service.

Using a Newsletter Service

The preceding section gives you a detailed, step-by-step procedure for using Outlook to send newsletters. I highly recommend using that approach (providing that your ISP will let you send enough copies at a time) until you just can't stand the overhead of maintaining the subscriber list in your Outlook Contacts.

If your list has grown too big, your ISP threatens to shut you down, and/or you have a religious objection to using Word and Outlook for your newsletter, you should consider using the services of a newsletter publisher to provide the infrastructure that you need.

Newsletter services fall into two categories:

✔ **Free services:** These typically append advertising to your newsletters. Rarely, you might be able to find a free service without advertising that really wants a newsletter covering your topic. See *Free*Lists (www.freelists.org) for an example.

The free service that I know best is Topica (www.topica.com). Log on and sign up to become a Topica Exchange member. Topica will try to sell you its Email Publisher service, but if you're persistent and wade through the Web site, you will find free advertising-laden newsletter services on offer.

 I know of very few people who stick with free newsletter services very long simply because the advertising can be so intrusive and so unpredictable.

✔ **Paid services:** These can be surprisingly cheap — as little as $25 per month, in some cases. Expect to get subscription services that include confirmation e-mails (so someone subscribing to your newsletter has to click a link in a message to confirm their subscription), templates, fully formatted (HTML) newsletters, bounce-back management (where messages that "bounce" with bad addresses are automatically removed from the list), and some archiving capabilities. Don't expect to get extensive support or any customization.

 Topica offers a highly regarded, bare-bones paid service (www.email-publisher.com, see Figure 61-7) that can handle large numbers of subscribers. Constant Contact (www.constantcontact.com) targets people and companies interested in e-mail marketing. ennectMail (www.ennectmail.com), which also offers extensive newsletter support, has an interesting comparison of the cost of electronic versus printed newsletters.

 Shop around! Prices for newsletter services vary all over the map, and discounts can frequently be had for the asking. See Table 61-1 for some eye-opening figures.

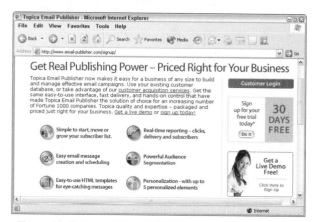

• **Figure 61-7: Topica's Email Publisher draws good reviews.**

Getting an ISSN

If your newsletter goes out beyond a small circle of friends, you should consider applying for an International Standard Serial Number (ISSN). The eight-digit ISSN number uniquely identifies a periodical, much as an ISBN number uniquely identifies books and other non-periodical publications.

Applying for an ISSN is easy, fast, and free. Drop by www.issn.org for instructions and an application form.

TABLE 61-1: COMPARATIVE COSTS OF NEWSLETTER SERVICES

Service	Price
Outlook	This is free although you have to find an ISP that lets you send messages with large numbers of addressees.
ennectMail	Base price is 5 cents per newsletter sent. If you send 2,000 short newsletters per week, that's around $400 per month.
Dundee	Base price is $25 per month plus 75 cents per 1,000 newsletters sent. If you send 2,000 short newsletters per week, it's less than $35 per month.

Growing Larger Gracefully

If your newsletter needs increase, you will no doubt find yourself moving from an Outlook-based approach to a paid newsletter service, and possibly moving from there to a major newsletter server. The reason? Money. See Table 61-1.

One company dominates the large-scale newsletter support software business: Lyris (www.lyris.com). More than a hundred companies offer Lyris-based newsletter services.

Lyris itself offers its own newsletter service, starting at $200 per month, ascending (steeply!) depending on how many newsletters you send and how many bytes they consume (see Figure 61-8).

 We at *Woody's Watch* have been using Dundee's Lyris service, www.dundee.net, for many years, and it's worked well for us. Dundee was the first company to license Lyris List Manager, so they've been at this game for quite some time.

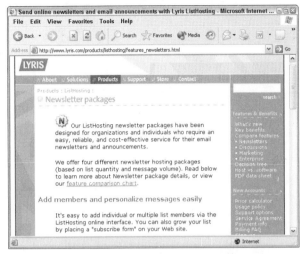

• **Figure 61-8:** Lyris makes the software used by most major newsletter service providers, and it offers the service directly.

Turning a Word Document Into a Presentation

Save Time By

- ✔ Converting a Word Table of Contents into a PowerPoint presentation
- ✔ Converting a presentation into a Word document — and making it legible

S o you have your report ready, and now you have to give a presentation on it. Fair enough. Happens every day.

Most people would crank up PowerPoint, type a title slide, bring up the report, and start copying across the points. You know the drill — select and copy in Word, paste and pray in PowerPoint. It's a tedious, error-prone process almost certainly guaranteed to result in a presentation that misses some high points and over-emphasizes others. There's a much better way.

Few people realize that a well-formatted Word document (which is to say, one with Heading 1, 2, and 3 styles — the kind folks usually use to create a Table of Contents, or TOC) can be transformed quickly and easily into a PowerPoint presentation. Even fewer realize that you can conversely take a presentation and turn it into a Word outline or TOC, even though PowerPoint unfortunately applies some truly bizarre formatting to the heading paragraphs.

This Technique shows you the tricks and the fixes.

Understanding Outline Levels

If you need to turn a Word document into a PowerPoint presentation, and your document uses the standard Heading 1, 2, and 3 styles, you're in luck. Converting the headings in the document into a presentation takes only a click.

 If you have a document that you want to turn into a PowerPoint presentation and it uses styles other than Heading 1, 2, 3 and so on, it's worth your while to change it over to the Heading styles.

The conversion process relies on a Word paragraph setting called the *Outline Level*. Each paragraph in a document has an Outline Level, which you can set from the Paragraph dialog box (choose Format⇨Paragraph; see Figure 62-1).

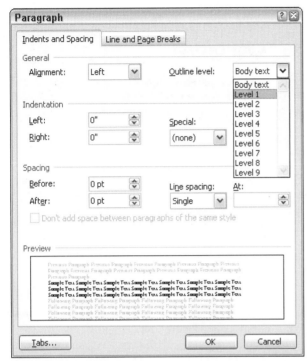

• **Figure 62-1: This Heading 1 paragraph is automatically assigned Outline Level 1.**

Outline Levels come into play inside Word when you look at a document in Outline view (choose View⇨ Outline; see Figure 62-2):

  ✔ The highest-level headings are assigned Outline Level 1.

  ✔ The next-lower level of headings are Outline Level 2, and so on.

  ✔ Run-of-the-mill text gets the lowest Outline level (*Body text*).

In Word's Outline view, changing the Outline Level of a paragraph is easy. For example, you can click and drag a paragraph to a higher level, select and push the Tab key to lower a level, or click inside a paragraph and assign the level from the drop-down box on the Outlining toolbar.

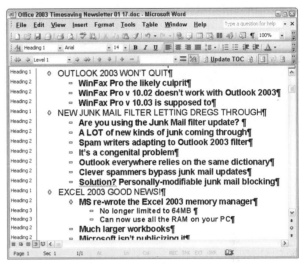

• **Figure 62-2: Outline view relies on Outline Levels for organizing paragraphs.**

 When you apply the Heading 1 style to a paragraph, Word assigns it an Outline Level of 1. Heading 2 corresponds to Outline Level 2, and Heading 3 corresponds to Outline Level 3. (Ah, New Math.) That's why it's fast and easy to change a document with Heading 1, 2, and 3 styles into a presentation.

When Word creates a Table of Contents, it usually builds the TOC based on both Heading styles and Outline Levels. So unless you've gone to great pains to create a custom Table of Contents, the TOC in your document should reflect the Outline Levels as well (see Figure 62-3).

 Word's Document Map (choose View⇨ Document Map), which appears in a pane on the left side of a document, also reflects the Outline Levels in the paragraphs.

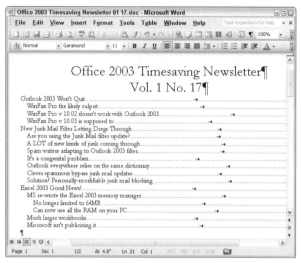

• **Figure 62-3: The Table of Contents also reflects Outline Levels.**

When Word converts a document to a PowerPoint presentation, it relies on Outline Levels. The converter starts at the beginning of the document; then

✔ The converter ignores all paragraphs at the lowest Outline Level (body text).

✔ When the converter encounters an Outline Level 1 paragraph, it creates a new slide and uses the contents of the paragraph as the slide's title.

✔ When it encounters an Outline Level 2 paragraph, it creates a high-level bullet point on the current slide and uses the contents of the paragraph for the text on the bullet point.

✔ When it encounters an Outline Level 3–9 paragraph, it creates a lower-level bullet point, using the contents of the paragraph for the bullet text.

In effect, if you have a document with Heading 1, 2, and 3 styles — and you haven't applied any Outline Levels manually — the Table of Contents of the document turns into the PowerPoint presentation, with each high-level heading in the TOC turning into a new slide.

Converting a TOC to a Presentation

Here's how to convert a well-formed document's TOC (or, more accurately, Outline Levels 1–9 paragraphs) into a PowerPoint presentation:

1. Open the document in Word.

Create a Table of Contents (choose Insert⇨ Reference⇨Index and Tables⇨Table of Contents and then click OK) to make sure that your outline levels are accurate. Alternatively, you can go into Outline view (choose View⇨Outline) or bring up the Document Map (choose View⇨ Document Map).

2. Choose File⇨Send To⇨Microsoft Office PowerPoint.

PowerPoint appears with a completely bare presentation (see Figure 62-4).

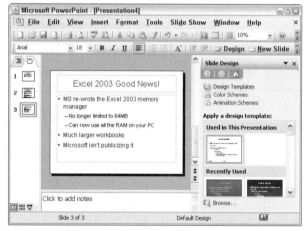

• **Figure 62-4: You get a minimalist presentation, with no title slide and no design applied.**

3. Verify that you have one slide in PowerPoint for each Outline Level 1 paragraph in Word.

If you encounter extra slides, click them one-by-one and press Delete to delete them. If you have one slide where you should have two, click the bullet point that should start a new slide and then click the Decrease Indent icon on the Formatting toolbar (the one with a bunch of lines and a left-pointing arrow) until PowerPoint creates a new slide.

 I've seen bugs in all versions of Office, but most distressingly in Office 2003, PowerPoint generates additional slides when there should be none and occasionally creates one slide where there should be more than one. Yes, Microsoft ran out of money when it built Office 2003. That's the only possible explanation for such sloppiness, eh?

4. Add a title slide by clicking the New Slide button on the Formatting toolbar, clicking the first sample in the Text Layouts pane on the right (it's called *Title Slide*), and then clicking and dragging the new title slide to the beginning of the presentation. Type the title of the presentation on the title slide.

The new title slide appears at the top of the heap (see Figure 62-5).

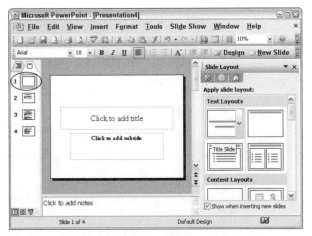

• **Figure 62-5:** Create and then drag a new title slide to the beginning of the presentation.

5. Apply a design by clicking the Design button on the Formatting toolbar and then choosing a design from the task pane.

In Figure 62-6, I apply the Mountain Top design.

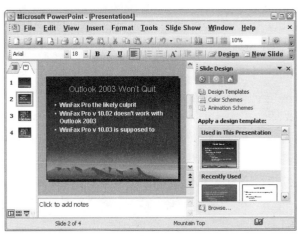

• **Figure 62-6:** Manually apply a design.

6. Edit and save your new presentation.

Converting a Presentation to a TOC

In the preceding section, I show you how to convert a Word document — basically, its Table of Contents — into a PowerPoint presentation.

Going the other way, PowerPoint makes it very easy to convert a presentation into the skeleton of a Word document — albeit a very bizarrely formatted document. In Word 2003, the resulting document is downright garish.

Here's how to convert a PowerPoint presentation into the heading points (or outline, or Table of Contents — they're basically all the same thing) of a Word document and then convert the document into something legible:

1. Open the PowerPoint presentation.

In Figure 62-7, I open the Connecting in Phuket presentation that appears in Technique 50.

2. Choose File⇨Send To⇨Microsoft Office Word.

PowerPoint responds with the Send to Microsoft Office Word dialog box, as shown in Figure 62-8.

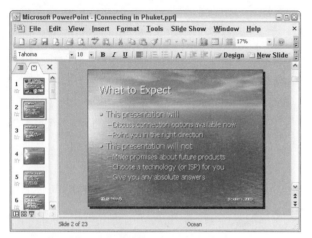

• **Figure 62-7: Start with the presentation.**

• **Figure 62-8: Send the outline to Word.**

3. Select the Outline Only radio button; then click OK.

Word comes up with a new document that includes a nearly illegible copy of the text on the slides (see Figure 62-9).

▶ Slide headings turn into Heading 1 paragraphs, but PowerPoint overrides your default Heading 1 formatting, setting its own style with a headache-inducing Tahoma 22 point shadow text.

▶ Main slide bullet points turn into Heading 2 paragraphs, but again PowerPoint overrides your Heading 2 format, setting it at Arial 14 point bold (which isn't too bad).

▶ Subordinate slide bullet points turn into Heading 3 paragraphs, with the style overridden in First Grade Crayola . . . uh, Tahoma 14 point shadow.

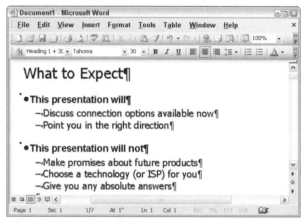

• **Figure 62-9: Quite possibly the worst automatically applied formatting I've ever seen — and PowerPoint does it whether you want it or not.**

4. Use this very convoluted way to apply your default Heading 1, Heading 2, and Heading 3 formatting to this bizarre document. Start by creating a new blank document by clicking the New icon on the far left of the Standard toolbar.

Word brings up a new, clean document.

5. Press Enter a few times; then go back to the top of the document and turn the first paragraph into a Heading 1 paragraph by clicking the drop-down arrow next to the Style box (the one that reads Normal) and choosing Heading 1. Go to the second paragraph and make it Heading 2. Make the third paragraph Heading 3, and the next one Heading 4.

6. Choose File⇨Save As. In the Save As Type box, choose Document Template. Type a name for the template and then click Save.

In Figure 62-10, I saved the template as Sane.dot, which is meant to be in stark contrast to the formatting applied automatically by PowerPoint.

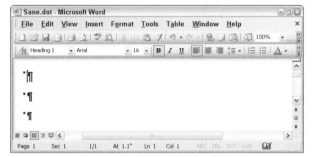

• **Figure 62-10:** Save a template with all your major Heading styles.

7. Go back to the PowerPoint-generated document. Choose Tools⇨Templates and Add-Ins, and then click the Organizer button in the lower-left corner.

Word responds with the Organizer dialog box (see Figure 62-11).

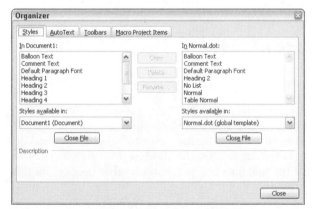

• **Figure 62-11:** The template Organizer allows you to copy styles from a template to a document.

8. On the right, under where it reads Styles Available In /Normal.dot, click Close File.

The Closed File button immediately changes into an Open File button.

9. Click Open File.

Word responds with a standard Open dialog box, which is looking at your Templates folder.

10. Choose the template that you saved in Step 6. Click Open.

As you might expect, I choose Sane.dot.

11. Select all the Heading styles on the right (Sane.dot) side of the Organizer dialog box; then click Copy.

12. Word asks whether you want to overwrite the bizarre heading styles in the PowerPoint-generated document. Click Yes to All.

Although there is no response from Word, the styles in the PowerPoint-generated document are overwritten nonetheless.

13. Click Close.

Word returns to the document, which now has reasonable heading formatting, but the headings still have manually applied bullets.

14. Select everything in the document by pressing Ctrl+A. Then choose Format⇨Bullets and Numbering⇨Bulleted, click the None sample, and click OK.

Word finally — finally! — has a decently formatted document, ready for you to flesh out (see Figure 62-12).

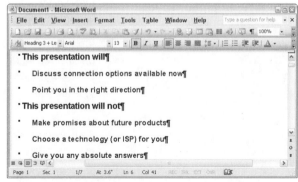

• **Figure 62-12:** That's the easy way to remove all the PowerPoint bizarre formatting.

Technique 63

Animating a Chart in PowerPoint

No doubt you've seen a PowerPoint presentation that includes a chart that goes zip-zip-zip, with lines or bars or pie slices appearing onscreen one piece at a time while the speaker tells a tale that explains the data as it unfolds. Done well, animated charts can paint a very compelling picture — one that's worth a thousand words (or perhaps two thousand bullet points).

Although you might think that it takes some sort of rocket scientist to stick a whizzing animated chart into a PowerPoint slide, you'd be wrong. In fact, far too few rocket scientists put animated charts in their presentations. Just about anybody with a good story to tell, an Excel spreadsheet to back it up, and a touch of pizazz can put together an absolutely killer animated slide in about 15 minutes.

Or you can lose hours trying to get past PowerPoint's bugs.

This Technique leads the way.

Building Charts in Excel

Excel charts in PowerPoint presentations can really make a point. Numbers talk. Bull . . . ets walk.

If you have the kind of data that lends itself to animation — bringing in one bunch of data, followed by another, then another — and you can use the step-by-step introduction of data on the slide to get across a compelling story. You have the makings of a presentation that people will talk about for days.

It all starts with the data.

Here's how to build a PowerPoint-ready graph (or *chart* if you want to use the official Microsoft terminology) in Excel:

1. **Start with a spreadsheet that shows the data you want to get across. If you want to change column headings so they show up differently on the chart's legend, now's the time to do it.**

In Figure 63-1, I open the Woodys Fruit Company Sales spreadsheet.

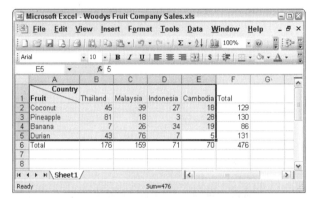

• **Figure 63-1: Create or open a spreadsheet with compelling data.**

2. **Select the data and then click the Chart Wizard icon on the Standard toolbar. (The Chart Wizard icon looks like a column graph.)**

Excel responds with Step 1 of the Chart Wizard (see Figure 63-2).

 When selecting data to form a column, bar, area, or line chart, selecting subtotals or totals is unusual. Generally, you want to select the data and the row and column headings. Pie charts, however, usually work with totals.

 Hold down the Ctrl key while you click to select cells that aren't next to each other.

3. **On the Standard Types tab, pick a chart type and subtype, clicking the Press and Hold to View Sample button to see a preview of how your presentation's chart will look. When you have the right kind of chart, click Next.**

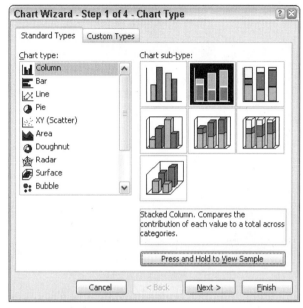

• **Figure 63-2: Choose a chart (chart) type here.**

4. **In Step 2 of the Chart Wizard, verify that Excel chose the right data and then click Next.**

You see Step 3 of the wizard.

5. **Avoid the temptation to type in a chart title; just click Next.**

Excel brings you to the final step of the wizard (see Figure 63-3).

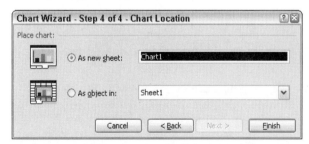

• **Figure 63-3: Always put the chart in a new sheet.**

6. **Select the As New Sheet radio button and then click Finish.**

Excel creates a new chart and puts it on its own sheet (see Figure 63-4). For now, there's no reason to format the chart — you can do that when you put it in the presentation itself (see the next section).

7. **Save the file.**

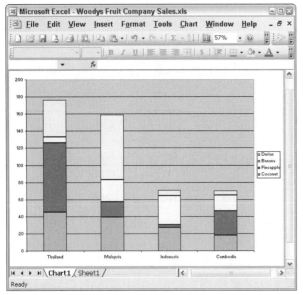

• **Figure 63-4:** The chart is ready to place on a PowerPoint slide.

Putting a Chart on a Slide

In the preceding section, I show you how to create a chart in Excel that's ripe for plucking and sticking into a PowerPoint presentation. That part's pretty straightforward. Unfortunately, the PowerPoint part in this section is riddled with bugs and gotchas. Follow along closely.

To put the Excel chart on a PowerPoint slide in a way that lets you modify the chart quickly and animate the chart's appearance, do the following:

1. **Open or create the PowerPoint presentation.**

If you have an existing presentation, click the slide that comes before the one that you want to hold the animated chart.

2. **Click the New Slide button on the Formatting toolbar.**

PowerPoint creates a new slide and brings up the Slide Layout task pane (see the right side of Figure 63-5).

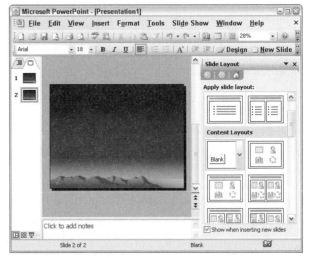

• **Figure 63-5:** Create a new slide with blank content layout.

3. **Click under Content Layouts to apply the blank layout to the slide.**

Because most animated charts are so big that they take up the entire slide (and then some!), I almost always choose the first Content Layout, the one called *Blank* (refer to Figure 63-5).

4. **Go back to your chart in Excel. Hover your mouse above the chart's legend, on the right, until the ToolTip reads Chart Area. Click once in the Chart Area and choose Edit⇨Copy.**

That copies the entire chart to the Clipboard (see Figure 63-6).

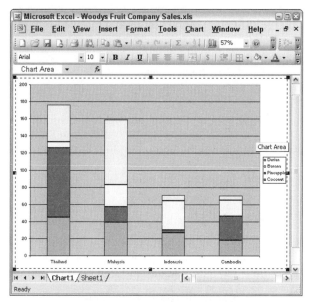

• **Figure 63-6: Copy the Chart Area to the Clipboard.**

5. **Move back to PowerPoint. Choose Edit⇨Paste.**

PowerPoint pastes a very squished, completely illegible copy of the chart onto the slide (see Figure 63-7).

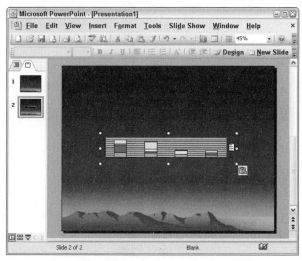

• **Figure 63-7: Paste the chart onto the slide.**

 Resist the immediate temptation to drag the resizing handles and make the chart bigger. If you do, the text will probably become completely illegible.

6. **Double-click the squished chart.**

That brings up Excel, with the still-squished chart showing (see Figure 63-8).

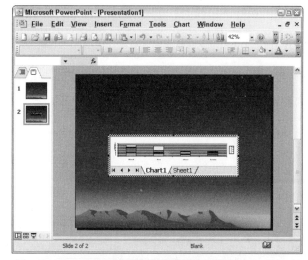

• **Figure 63-8: Double-click the squished chart to bring up Excel inside PowerPoint.**

7. **Click and drag the resizing handles in the corners to maximize the chart on the slide.**

You can even let the Excel sheet navigation area — where it reads Chart1 and Sheet1 — flop off the bottom of the slide (see Figure 63-9).

8. **Click once on the slide, outside the chart area.**

You see the slide in all its glory, ready to be animated (see Figure 63-10). I explain how to animate the chart in the next section.

 When you leave Excel and go back into PowerPoint, the Excel navigation buttons disappear.

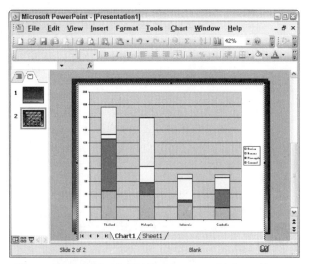

• **Figure 63-9:** Resize inside Excel to get a high-quality chart on a slide.

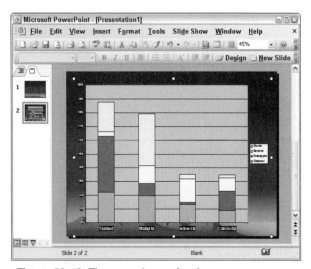

• **Figure 63-10:** Time to animate the chart.

If you want to change anything about the chart — fonts, colors, data order, the legend, whatever — double-click the chart and use Excel's wide array of formatting options. In Figure 63-10, I went back into Excel by double-clicking the chart, right-clicking each of the axes in turn, choosing Format Axis, and then turning the fonts white so they would be legible on the slide.

Animating the Chart

In the first section of this Technique, I show you how to create a chart in Excel that's suitable for animating. In the second section, I explain how to put that chart on a slide. In this section, I (finally!) show you how to automate pieces of the chart that so they appear, with each piece arriving at the command of your click.

Here's how to animate the chart:

1. **Open the presentation, go to the slide that contains the chart you want to animate, and click the chart.**

The chart should have selection dots around it (refer to Figure 63-10).

2. **Choose Slide Show⇨Custom Animation.**

The Custom Animation task pane appears (see the right side of Figure 63-11).

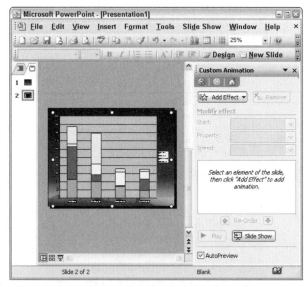

• **Figure 63-11:** Set chart animation with the Custom Animation task pane.

3. You must select one animation to be used for all the pieces of the chart. (For example, you can't use Wipe for some parts of the chart and Checkerboard for others.) To pick the global animation, choose Add Effect⇨Entrance and pick an entrance animation.

You can choose an animation from the list offered (which looks something like Figure 63-12) or choose More Effects to see many dozens more.

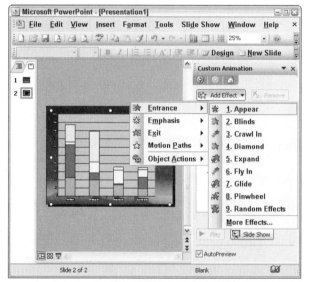

• **Figure 63-12:** You must choose a custom animation for the chart as a whole.

 Microsoft doesn't document it anywhere — in fact, I don't think this has ever been documented before — but if you want to animate pieces of the chart, you *cannot* pick any of the animations in Table 63-1. If you do, PowerPoint accepts what you've chosen, but doesn't let you animate the chart (see Step 5). As far as I can tell, this is a bug. It's certainly infuriating — and the source of many wasted hours.

PowerPoint shows your custom animation in the task pane. In Figure 63-13, I chose the Appear animation.

TABLE 63-1: BUGGY ANIMATIONS

Peek In	Crawl In	Fly In
Faded Zoom	Ascend	Descend
Grow & Turn	Spinner	Center
Compress	Ease In	Rise Up
Stretch	Zoom	Boomerang
Credits	Fold	Light Speed
Pinwheel	Spiral In	Swivel
Bounce	Curve Up	Float
Glide	Magnify	Sling
Thread	Revolve	Expand

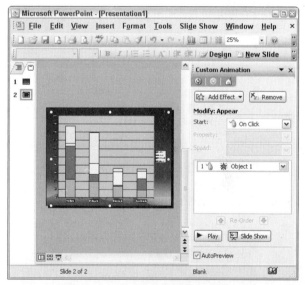

• **Figure 63-13:** The entrance animation for the entire chart appears in the task pane.

4. Click the down arrow next to Object 1 (in the task pane on the right side of the screen) and choose Effect Options. In the Appear dialog box that appears (see Figure 63-14), click the Chart Animation tab.

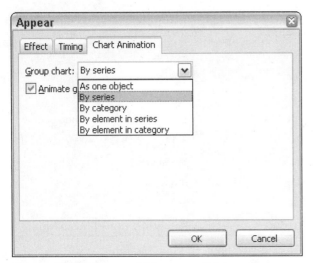

• **Figure 63-14:** Choose which groups of data appear onscreen.

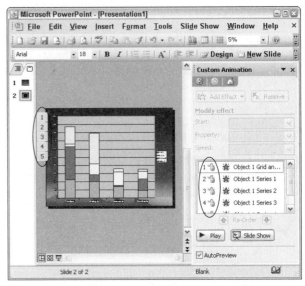

• **Figure 63-15:** PowerPoint identifies five different animations — for the chart itself and then for each of the sets of stacked bars.

5. Click the down arrow next to Group Chart. If As One Object is your lone option, you chose one of the buggy entrance animations in Table 63-1. Click Cancel (which kicks you back to the Custom Animation task pane) and then click Remove to get rid of the buggy animation. Then go back to Step 3, repeat Step 4, and pick a good animation.

Yep. You guessed it. Microsoft ran out of money when it was debugging PowerPoint.

6. In the Appear dialog box, choose one of the four Group Chart options as explained in Table 63-2. Click OK.

In Figure 63-14, I choose By Series. Excel returns to the chart, with all the animation points ready (see Figure 63-15). Different animation points are set for the chart's grid lines than for each of the sets of stacked bars. That means that you have to click for the grid lines to appear, click again to bring in the first set of stacked bars, click again for the second set, and so on. The animation visual effect (fly, bounce, float, whatever) is the same for each of the components.

7. Click the Slide Show button on the task pane (or press F5) to run the slideshow. Watch how the elements of the chart appear as you click the mouse.

As soon as you run through the animation, the Add Effect button (in Figure 63-15) becomes the Change button.

8. If you feel so inclined, click the Change button on the Custom Animation task pane and return to Step 3. You can also double-click the chart to go back to Excel and change any details about the chart itself.

9. Save the animated presentation.

Congratulations!

TABLE 63-2: GROUP CHART OPTIONS

Option	What It Means in a Stacked Bar (Column) Graph
By Series	When you first click, shows all the bottom bars. When you click a second time, shows all the next group of bars, sitting on top of the bottom bars. When you click a third time, shows all the next group of bars, and so on.
By Category	When you first click, shows all the bars, stacked on top of each other, for the first item on the x axis. When you click again, shows all the bars, stacked, for the second item. And so on.
By Element in Series	On the first click, shows the bottom bar for the first item on the x axis. On the next click, shows the bottom bar for the second item on the x axis. On the next click, shows the bottom bar for the third item. When you reach the end of the x axis, shows the second bar for the first item, stacked on top of the bottom bar. And so on.
By Element in Category	On the first click, shows the bottom bar for the first item on the x axis. On the second click, shows the second bar stacked on top of the bottom bar for the first item. Then shows the third bar, and so on. When you reach the top of the first item, shows the bottom bar for the second item on the x axis.

Running Fine-Grain Animation

The preceding sections show you how to animate the major components of a chart.

PowerPoint actually has the ability to animate every single detail in a chart — every bar, point, line, label, legend . . . any detail that you can see on the slide can be brought in with its own animation, under your control. The procedure involves a lot of nit-picking detail, but if you're persistent, anything's possible.

Here's how:

1. **Follow the steps in the first two sections of this Technique to put a chart on a PowerPoint slide.**

2. **Right-click the chart and choose Grouping⇨ Ungroup.**

PowerPoint shows you the warning in Figure 63-16.

• **Figure 63-16: Convert the chart to a drawing object only if you have the original data safely tucked away.**

3. **Click Yes.**

A bug in PowerPoint (tell me if you've heard this one before) prevents it from ungrouping the chart. So you have to do all this a second time.

4. **Right-click the chart again and choose Grouping⇨Ungroup again.**

This time the chart explodes. Or implodes. PowerPoint breaks the chart down into its zillions of components (see Figure 63-17).

5. **Click once outside the chart to deselect all the pieces. Then choose Slide Show⇨Custom Animation to bring up the Custom Animation task pane.**

6. **Select individual elements that you want to animate (hold down Ctrl while you click them) and then click the Add Effect button to set the animation that you want.**

The pieces of the chart are numbered in a more-or-less logical way, which you might helpful when chasing down recalcitrant pieces (see Figure 63-18).

From that point, you can save, modify and run the presentation to your heart's content.

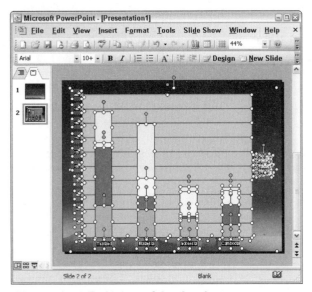

• **Figure 63-17:** Each piece of the chart becomes an independent picture.

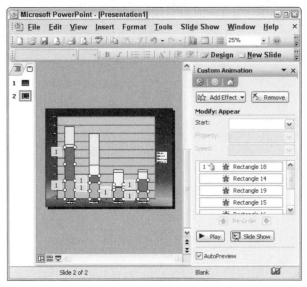

• **Figure 63-18:** You can choose any conceivable piece of the chart and animate it.

Technique 64

Rotating Text in a Word Document

For more than a decade now, I've been amazed at how hard it can be to do really simple, everyday stuff in Office.

One of my favorite examples is rotating text in a Word document. Everybody, sooner or later, needs to rotate some text in a doc, whether it's to emphasize a word or two, create an ad, or even to print a name tent that you fold and put on the table in front of participants at a conference.

As long as you need to rotate the text by 90 degrees, Word has some (clumsy!) tools that will help. But if you need to rotate text by 45 degrees — or even 180 degrees — your choices are incredibly poor.

Unless you know the trick.

This Technique steps you through the Word-only solutions (which work in certain limited circumstances) and then shows you how to solve almost any problem (by using Excel).

Rotating Text with Word Tools

If you need to rotate text in a Word document, your choices don't look very good, both literally and figuratively:

✔ **Try WordArt.** Choose Insert➪Picture➪WordArt. From the WordArt Gallery, you can choose from a handful of designs. Click a design, click OK, type the text that you want to use, click OK again, and the WordArt appears (see Figure 64-1). To adjust the angle of rotation, click the WordArt, choose Format➪WordArt➪Size, and change the Rotation number.

✔ **Put text in a table cell.** Drawing a table can be a monumental hassle, particularly if you're trying to put the rotated text in line with other text. After you create a table, type the text in a cell, choose Format➪ Text Direction and rotate the text by plus or minus 90 degrees (see Figure 64-2). Those are your only choices: You can't even invert the text.

• **Figure 64-1:** WordArt rotated text tends to be garish and hard to control.

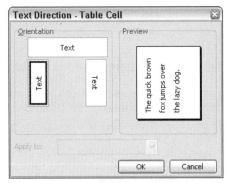

• **Figure 64-2:** Table cells let you rotate only by plus or minus 90 degrees.

✔ **Use a text box.** Any AutoShape with text inside (see Technique 11) can have the text rotated, but just like with table cells, your only options are plus or minus 90 degrees.

✔ **Take a picture.** This is a quick-and-dirty approach (see the following steps) that might be usable if you don't need a particularly good quality rendition of the text.

Here's how to take a picture of text in a document and then rotate the picture:

1. In Word, open or create a document. In Print Layout view (choose View➪Print Layout), type the text you want to rotate in your document.

2. Select the text you want to rotate and press Ctrl+X (or choose Edit➪Cut).

That puts the text on the Clipboard.

3. Choose Edit➪Paste Special, select Picture (Windows Metafile), and then click OK.

Word inserts a picture of the text into your document. Unfortunately, it's a big picture, which you need to crop.

4. Right-click the picture and select Show Picture Toolbar.

5. Click the Crop icon on the Picture toolbar (it looks like two overlapping carpenter squares). Then click and drag the sizing handles around the picture, cropping out all the white space (see Figure 64-3).

• **Figure 64-3:** Crop off all the excess white space in the picture.

6. Click the Text Wrapping icon on the Picture toolbar (it looks like a dog) and choose Tight.

The picture gets a green rotation handle above the top of the text (see Figure 64-4).

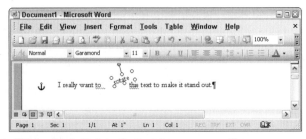

• **Figure 64-4:** Rotate the text however you like.

7. Click the rotation handle and rotate the text.

 You can click and drag to move the text, too.

The result isn't very true to the original font, but if you need something really quick, it might suffice.

Making a Name Tent

If you want a quick *name tent* — a piece of paper that you can fold and use to identify people sitting at a table — Word can do it:

1. Create a new document. In Print Layout view (choose View⇨Print Layout), make things more visible by clicking the Zoom setting on the Standard toolbar and choosing Whole Page.

2. Choose Table⇨Insert⇨Table. In the Insert Table dialog box, tell Word that you want 2 columns and 1 row. Set the Fixed Column Width to Auto and then click OK.

Word creates a small, two-cell table at the top of the page.

3. Click the lower, horizontal line (the bottom line of the table) and drag it to the bottom of the page (see Figure 64-5).

4. Choose Table⇨Select⇨Table. First choose Format⇨Borders and then choose Shading⇨Borders. Click None and then click OK.

Although you probably still see borders, the borders on the table are toast.

 Technically, the borders are called *table gridlines,* but they won't be printed.

5. Click in the first cell and then choose Format⇨Text Direction. Click the Text sample box on the right and then click OK.

That sets up the first table cell to read from top to bottom.

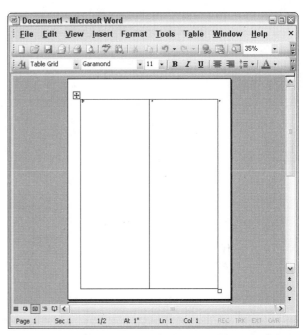

• **Figure 64-5:** Make the table fit the printable part of the page.

6. Click in the second cell and choose Format⇨Text Direction. Click the Text sample box on the left and then click OK.

The second cell reads from bottom to top.

7. Click in the first cell, and type the text that should appear on the name tent. Select the name and format it however you like.

To center the name, choose Table⇨Table Properties. On the Table tab, click Center. On the Cell tab, click Center, and then click OK.

8. Select the text in the first cell, press Ctrl+C (or choose Edit⇨Copy), click inside the second cell, and press Ctrl+V (or choose Edit⇨Paste).

To center the name, use the procedure in Step 7. The result is in Figure 64-6.

9. Choose File⇨Print, and your name tent appears on the printer.

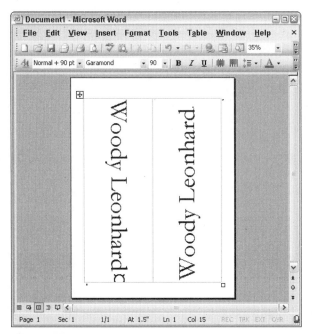

• **Figure 64-6:** The final name tent, ready for printing.

Rotating Any Text

If the two preceding sections left you with the impression that Word is singularly ill-equipped to produce text at any angle beyond zero degrees — simple left-to-right — well, you're absolutely correct.

In fact, if you don't know the trick, you can lose an enormous amount of time trying to rotate text in Word, coming up only with something that's just barely legible. I know. Been there. Done that.

The trick: Use Excel. Unlike Microsoft's flagship word processor, its flagship spreadsheet program rotates text with ease, and the result looks very good indeed. Here's how to stick an Excel-rotated word or phrase into a Word document:

1. **Create or open the Word document where the rotated text is supposed to go. In Page Layout view, type any text that goes before or after the rotated text.**

In Figure 64-7, I have all the text before and after the location where I want to put the rotated text.

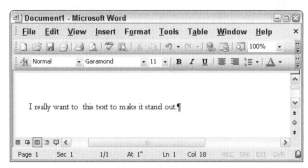

• **Figure 64-7:** Click where you want the rotated text.

2. **Click (place your cursor) where you want the rotated text to appear. Choose Insert⇨Object⇨Create New.**

Word brings up the Object dialog box, as shown in Figure 64-8.

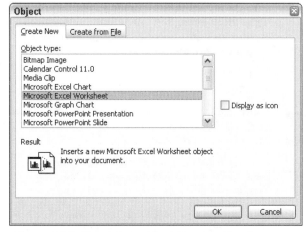

• **Figure 64-8:** To rotate text best, insert an Excel worksheet.

3. **Choose Microsoft Excel Worksheet and then click OK.**

Word sticks an entire spreadsheet in your document (see Figure 64-9). Hang on. This isn't as bad as it looks.

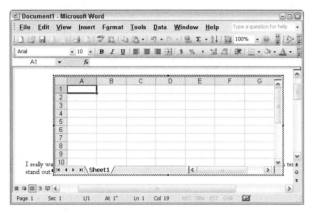

• **Figure 64-9: Yes, that's an entire spreadsheet in your document.**

4. Click in cell A1 and type the text that you want to appear in your document. Press Enter. Format it with whatever font you like (choose Format⇨Cells⇨Font).

The text appears in the upper-left cell (A1) of the spreadsheet (see Figure 64-10).

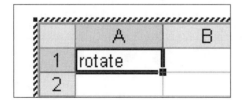

• **Figure 64-10: The text destined for Word goes in cell A1.**

5. Right-click cell A1 and choose Format Cells⇨Alignment.

Excel (working inside Word) responds with the Format Cells dialog box, as shown in Figure 64-11.

6. Under Orientation, click and drag the Text line or set a rotation angle in the Degrees box; then click OK.

Word appears with the text rotated inside the cell (see Figure 64-12). The text might look blurry on your screen, but in fact, it's very high quality and prints with absolute fidelity.

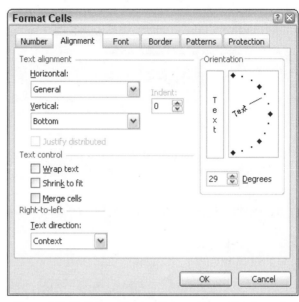

• **Figure 64-11: Rotate the text however you like from the Excel Format Cells dialog box.**

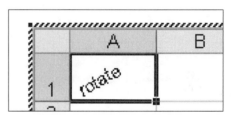

• **Figure 64-12: The text is rotated, but it's still in an Excel spreadsheet cell.**

7. Make cell A1 as small as you can without bumping into the text.

Excel automatically adjusts the width of the A cell if you move your mouse slowly to the right of the cell with the A, until it turns into a + sign with arrows on the right and left. Then double-click.

8. Do the same with the horizontal line below the 1.

The trimmed cell looks like Figure 64-13.

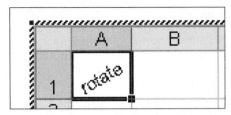

• **Figure 64-13:** Squeeze out the excess white space.

9. Resize the spreadsheet. Click the resizing handles on the corners of the spreadsheet, collapsing it so that only cell A1 shows.

As improbable as it looks, Figure 64-14 shows how the condensed spreadsheet appears.

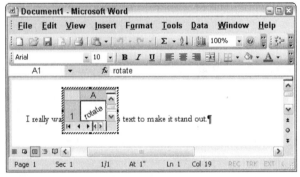

• **Figure 64-14:** Shrink the spreadsheet down to a single cell.

10. Click in your document, outside the spreadsheet.

The rotated text appears in line with your other text (see Figure 64-15). You might see boxes or other screen artifacts around the rotated text, but they don't show up on the final printed sheet. And when the text prints, it's absolutely perfect.

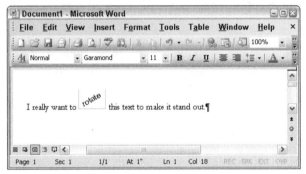

• **Figure 64-15:** The final text.

Thanks to *Woody's Office Watch* reader Kevin Hardie for helping me crack this surprisingly difficult time-saving problem!

Part VIII

The Scary (Or Fun!) Stuff

The 5th Wave   By Rich Tennant

"We're here to clean the code."

Technique

65

Taking Over Word's Show/Hide

Almost every day, I get a message complaining about Word breaking out in dots. Dots run all over the page, making it impossible to stare at the screen for more than ten seconds without getting a headache (or at least a flashback to high school and a terminal case of acne).

The dots appear onscreen when you click Word's Show/Hide icon on the Standard toolbar. It's the one that looks like Word's paragraph mark, ¶ — better known to the cognoscenti as a *pilcrow.* When you click the Show/Hide icon, every space in your document gets a big, fat, space dot stuck right in the middle. You can conveniently click it again to toggle it off, but then you lose the good stuff you still want to see, as I explain in this Technique.

Some people love looking at the dots, particularly if they have to get rid of extra spaces in a manuscript. But most people hate the dots. I fall into the latter camp, as do about 99 percent of the people I know.

This Technique shows you how to write a small macro that not only gets rid of the dots but also actually makes Show/Hide do something quite useful.

Seeing Word's Critical Marks

In Technique 15, I show why it's absolutely vital for Word users to show these three critical formatting characters onscreen:

✔ **Paragraph marks:** You need to see paragraph marks all the time because Word stores paragraph formatting in the paragraph mark. If you've ever seen Word suddenly start right-justifying your paragraphs, or making everything **bold** or *italic* or ***both,*** or sticking bullets or numbers on all the lines, you've experienced the effects of formatting that's stored in the paragraph mark. If you can't see the paragraph mark, you don't stand a snowball's chance in Phuket of understanding what's going on.

✔ **Tabs:** You must have Word show you Tab characters. If Tab characters stay invisible, the text that you type or copy can flip-flop all over the screen like an accordion playing *Flight of the Bumblebee,* and you'll never have a clue why the text (mis)behaves the way it does.

✔ **Picture anchors:** You should have Word show you picture anchors. The minute you click and drag a floating picture, the location of its anchor controls its destiny. When an anchor moves, your picture does, too — and if you can't see the anchor, you have absolutely no idea why a particular picture starts flying across the page.

Straight out of the box, Word includes an easy way to show you all three of these critical marks. Simply click the Show/Hide icon on the Standard toolbar — the one that looks like a backward P (a pilcrow, ¶) — and Word shows you paragraph marks, Tab characters, and picture anchors. But it also shows you big dots, right in the middle of every space in the document (see Figure 65-1).

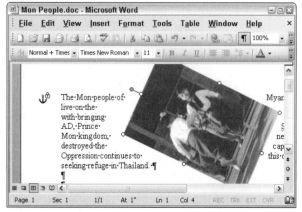

• **Figure 65-1:** The formatting marks are great, but who needs all the dots?

The dots can help editors (and you) find extra spaces buried in documents — most frequently, two spaces after a period (see the sidebar, "One Space or Two?"). But for most people, most of the time, the dots are so bad that one click of the Show/Hide icon is immediately followed by another click of the Show/Hide icon (turn it off!), thus obscuring the critically important paragraph mark, Tab characters, and picture anchors.

One Space or Two?

When I learned to type — on a manual typewriter, no less — my teacher taught me to put two spaces after every period. That's not surprising. Since typewriters first appeared, two spaces after the period has been the de facto standard. Even Mark Twain used two spaces (see `www.mytypewriter.com`).

Times have changed. The standard for published work is one space after the period, and most publishers want the extra spaces expunged (see `www.press.uchicago.edu/ Misc/Chicago/cmosfaq/cmosfaq.OneSpaceorTwo. html`). That doesn't mean *you* have to use just one space. But if you want to publish what you write, you'll save yourself a lot of time by sticking to a single space.

The next section in this Technique shows you how to create a macro that takes control of the Show/Hide icon, making it show you only those formatting characters you need to see — with nary a dot in sight.

 A *macro* is just a computer program. Nothing more, nothing less. All Office applications allow you to write your own programs — your own macros — which you can run in a myriad of different ways.

Building a Better Show/Hide

I have one macro that I use on every PC I own. I hook it up so it runs every time I click the Show/Hide icon in Word. In the next section, I explain how to write the macro and make it work in place of Word's standard Show/Hide function. In this section, I explain what the macro does when you click the Show/Hide icon. (You can also find these settings by choosing Tools➪Options➪View.)

✔ **Show All:** Turns off Show All, which has Word show paragraph marks, Tab characters, picture anchors, and all those ugly dots in place of spaces.

✔ **Show Spaces:** Turns off Show Spaces, which also makes Word show you all those ugly dots.

✔ **Field results:** Tells Word to start showing field results if Word currently shows *field codes* (those small directives like {date} that go out and retrieve stuff) for the entire document. This doesn't change the setting for individual fields, though, so if you're looking at one specific field code, clicking the Show/Hide icon won't change anything.

✔ **Hide critical marks:** Tells Word to hide paragraph marks, Tab characters, and picture anchors if Word currently shows paragraph marks.

✔ **Show critical marks:** Tells Word to show paragraph marks, Tab characters, and picture anchors if Word doesn't currently show paragraph marks.

Writing the Macro

The preceding sections in this Technique explain why and how the macro works. This section gets down to the nitty-gritty.

If you've never written a Word macro before, this is an excellent first effort. Typing the macro commands takes a little bit of time, but Word helps. Even if you mess up beyond all hope, removing everything you've done takes only two clicks.

Here's how to write a macro that takes over the Show/Hide icon:

1. **Choose Tools⇨Macro⇨Macros.**

Word shows you the Macros dialog box, as shown in Figure 65-2.

 If you have trouble bringing up the Macros dialog box, or if any of the buttons you need appear grayed out, someone has possibly locked you out of your global template, normal.dot. Check with your network administrator — and complain loudly that you want to be able to control your own Word destiny!

• **Figure 65-2: Create a new macro called** ShowAll.

2. **Type ShowAll (all one word) in the Macro Name box and then click the Create button.**

 Macro names can't have any spaces or weird characters. (Numerals are okay.)

ShowAll is the name of the macro that Word already has assigned to the Show/Hide icon. By telling Word to create a new macro called ShowAll, you're also telling Word that you want this new macro to run in place of the old one every time you click the Show/Hide icon.

Word cranks up the Visual Basic Editor (VBE; see Figure 65-3).

• **Figure 65-3: The VBE, where you get to write your own programs.**

3. **Select everything between** Sub ShowAll() **and** EndSub **and then delete it.**

Start from a clean slate (see Figure 65-4).

• **Figure 65-4: Get rid of the old** ShowAll **macro.**

4. **Type the lines of code shown in the upcoming Listing 65-1.**

As you type, you discover that VBA helps do some of the typing for you. Try using the Tab key to accept suggestions from VBA as you type. Ultimately, the program looks like Figure 65-5.

5. **Go back to Word and click the Show/Hide icon.**

As you click the button repeatedly, Word cycles between showing the formatting marks (paragraph marks, Tab characters, and picture anchors) and not showing any formatting marks. Those ugly dots for spaces never appear.

6. **When you're satisfied that the macro works properly, from inside Word, choose File⇨Exit.**

Your macro is saved automatically; then both VBA and Word quit.

From this point on, every time you click the Show/Hide icon, Word runs your macro, cycling between showing and not showing the important formatting marks.

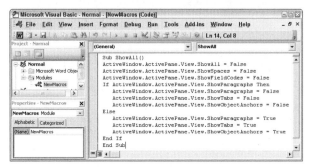

• **Figure 65-5: The entire ShowAll program.**

 If you ever decide to get rid of the macro, choose Tools⇨Macro⇨Macros, click ShowAll once, and then click Delete. That's all there is to it. Your macro is gone forever, and Word reverts to its old, ugly behavior.

Special thanks to Guy Wells for help with the macro.

LISTING 65-1: THE SHOWALL MACRO

```
Sub ShowAll()
ActiveWindow.ActivePane.View.ShowAll = False
ActiveWindow.ActivePane.View.ShowSpaces = False
ActiveWindow.ActivePane.View.ShowFieldCodes = False
If ActiveWindow.ActivePane.View.ShowParagraphs Then
    ActiveWindow.ActivePane.View.ShowParagraphs = False
    ActiveWindow.ActivePane.View.ShowTabs = False
    ActiveWindow.ActivePane.View.ShowObjectAnchors = False
Else
    ActiveWindow.ActivePane.View.ShowParagraphs = True
    ActiveWindow.ActivePane.View.ShowTabs = True
    ActiveWindow.ActivePane.View.ShowObjectAnchors = True
End If
End Sub
```

Technique

66

Inserting Unformatted Text in Word

It seems like I spend my life copying and pasting.

I grab text from documents, from Web pages, from spreadsheets, from old text files, from every imaginable place, and then paste, paste, paste into Word. It's like I press Ctrl+C (which copies text to the Clipboard) and then Ctrl+V (which pastes text from the Clipboard) in my sleep. The Ctrl, C, and V keycaps on my keyboard are nearly worn out. True fact.

But there's a teensy-tiny problem with pasting. Usually when I paste something into a document, I don't want the formatting from the old location to come along for the ride. Tag-along formatting really screws up my documents — if not now, then a day or a week or a month down the road.

That's why one of my favorite timesaving techniques of all time involves a little macro that strips the formatting from text before pasting it into my document.

Word Pasting 101

If you're like most folks, when you paste text in a Word document, you want the pasted text to take on the formatting in the document. Rarely do you want to keep the formatting from the text source. You can futz with the Paste Options Smart Tag and hunt and peck your way around the problem. Or you can override Office's built-in settings, solving the problem once and for all.

Word victims (like me!) commonly paste in one of four ways:

✔ **Press Ctrl+V.** This method is by far the fastest, easiest way to paste and the number-one choice of power users.

✔ **Click the Paste icon on the Standard toolbar.** This method is slow (gotta use your mouse) and error-prone (it's hard to hone in on that little icon, which looks like a clipboard with a document). However, those who haven't memorized the Ctrl+V key combination use it most frequently: It's the number-one choice of new Office users.

✔ **Choose Edit⇨Paste.** Most newbies get over this bad, slow habit quickly.

✔ **Use the Insert key.** The least common method of the bunch, you can tell Word that you want to use the Insert key to paste by choosing Tools⇨Options⇨Edit and marking the Use the INS Key for Paste check box (see Figure 66-1). Using the Insert key is a disaster waiting to happen because it sends you into *overtype* mode (gobbling up any text you've already typed, even if you press the key accidentally, which is easy enough to do). If you make the Insert key paste, you don't have to worry about being sporadically thrust into the overtype twilight zone.

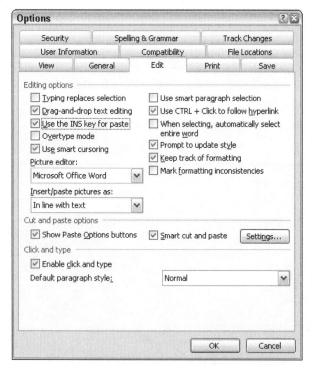

• **Figure 66-1: Tell Word to use the Insert key for pasting instead of wigging out to overtype mode.**

Yes, there are other ways to paste: click and drag; right-click and choose Paste; Shift+Insert; choose Edit⇨Paste Special; and click Paste in the Office Clipboard task pane. But the four pasting methods in the preceding bulleted list cover the lion's share of pasting, at least in my experience.

Most of the time when you paste, Word displays a special Paste Options Smart Tag near the bottom-right corner of what you've pasted (see Figure 66-2).

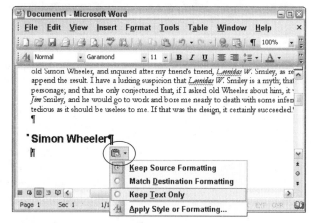

• **Figure 66-2: The Paste Options Smart Tag.**

 Although the Paste Options Smart Tag appears most of the time, I've hit situations where it adamantly refuses to appear: I can paste, undo, and paste again — and the Smart Tag still doesn't show up. It appears to be an intermittent bug, which hasn't been documented anywhere I know.

If you click that Smart Tag, you can choose to

✔ **Keep Source Formatting:** That sounds simple, but it isn't because the results depend on whether you selected a paragraph mark when you copied the text (and the paragraph mark can be in a Word document, a formatted e-mail message, or an HTML/Web page). If you select the paragraph mark, knowingly or not, all the paragraph formatting follows in addition to the paragraph mark and the paragraph's style. To add insult to injury, the paragraph's style is added to the document's list of styles. If you didn't select the paragraph mark, you get only the character formatting inherited from the paragraph's style. And if you selected a section break accidentally when you copied. . . . Whoa, Nelly.

✔ **Match Destination Formatting:** Word applies all of the formatting in effect at the current cursor location to everything that's copied. Paragraph marks take on the paragraph style at the current cursor location. Text takes on all the formatting in effect at the cursor location — whether from paragraph or character styles or from manually applied formatting — but manually applied formatting in the copied text is maintained.

✔ **Keep Text Only:** If a paragraph mark is at the end of the copied text, it's thrown away. The text — no pictures, no formatting, no styles — gets copied across. Paragraph marks are copied, too: They take on the paragraph style at the current cursor location.

Predictably, Keep Source Formatting — the option that causes the greatest possible havoc, and the one least likely to produce the desired result — is the default.

Writing a Pasting Macro

In the preceding section, I explain how Word has an annoying habit of carrying along all the baggage — er, all the formatting — when you paste stuff into a Word document.

I know an easy way to tell Word that you don't want to copy anything except the raw, plain, unadorned text. In fact, all it takes is a two-line macro. Here's how to write it:

1. **Start Word.**

2. **Choose Tools⇨Macro⇨Macros.**

Word brings up the Macros dialog box (see Figure 66-3).

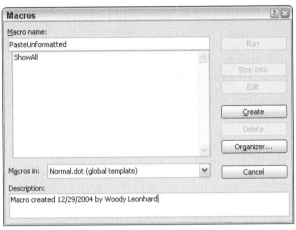

• **Figure 66-3: Create a new macro called** `PasteUnformatted`.

 If you have trouble bringing up the Macros dialog box, or if any of the buttons you need appear grayed out, someone has possibly locked you out of your global template, `normal.dot`. Check with your network administrator — and complain loudly that you want to be able to control your own Word destiny!

3. **In the Macro Name box, type a name for the macro, such as** `PasteUnformatted`. **In the Macros In box, choose Normal.dot. Then click Create.**

 Macro names can't have any spaces or weird characters. (Numerals are okay.)

Word takes you into the Visual Basic Editor (VBE; see Figure 66-4). It isn't nearly as scary as it looks.

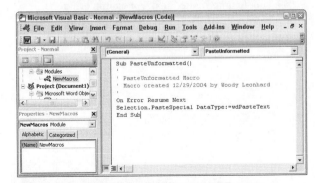

• **Figure 66-4: Type the macro into the VBE.**

4. **Between the line that reads** `Sub`
`PasteUnformatted()` **and the line that**
reads `End Sub`, **type these two lines. (Note**
that the command starting with `Selection`
and ending with `wdPasteText` **must appear**
on one line.)

```
On Error Resume Next
Selection.PasteSpecial
    DataType:=wdPasteText
```

Comment lines begin with apostrophes (you
can see these in Figure 66-4) and don't affect
the program. You can include as many comments as you like.

The first command tells Word to ignore any
errors that it encounters. The second command
tells Word to run an Edit⇨Paste Special, pasting
the contents of the Clipboard as plain text.

5. **Choose File⇨Close and Return to Microsoft**
Word.

Word reappears.

6. **Test the macro by copying anything you like to**
the Clipboard, choosing Tools⇨Macro⇨Macros,
and double-clicking PasteUnformatted.

Word pastes the unadorned text into your document. After you know the macro is working, you
need to find a way to make it work, other than
this long string of menu commands. The next
section has all the details.

This is a very fast, very specific macro: It pastes
only unformatted text. For example, if you
copy a picture to the Clipboard and then run
this macro, Word ignores the picture and
nothing gets pasted. It's all text, all the time.

Assigning a Shortcut to the Pasting Macro

In the preceding section, I show you how to write a
macro that pastes plain, simple text — no pictures,
no formatting, no styles. Just text.

In this section, you get to grapple with the question
of how you want to run the `PasteUnformatted` macro.
You have a couple of viable options:

- ✔ You can hook up this `PasteUnformatted` macro
  to its own toolbar icon or to a special key combination (see Technique 68).

- ✔ You can tell Word to run `PasteUnformatted`
  whenever you press Ctrl+V. If you paste any
  other way (clicking the Paste icon, choosing
  Edit⇨Paste, right-clicking and choosing Paste, or
  pressing the Insert key), Word pastes normally.

The second approach is what I prefer because
it runs fast and saves time — especially if you
follow the instructions in the first section of
this Technique to make the Insert key paste
normally, instead of going into overtype
mode. It's the best use of the Insert key I
know. If you also set up Ctrl+V to paste unformatted text, you then have two quick ways to
paste: Ctrl+V pastes unformatted text, and the
Insert key pastes normally.

To make `PasteUnformatted` run whenever you press
Ctrl+V

1. **Choose Tools⇨Customize⇨Commands.**

Word brings up the Customize dialog box, as
shown in Figure 66-5.

2. **Make sure that Save In shows Normal.dot and**
then click the Keyboard key.

You see the Customize Keyboard dialog box, as
shown in Figure 66-6.

3. In the Categories box, choose Macros. In the Macros box, choose PasteUnformatted. Click in the Press New Shortcut Key box and then press Ctrl+V.

Word warns you that the Ctrl+V key combination is currently assigned to `EditPaste`.

4. Click the Assign button.

Word moves Ctrl+V to the Current Keys box.

5. Click the Close button twice.

After the key combination is assigned, whenever you press Ctrl+V, Word runs `PasteUnformatted`, slapping the text, the plain text, and only the plain text into your document.

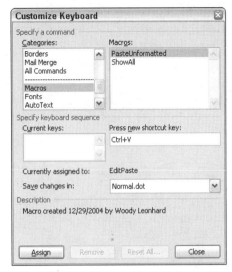

• **Figure 66-6:** Set Ctrl+V to run `PasteUnformatted`.

If you ever want to get Ctrl+V back so that it runs the standard Word paste, do the following:

1. Choose Tools⇨Customize⇨Commands.

You get the Customize dialog box; refer to Figure 66-5.

2. Make sure that Save In shows Normal.dot and then click the Keyboard key.

Word brings up the Customize Keyboard dialog box; refer to Figure 66-6.

3. In the Categories box, choose Edit. In the Commands box, choose EditPaste. Click in the Press New Shortcut Key box and then press Ctrl+V.

4. Click the Assign button.

5. Click the Close button twice.

• **Figure 66-5:** Go this way to assign a macro to a key combination.

67 Technique

Inserting Unformatted Text in Excel

Although Microsoft would have you think that all the Office applications work well together, that's actually not the case. Cutting and pasting within Excel is a breeze, but cutting and pasting between Excel and other applications can become a big headache — unless you use the macro that I show you how to create in this Technique.

When you paste text into a Word document, you usually want to paste unformatted text. That's what Technique 66 is all about. In Excel, the situation isn't so clear-cut. Copying cells within Excel and copying text from sources outside Excel work quite differently:

- **Copying and pasting cells within Excel:** Most cutting and pasting in Excel deals exclusively with Excel cells. Excel knows that if you copy a bunch of cells, you probably want to paste the copied cells into new cells, cell by cell. When you choose Edit⇨Paste Special to copy and paste cells within Excel, you see the dialog box shown in Figure 67-1. It's designed to work with the data typically crammed into Excel (and is a far cry from the dialog box you get when you Paste Special in Word). Although you have a lot of options for pasting cells, the process works smoothly if you know what you want to do, because Excel is comfortable working within its own boundaries.

- **Copying and pasting text from outside Excel:** When you copy text onto the Clipboard (from Word, a Web page, or any other source) and paste it into Excel, Excel has to deal with the same fundamental questions as Word — namely, how you want the content to appear. When you copy *text* to the Clipboard and then choose Edit⇨Paste Special in Excel, you get the options shown in Figure 67-2. If you find yourself frequently copying text from various sources into your spreadsheets, you probably want to strip formatting from the text before putting it in the spreadsheet. The rest of this Technique is devoted to creating a macro that delivers just that — and in a matter of seconds.

When Excel pastes text into a spreadsheet, it puts one paragraph in the first target cell, the next paragraph in the cell below it, and so on. If you copy five paragraphs to the Clipboard, click cell A1, choose Edit⇨Paste Special, and then choose one of the Text options, cells A1 through A5 each contain the contents of the first through fifth paragraphs.

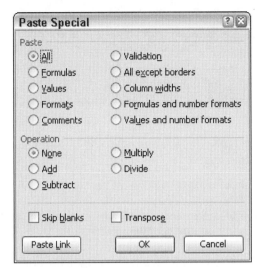

• **Figure 67-1: When copying cells to cells, the question becomes how to paste it.**

• **Figure 67-2: When you copy text to cells, Excel has to deal with formatting.**

Recording a Macro

Macros are just programs attached to Office documents. In theory at least, you record a macro to perform a specific task, and then play it back to repeat the task. In practice, life is rarely that simple.

Although you have a dozen ways to write macros for Excel, if you've never created an Excel macro before,

using the macro recorder has one big advantage: The workbook that Excel uses to store macros — personal.xls, sometimes called the *Personal Macro Workbook* — doesn't even exist unless and until you do something (such as recording a macro) to create it. By using the macro recorder, Excel takes care of all the messy details of getting personal.xls going.

> I rarely recommend that people use the macro recorder except when they're in a tight spot — specifically, the first time you set up an Excel macro, or when you can't figure out what in the %$#@! Visual Basic for Applications (VBA) calls a particular action. The recorder isn't able to record most actions the way you want them to be played back, and it isn't the recorder's fault. For example, say you have a column of numbers in Excel that ends at cell B6. If you're recording a macro and you click cell B7, there's no way the recorder can know whether you want to jump to the first empty cell in column B or whether you just want to go to B7. For tips on writing a macro in Excel without the recorder, see Technique 68.

In the specific case of stripping formatting from text prior to placing it in an Excel spreadsheet, the recorder works like a champ. Here's how to record the macro that does the trick:

1. **Copy some text from Word or Internet Explorer to the Clipboard.**

2. **In Excel, choose Tools⇨Macro⇨Record New Macro.**

Excel shows you the Record Macro dialog box, as shown in Figure 67-3.

3. **In the Macro Name box, type a name for the macro. In the Shortcut Key box, type a key that you would like to use as a shortcut. In the Store Macro In box, choose Personal Macro Workbook.**

In Figure 67-3, I call the macro PasteUnformatted, and I tell Excel to run PasteUnformatted every time I press Ctrl+Shift+V.

• **Figure 67-3:** Set up the macro recorder here.

 This dialog box won't let you overwrite existing shortcut key combinations, so Ctrl+V — the usual paste key combination — isn't an option. If you try to type Ctrl+V, Excel changes it to Ctrl+Shift+V.

4. Click OK.

The macro recorder starts. Excel shows you the most bizarre toolbar in all of Officedom: a stunted thing with two buttons called (I kid you not) the Stop Recording toolbar (see Figure 67-4). As long as you can see the Stop Recording toolbar, the macro recorder is working, recording everything you do.

• **Figure 67-4:** The Stop Recording toolbar.

5. Choose Edit⇨Paste Special. Choose Text and then click OK.

Excel dutifully pastes the text held on the Clipboard into the Excel spreadsheet (see Figure 67-5).

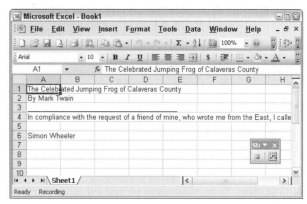

• **Figure 67-5:** Perform an unformatted paste with the macro recorder running.

6. Click the first button on the Stop Recording toolbar.

Excel stops recording the macro.

7. From the Excel menu bar, choose File⇨Exit.

8. When Excel asks whether you want to save the changes you made to Book1, click No.

9. When Excel asks whether you want to save the changes you made to the Personal Macro Workbook, click Yes.

Your new macro, PasteUnformatted, gets saved in personal.xls.

How Does personal.xls Work?

personal.xls is a weird workbook that Excel sticks in its XLStart folder, typically C:\Program Files\Microsoft Office\OFFICE11\XLSTART, the same place where Excel puts book.xlt, the default workbook. (I talk about book.xlt in Technique 34.) In most circumstances, personal.xls contains only macros. And in many cases, it has only recorded macros because macro programmers tend to prefer to stick their own templates in XLStart.

When Excel starts, it automatically opens everything in the XLStart folder. Because personal.xls is in the right place at the right time, it comes along for the ride. That's why you can get at recorded macros whenever Excel is running.

Editing an Excel Macro

In the preceding section, I show you how to record a macro. The steps are basically the same in Word and Excel.

Recording a macro is largely ineffectual in PowerPoint, and the Outlook macro recorder is just the Word macro recorder.

However, if you want to look a macro that you recorded in Excel, you have to jump through some relatively strange hoops. Here's how:

1. **Start Excel.**

When Excel starts, it opens all the workbooks in the XLStart folder. If you've ever recorded a macro in Excel, the recorder created a `personal.xls` in the XLStart folder, so it gets opened, too. (See the sidebar, "How Does personal.xls Work?")

`personal.xls` is a hidden file: Excel doesn't show you anything about `personal.xls` unless you specifically go in and tell Excel to unhide it. Making a file hidden *isn't a security technique:* Anybody who bumps into the Window menu can unhide a file. Rather, hiding is a method to keep extraneous workbooks out of the way.

2. **Choose Window⇨Unhide.**

Excel shows you the Unhide dialog box, with `personal.xls` notably present (see Figure 67-6).

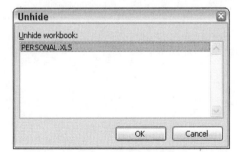

• **Figure 67-6:** Before you can do anything with `personal.xls` or its macros, you have to unhide it.

3. **Click** `personal.xls` **and then click OK to unhide the file.**

Excel returns with `personal.xls` showing.

4. **Choose Tools⇨Macro⇨Macros.**

You see the Macro dialog box, as shown in Figure 67-7.

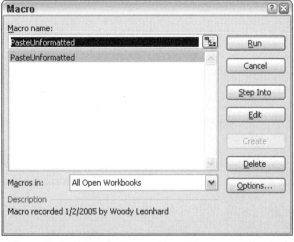

• **Figure 67-7:** Excel allows you to open a macro only when the workbook containing the macro is unhidden.

5. **Click the Edit button.**

The Visual Basic Editor (VBE) kicks in, with Module1 from `personal.xls` showing (see Figure 67-8).

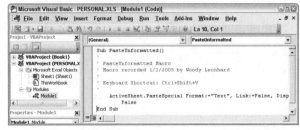

• **Figure 67-8:** What the `PasteUnformatted` macro really looks like.

6. If you want to make changes to the macro, you can at this point. For example, you can delete this extraneous code without any problems:

```
, Link:=False, DisplayAsIcon:= _
        False
```

7. When you're done making changes, choose File⇨Close and Return to Microsoft Excel.

8. When you're back in Excel, choose Window⇨Hide to hide `personal.xls`.

If you don't hide `personal.xls`, every time you start Excel, it will show `personal.xls` on the screen, and you have to do the extra work of choosing File⇨New to start a blank workbook.

Technique

68

Printing a Bunch of Spreadsheets — Fast

Save Time By

- ✔ Writing a macro to print all the spreadsheets you select in a folder
- ✔ Running the macro with a couple of clicks
- ✔ Discovering a few tricks for your own macros

I must get mail from a dozen readers every month with the same question: How do you print a folder full of spreadsheets?

The question comes under many guises. These folks need to print invoices or stock inventory forms or employee evaluations or real estate appraisals or statements or aged receivables or just about anything you can imagine (taking a breath now), and they need to print them by the bucket. Paperless office? HA! Maybe where you work, it's paperless. Everyplace I've seen is drowning in paper. Hard copy rules. What to do?

Write a macro!

Printing is precisely the kind of problem that's well suited for a macro: repetitive, easily defined, and booooooooring. It takes forever to click, click, click, open, file, print, close, and open again. And it's so easy to skip a spreadsheet or to print one twice.

This Technique shows you how to write, from scratch, a Visual Basic for Applications (VBA) macro that runs in Excel. The macro itself is fairly simple but is also a huge timesaver for people who have to print large numbers of spreadsheets in batch jobs. The methods that I use to create the macro should show you, via a very concrete example, how you can start to use VBA to automate repetitive jobs that you encounter every day.

 Most of what you read about macros either states or implies that macros are good at automating repetitive tasks (thus saving you time). That's only part of the story. In fact, macros can do everything that Excel (or Word) can do, and then some. VBA is a powerful, full-fledged programming language. The fact that VBA sits inside Excel, Word, and Access (and to a lesser extent, PowerPoint and Outlook) shouldn't deter you. Behind those pretty faces beats the heart of a powerful programming beast. For more info about VBA, pick up a copy of *VBA For Dummies,* 4th Edition (John Paul Mueller, Wiley).

Setting Up Excel for Macros

In Technique 67, I explain why the easiest and fastest way to get started with Excel macros involves the wimpy, under-aspirated Excel macro recorder. Refer to the details there if you're curious, but if you haven't yet created any macros in Excel, you need to run the recorder once to get Excel set up properly — specifically, to make sure `personal.xls` is ready to go.

 As I explain in Technique 67, `personal.xls` is a hidden file, stored in the XLStart folder. Every time you start Excel, it opens all the files in the XLStart folder. Thus, any macro you put in `personal.xls` will be available every time you start Excel.

1. **Start Excel. Choose Tools⇨Macros⇨Record New Macro.**

Excel shows you the Record Macro dialog box, as shown in Figure 68-1.

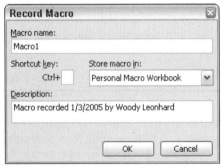

• **Figure 68-1: The fast, sure way to create the file** `personal.xls`.

2. **Make sure that Store Macro In shows Personal Macro Workbook, and then click OK.**

Excel starts the macro recorder and shows you that bizarre, tiny toolbar called Stop Recorder (see the bottom-right of Figure 68-2).

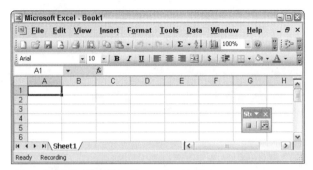

• **Figure 68-2: The Stop Recorder toolbar.**

3. **Press the Tab key.**

This puts your cursor in cell B1.

 Actually, you can do just about anything in Excel — create a chart, set headers and footers, you name it — as long the macro recorder recognizes what you've done.

4. **Click Stop Recording on the Stop Recorder toolbar. It's the first button.**

You now have a new macro called `Macro1`. It only moves the cursor to cell B1, but that's okay.

5. **Choose File⇨Exit.**

6. **When Excel asks whether you want to save the changes you made to the Personal Macro Workbook, click Yes.**

`personal.xls` is all set up and ready to go.

Building the PrintWorkbooks Macro

In the preceding section, I show you how to create a spreadsheet called `personal.xls`. Although Excel uses `personal.xls` to hold recorded macros, you can use the same file for your own porpoises. Or whales. Talk about bloated code! (Sorry. Sometimes I start to channel Groucho, and it hurts.)

Here I show you how to write a macro that you can use to print all the workbooks in a folder. To write the `PrintWorkbooks` macro

1. **Start Excel. Choose Window⇨Unhide.**

You see the Unhide dialog box, as shown in Figure 68-3.

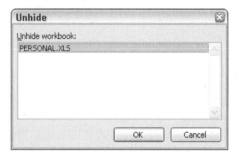

• **Figure 68-3: Start by making** `personal.xls` **visible.**

2. **Choose PERSONAL.XLS and click OK.**

Excel shows you `personal.xls`, which looks like any other empty workbook.

3. **Press Alt+F11.**

Of the many ways to bring up the Visual Basic Editor (VBE; see Figure 68-4), Alt+F11 is the fastest.

 A brief introduction: The upper-left pane of the VBE is the *Project Explorer window,* which lets you move from workbook to workbook. The lower left is the *Properties window,* which occasionally holds important information about the items you've selected. On the right is the *programming window* (also known as the code or Module window), where you type your VBA program.

4. **In the Project Explorer window (upper left), drill your way down to the program module called Module1 in** `personal.xls`**.**

The macro that you recorded appears onscreen (refer to Figure 68-4).

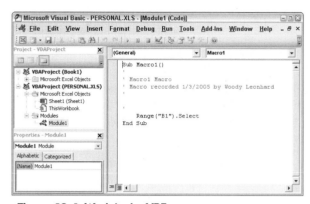

• **Figure 68-4: Work in the VBE.**

 A lot of the terminology that you see onscreen at this point is typical computer gobbledygook. Don't let it throw you. All you really need to know is that every `.xls` file (called a *VBAProject* for no apparent reason) can contain custom dialog boxes (called *UserForms,* for no apparent reason) and programs (called *procedures,* which they are, sorta). The custom dialog boxes and programs are grouped together into *modules,* which can be helpful if you're writing huge systems. You can break the giant system down into lots of modules, and program each one separately — but for most people, modules just get in the way. If you want to write a program (a macro) that you can use in any worksheet, put it in a module that's inside `personal.xls`, the big kahuna of projects.

5. **To put a new macro (er, program, uh, procedure) in the module called Module1, choose Insert⇨Procedure.**

VBA brings up the Add Procedure dialog box, as shown in Figure 68-5. It's automatically set to be a `Public` (that is, available everywhere) `Sub` (a subroutine or program).

6. **In the Name box, type** PrintWorkbooks **(all one word, no spaces), and then click OK.**

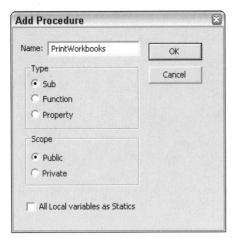

• **Figure 68-5:** Create a new macro here.

VBA creates a new subroutine called `PrintWorkbooks`, adorning it with the obligatory `Public Sub` and `End Sub` statements (see Figure 68-6).

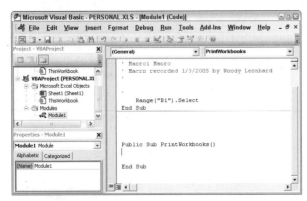

• **Figure 68-6:** The beginning of this subroutine is `PrintWorkbooks`.

7. **Start by typing two lines after the `Sub` line, which establish the variables that I use in the macro:**

```
Dim i As Integer
Dim FileNames As Variant
```

 Note how VBA helps you as you type. As soon as VBA identifies a word that you want to type, press the Tab key, and VBA autocompletes the text.

The variable `i` is set up as an integer. `FileNames` is established as a `Variant`, which is sort of a catch-all kind of variable that can be almost anything — text, number, array, and much more (see Figure 68-7). (VBA calls this *dimensioning* — `Dim` — but that's another bit of archaic, arcane computer jargon.)

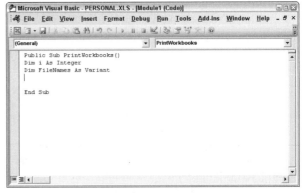

• **Figure 68-7:** Set up the variables for the program.

LISTING 68-1: THE PRINTWORKBOOKS MACRO

```
FileNames = Application.GetOpenFilename(,,"Choose workbooks",,True)
If IsArray(FileNames) Then
    For i = 1 To UBound(FileNames)
        Workbooks.Open FileNames(i)
        ActiveWorkbook.ActiveSheet.PrintOut
        ActiveWorkbook.Close (False)
    Next i
End If
```

8. **Type the rest of the macro shown in Listing 68-1.**

The final macro looks like Figure 68-8.

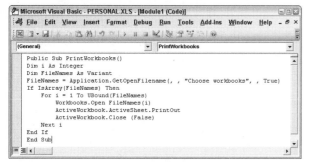

• **Figure 68-8: The** `PrintWorkbooks` **macro.**

Here's how the macro works. First, it uses a Windows function called `GetOpenFilename` to show a built-in Windows dialog box that lets the user choose multiple files. If the user picks any files at all, `FileNames` turns into an array of the names of the files that were chosen. (That's why it was declared as a variant.) For each file that the user chose, the macro opens the file, prints it (actually, prints the worksheet in the workbook that was active the last time the workbook was closed), and then closes the workbook without saving changes — that's what the `(False)` entry does.

If you're ever curious about what a particular VBA command does, click the command once and then press F1. Visual Basic Help appears, and although it's deficient in many ways, at least it will get you started.

Can't figure out which command to use? Yeah, that's a huge problem. Of the many tricks, the number-one timesaver goes by the unlikely name of the Object Browser. (It seems like everything in VBA is an object, eh?) To use the Object Browser, press F2. Choose Excel from the top drop-down list, type an associated name in the second drop-down box (if all else fails, try Application), and then press Enter.

Making Your Variables Typo-proof

Unless you change things, VBA lets you create new variables on-the-fly while you're typing a program. That's dangerous. Say you have a variable called `FileNames`, which you use throughout a program — except once, where you accidentally type it as `FileName`. Excel lets you create the new variable called `FileName` at the location where you misspelled it. As a result, your program has two different variables — `FileName` and `FileNames` — and it's deucedly difficult to find or correct the error.

The solution? `Option Explicit`. When you have an `Option Explicit` statement at the beginning of a module, Excel requires you to declare your variable names before you use them. So, for example, you have to declare `FileNames` as a variant (see Step 7 in this section). Later, when you're typing your program, the minute you accidentally type `FileName`, Excel looks and can't find any declaration for `FileName`. It immediately flags your mistyping as a mistake, and all is right with the world.

I strongly recommend that everyone take a moment to do the following. Choose Tools⇨Options; on the Editor tab, mark the Require Variable Declaration check box. That way, all new modules will automatically get an `Option Explicit` as soon as they're created.

Running and Testing the Macro

Here's how to *debug* (test) the `PrintWorkbooks` macro, which I showed you how to develop in the preceding section:

1. **With your cursor anywhere inside the** `PrintWorkbooks` **macro, choose Debug⇨ Step Into (or press F8).**

VBA starts to run your program. The first line — `Public Sub PrintWorkbooks()` — gets run. VBA highlights it and puts an arrow next to that line, to show it's the one being run (see Figure 68-9).

2. **Press F8.**

VBA jumps down to the next executable line, the one that starts `FileNames =`.

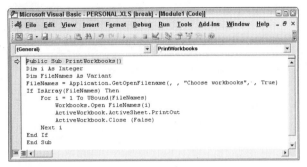

• **Figure 68-9:** Run in debug mode, one line at a time.

3. **Press F8.**

VBA runs the `FileNames =` line and opens the Choose Workbooks dialog box (see Figure 68-10).

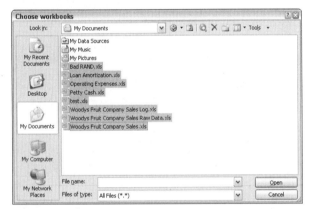

• **Figure 68-10:** The `GetOpenFilename` command opens this dialog box onscreen, allowing you to choose multiple files.

4. **Choose any files you wish to print, and then click Open.**

VBA returns to the next line in the program, the one that starts with `If IsArray()`.

5. **Press F8.**

Assuming that you chose some files to print (and thus `FileNames` is an array filled with the names of the files you chose), VBA moves on to the `For i = 1` line, which is highlighted with an arrow next to it.

6. **Continue pressing F8.**

VBA steps through each line in the program, runs it, and then goes on to the next line. Keep pressing F8 until you're comfortable that the macro works properly.

7. **When you're sure the macro works correctly, choose Run⇨Reset.**

That stops the macro.

8. **Choose File⇨Close and Return to Microsoft Excel. Back in Excel, chose Window⇨Hide to hide** `personal.xls`**. Then choose File⇨Exit. When Excel asks whether you want to save changes in your Personal Macro Workbook, click Yes.**

Excel is back to normal, and your `PrintWorkbooks` macro will be available whenever you start Excel again.

Assigning the Macro to a Button

You can always run a macro by choosing Tools⇨Macro⇨Macros, selecting the macro, and then clicking Run.

However, setting up any macro so it runs when you click a button on a toolbar is a much faster way. Here's how:

1. **Start Excel and make sure that your macro is available. (It will be if it's in** `personal.xls`**.) Then choose Tools⇨Customize⇨Commands.**

Excel shows you the Commands tab of the Customize dialog box, as shown in Figure 68-11.

2. **On the left, under Categories, select Macros. On the right, click Custom Button, drag the cursor to a convenient location on an Excel toolbar, and then drop it.**

In Figure 68-12, I drag the custom button to the right of the ? (question mark) icon on the Standard toolbar. You're stuck with the smiley face icon for a moment. Patience, patience.

• **Figure 68-11:** Use the Customize dialog box to put a button on a toolbar.

• **Figure 68-12:** The smiley face shows where the new custom macro button will appear.

3. **Right-click the smiley face button and choose Assign Macro.**

Excel brings up the Assign Macro dialog box, as shown in Figure 68-13.

4. **Select PERSONAL.XLS!PrintWorkbooks and then click OK.**

The macro PrintWorkbooks is now assigned to the button; if you click the button, Excel runs PrintWorkbooks. You go back into the Customize dialog box.

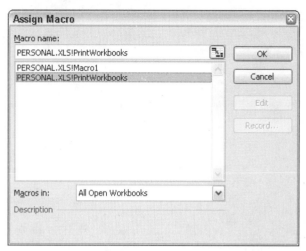

• **Figure 68-13:** Assign the PrintWorkbooks **macro to the smiley face.**

5. **Right-click the smiley button on the toolbar and type a new name in the Name box.**

6. **Right-click the button and choose either Change Button Image or Edit Button Image.**

Pick a new picture from the choices on offer. Get rid of that smiley face, replacing it with something you can remember (and stomach).

7. **In the Customize dialog box, click the Close button.**

From that point on, every time you click the button, Excel runs the PrintWorkbooks macro.

If you ever want to get rid of the button or move it, choose Tools➪Customize. Then either click and drag the button off the toolbar (which deletes it completely) or drag it onto a different toolbar of your choosing.

Technique

69

Protecting Your Privacy

Save Time By

- Keeping personal information out of documents you distribute
- Ensuring that old comments and versions of a document don't get out

You probably know — or at least have a sneaky suspicion — that the documents, workbooks, and presentation files that you work on contain all sorts of buried information about you. It's true.

Ask Tony Blair, whose governing team in the UK was shaken — not stirred — about a publicly posted Word document highlighting intelligence about Iraqi weapons. Among the many scandals that ensued regarding this document, the British government could hardly have been pleased to discover that buried in the text was a list of the people who modified the document. (See Richard Smith's analysis at www.ComputerBytesMan.com/privacy/blair.htm.)

This Technique isn't as much a timesaver as a buttsaver. Read it and you'll see why.

Seeing the Hidden Stuff

The Internet must have millions of Word doc files available for downloading. And the vast majority of them abound with hidden, personal, and sometimes embarrassing information.

Want to go doc Dumpster Diving? Here's how:

1. Find a Word document that might contain some interesting tidbits.

You might have one sitting on your hard drive, or you can look for one on the Internet with a tool like Google's Advanced Search.

2. Double-click the file to open it in Word. Choose File⇨Properties⇨ Summary.

Word brings up the Summary information, which usually includes the name of the so-called official author (see Figure 69-1).

• **Figure 69-1:** Occasionally the Summary tab brings up some interesting information.

3. **Click the Custom tab.**

If the Word doc was sent attached to an e-mail message and the sender used Outlook 2002 or 2003, Outlook brands the file with the sender's e-mail address and the subject of the e-mail message.

4. **Close the document. Don't save any changes.**

In order to see the information buried inside the document, you have to close it first.

5. **Choose File⇨Open. In the Files of Type box, choose Recover Text from Any File. Then navigate to the file and open it again.**

Word brings up a Show Repairs dialog box saying that errors were detected. Ignore it and click the Close button.

6. **Scroll down in the document. You usually find the most interesting information past the normal text.**

In Figure 69-2, I see who made changes to the document. I can also see where they stored the file.

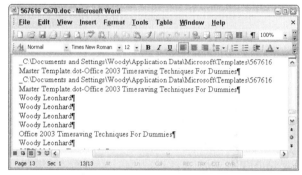

• **Figure 69-2:** A list of the people who modified the file and where it was stored at the time.

 There's nothing illegal, immoral, or fattening about doc Dumpster Diving. Everything you see was posted on the Internet, and made available for wide distribution. The only difference? You now know where to look for the, uh, more intriguing stuff.

 Moral of the story: Don't post Word documents on the Web and don't distribute them outside of your organization. Instead, use a *PDF*, which is the format that Adobe Acrobat developed, or some alternative such as an RTF file (which Word can produce directly). See a detailed discussion of PDF and various tools available to put it to work at www.woodyswatch.com/wowmm/ archtemplate.asp?v4-n15.

Zapping the Embarrassing Stuff

Considering that Microsoft itself posts all sorts of embarrassing information hidden in Word documents on the Internet, you'd think it would be easy to get rid of the hidden stuff.

And, of course, you'd be wrong.

Throughout this book, I emphasize how important it is to use the tools at your disposal to keep your personal information out of documents. Unfortunately, the tools don't cover all the bases in Office 2003 (and none of them are turned on by default). The tools only scratch the surface in Office XP, and Office 97 and 2000 basically have no privacy tools at all.

Word 2003 goes a long way toward removing hidden information, particularly if you follow my recommendations in Technique 16 and change Word's default security settings for all new blank documents.

In early 2004, Microsoft released a Hidden Data Removal Tool that removes most (but not all) hidden data in Office 2003 and XP documents (Word `.doc`, Excel `.xls`, and PowerPoint `.ppt`/`.pps` files). It's a snarly, buggy program (see `www.woodyswatch.com/office/archtemplate.asp?v9-n01`) that nonetheless removes most potentially embarrassing data, most of the time. You can get a copy at `www.microsoft.com/downloads/details.aspx?FamilyId=144E54ED-D43E-42CA-BC7B-5446D34E5360`.

If you're using Word 2000 or earlier, you can do a little bit to remove some of this embarrassing hidden information — for example, you can manually delete the information in a document's Properties box — but in many cases, you're up the proverbial creek. In particular, Word 97 and 2000 bury the names of the last ten people who edited the document — *and there's nothing you can do about it.*

Hidden revision tracking names only touch the tip of the iceberg. Wary Word 97 and 2000 users — and Word 2003 and 2002 users who don't run the Hidden Data Removal Tool — must also watch out for

✔ **Fast Saves:** This buggy-whip-era feature can leave huge chunks of embarrassing data in your documents by storing the *deltas* — the changes you make to a document — while leaving the original, edited, and even deleted data intact. I talk about it, and insist that you disable it, in Technique 15.

✔ **Track Changes:** While doc Dumpster Diving not too long ago, I found a Word doc on the Internet from a big-time security researcher, whose company had forgotten to accept changes to his document before posting it. To get rid of all tracked changes in a document, choose View⇨Markup, click the down arrow next to the Check icon, and choose Accept All Changes in Document.

✔ **Comments:** You have to delete Comments, or anybody who gets a copy of your document can see them with no problem at all. To get rid of all Comments in a document, choose View⇨Markup, click the down arrow next to the X icon, and choose Delete All Comments in Document.

✔ **Versions:** If you (or someone who's worked on your document) has a doc set up to save multiple versions — either manually or automatically — every single version is available to anyone who opens your document. Choose File⇨Versions to see whether you have a list of Existing Versions. If you do, save the current, latest version of the file by choosing File⇨Save As and giving the doc file a new name. The new file won't include the old versions.

Microsoft has a lengthy list of steps that you can take to meticulously remove all the hidden junk that Word and Outlook stick in your doc files. It's at `msdn.microsoft.com/library/en-us/dnword2k2/html/odc_protectword.asp`. **Required reading.**

I, personally, use and swear by Metadata Assistant, which is a $79 document cleanser that gets rid of all the potentially embarrassing information that I know about. It runs inside Word, Excel, and PowerPoint, so you can clean a document by clicking a menu or you can run it on a folder full of docs. It also watches as you're sending out messages to see whether any Office docs are attached, offering to clean them as they go. This is one, slick product (with 1,000,000 users) that works with Office 97 to 2003. See `www.payneconsulting.com` for details.

Printing Personalized Greetings in Batches

Technique 70

I'll never forget the first time I tried to use Word version 1.1 to print a Christmas newsletter and envelopes for all my Christmas cards. I spent days — *days* — trying to get Word to work right. The whole experience left me so frustrated I almost gave up on Word for good.

In retrospect, I probably should've.

Over the years, Word's gotten a little bit better, and now Outlook provides a way to store all the names and addresses. But some of the old glitches are still there and, frankly, it all seems to be strung together with baling wire and chewing gum. I frequently wonder whether anybody at Microsoft has ever used Office to print greeting cards, newsletters, and envelopes. I doubt it.

This Technique covers all the tricks that I've gleaned for printing cards, newsletters, and envelopes. Many of the tricks apply to any printed newsletter, form letter, or list — or anything else that requires a mail merge.

Understanding Mass Mailing

Every year I get hundreds — sometimes more than a thousand — messages from *Woody's Office Watch* readers about surviving Christmas, Hanukkah, Kwanzaa, 'Id al-Fitr, Visaka Puja, New Year's, and other holiday greeting card times. (Okay, okay. I'll stop trying to be politically correct, and use the term *greeting card* in its generic sense. Great Pumpkin anybody? Sheesh.)

The cause of all the Office mass-mailing angst: Word and Outlook, and the way they're hooked together. You folks have spent hundreds of dollars (euros, shekels, ringgit, riyals, escudos, baht, pounds, kyat, you name it) for the fanciest word processor and information manager on the planet, but you can't get it to do something as simple as printing greeting cards.

Believe me, you aren't alone.

This Technique includes all the details you need to

- ✔ **Set up a mailing list.** This consists of Outlook Contacts who are specifically earmarked for receiving cards and/or e-mail messages.

- ✔ **Print customized cards or newsletters.** These can contain personalized information (such as a *Dear Cliff, Carolyn, Zane & Joel* line) drawn from the Outlook Contacts entry.

- ✔ **Print custom envelopes.** You can make these go with the cards or newsletters.

- ✔ **Send e-mail messages instead.** After all, some people prefer bit-based greetings.

Don't let the greeting-card bias throw you. The steps in this Technique also work if you want to print and mail a small-circulation, hard copy newsletter, advertisement, or brochure to your customers, any time of year. Ho, ho, ho.

I've used the methods in this Technique to run print mailings, delivered through the U.S. Postal Service, up to about 5,000 pieces. It ain't easy, but it can be done.

Before you start, you need to understand two givens:

- ✔ **Spending upfront time:** The first time you use a computer to send out cards, newsletters, or messages, prepare to invest a lot of time and effort. With rare exceptions, doing it all by hand the first time is almost always faster and easier. You won't start seeing the timesaving benefits of automating the process until the second time you do it — or maybe even the third.

- ✔ **Massaging Word and Outlook:** Mass mailings (or e-mailings) set up this way require two very different Office programs (Outlook and Word) as

well as a key Office feature — Word's mail merge. The programs don't work the same way, and the merge doesn't do a great job of bridging the gaps. You're doomed to failure if you don't use Word and Outlook in the correct order. Follow the steps here, and avoid the temptation to jump back and forth between Word and Outlook.

Entering and Updating Contacts

Every good mail merge starts with a clean mailing list. If you're lucky, most of your card recipients are already in your Outlook Contacts list, and their mailing addresses (or e-mail addresses) are accurate and up-to-date. If you aren't so lucky, you have a lot of typing in your future.

If you already have your address list set up in Excel or Access or even in a Word table, consider transferring them to Outlook. You'll save yourself a lot of time and headache in the long run because you don't have to maintain two separate sets of addresses. Word is capable of running mail merges with the names coming from Excel, Access, or even Word. But it's a whole lot simpler if you work from Outlook's Contacts (if you know the tricks).

Heed this school-of-hard-knocks advice:

- ✔ **Set the personal greeting in Outlook Contacts.** If you want to print a personal greeting on each card or newsletter, or add a personal greeting to each e-mail message, you have to stick the greeting in every Outlook Contact destined to receive a card or message. For example, if you want your holiday newsletter to begin *Dear Cliff, Carolyn, Zane & Joel,* you must have an entry on the family's Contact card that reads *Cliff, Carolyn, Zane & Joel.* Otherwise, Word won't be able to generate the name you want.

Most of my Christmas cards go out to friends, and I usually greet them by their first names. I've found that the best way to get a decent salutation is to use the First Name field on each Contact for the names of the people I want to list by name in my Christmas cards and family newsletters. (For example, the First Name field for Cliff's family reads *Cliff, Carolyn, Zane & Joel.*) I leave the First Name field for companies blank.

✔ **Separate regular cards from e-mails.** Set up separate categories for hard copy Christmas card recipients and e-mail Christmas card recipients. That makes it easy to separate the different classes of recipients when you run a merge.

 Personally, I use three categories for Christmas cards. The Envelope Only group consists of companies and business associates who require a printed envelope for their card but don't get my (captivating!) family newsletter. The Wired group gets an e-mail message. And the Whole Enchilada group gets a printed newsletter and envelope.

 If you use this Technique to print company newsletters or custom reports, you should spend some time thinking about the different categories of Contacts you need. In Technique 61, I talk about setting up newsletter subscribers with a Newsletter category. Pick a category or two (or three or ten) that work for you and your situation.

Here's how to set up your greeting card categories:

1. **Establish your card categories by starting Outlook, moving to Contacts (typically by choosing Go⇨Contacts), and then choosing Edit⇨Categories.**

Outlook responds with the Categories dialog box.

2. **Click the Master Category List button.**

You see the Master Category List in Figure 70-1.

3. **One by one, add the categories that you want to use for your Christmas card lists by typing the category name and clicking Add.**

In Figure 70-1, I add the _XmasBus category for the Envelope Only business contacts, _XmasMsg for my wired friends who should receive e-mail messages, and _XmasCard for those folks who get the full hard copy treatment.

 Putting an underscore (_) at the beginning of the category name assures you that the name will float to the top in any alphabetized list. That can be very handy.

• **Figure 70-1: Add your Christmas card categories to the list.**

 Although nothing is wrong with using the prebuilt Holiday and Holiday Cards categories, I always have a hard time remembering who belongs to which group. For example, if Bill Gates is one of my Contacts, should he go in the Holiday or the Holiday Cards category or both? By using my custom categories, it's easy to decide: Bill goes in the _XmasCard category, so I can send him news each year on how the family is doing. Hey, maybe he'll invite me to his annual retreat. . . .

4. **After you add the categories that you need, click OK twice to go back to Outlook.**

 If you use a handheld computer (or any other computer that's synched to your Outlook Contacts) make sure that its software is smart enough to maintain these custom categories. Some software clobbers the categories, either going into the handheld or coming back out. Make a test run by setting a custom category on one Contact (see the next series of steps), synching with your handheld, and then synching back. If your handheld is going to blast away your custom categories, it's better to find out before you go to all the work of assigning categories to everybody in your Contacts list.

After you set up your categories, you can add Contacts to those categories in one of two ways:

✔ **Adding existing Contacts:** Click and drag Contacts to the appropriate category.

 You can assign a whole bunch of Contacts to a category by choosing View➪Arrange By➪ Categories. Then select the Contacts that you want to add and click and drag the bunch onto the appropriate Categories entry (see the upcoming Figure 70-2).

✔ **Adding new Contacts:** As you add people to your Contacts list, you can assign categories to the contact while you're at it. Just click the Categories button at the bottom of the Contact's record and mark the checkboxes in the Categories dialog box that appears.

Checking Contacts

In the preceding section, I talk about creating good Contact records for everyone on your greeting card list. In this section, I show you how to double-check your Contacts and make sure that all the data is in place.

After you have the new Contacts entered, take a few moments to make sure you have all your Contacts correctly assigned to each category. Here's the fast way:

1. **Bring up your Contacts list (choose Go➪ Contacts). Choose View➪Arrange By➪ Categories.**

Outlook shows you a list of all your Contacts, arranged by category (see Figure 70-2).

2. **To show or hide the list of individual contacts in each category, click the + or – button to the left of the category name.**

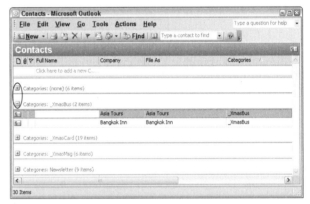

• **Figure 70-2:** The bird's eye view of all your Contacts and their categories.

3. **Scan each category's list. If you find a Contact who should not be in a particular category, right-click the Contact, choose Categories, and clear the check box next to the offending category.**

If you find many Contacts who should be in one particular category, Ctrl+click or Shift+click to select them all. Then right-click, choose Categories, and enable the check box next to the category you want to add the Contacts to.

With the categories nailed down, make sure that the folks who will receive your holiday e-mail greetings have valid e-mail addresses, and that those destined to receive snail mail have mailing addresses the postal people can understand. To scan quickly

1. **If you just finished the preceding steps, you can see your Contacts in category view. If not, bring up your Contacts list (choose Go⇨Contacts). Choose View⇨Arrange By⇨Category.**

   Outlook shows you your Contacts in category view (refer to Figure 70-2).

2. **Right-click one of the field names (Full Name, Company, File As, and so on) and choose Field Chooser.**

   Outlook brings up the Field Chooser dialog box (see Figure 70-3).

• **Figure 70-3:** Add a new field to category view.

3. **Select Mailing Address and drag it to the left of the File As field up on the bar. When you see a red arrow indicating that the Mailing Address field will be inserted (see Figure 70-4), release the mouse button.**

   Outlook makes the Contacts' mailing addresses visible.

4. **Click the drop-down arrow at the top of the Field Chooser dialog and choose E-mail Fields.**

5. **Click the E-mail field and drag it to the left of the File As field.**

   Outlook shows you the e-mail address for each of your Contacts.

• **Figure 70-4:** Show the mailing address for each of your Contacts.

6. **Look at each Contact in your card categories and make sure you have a valid mailing address or e-mail address.**

   Cleaning up the data now is much easier — before you try to print envelopes or create e-mail messages (see Figure 70-5).

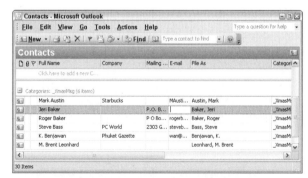

• **Figure 70-5:** Everyone in your _XmasMsg category should have a valid e-mail address.

Printing Personalized Newsletters

In the preceding sections, I show you fast and accurate ways to get your Christmas card list into Outlook. In this section, I explain how to print newsletters.

If your printer has an automatic envelope feeder, you might think about interleaving newsletters and envelopes. That is, print the envelope for the Ables, then the family newsletter for the Ables, then the envelope for the Bakers, then the newsletter for the Bakers, and so on. Don't do it. Word's support for attaching envelopes to documents is a pain in the neck, and if just one envelope or newsletter gets screwed up, recovering from the problem can take an Act of Congress.

Here's how to perform a mail merge — for family newsletters, company newsletters, flyers, or anything else that strikes your fancy. Be very careful to follow these steps precisely:

1. **Follow the steps in the preceding sections to get your newsletter contacts in good shape, assigned to the correct category, and with thoroughly vetted mailing addresses. Then shut down Outlook.**

If you use the categories that I suggest, you will be working with the _XmasCard category.

2. **Start Word. Put together the static part of the newsletter — the part that will be the same for everybody in the mailing.**

Don't worry about the *Dear Cliff, Carolyn, Zane & Joel* part just yet. Work on the stuff about the cat going in for its first round of psychotherapy and how the neighbor's cattle keep eating your petunias.

Microsoft publishes holiday family newsletter templates every year at `www.office.microsoft.com`. By all means, pick up a

template or a piece of art — but *don't* follow its advice on running holiday card mail merges! MS hasn't gotten it right yet, despite trying for ten years.

Do *not* run the Mail Merge Wizard in Word. Word will let you use Contacts in a merge 'til the cows come home, but the glue that binds Word and Outlook isn't smart enough to show Word the categories. Yeah, Microsoft ran out of money.

3. **When you're done with the static part of the newsletter, close the document and shut down Word.**

WordMail has a reputation for gumming up the works when you try to do anything complicated with Outlook while Word is running. The easiest, most reliable solution is to just say No to Word.

4. **Start Outlook. Bring up the Contacts list (choose Go⇨Contacts). Choose View⇨Arrange By⇨ Categories. Click the + sign next to the category that you want to send newsletters to. Then select all the Contacts in the category by clicking the first Contact in the category, holding down the Shift key, and clicking the last.**

5. **Choose Tools⇨Mail Merge.**

Outlook brings up the Mail Merge Contacts dialog box (see Figure 70-6).

6. **Under Contacts, select the Only Selected Contacts radio button. Under Document File, click the Browse button and choose the Word document that you created. Click OK.**

If you get weird messages about *The process cannot access the file because it is in use by another process* — or gobbledygook of that ilk — chances are good that you didn't follow my instructions precisely and left Outlook running while working in Word (or vice versa). Be careful. Thar be tygers here. Close Word if you're working in Outlook. Close Outlook if you're working in Word. Then try again.

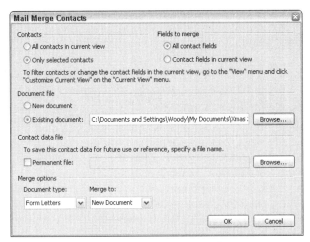

• **Figure 70-6:** If you want to be able to select your Contacts by category, run the mail merge from inside Outlook and not Word.

After Outlook spins its wheels for a bit, it opens the static document in Word, attaches the merge data from your Contacts list to the document, and shows the Mail Merge toolbar.

7. Immediately choose File⇨Save As and save the document with a new name.

8. With the saved document still open, start by typing Dear and a space where you want a salutation line to appear (so you see *Dear Bill* on one newsletter and *Dear Cliff, Carolyn, Zane & Joel* on another one).

9. Click the Insert Merge Fields icon, which sits immediately to the left of the Insert Word Field button.

Word brings up the Insert Merge Field dialog box (see Figure 70-7).

10. Select the First_Name line, then click the Insert button. The Cancel button turns into a Close button. Click Close.

Word puts a *merge field* — a placeholder that's filled in with each Contact record, in turn — into the document. The chevrons (<< >>) surround

the merge field, indicating that the data gets pulled from Contact records (see Figure 70-8).

11. Type a comma.

This inserts a comma at the end of Dear <<First_Name>>.

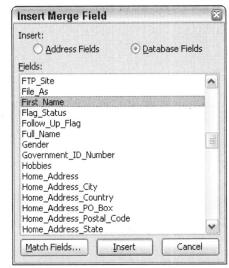

• **Figure 70-7:** Choose the field(s) that you want to pull from the Contact record.

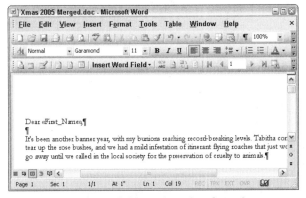

• **Figure 70-8:** Merge fields retrieve data from the merge records — in this case, from each Contact's record.

12. Click the ABC icon, found to the right of the big Insert Word Field button.

Word performs the merge, showing you the result of merging with the first Contact in your selected category (see Figure 70-9).

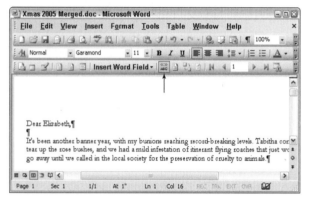

Dear Elizabeth,¶
¶
It's been another banner year, with my bunions reaching record-breaking levels. Tabitha con
tear up the rose bushes, and we had a mild infestation of itinerant flying roaches that just wc
go away until we called in the local society for the preservation of cruelty to animals.¶

• **Figure 70-9:** The results of merging with my first _XmasCard contact, Elizabeth Sharp.

13. To see how the rest of your merged newsletters will look, click the right and left buttons flanking the number 1 on the Mail Merge toolbar.

14. Flip back and forth between looking at the merge fields and the merged documents themselves by clicking the ABC icon. Insert merge fields to your heart's content, clicking to the right and left of the 1 to make sure that all your merged newsletters look right.

15. When you're happy with the result, choose File⇨Save. Then click the Merge to New Document button, which is way out on the right end of the Mail Merge toolbar.

Word asks whether you want to merge all the records or just some of them.

16. To merge all the records, click the All button and then click OK.

Word produces a big document called Letters1, with one page for each record in your selected Contacts category.

17. Save the document with a new name.

18. Print a sample page by choosing File⇨Print, selecting the Current Page radio button, and clicking OK. If the sample looks good, make sure you have enough paper on hand and then go ahead and print the document.

 If you're printing a lot of newsletters, expect all sorts of problems — printer jams, the ink or toner going *kaput,* a playful spider suddenly deciding to make your fuse box his home. If your print run gets clobbered, don't fret. Simply pry out the spider's remaining seven legs, open the final merged document, locate the bad newsletter (probably via Edit⇨Find), and then reprint any botched copies by choosing File⇨Print and selecting the Current Page radio button of the Print dialog box.

Printing Envelopes

In the preceding sections, I show you how to set up a Contacts list with appropriately defined categories, and then run a mail merge to produce newsletters (or brochures, flyers, whatever). In this section, I struggle with envelopes, which are far more difficult than they should be.

To print envelopes

1. Start Outlook. Bring up the Contacts list (Go⇨Contacts). Choose View⇨Arrange By⇨ Categories. Click the + sign next to the category that needs envelopes. Then select all the Contacts in the category by clicking the first Contact in the category, holding down the Shift key, and clicking the last.

 If you use the categories that I suggest at the beginning of this Technique, you need to run two sets of envelopes — one for the folks in the _XmasCard category and one for the folks in the _XmasBus category.

2. **Choose Tools⇨Mail Merge.**

You get the Mail Merge Contacts dialog box, as shown in Figure 70-10.

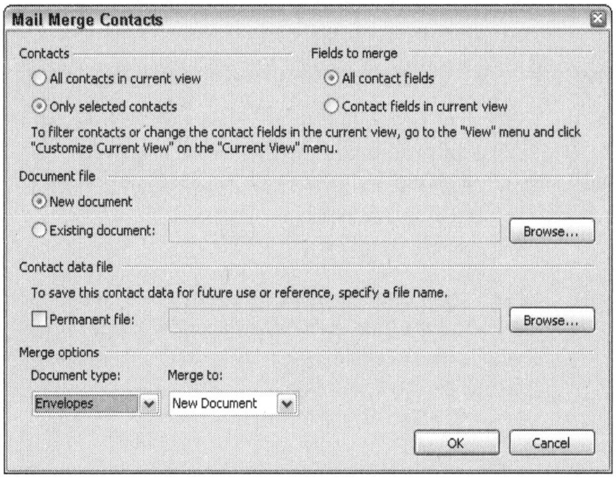

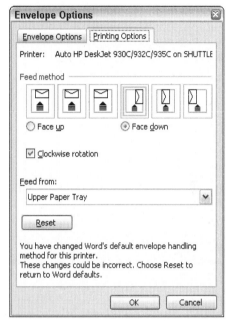

• **Figure 70-10:** Don't worry about choosing a document file; if you want envelopes, just pick Envelopes.

3. **Under Contacts, make sure that the Only Selected Contacts radio button is selected. Then at the lower left, under Document Type, choose Envelopes. Click OK.**

Outlook cranks up Word, presenting you with the rather strange warning about the Setup button.

4. **Click OK.**

Word throws you back into a generations-old interface: the Mail Merge Helper.

5. **Under Number 1 of the Mail Merge Helper, click Setup.**

Word shows you the Envelope Options dialog box (see Figure 70-11). *Hint:* It's the same dialog box you would see if you chose Tools⇨Letters and Mailings⇨Envelopes and Labels⇨Options.

6. **Make any changes that you need to make to the envelope printing options. (If you've been**

printing envelopes on this machine all the time, you don't need to make any changes.) Click OK.

The Mail Merge Helper dialog box returns.

• **Figure 70-11:** Change envelope printing settings here.

7. **Click Close to get rid of the Mail Merge Helper.**

Word shows you the skeleton of an envelope, as in Figure 70-12. It's pretty bizarre — and if you can't see paragraph marks (Technique 15), you won't even know what's there.

8. **In the upper-left corner of the skeleton, type the return name and address.**

You can also add a picture, WordArt, or anything else that strikes your fancy.

9. **Click once in front of the paragraph mark in the middle of the envelope. Then click the Insert Merge Fields icon on the Mail Merge toolbar, found to the left of the big Insert Word Field button.**

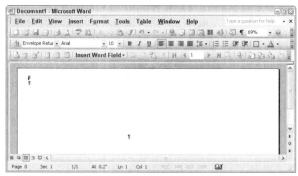

• **Figure 70-12:** An envelope skeleton with the Mail Merge toolbar.

10. If you're sending envelopes to individuals, click the Full_Name field, click Insert, and then click Close. If the envelopes are headed to companies, click the Company field, click Insert, and then click Close.

That puts a <<Full_Name>> merge field at the top of the addressee location.

11. Press Enter.

12. Click the Insert Merge Fields icon again. Click the line that reads Mailing Address, click Insert, and then click Close.

This is an enormously convoluted way to set up the merge envelope shown in Figure 70-13.

• **Figure 70-13:** Word makes it exceedingly difficult to put together a simple merge envelope.

13. Click the ABC icon (located to the right of the big Insert Word Field button).

Word runs the envelope merge and shows you the result of merging with the first Contact in your selected category.

14. To look at your merged envelopes, click the right and left buttons flanking to the number 1 on the Mail Merge toolbar.

15. Flip back and forth between looking at the merge fields and the merged envelopes by clicking the ABC button.

16. When the result looks good, choose File⇨ Save. Then click the Merge to New Document icon (found on the right end of the Mail Merge toolbar).

Word asks whether you want to merge all the records or just some of them.

17. To merge all the records, click the All button and then click OK.

Word produces a big document called Envelopes1, with one envelope for each record in your selected Contacts category.

18. Save the document with a new name.

19. Print the document and watch the envelopes come flying out of your printer.

E-mailing Holiday Greetings

Sending out a holiday newsletter over e-mail requires the same steps as sending out any other electronic newsletter. See Technique 61. You need to work with the category that you've chosen for your holiday e-mails, of course — the ones I put in _XmasMsg earlier in this Technique.

Technique 71

Creating Versatile Watermarks

Save Time By

- Making Word document watermarks quickly and easily
- Modifying and customizing the built-in watermark text
- Running watermarks on the first page only

You know all about Word watermarks, right? Typically, you put a watermark on a document that reads DRAFT or CONFIDENTIAL or some such, usually slanted across the page, almost always in a light gray color.

As long as you can live with Word's built-in choices for font and color and you want the text to run at a 45-degree angle (or boringly horizontal), putting a watermark in a document only takes a couple of clicks. Surprisingly, though, customizing a watermark isn't that much more difficult. You can use text of your own choosing, or run the text at a slightly greater or lesser angle, or format it with a picture fill or a gradient color. You can even choose a different watermark for the first page of a document. Fun stuff.

This Technique takes you through the steps.

Setting a Standard Watermark

In the simplest case, putting a watermark on a document — grayed-out text such as DRAFT or DO NOT COPY that sits underneath the text of the document — couldn't be easier:

1. **Open the document to which you want to add a watermark.**

2. **Choose Format⇨Background⇨Printed Watermark.**

   Word shows you the Printed Watermark dialog box (see Figure 71-1).

3. **Select the Text Watermark radio button.**

   Picture watermarks also work well and can serve as a very professional adjunct to a well laid-out letterhead (see Technique 23). The fancy manipulation methods in the remainder of this Technique apply only to text watermarks.

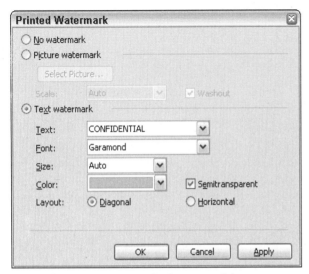

• **Figure 71-1: Adding a standard watermark is easy.**

4. Choose the boilerplate text that you want to appear in the watermark or type your own text in the Text box.

You get to choose from boilerplate watermark text entries, such as CONFIDENTIAL, DO NOT COPY, SAMPLE, and URGENT. If you don't find precisely what you want, type your own entry. You can always change it later (see the next section).

5. Change the Font, Size, Color, and/or Layout if you like. Then click OK.

Word creates the watermark according to your specifications (see Figure 71-2).

 Unless you change it, a watermark prints on every page in the document, precisely as you see onscreen. If you want a watermark only on the first page of a document, see the upcoming section, "Making Watermarks Appear on the First Page Only."

For most people, watermarks end there. For you timesavers, you've only just begun.

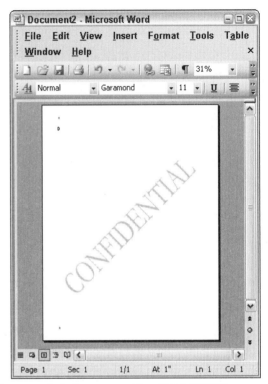

• **Figure 71-2: A document with a** CONFIDENTIAL **watermark.**

Modifying Watermark WordArt

You probably think that a Word watermark is some sort of weird internal thing that Word carries along with the document — say, something like the document formatting or page setup. Not so. A watermark is just a piece of WordArt that Word sticks in the document's header.

 I talk about WordArt in Techniques 23 and 64. Also find extensive coverage at www.uwec. edu/help/Office00/edwordart.htm.

Admittedly, a watermark doesn't look like WordArt sitting in the header — after all, you're accustomed to seeing page headings in headers — but in fact, the watermark is just a WordArt picture that's anchored to the document's (first page) header.

Because a watermark is a simple piece of WordArt, you can modify it with very little effort:

1. **If you have a document with a watermark handy, open it. Otherwise, follow the steps in the preceding section to create one.**

It's much easier to see what's going on if you set the Zoom to Whole Page.

2. **Choose View➪Header and Footer.**

Word shows you the headers and footers in the document.

3. **To select the watermark, hover your cursor over the watermark until it turns into a four-headed arrow; then click once.**

As you can see in Figure 71-3, the watermark is a picture with sizing handles on the edges and corners, a rotation dot at the top, and an extruding square at the bottom. The anchor for the watermark is attached to the first paragraph mark in the header. (I talk about picture anchors in Technique 24.)

4. **Modify the watermark.**

➤ **Move it:** Click it and drag it.

➤ **Enlarge/reduce it:** Click and drag the resizing handles on the edges or corners.

➤ **Rotate it:** Click the rotation dot and drag.

➤ **Change the slant of the characters:** Click the extruding square at the bottom and drag it.

5. **To change the text in the watermark, double-click the watermark.**

Word brings up the Edit WordArt Text dialog box, as shown in Figure 71-4.

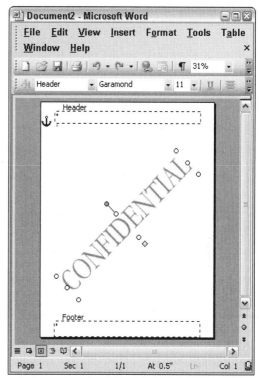

• **Figure 71-3: The watermark's anchor, rotation dot, and extruding square.**

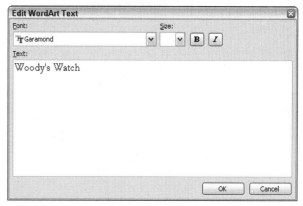

• **Figure 71-4: The watermark is WordArt, and all the WordArt tools are available.**

6. Type your new text for the watermark, format it if you like, and then click OK.

Your modified text appears in the watermark (see Figure 71-5).

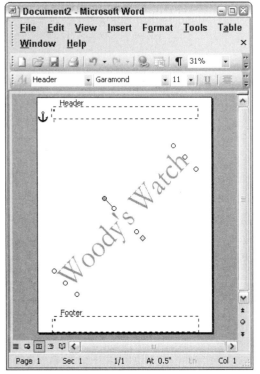

• **Figure 71-5:** Changing the text is very fast and easy — you aren't limited to the boilerplate choices.

7. To add fill effects to the watermark (say, using a picture of a flag to fill in the text, or applying gradient shadings), choose Format⇨WordArt⇨ Colors and Lines. In the Color drop-down box, pick Fill Effects. From there, the choices are nearly limitless (see Figure 71-6).

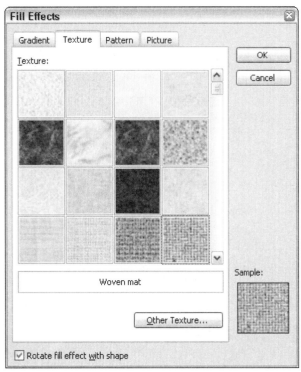

• **Figure 71-6:** Choose textures or pictures to fill your watermark.

Making Watermarks Appear on the First Page Only

Because the watermark is anchored to the paragraph mark in the header, setting up a document so the watermark only appears on the first page of the document is easy:

1. Create a watermark by using the steps in the first section in this Technique.

Don't bother customizing the watermark just yet. (Word has a bug that eliminates your customizing when you place a watermark only on the first page.)

2. Click View and make sure that Header and Footer is not selected.

If Header and Footer is selected, click it again. You want to be in the body of the document — not the header or footer.

3. Choose File⇨Page Setup⇨Layout.

Word shows you the Layout tab of the Page Setup dialog box, as shown in Figure 71-7.

• **Figure 71-7:** Make Word show different first page headers.

4. Enable the Different First Page check box and then click OK.

5. Choose Insert⇨Break. Choose Page Break and click OK.

You now have a two-page document with the same watermark on both the first and second pages.

6. Click the second page. Choose View⇨Header and Footer.

7. Hover your mouse cursor over the second page's watermark until it turns into a four-headed arrow. Then click once to select the watermark.

8. Press Delete.

The watermark disappears from the second (and subsequent) pages.

9. Go back to the first page and edit the watermark any way you like.

The watermark appears on the first page only.

 You can use the same steps to create two different watermarks — one for the first page and the other for all subsequent pages — in a document. You can also delete the watermark on the first page but leave it on the second and all subsequent pages.

Technique 72

Building (And Stealing) E-mail Stationery

Save Time By

- Using prebuilt stationery — quickly
- Making your own stationery
- Stealing stationery from incoming messages

I've always detested e-mail stationery. That is, I used to detest e-mail stationery until I got a message from somebody who works for one of the big, computer PR agencies, and his stationery bowled me over — simple, clean, good-looking, functional.

I immediately stopped using my old plain-text signatures and jumped over to formatted e-mail, specifically so I could use Outlook stationery. That's big jump for an old buzzard like me. Until I made the leap, I, too, grumbled about the bloated messages and cutesy formatting that so frequently accompanies formatted e-mail.

Yeah, I'm nostalgic. I miss those funny ASCII-art pictures of cavorting chipmunks and guys peeking over the tops of walls — and guys peeking over tops of walls looking at cavorting chipmunks. But this is progress. And the thought of stealing a bit of stationery from Microsoft's PR agency . . . well, it was just too good to pass up.

Here's how to build, buy or, uh, borrow some stationery of your own.

Using Built-in Stationery

The world of e-mail message senders falls neatly into two camps:

- **The old buzzards:** These curmudgeons insist that the only good e-mail is a plain, text e-mail. Plain ol' ASCII text e-mail is fast, small, and reliable. And although it can be read by any e-mail program on the planet, it's also booooring. Plus, it's hard for novices to understand *why* those messages have _all_ of those funny ;-) character things in them <gd&rvvf>.

- **The young buzzards . . . er, Turks:** These hipsters frankly don't care whether their messages take 20,000 bytes instead of 7,000. Formatted e-mail (also known as *HTML e-mail*) gives you the opportunity to use **bold** and *italic* text, change fonts around, use color, add pictures, and the like. But it's also big, slow, and prone to occasional problems (from e-mail programs that don't work right, and there are some). And don't forget formatted e-mail's worst sin: an appalling tendency to bring out the *cute* in those who use it. Bah.

If you want to use Outlook stationery, you have to use formatted e-mail. That means you tread perilously close to the line that separates believers in the utilitarian nature of e-mail from those who never got beyond AOL Instant Messenger. ☺

Each specific stationery holds up to five different items:

- ✔ A default message font (style, size, treatment, and color)

- ✔ Fonts for headings and links

- ✔ A background color

- ✔ A picture (which typically repeats along the left and/or right edges of the message)

- ✔ Boilerplate text

Note, however, that Outlook's tools for constructing stationery don't support all the above items, and none of Microsoft's built-in stationery includes all five items.

Here are the two completely different — and maddeningly different — ways of choosing a default stationery for new Outlook messages:

- ✔ **Use Outlook.** If you set the default stationery in Outlook, a set of rudimentary tools lets you edit the stationery's background and picture, but no tools are available for specifying the font that's used when replying to or forwarding messages.

- ✔ **Use Word.** If you set the default stationery in Word, you have more choices for the stationery because you can also use Word Themes. On the other hand, there's stationery available in Outlook (such as the Notebook, which I like!) that simply isn't available in Word. In Word, you get better tools for changing the font that's used when you reply to or forward a message, but there are no tools at all for changing the background or picture. Most damning, you can set

default stationery in Word that isn't available in Outlook — or even in parts of Word. It's a bizarre situation.

 In general, you're better off setting the default stationery in Word. But if you run into problems or you can't find the stationery you want in Word, hop over to Outlook and try to sort it all out there.

Setting up stationery in Word

To set the default stationery in Word — and not Outlook

1. **Start Word.**

2. **Choose Tools⇨Options⇨General. Then click the E-Mail Options button in the lower-right corner.**

3. **Click the Personal Stationery tab.**

   Word shows you the Personal Stationery tab of the E-mail Options dialog box, as shown in Figure 72-1.

• **Figure 72-1: Set the default stationery using Word from this deeply buried dialog box.**

4. **Click the Theme button.**

Word shows you the Theme or Stationery dialog box, as shown in Figure 72-2. This is a very strange dialog box because it combines Word Themes with some (but not all) built-in Outlook stationery as well as stationery that you create manually (see the last section in this Technique).

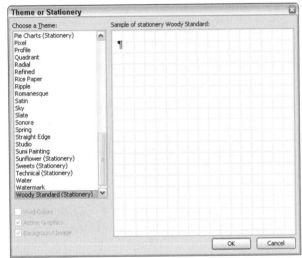

• **Figure 72-2:** A very odd mixture of options available for default stationery.

5. **Under Choose a Theme, pick the stationery you want for your default in Outlook.**

6. **Click OK three times to return to Word.**

That sets the default stationery for new e-mail messages.

Setting up stationery in Outlook

To use a piece of existing stationery as the default for new Outlook messages by using Outlook

1. **Choose Tools⇨Options⇨Mail Format. Click the Stationery Picker button.**

The Stationery Picker (see Figure 72-3) shows you previews of some — but not all — of the stationery that ships with Outlook. It does, however,

include some stationery that's missing in Word's Theme or Stationery dialog box.

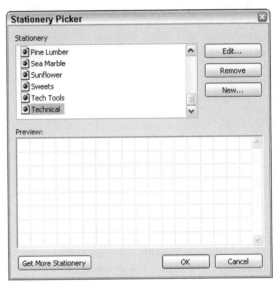

• **Figure 72-3:** Use the Stationery Picker to preview stationery background and pictures.

2. **When you find stationery that you like, click OK.**

If you're using Office 2003, don't bother clicking the Get More Stationery button. As this book went to press, anyway, Microsoft had a dozen pieces of stationery available for download from its Web site, but none of the stationery will install unless you have Office 2000 or Office XP. Microsoft will, however, *sell* you additional pieces of stationery. How nice. Look for the Office Personal Portfolio add-on package at a store near you.

In Figure 72-4, I choose the Notebook stationery.

3. **Click OK to return to Outlook.**

4. **Click the New button to compose a new e-mail message.**

If you specified one of the uninstalled pieces of stationery as your default, Outlook shows you a warning message. If you don't get the warning, you're done. If you do, keep going.

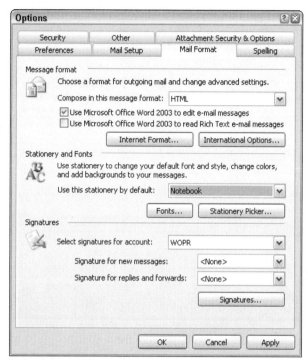

 I can't imagine that anyone would attempt to copyright the background of e-mail stationery, but stranger things have happened. If you swipe stationery, make sure you aren't taking anything that's owned by someone else, okay?

To make an inbound message's stationery available to your copy of Outlook

1. **Double-click the message to open it.**

2. **Choose File⇨Save Stationery.**

Outlook shows you the Create New Stationery dialog box (see Figure 72-5).

• **Figure 72-4: Pick the stationery you want to use for new messages.**

5. **Click Yes.**

The Windows Installer kicks in. You might need to supply your Office CD. When it's done, Outlook comes up with a new message, ready for you to type.

 To use a different stationery for one new message, you don't need to change the default. Just go into Mail (Go⇨Mail), choose Actions⇨New Mail Message Using⇨More Stationery, and choose the stationery that you like.

Stealing Incoming Stationery

It's very easy to, uh, recycle stationery from an inbound message. You won't get the text or any pictures, but you do get the background, font settings, and the like.

• **Figure 72-5: Pilfering stationery is just that simple.**

3. **Type a name for your new stationery and click OK.**

From that point on, the new stationery is available in the same way as all the existing stationery: You can make it the default or modify it at will. The new stationery is even available from inside Word.

Creating Your Own Stationery

Creating your own stationery — either by starting from scratch, or by modifying an existing sample — isn't difficult at all:

1. **Choose Tools⇨Options⇨Mail Format and then click the Stationery Picker button.**

The Stationery Picker arrives (refer to Figure 72-3).

2. **Click New.**

You see the Create New Stationery dialog box (refer to Figure 72-5).

3. **Type a name for your new stationery, select the radio button that reflects what you want to do, and then click Next.**

▶ **Start with a Blank Stationery:** This option lets you supply font formatting and a background picture or color that's applied uniformly on the stationery.

▶ **Use This Existing Stationery As a Template:** As a starting point, Outlook pulls the font and background from the stationery you specify.

▶ **Use This File As a Template:** As a starting point, Outlook takes the font and background from the HTML file that you pick.

Oddly, some of the built-in stationery (such as Notebook) isn't available for creating new stationery. On the other hand, stationery that you pilfer is available both as a Use This Existing Stationery as a Template choice, and in the Use This File as a Template box.

Outlook brings up the Edit Stationery dialog box (see Figure 72-6). You can change only the background picture or the background color — not both.

4. **Change the default font, if you like.**

5. **If you want a simple signature at the bottom of each new message, you can type one in the Preview box.**

Most people want to add a *signature* to their new stationery — a blurb that appears at the bottom of every message. Believe it or not, the *worst* place to create an Outlook e-mail signature is in Outlook. The best place is in Word.

6. **When you're done, click OK twice.**

Outlook sets your new stationery as the default (refer to Figure 72-4).

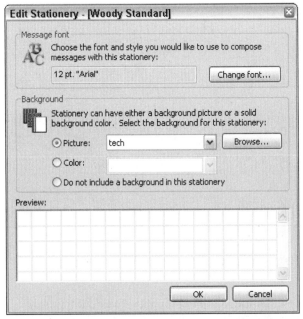

• **Figure 72-6:** Pick a default font and choose between a background picture and a background color.

Index